Loren's book provides a way for companies to quickly and efficiently use Assistive Technology to make basic spreadsheets accessible. His approach is direct and easy to follow, hands-on, and practical. His innovation, Assistive Portals, opens the door to making graphical interfaces embedded in decision analysis spreadsheets readily accessible to individuals with visual impairments. While making technology accessible is a difficult challenge for the business world, this book brings it well within reach. More importantly, making something accessible doesn't require watering it down. We think these ideas warrant serious attention and represent a milestone in leveling the playing field for individuals with disabilities."

Crista Earl, Director of Web Operations/American Foundation for the Blind

"XML and spreadsheets are not usually thought of in the same breath. Loren's concepts and implementation of Spreadsheet Portals using the IBM WebSphere tools combines these two in an elegant and natural manner, and makes best use of what these technologies have to offer. It's not everyday that you get a clear and lucid explanation of best practices, new ideas and wealth of information all wrapped up into a single book. In a fast paced world where on demand business decisions are being made in Internet time, Excel Best Practice for Business is a "must-read" for today's busy professionals working with quantitative information."

Tom Inman
Vice President, WebSphere Foundation & Tools
IBM Software Group
URL: www.ibm.com/websphere

Excel Best Practices for Business

Excel Best Practices for Business

Loren Abdulezer

WILEY

Wiley Publishing, Inc.

Excel Best Practices for Business

Published by
Wiley Publishing, Inc.
10475 Crosspoint Boulevard
Indianapolis, IN 46256
www.wiley.com

Copyright © 2004 by Wiley Publishing, Inc., Indianapolis, Indiana

Published simultaneously in Canada

Library of Congress Control Number: 2003105683

ISBN: 0-7645-4120-X

Manufactured in the United States of America

10 9 8 7 6 5 4 3 2 1

1B/SZ/RQ/QT/IN

About the Author

Loren Abdulezer (Brooklyn, NY) President of Evolving Technologies Corporation, is an experienced IT professional who has worked with several Fortune 500 companies, such as JP Morgan Chase, IBM, Procter & Gamble Pharmaceuticals, and Pfizer. Over a five-year period at JP Morgan Chase, he has consulted on MIS/Web reporting, Java and object-oriented programming, Internet security, and business continuity planning. He has played an integral, hands-on role in the implementation and deployment teams for a variety of strategic technologies for the bank including the first wireless Internet application and a Public Key Infrastructure/Smart Card initiative.

Credits

ACQUISITIONS EDITOR
Greg Croy

PROJECT EDITOR
Susan Christophersen

TECHNICAL EDITOR
William Good

COPY EDITOR
Susan Christophersen

EDITORIAL MANAGER
Carol Sheehan

**VICE PRESIDENT AND
EXECUTIVE GROUP PUBLISHER**
Richard Swadley

VICE PRESIDENT AND PUBLISHER
Andy Cummings

EDITORIAL DIRECTOR
Mary Corder

PROJECT COORDINATOR
Kristie Rees

**GRAPHICS AND PRODUCTION
SPECIALISTS**
Beth Brooks
Carrie Foster
Joyce Haughey
LeAndra Hosier
Michael Kruzil
Kristin McMullan
Barry Offringa
Lynsey Osborn
Heather Pope

QUALITY CONTROL TECHNICIANS
Laura Albert
Carl William Pierce
Dwight Ramsey
Brian Walls

PERMISSIONS EDITOR
Carmen Krikorian

MEDIA DEVELOPMENT SPECIALIST
Greg Stafford

PROOFREADING AND INDEXING
TECHBOOKS Production Services

To my wife, Susan, for being my inspiration, best friend, and partner in life.

Preface

There's a very large community of business professionals who regularly work with spreadsheets. They are not spreadsheet experts and don't claim to be. They don't have enough time; they're too busy meeting deadlines. The budget implications take precedence over the details of preparing a well-designed budget spreadsheet.

However, this "business before technology" attitude comes at a price. All too often, business professionals are caught short of time and find themselves designing spreadsheets inefficiently. Many business people have told me that they know they are not preparing spreadsheets as well as they could and should be doing. They work hard (perhaps too hard) to meet deadlines. The process feels like, and often is, an exercise in "electronic pencil pushing." Once done, they move on to the next task at hand and promptly forget their work until exactly one month rolls by. Then they repeat the whole process, inefficiently resorting to "one-offs."

This state of affairs would not be so bad were it not for the fact that the current business and economic climate demands greater efficiency. Furthermore, business decisions must now be performed according to "Internet time." Crucial decision-making in a shortened time frame, coupled with the critical consequences of those decisions, increases risk exposure to businesses and thereby the likelihood of fallout for individual business managers. No one can afford to be wrong in today's warp-speed and closely watched business environment.

How do we meet these challenges? Corporate practices relating to spreadsheets often amount to leaving people to their own devices to work their way through the task, picking up what they can from books and colleagues, repeating what worked the last time, and if necessary, force parts of their spreadsheet to work in order to complete their spreadsheet.

My starting point for addressing spreadsheet practices and features consists of what you need to be able to do in the day-to-day business setting. In the process of explaining techniques and practices, I introduce spreadsheet features where they are needed and have a clear purpose. I point out the "gotchas" and stubbornly refuse to sweep details under the rug. Providing techniques and guidance for real business situations is what this book is all about.

Because this is a book about techniques, you'll find plenty of "Take-Aways" on the accompanying CD that you can immediately put to use. The examples illustrated throughout *Excel Best Practices for Business* all incorporate Excel 2003. Fortunately, best practices are largely independent of which version of Excel you happen to be using. You need to be aware that Excel 2003 introduces many new XML-related features not found in the earlier versions of Excel. These XML- and Web-related features play an important role in Chapter 12, "Spreadsheet Portals, XML, and Web Services." To gain full benefit of these capabilities, you need to work with Excel 2003.

From a stylistic standpoint, I favor providing industrial-strength spreadsheet examples and try to present concepts from a mature business perspective. I want you to be able to pinpoint where and when specific techniques and practices come into play. An added benefit of these full-featured spreadsheets is that they are rich in "mini-techniques" that often are unrelated to the main theme or purpose of the spreadsheet. My hope is that you can harvest these components and use them within your spreadsheets. Finally, these full-featured spreadsheets can be turned into production-quality spreadsheets. Whenever possible, I outline features that you may want to incorporate to ready them for a production environment.

Now, you'd better hold on to your hat, because Excel is getting a second wind. Fanning the sails is XML. Microsoft has decided to embrace XML and integrate it heavily with Excel 2003 and Office 2003. This is a smart move on Microsoft's part. In the coming years, XML *will be* the ubiquitous medium for virtually all electronic data exchange for business. This development will catapult Excel to center stage, and *Excel Best Practices for Business* readies you for this by introducing the topic of Spreadsheet Portals, among other things.

Also important is the need to make the contents of spreadsheets accessible to individuals with disabilities. For federal agencies, making electronic information accessible has been mandated by law under Section 508 of the Rehabilitation Act. To address this need, a significant amount of the text (Chapter 13) is devoted to the topic of Assistive Portals, which provide an elegant means to grapple with the serious challenges faced by users and preparers of accessible-friendly spreadsheets. To serve as a hands-on example, the basics of setting up screen reader software are included, along with simple, practical methods for making spreadsheets accessible.

Almost every chapter compiles information that you may not easily find elsewhere. I have prepared much of this information in a form intended for easy reading and reference. Also, you'll find a cross-reference listing (Appendix C) of many of the specific best-practice techniques that the book highlights.

Chapter 8, "Analyzing Data," is a good deal more mathematical than the rest of the book. A second track that is largely non-mathematical in nature is also provided, allowing you to obtain beneficial information and useful tools for data analysis. The technical rigor in selected portions of the chapter is needed to place the validity of certain topics on firm ground. In particular, the section on the quantification of uncertainty involves a methodology borrowed from mathematics and physics called "Addition in Quadrature." This method is applied to financial analysis and is fully integrated with spreadsheets. Financial analysts, MBAs, and actuaries will need the mathematical rules that formally spell out this body of knowledge. For this reason, I felt it necessary to include these topics, even though some of you will find it reaching beyond your needs or interests.

Throughout this book, you may encounter unfamiliar topics. My goal has been to provide enough initial knowledge to bring you to the doorstep of a discipline that you may then feel encouraged to explore on your own.

I purposely pose questions and prod you to look at things from a new perspective and think outside the box. I am confident that as you make your way through the techniques presented here, you will select the styles, methodologies, and practices that work best for you.

Loren Abdulezer
September 2003

Acknowledgments

Fashioning a roughly written manuscript into a polished document ready for prime time is no small undertaking. It takes more than technical skills and a mechanized process to produce a quality book. I am impressed with the clarity of thought and insight to the big picture that the Editorial team at Wiley brought to the table. I am also impressed with the care and dedication they bring to each and every published title. If I didn't know that Wiley is one of the major publishers in the industry, I could easily be convinced that my book is the only one they're publishing. Major kudos to Greg Croy and Susan Christophersen for having done an outstanding job. I feel fortunate to have gotten Bill Good to serve as Technical Editor/Reviewer. Jason Marcuson helped me to crystallize some essential topics. I also want to thank Andy Cummings and Bob Ipsen. It has been a marvelous experience working with the Wiley team.

I owe special gratitude to my wife, Susan, for immediately seeing before anybody else the value of this rather substantial undertaking, and for her constant encouragement and support in every way possible. This book would not be a reality without her involvement.

All the people listed here in some way or another, large or small, have contributed in a substantive way to *Excel Best Practices for Business*. In all cases, however, each of you pushed me to expand my horizons and further address topics particularly germane to this book. Thank you Barry Wexler, Bill Good, Crista Earl, David Wong, Don Shea, Howard Dammond, Iris Torres, Jamie McCarron, Jason Molesworth, Jim Meyer, Jim Parker, Jim Rees, Jim Shields, Joe Marino, John Picard, Joseph Rubenfeld, Karen Gorman, Karen Luxton-Gourgey, Kevin Gordon, Larry Gardner, Larry Litowitz, Lenny Vayner, Leslie Wollen, Luis Guerrero, Lynette Tatum, Madalaine Pugliese, Marilyn Silver, Mary Ellen Oliverio, Michael Tobin, Mike Ciulla, Mike Mazza, Mike Wu, Nancy and Bob Stern, Neila Green, Noah Ravitz, Peggy Groce, Ralph Chonchol, Russ Logar, Stanley Sandler, Vis Hariharan, Vita Zavoli, Yatin Thakore, and in memoriam, Harry Picard.

Special thanks go to the American Foundation for the Blind, the Computer Center for Visually Impaired People at Baruch College, and the NYC Department of Education/Educational Vision Services, for their assistance and feedback on the chapter on Assistive Technologies. I also want to thank the team at Freedom Scientific and in particular Eric Damery and Bill Kilroy for their technical assistance.

Contents at a Glance

Contents

Introduction

How to Use This Book

Although the cover lists this book as being intended is for intermediate to advanced users of Excel, rest assured that even if you consider yourself a beginner, the book can serve as a wonderful learning tool for you as well. You will probably want to have some additional source of information at your disposal, however. Because this book focuses on spreadsheet construction and best practices within the business setting, there are bound to be gaps on basic spreadsheet concepts that a more seasoned Excel user could fill in without resorting to supplementary material.

Regardless of your level of Excel expertise, use this book to get you on the road to practicing techniques that will regularly prove useful. Packed within it is valuable information that is otherwise hard to gather in one place. Just make sure you have additional sources of information. There are plenty of books, including *Excel 2003 Bible* by John Walkenbach, Wiley Publications. You'll also find many "Take-Aways" and spreadsheet examples included in the book and on the CD-ROM. So, even if you are not a seasoned Excel user, you can make good use of the material provided.

For those of you who are in the intermediate to advanced range, you should take what you already know and find ways to extend or improve it. To that end, I've taken a three-pronged approach by providing the following:

- ◆ Tidbits, facts, and techniques that are helpful in promoting best practices.

- ◆ Ways to approach things differently from what might be conventional wisdom or common practices.

- ◆ New material that has not generally appeared in published form. Starting with Excel 2003, a whole host of new features have become available, resulting in potential new uses of spreadsheet technology. You will see some of these in action when you come across Part III of this book.

This book can be profitably read with and without a computer at hand. At some point, I assume you are going to be working out examples on your computer.

It would be ideal if you could read the book from cover to cover. Of course, I know this is not going to happen. I have tried to prepare the book so you could get the most out of it regardless of how many chapters you read. In my mind, this means there's got to be something useful in every chapter. It also means that if you go to one of the later chapters, you should not feel suddenly stranded. I like to think I provided enough road signs and a clear enough map. To help you along I've included in Appendix C a list of techniques covered in *Excel Best Practices for Business* and where they can be found in the book.

Though you are free to lunge into any chapter or topic the moment you take the book home, I would suggest that you thoroughly read Chapter 1 and Appendix A first. The examples throughout the book use the settings and conventions described in the setup and foundation material.

I encourage you to innovate and develop your own practices and techniques.

What You Need to Use This Book

Excel 2003 and, for that matter, Office 2003, for the first time introduces a comprehensive suite of features related to XML not found in the earlier versions of Excel. To make use of XML, the Web-savvy capabilities, or Spreadsheet Portals, you absolutely will need Excel 2003 and not an earlier version. Most of the online examples detailed in Chapter 12 will not work with earlier versions of Excel.

Beyond these restrictions, essentially all other book examples will work perfectly well with Excel 2002 (or Office XP). Thankfully, most of the practices and techniques described in this book are not dependent on the specific version of Excel used. As you progress to earlier versions of Excel, increasingly fewer of the examples will work as presented. Table A-1 in Appendix A summarizes what general features work with various versions.

What This Book Covers

Let me state flat out: This book is about spreadsheet techniques and best practices in business. It is not meant to be an encyclopedic reference on Excel.

Concerning XML

In many regards, Excel 2003 is like its predecessors. In one regard there stands a clear exception. Substantial XML support is entirely new to Excel 2003 and is tightly integrated with the product. This new XML capability has generated a lot of excitement and is a principal focus of Chapter 12 (Spreadsheet Portals, XML, and Web Services).

Thankfully, there's very little formal knowledge of XML that you need to know in order to profitably use the XML features of Excel 2003. While such knowledge of XML is "nice to have", it is definitely NOT a "must have" prerequisite. If you are familiar with HTML and can understand that XML is similar, except that XML allows you to define your own vocabulary rather than restricting yourself to a lexicon of hardwired tags, then you'll have enough of an understanding to put XML to use in Excel 2003.

Concerning macros

It is not until Chapters 12 and 13 that Excel macros play any significant role. Other than these last two chapters, there is no need to acquire knowledge of macros. In presenting macros in Chapter 12, I introduce what you need to know about macros as if you are learning it for the first time. Should you feel you need more extensive information on macros and VBA, go to John Walkenbach's *Excel 2003 Power Programming with VBA* (Wiley Publishing, Inc.).

You should be aware that if you have your Excel security settings set to High, you will not be able to run the macros. Setting the security level to Medium will allow you to run macros but prompt you with a dialog box to ask your permission to use them for the duration of your session. This is the setting that I recommend that you use for the book.

Conventions Used in this Book

Listed below are the various conventions used in the book.

Spreadsheet functions and cells

The built-in Excel worksheet functions (such as SUM or RAND), as well as standard Excel Add-In functions (such as RANDBETWEEN), all appear in UPPERCASE format. User-defined names assigned to cell ranges appear in a mixed case (for example, SomeValueDefinedForACell).

Using keystroke sequences and menu command sequences

Isolated keystrokes are identified by the name as it appears on the keyboard: Alt, Ctrl, and so on. Keystroke combinations are signified by a plus sign, as in Ctrl+Alt+Del (the DOS reboot sequence).

Menu command sequences, such as clicking File to open that menu and then clicking Save to save a document, are signified as follows: File → Save.

Macintosh users should consult Appendix B to better map actual experiences with the book description.

Using the R1C1 convention

This book reintroduces the use of the R1C1 style for representing Excel formulas. Excel spreadsheets and their formulas can be rendered using either the A1 Style or R1C1 Style. Although you may be used to using the A1 Style, you will find some compelling reasons, discussed in Chapter 1, for adopting the R1C1 Style. To give you the benefit of easily switching back and forth, I have provided on the CD-ROM a SwitchTool that will allow you to go back and forth between notation styles at the click of a button. Additionally, where appropriate, named ranges and references are used instead of cell coordinates, thus rendering the A1-vs.-R1C1 debate essentially moot.

Icons Used in the Book

Following are descriptions of some visual cues used throughout this book to draw your attention to specific issues.

Practical techniques to get in the habit of using regularly to promote effective and efficient spreadsheet preparation and maintenance.

Ideas or issues that require some special awareness or workaround.

When you see this icon, read carefully. Some actions you might be about to take could be disastrous. Some things you may not know could hurt you. In cases such as these, ignorance is definitely not bliss.

Occasionally you'll see a reminder in this fashion to make use of tools or examples that you'll find on the CD-ROM accompanying this book.

How This Book Is Organized

This book is organized in three parts. Part One, "Best Practice Essentials," discusses the process of managing the Excel environment. The basic Excel worksheet functions, along with explanations of their intended purpose and typical usage, are explained, and basic spreadsheet construction practices for both simple and complex spreadsheets are introduced.

Part Two, "Spreadsheet Ergonomics," builds upon the background material introduced in the first few chapters, with emphasis on best practice techniques. This portion of the book arms the reader with potent techniques and methodologies for doing anything and everything that has to do with their spreadsheet data.

The chapters in Part Three are all single topic chapters and can be read in any order. The focus within these chapters is all on technique. They put to use and extend all the material presented in Parts One and Two.

The last part of the book contains the appendixes. Appendix A presents information concerning the suitability of various versions of Excel you might be using, along with some setup guides. Of particular importance is the use of `monospace` fonts. You'll also find information and tools concerning the notation style of referencing cells using row and column numbers (Chapter 1 describes this as well). Appendix B contains information relevant to Excel users working with the Macintosh platform.

Part I

Best Practice Essentials

Chapter 1

A Foundation for Developing Best Practices

IN THIS CHAPTER

- ◆ Understanding alternative ways to represent cells (R1C1 notation style compared to the traditional A1 style)

- ◆ Alternative approaches to computing numbers

- ◆ Getting a firm grounding on absolute, relative and hybrid cell references and when to use each

- ◆ Specifying cell ranges and incorporating those within functions such as SUM

- ◆ Understanding rapid and efficient navigation techniques in large spreadsheets

- ◆ Defining user names (in rapid fire succession)

THIS CHAPTER IS INTENDED TO ARM you with the foundation for best practices including basic components and spreadsheet functions you need to know. The chapter begins with a discussion of important concepts and spreadsheet functions that you will be working with regularly and presents the best way to use these. Included are the gotchas, the tips, cautionary tales, and revelations that uncover new avenues for developing your spreadsheets.

Some important and useful Excel functions are introduced, but focus is on their usage rather than giving a formal treatment.

Preliminaries

This is a book about best practices. In my mind, the notion of *best practices* conjures up an image of working smartly and efficiently when using spreadsheets. To be sure, there is no shortage of "esoterica" or sophistication in this book, but there is plenty of time for that later. Sophisticated techniques that are effective and useful are not generally built upon more esoteric concepts. Rather, they take hold most easily when built on solid foundations.

3

Moreover, a surprising amount of sophistication comes from simple and basic stuff. This will become evident as you explore the later chapters. If you're curious, thumb ahead and glance at the Chapter 7, "Creating and Using Smart Data," to see what I mean. You'll better appreciate the things you can do, though, if you give me a chance to mold the way you think about spreadsheets and their use. I therefore focus on simple and basic spreadsheet concepts in the early chapters.

Many, if not all of the topics covered in the opening portions of this book may already be well known to you. My purpose for presenting these "foundation" topics is to get you to characterize and think about things a certain way. So, if you're already familiar with the topics, this should be an easy and quick read.

Indulge me. Read through the early chapters even if you know spreadsheets backwards and forwards. Getting into the deeper and more involved discussions, later in the book, will occur more naturally if you do. I'm also willing to bet you'll acquire a thing or two in the early chapters that you'll be happy to carry in your hip pocket.

Enough of the pep talk. Let's get on with Excel best practices.

Working with Different Ways To Compute a Number in Excel

Often, what people are taught about spreadsheets is the lowest common denominator, just enough to squeak by. These skills can be readily acquired through corporate and continuing education courses. Most people who regularly work with spreadsheets tend to adopt, learn and share common practices—which are not always synonymous with best practices. My goal in writing this book is to get you to elevate the bar, to go beyond the common denominator so that your ability to manipulate spreadsheets is on par with your natural abilities. Spreadsheets are intimidating, so many of us are afraid to go beyond what others have taught us. I would like to reconnect your good business instincts with your ability to handle spreadsheets, and I have no doubt that you'll be able to achieve and exceed your expectations.

This chapter introduces you to the various ways you can put to use in your formulas absolute, relative and hybrid expressions. You will also be shown the practical benefits of using one approach over another.

Also, you will find out that the built-in Excel functions are not only about performing arithmetic and mathematical calculations. You will see that Excel introduces specific functions of a spatial nature. Other Excel functions have a temporal nature to them. As I go through this list, it should not surprise you that some Excel functions perform computations specifying precision and fuzziness (and this has nothing to do with "Fuzzy Math"). Did you think I was going to end there? Would it interest you to know that there are Excel functions that can edit text? I'm not talking about functionality, as in features of the Excel product; I am specifically talking about Excel functions that utilize these features in their computations.

The point is, more computational facilities are at your disposal than just straight-forward arithmetic. You should be thinking about Excel functions in this purposeful and tantalizing manner, rather than as a boring laundry list of computing functions.

Understanding Alternative Ways to Represent Cells

Spreadsheets organize information into rows and columns like the one contained on your CD-ROM (open the sample spreadsheet, ch01-01.xls).

The intersection of a row and column is referred to as a spreadsheet *cell*. In Figure 1-1, a cell has been selected on row 13 and column 2. A shorthand notation for designating this cell position is R13C2. Excel understands this notation, so you can use it directly in your formulas. Excel also understands a different way of expressing formulas, which involves having columns that use letters instead of numbers. This section explains that approach and discusses the implications and benefits of both types of notation.

Excel provides two basic ways to display formulas appearing in spreadsheet cells. One of them is referred to as an "A1" style and the other as "R1C1." In much the same way as a fashion statement, these styles affect only the outer appearance of a spreadsheet. The underlying content remains unaffected no matter how often you switch back and forth between the two modes (yes, you can switch back and forth). What follows is information about these two approaches, what they offer, and how they differ.

 Appendix A discusses Excel Options settings that you can adjust, including telling Excel whether you want your fashion garb to be R1C1 or A1. Actually, the CD-ROM with this book contains a spreadsheet tool that will make switching back and forth as often as you like very easy.

The traditional approach: The A1 style

Most people are already familiar with the A1 style of representing spreadsheet cells. In this scheme, columns appear as letters and rows as numbers. Out of the box, Excel is loaded with the default setting switched to A1.

There are some consequences associated with using columns as letters and rows as numbers. When referring to a relative reference (say, two columns over to the right and two rows down), you must specify fixed absolute position in space (the actual column letter and row number). If you copy a cell and paste it to other locations on the spreadsheet, the formula, as it is written, changes. The exact formula is dependent upon the cell you paste to. You're giving yourself the burden of translating column letters and row numbers in your head.

	1	2	3	4	5	6
1	[FILL-IN YOUR NAME] COMPANY					
2	Web Page Statistics					
3	For the prior 7 days					
4						
5		Page Views	Visits			
6	Day 1	55223	17641			
7	Day 2	40694	14156			
8	Day 3	24946	8281			
9	Day 4	52701	16631			
10	Day 5	59495	18902			
11	Day 6	57235	18174			
12	Day 7	55416	18546			
13						
14						
15						

Figure 1-1: A sample spreadsheet

Suppose you see two formulas. The one in cell DC91 is

=CR98+CX66

There's another cell, EG62, which contains the formula:

=DV69+EA36

Now for the pop quiz. Giving these just a quick visual inspection, do you see them as equivalent formulas (that is, could you have done a simple copy-and-paste to get the second formula from the first)? I am willing to bet that most spreadsheet users wouldn't want to be caught thinking about such a question.

If you do give it a little thought, you will see that in the first formula, CR98 is 7 rows below DC91 as well as 11 columns to the left of DC91. In the second expression of the formula, CX66 is 25 rows above DC91 and also 5 columns to the left of it.

In the second formula, DV69 is 7 rows below EG22, as well as 11 columns to the left of EG62. So, the first expression lines up. The second expression, EA36, is 26 rows above EG62 as well as 6 columns to the left of EG62.

Whew! That was a bit of mind twisting. Not only did I have to think about this twice, I had the editors breaking their heads when proofing the cell references by hand.

Oh, after all that, you do know whether the formulas were equivalent, don't you?

If you instead used row and column number referencing (that is, the R1C1 style in the Excel Options), you find would it immediately evident that these formulas are not the same. In terms of row and column references, you would see that the first formula is

=R[7]C[-11]+R[-25]C[-5]

and the second formula is

=R[7]C[-11]+R[-26]C[-6]

Although the first expression (R[7]C[-11]) matches perfectly, the second expression doesn't. Just looking at the formulas is all you need to do. There is no mental translation.

In this example, using the R1C1 style, it was easy to see that the second expression in the formulas doesn't line up in terms of the number of row offsets or column offsets.

Does the R1C1 approach scale well?

What if the formulas were more complex, having more than two expressions as well as incorporating mathematical functions going well beyond the simple arithmetic of addition and subtraction? The answer is that you would still be fine using the R1C1 style of cell referencing.

Understanding how these two approaches differ

So, why is the alphabetic notation for columns potentially unwieldy when compared to the numeric referencing of columns? There are several reasons:

◆ Imagine giving someone driving directions using east/west directions in miles and north/south directions in kilometers. Do you think it's a good way to give directions? Why use numbers for rows and letters for columns? Complicate this by the fact that rows are labeled in Base 10 notation and columns in Base 26 (twenty-six letters in the alphabet). This situation forces you to use two different numbering or labeling systems.

◆ Try taking any of your typical spreadsheets and swapping the rows for columns and columns for rows. Compare the formulas between the two spreadsheets. It may not be immediately evident which formulas correspond to which. If Excel didn't provide a "Transpose" capability when copying and pasting cells, you could quickly get lost in comparing and rewriting formulas.

◆ In the A1 style of cell referencing, relative references in formulas must specify the *actual* position of a cell relative to the current cell being computed. Does that sound convoluted enough? Other than the fact that you're just used to it; why would you want to use an absolute cell position for a relative reference? Doing so only introduces an artificial artifact.

Take it one step further. When you copy and paste a cell involving relative references, each new formula, although similar in structure, is dependent upon the location it is copied to whenever relative cell references are involved in the formula. Wouldn't it seem preferable and logical to have the replicated formulas remain the same as the original formula they were copied from?

What do you give up by using the Row and Column notation?

Making the switch to using row and column numbers does come with a price, albeit a small one. For example, the R1C1 style forces you to put an *R* in front of the row number and a *C* in front of the column number. There are some other mental adjustments I want you to think about:

- In the "matrix style" of rows and columns, cells are written with the row followed by the column. The A1 style, by comparison, displays the column first as a letter. If you're already used to the A1 style, there a definite readjustment in thinking "row, column" rather than "column letter, row."

- There is another adjustment, though I wouldn't call it giving up something, but rather an even trade. Absolute references in the A1 style are designated by a $ symbol — for example, $B$23. In R1C1 parlance, this refers to row 23, column 2, hence R23C2. As the example shows, in the R1C1 style you drop the $ notation, because you don't need it for absolute references. When a relative reference is involved, you place brackets around an "offset" number. As an example, if you want to specify the cell to your immediate right, you use RC[1]. It doesn't matter which cell you are in. If you copy and paste cells that use RC[1], the expression RC[1] remains unaltered in the pasted cell regardless of where you paste it.

    This way of referencing forces you to start thinking about the position of spreadsheet cells visually. For example, think of R[3]C[1] as one cell over to the right, three cells below.

- Excel allows you to compute the sum of a whole row or column. Using the A1 style, if you want to take the sum of all cells in row 5, you write SUM($5:$5) in absolute coordinates or SUM(5:5) in relative coordinates for the cell you happen to be in. If you were to switch this to the R1C1 style, you would write SUM(R5) in absolute coordinates and SUM(R[2]) in relative coordinates if you happen to be anywhere in the third row. Understandably, the usage of the R1C1 style for representing a whole row using absolute coordinates can be confusing if you are used to the A1 notation, because R5 looks like an A1 notation. Make no mistake about it. R5 in the R1C1 style refers to all of row 5. How hard can that be to get used to?

In summary, you're not really giving up anything. You're just making some mental adjustments to think about things a little differently.

What do you gain by using the Row and Column notation style?

Here's what you gain by switching to the Row and Column notation:

◆ It buys you mental brevity. When you copy and paste formulas, the pasted formulas remain unchanged regardless of where you paste them. This eases the level of spreadsheet complexity. The one thing you don't want to have to be doing is thinking about many different versions of the same formula. You have to think about only one formula; there's no mental translation involved.

You can quickly spot altered formulas, however slight the variations may be. Just use your arrow keys on the keyboard to quickly pass over cells that should be identical. If one of them is different, the formula will not appear the same as the others.

◆ You begin to think about the relationship between cells visually. After all, one of the major appeals of using a spreadsheet is to visually spread out your numbers onto rows and columns, in much the same way as you would think about laying out cards and arranging them on a table.

◆ You think more clearly about your formulas. Imagine that you are preparing a report that summarizes projected financial data for a ten-year period. Different groups of data exist for each of the ten years. As an example, open the file ch01-02formulacompare.xls (or just look at Figure 1-2). If the categories are arranged in groups of ten columns (one column for each of ten years), your formula could appear as:

```
=L7+V7+AF7+AP7+AZ7
```

when using the A1 Style. If instead, you choose to use the R1C1 Style (if you have the spreadsheet open, try clicking the R1C1 Style button), the formula becomes:

```
=RC[10]+RC[20]+RC[30]+RC[40]+RC[50]
```

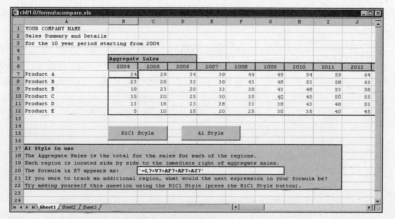

Figure 1-2: Formulas using the "A1 style"

As you can see, each successive term in the formula points to a cell 10 columns further to the right (Figure 1-3). This formula is a lot easier to understand and visualize than is the A1 style of the same formula.

This is the formula for R7C2. What about the formula for row 7, column 3? The formula is

```
=RC[10]+RC[20]+RC[30]+RC[40]+RC[50]
```

Notice any similarity? Why not check the formula in the cell immediately below R7C3? The formula is

```
=RC[10]+RC[20]+RC[30]+RC[40]+RC[50]
```

In fact, all the formulas that compute the aggregate sales for any product during any given year are identical. They are also easy to read and understand.

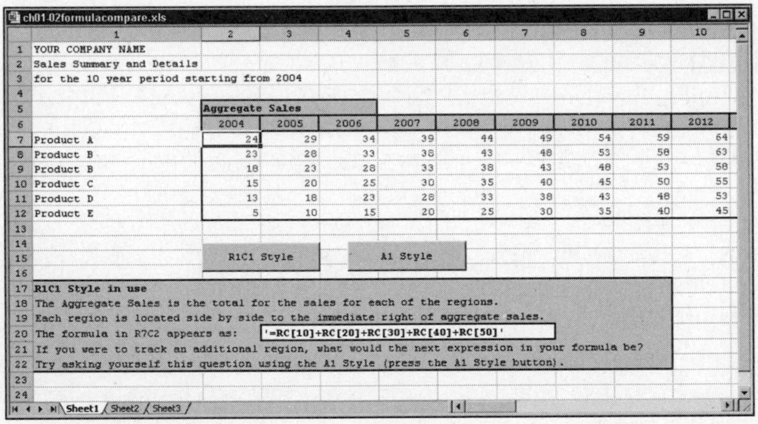

Figure 1-3: Formulas using the "R1C1 style"

Try pressing the A1 style button. Inspect the formulas in the different cells. Do the formulas appear identical? Is it clear that you're shifting over in columns of 10 with each additional expression in the formula? Would you know what to type in for the next expression (that is, what column letter to use) if you were to add yet another category?

If you never used spreadsheets before in your life, and you looked at this example, which approach do you think would make more sense and enable you to better manage increasingly complex spreadsheets? What would the kid who just graduated from college, and is not wedded to any particular style, think? If he or she would pick the R1C1 style, would that gained simplicity give that person a competitive edge?

The correct answer in any scenario is that you decide what's best for you. All I can do is lay the cards on the table and present options and ways to think about these things.

Is there any happy medium between these choices?

Yes, there is a happy medium. There is no reason for you to deny yourself the availability of both approaches. You have seen that you can switch between one mode and the other at a press of a button (see Figures 1-2 and 1-3).

 I've provided a SwitchTool spreadsheet (ch00-02switchtool.xls on the CD-ROM) for your use. You can switch back and forth at the click of a button.

You should be aware that Excel really doesn't care which way you represent cells. The underlying representation of cells has nothing to do with the way you represent and label the data. So, you can switch the mode or context from the R1C1 to A1 (and vice versa) as often as you like, and save your spreadsheet files in either mode.

Even better: Using names instead of coordinates for cell referencing

To make matters better, there is yet a cleaner and more elegant approach to complex spreadsheets that definitely promotes best practices. The approach is to define descriptive names and use the names instead of cell references directly in your formula. To see for yourself, try this: Which of the following three formulas would you prefer to use to compute current assets?

```
=B$24+B$35+B$40+B$45+B$50
=R24C-R35C+R40C+R45C+R50C
=Cash+MktbleSecurities+Receivables+Inventory+PrepaidExpenses
```

Although an extra step is required in terms of defining named ranges, the payoff is definitely there. To begin with, your formulas incorporate meaningful words rather than use cryptic cell references. The formula not only is readable to you and third parties but also is equally well understood by the computer. Getting everyone (the computer included) to be using the same referencing scheme is a definite plus.

As if this is not enough justification, you have the added benefit of getting the computer to validate that you are using properly defined expressions. If you accidentally misspell a word such as *Inventory* by spelling it, for example, *Inventorx*,

Excel will evaluate the cell to be #Name?. You'll know right away that it's wrong. This wouldn't happen if you had used a cell reference such as R39$C instead of R40$C or R39C instead of R40C.

The use of named references does not involve any context mode switching, and no Excel setting is required. It's just there for you to use.

Using named references is definitely the way to go!

Computing a Number in Excel

Spreadsheet cells have a variety of properties. In terms of plain-vanilla spreadsheet cells, one of three basic options is allowed for any spreadsheet cell:

◆ **Option 1:** The cell can be blank.

◆ **Option 2:** The cell can contain a fixed value. This fixed value can be a number, a date, or some text label. If this value is fixed, the cell has no formula. Also, the value of the cell will be visually displayed on the spreadsheet.

◆ **Option 3:** A cell can possess a formula that is used to dynamically compute a value that will be displayed in the cell. Formulas always start with an equal (=) symbol.

Arbitrarily pick any cell, say row 14, column 1. If this cell holds the formula

```
=2+3
```

it maintains an internal formula but displays the value 5. There is a fundamental distinction between fixed values (for example, 5) and equivalent formulas (such as =2+3 or =5). In a formula, Excel will try to compute formulas and then display the value rather than just simply retrieve the value. You will see that formulas can and do get more complicated.

Excel formulas can use mathematical functions. For instance, you can obtain the square root of 200 using the following formula:

```
=SQRT(200)
```

The value that Excel displays will be 14.14213562. Certainly, you can combine mathematical expressions to build more complicated formulas. As an example, you can add 10 to the square root of 200 with the following formula:

```
=SQRT(200)+10
```

The value displayed will be 24.14213562. Clearly, this is neither a very complicated nor interesting formula. Probably, some of you are thinking "I'm not interested in square roots. That's what mathematicians use. I don't have the time to get involved with stuff like that." Basically, you're right. Throughout most of this book you will hardly touch upon square roots and other similar mathematical constructs except where it's really appropriate. When you do, you'll be supplied with all the information you need.

In addition to conventional mathematical expressions, Excel formulas can incorporate values already computed in other spreadsheet cells. Here, things start to get interesting. The real goal is to get you to understand the options available to you when entering Excel formulas and the subtleties involved with cell references.

Cell references in Excel are generally not well understood. This is why people are easily stymied when it comes to understanding and using formulas in Excel. It's worth the time to really nail down this topic. It will pay off in handsome dividends.

As you build formulas, you can refer to the contents of other spreadsheet cells. You can do so by identifying which cell you want based on its *specific* row and column. This is known as an *absolute* cell reference.

You can also do so by identifying, in terms of the number of rows and columns, *how far away* the cell is. This is known as a *Relative* cell reference.

You can also make use of a *hybrid* cell reference, in which the row is fixed but the column offset is relative (or vice versa).

For an illustration of the contrast among these three types, look at Figure 1-4.

	1	2	3	4
1	Description	actual	formula used in	Comments
2		computation	computation	
3				
4	ten	10	10	plain value
5	square root of 200	14.14213562	=SQRT(200)	simple formula
6	diferent ways to compute	24.14213562	=R5C2+R4C3	Absolute rows, columns
7	ten + square root of 200	24.14213562	=R[-2]C+R[-3]C	Relative rows, columns
8		24.14213562	=R5C+R4C	Abs. rows, Rel. columns
9		24.14213562	=R[-4]C2+R[-5]C2	Rel. rows, Abs. columns
10				

Sheet1 / Sheet2 / Sheet3 /

Figure 1-4: Absolute vs. relative vs. hybrid cell reference usage in Excel formulas

Rows six through nine of column 2 show alternative ways to compute the value of ten plus the square root of 200. They all produce the identical results, but each one is computed in a slightly different manner. Column 3 displays the formulas used for column 2 so that you can see what they look like; column 4 provides some explanation.

The value of 10 is occupied in the cell R4C2. It is a plain value.

In R5C2, the square root of 200 is computed using this formula:

```
=SQRT(200)
```

The cell displays the value that results from the computation.

The number in row 6 is computed using the sum of pure absolute cell references R5C2 and R4C2:

=R5C2+R4C2

Row 7 contains a slightly different kind of formula, which employs "relative" references. The formula used is

=R[-2]C+R[-3]C

Basically, the formula in row 7 column 2 is saying: "Give me the value of the cell two rows directly above me and in the same column (this happens to be 14.14213562) and add to this the value of the cell three rows directly above me and in the same column as I am (which happens to be the value 10)."

The bracketed numbers immediately after the row reference indicates a "row offset." So, R[-1]C would refer to the neighboring cell to the immediate north. By comparison, R[1]C refers to the neighboring cell directly below or to the south. By the same token, R[2]C refers to the cell two rows directly below (to the south).

The relative reference in row 7 column 2 could explicitly state the "column offset" of zero in addition to the row offsets. This would make the formula more verbose than it needs to be. In this case, the formula would appear as

=R[-2]C[0]+R[-3]C[0]

The column offset happens to be zero, since the cells being referred to by the formulas are in the same column as the formula for R7C2. Excel is happy to drop off the bracketed zeros, because doing so will make formulas easier to read. Had the formula been referring to a cell to the immediate left (west), the column offset would be a negative number. Had the formula been referring to a cell to the immediate right (east), the column offset would be a positive number.

Thus, the way to refer to a cell directly above and to the immediate right (that is, northeast) would be referenced by R[-1]C[1]. Had there been a greater separation between the cells, the offsets of rows and columns would have had to be increased accordingly.

This way of thinking about cell references takes a little getting used to. When you get comfortable using offsets, you'll find yourself thinking about formulas visually rather than in terms of abstract formulas.

At this point you might be asking, "Can I mix relative and absolute cell references?" The answer is a resounding yes. When a formula is composed of a compound formula involving multiple references, it uses the cell value and doesn't care how the cell was referenced.

As an example, take a look at the formula in row 8.

=R5C+R4C

Here you have such a mixture. The rows are listed in absolute references (notice that the numbers 5 and 4 do not have brackets around them, so they must refer to rows 5 and 4, respectively). The columns are relative references. In relative references, you don't have to show the brackets if your offsets are zero. Had you decided to provide the column offsets using bracketed expressions, you would have:

```
=R5C[0]+R4C[0]
```

Another possible formula appears in row 9. In this case, the row references are kept relative and the columns are absolute. It takes the form:

```
=R[-4]C2+R[-5]C2
```

Most of the time, you will be working with pure relative references. There are a couple of reasons for this.

1. Excel will let you build spreadsheet formulas by "clicking" the cells you want to reference. As you click cells, Excel inserts them into the edit line of your formula as relative cell references. So unless you want to change these references, the formulas you build will tend to be based on relative references.

2. Relative cell references are mostly a good thing because they make replicating formulas to other portions of your spreadsheet easy.

When entering and editing an Excel formula, you can switch selected portions of your formula from relative to absolute to hybrid by pressing the <F4> key.

Best Practice Topic: Evolving a strategy toward Absolute vs. Relative vs. Hybrid cell references

Rather than just state a pre-established set of guidelines regarding the use of alternative types of cell references, I want to present some scenarios and have you formulate your own judgments concerning the merits of the various choices among absolute, relative and hybrid cell references.

Consider the following: You have a variety of items. For argument's sake, let's say there are ten such items and you may be purchasing these items. Although each of these has a listed cost, you are entitled to a 20% discount. The items are arranged (see Figure 1-5) in a vertical column.

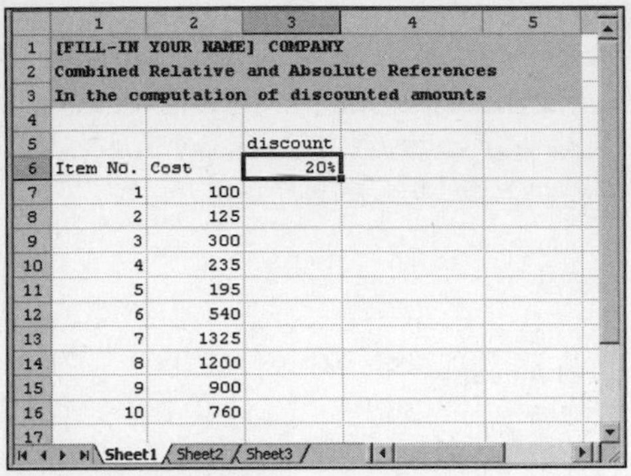

Figure 1–5: Preparing a schedule to compute
discounted amounts

A natural step in the cost analysis is to compute the discount amount for each of the ten items. In the cells to the immediate right of each of the ten items, you can write a formula in column 3 that looks like:

```
=RC[-1]*0.2
```

or

```
=RC[-1]*20%
```

or

```
RC[-1]*20/100
```

They'll all work. However, they are hard-wired to 20%. This may be correct for your discount percentage today. Next week you might need to adjust your discount percentage. That would mean that you would have to rework your formulas every time the discount changes. You don't want to have to change this by hand, for two good reasons:

1. In the first place, it is time consuming to hunt everywhere to change the 20% discount factor to something else.

2. Even if you have the time to make manual changes, chances are that as the complexity and size of your spreadsheet increases, the likelihood of missing a number you need to change, or making a mistake when hand editing, increases.

So a better way to approach this is to reference the item cost using a relative reference, and reference the discount rate using an absolute cell reference. The discount rate could be parked into a place like R6C3 (see Figure 1-6).

Where possible, try to use global references. Single global numbers in isolated cells are easily identified and maintained. It will serve your purpose even better if you assign a name to use in place of cell coordinates.

Then you could use a formula like:

Formula 1-1: First Attempt at Computing Discounted Amounts

```
=RC[-1]*R6C3
```

	1	2	3	4	5
1	[FILL-IN YOUR NAME] COMPANY				
2	Combined Relative and Absolute References				
3	In the computation of discounted amounts				
4					
5			discount		
6	Item No.	Cost	20%		
7	1	100	20	=RC[-1]*R6C3	
8	2	125	25	=RC[-1]*R6C3	
9	3	300	60	=RC[-1]*R6C3	
10	4	235	47	=RC[-1]*R6C3	
11	5	195	39	=RC[-1]*R6C3	
12	6	540	108	=RC[-1]*R6C3	
13	7	1325	265	=RC[-1]*R6C3	
14	8	1200	240	=RC[-1]*R6C3	
15	9	900	180	=RC[-1]*R6C3	
16	10	760	152	=RC[-1]*R6C3	
17					

Sheet1 / Sheet2 / Sheet3 /

Figure 1-6: Combined relative and absolute references

The formula for computing discounted amounts is more easily maintainable. The discount percentage is now:

◆ A single global number. (If you were to update/alter the number, every reference to the discount percentage would be immediately updated.)

◆ The number is visible and accessible for easy updating.

This way has a decisive advantage. When the number has changed, you know it has changed and you know what the new value is.

So far, so good. It's time to throw in a little more complexity. The likelihood is that you might need to evaluate the financial impact of more than one discount rate. You have two strategies available:

1. Compute your values using the first rate (and if necessary, print it). Compute your values again with the alternative rate. After all, the formulas are set up so that the discount rate only appears in one (globally referenced) cell. Changing it in this one location is easy. Spreadsheets are great for this purpose. You can interactively try different values and see what their impact would be. This is often referred to as a "what if?" scenario.

What I describe is a kind of manual approach to a what-if scenario. Excel sports a special-purpose facility called a Scenario Manager. To get an idea of what you can do with Scenario Manager, look at Figure 1-7.

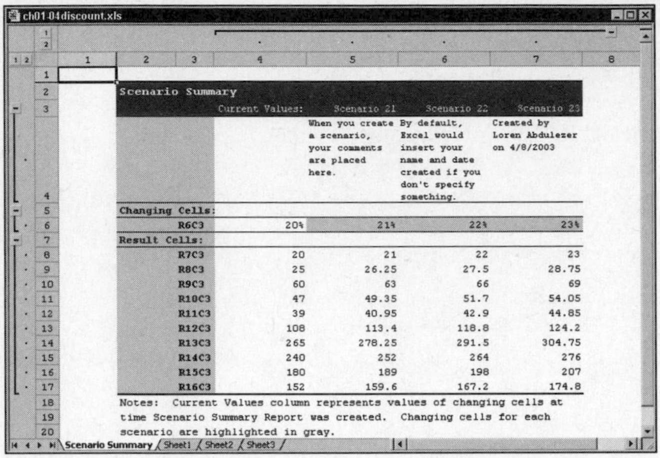
ch01-04discount.xls

Scenario Summary

	Current Values:	Scenario 21	Scenario 22	Scenario 23
		When you create a scenario, your comments are placed here.	By default, Excel would insert your name and date created if you don't specify something.	Created by Loren Abdulezer on 4/8/2003
Changing Cells:				
R6C3	20%	21%	22%	23%
Result Cells:				
R7C3	20	21	22	23
R8C3	25	26.25	27.5	28.75
R9C3	60	63	66	69
R10C3	47	49.35	51.7	54.05
R11C3	39	40.95	42.9	44.85
R12C3	108	113.4	118.8	124.2
R13C3	265	278.25	291.5	304.75
R14C3	240	252	264	276
R15C3	180	189	198	207
R16C3	152	159.6	167.2	174.8

Notes: Current Values column represents values of changing cells at time Scenario Summary Report was created. Changing cells for each scenario are highlighted in gray.

Scenario Summary / Sheet1 / Sheet2 / Sheet3

Figure 1-7: Scenario Summary produced by the Excel Scenario Manager

There are too many caveats on the usage of this facility. My chief goal right now is to keep you focused on the use of absolute, relative, and hybrid cell references in Excel formulas.

2., The Scenario Summary, shown in Figure 1-7, is actually food for thought. Instead of trying to experiment with different values for the discount percentage one at a time (which is what you would do when you generate each scenario anyway), think about how you would write the formulas to compute discount amounts for multiple discount rates placed side by side.

To make this accommodation for the second strategy, you need to make some alterations to Formula 1-1. Think of doing a side-by-side comparison of discounted amounts based on differing percentages. The one that already incorporates the 20% baseline is a series of numbers running down column 3 from rows 7 through 16. Imagine placing an alternate discount percentage on row 6 column 4 and having the computed numbers running down column 4 from rows 7 through 16.

These sets of computations share two features:

1. The discounted amount resides on the same row as the item to be discounted. Specifically, the item to be discounted resides in column 2. You'll want to think of the item to be discount in terms of its absolute column reference.

2. The discounted amount resides on the same column as the discount percentage. Specifically, the discount percentage in this layout (see Figure 1-8) is always placed on row 6; this is an absolute.

The resulting formula to compute the discounted amount should be

Formula 1-2: Hybrid Formula

```
=RC2*R6C
```

Figure 1-8 shows how the spreadsheet with the revised formulas should appear. Note that the formulas (appearing in column 4) used for computing the discounted amount based on the alternate discount percentage are completely identical to the formulas (appearing in column 3) based on the original discount percentage. Additionally, if you want to do a side-by-side comparison with three or more discount rates, you need only to keep putting your discount rates side by side across row 6. Then replicate your formula (=RC2*R6C) across all your discounted amounts.

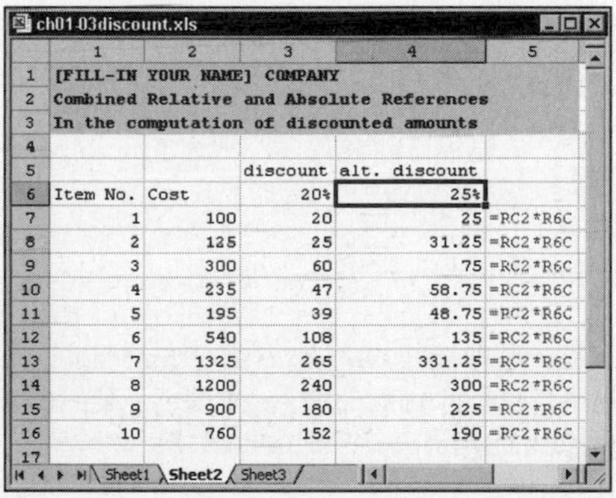
ch01-03discount.xls

	1	2	3	4	5
1	[FILL-IN YOUR NAME] COMPANY				
2	Combined Relative and Absolute References				
3	In the computation of discounted amounts				
4					
5			discount	alt. discount	
6	Item No.	Cost	20%	25%	
7	1	100	20	25	=RC2*R6C
8	2	125	25	31.25	=RC2*R6C
9	3	300	60	75	=RC2*R6C
10	4	235	47	58.75	=RC2*R6C
11	5	195	39	48.75	=RC2*R6C
12	6	540	108	135	=RC2*R6C
13	7	1325	265	331.25	=RC2*R6C
14	8	1200	240	300	=RC2*R6C
15	9	900	180	225	=RC2*R6C
16	10	760	152	190	=RC2*R6C
17					

Sheet1 Sheet2 Sheet3

Figure 1-8: Correct use of replicating hybrid formulas

Clearly, if the spreadsheet you build is arranged differently than the one in this chapter, the formulas will be different. However, the logic remains identical.

More useful information about working with formulas

Shortly I discuss the functions SUM, SUMPRODUCT, and others. First, I explain some details on entering formulas, changing cell references, and designating any range of cell names of your choosing so that formulas can be easier to write, read, and validate.

ENTERING FORMULAS

You may have noticed that the mathematical functions such as SQRT and cell references have been appearing in uppercase format. This is no accident. Excel likes to convert and store its worksheet functions and cell references that way. What happens if you enter them in lowercase? Go ahead and try it. Enter something like the following set of formulas, each in separate rows, one below the other:

```
=now()
=row()
=row(r[1]c)
=sqrt(18)
=power(2,3)
=rand()
=sum(r[-5]c:r[-1]c)
=max(r[-6]c:r[-2]c)
=average(r[-7]c:r[-3]c)
=average(10,20,30,70,80,90)
```

After you've entered these expressions, go back and click on each of these cells to see whether these spreadsheet functions and cell references appear in uppercase format.

Okay, Excel doesn't really care how you enter formulas; it converts them to uppercase regardless. What's the big deal? You can use this to your advantage. Consider typing in the formula:

```
=average(1,2,3,4,5)+random()
```

The result you get is #NAME?. Obviously, something is wrong with this formula; otherwise you would get a computed number, not a quizzical error message. You have two functions in your formula: average and random. Which of these two is the offending function? Maybe it's both.

If you select the cell where you just entered this formula, you will see the text shown in the Excel Formula Bar in Figure 1-9.

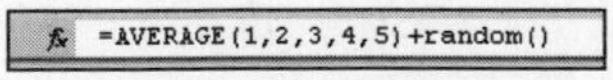

```
ƒx  =AVERAGE(1,2,3,4,5)+random()
```

Figure 1-9: The function with the error is not
automatically converted to uppercase.

Notice that Excel converted the AVERAGE function to uppercase. However, it didn't do anything with "random." This is because Excel does not have a "random" function. Had you written the function as RANDOM, Excel would have kept it that way, in which case you'd be staring at two expressions in uppercase form, not knowing which one is the offender.

Enter the Excel functions in your formula in lowercase form. If the functions are understood by Excel, they will be converted to uppercase. Those functions not understood by Excel will remain in lowercase. This practice enables you to spot naming errors in your formulas when they occur.

If you want to go ahead and fix the formula, you can edit the formula to

```
=AVERAGE(1,2,3,4,5)+rand()
```

ENTERING AND EDITING FORMULAS

Perhaps it's time to begin discussing easier ways to enter formulas. Open the sample spreadsheet, ch01-01.xls (Figure 1-10).

	1	2	3	4	5	6
1	[FILL-IN YOUR NAME] COMPANY					
2	Web Page Statistics					
3	For the prior 7 days					
4						
5		Page Views	Visits			
6	Day 1	55223	17641			
7	Day 2	40694	14156			
8	Day 3	24946	8281			
9	Day 4	52701	16631			
10	Day 5	59495	18902			
11	Day 6	57235	18174			
12	Day 7	55416	18546			
13						
14						
15						

Figure 1-10: Sample spreadsheet with Web log data

If you want, you can enter a formula into R13C2 such as the total Page Views over the seven-day interval. You could enter the following (see Figure 1-11):

 The following formula is included in your Take-Away text file takeaway.txt:
```
=r6c2+r7c2+r8c2+r9c2+r10c2+r11c2+r12c2
```

This formula produces a count of 345,710 for Page Views over the seven-day period.

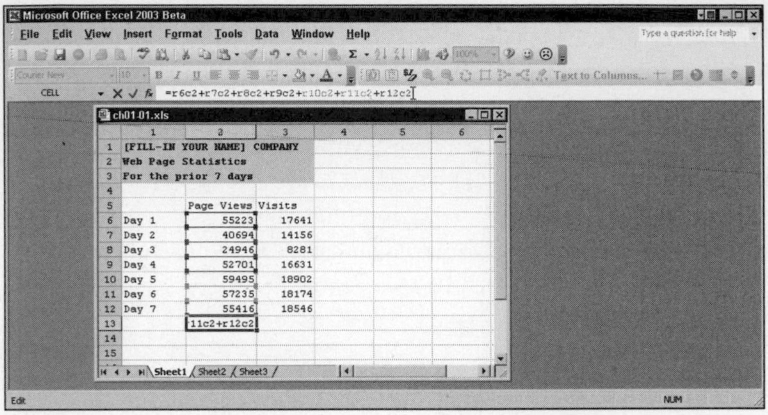

Figure 1-11: Cells in the formula line are visually highlighted.

You should notice that as you type in the formulas, the cells or ranges of cells you specified in your formula become highlighted in colored borders and the colors are matched with the cell references as you are editing or typing in the formulas. This is a useful aid for two reasons:

◆ It can give you easy visual feedback of what you've just typed in.

◆ If you have a typographic error in your formula, strange things will happen to the highlighting (Figure 1-12); or what you expect to be highlighted will not be highlighted at all.

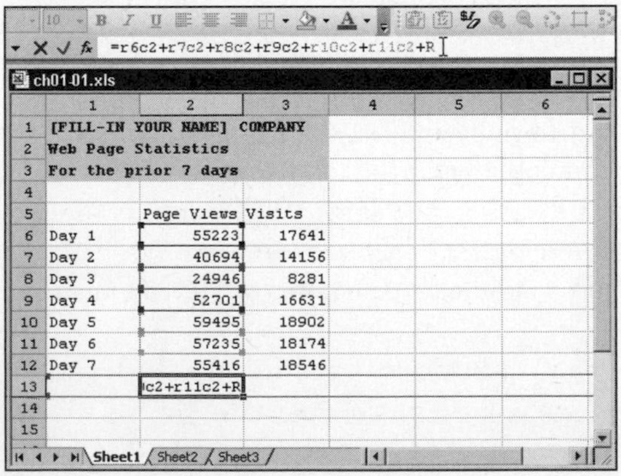

Figure 1-12: A formula entered with an error is highlighted differently.

This technique of clicking in the edit line and seeing the corresponding high-lighted cells within the worksheet will prove helpful when you prepare and analyze more complex spreadsheets.

The technique of visually highlighting cell references in a formula (as shown in Figures 1-11 and 1-12) need not be applied only to new formulas you are entering. You can also click the Excel Formula Bar for any cell. This is especially useful when you receive a spreadsheet from a third party and want to quickly inspect where it is gathering its numbers.

While you're at it, you're likely to have the occasion to write some nested formulas. As you type away in the edit line, when you enter a closing parenthesis, Excel momentarily highlights the corresponding opening one (see Figure 1-13). This feature helps you both to see what your expressions contain as well as to balance the parentheses (that is, ensure that the number of opening parentheses matches the number of closing ones).

Figure 1–13: As you enter the closing parenthesis on the right, the corresponding opening parenthesis is momentarily highlighted (in this case, between IF and RC[1]).

Unfortunately, the corresponding balanced parenthesis is highlighted for only a brief moment. Sometimes Excel formulas can contain heavily nested expressions. A technique I often use is to go to the edit line, backspace or delete one of the closing parentheses, and immediately re-enter it. This way, I can see where the opening parenthesis is located.

Excel sports another feature to aid in the editing of formulas. The logical formula structure is highlighted in a hovering text message (see Figure 1-14).

Be sure to enable the Function tooltips feature on your Excel Options... General tab. For further information, consult Appendix A.

Figure 1–14: Hovering text helps to identify formula structure.

This use of the hovering text is definitely helpful in keeping your bearings when entering formulas. It zeroes in on the selected portion of the Excel formula, freeing you from being distracted by the rest of the line.

SELECTING CELLS AND SPECIFYING CELL RANGES IN EXCEL FORMULAS

Many Excel functions are capable of performing computations on ranges of cells. Most prevalent of these is the familiar SUM worksheet function. Ranges of cells in such formulas are separated by a colon (:) symbol. Examples of this usage include:

```
=SUM(R1C1:R10C4)
=SUM($A$1:$D$10)
```

The preceding examples include equivalent formulas in both the R1C1 and A1 notation (see the section "Understanding Alternative Ways to Represent Cells," earlier in this chapter). Where possible, I present both these notations or else use named ranges, as appropriate. For cases in which the context is clear and has little or no dependency on the cell-referencing notation, I may use only one notation style.

With regard to screen shots, I use only one of these notations. The choice is based on whatever makes most sense. Quite often, the screen shot illustrates something independent of the notation.

 You have the SwitchTool spreadsheet to change modes on your spreadsheets at the press of a button. Therefore, don't worry about the format.

I discuss the Excel SUM function in other places and in different contexts throughout this book. Here, I'm just using it as a representative function that accepts multiple cell ranges for its input.

Take a look at the three examples in Listing 1-1.

Listing 1-1: The same formula shown three different ways

```
=SUM(R1C1:R10C4,R4C6:R14C6)
=SUM($A$1:$D$10,$F$4:$F$14)
=SUM(OverHeadAndAdminExpenses,OperatingExpenses)
```

As you can see, Excel functions such as SUM can accommodate multiple cell ranges, each separated by a comma. The following representative formulas (see Formulas 1-3 and 1-4) show that the SUM function can accommodate a variety of input arguments. I provide the same examples in both the R1C1 notation and A1 notation:

Formula 1–3: Example of Input Arguments for the SUM function in R1C1 Notation

```
=SUM(R21C1:R30C1)
=SUM(R[-10]C:R[-1]C)
=SUM(R21C1:R30C1,R[-10]C:R[-1]C)
=SUM(R[-10]C:R[-1]C,C[1],R4,R5,R6)
=SUM(OneUserDefinedRange,AnotherDefinedRange,StillAnotherUserDefined
Range)
=SUM(OneUserDefinedRange,R[1]C[1],3,4,5,R1C1:R10C3,3.14159)
```

Formula 1–4: Same Formulas as that in Formula 1–3, represented here in A1 Notation

```
=SUM($A$21:$A$30)
=SUM(A11:A20)
=SUM($A$21:$A$30,A12:A21)
=SUM(A13:A22,B:B,$4:$4,$5:$5,$6:$6)
=SUM(OneUserDefinedRange,AnotherDefinedRange,StillAnotherUserDefined
Range)
=SUM(OneUserDefinedRange,B25,3,4,5,$A$1:$C$10,3.14159)
```

Notice that valid cell ranges can include literal values (such as a number), user defined named ranges, cell references (whether relative, absolute or hybrid). Note that a cell range can reference a rectangular swatch; not just only a single row or column.

Keep in mind that named values in Excel need not be restricted to individual cells, but can be indicative of a range of cells for any individual name. As indicated in Listing 1-1 (appearing earlier in the chapter), OverHeadAndAdminExpenses could be defined to range over the cells A1 through D10. OperatingExpenses might correlate to F4:F14; making the third formula equivalent to the first two. There are certainly other possible combinations of valid formulas equivalent to the formulas shown in Listing 1-1. Consider:

```
=SUM(R1C1:R10C4, OperatingExpenses)
=SUM($A$1:$D$10,OperatingExpenses)
```

OVERLAPPING RANGES

What happens if the ranges separated by commas happen to overlap? Would those overlapping regions be counted more than once? While you to ponder this question, consider another one, which may help: What amount would be computed for the following?

```
=SUM(1,3,1,2)
```

The computed sum in this case doesn't involve cell positions; it just involves literal values. There is no confusion. The result is 7. Ask yourself what SUM is doing. The answer: It is separately evaluating each of the expressions separated by commas and adding up the numeric value of each of the results.

If you're summing regions that overlap, the overlapped regions can get counted more than once.

The situation is no different when cell references are brought into the picture. Look at Figure 1-15. The formula:

=SUM(B3:E12,D9:H20)

would first evaluate the sum of B3:E12 (which is 10500), and then evaluate the sum of D9:H20 (which is 10003), and then add these together to get a total of 20503. So, if the numbers are represented more than once, they will be counted more than once.

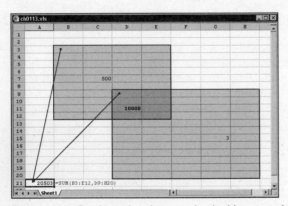

Figure 1-15: Overlapped regions can be double counted.

Keyboard and cursor navigation tips

Although the use of spreadsheets and the windowing environment is intuitive, people sometimes find it not so easy to manage large spreadsheets that may have many thousands of rows of data. There are some things you can do to facilitate moving about on a large spreadsheet and manage formulas. These are essentially trivial, but practical nonetheless.

Open the file ch01-05navigation.xls (see Figure 1-16).

The screen shot shows the beginning and end portions of data that spans 1,000 rows. When you open the file on your CD that accompanies the book, it appears without the horizontal split pane shown in the figure. The file contains data that's actually used in a later chapter (Chapter 9, "How Not to Get Stuck in the M.U.D."), where you'll be addressing some very thorny issues on data ambiguity. The data, as you can see, is a string of numbers. The numbers actually represent dates without a delimiter to separate days, months, and years. Take a look at the first two entries. If you knew the dates follow the sequence of day-month-year, you could unambiguously interpret 122952 as 12/29/1952. Likewise, you could see that 3643 would be 3/6/1943. The way you reason this out is dependent, in part, upon the length of the string of characters that make up the date string. Does this problem seem intriguing? If you want, you can jump ahead to Chapter 9 to get a sneak peak.

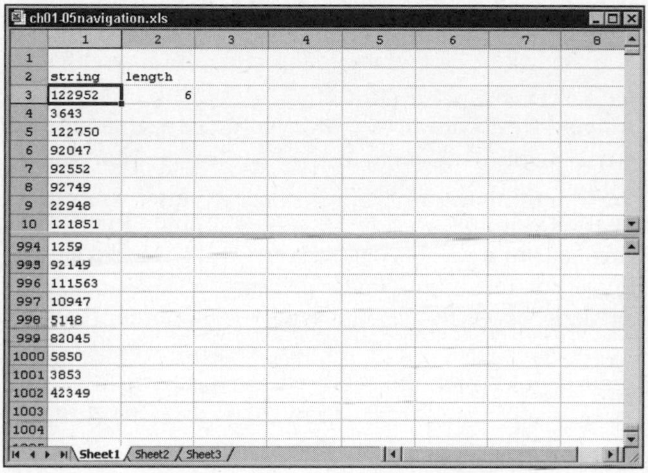

Figure 1–16: Spreadsheet with continuous stream of data for 1,000 rows

Right now, I want you to deal with the much more mundane task of quickly filling in the needed first steps, the first of which is to compute the length of each of the 1,000 strings. The focus here is in nailing down a rudimentary mechanical technique so that when you turn to large, complex, and challenging problems, you'll be slicing through the data as easily as a hot knife cuts through butter.

The worksheet function used to compute the length of a string of characters is called LEN. With the string data in the first column, the formula to compute the string length from the second column is

```
=LEN(RC[-1])
```

This is obviously a simple formula. The key is to replicate it a thousand rows down. One way of doing so is to select the cell in the second row containing your length formula and scroll all the way down until you reach the last piece of data, which happens to be on row 1002. Press Shift and click Select and Fill Down (Ctrl+D). Not particularly hard, right? But ask yourself some questions:

◆ How many mouse clicks or key presses did you need to scroll down?

◆ What if the number of lines of data were closer to fifteen thousand than one thousand?

Think of some of the shorter steps you could have done. You could grab the vertical scroll bar and pull it all the way down to get to the last row of data. The "last row" happens to be the last row of the worksheet. In any given situation, what guarantee do you have that the specific data you are working on extends all the way down to the bottom of the spreadsheet?

THE PROBLEM: TRYING TO KEEP TRACK OF YOUR DATA

The real spreadsheets that you work with, as opposed to the simplified example from this book, might be chock full of data spread over many columns. And when you scroll down to the bottom the last piece of data you're looking for, you might not find it there. You think it's very near the last row of the spreadsheet, so you press PgUp several times. To no avail; it's not there. Now you go back to manually scanning by moving the vertical scroll bar. You spot the last line of data. You've wasted 15–20 seconds searching for that last cell.

To avoid that delay the next time around, you make a mental note of what row it appears in. Say that row happens to be 3874. Chances are, if it's that far down, your spreadsheet is complex and you're working under pressure.

The last thing you want to do is to tax your memory with information that has nothing to do with the underlying spreadsheet and interpretive analysis of its data. Also, when you put down your spreadsheet and reopen it next month to add or update data, do you really think you're going to have row 3874 at the forefront of your thoughts? So there you go chasing after that row of data again, probably along with others as well.

I'm sure you've guessed that I have a simple solution in mind. I do. If it's that simple, why go through all the coy disguises? Why not flat-out state it and be done with it? The answer is that the simple solution is not the moral of the story. The tendency and common practice among many people in business is to apply a "one-off" approach to everything. Nowhere is this more true than in how people use spreadsheets in the business environment.

THE SOLUTION

Here's the simple solution: I previously said, the string of dates in column 1 was contiguous. Select the first cell containing data in column 1, press Ctrl+Down Arrow and you're instantly brought down to row 1002 (or whatever row the last contiguous piece of data happens to reside in). Now press the right arrow key once. You're now 1,000 rows directly below R2C2, which contains the length formula you want to replicate. Now press Shift+Ctrl and, keeping those keys down, also press the Up Arrow key. The addition of the Shift key in this action allows you to select all the intervening cells you just navigated. With all the intervening cells selected (the top cell of which having the formula you want to replicate), click Fill Down (or press Ctrl+D) and you're done.

A REAL-WORLD COMPLICATION ... AND WHAT TO DO ABOUT IT

Let me add a little complication. Suppose that you want to do the same and select all the cells in the range, but the string of data in column 1 is not contiguous. You might have two or three cells that are empty. Well, you could quickly "arrow over" to the last piece of data before hitting the empty cell. This could be useful to identify where the breaks are in an otherwise continuous chain of data. Suppose there are significantly more than two or three breaks? What if 10 percent of the many hundreds or thousands of lines have empty cells and for the most part are randomly placed? The technique to moving across the cells using the arrow key as presented wouldn't be very useful. So, you need to improvise. After going down a screenful or two and seeing that this method is too slow, just select the cell one column over to the right (that is, press the right arrow key once to place yourself on to column 2, which is now essentially empty). Press Ctrl+Down Arrow. This action brings you down to row 65536, the bottom of the spreadsheet. Move one column to the left. Press Ctrl+Up Arrow to move to the very last piece of data in column 1. This is where you were trying to go. Move one column over to the right. Press Ctrl+Shift+ Up Arrow and click Fill Down (or press Ctrl+D).

What advantages have you gained by this?

- ◆ You virtually eliminate any guesswork in finding, selecting, moving data for copying, pasting, moving, or otherwise manipulating large blocks of data.

- ◆ The overhead for managing large blocks of data remains constant regardless of how large your spreadsheet grows.

- ◆ By traversing the spreadsheet with lightning speed and removing the burden of thinking about cell locations and placing artificial visual markers, you are freer to focus on the important things in your spreadsheets.

The keystroke-based cell navigation technique will be useful while you are in the process of entering formulas that use cell references spanning many rows and columns. From the Excel Formula Bar, you can click in cells and navigate your spreadsheet using these keystroke techniques. As you move about, the Formula Bar will be populated with the corresponding cell ranges. They will be a definite time saver and reduce errors.

User-defined names within Excel spreadsheets

The feature of user-defined names is an important part of Excel. You likely already know how to use this feature, but I go over the bare-bone basics just in case.

There are two techniques for defining a batch of names.

USING KEYSTROKES TO DEFINE A SEQUENCE OF NAMES

Sometimes it is easier and quicker to define user names by navigating the user menu through keystroke sequences than by using the mouse. If your named ranges are single cells, you might want to try the following steps. (I am assuming that you are using the default Excel Edit Options, which involves moving your selection down after pressing Enter. Appendix A has more on setting Excel Options).

1. Group the cells to be named together, generally in a column.

2. Pre-label the cells. The labels can be to the immediate left of the cells to be defined.

3. For each cell to be defined, press the following keystroke sequence:

   Alt+i+n+ENTER+ENTER+ENTER

As you type in the keystrokes given in Step 3, the Excel menu will automatically pull down. Excel will "guess" and insert a suggested name in the edit line of the Define Name window (see Figure 1-17).

Note that in column A, a list of labels starts in row 2. These are the names you'll be giving to the cells you define. Obviously, the choice of names is up to you. As you can see in Figure 1-17, the name being defined for the cell B5 is TaxRate4, which matches the label to its immediate left. This is no accident. Excel picked up the name from the label, sparing you the drudgery of entering it. For the nine or ten names you have pre-listed, press the repetitive keystrokes in Step 3 of the preceding list and you'll quickly be done with defining user names.

 This technique of rapid name definition does not apply to named ranges spanning multiple cells for a given name.

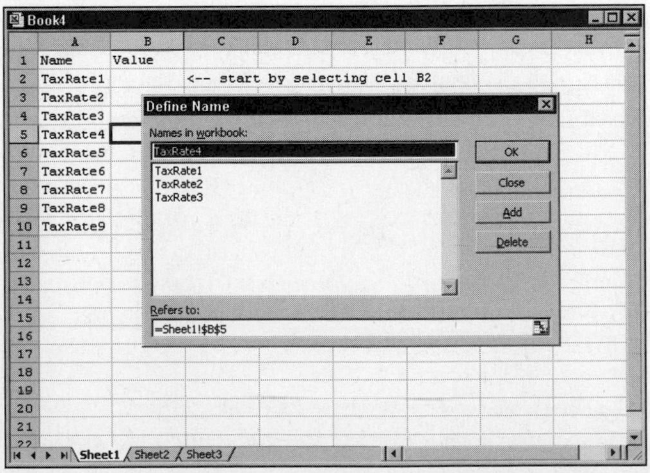

Figure 1-17: Using labels to generate user-defined names

Is there a limit to how many names you can define this way? There really isn't; however, if you'll be defining a great many names, such as hundreds, you may want to consider using an Excel Macro/VBA facility to automate this process. This lies beyond the scope of this book. Applying a visual marker to identify named cells is a good practice. You can apply cell shading, borders or even sticky notes.

USING CTRL+SHIFT+F3 TO DEFINE A BATCH OF NAMES

There's a more rapid and efficient way to define a group of names. You can select the labels and the group of cells to be given names and press Ctrl+Shift+F3. You will then be presented with a dialog box like the one shown in Figure 1-18.

This technique is much easier to perform than the one shown in the previous section, but it does not afford as much flexibility. In the previous method, as you create new names, you can pause momentarily to decide whether you want to tweak the name that Excel suggests.

Both of these methods are effective. Use whatever works for you.

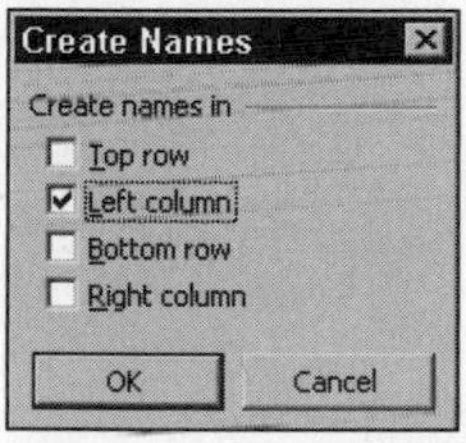

Figure 1–18: Batch creation of names

Excel Functions

Now that you're armed with a little bit about how to express formulas, I want to spend some time discussing Excel functions.

Excel has two very powerful features in it. It's got a terrifically efficient computing engine and is also a powerful tool for visually communicating numerical information. This combination makes Excel particularly potent and vital in business.

Obviously, there's a lot more to Excel than just these two facets. But without these, Excel would be just another faceless application that we would all tire of quickly.

When I speak about the computational engine, I am referring to both the raw number crunching capacity and the range of special-purpose and general functions it possesses.

Number crunching is not always about benchmarks such as how many multiplications can be performed each second. To be sure, Excel on a desktop computer is not going to outperform a supercomputer in sheer number-crunching capacity. One thing it does "excel" at, though, is its unwavering ability to take complex relationships (with multitudes of formulas, each of which can be dependent upon other computations) and combine them with large quantities of data to immediately produce correct results. This ability to alter a formula in just one or two cells and at the turn of a dime, transforming the overall flow of numbers through spreadsheets, is what sets Excel apart from so many other software packages.

Programming without programming

Excel allows business people to do *programming without programming*. Programming is done visually on the screen, using formulas as your paintbrush and the grid of cells as the canvas. Excel represents programming and software development at its best. Those of you familiar with software development suites and modern programming languages would be hard pressed to come up with conventional programming tools that's as near-universally accepted, flexible, sophisticated, and easy to use, or one that makes the sharing and communication of ideas as easy.

Meanwhile, every spreadsheet is a full-fledged program in its own right. The programming can be as simple as adding a few numbers in a column or as complex as analyzing the monthly sales and financial trends of stores in hundreds of shopping malls throughout the country collected over a five-year period and broken out by NAICS/SIC codes, demographic regions, square footage of leased properties, and so forth.

The essential point is that both extremes, the simple and complicated; are handled by the exact same software tool (Excel). You just don't find many software programs that competently handle both ends of the spectrum.

This is the mental picture I want you to use when thinking about spreadsheets.

I cover only a few Excel functions in this chapter, but introduce others in the next several chapters, in the context in which those functions are used.

Types of Excel formulas you will encounter

My purpose here is twofold: to make you aware of a variety of spreadsheet functions and categories of functions, and to present enough information on some of these functions to keep from interrupting later chapters to explain them there. If you need an encyclopedic presentation of spreadsheets, you'll need to look elsewhere, be it through the Excel Help menu or one of the many books on Excel formulas, such as Excel 2003 Formulas, by John Walkenbach (published by Wiley Publishing, Inc.). You may also find some useful information and links on my Web site, at http://www.evolvingtech.com/excel.

Excel functions come in a variety of sizes and shapes, which can be viewed within the context of three broad groups. The following list includes these groups and some representative functions for each.

- ◆ Functions requiring no inputs

    ```
    =RAND()
    =TODAY()
    =TRUE()
    =ROW()
    ```

◆ Functions that operate on a single value

```
=TRIM("  Remove extra spaces at start and end of string   ")
=INT(99.44)
=DAY("1/28/2004")
=ROW(Some_TaxRate_I_Defined)
```

◆ Those that can accept more than one input value or argument

```
=SUMPRODUCT(A1:A10,D1:D10)
=MID("pick four characters starting the 6th character,6,4)
=OFFSET(SA$1,3,4)
```

Some Excel functions are "overloaded" and can overlap these categories.

Some important functions and how they're used

Somewhere along the way in this chapter and other portions of this book, you'll pick up some useful information on a variety of Excel functions. Don't concern yourself too much with a formal knowledge of these functions. Instead, focus on the hands-on approach, paying attention to the "gotchas" and subtleties. Think about when and where you would be using these functions. Make no mistake — the functions described here are all put to use somewhere in this book. Chances are good that many of them will become directly relevant to how you use spreadsheets in your line of work.

NO-INPUT FUNCTIONS

No-input functions are just what the name says. Being independently minded creatures, they don't need to be fed any special parameters to work properly. The most independently minded functions of this type are `TRUE()`, `FALSE()`, and `PI()`.

These functions stubbornly return the same values no matter where or when they perform a computation. You can imagine what `PI()` returns. The function `TRUE ()` returns the value `TRUE`; `FALSE()` returns `FALSE`. Why do you need a `TRUE()` or `FALSE()` function in Excel? It turns out there are good uses, but they are not as you might expect. Rather than use one of these functions in a "finished formula," you might use it as a placeholder in a complex formula in preparation, thereby aiding in testing and validation. Consider the formula:

```
=IF(SomethingUsuallySmall>100000,ExceptionalSituation,UsualSituation)
```

`SomethingUsuallySmall` is a placeholder for a number that is, well, usually small. So how often is it going to be over 100,000? Not very often. As a consequence, the `ExceptionalSituation` is almost never run. In building your spreadsheet, you may have a whole bunch of computations that behave differently when the `ExceptionalSituation` is returned. You may want to temporarily force things so that the `ExceptionalSituation` prevails. You can do this by replacing `SomethingUsuallySmall>100000` with the value `TRUE` or the function that generates TRUE. Your formula might look like:

```
=IF(TRUE(),ExceptionalSituation,UsualSituation)
```

Of course, you'll change `TRUE()` back to `SomethingUsuallySmall>1000000` later. Previously, I allude to more than one kind of use for `TRUE` and `FALSE`. Near the end of this chapter you will see that TRUE/FALSE are sometimes needed as special parameters for certain Excel functions.

EXCEL FUNCTIONS HAVING A SPATIAL NATURE

Other no-input functions are not so independently minded. For some functions, it may not matter *when* you call them, but it does matter *where* they are called from. In particular, consider the functions: `=ROW()` and `=COLUMN()`.

These functions report the row and column number of the cell that happens to be making the call. At first glance, the actual row or column number of a cell may not seem that important. Harnessing the positional arrangement can be important.

Consider setting up a table that has a user-defined name called `StartPosition` situated in the top-left corner. In the cells below it, you may be computing values that are dependent on how far below they are in relation to the `StartPosition`. You might use a formula like this:

```
=(ROW()-ROW(StartPosition))*SomeFinancialPenaltyUsefulForYourSpreadsheet
```

Pay attention to the fact that when an input is provided to the `ROW` or `COLUMN` functions, it uses the cell position of that referenced name or cell, rather than its own. `ROW` is one of those "overloaded" functions referred to earlier in this chapter. When no input is provided, the `ROW` function uses its own cell position.

You can probably write an equivalent formula without involving rows. Your table could have been flanked on the left with a vertical column of numbers instead. Because of space and presentation constraints, you may not be free to place a separate vertical column of numbers. The strategy used in computing with rows is to create an "in-lined" numbering system. Instead of relying on an explicit set of numbers that increment by 1 with each row, the `ROW()-ROW(StartPosition)` term accomplishes the same inside the formula. There is an advantage with this technique; as you insert or delete intervening rows and columns, the count on these positional arrangements remains correct. You will see this technique being used in the Data Viewer tool of Chapter 8, "Analyzing Data." Most typically, this technique of in-lined counting is used with the Excel `OFFSET` function.

EXCEL FUNCTIONS HAVING A TEMPORAL NATURE

Previously I spoke about no-input functions that depend on where they're being called. What about *when* they are called? Spreadsheets can include temporal aspects in their formulas. I would like to call your attention to two Excel functions that serve that purpose: TODAY and NOW. To understand the difference between the two, think of TODAY as returning INT(NOW()). The function NOW returns a numeric representation of the current date and time. The hours, minutes, seconds, and fraction of a section form the decimal portion of this numeric quantity. When the function INT is applied to NOW, it lops off the fractional portion, leaving whole numbers that represent the exact calendar date that would be computed using the TODAY function.

For the moment, pay attention to the fact that spreadsheets can be armed with the sense of time. You can, for instance, have a spreadsheet that computes how many days you have left until a note or bond matures. This is not a hypothetical date computation, but rather a *real-time* computation.

EXCEL FUNCTIONS THAT DEPEND ON WHEN AND WHERE THEY ARE CALLED

I suppose by now you must be wondering about no-input functions that change *when* and *where* they are called. On that possibility, let me tell you about the RAND function.

The RAND function is about as fickle as you can get. It tries not to repeat itself or show any discernable pattern other than providing a decimal number between zero and one. You should be aware that the RAND function is really a pseudo random function that only approximates a true random function.

If you need more mathematical horsepower in a spreadsheet environment, you may want to consider using a tool such as Mathematica Link for Excel coupled with Mathematica (products of Wolfram Research).

 The Excel RAND function is not a strong enough random number generator to be useful for cryptographic routines.

Random numbers can serve many useful purposes. You might, for instance, want to spot-check products by their SKU number or warehouse location and need to generate a list. The RAND function obviously generates random numbers, but it's constantly changing. Besides, the numbers are between zero and one. This may not be the range you're looking for.

On both these counts, easy fixes exist. To fix the range problem, "magnify" the random number; that is, perform an arithmetic manipulation to multiply the random numbers by a magnification factor. This magnification factor is the numerical difference between the UpperLimit and LowerLimit.

```
=LowerLimit+(UpperLimit-LowerLimit)*RAND()
```

The spreadsheet file ch01-06random.xls (Figure 1-19) shows this specific formula being used to generate the test values.

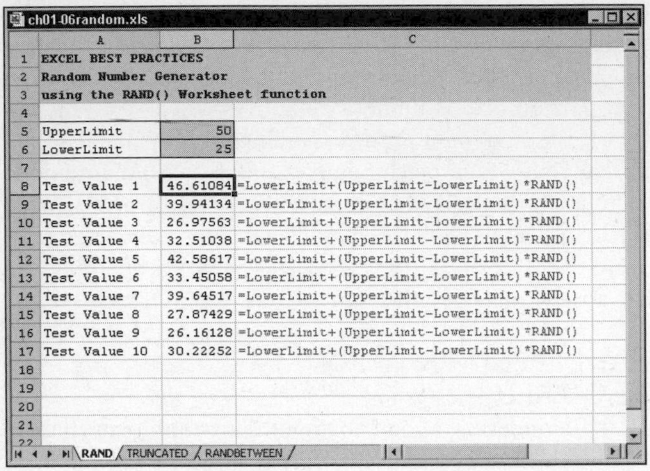

ch01-06random.xls

	A	B	C
1	EXCEL BEST PRACTICES		
2	Random Number Generator		
3	using the RAND() Worksheet function		
4			
5	UpperLimit	50	
6	LowerLimit	25	
7			
8	Test Value 1	46.61084	=LowerLimit+(UpperLimit-LowerLimit)*RAND()
9	Test Value 2	39.94134	=LowerLimit+(UpperLimit-LowerLimit)*RAND()
10	Test Value 3	26.97563	=LowerLimit+(UpperLimit-LowerLimit)*RAND()
11	Test Value 4	32.51038	=LowerLimit+(UpperLimit-LowerLimit)*RAND()
12	Test Value 5	42.58617	=LowerLimit+(UpperLimit-LowerLimit)*RAND()
13	Test Value 6	33.45058	=LowerLimit+(UpperLimit-LowerLimit)*RAND()
14	Test Value 7	39.64517	=LowerLimit+(UpperLimit-LowerLimit)*RAND()
15	Test Value 8	27.87429	=LowerLimit+(UpperLimit-LowerLimit)*RAND()
16	Test Value 9	26.16128	=LowerLimit+(UpperLimit-LowerLimit)*RAND()
17	Test Value 10	30.22252	=LowerLimit+(UpperLimit-LowerLimit)*RAND()
18			
19			
20			
21			

RAND / TRUNCATED / RANDBETWEEN

Figure 1-19: Generating random numbers between an upper and lower limit

Note that the preceding formula contains user-defined names rather than cell references. This method makes the formulas much easier to read. Also note that the identifying information appears at the top of the spreadsheet (see more about this in Chapter 2, "Mastering Spreadsheet Construction Techniques").

Okay, you have a pretty spreadsheet, but it's not quite what you want. Suppose the lower and upper limits represent monetary amounts, using U.S. dollars as the currency. You want the generated values to be in terms of dollars and cents. You don't need all the extra digits. Your first inclination might be to just "format away" the problem; that is, change the formatting of the generated numbers to display information to only two decimal places. This method is not a solution, though, because after you copy and paste values, you still have to contend with the extra digits.

EXCEL FUNCTIONS INVOLVING PRECISION AND FUZZINESS

You can use the `ROUND` worksheet function to round the generated random numbers to two decimal places as is done on the second tab of your spreadsheet workbook, called `TRUNCATED` (see Figure 1-20).

The formula used is

```
=ROUND(LowerLimit+(UpperLimit-LowerLimit)*RAND(),2)
```

In Figure 1-20, the Test Value 6 shows as `42.7` rather than `42.70`. Nothing is wrong with this number. Both `42.7` and `42.70` represent the same value. For some people, however, showing numbers this way, especially for published reports, can create an eyesore. These people want everything to line up or add up to exactly 100 percent. The usual tendency is for people to adjust these formatting details at the outset so that they don't have to think about it later. Okay, so you can adjust the formatting for the generated list to two decimal places, and whisk away the problem. For the generated random numbers, this doesn't present a problem. But what about percentages that must add up to exactly 100%?

	A	B	C
1	EXCEL BEST PRACTICES		
2	Random Number Generator		
3	rounding to two decimal places		
4			
5	UpperLimit	50	=UpperLimit
6	LowerLimit	25	=LowerLimit
7			
8	Test Value 1	30.78	=ROUND(LowerLimit+(UpperLimit-LowerLimit)*RAND(),2)
9	Test Value 2	26.96	=ROUND(LowerLimit+(UpperLimit-LowerLimit)*RAND(),2)
10	Test Value 3	33.62	=ROUND(LowerLimit+(UpperLimit-LowerLimit)*RAND(),2)
11	Test Value 4	45.01	=ROUND(LowerLimit+(UpperLimit-LowerLimit)*RAND(),2)
12	Test Value 5	42.43	=ROUND(LowerLimit+(UpperLimit-LowerLimit)*RAND(),2)
13	Test Value 6	42.7	=ROUND(LowerLimit+(UpperLimit-LowerLimit)*RAND(),2)
14	Test Value 7	35.34	=ROUND(LowerLimit+(UpperLimit-LowerLimit)*RAND(),2)
15	Test Value 8	35.46	=ROUND(LowerLimit+(UpperLimit-LowerLimit)*RAND(),2)
16	Test Value 9	40.19	=ROUND(LowerLimit+(UpperLimit-LowerLimit)*RAND(),2)
17	Test Value 10	31.55	=ROUND(LowerLimit+(UpperLimit-LowerLimit)*RAND(),2)
18			
19			
20			
21			
22			

Figure 1-20: Rounding to two decimal places

Believe it or not, people make the mistake all the time of displaying numbers using one level of precision and storing it internally in another. I discuss this issue at greater length in Chapter 3, "Your Handy Reference for Manipulating Data."

Separate your raw data and analysis from your presentation portion of your spreadsheet. Retain the needed numerical precision throughout your computations until you get to the presentation layer, where you can make needed formatting adjustments.

Let me say a word or two for now about rounding. ROUND has the following syntax:

```
ROUND(number, num_digits)
```

As you've seen, rounding numbers to two decimal places is achieved by using the value 2 for num_digits. To zero decimal places or whole numbers, you would use 0 for num_digits. Suppose you want to round numbers to the nearest hundred or thousand? You'll notice that rounding works in exponents of 10 though in an inverted pattern. To round to the nearest 1,000, you would use -3 for num_digits. Figure 1-21 shows this in action.

Note how the rounding goes up to 1,540 and then back down again to 1,500.

Another function, CEILING is similar to ROUND in some regards. Rather than specify the number of digits, you specify the actual amount you want to round to. The rounding in CEILING *always* rounds up. For example, CEILING(67,15) returns

75. If you want to explore more on the CEILING function, look at the second tab of the file ch01-07round.xls on your CD-ROM. You may also want to explore the FLOOR worksheet function (information on this can be searched from the Excel Help menu).

	A	B	C	D	E
	EXCEL BEST PRACTICES				
1	EXCEL BEST PRACTICES				
2	Example Computations				
3	involving rounding				
4					
5	number	num_digits	Result	Formula	
6	1539.86193	3	1539.862	=ROUND(1539.86193,3)	
7	1539.86193	2	1539.86	=ROUND(1539.86193,2)	
8	1539.86193	1	1539.9	=ROUND(1539.86193,1)	
9	1539.86193	0	1540	=ROUND(1539.86193,0)	
10	1539.86193	-1	1540	=ROUND(1539.86193,-1)	
11	1539.86193	-2	1500	=ROUND(1539.86193,-2)	
12	1539.86193	-3	2000	=ROUND(1539.86193,-3)	
13	1539.86193	-4	0	=ROUND(1539.86193,-4)	
14	-1539.86193	3	-1539.862	=ROUND(-1539.86193,3)	
15	-1539.86193	2	-1539.86	=ROUND(-1539.86193,2)	
16	-1539.86193	1	-1539.9	=ROUND(-1539.86193,1)	
17	-1539.86193	0	-1540	=ROUND(-1539.86193,0)	
18	-1539.86193	-1	-1540	=ROUND(-1539.86193,-1)	
19	-1539.86193	-2	-1500	=ROUND(-1539.86193,-2)	
20	-1539.86193	-3	-2000	=ROUND(-1539.86193,-3)	
21	-1539.86193	-4	0	=ROUND(-1539.86193,-4)	

ROUND / CEILING / INT /

Figure 1-21: Example computations involving rounding

There is another function you need to know about. It's called INT. As would be expected for positive numbers, it literally lops off the decimal digits. INT(2.9) becomes 2. Negative numbers are treated somewhat differently. They are chopped down to the next lower number. The third tab of the file ch01-07.xls shows some examples of this.

Reversing the signs of computation (that is, flipping positives to negatives and vice versa) may not behave as expected, as the following example shows:

INT(2.9) returns 2, whereas INT(-2.9) returns -3

This is an important subtlety.

EXCEL ADD-IN FUNCTIONS

The random list generator that brought on this whole discussion may still not be quite satisfactory for your needs. You might want to pick whole numbers and dispense decimal points, rounding, and RAND altogether. There's an Excel Add-In function called RANDBETWEEN. RANDBETWEEN takes two inputs, a lower limit and an upper limit. Both these numbers must be integers. RANDBETWEEN returns an integer randomly chosen within this range.

I use the term *Add-In* as opposed to worksheet because to use the function, you must tell Excel to load a supplemental module called the Analysis ToolPak (see Figure 1-22). You can load supplemental modules from the Excel Tools: Add-Ins menu. See Figure 1-23 for an example of using RANDBETWEEN.

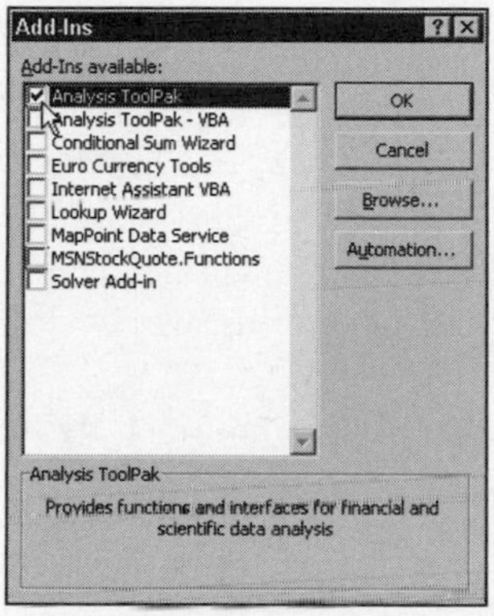

Figure 1-22: Selecting Excel add-ins

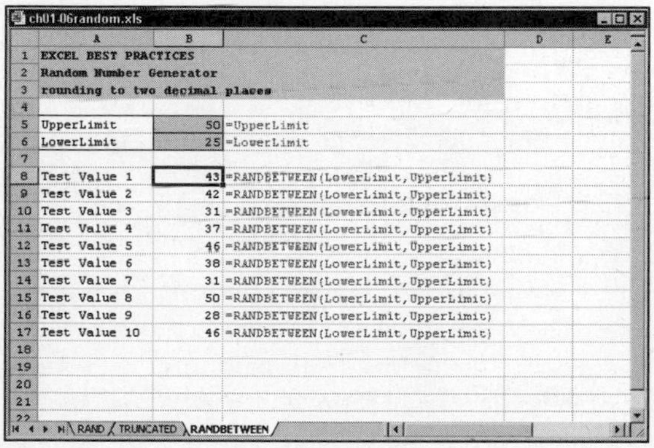

Figure 1-23: Usage of RANDBETWEEN

When you tell Excel to load an Add-In, it does so every time you fire up Excel from that point on, with one exception. Sometimes your Excel may be loaded off of a network rather than from your local machine. The settings for your copy of Excel may be preset and unchangeable, and the changes you make to your settings may not be retained. If this is the case, you've got a bigger set of issues than keeping RANDBETWEEN in the sights of Excel. If your Excel configuration is pre-set, changes you make to your settings will be forgotten the moment you quit Excel.

If you are sharing your spreadsheet with a colleague or third party and the spreadsheet uses RANDBETWEEN or some other Add-In function, make sure that user has the appropriate Add-In modules loaded.

Assuming that you have no problems getting your copy of Excel to automatically work with RANDBETWEEN, you still may have a problem down the road. Suppose that you want to share your spreadsheet with a colleague and your spreadsheet happens to use RANDBETWEEN or some other function in one of the other modules. Your colleague may not have that module loaded on his or her machine. Think carefully about your usage of Add-In functions if you plan on sharing work with others.

There are still two issues looming on the random-number list generator. They're actually quite easy to solve. The first issue is that anytime something changes in the spreadsheet, the random numbers are recalculated. Because the formulas are constantly changing the values returned, you can't preserve the numbers within the formulas. Aha! There's no need to preserve the numbers within the formulas. Just copy and paste the values to an adjacent column or wherever is appropriate. That was an easy fix. The next issue is a little more involved and context based.

REAL WORLD USE OF RANDBETWEEN

Selecting random in a range is straightforward. Not everything in the world is going to be listed as a continuous range of numbers like the kind you might generate from the previously shown worksheets. If you are looking for "items" in a list, then you can use one of the lookup functions that Excel provides and combine that function with your random-number generator.

Imagine, for example, that you are auditing credit card transactions for a business for the month of December 2003. There are 800 transactions for this period. You have the responsibility of spot-checking or auditing the amounts of 20 randomly selected items from the list of recorded transactions. As you can see in Figure 1-24, there are two principal regions in the spreadsheet. On the right side is a table containing all 800 transactions, including date and dollar amount. If you open the file ch01-08sampling from the CD with this book, you can see that the transaction data has a name, Table01, which extends from G8 through I808 (in R1C1 notation the cell coordinates are R7C7:R809C9). The left side of the spreadsheet contains the data being used for testing. The transaction IDs were randomly selected between 1 and 800 using this formula:

```
=RANDBETWEEN(LowerLimit,UpperLimit)
```

MORE EXCEL SPATIAL FUNCTIONS

The smaller list of transaction IDs that will be used for audit testing were given a user-defined name, TransID (which extends from A7 through A26). After the values were generated, the cells were copied and pasted (values only) so that the original formulas were obliterated. This ensures that the values won't continue to change. On the next two columns, table lookups for specific transaction data are performed. The function used for this purpose is VLOOKUP. As it is used in ch01-08sampling.xls, VLOOKUP takes the following form:

```
VLOOKUP(value_to_lookup, table_or_range_of_data, column_number)
```

The formula for looking up the transaction amounts is

```
=VLOOKUP(TransID,Table01,3)
```

The number 3 appears in this formula because the transaction amount is found on the third column of Table01.

You should be aware that there is also an HLOOKUP function that is like VLOOKUP turned sideways. Both of these functions are overloaded.

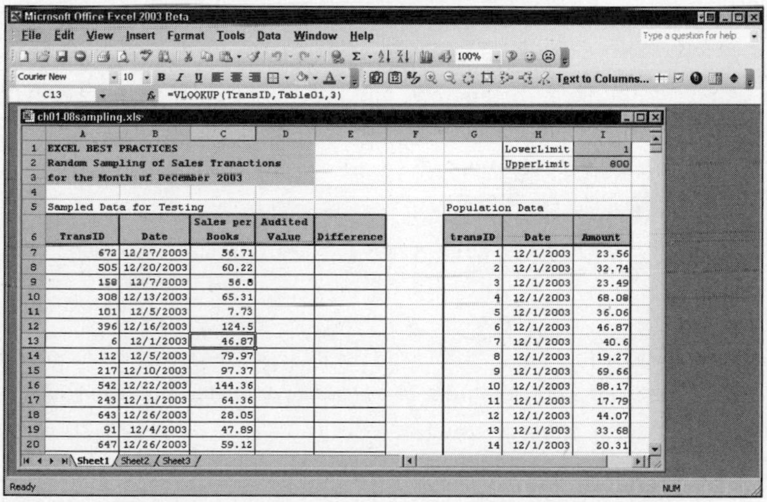

Figure 1-24: Worksheet for comparing audited values to book values

I want to turn your attention to some potential trouble spots with VLOOKUP. If you're the list of items you are searching is "out of sequence," the value returned by VLOOKUP may not be what you are looking for.

In this example, the lookup values in Table01 starts from an ID of 1 and ends with 800. It follows a nice, structured order. What if lines 6 and 8 were switched (including the ID, date, and transaction amount)? The data is still correct; it's just presented in a different sequence. (See Figure 1-25, in which the relevant information is highlighted.) While looking up the number 6 in Table01, VLOOKUP finds 5, and then immediately stubs its toe when it reaches the number 8. This out-of-sequence number causes VLOOKUP to stumble and fall out of the computation prematurely, holding the data for the value 5. The transaction amount having the ID of 5 is 36.06. This is not, of course, the number that you're looking for.

	A	B	C	D	E	F	G	H	I
1	EXCEL BEST PRACTICES							LowerLimit	1
2	Random Sampling of Sales Transactions							UpperLimit	800
3	for the Month of December 2003								
4									
5	Sampled Data for Testing						Population Data		
6	TransID	Date	Sales per Books	Audited Value	Difference		transID	Date	Amount
7	672	12/27/2003	56.71				1	12/1/2003	23.56
8	505	12/20/2003	60.22				2	12/1/2003	32.74
9	158	12/7/2003	56.8				3	12/1/2003	23.49
10	308	12/13/2003	65.31				4	12/1/2003	68.08
11	101	12/5/2003	7.73				5	12/1/2003	36.06
12	396	12/16/2003	124.5				8	12/1/2003	19.27
13	6	12/1/2003	36.06				7	12/1/2003	40.6
14	112	12/5/2003	79.97				6	12/1/2003	46.87
15	217	12/10/2003	97.37				9	12/1/2003	69.66
16	542	12/22/2003	144.36				10	12/1/2003	88.17
17	243	12/11/2003	64.36				11	12/1/2003	17.79
18	643	12/26/2003	28.05				12	12/1/2003	44.07
19	91	12/4/2003	47.89				13	12/1/2003	33.68
20	647	12/26/2003	59.12				14	12/1/2003	20.31

Figure 1–25: VLOOKUP is easily confused if the data being looked up is out of sequence.

This problem can be easily fixed, fortunately. Add an additional parameter called FALSE to your formula. The revised lookup formula is

```
=VLOOKUP(TransID,Table01,3,FALSE)
```

This formula returns the result of 46.87 and is the result you would expect.

 If you are using VLOOKUP or HLOOKUP and the table you are searching is not in strict numeric order, you may need to place the parameter FALSE in your formula.

Closing Thoughts

I hope that this chapter got you on the road to understanding differences among absolute, relative and hybrid cell references, along with ways to put them to use. Also illustrated in this chapter were different ways to write your formulas using A1 notation, R1C1 notation and user-defined names. To assist you in this process, you now have at your disposal a "SwitchTool" spreadsheet, and keystroke techniques for defining names in rapid succession and navigating/managing larger spreadsheets.

You have been introduced to a view that Excel functions can be used for more than just plain-vanilla arithmetic calculations. From a hands-on perspective, you have seen a variety of spreadsheet functions in action, including TRUE, FALSE, ROW, COLUMN, TODAY, NOW, RAND, RANDBETWEEN, ROUND, CEILING, INT, and VLOOKUP.

What should start to emerge is that powerful things you can do with spreadsheets begin to happen when you combine things. When RANDBETWEEN and VLOOKUP were combined, it became possible to randomly select items that did not match the format of random integers.

There are subtleties in functions that you should now be aware of, such as when you may need to insert a FALSE parameter in the lookup functions. This kind of knowledge should help you steer clear of sand traps that frequently snag people. When people do get snared, they consume and waste precious time coming up with a fix. More often than not, the fix is a quick fix. Pretty soon, people fall into the habit of doing things in a "one-off" style. This habit is a slippery slope.

The tips, cautionary notes and discussions presented in this chapter and throughout the book should help you to avoid this one-off style; whether in the writing of spreadsheet formulas or the construction of spreadsheets. Chapter 2 continues and expands on best practices for spreadsheet construction.

Chapter 2

Mastering Spreadsheet Construction Techniques

IN THIS CHAPTER

- ◆ Understanding the fundamental concepts of creating spreadsheets

- ◆ Building a spreadsheet: A step-by-step example

- ◆ Interpreting the results and fixing problems

- ◆ Making the spreadsheet look professional

- ◆ Understanding issues and techniques for working with complex spreadsheets

THIS CHAPTER PROVIDES YOU with basic spreadsheet construction techniques. It gives you both a conceptual and hands-on perspective on how to go about constructing spreadsheets. The emphasis is on the mechanical process and the hidden bumps in the road.

You will see that simple spreadsheets lend themselves to a systematic process from inception to the finished product. These steps are outlined and immediately followed by a worked-out construction example.

You are going to see the use of Excel templates. Along the way, you'll collect many practical tips and techniques (not to mention how to spot the hidden sandpits and other traps).

The construction of simpler spreadsheets is complemented by an interesting perspective on complex spreadsheets. Insight can be gleaned from identifying what made a spreadsheet suddenly turn complex. This, in turn, further helps to pick a strategy or tool to better manage the complexity.

Next, you are introduced to the use of layering for when you construct larger spreadsheets. In a sense, you can think of this method as a "blueprint." The framework, as described, is implemented in later chapters of the book.

One Size Does Not Fit All

Depending on the complexity, spreadsheet construction can proceed along a number of different paths. I will first outline a nice way to prepare simple and clean spreadsheets that can be quickly assembled. When thinking about more complex spreadsheets, additional factors need to be brought into the mental equation. I address some of the things you need to start thinking about, but defer full-blown applications to the chapters on dealing with spreadsheet ergonomics (in Part II) and special topics (in Part III).

Understanding Simple Spreadsheets

In the next section, I walk you through a detailed example of the process of building an actual spreadsheet, mostly to get you to develop a style you can settle into that will allow you to proceed quickly and maintain a certain quality of standards in your work. The actual formulas used in the spreadsheet example are of almost no consequence. Pay attention, instead, to the process and the flow of building the spreadsheet and the things that are done to facilitate the spreadsheet construction.

Before you work your way through the example, here is an overview the fundamental motions to go through when you create new spreadsheets:

1. **State your goal(s).**

   First, you're going to have some original goal, which essentially will be unchanging.

2. **Sketch a rough outline.**

   The outline should contain how you want your spreadsheet to look. It will easily suffice to write out a few notes, schematics, or both on a single sheet of paper. Basically, you want to identify the important inputs and outputs and perhaps a placeholder for something that would perform a computation to get to the output from the input.

3. **Procure sample or representative data.**

   Start thinking about where you're going to get the data for use in your computations. You would do well to have a couple of "Use Cases" in mind. Sometimes, computations can get a little hairy. Knowing the results of one or several sample computations will go a long way toward constructing your worksheet.

4. **Start building spreadsheet (with formulas).**

   At this point you should be more than ready to begin the spreadsheet. With a blank spreadsheet or a pre-built template, start entering the basic labels of the inputs and outputs as well as some sample/representative data. Don't yet worry about completeness or correctness of any of the formulas. Just have it follow along the lines of what you'd do on your paper scratch pad. Indeed, you should start thinking of your spreadsheet as an electronic scratch pad. Excel provides the ability to move and rearrange cell contents as well as insert/delete rows and columns. You should be putting this capability to use.

Now that you have some labels and some input numbers, start entering some of the spreadsheet formulas. Get them working to produce numbers that you know should be correct. If necessary, hardwire the formulas. There will be time to go back and clean up. Do you have all the information you need to complete the computation(s)? Perhaps, you need to insert a couple of rows in your spreadsheet for intermediate calculations.

These interim calculations could be simply be for your personal edification (and help you verify a complex chain of calculations), or you could present these interim results as part of your final spreadsheet. They may be appropriate subtotals that are to be incorporated into the final results. For example, if your final result is a net gain or loss, you may have one set of computations for the revenue side and another set of computations for the expense or cost side. The final result is obtained by subtracting the expense/cost portion from the revenue portion.

Presenting these interim numbers not only provides a helpful way to work through and validate the computation but also serves to represent meaningful accounting information that may well be worth presenting in the final spreadsheet.

5. **Focus on getting correct results.**

Don't labor too much over how you want to present the final results. Concentrate at this stage on getting correct results and validating your formulas. You may have one way at arriving at a number and getting your expected results. In reality, you know that you want to use an entirely different way of computing your results for the completed spreadsheet. It may be a simplification of some "megaformula." Insert more rows and/or columns in your spreadsheet to accommodate your new calculations. Don't be too quick to throw away your first set. In particular, if a quantity you're computing is calculated in two different ways, then when you subtract one number from the other, the results should always be zero, right? If this is not the result you get, then somewhere, there may be an error in the logic that you need to identify.

6. **Refine the spreadsheet's appearance.**

After you have gained confidence in your basic spreadsheet model or set of computations, start refining the appearance of your spreadsheet. You should veer toward a consistent but easily modifiable and reproducible look and feel, or branding. This appearance should be characteristically the same throughout all your spreadsheets. The uniformity will not only set up expectations amongst your colleagues but also help you to go past the mechanics of production and focus your efforts where they're needed most — getting the numbers right.

So, for uniform appearance, think about what elements you would want to have in every spreadsheet you produce. I make the assumption that the spreadsheets you prepare will at some point or another be reviewed by some third party, whether your manager or boss, colleagues within your company, or some auditor or adversarial party at a later date. In the latter case, there's a good chance you may not be anticipating such scrutinizing at the time that you're preparing the spreadsheet. Sorry for the sinister tone, but business is business regardless of how well intentioned and conscientious you may be.

Sometimes the numbers can be rock solid, but if the presentation isn't up to par, your ability to convince others of your findings will be needlessly weakened. The converse is true and even more extreme. If your spreadsheets look great and convincing but lack the rock-solid correctness, there is the potential that the spreadsheet will be applied in a manner in which it wasn't originally intended. This result could be costly. The shortcomings may not be discovered until well after the fact.

7. Rework spreadsheets for maintainability.

After you get past the stage of establishing the basic spreadsheet appearance and computational correctness, you should rework the spreadsheet to make it easy to maintain. To do so, ask yourself these questions:

* Can the formulas be simplified?

* How about assigning names to important cell ranges and substituting those names into the formulas? (Six months from now you'll be thankful that you put in names instead of cell references)

* Is something in your spreadsheet bound to change? The obvious item that comes to mind is the range of dates. You may also have some scalability issues looming. Your spreadsheet in its current incarnation may need to track only a small number of items, perhaps ten or so; or, it might be suited only to summarizing data that spans a week or two, not months or years. The purpose of your spreadsheet may change over time. You may want to rework portions of your spreadsheet as a preemptive measure.

* Do you want to be a victim of your own success? Your spreadsheet might work so well for your department that a manager saddles you with the burden of preparing a consolidated spreadsheet across multiple departments. You don't want to be dealing with two issues: increased complexity and getting into the habit of preparing one-offs (a different implementation for each department).

For the time being, this is enough to be thinking about in advance. It's time to get some hands-on involvement and work through the process of preparing the spreadsheet.

Building a Spreadsheet: A Simple Example

The spreadsheet example that follows is not very involved. It's meaty enough that the important elements of spreadsheet construction come into play. As noted previously, you should pay little or no attention to the spreadsheet formulas used. Focus your energies instead on the issues that crop up during the spreadsheet construction process.

BACKGROUND DESCRIPTION

You have a situation in which shares in a public company were bought some time in the past. At any point in the future, perhaps today, you would like to know how fast your investment has been growing. The situation is complicated by the fact that you have to take into account the commission fees from when you originally purchased the stock as well as for when you will sell them. These commissions affect the profitability of your investment.

STEP 1: STATE YOUR ORIGINAL GOAL

First, you need to define your goal, which is simple enough: Calculate the (annual) net rate of growth of your investment. Next, you need to follow the remaining steps:

STEP2: DEVELOP A ROUGH OUTLINE IDENTIFYING THE IMPORTANT INPUTS/OUTPUTS

On the input side, you have several basic pieces of information for the computation:

- ◆ Stock price at date of purchase

- ◆ Current stock price (as of today)

- ◆ Date of original purchase

- ◆ Current date

- ◆ Number of shares bought

- ◆ Brokerage commission paid for original purchase

- ◆ Brokerage commission upon selling

On the output side, you need to see the net rate of growth for your stocks on an annual basis.

STEP 3: DETERMINE THE DATA TO USE IN YOUR COMPUTATIONS

For this example spreadsheet, pick a security of your choosing, such as one that you have been following and for which you know the price of the stock as of a specific date. Certainly, if you already bought shares in a public company and want to use that data, go ahead. Because I don't know which one you're thinking of, I'll go ahead and pick one for which I already have data.

- Stock symbol: `ORB`
- Company: `Orbital Sciences Corporation`
- Purchase date: `8/5/2002`
- Purchase price: `$3.26`
- Shares bought: `100`
- Brokerage commission paid: `$29.95`

STEP 4: CREATE YOUR INITIAL SPREADSHEET

If you haven't already done so, take a look at Appendix A for information regarding spreadsheet settings. Although you're free to choose any settings you want, I strongly urge that you consider and adopt the use of `monospace` fonts when and wherever possible. All the examples in the book use `monospace` fonts.

Open a new spreadsheet and start putting in the data that roughly corresponds to your intended layout. Place basic labels for the inputs and outputs. Your spreadsheet should look something like Figure 2-1.

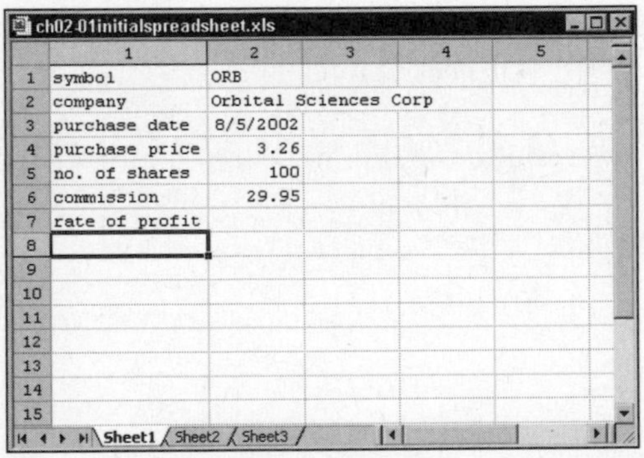
ch02-01initialspreadsheet.xls

	1	2	3	4	5
1	symbol	ORB			
2	company	Orbital Sciences Corp			
3	purchase date	8/5/2002			
4	purchase price	3.26			
5	no. of shares	100			
6	commission	29.95			
7	rate of profit				
8					
9					
10					
11					
12					
13					
14					
15					

Sheet1 / Sheet2 / Sheet3

Figure 2-1: An initial spreadsheet

MOVE AND REARRANGE

Your rate of growth on investment will be based on three things: (1) the total amount you've spent; (2) the total amount you will put into your pocket when all is said and done; and (3) the duration of time your money was invested in the stock.

Total in your pocket? Does this mean that you have to take into account taxes? To keep things simple for this example, pretend that you already have a tax-protected retirement account at a major investment firm. So, tax calculations won't be playing a role in this example.

Although you might have some tax sheltering, it's not going to protect you from the brokerage commission that comes into play both from when you bought the securities *and* when you sell it. It looks as though you need to insert a second line to accommodate the commission at the time you sell. To track the growth of your investment, you also need to know the selling price (or current price as of today) and the selling date. Your spreadsheet should look like Figure 2-2.

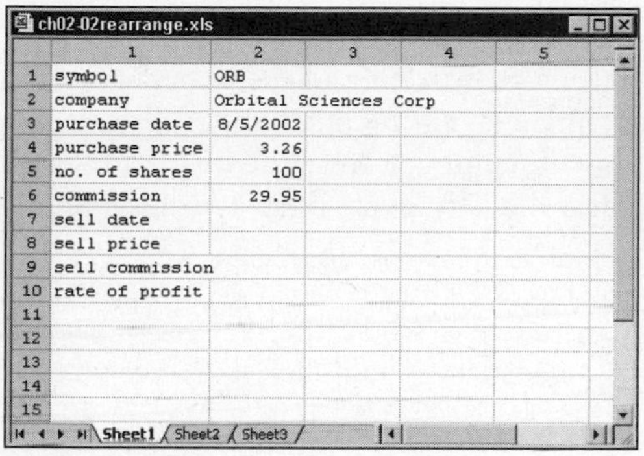

Figure 2-2: Some basic rearrangement to your initial spreadsheet

START ENTERING FORMULAS

In words, your formula for investment growth is

```
investment growth = total in your pocket - total amount spent
```

The total amount spent is

```
total amount spent = (initial stock price * number of shares) + buy commission
```

The total in your pocket is

```
total in your pocket = (selling price * number of shares) - sell commission
```

Notice that the buy and sell commissions have opposite signs (plus versus minus). The sell commission has a negative sign because it reduces the total that will go into your pocket.

Although the amount that you pay for brokerage commissions for buying and selling are likely to be the same, it is certainly possible for them to be different. For example, you might be selling additional securities in the same sell order. It would then make sense to prorate your commission among the shares that you buy or sell during any particular order. Unless you feel strongly about doing otherwise, stay with two different commissions rather than a single number.

You now have the conceptual basis for calculating investment growth, but what about the rate of growth? Your rate of growth should be as follows:

```
growth rate = investment growth / time elapsed
```

and

```
time elapsed = date of sale - date of purchase
```

When I presented an outline, earlier in this chapter, one of the items was: "Do you have all the information you need to complete the computation(s)?" This is the question you should be asking yourself now. Though you have the inputs that will drive the spreadsheet, you still need to insert a few more lines and appropriate labels for items like investment growth.

As silly as it may seem, sometimes it makes sense to manually type the pseudo formulas, entering them as placeholders in the cells where the real formulas are slated to go. Figure 2-3 shows what your spreadsheet should look like after you do this.

	1	2	3	4	5	6	7	8
1	symbol	ORB						
2	company	Orbital Sciences Corp						
3	purchase date	8/5/2002						
4	purchase price	3.26						
5	no. of shares	100						
6	commission	29.95						
7	sell date							
8	sell price							
9	sell commission							
10	total spent	(initial stock price * number of shares) + buy commission						
11	total in your pocket	(selling price * number of shares) + sell commission						
12	investment growth	total amount spent - total in your pocket						
13	elapsed time	date of sale - date of purchase						
14	rate of profit	investment growth / time elapsed						
15								

ch02.03addsomeformulas.xls — Sheet1 / Sheet2 / Sheet3

Figure 2-3: After further rearrangement with pseudo formulas

For the time being, shade any cells that you know will require data you haven't supplied or will have formulas that compute values.

Mark up spreadsheet cells that require further attention. You can do this by shading the particular cells. While you're at it, enter pseudo formulas where the real formulas will ultimately go.

One by one, fill in the empty cells with formulas or values. You can use any data you have collected so far, as suggested previously. The selling price for the security I'm using in this example was, on the close of 3/27/2003, $5.51 a share. You can use static data of this kind to help complete the model even though the data will be changing.

Unless you have different information, you can assume that the selling commission is the same as the original commission you paid. In the gray cell where you will be placing the formula for commission, enter an equal symbol (=) and click your mouse on the commission value of 29.95, three rows above. Alternatively, you can enter the following formula into R9C2:

```
=R[-3]C
```

As you place actual formulas for the assumptions, go ahead and remove the shading for those cells (Figure 2-4).

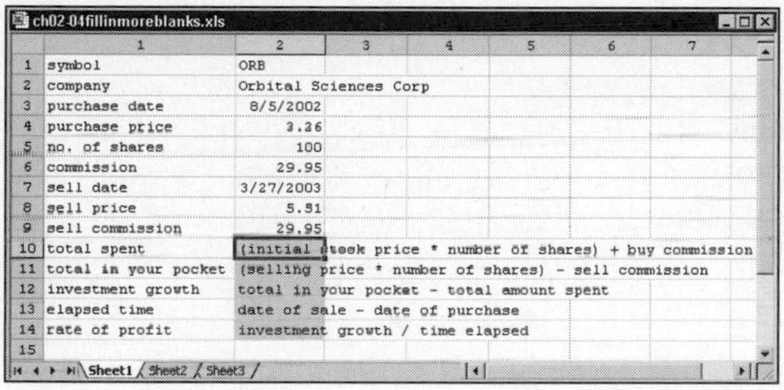

Figure 2-4: Narrative assumptions specified shown in the gray shaded background will be replaced with actual formulas.

FORGE AHEAD TO PRODUCE THE NUMBERS

Your pseudo formulas are as follows:

```
(initial stock price * number of shares) + buy commission
(selling price * number of shares) - sell commission
total in your pocket - total amount spent
date of sale - date of purchase
investment growth / time elapsed
```

These will be replaced with:

```
=(R[-6]C*R[-5]C)+R[-4]C
=(R[-3]C*R[-6]C)-R[-2]C
=R[-1]C-R[-2]C
=R[-6]C-R[-10]C
=R[-2]C/R[-1]C
```

Watch out for some quagmires! Whenever you enter a formula that references a cell with a date, Excel in its infinite wisdom tries to coerce the resulting cell value to have a date format.

Excel will sometimes try to change the formatting of your cell without consulting you. This typically happens when computations in your formulas involve dates or other cells that contain dates. You may have to reset the formatting of your cell so that the quantity displayed in your cell is restored to its original format.

In this specific situation, when the difference between two dates is computed to obtain the elapsed time, Excel forces the elapsed time to be formatted as a date. This makes things very confusing (Figure 2-5).

	1	2	3	4	5	6	7
1	symbol	ORB					
2	company	Orbital Sciences Corp					
3	purchase date	8/5/2002					
4	purchase price	3.26					
5	no. of shares	100					
6	commission	29.95					
7	sell date	3/27/2003					
8	sell price	5.51					
9	sell commission	29.95					
10	total spent	355.95	=(R[-6]C*R[-5]C)+R[-4]C				
11	total in your pocket	521.05	=(R[-3]C*R[-6]C)-R[-2]C				
12	investment growth	165.1	=R[-1]C-R[-2]C				
13	elapsed time	8/21/1900	=R[-6]C-R[-10]C				
14	rate of profit	investment growth / time elapsed					
15							

Figure 2-5: The date 8/21/1900 doesn't seem very realistic. (It's not!)

The date of 8/21/1900 doesn't look very realistic. You can fix this by adjusting the formatting so that it is not forced to appear as a calendar date when it should instead be a duration. Because the elapsed time should be a pure number, you could copy the cell directly above it and paste the format (with luck, you already have your toolbar set up so that you can use the Paste Format toolbar icon to directly paste the format). You should obtain 234 as the number of days for this duration (that's how many days passed between August 5th and March 27th). The computed number of days is dependent on the purchase date and sell date. Obviously, if you supply different dates than the ones shown in the example, your results will differ.

You may encounter a situation in which you expect to be modifying a formula many times. This may be because you are experimenting with variations on the formula. If such formulas involve date arithmetic, Excel may alter the formatting of your cell without consulting you. Restoring the original format using the Excel Format Cells... menu can be tedious and time consuming. A better practice would be to copy a nearby cell that is already formatted correctly and paste the format to your current cell whose formatting was rudely altered by Excel. Consult Appendix A on the setup of toolbars so that you can bypass the Excel menus to accomplish this.

STEP 5: ENSURE THAT THE NUMBERS ARE CORRECT

Finally, complete the last formula to compute: (investment growth) / (time elapsed) (Figure 2-6).

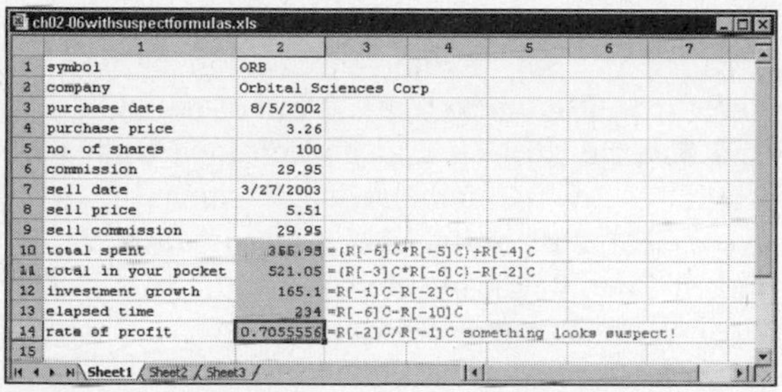

Figure 2-6: Computation of investment growth / time elapsed

INTERPRETING THE NUMBERS FOR PLAUSIBILITY (AND FIXING ANY HARDWIRED FORMULAS)

At first glance, the results of the computation don't appear to make sense. How can it be? The shares were originally bought at $3.26 apiece. The price has gone up to $5.51 apiece. Yet the rate of profit is 0.71.

Actually, the formula is correct. It's the terminology and interpretation that's fuzzy. The correct interpretation is that over the course of the investment lifetime (of 234 days), the investment was earning on average 71 cents a day. After 234 days, the net increase on the investment is $165. The term *rate of profit* is not a good term to unambiguously describe this result. If you are looking for annual growth rate, state it as such. Then annualize the 71 cents a day and restate it in terms of percentage increase based on principal (Figure 2-7).

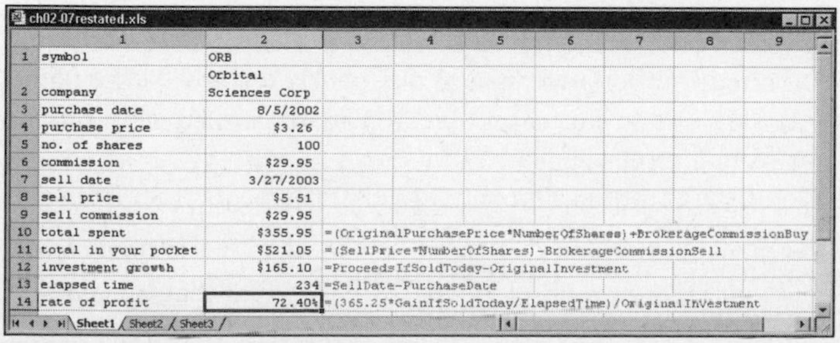

Figure 2-7: Restated spreadsheet

STEP 6: REFINING YOUR SPREADSHEET'S APPEARANCE

At this point you can begin to develop a sense of confidence in the numbers. The visual presentation of the spreadsheet results, however, is in need of improvement. If the spreadsheet were to be presented as is to your company management, it might not be viewed as a professional product.

The numbers are certainly accurate. The annual profitability of 72%, if it's still maintained by the time you present your report, looks great. If the appearance is not up to par, management might not be too quick to share your overflowing sense of confidence and optimism in the numbers, however. Management types are often stodgy—but for good reason! Your objective is to keep them from being distracted by lackluster or unprofessional appearance so that they will zero in on the numbers. The more consistent and structured you are in the presentation portion of your spreadsheets, the more management will buy into the validity of them.

How many times have you looked at a spreadsheet and had no idea what was really going on? Do you want people to say the same when it comes to your spreadsheets? I suspect not. To avoid that possibility, give the spreadsheet the appearance of structure and an ordered flow. Begin by inserting four lines at the top of the worksheet. In the first three lines of your spreadsheet, answer the questions *WHO?*, *What?*, and *when?*

If, at a glance, your spreadsheets immediately communicate who, what, and when, people using your spreadsheet are automatically a step closer to understanding what the spreadsheet is meant to convey. This puts you ahead of the competition if your competitors neglect to do this.

Specifically, in the corporate setting, it is a good practice to always place the appropriate branding information in the first line. Generally this is the COMPANY NAME. Unless the Corporate Identity manuals for your company or branding practices dictate otherwise, it is a good idea to display the company name in UPPER-CASE form for all the letters (not just the first letter of each word).

The second line of your spreadsheet should identify what is contained in your report or spreadsheet. My style is to generally capitalize the first letter of all major words in this line.

The third line should tether your report/spreadsheet to a specific date, range of time, or some other set of circumstances that would differentiate it from other similarly prepared reports. My style is to not capitalize any of the words here unless they are proper names or formal terms.

These three lines of identifying information should generally be distinct from the spreadsheet contents. My style is to leave a blank line separating the identifying information for the spreadsheet contents. I also like to shade the identifying information and show its text in boldface. This format contributes to the perception that the spreadsheet is structured as indeed it is. At a quick glance, anyone can answer the questions *WHO, What,* and *when.*

Make the terminology in your computations consistent with your computations. You may have noticed that in the description of the spreadsheet construction I vacillated between "elapsed time" and "time elapsed." I'm sure this was unnerving for some readers. If you found it distasteful, imagine how people will react to your spreadsheets if they find you making similar faux pas. I'm sure it's never been your practice. It doesn't hurt to keep you on your guard.

The spreadsheet should appear as that shown in Figure 2-8.

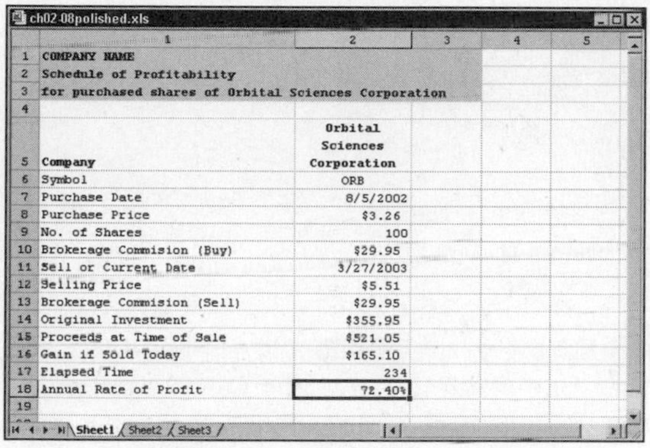

Figure 2–8: Improved spreadsheet appearance

Notice some additional changes:

♦ `Orbital Sciences Corp` has been changed to its proper name, `Orbital Sciences Corporation`.

♦ The appearance of the Orbital Sciences Corporation in the cell `R5C2` has been formatted with word-wrap enabled and text centered.

♦ Cells in row 5 appear in boldface format.

♦ Items in the first column are consistently capitalized.

♦ Monetary amounts are formatted so that numeric quantities appear in U.S. Currency format to two decimal places. Note that Currency is a specific type of number format that you can specify within Excel.

There are additional changes to make to facilitate the professional appearance of spreadsheets when printed. One is to create a custom footer. From the Excel View menu, select the Header and Footer option. Select the Custom Footer button and enter information appropriate for your worksheet (see Figure 2-9 for an example).

Obviously, the information you are going to be entering is specific to your worksheet. A common practice among companies is to place copyright information along with a disclaimer and/or confidentiality info in the printed spreadsheet. If this is the standard practice within your company, here are some thoughts that may prove useful. The confidential info disclaimer is a brief line or phrase that your lawyers would prepare. Sometimes, the confidentiality info can be lengthy. It all depends upon what the corporate lawyers dictate. You can ameliorate the situation by breaking out the legal disclaimer onto multiple lines. Excel will let you do this.

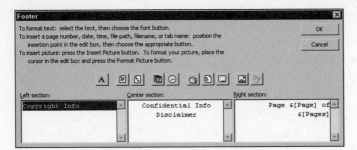

Figure 2–9: Representative information for custom footer

To indicate the page number info, make use of the second and third button icons appearing in the middle of Figure 2-9. One of these shows the pound symbol (#) and the other shows two plus signs (+ +). Click these buttons to insert, respectively, the current page number and total number of pages for your worksheet.

When you prepare your custom headers and footers, as well as any other page setup info, you quite possibly will want the identical information on all your worksheets. Excel doesn't automatically give you such a facility for replicating the page settings across worksheets. There are two ways to accomplish this replication, as explained in the next two sections.

THE REPEAT FEATURE

One way to make Excel repeat an action is to use its "Repeat" feature for each worksheet. Excel has the capability to remember the very last thing you just did. The very last action you performed could be the pasting of cell contents (including the specific Paste... Special options you've selected), inserting or deleting of rows, or, in the current spreadsheet example, the repetition of the page setup. Immediately after you've made your custom footer, click the OK button to close the dialog box; then, click the tab for your second worksheet. Now press Ctrl+Y, or open the Excel Edit menu and select the Repeat option, which now specifies Repeat Page Setup (see Figure 2-10) because that's the previous action that you just performed. If you have additional worksheets, you can immediately continue the repeat process for each of them.

Sometimes, you may have thought that you've completed all your page setups and gone on to perform some other action. You then realize that you still have another worksheet needing the same custom headers and footers. Do you have to go through the painstaking setup again? The answer is no.

Here's how you get around it. Go to a worksheet that already has the custom page setting the way you like it. Get to the Custom Footer or Header dialog box (refer back to Figure 2-9). Tweak it ever so slightly. You could, for example, type in a space at the end of one of the sections. Press the OK button. Go back to remove that space. Press OK once more to accept the changes.

Edit		
Can't Undo	Ctrl+Z	
Repeat Page Setup	Ctrl+Y	
Cut	Ctrl+X	
Copy	Ctrl+C	
Office Clipboard...		

Figure 2–10: Repeating the page setup

Basically, you forced Excel to remember the complete page settings even though there was no net change to your settings. Now you can merrily go on your way using Ctrl+Y to clone or replicate the page setup info for the additional worksheets.

TIP   Sometimes you can trick Excel into repeating more than what you just did. Excel tracks your steps. Often, it will remember all the settings in a dialog box and not the specific item you checked in the dialog box.

You can also trick Excel into repeating something that you basically didn't change. Go to your dialog box and change something ever so slightly. Go to the same dialog box and undo that action; for example, uncheck an option you just checked. Now, Excel will "remember" everything in the dialog box and is ready to repeat it right away. This is a great way to clone something with all the attributes, in a pinch. You will have the occasion to use this when you work with conditional formatting, a topic covered in Chapter 7, "Creating and Using Smart Data."

I don't want people to be thinking that "tricking" Excel is a "best practice"; it's not. Workarounds are not the kind of solutions I want to promote. The specific workaround does work, however, and will spare you the drudgery of manually editing page setup for additional worksheets and reduce the likelihood of making mistakes.

EXCEL TEMPLATES

I stated earlier that there are two things you could do to counter the fact that Excel won't immediately replicate the page settings for each of the worksheets. The previous section describes one approach. Here is another. If you're planning to prepare a consistent appearance for all or many of your spreadsheets, it would serve your purposes well if you built them from a standard spreadsheet template. In this manner, you could incorporate all the features and formatting that you generally want.

Simply build your prototype spreadsheet with all the formatting and text that you would like to see in your spreadsheets. Then, from the Excel File menu, select Save As and then select Template for the Save as type option (Figure 2-11).

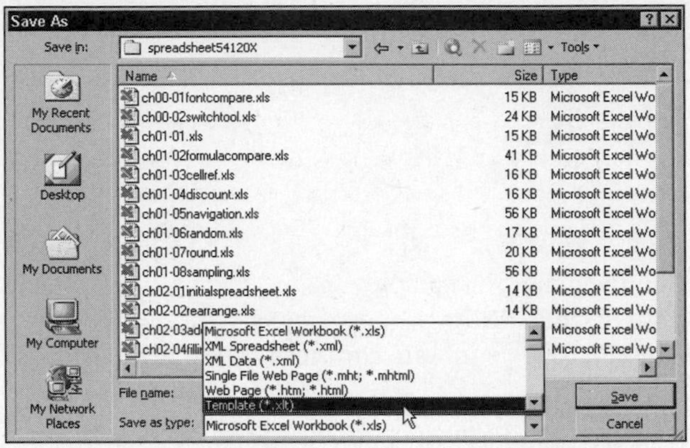

Figure 2-11: Saving a spreadsheet as an .xlt template

The next time you open a new spreadsheet, you have the option of creating it from the template file.

I have some thoughts to offer. It is not uncommon to prepare spreadsheets that make use of a large number of columns. For example, you might be preparing a 36- or 48-month projection with figures computed for each month. When you print such a document, you'll want to adopt print settings such as the following:

- Use both horizontal and vertical print titles so that the top and left side of every printed page contains identifying information. Also use the Freeze Pane feature to split the page that matches the print titles (see Appendix A for its setup). In this manner, the screen appearance of your worksheet will match your printed document.

- Use the "Z" pattern (see the top figure in Figure 2-12): Select the option to print across and then down (Excel generally uses a page default setting of printing down then across). It will be easier for people to work with the printed document if the page sequence flows from left to right then down.

- These wide and large documents tend to be more readable and use fewer printed pages when they are set to print in Landscape mode instead of Portrait mode.

- To print with fewer pages, you can set print magnification to less than 100%. Unless you are planning on having a magnifying glass handy, don't set your magnification below 75%.

◆ If you really need to squeeze space, steal it from the margins. The left and right margins generally provide three-quarters of an inch of space on either side (assuming the use of U.S. Letter Size). You can try setting this to one-half inch for each side. I've never come across a laser printer that has had difficulties with this.

The top and bottom margins are a slightly different story. When your spreadsheet has headers and footers, grabbing the extra vertical space could present a challenge. In my spreadsheets, I generally have custom footers. Unless I have to do otherwise, I restrict all the header/foot information to just the footers. This way, if I need to grab some extra vertical space, I'm free to take it from the top of the page.

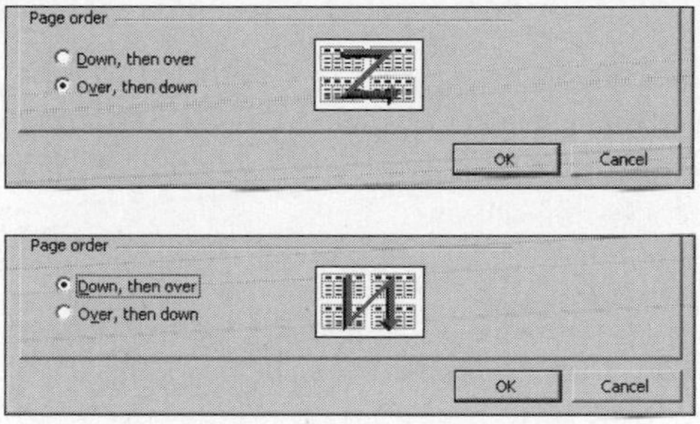

Figure 2–12: Follow the "Z" pattern, not the "inverted N" pattern, for spreadsheets with many columns.

I could go on and on, but these are the chief practical elements and concerns when preparing simple spreadsheets.

Some closing remarks on simple spreadsheets

I remember discussing with a colleague some computational problem that involved a bunch of adding, multiplying, and dividing. During the conversation, my friend popped open the Windows Calculator tool to compute some ballpark estimates. I inquired, "Why not use a spreadsheet?" My friend agreed that doing so would make sense, but then proceeded to continue using the desktop calculator tool. My friend, who wouldn't think twice about doing something complex on a spreadsheet, was hard pressed to open one for simple calculations. Why is this true of so many people?

Basically, it boils down to how often people work with spreadsheets. If you use spreadsheets a lot, chances are you're going to invent new uses for it all the time and will be predisposed to "work through" problems using the spreadsheet as your electronic scratch pad to formulate and figure things out. If you're like my friend who equates spreadsheets with "big" projects, then you will be finding it "rougher" to do those "big" projects.

A very essential and often overlooked spreadsheet skill is the ability to manage, manipulate, and work through the numbers in extremely small increments. It is exactly what you do with a calculator, but calculators work differently than spreadsheets. *The net result is that people do not become facile with spreadsheets simply because they don't engage in the fundamental skill-building activities.*

After you get into the habit of using Excel as your electronic scratch pad, you will develop the skill of thinking through problems and quickly become adept at rearranging numbers and trying alternative computations. In short, these skills will enormously reduce the difficulties you'll encounter when you get to the big spreadsheet projects.

Complex Spreadsheets

Complex spreadsheets and best practices for them are the topics that occupy most of this book. Therefore I characterize them in this chapter only to let you know what makes something "complex." I also want to alert you to things that you might want to consider in dealing with the specific complexity. Finally, I want to get you thinking about an overall design pattern when it comes to large and complex spreadsheets.

Determining what makes a spreadsheet complex

The techniques that apply to simple spreadsheets are generally applicable to the complex ones. There are more things you'll want to address when it comes to complex spreadsheets. I outline some of them here so that you'll have some time to mull over them before you get to the later chapters.

First, I want to distinguish between natural and artificial complexity. Artificial complexity is introduced when your spreadsheet incorporates decisions and logic that is determined outside the spreadsheet. It takes the form of what I call "off-spreadsheet analysis." I take up this topic later in the book.

When does a spreadsheet suddenly become complex? The mere process of asking and answering this question can give vital clues on how to deal with the complexity. Complexity becomes a factor in situations such as the following:

◆ Computations, however few or many, become hairy or may be subject to more than one kind of interpretation. There are strategies for dealing with convoluted formulas (the so-called "megaformulas"). You can use a divide-and-conquer approach to break out multi-line formulas into separate cells to isolate each part of the logic.

◆ If the introduction of a separate verification/validation process becomes necessary, it is a signal that the spreadsheet is complex. To deal with this situation, Excel provides some formula auditing facilities that allow you to examine how formulas for cells you designate are computed. Included is the ability to examine, step by step, every computation and subcomputation that Excel makes for an isolated cell. The topic of verifying and validating spreadsheets, as a whole, is addressed at length in Chapter 11, "Spreadsheet Auditing: Challenging the Numbers of Others."

◆ If there is a need to incorporate a change-management process along with some version control, it is an indication that the spreadsheet has become complex. Excel provides some change-tracking facilities that can be helpful in sharing files in which colleagues make minor alterations to the spreadsheet. There are steps you can take beyond the out-of-the-box facilities provided by Excel. Some of these are discussed in Chapter 11.

◆ When documentation exists regarding numeric assumptions and formulas used and is considered an integral part of the spreadsheet (that is, this documentation gets distributed to whomever receives the spreadsheet), it is an indicator that the spreadsheet is complex. This kind of documentation is often found with financial projections and forecasts. The objective of such documentation is to provide enough information to enable a third party to take the same base data and build an equivalent spreadsheet and replicate the same results.

◆ A spreadsheet can involve a formal publication process whereby there are specific parties who are allowed to make changes to the spreadsheet. The nature of the changes can be restricted by role. Excel provides facilities for protecting different parts of a spreadsheet using passwords. From a publishing standpoint, companies and organizations are free to create their own workflow or incorporate the spreadsheet into a Content Management or Document Management System.

◆ There may be a need to employ specialized formulas found in one of the Excel Add-In modules, a Visual Basic Application, or some third-party tool such as MathematicaLink for Excel (a product of Wolfram Research) or CrystalBall (a product of Decisioneering, used for Monte Carlo simulations and risk analysis). This topic lies beyond the scope of this book; however, you can find some links and information on this topic at my Web site (www.evolvingtech.com/excel).

◆ Spreadsheets become complex when scalability issues play a prominent role. The sheer size of a spreadsheet can be enough to warrant making specific accommodations to deal with scalability. Size is not the only factor that alters a spreadsheet's scalability. If you had been actively using spreadsheets in the late 1990s, you may have dealt with the Year 2000 problem.

A real problem that occurs with spreadsheets is that they are designed one way, without scalability in mind, because it was not needed or anticipated at the time of creation. Things can change and suddenly the spreadsheet needs major reworking to accommodate the change.

◆ A clear indication that a spreadsheet is complex is when formalization helps you to simplify the spreadsheet. With simple spreadsheets, you can "fly by the seat of your pants." As is often the case with simple spreadsheets, creating and using named references may not buy you all that much in terms of efficiency or ease of use. If you're just adding two numbers, and there are descriptive labels right next to them, it may not be necessary to rework the formulas using named references. However, at some point a spreadsheet could grow in complexity and really benefit by having named references, separate areas for storing commonly referenced information, and a means of accessing such information by a named reference instead of by cell coordinates.

◆ Excel provides for "shared workbooks" that allow several people in a networked environment to simultaneously access and edit a workbook.

◆ There is one more yardstick to determine whether a spreadsheet is "complex." Determine whether the lifetime of active management of the spreadsheet exceeds the personnel turnover rate (that is, something in the spreadsheet needs to survive from one person to the next). Even if nothing in the spreadsheet is inherently complex, it should be treated as complex if you have to make special accommodations when people are not expected to be around long enough to transfer knowledge.

Creating a "blueprint" for large or complex spreadsheets

I want to keep this short and simple; throughout the book examples, you're going to see this in action, over and over again. You should be thinking about constructing larger spreadsheets in terms of an easy-to-follow design pattern called "layering," shown in Figure 2-13. No rocket science is involved.

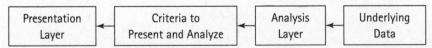

Figure 2-13: Layering your spreadsheets

In your spreadsheet, think of the Presentation Layer as Sheet1 of your Workbook tabs. Ideally, the Presentation Layer should be largely devoid of any of the heavy-duty computations. That activity should be carried out elsewhere in the spreadsheet.

Depending on how you want to structure your spreadsheet, you can choose to provide the consumer of the spreadsheet with some abilities to adjust the presentation. These could be in the form of buttons or spinner controls (see Appendix A for the topics of Excel setup and configuration). Such controls can allow the user to adjust values or otherwise modify how and what is presented in the spreadsheets.

Behind the scenes, you will be actually managing the information that is used in controlling the spreadsheet behavior. If, for example, your spreadsheet is displaying a graph of profitability by product code, your button or spinner control can be adjusting the lookup value to retrieve the data that gets graphed. Ideally, this behind-the-scenes activity is shielded from the user.

If you noticed, I put the shoe on the other foot, so to speak. You're designing the spreadsheet. You understand its inner workings. The people you're distributing the spreadsheet don't. A naive user could fiddle around and break the spreadsheet formulas without realizing it. It's in everyone's best interest if end users are shielded from the program's complexity and the complex parts are not in harm's way. You may want to keep tabular and lookup information used to manage the spreadsheet behavior in a separate location, perhaps Sheet2 of the spreadsheet workbook.

Somewhere in your spreadsheet, the difficult calculations and analyses are going to be performed. You may be doing things such as calculating correlation coefficients, some detailed statistical analysis, or whatever. This analysis layer forms the heart of your computation engine. It is often a good idea to segregate this Analysis Layer from the two prior layers. You might choose to put this Analysis Layer in Sheet3 of your workbook.

It is very tempting to let the raw data that your spreadsheet uses cohabitate with the Analysis Layer. *Don't do it.* When you mingle the two, you place yourself on the precipice of a very slippery slope. Here are some of the issues that may result:

◆ Heavy-duty calculations are computationally expensive. If you mix the calculation engine with all the data, you'll quickly find yourself performing some calculation on every row of data rather than a select few. Keep your complex calculations to a minimum. Just perform them for the ones that are to be displayed in the Presentation Layer. You will see this in later chapters. The Data Viewer tool in Chapter 8, "Analyzing Data," provides an excellent example of how this works. Also, in Chapter 12, "Spreadsheet Portals, XML, and Web Services," I show you how to do this. For those of you using versions of Excel earlier than Excel 2003, don't despair. The essential features of Spreadsheet Portals, although greatly enhanced by XML and Web Services, are not dependent on these technologies. You will have a working implementation that shuttles data from the Underlying Data Layer to the Analysis Layer, munches on it, and punts it over to the Presentation Layer — with all these actions occurring under a defined control mechanism that manages who gets what, and when.

◆ If the underlying data becomes mixed with the Analysis Layer, you may find updating your data to be difficult.

◆ When you mix the Data and Analysis Layers, if you then replicate cells and have portions of the replicated content spilling over to other portions on the same worksheet, you might wind up compromising your data or your formulas.

These are three good reasons that should be enough to deter you from mingling your Analysis Layer with your Underlying Data Layer.

To summarize info about your Analysis Layer:

- The calculation engine in your Analysis Layer should perform a limited set of very specific calculations.

- The calculation engine should operate on only a limited portion of data rather than the whole dataset.

- The calculation engine doesn't determine what data is to be calculated. It knows only to perform calculations for a specific set of rows/columns or data values. Whatever is in that predefined set of cells is what's going to be used in the calculations. I call these limited number of cells the *analysis data* to distinguish them from the much larger number of cells containing the *underlying data* or *source data*.

- The calculation engine "expects" analysis data to conform to a certain format or structure. When the data is somehow transferred from the Underlying Data Layer to the Analysis Layer, there may need to be some massaging or cleanup of the data to make it suitable for the calculation engine. For instance, the Underlying Data Layer may contain a long list of employee names. All too often, employee names may have trailing or leading spaces. These may need to be removed.

- The calculation engine relies on some external mechanism (sitting between the Analysis Layer and the Presentation Layer) to determine what data gets pulled in for analysis and punted over to the Presentation Layer.

In principle, all these layers could be folded into a single worksheet. Unless your spreadsheet is really simple, this would not be a good practice to place everything in one worksheet. Even if you were in just the very early stages of prototyping your spreadsheet, it would be a far better practice to separate these layers onto separate worksheets. Depending on your needs, you could fold the mechanism that manages what data gets analyzed and presented to either the Presentation Layer or the Analysis Layer. However, you should really stay away from mixing your underlying data with your analysis data. For large and complex spreadsheets, this is the golden rule.

Closing Thoughts

If you worked through the example in this chapter, you have seen that the process of constructing a spreadsheet isn't tightly intertwined with the formulas and Excel functions you use. If you haven't previously adopted a style in the construction of spreadsheets, this chapter will get you a good deal closer. If you started this chapter already possessing your own, the exposition I have presented may have given you some new ideas to further improve your own spreadsheet construction techniques.

When I think of complex spreadsheets, I tend to think about the moment in time, or event, or contributing factor that changed, thereby causing them to go from simple to complex. After I know what is different, I can evolve a strategy for better managing that complexity. I provided some specifics regarding out-of-the-box features of Excel that may aid you (such as Formula Auditing), as well as alluded to the specific chapters of this book that address these topics in more depth.

It is not always possible to define the singular moment that makes a spreadsheet suddenly complex. By that I don't mean the situations when you have more than one kind of complexity in a spreadsheet. Rather, I have in mind the times when you may be handed an already constructed spreadsheet and told, "Here, you know what to do with this...." Dealing with that type of situation to make such a spreadsheet more workable is the topic of Chapter 10, "Going for the Facelift: Spreadsheet Makeovers."

One important topic introduced in this chapter was the layering of your spreadsheets when they get large. All too often I hear of people recovering from their "monster" spreadsheets. The use of the layering technique is an essential topic if you anticipate having to construct large spreadsheets. I introduced the basic design pattern here. You will see this technique repeatedly implemented throughout the book.

Chapter 3

Your Handy Reference for Manipulating Data

IN THIS CHAPTER

- ◆ Tidying up your data
- ◆ Introducing Excel functions for data manipulation
- ◆ Sorting, block-sorting, and scaffolding
- ◆ Working with techniques for data surgery and data manipulation

CHAPTER 1 INTRODUCES YOU to the syntax of a variety of Excel functions. In this chapter, I bring into play what I call the semantics of Excel functions. This is one of those chapters in which it's all about rolling up your shirtsleeves and getting to work. Though I summarize concepts, I mostly focus on ways to parse and manipulate data.

You will get a sampling of various functions for manipulating data. Many of these functions, you will soon discover, bear a striking similarity to others. Where possible, I compare and contrast these and give you an idea of when and where one function might be preferred over another.

I then show you special techniques for sorting data. One of these techniques relates to sorting more than three columns (or rows). The other deals with block sorting.

I then show you how to convert tabular spreadsheet data to a format suitable for importing the data to a relational database. I provide you with a tool to do this and explain how it works. You will see that some of the string manipulation functions introduced early on in the chapter in action.

Excel String Manipulation Functions You Need to Know

There are some broad categories of Excel functions that will help you manipulate data.

First, you may want to compare one piece of data to another to assure that the group of data is uniformly identical. Two mechanisms are available: the EXACT function and the equality operator =.

69

There are functions that will allow you to locate pieces of information inside a string of characters. These include FIND and SEARCH.

As you will see, many Excel functions are similar to one another, but there are subtle and important differences. In this chapter, I try to clue you in on some of these distinctions.

Some functions allow you to perform "surgery" on strings of data and even "lobotomize" the data. In this manner you can cleave and restructure data to suit your needs. Surgical functions can include LEFT, MID, RIGHT, SUBSTITUTE, REPLACE, REPT, CLEAN, and TRIM.

There are times you will need to take apart string data and convert portions of them to numbers suitable for doing calculations. Functions such as VALUE will allow you to accomplish this. You may also want to construct cell references from string segments.

You will come to understand the differences between CONCATENATE and the & operator. Moreover, you will see that when you combine concatenated expressions with the INDIRECT function, you can dynamically alter which data flows through your formulas.

Sorting Techniques

Not everything that has to do with data is wrapped up in Excel functions. Sometimes you'll need to organize and rearrange data. To this end, you can go beyond Excel's imposed limit of sorting a maximum of three criteria.

Excel likes to do sorting on a row-by-row basis, but sometimes you'll want to sort and move blocks of data instead of individual rows. The following chapter delves more further into data rearrangement, and discusses PivotTables and useful things you can do with filtered data.

I hope that this chapter will arm you with a battery of techniques that will be handy when you're down in the trenches working with data.

First Steps to Tidying Up Your Data

When you first receive a new set of data, you will likely want to organize and compare values. Rearranging information in a consistent manner is dependent on the data being in as close to a pristine state as possible. It may become necessary to tidy up your data.

Sometimes you have lists of data whose common elements should be *exactly* identical (as opposed to *almost* identical). You might see an employee name repeatedly appearing that contains the first name, middle initial, and last name, but even so, the various cells may not be identical. You might, for instance, have:

```
John A. Doe
John A  Doe
John A Doe
```

The name John A Doe is almost the same in all three instances. Each instance refers to a person with the exact same name and differs only in appearance or lexical structure. As far as Excel is concerned, they are all different entries. If you tried to count the number of occurrences using the COUNTIF function, you might not get an accurate count.

You would need to do two things:

♦ Test to see whether data matches up properly.

♦ Clean up the data.

If you are importing data for which you already know the kinds or corrections that need to be made, you can just proceed to the cleanup, wholesale style and make changes in a single sweep. Of course, at some point you will (or should!) test the data to verify that it matches up properly.

If you already have data being actively used in your spreadsheets, then step 1 is particularly important. If you see discrepancies, some simple manual editing of the few aberrant entries might suffice after you've determined where they occur.

Two mechanisms are available for testing whether two pieces of data match up. One of these is the Excel function EXACT. It is case sensitive. The other is the equality operator =, which is not case sensitive. To get a better idea of what is case sensitive and what is not, look at Table 3-1. Also, take a look at the third tab (EQUALITY) of ch03-01datacompare.xls on your CD-ROM.

TABLE 3–1 REPRESENTATIVE COMPARISON OF VARIOUS EXCEL FUNCTIONS

Excel Formula or Operation	Value Displayed	Comments
=EXACT("John A Doe","john a doe")	FALSE	EXACT function is case sensitive.
="John A Doe"="john a doe"	TRUE	The equality operator is not case sensitive. Also note that = appearing inside a formula is not the same as the = that starts off the formula.
=VLOOKUP("jOhN a DoE",SomeDataset) =VLOOKUP("john a doe",SomeDataset)	Returns the same results with either formula.	VLOOKUP is not case sensitive.

Continued

TABLE 3-1 REPRESENTATIVE COMPARISON OF VARIOUS EXCEL FUNCTIONS
    (Continued)

Excel Formula or Operation	Value Displayed	Comments
Using the Excel sorting feature		Sorting is not case sensitive unless it is enabled from the button Options from the Sort Dialog Box.
=SUBSTITUTE("aBbB","B","x")	axbx	SUBSTITUTE is case sensitive.
=FIND("a","AAAaaa")	4	FIND is case sensitive
=FIND("A","AAAaaa")	1	Note that finding an
=FIND("","AAAaaa")	1	empty string does not return an error.
SEARCH("a","AAAaaa")	1	SEARCH is not case sensitive.

It feels silly to use EXACT or the equality operator to test whether just two cells match up. This may be true when you're displaying data using monospace fonts and you have only two cells, one directly below the other. If you have hundreds or thousands of cells, eyeballing the data is definitely prone to error.

The Sentinel LookAhead Technique

Sometimes it is helpful to know where the next change occurs in a long list of data. There is a methodology that you can use called the Sentinel LookAhead Technique. I provide you with an example of its usage in the file ch04-01datacompare.xls. Open this file and go to the LONGLIST tab (if you don't have your computer and the CD-ROM available right now, then see Figure 3-1). Column 1 shows a list of almost identical names. Because the variations in the name occur infrequently, you would have to do a lot of scrolling to spot where the next change occurs. The LookAhead technique applied in both columns 3 and 4 reports the row in which the next variation in the list (column 1) occurs without needing manually scroll down the worksheet.

You can quickly see that after row 12, you have to scroll down to row 878 to see a variation in the data (John A Doe appears in lowercase). If you ignore case sensitivity, the data actually changes when you cross row 1142. This LookAhead facility can be extremely useful when you are working with thousands of lines of data and will help you to tidy up your data by pinpointing and eliminating the variations.

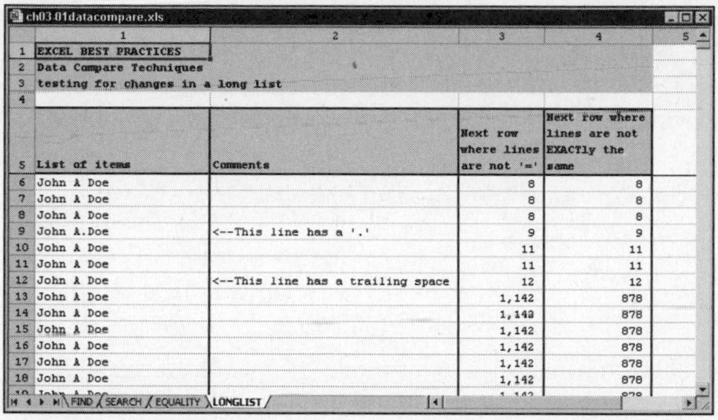

ch03-01datacompare.xls

	1	2	3	4
1	EXCEL BEST PRACTICES			
2	Data Compare Techniques			
3	testing for changes in a long list			
4				
5	List of items	Comments	Next row where lines are not '='	Next row where lines are not EXACTly the same
6	John A Doe		8	8
7	John A Doe		8	8
8	John A Doe		8	8
9	John A.Doe	<--This line has a '.'	9	9
10	John A Doe		11	11
11	John A Doe		11	11
12	John A Doe	<--This line has a trailing space	12	12
13	John A Doe		1,142	878
14	John A Doe		1,142	878
15	John A Doe		1,142	878
16	John A Doe		1,142	878
17	John A Doe		1,142	878
18	John A Doe		1,142	878

Figure 3-1: Spotting the row where the next change occurs

Though you can retrofit the sample spreadsheet from the CD to work with your data, it may be simpler to just lift the essential formulas and apply it directly in your spreadsheets. I give you the basic formula, explain how it works, and show you variations on the formulas for extra flexibility.

Here is a formula you can use to perform the equality comparison:

```
=IF(RC1<>R[1]C1,ROW(),R[1]C)
```

Alternatively, you can use:

```
=IF(NOT(RC1=R[1]C1),ROW(),R[1]C)
```

Basically, you're asking Excel to compare the values of the cell in column 1 on your current row with the one immediately below it. If they don't match, they return the current row number; otherwise, report the row identified in the cell immediately below. This has the effect of looking ahead for the next change and percolating it up to the current cell location. Keep in mind that if the data you are comparing does not reside in column number 1, you will need to adjust your formula slightly. If, for instance, your data resides in column 23, you can use the formula:

```
=IF(RC23<>R[1]C23,ROW(),R[1]C)
```

Sometimes, you will be constantly inserting and deleting rows as you update your data. The Sentinel LookAhead formulas immediately above and below can get disrupted, because they reference lines that were just inserted or deleted. You will want to restore these altered formulas to their original state. If you really don't want to be snagged by this kind of issue, you can write your compare formula so that it won't require any changes upon inserting or deleting rows, as follows:

```
=IF(OFFSET(R1C1,ROW()-1,0)<>OFFSET(R1C1,ROW(),0),ROW(),
                              OFFSET(R1C1,ROW(),COLUMN()-1))
```

Granted, this is a long one-line formula. It is more robust than the earlier versions. It is included in your takeaway.txt file on the CD, so you can just copy from the file and paste it to the edit line in your Excel formula bar.

If the data you are comparing does not reside on column number 1, you need to adjust your formula slightly.

If, for instance, your data resides in column 23, you can use the formula:

```
=IF(OFFSET(R1C1,ROW()-1,22)<>OFFSET(R1C1,ROW(),22),ROW(),
                    OFFSET(R1C1,ROW(),COLUMN()-1))
```

The formula replaces the column offset of 0 to an offset of N-1. N, in this case, is 23. So the column offset of N-1 is 22. Once again, this formula is included in your takeaway.txt file.

My personal style is not to do an unnecessary amount of "formula hacking" when I'd rather be immersing myself in the data. I am willing to put up with the occasional imposition of reworking formulas around the rows I just inserted or deleted.

As a result, I don't usually need to use OFFSET for this kind of data validation. However, should I need to assure myself that formulas remain unchanged when inserting or deleting rows, I wouldn't hesitate to use OFFSET in the manner just described (and neither should you). Near the end of Chapter 10, "Going for the Facelift: Spreadsheet Makeovers," you can see how the technique of formula invariance using OFFSET really pays off. I also explain the technique in greater detail.

 If you have a limited amount of time and resources available, focus more on getting familiar with your data and making sure that it is well stated than on fancy editing formulas and formatting touches.

I've shown you how to identify where variations occur. Because the changes shown here were both few and easily located, it would suffice to manually correct them. More often than not, the changes may be too numerous to fix by hand. Furthermore, you need to learn automate your tasks. I go into automation more thoroughly in later chapters, particularly Chapter 9, "How Not to Get Stuck in the MUD (Messed-Up Data)."

Other Functions for Effective Data Manipulation

Before moving on to sorting techniques and a detailed application involving data manipulation, there are some Excel functions and information associated with their use that it will help you to know about.

The & joining operator and CONCATENATE

Both the & operator and CONCATENATE accomplish similar tasks. The & operator is a binary infix style operator that sits between two expressions; in much the same way that + sits between two numbers. By comparison, CONCATENATE is a prefix style operator, separating each of its arguments (input parameters) by commas (,). Both sets of operators always return string expressions. Does that mean that these functions can't be used for numeric calculations or computations not involving strings? Not at all. Keep reading.

You might recall from Chapter 1, "A Foundation for Developing Best Practices" (refer to Figure 1-17, in that chapter) that a variety of names were defined containing the same base expression but differing slightly. These were names such as TaxRate1, TaxRate2 and so forth. Suppose you want to work out a single computation in which you switch among these names inside your formula. How would you do this? Here are three options:

Option 1 – Hardwired Formulas

=CHOOSE(MyNumber,TaxRate1,TaxRate2,TaxRate3)

This approach isn't bad, except that:

- ◆ The maximum number of arguments that can be accepted as input for Excel functions is 30. In the example using CHOOSE, only 29 variables at most can be used (the variable MyNumber eats up one of the 30 available slots). If you were to attempt to use more than a half a dozen or so variables as inputs, the formula would quickly become unwieldy.

- ◆ The names or cell references used as inputs for CHOOSE are hardwired. If these names used in your CHOOSE formula were changed someday, you may have to perform surgery to directly edit the formula using CHOOSE. This is definitely not a good practice.

Option 2 – Use some type of lookup function

You could have a formula like this:

=OFFSET(BasePositionOfTaxRateTable,MyNumber,0)

or this:

=VLOOKUP(MyNumber,SomeListOfTaxRatesInALookupTable,2)

These types of formulas definitely get around the limitation of the number of values to pick from, as you can easily surpass the limitation of 29. You also have the advantage of not requiring a uniquely defined name from each and every value you can conceivably pick.

The key factor that you are banking on is that all the values you expect to be selecting from are *arranged together* and that their *positional arrangements are unchanging.* Most of the time, this will work fine, especially if you keep such tables out of harm's way when it comes to naive consumers of your spreadsheets.

You can't always guarantee that the data you might want to retrieve all reside in a single area of your spreadsheet. For this case, I give you a third option.

Option 3 – Dynamically construct the name or cell reference

This option is interesting. Consider the following:

```
=INDIRECT("TaxRate"&MyNumber)
```

Here, I have introduced the Excel function INDIRECT. This function retrieves the value of whatever string name it is given. INDIRECT expects a single string expression. It gets it. The fact that the single string expression is constructed out of a fixed or static part ("TaxRate") and a changeable part (MyNumber, resulting in "TaxRate1" or "TaxRate2" or something else) is what makes this function extraordinarily flexible. The name INDIRECT is not super intuitive, but the function works well.

This option is very much like Option 1 except it removes the imposed limitation of 29 items to pick from. As you can see in this example, the string expression "TaxRate" is hardwired into the formula. This dependency should be removed. It would be preferable to point to some value that is not part of the cell's formula. Consider:

```
=INDIRECT(SomeNamedValue&MyNumber)
```

where SomeNamedValue happens to have the value "TaxRate" or whatever static string value that you deem appropriate. Now the hardwired dependency has been totally extricated from the formula.

It is generally better to keep hardwired values and parameters isolated, exposed, and easily editable than to bury them deep inside a complex formula.

USING INDIRECT WITH CONCATENATE

Here is how the formula from the previous section:

```
=INDIRECT(SomeNamedValue&MyNumber)
```

would appear if you use CONCATENATE instead of the & operator:

```
=INDIRECT(CONCATENATE(SomeNamedValue,MyNumber))
```

As long as you are using 30 or fewer arguments as input, both CONCATENATE and & will work equally well. If you have the occasion to use more than 30 inputs to concatenate, your only option is to use the & operator.

Some more functions for data manipulation

To facilitate data manipulation, it will be helpful for you to know about more Excel functions and be provided with some sample computations. These examples illustrate the syntax usage and show you the computed results.

LEFT, MID, AND RIGHT

No doubt you can guess what LEFT, MID, and RIGHT do. Representative examples include:

```
=LEFT("Now is the time.",5)          returns 'Now i'
=MID("Now is the time.",5,2)         returns 'is'
=RIGHT("Now is the time.",5)         returns 'time.'
```

 You should be aware that Excel has double-byte versions of these functions, called LEFTB, MIDB, and RIGHTB. There are plenty of others. Such functions are designed to accommodate double-byte character set (DBCS) languages.

REPT, REPLACE, AND SUBSTITUTE

These three functions are used for placing specific string sequences within a string of characters. Here are some representative examples of these functions:

```
=REPT("*",3)&"Header"&REPT("*",3)     returns '***Header***'
=REPLACE("Now is the time.",5,2,"was")  returns 'Now was the time.'
=SUBSTITUTE("AbAbcA","A","x")         returns 'xbxbcx'
=SUBSTITUTE("AbAbcA","A","x",2)       returns 'AbxbcA'
```

The SUBSTITUTE function is case sensitive. If the optional argument of the occurrence number is provided, it will substitute only that for that occurrence.

LOWER, UPPER, AND PROPER

You use these functions to adjust the capitalization of characters in a string. Here are some representative examples of these functions:

```
=LOWER("ThiS iS a TItle")            returns 'this is a title'
=PROPER("ThiS iS a TItle")           returns 'This Is A Title'
=UPPER("ThiS iS a TItle")            returns 'THIS IS A TITLE'
```

Notice that PROPER forces the phrase into uppercase for the first letter of every word and into lowercase for all others.

LEN AND TRIM

LEN allows you to determine the length of a string of characters. TRIM allows you to remove excess character spaces between words as well as remove the leading and trailing spaces for the phrase. Here are some representative examples of these functions:

```
=LEN("Now is the time.")            returns 16
=TRIM("  Too    many   spaces   ")  returns 'Too many spaces'
```

CHAR, CODE, AND CLEAN

Have you ever been given exported data from a database such as Access, brought it into a spreadsheet, and seen little square boxes along side portions of the text? One way of getting rid of the little "gremlins" is to go the edit line of your Excel formula bar and physically delete the offending character. Manual editing of this nature is tedious, time consuming and prone to error. You can use the CLEAN function to exterminate the gremlins (that is, non-printing characters).

There's more to a character than meets the "i"

What are some of these non-printing characters and how are they generated in the first place? If you look at any of the typical spreadsheet formulas you might create or find in most books, you will see they don't have tabs, carriage returns, or line feeds embedded as an integral part of the formulas. Tabs, carriage returns and line feeds are some of the nonprintable characters.

Okay, pull back one step to get to the basics. When you communicate information you use an alphabet from a language such as English. Normally, you associate this with 26 letters. To communicate information using documents, you need more than 26 letters. Certainly you would want to have digits; so you add another ten for 0 through 9. Surely you will need decimal points, commas, and the dollar symbol. These also double as punctuation marks for currency and narrative sentences.

If you're going to have proper sentences, you need to distinguish between upper- and lowercase characters. Your alphabet soup has grown by leaps and bounds. You need to establish some order for this. To get computers to all work together and share data unambiguously, organizations such as the American National Standards Institute and the International Standards Organization defined standards that are commonly accepted. These standards map an ordered list of character symbols to a sequence of digits. This mapping allows computers to exchange information using digits, which then can be meaningfully interpreted by their character equivalents.

Excel has functions that map an ordered structure of characters to a number sequence and will produce the character symbol that corresponds to the known number code. Here are some sample computations:

```
=CHAR(65)                          returns 'A'
=CHAR(66)                          returns 'B'
=CHAR(67)                          returns 'C'
=CHAR(97)                          returns 'a'
=CHAR(98)                          returns 'b'
=CHAR(99)                          returns 'c'
=CHAR(32)                          returns ' '
=CODE("a")                         returns 97
=CODE("A")                         returns 65
=CODE(" ")                         returns 32
```

A character space that normally separates words can be generated using CHAR(32). To generate a tab character, you use CHAR(9). A carriage return can be generated using CHAR(13); a linefeed by using CHAR(10). Generating tabs, carriage returns and linefeeds may not be all that beneficial inside the spreadsheet. However, when a spreadsheet file is saved as text or its contents are exported, the appearance of this character encoding could be relevant to other programs.

VALUE AND TEXT

VALUE will convert a text string appearing as a number to its numerical representation. TEXT performs the reverse. It takes a number (which may be a computed value) and turns it into a string of text which conforms to a designated format pattern. Here are some representative examples of these functions:

```
=VALUE("$1,000,000")               returns 1000000
=TEXT(2000*3000,"$###,##0")        returns '$6,000,000'
```

Notice the single quotes around the $6,000,000. They are there because the expression the number computed by multiplying 2000 times 3000 (which is 6000000) has actually been converted to a text string replete with all the commas and the $ symbol. It is no longer a number. You will have the opportunity to use TEXT later in the chapter, when you convert a date value to a formatted text representation.

Useful Sorting Techniques

Not everything in Excel is concerned with functions and formulas. In spreadsheets you need to be organizing your data. Drag and Drop Editing is fun when you're moving data over a few rows and columns, or perhaps a screenful or two. Obviously, you will want to go beyond manual editing after you start managing more than a screenful of information.

Chances are you are already familiar with the data-sorting features of Excel. You may not be familiar with sorting data using more than three criteria or columns are involved. Also, you may not have attempted "block sorting." I cover these topics next.

Sorting with more than three columns (or rows)

Out of the box, Excel allows you to sort using only, at most, three columns (or rows) as your sort criteria. This works well when you have a simple list composed of name, age, and ZIP Code, for example, with each of these residing on a separate column in your worksheet. But what if you need to organize your data using more than three criteria?

The technique I discuss here allows you to perform a sort involving more than three criteria. This methodology applies equally well to sorting either columns or rows (though I only discuss the sorting of columns).

Although Excel limits how many columns you use as criteria for sorting, an easy workaround exists that involves an additional step anytime you need to use more than three criteria. It boils down to multiple passes for sorting.

METHODOLOGY

Here are your steps when sorting by more than three criteria:

1. For your given set of data residing on a single worksheet, identify the criteria (columns) you are using for you sort. Order these from the one starting from the highest priority criteria to the lowest. Keep a tally of the number of sort criteria available for sorting. Call this number "N." You will identify sort criteria from 1 through N, with 1 being the criterion having the highest priority and N, the lowest.

2. Select all the data on your worksheet that you will sort. Open your sort dialog box. If N > 3, place the criteria or column associated with N in the third (bottom) entry of your sort dialog box. Place the criteria or column for N–1 in the second (middle) entry of your sort dialog box. Place the criteria or column for N–2 in the first (top) entry of your sort dialog box. Assure that the Ascending/Descending attributes are accurately set for each of the search criteria. Press the OK button.

3. You no longer need to consider additional sorting for the three criteria you just sorted by from your list, so your new value for N is three less than it was in Step 2. If your new value for N is still greater than 3, repeat Step 2; otherwise, go to Step 4.

4. If the number of remaining sort criteria is three, place the third criteria in the third (bottom) entry of your sort dialog box. Then place the second criteria in the second (middle) entry of your sort dialog box. Then place the first criteria (one having the highest priority) in the first (top) entry of your sort dialog box.

If the number of remaining sort criteria is only two, place the second criteria in the second (middle) entry of your sort dialog box. Then place the first criteria (one having the highest priority) in the first (top) entry of your sort dialog box. Clear the bottom entry (set it to "none").

If the number of remaining sort criteria is only one, then obviously place the remaining criteria (one having the highest priority) in the first (top) entry of your sort dialog box. Clear the middle and bottom entries (set them to "none").

Assure that the Ascending/Descending attributes are accurately set for each of the search criteria. Press the OK button.

A WORKED-OUT SORTING EXAMPLE

For this example, I want you to open a file (ch04-01censusdata_4K.xls) that you'll be using with PivotTables in Chapter 4, "Compiling, Managing, and Viewing Your Data." If the file is not immediately available to you, just look at Figure 3-2.

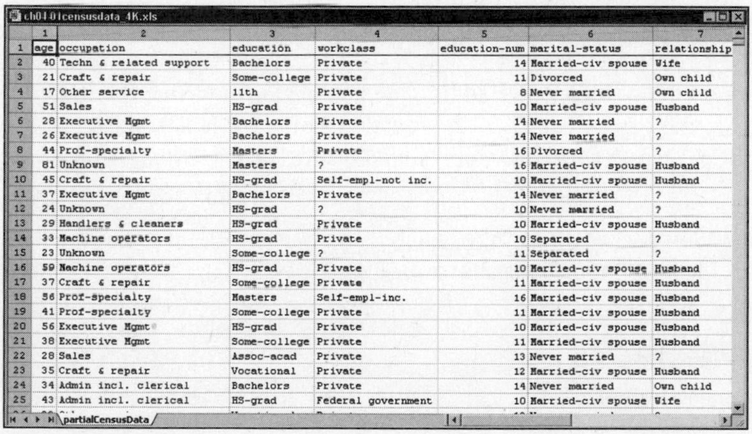
ch04-01censusdata_4K.xls

	1	2	3	4	5	6	7
1	age	occupation	education	workclass	education-num	marital-status	relationship
2	40	Techn & related support	Bachelors	Private	14	Married-civ spouse	Wife
3	21	Craft & repair	Some-college	Private	11	Divorced	Own child
4	17	Other service	11th	Private	8	Never married	Own child
5	51	Sales	HS-grad	Private	10	Married-civ spouse	Husband
6	28	Executive Mgmt	Bachelors	Private	14	Never married	?
7	26	Executive Mgmt	Bachelors	Private	14	Never married	?
8	44	Prof-specialty	Masters	Private	16	Divorced	?
9	81	Unknown	Masters	?	16	Married-civ spouse	Husband
10	45	Craft & repair	HS-grad	Self-empl-not inc.	10	Married-civ spouse	Husband
11	37	Executive Mgmt	Bachelors	Private	14	Never married	?
12	24	Unknown	HS-grad	?	10	Never married	?
13	29	Handlers & cleaners	HS-grad	Private	10	Married-civ spouse	Husband
14	33	Machine operators	HS-grad	Private	10	Separated	?
15	23	Unknown	Some-college	?	11	Separated	?
16	59	Machine operators	HS-grad	Private	10	Married-civ spouse	Husband
17	37	Craft & repair	Some-college	Private	11	Married-civ spouse	Husband
18	56	Prof-specialty	Masters	Self-empl-inc.	16	Married-civ spouse	Husband
19	41	Prof-specialty	Some-college	Private	11	Married-civ spouse	Husband
20	56	Executive Mgmt	HS-grad	Private	10	Married-civ spouse	Husband
21	38	Executive Mgmt	Some-college	Private	11	Married-civ spouse	Husband
22	28	Sales	Assoc-acad	Private	13	Never married	?
23	35	Craft & repair	Vocational	Private	12	Married-civ spouse	Husband
24	34	Admin incl. clerical	Bachelors	Private	14	Never married	Own child
25	43	Admin incl. clerical	HS-grad	Federal government	10	Married-civ spouse	Wife

partialCensusData

Figure 3-2: Spreadsheet to be sorted using more than three columns

Fourteen columns are in this spreadsheet. The first row is your Header row.

1. To keep things simple, sort the data using the first four columns, with highest priority given to `age`, followed by `occupation`, then `education`, and finally by `workclass`. In a real world situation, you pick which columns you want to use for sorting and set the priority. Following the steps outlined in the preceding "Methodology" section. For the example in this section, N = 4.

2. The spreadsheet contains 4,001 rows and 14 columns. Select all the cells (`R1C1:R4001C14`) and open your sort dialog box. Because N is greater than 3, place the "Nth" item ("workclass"), which has the lowest sort

priority, as the bottom entry. Place the criteria that corresponds to N–1 ("'education") as the middle entry. Place the criteria that corresponds to N–2 ("occupation") as the top entry. This scheme should correspond to that shown in Figure 3-3.

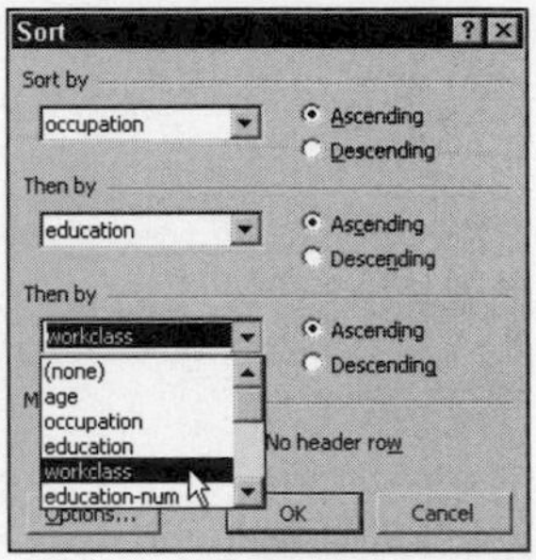

Figure 3–3: The first pass through the sort

Assure that the Ascending/Descending attributes are accurately set for each of the search criteria. Press the OK button.

3. You no longer need to consider additional sorting for the three criteria you just sorted by from your list, so your new value for N is three less than it was in Step 2. Only one item is left to sort ("age"). Proceed to Step 4.

4. Set the top "Sort by" entry to "age" and clear the middle and bottom entries (set them to "none"), as shown in Figure 3-4.

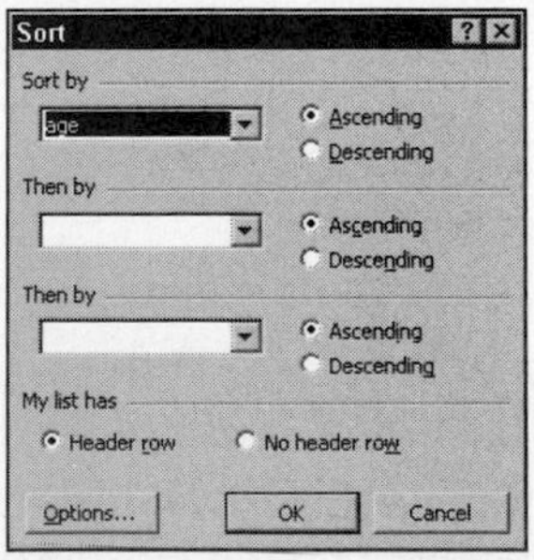

Figure 3–4: The second pass through the sort

Assure that the Ascending/Descending attributes are accurately set for each of the search criteria. Press the OK button.

Now your spreadsheet is properly sorted with four columns, starting with `age`, then `occupation`, followed by `education`, and finally by `workclass` (see Figure 3-5).

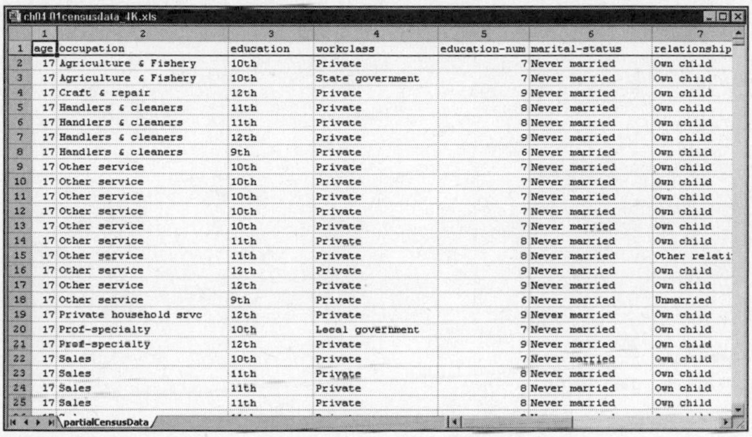

	1	2	3	4	5	6	7
1	age	occupation	education	workclass	education-num	marital-status	relationship
2	17	Agriculture & Fishery	10th	Private	7	Never married	Own child
3	17	Agriculture & Fishery	10th	State government	7	Never married	Own child
4	17	Craft & repair	12th	Private	9	Never married	Own child
5	17	Handlers & cleaners	11th	Private	8	Never married	Own child
6	17	Handlers & cleaners	11th	Private	8	Never married	Own child
7	17	Handlers & cleaners	12th	Private	9	Never married	Own child
8	17	Handlers & cleaners	9th	Private	6	Never married	Own child
9	17	Other service	10th	Private	7	Never married	Own child
10	17	Other service	10th	Private	7	Never married	Own child
11	17	Other service	10th	Private	7	Never married	Own child
12	17	Other service	10th	Private	7	Never married	Own child
13	17	Other service	10th	Private	7	Never married	Own child
14	17	Other service	11th	Private	8	Never married	Own child
15	17	Other service	11th	Private	8	Never married	Other relati
16	17	Other service	12th	Private	9	Never married	Own child
17	17	Other service	12th	Private	9	Never married	Own child
18	17	Other service	9th	Private	6	Never married	Unmarried
19	17	Private household srvc	12th	Private	9	Never married	Own child
20	17	Prof-specialty	10th	Local government	7	Never married	Own child
21	17	Prof-specialty	12th	Private	9	Never married	Own child
22	17	Sales	10th	Private	7	Never married	Own child
23	17	Sales	11th	Private	8	Never married	Own child
24	17	Sales	11th	Private	8	Never married	Own child
25	17	Sales	11th	Private	8	Never married	Own child

Figure 3-5: Spreadsheet data sorted by four columns

Block-sorting

This technique requires little brainpower but is nonetheless useful. Don't you love it when things are easy?

Suppose you have a mailing list similar to the one appearing in Figure 3-6, which needs to be sorted by Customer ID. Basically, you're looking to do a vertical rearrangement by the Customer ID. When you attempt to perform a sort, Excel wants to do the sorting for individual rows or individual columns. No immediate way is available to say "move all the customer information for customer number 27, including the name, address, city, state and ZIP, directly below the information for customer number 26." Any ideas on how to do this? See the next section for one.

ERECT A SCAFFOLDING

The technique you can use is to erect a "scaffolding" that binds all the supplementary information (name, address, city, state, ZIP) to the Customer ID. When the scaffold is built, do the sorting using the scaffold as the sort key.

Figure 3-7 shows what the scaffolding looks like.

The formula for each of the numbers appearing in the scaffold (that is, column 3) is really simple:

```
=IF(RC[-2]="Customer ID",RC[-1],R[-1]C)
```

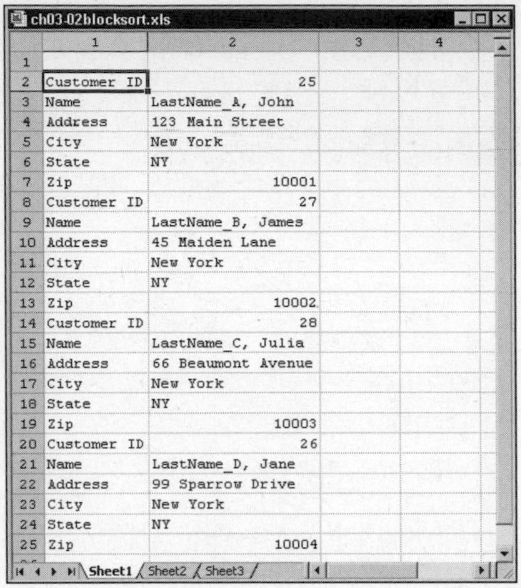

ch03-02blocksort.xls

	1	2	3	4
1				
2	Customer ID	25		
3	Name	LastName_A, John		
4	Address	123 Main Street		
5	City	New York		
6	State	NY		
7	Zip	10001		
8	Customer ID	27		
9	Name	LastName_B, James		
10	Address	45 Maiden Lane		
11	City	New York		
12	State	NY		
13	Zip	10002		
14	Customer ID	28		
15	Name	LastName_C, Julia		
16	Address	66 Beaumont Avenue		
17	City	New York		
18	State	NY		
19	Zip	10003		
20	Customer ID	26		
21	Name	LastName_D, Jane		
22	Address	99 Sparrow Drive		
23	City	New York		
24	State	NY		
25	Zip	10004		

Sheet1 / Sheet2 / Sheet3

Figure 3-6: Prototypical mailing list to be sorted by Customer ID

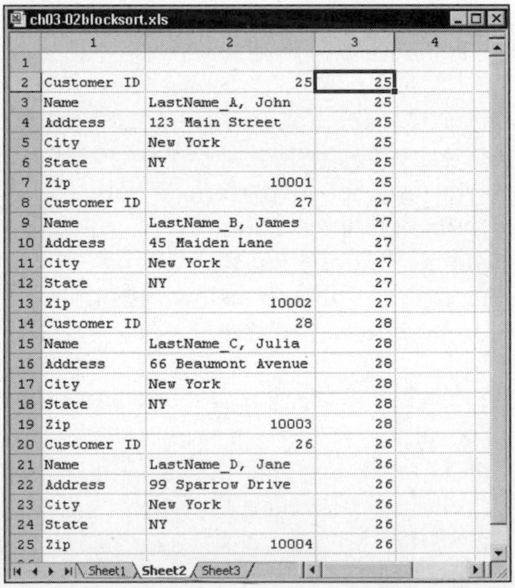

ch03-02blocksort.xls

	1	2	3	4
1				
2	Customer ID	25	25	
3	Name	LastName_A, John	25	
4	Address	123 Main Street	25	
5	City	New York	25	
6	State	NY	25	
7	Zip	10001	25	
8	Customer ID	27	27	
9	Name	LastName_B, James	27	
10	Address	45 Maiden Lane	27	
11	City	New York	27	
12	State	NY	27	
13	Zip	10002	27	
14	Customer ID	28	28	
15	Name	LastName_C, Julia	28	
16	Address	66 Beaumont Avenue	28	
17	City	New York	28	
18	State	NY	28	
19	Zip	10003	28	
20	Customer ID	26	26	
21	Name	LastName_D, Jane	26	
22	Address	99 Sparrow Drive	26	
23	City	New York	26	
24	State	NY	26	
25	Zip	10004	26	

Sheet1 / Sheet2 / Sheet3

Figure 3-7: Mailing list with scaffolding on the side

Follow these steps:

1. Create your scaffold formula (from the top).

   Start at the top of the scaffold, which is at row 2 column 3. Retrieve the value of the label two cells over to the left (RC[-2]). Depending on which row the calculation is being done in, you will get either Customer ID, Name, Address, City, State, or Zip. If you get Customer ID, it signals the start of a new record; in which case, grab the actual Customer ID number that happens to be one cell over to the left (RC[-1]). If the label you just retrieved is not the Customer ID, then you're still on the same record number as that of the cell one row above you on the scaffold (R[-1]C).

Before I forget, because your scaffolding formula looks at the value of the cell immediately above it, you cannot start the formula for your scaffold on row 1. If the data you want to block-sort begins on row 1, insert a new row so that the data begins on row 2; then start your scaffolding.

2. Replicate the scaffolding formula by copying and pasting the formula.

   The scaffolding formula is just replicated down the column. Note that nothing has been sorted yet. The sequence of records is 25, 27, 28, 26.

3. Select *both* your data and scaffold for sorting.

   Select all your data from the top-left corner all the way to the bottom-right of your scaffold.

Remember, If there's lots of data, use the navigation techniques provided in Chapter 1.

4. Perform the sort.

   After your data is selected, go to the Excel Data menu and select Sort.

   Make sure that you specify "No header row" (see Figure 3-8).

   After you have specified "No header row," select the scaffold column (in this case, column 3) for your Sort by criteria. Then press the OK button.

   As you look down the scaffolding after performing the block-sort, you see that the Customer IDs are now in sequential order (see Figure 3-9).

5. If you don't wish to keep the scaffolding, feel free to remove it by clearing the cell contents (selecting the cells in the scaffold and pressing the Delete key will accomplish this).

   Keep in mind that the customer numbers (or whatever you want to sort by) do not have to be numbers. They can be labels of any kind; just as long as you can use them as your basis for sorting.

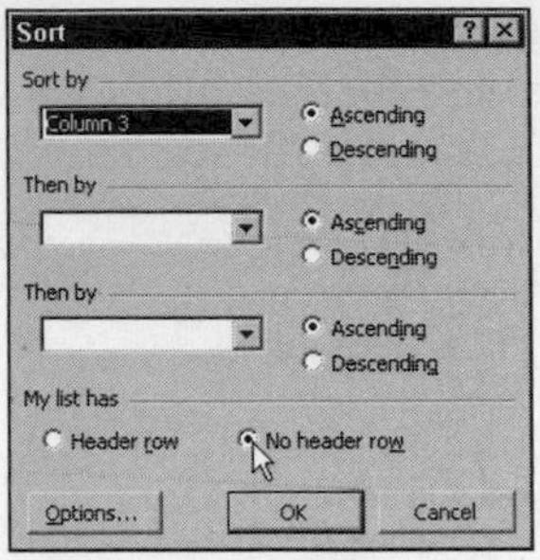

Figure 3-8: Remember to select "No header row" before picking the scaffolding column to sort by.

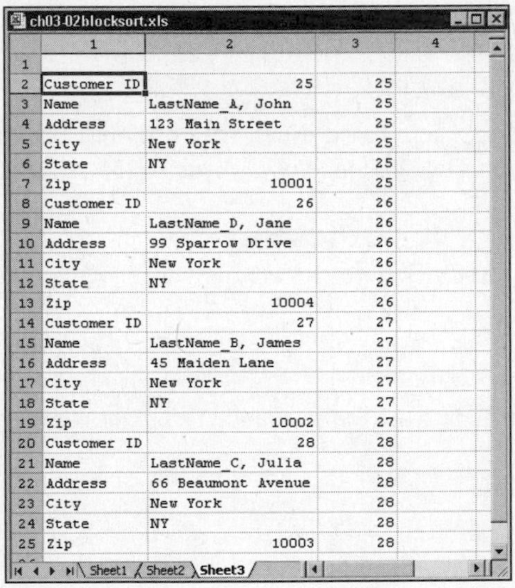

ch03-02blocksort.xls

	1	2	3	4
1				
2	Customer ID	25	25	
3	Name	LastName_A, John	25	
4	Address	123 Main Street	25	
5	City	New York	25	
6	State	NY	25	
7	Zip	10001	25	
8	Customer ID	26	26	
9	Name	LastName_D, Jane	26	
10	Address	99 Sparrow Drive	26	
11	City	New York	26	
12	State	NY	26	
13	Zip	10004	26	
14	Customer ID	27	27	
15	Name	LastName_B, James	27	
16	Address	45 Maiden Lane	27	
17	City	New York	27	
18	State	NY	27	
19	Zip	10002	27	
20	Customer ID	28	28	
21	Name	LastName_C, Julia	28	
22	Address	66 Beaumont Avenue	28	
23	City	New York	28	
24	State	NY	28	
25	Zip	10003	28	

Sheet1 / Sheet2 / Sheet3

Figure 3-9: Data is now properly block-sorted.

Data Surgery and Data Manipulation

Are you ready to shift into high gear? I want you to be able to do things concerning manipulating data. I'm not talking about clever formulas; I'm talking about doing really useful things in the real world.

When people speak about spreadsheets and databases, the typical mindset is to think about exporting data from the database and bringing it into Excel. The reality is that much database information actually originates from spreadsheets and other sources. The last part of this chapter provides a tool to help tackle the conversion of financial and spreadsheet data to a form suitable for consumption by a standard relational database. I dissect that tool piece by piece, isolating the data manipulation logic and design decisions. I cap it all off with a discussion of additional enhancements and extensions to turn this tool into an industrial-strength facility.

A scenario

Imagine that you are a financial analyst who's tracking sales data of commercial stores for several shopping malls that are part of your portfolio. You are given monthly sales data in the form of one huge spreadsheet stretching out year after year over a period of five years (see Figure 3-10 or go to the Sheet2 tab of the ch03-03sqlscriptgenerator.xls file on your CD-ROM). Actually, the spreadsheet as shown in Figure 3-10 is in pretty good shape. Chances are, a third party informally sending you data may not be so meticulous and keep up with your standards to assure consistent layout, appearance, formatting, and correctness.

The data you are given, though nicely presented on a spreadsheet, really needs to be brought into a relational database. Somehow you have to find a reliable way to bring that data into the database so that it can be analyzed and compared to similar datasets for other companies.

ch03-03sqlscriptgenerator.xls

	1	2	3	4	5	6	7		61	62	63	64
1	TID	Tenant Name	Property	Suite	Jan-99	Feb-99	Mar-99		Sep-03	Oct-03	Nov-03	Dec-03
2	T01	Tenant 01	1A	100	9340	8950	10280		12550	11830	13990	15040
3	T02	Tenant 02	1A	101	9170	8960	9800		12810	11670	13410	14670
4	T03	Tenant 03	1A	102	9410	9280	9760		13330	11790	13130	14960
5	T04	Tenant 04	1A	103	9450	9100	9920		11970	11540	13600	14690
6	T05	Tenant 05	1A	104	9130	8860	9220		11890	12260	13070	14720
7	T06	Tenant 06	1A	105	9700	8820	9190		13070	11400	13290	13530
8	T07	Tenant 07	1A	106	9610	8930	10090		12950	12530	13590	13590
9	T08	Tenant 08	1A	107	9860	9170	9570		12230	12680	13790	13750
10	T09	Tenant 09	1A	108	9520	9280	9820		12480	11850	13080	14220
11	T10	Tenant 10	1A	109	9190	9040	9450		11930	12450	13000	15010
12	T11	Tenant 11	1B	201	9040	9260	9160		12880	11460	12840	14850
13	T12	Tenant 12	1B	202	9530	8670	10140		12140	11830	13510	13860
14	T13	Tenant 13	1B	203	9530	9620	9770		13350	12540	12970	13870
15	T14	Tenant 14	1B	204	8920	8630	9460		12130	11480	12720	14420
16	T15	Tenant 15	1B	205	9510	9270	9570		11890	12100	13130	15010
17	T16	Tenant 16	1B	206	9970	8890	9420		12720	11830	13460	14140
18	T17	Tenant 17	1B	207	9840	9060	9450		12450	11830	13670	14640
19	T18	Tenant 18	1B	208	9760	9300	9520		13360	12640	13530	14490
20	T19	Tenant 19	1B	209	9230	8820	10150		12520	12280	14030	14200
21												
22												
23												

Sheet1 \ Sheet2 \ Sheet3 /

Figure 3-10: Five years of sales data to be converted to SQL scripts

Assume for the moment, though, that the spreadsheet holding the sales data is, after your clean-up efforts, in good shape. Are you ready to do data analysis on it? As previously stated, not all the data analysis is going to be done entirely inside a spreadsheet. Being a financial analyst, you have access to your company's massive database, loaded with reams of proprietary financial and economic data, high-end analytical tools, and a wealth of competitors' analyses/data that rivals the data the competitors keep on their own portfolios. Your immediate goal is to get the spreadsheet information into the database.

Getting the data into a database presupposes the existence of a defined table. The schema for such a database table (which I've named SALESDATATABLE for this example) and representative data for such a record are shown in Table 3-2.

TABLE 3-2 DATABASE SCHEMA FOR THE SALESDATATABLE

FieldName	Type	PrimaryKey?	Sample Value
TENANTID	VARCHAR, Not Null		Tenant 01
PROPERTY	VARCHAR, Not Null		1A
SUITE	VARCHAR, Not Null		100
RECORDID	VARCHAR, Not Null	YES	T0136161
SALESDATE	DATE, Not Null		1-Jan-1999
SALES	NUMBER, Not Null		9340

This table schema is simple to define in a standard SQL database such as DB2 or Oracle. Those of you who want to learn more about Structured Query Language (SQL) and relational databases can check out *SQL Bible,* by Alex Kriegel and Boris Trukhnov (Wiley Publishing, Inc.), or *SQL: The Complete Reference,* by James R. Groff and Paul N. Weinberg (McGraw-Hill Osborne). Alternatively, if you want to do an online search for books related to SQL databases (or for that matter, any other topic), you can go to http://www.evolvingtech.com/webservices/etcFrame.html and type **SQL Database** in the line above the Run Search button on the Web page, and then press Enter or the Run Search button.

Using the Sample Value data shown in Table 3-2, the SQL statement used to create a new database record would appear as:

```
insert into SalesDataTable values ('Tenant 01','1A','100',
                                   'T0136161','1-Jan-1999',9340);
```

Relational databases will have no trouble loading records prepared in this manner. You could use an interactive tool like SQL*Plus or write some Java code that uses JDBC to make the connection and insert the records. A more traditional approach would be to prepare a raw data file, along with a control loader file, and use a database vendor-supplied tool (such as SQL*Loader) to perform the load.

The traditional approach

If you go this route you will have to prepare a control document that dictates how data is to be loaded into the database. You will also have to export your spreadsheet into one or more text files that conform to the control document specifications. A common format that might be used is a comma-separated variables, or CSV, file. The resulting CSV file would look much like the SQL statement without the "insert into SalesDataTable values" and the enclosing parentheses.

If all you had to do were to move a continuous serial stream of sales data, doing so would be easy. However, each database record has to take into account the sales amount along with the month and year, property, suite number, and the tenant name or ID. If you think you can further normalize the table so that you don't have to repeat the data pertaining to property and suite, think again. Just because the property and suite remain constant for the 19 tenants in your spreadsheet doesn't mean that they're going to stay the same for all tenants over all time.

Another item you need to take into account is that the database schema requires that the RecordID be unique, because it is the primary key. The RecordID is not in the spreadsheet data and will have to be created. You have to think about creating such a unique ID. A meaningful one could be a combination of the tenant ID along with the sales date.

So, if you want to go the traditional route of using a conventional SQL Loader tool, you've definitely got your work cut out for yourself.

The alternative approach

In this section I provide a different approach that harnesses the ability of Excel to gather, construct, and format the data in a manner well suited to directly pumping records into the database.

I do not profess this to be a better approach. I want you to understand what is possible and then weigh the options. In the end, it's your choice and comfort level that will determine what you will do. The flexibility, ease of setup, and direct inter-activeness afforded by this approach make it well suited for small- to medium-sized datasets. To turn this into an "industrial strength" facility, you should consider suggested enhancements located at the end of this chapter.

As you look at Figure 3-10, you should have no trouble reading the spreadsheet information. The story is different with relational databases. Databases store data point by point, taking into account all related items. For this reason, the database has to acquire the information a record at a time. It performs a sequence of operations such as the following:

```
insert into SalesDataTable values ('Tenant 01','1A','100',
                            'T0136161','1-Jan-1999',9340);
insert into SalesDataTable values ('Tenant 01','1A','100',
                            'T0136192','1-Feb-1999',8950);
insert into SalesDataTable values ('Tenant 01','1A','100',
                            'T0136220','1-Mar-1999',10280);
insert into SalesDataTable values ('Tenant 01','1A','100',
                            'T0136251','1-Apr-1999',9780);
```

What you need is a spreadsheet that reads off the values from sheets of data like the one shown in Figure 3-10 and converts it into SQL statements. Open the ch03-03sqlscriptgenerator.xls file on your CD-ROM and look at the Sheet1 tab (or see Figure 3-11).

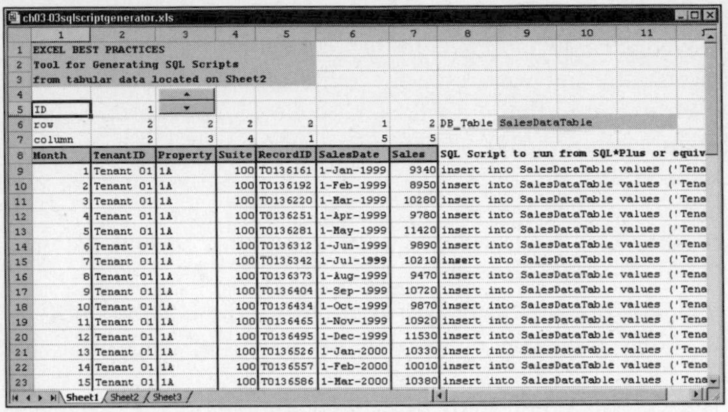

Figure 3-11: Tool to generate SQL scripts

This tool reads the sales data contained on a separate worksheet (which happens to be located in the Sheet2 tab) and constructs the SQL script for each of the recorded sales. The individual SQL scripts are the verbiage appearing on the right side of Sheet1, starting on column 8. The general notion is that you can select these SQL Scripts with your mouse and then copy and paste them directly into a standard database tool such as SQL*Plus. Depending on how many rows you will be inserting at a time, you may have to adjust the buffer setting in your database tool or restrict how many rows you will paste at a time. More likely, you will take all the content generated by the spreadsheet, save it to an .sql file, and run it with a standard database tool.

Anatomy of the SQL Generator Spreadsheet Tool

Chapter 2, "Mastering Spreadsheet Construction Techniques," shows you how to construct a spreadsheet from scratch. It doesn't pay much attention to the formulas. Here, I show the detailed anatomy of the spreadsheet, highlighting the formulas used and alerting you to some key design decisions you would make to construct a similar tool.

From a design-decision standpoint, you will find that you won't be able to avoid some complexities. You have a number of choices as to where you're going to place that complexity.

THE SPINNER CONTROL
This tool introduces some new features not shown in Chapters 1 and 2. For starters, the Up/Down arrows of the spinner control button are prominently positioned in the spreadsheet. This controls which dataset is retrieved (there is one for each tenant). Basically, you're retrieving 60 records at a time, thereby getting five years' worth of data for each tenant at a time. Try clicking the Up/Down arrows. Notice that the ID changes in increments of 1 and maxes out at 19. You can adjust the settings for the Spinner by right-clicking it (Figure 3-12).

Figure 3-12: The spinner control can be customized.

The Cell Link is set to R5C2, which is the location that tells the spreadsheet which row of tenant data in Sheet2 to convert to SQL. In the context of this example, I have provided a very limited set of data (only one tenant at a time). You can revise this spreadsheet to retrieve all the data for all the companies at one time. Doing so for about 1,000 data points is not so bad. You will start to run into problems when you have a hundred or so companies, each with many hundreds of data points. To be safe, you would do well to stay under 10,000 rows of generated SQL statements at a time. If you find yourself pushing beyond this, you should be definitely considering other alternatives.

READER OFFSETS

When you look at the sales data on Sheet2, you see that the first cell containing TenantID information starts at row 2, column 2. Look at Figure 3-13. Notice that the row and column values shown in Figure 3-13 correspond to the physical starting positions of the TenantID data in Sheet2.

You are about to face one of those "complexity" issues I spoke of. You have a choice. The row and column numbers appearing in Figure 3-13 indicate start positions, not offsets.

If they were offsets, each of the numbers would be a value of 1 less than the start position. So you would see (1,1) for TenantID, (1,2) for Property, (1,3) for Suite, (1,0) for RecordID, (0,4) for SalesDate, and (1,4) for Sales instead of (2,2), (2,3), (2,4), (2,1), (1,5), and (2,5), respectively.

If you use offsets instead of the cell positions, formulas such as that shown in Listing 3-1 will be simpler (you won't have the dangling –1 appearing repeatedly. However, the visual appearance of offset values shown in rows 6 and 7 of Figure 3-13 is, for some people, unintuitive and makes the spreadsheet harder to understand and use.

Using the cell positions is more intuitive, but the complexity has to be parked somewhere. In this case, the formulas are slightly more complex, because they now have to contend with the –1 term throughout the formulas.

This is a trade-off decision. There is no absolute answer regarding which of these two are better decisions. In this instance, I favored using start positions instead of offset because I felt that the spreadsheet would be easier to use by other people. I also know that I can manage the increased complexity in the formulas.

The equivalent can be said about `Property`, `Suite`, `RecordID`, `SalesDate`, and `Sales`. These start positions combined with the `ID` (adjusted every time you click the spinner control button) and the `Month` number provide enough information to triangulate and pinpoint the individual pieces of data.

6	row	2	2	2	2	1	2
7	column	2	3	4	1	5	5
8	**Month**	TenantID	Property	Suite	RecordID	SalesDate	Sales

Figure 3–13: Row and column values correspond to the starting positions of the respective data items.

Take a look at the formula for retrieving the Tenant Name (`TenantID`) presented in Listing 3-1.

Listing 3–1: Formula for Retrieving TenantID

```
=OFFSET(Sheet2!R1C1,R6C-1+ID-1,R7C-1)
```

Don't be put off by `OFFSET`. Take your time and look at what this formula is doing. The data you want is contained in Sheet2. You can change Sheet2 to a more appropriate name by selecting the Sheet2 worksheet on the bottom tab, double-clicking it, and renaming as desired. Your `OFFSET` formula will reflect this change automatically. Right now, I want you to stay with Sheet2 so that you can follow the examples in this chapter.

RETRIEVING THE SALES DATA

The `OFFSET` originates at `R1C1` or, in other words, the top-left corner of the worksheet. The first piece of data for the `TenantID` on Sheet2 begins on row 2 and column 2. The second `TenantID` appears on row 3 and column 2. The third `TenantID` appears on row 4 and column 2. To simplify the `OFFSET` formula, what's being done is:

```
=OFFSET(R1C1,1,1)        this returns the contents of R2C2
=OFFSET(R1C1,2,1)        this returns the contents of R3C2
=OFFSET(R1C1,3,1)        this returns the contents of R4C2
...
```

The R1C1 corresponds to Sheet2. I temporarily eliminated its appearance in the formula to remove the clutter. This should make it easier for you to see what's happening behind the scenes. In this context of Sheet2, R2C2 is the name of the first tenant (Tenant 01), R3C2 is the name of the second tenant (Tenant 02), R4C2 is the name of the third tenant (Tenant 03), and so forth.

I'll use a slight of hand to recast the formulas.

```
=OFFSET(R1C1,2-1,2-1)       this returns the contents of R2C2
=OFFSET(R1C1,3-1,2-1)       this returns the contents of R3C2
=OFFSET(R1C1,4-1,2-1)       this returns the contents of R4C2
...
```

Notice that the first integers in the offsets now match the cell positions. As an example, the 4 and 2 of OFFSET(R1C1,4-1,2-1) map to R4C2. I am paying a price to see information this way (I still have to include –1 for each of the offsets. This is why you see –1 appearing in Listing 3-1.

Once more, I wave the magic wand to recast the formulas:

```
=OFFSET(R1C1,2-1+ID-1,2-1)  returns the contents of R2C2 When: ID=1
=OFFSET(R1C1,2-1+ID-1,2-1)  returns the contents of R3C2 When: ID=2
=OFFSET(R1C1,2-1+ID-1,2-1)  returns the contents of R4C2 When: ID=3
...
```

Now, given the first row and column positions for TenantID (which happen to be 2 and 2, respectively), I need only to have the ID number to retrieve the respective tenant name.

It seems like a lot of work to retrieve a value.

NOW, TO REAP THE BENEFITS

Here is where the savings begin. The formulas used in Sheet1 to retrieve the data all start taking on similar structure. Starting at row 9, column 2 and proceeding all the way down through row 68, the formula used for retrieving the Tenant Name (Listing 3-1) is unchanging. Now, take a look at the formula for retrieving the respective property (open your spreadsheet and inspect each of the formulas in row 9, column 3 through row 68).

Listing 3-2: Formula for Retrieving the Property Info

```
=OFFSET(Sheet2!R1C1,R6C-1+ID-1,R7C-1)
```

Do you notice any similarity between Listing 3-1 and Listing 3-2? Now, take a look at the formula for retrieving the respective suite (same set of rows but in column 4).

Listing 3-3: Formula for Retrieving the Suite Info

```
=OFFSET(Sheet2!R1C1,R6C-1+ID-1,R7C-1)
```

What similarities do you find among Listing 3-1, Listing 3-2, and Listing 3-3? They're all exactly the same formula! Talk about mental brevity: The same formula for 180 cells representing three different types of data (tenant ID, property, and suite).

WHAT HAPPENS NEXT

Now I'm jumping ahead to the generated SQL statements. The formula used for rows 9 through 68 in column 8 is given in Listing 3-4.

Listing 3-4: Formula for Generating SQL Statements

```
=IF(RC[-1]=0,
    ";",
    "insert into "&DB_Table&" values
        (
        '"&TenantID&"',
        '"&Property&"',
        '"&Suite&"',
         '"&RecordID&"',
        '"&SalesDate&"',
        "&Sales&"
        );"
)
```

I've spread the formula out over several lines to make it easier to read. The formula is pulling all the values for TenantID, Property, Suite, RecordID, SalesDate and Sales and is constructing an SQL Statement out of them. Listing 3-5 identifies the cell ranges for these names.

Listing 3-5: User-Defined Names and Their Cell Ranges

```
TenantID  is a User Defined Name having the cell range of R9C2:R68C2
Property  is a User Defined Name having the cell range of R9C3:R68C3
Suite     is a User Defined Name having the cell range of R9C4:R68C4
RecordID  is a User Defined Name having the cell range of R9C5:R68C5
SalesDate is a User Defined Name having the cell range of R9C6:R68C6
Sales     is a User Defined Name having the cell range of R9C7:R68C7
```

CONTENDING WITH EXCEL'S WAY OF REPRESENTING DATES

I want you to pay attention to two things in particular. The Sale Dates shown in the Sheet2 (refer to Figure 3-10) are all formatted by Excel the way Excel automatically represents dates. Excel takes a date that you enter manually and turns it into a serial number. At the same time, it also formats the display so that this "numerical" date is rendered as calendar dates based on the geographic locality set when Excel is installed. This is not too different than the spreadsheet construction example of Chapter 2.

If the `SalesDate` data appearing on Sheet1 were directly retrieved from Sheet2, the way the other quantities are, the retrieved date info would appear as a numerical serial number rather than as a natural-looking calendar date. Ignoring, for the moment, how a natural-looking calendar date would be represented, the database may not be able to correctly interpret the numerical representation of the date.

Rather than get this:

```
insert into SalesDataTable values ('Tenant 01','1A','100',
                                  'T0136161','1-Jan-1999',9340);
```

you would get this:

```
insert into SalesDataTable values ('Tenant 01','1A','100',
                                  'T0136161','36161',9340);
```

Not only might you be unhappy about seeing a date as 36161, but also the database that's loading the data would not know what to make of it.

Fortunately, this problem is easy to fix. It requires the use of the Excel `TEXT` function.

Consider the following:

```
=TEXT(36161,"d-mmm-yyyy")
```

This function returns `1-Jan-1999`, which is exactly the way the database would like to see it. You could modify the formula that constructs the SQL statement (Listing 3-4). Doing so would make the formula in Listing 3-4 all the more complex. The sales date information is already being extracted from Sheet2 and placed into the `SalesDate` defined region. So rather than make the formula in Listing 3-4 more complicated and error prone, you could perform the `TEXT` conversion in the column for `SalesDate`. The formula for `SalesDate` becomes as shown in Listing 3-6.

Listing 3-6: Retrieve Sales Date as a Serial Number and Convert it to a String

```
=TEXT(OFFSET(Sheet2!R1C1,R6C-1,R7C-1+Month-1),"d-mmm-yyyy")
```

This formula bears a striking resemblance to Listing 3-1, 3-2, and 3-3. It takes the numeric date value retrieved by the `OFFSET` function and converts it to a text string that conforms to the format of `d-mmm-yyyy`. When the individual sale dates are pulled into the constructed SQL Statement, no conversion is necessary for the date information.

Look once more at Listing 3-6. Something new appears to have crept in. Now there is a `Month` number. `Month` is a User Defined Name having the cell range of `R9C1;R68C1`. `Month` is the column of numbers on the left side of Sheet1 that starts at the value 1 and works its way up to 60 (there are 60 months in a five-year interval).

Things you might do to enhance this tool

The tool presented is very flexible. You could adapt it for many purposes. Here are things you might want to do if you plan on extending or enhancing this tool.

◆ Enable retrieving data for more than one company at a time.

◆ Create a placeholder to write the name and location of a separate spreadsheet that contains the data you want to convert. This prevents your having to copy and paste the spreadsheet data from elsewhere into this tool.

◆ Modify the formula that generates the SQL Statement to make it easy to convert to other formats (such as CSV).

◆ Add some error-handling capabilities. There are times when data you'll want to convert doesn't conform to what the database expects to load. This method has two substrategies:

    a. When you have situations such as missing pieces of data, have the record generate output in a manner that won't trip up the database. It would be better to have an empty line that the database will skip than to have an incomplete line where required fields are missing.

    b. Consider setting up an alert facility so that you know when the data you want to import will contain bad or skipped records, and pinpoint where and what they are. Chapter 7, "Creating and Using Smart Data," may give you some ideas on how to go about this.

Implementing the preceding enhancements to the SQL Script Generator lies beyond the scope of what's covered in this book. Besides, I've got plenty of nifty things to tell you about without it!

Closing Thoughts

Data manipulation, as you can see, is a broad and extensive topic. It is filled with minutia in terms of countless numbers of Excel functions, nuances in case sensitivity, and multiple ways of doing almost exactly the same task. The devil may be in the details, but the heavens are charted by simple and effective strategies such as the scaffolding technique to perform a block-sort.

You have seen how you can take an otherwise complex and messy task (such as converting tabular spreadsheet data to a form suitable for direct consumption by a relational database) and break it down into simple parts.

This strategy makes each part more manageable because the constituent components need only to deal with their own respective tasks. For example, the formulas that construct the actual SQL statements do not worry about where to get the data. The parts that retrieve the data make no assumptions about where the underlying data physically resides. They read this off a table of start positions. The table is just a list of row and column positions that are easily eyeballed by a person and quickly updated by hand.

This separation of responsibility represents and exemplifies good practices. With luck, you will be able to take and apply similar practices in your endeavors. Your ability to accomplish this will be limited if you don't confront challenges and steer their resolution toward your advantage. Specifically, when you perform large-scale data manipulations, you are likely to find complexities that will make your work harder. You will not be able to sweep these under the rug. You may need to "park them" in one place or another within your spreadsheet. You saw this type of situation in the data conversion example of this chapter. A choice had to be made between representing the read-off table data as offsets or physical cell positions. One approach made the formulas easier to write but notched up the difficulty of working with the spreadsheet. The other approach brought the exact reverse. Trade-off decisions are never easy; nonetheless, they still need to be made and you have to live with the decisions.

If I could drive home one lesson from this chapter, it would be that successful data manipulation is synonymous with being immersed in the data. As this book progresses, I continue hammering away at this theme. Look to Chapter 4 to get you comfortable with touching, viewing, and working with data in every way conceivable. You'll encounter things such as PivotTables and Excel data filters, and you'll be working with Add-Ins such as the Solver to further strengthen your analytical capabilities.

Chapter 4

Compiling, Managing, and Viewing Your Data

IN THIS CHAPTER

- ◆ Moving and converting data from external sources to Excel for financial statement presentations
- ◆ Grouping data in PivotTables
- ◆ Charting PivotTable data
- ◆ Using Pivot Formulas
- ◆ Preparing data for PivotTables
- ◆ Web publishing of PivotTables

Preliminaries

This chapter is all about improving your ability to work with data. So, what is it you want to do with the data?

- ◆ You want to ease the process of converting third-party information to a consistent and uniform format, making it easier to use and analyze.
- ◆ You want to become facile in looking at large amounts of data, quickly. You want to characterize it, find hidden relationships, and drill down to the underlying detail.
- ◆ You want to compute a variety of descriptive statistical measures on grouped data without cluttering your spreadsheet.

Third-party information can be provided in electronic form but it may not be suitable for immediate use inside a spreadsheet. Though you can copy and paste the data into your spreadsheet, how it comes out could be anything but clean. In this chapter I show you how you can take data, such as PDF versions of financial accounting statements, and prepare them for use within a spreadsheet.

You may have enumerated data, and lots of it. Think of a collection of census data laid out over thousands of rows in a spreadsheet. Each line could represent the data for an individual surveyed. It's one thing to sort such data (you've seen this in the previous chapter). It's entirely another to tally the totals broken out by any sequence of categories. PivotTables will give you "a handle" on this. Think of PivotTables as your mechanism for "folding and unfolding" multidimensional data. You will find that you can quickly and easily characterize data for each of these folds. This chapter should give you a feel for how to use PivotTables and, more important, help you with practical ways of converting and getting your data into PivotTables for meaningful analysis.

The Number Line-Up

On numerous occasions I find that the data I want to analyze using a spreadsheet exists in electronic form, but not on a spreadsheet. There's a wealth of such electronic information available on the Internet. Common publishing formats include HTML, plain text, and PDF (Portable Document Format). The new kid on the block is XML.

Excel has no problems opening and reading HTML pages and converting them to spreadsheet format. It also has no problems in taking the data of a spreadsheet and saving it to HTML. Chapter 12, "Spreadsheet Portals, XML, and Web Services," discusses XML and its kin, so I'm not covering them here.

For opening and reading PDF files, the situation is not quite the same. PDF files are important because a lot of financial data is published in PDF format.

One of the nice features of PDF files is that their contents can easily be copied from a PDF viewer such as Acrobat Reader and pasted to other documents, such as an Excel spreadsheet. This is great, but there are some caveats and wrinkles to deal with along the way. Getting your numbers to line up, validating their correctness, and putting them into a state in which they are fully acclimated in the spreadsheet are what this section is all about.

Copying and pasting columnar data

Think about a financial statement, such as a balance sheet, and how it might appear in a PDF file. Such a report will likely have some text – the report title, narrative descriptions concerning the various kinds of assets and other balance sheet accounts, dates for the accounting period, and, of course, the numerical data replete with all the currency symbols and system separators such as commas and decimal points (see Figure 4-1, which displays a PDF file from an Adobe Acrobat Reader).

Aside from observing the pretty thumbnails, note that one of the columns has a rectangular outline that is being made by an I-bar style cursor. To select a column like this, just press Ctrl+click. With the mouse button down, drag to create the outline surrounding the column of text you wish to select. When you depress the mouse button, the vertical column of text will be selected. You can copy and paste this directly to your spreadsheet.

You just won half the battle. Your spreadsheet now contains numbers that you can use in computations such as summing a group of numbers. Go ahead and try this on a PDF document of your choosing. Alternatively, you can use the file orb10Q.pdf that is on the CD-ROM with this book. This is a PDF file of a 10-Q Statement filed with the SEC and is a publicly disclosed record.

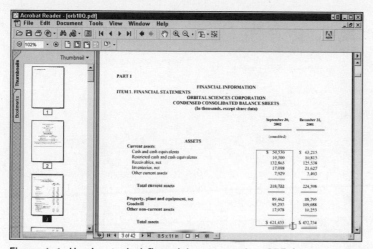

Figure 4–1: Here's a typical financial statement in a PDF document. Notice the individual column being selected by pressing Ctrl plus clicking and dragging.

When you copy and paste, there are several things you may notice. Dates, such as at the start of the balance sheet, appear to take up two lines. You might want to represent date information in your spreadsheet in one cell instead of having the month and day on one row and the year on another. Except for share data, the financial statement represents numbers as multiples of thousands of dollars. You may want to convert these to exact dollar amounts rather than multiples of thousands. Some descriptions, such as those of common stock, take up two lines. You may want to abbreviate such descriptions and put them on one line. The numbers may be expressed in multiples of thousands of dollars. You may want to show actual dollars or may want to do some currency conversion. If you are a financial analyst or expect to be doing some pretty exacting work, all these soft conversions may leave you a little uncomfortable.

I have provided a Take-Away that will give you precise control to help convert financial data, typically found in PDF files, over to a spreadsheet. Open the file ch04-02PDFconvert.xls (located on the CD with this book), or see Figure 4-2.

In Figure 4-2 you can see the top and bottom portions of the balance sheet in finished form. Dates appear in single cells instead of occupying two rows. The accounting convention of placing parentheses around negative numbers is followed. Negative numbers are also colorized. Numbers having a zero value are indicated by a hyphen (-). Numbers are expressed in full dollar amounts rather than in multiples of thousands (also, the line originally stating "in thousands, except share data" has vanished). These changes happen by formula control. For example, if you want to go back to showing the numbers in thousands, reduce the Factor' (see upper-right corner of Figure 4-2) from 1000 to 1. The numbers will be expressed in multiples of 1000, and the line stating "in thousands, except share data" will reappear.

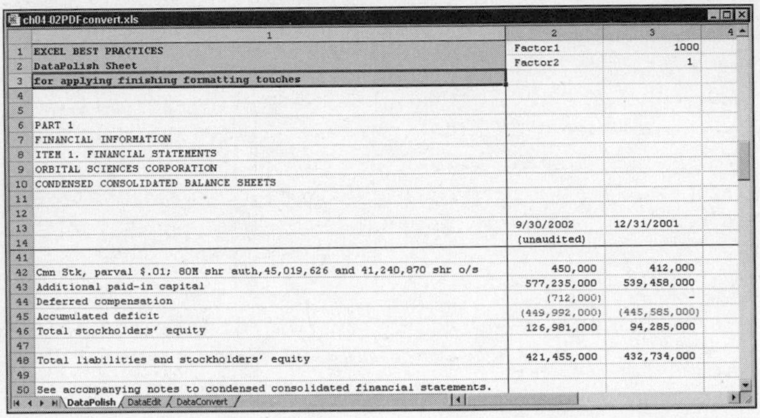
ch04-02PDFconvert.xls

	1	2	3	4
1	EXCEL BEST PRACTICES	Factor1	1000	
2	DataPolish Sheet	Factor2	1	
3	for applying finishing formatting touches			
4				
5				
6	PART 1			
7	FINANCIAL INFORMATION			
8	ITEM 1. FINANCIAL STATEMENTS			
9	ORBITAL SCIENCES CORPORATION			
10	CONDENSED CONSOLIDATED BALANCE SHEETS			
11				
12				
13		9/30/2002	12/31/2001	
14		(unaudited)		
41				
42	Cmn Stk, parval $.01; 80M shr auth,45,019,626 and 41,240,870 shr o/s	450,000	412,000	
43	Additional paid-in capital	577,235,000	539,458,000	
44	Deferred compensation	(712,000)	-	
45	Accumulated deficit	(449,992,000)	(445,585,000)	
46	Total stockholders' equity	126,981,000	94,285,000	
47				
48	Total liabilities and stockholders' equity	421,455,000	432,734,000	
49				
50	See accompanying notes to condensed consolidated financial statements.			

DataPolish / DataEdit / DataConvert

Figure 4-2: PDF Conversion Take-Away (note the three tabs: DataPolish, DataEdit, and DataConvert)

How does this tool work, and is it super-automated?

Effective use of this tool does entail some effort, but the effort is well spent. Here are some important features:

- You have the opportunity to line up the numbers and text that you transfer to the DataConvert worksheet. Where various numbers are aggregated as totals, you have the ability to validate that the reported totals match what you would compute arithmetically. This proofing capability will help to assure that the numbers you transfer and convert are airtight.
- You can make editorial changes to the text of the financial statement in the DataEdit worksheet and alter the final appearance in the DataPolish worksheet. All these post-transfer changes leave your original data as it was entered in the DataConvert worksheet.
- You can convert the numbers in the statement to a different denomination (for example, actual dollars versus thousands of dollars) or apply a different currency.
- If you are converting similar financial statements for multiple accounting periods, you can keep their format consistent and uniform in appearance.

HOW THE CONVERSION TOOL IS ORGANIZED

The spreadsheet has three worksheet tabs: DataConvert, DataEdit, and DataPolish. The starting worksheet begins with the rightmost tab (DataConvert) and ends with the leftmost tab (DataPolish). There is a very good reason for the tabs' appearance in this order. Any end user or consumer of a spreadsheet will typically expect to see the spreadsheet results in the leftmost tab. This is why all the presentation layers appear in the leftmost worksheet tabs.

I urge you to get used to associating left tabs with presentation, middle tabs with analysis, and right tabs with the underlying source or raw data. This is a practice you should follow religiously. Obviously, you could keep everything in one worksheet if your spreadsheet is super simple. If you plan to do so, consider whether it makes sense to separate your data from the analysis/presentation portions.

DATACONVERT WORKSHEET

Figure 4-3 shows the DataConvert worksheet populated with data. If you're starting with a new financial statement, clear out the contents in columns 1, 3, and 4. These are the columns into which you'll paste your copied text and columns of numbers.

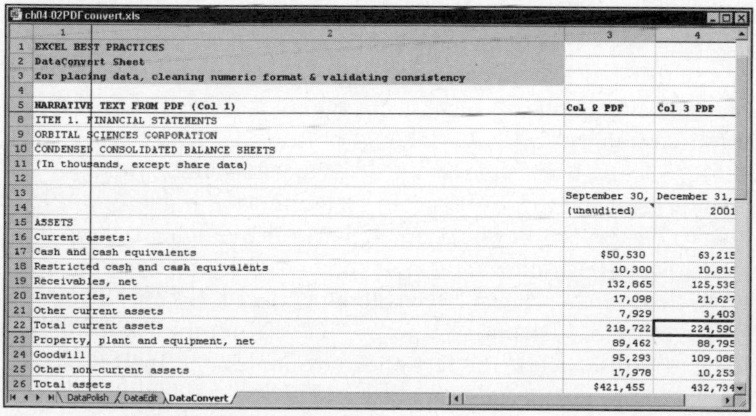

	1	2	3	4
1	EXCEL BEST PRACTICES			
2	DataConvert Sheet			
3	for placing data, cleaning numeric format & validating consistency			
4				
5	NARRATIVE TEXT FROM PDF (Col 1)		Col 2 PDF	Col 3 PDF
8	ITEM 1. FINANCIAL STATEMENTS			
9	ORBITAL SCIENCES CORPORATION			
10	CONDENSED CONSOLIDATED BALANCE SHEETS			
11	(In thousands, except share data)			
12				
13			September 30,	December 31,
14			(unaudited)	2001
15	ASSETS			
16	Current assets:			
17	Cash and cash equivalents		$50,530	63,215
18	Restricted cash and cash equivalents		10,300	10,815
19	Receivables, net		132,865	125,536
20	Inventories, net		17,098	21,627
21	Other current assets		7,929	3,403
22	Total current assets		218,722	224,590
23	Property, plant and equipment, net		89,462	88,795
24	Goodwill		95,293	109,086
25	Other non-current assets		17,978	10,253
26	Total assets		$421,455	432,734

Figure 4-3: DataConvert worksheet

Note where the split-pane lies in Figure 4-3. This split serves a useful purpose. Also note that the display of text in column 1 spills all the way over into column 2. Also, there appears to be nothing in column 2.

As you scroll over to the right, the "spillover" in column 2 will be replaced by the additional columns for revising your numbers (see Figure 4-4).

You will see some sticky notes that I've left for you to read in the spreadsheet. The columns of numbers pasted into columns 3 and 4 are repeated on the immediate right, stripped of commas, dollar symbols and other formatting. It is these "cleaned" numbers in columns 5 and 6 that are used in the DataEdit and DataPolish worksheets.

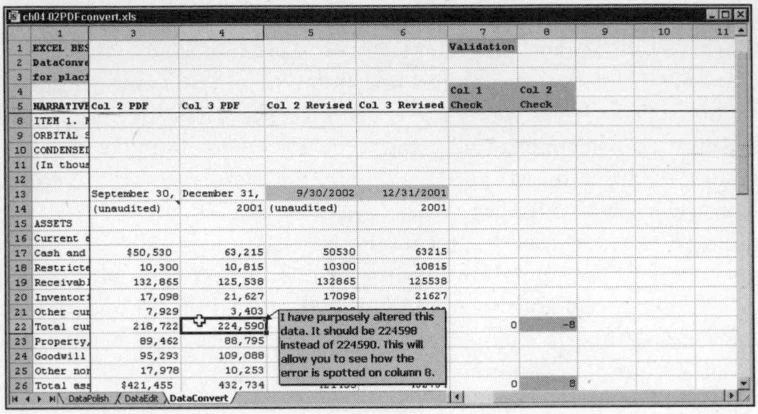

Figure 4-4: Number revision and proofing

The numbers you transfer from your PDF file to columns 3 and 4 are, it is hoped, correct. Nothing guarantees this. You can see in Figure 4-4 that I purposely altered a number to create a mistake. This will allow you to see how the error is automatically flagged in column 8. In columns 7 and 8, you can write in your own formulas to do an independent check that the numbers are consistent. The basic strategy is to take the numerical difference between a resulting number and all the numbers that contribute to it. If this numerical difference is not zero, it is flagged in bright red.

Take, for instance, the number 224590. It should be the sum of 63215, 10815, 125538, 21627, and 3403. It's been shortchanged by a value of 8. This "–8" is shown in red. Also note that 224590 (or 224598) feeds into the value of 432734 (last row of Figure 4-4). The arithmetic check on value for this number reveals that this total is overstated by +8. All other things being constant, when you see this flip-flop behavior, the first number flagged needs to be adjusted. Go ahead and fix the number in row 22, column 3 (changing it to 224598 will return a zero difference and the red flags will disappear). The rest of the examples and figures in this chapter reflect that this correction has been applied.

One of the nice features in this worksheet is that you can move (that is, drag and drop) the cells in columns 3 and 4 without affecting the formulas in columns 5 and 6.

DATAEDIT WORKSHEET

As does the DataConvert Worksheet, DataEdit uses column 2 as a spillover column. It picks up the cleaned and validated numbers from DataConvert and places them into columns 3 and 4. Scrolling over to the right, you can apply editing changes.

Any changes you make in columns 5, 6, and 7 will be highlighted in a tan color if there is text and a yellow color if the cell contains only a space (see Figure 4-5). Placing an isolated space in column 5 of this worksheet will result in an empty cell in the text column (column 1) of the DataPolish worksheet. In this manner you can remove unwanted lines from the financial statement that has been restated in the form of a spreadsheet.

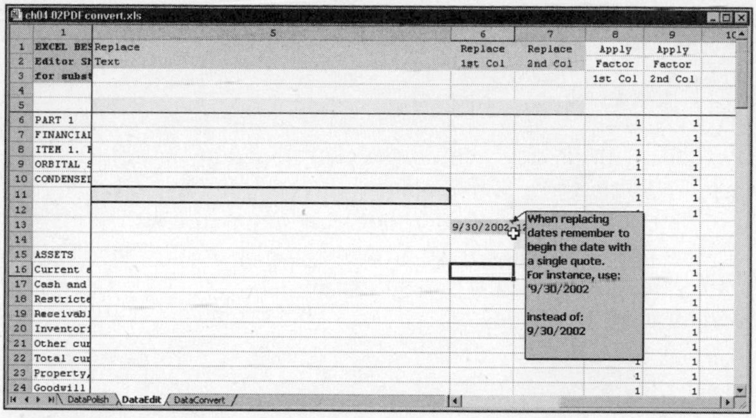

Figure 4-5: Changes you make in columns 5, 6, and 7 will be incorporated into the text and numbers that reside in columns 1, 3, and 4 (partially hidden in the screenshot but fully visible in the spreadsheet).

A chief benefit of using the DataEdit worksheet is that changes you make are isolated and not mingled with your source data or your final results. This kind of construct is known as a "Data Overpass." I discuss it at greater length in Chapter 9, "How Not to Get Stuck in the MUD (Messed-Up Data)."

DATAPOLISH WORKSHEET

The DataPolish worksheet, as shown in Figure 4-2, pulls together, in three contiguous columns, the finished financial statement redone as a spreadsheet. Places where you've deleted text using a space mark are now empty cells. You can now select the contents of this worksheet and then copy and paste the values and format (using Paste Special) into any other spreadsheet.

You may have noticed that at the top-right corner of the worksheet are a couple of "Factors." These provide a financial conversion factor. The financial quantities in columns 2 and 3 of this worksheet use these as a multiplying factor. They allow you to adjust the numbers by any numerical factor of your choosing. You could change the statement from thousands of dollars to actual dollars. Alternatively, you could use some currency conversion ratio of your choosing. You can choose which of these two factors you want to apply on a line-by-line, cell-by-cell basis. This technique affords great flexibility. The way to tell Excel which factor you want to use is to "tag" the values in your DataEdit worksheet. Look back at columns 8 and 9 of Figure 4-5. Each occurrence of "1" tells Excel to use the first factor in its financial conversions on the DataPolish sheet. If instead you wish to apply Factor2, replace the 1 with a 2. If you wish to have no factor applied at all, leave the cell blank. Figure 4-5 shows the occurrence of such blank cells because conversion factors are neither wanted nor needed for the rows containing dates.

I hope that you have found this to be a good Take-Away tool for your use. Even if you don't intend to be converting PDF-based financial data to spreadsheet, you at least have some working best practice examples to follow.

Putting Data into Perspective with PivotTables

The world is a sea of data with its ebbs and flows. If someone dips into this ocean of data and scoops out a bottle's worth and hands it to you, you have a finite, but still large, amount of data to comprehend. Your bottle, although it doesn't contain the whole ocean, still contains the same trace elements and shares the same basic ingredients. All in all, your "limited" dataset is still quite complex.

So, how do you analyze what you've got?

Enter the PivotTable

The key feature that makes PivotTables interesting and useful is that large amounts of data can be quickly and easily "folded" in revealing ways. Folding data? That's a rather intriguing way of looking at things. A good example to look at is census data. As you can imagine, there's lots of it. Thankfully, census data is a matter of public record. You can get all the data you want by going to

```
http://dataferrett.census.gov/TheDataWeb/index.html
```

Rather than have you fetch the information, I've included several thousand rows of such data in the file ch04-01censusdata_4K.xls, which is located in the CD-ROM. Open this file, or see Figure 4-6.

	1	2	3	4	5	6	7
1	age	occupation	education	workclass	education-num	marital-status	relationship
2	40	Techn & related support	Bachelors	Private	14	Married-civ spouse	Wife
3	21	Craft & repair	Some-college	Private	11	Divorced	Own child
4	17	Other service	11th	Private	8	Never married	Own child
5	51	Sales	HS-grad	Private	10	Married-civ spouse	Husband
6	28	Executive Mgmt	Bachelors	Private	14	Never married	?
7	26	Executive Mgmt	Bachelors	Private	14	Never married	?
8	44	Prof-specialty	Masters	Private	16	Divorced	?
9	81	Unknown	Masters	?	16	Married-civ spouse	Husband
10	45	Craft & repair	HS-grad	Self-empl-not inc.	10	Married-civ spouse	Husband
11	37	Executive Mgmt	Bachelors	Private	14	Never married	?
12	24	Unknown	HS-grad	?	10	Never married	?
13	29	Handlers & cleaners	HS-grad	Private	10	Married-civ spouse	Husband
14	33	Machine operators	HS-grad	Private	10	Separated	?
15	23	Unknown	Some-college	?	11	Separated	?
16	59	Machine operators	HS-grad	Private	10	Married-civ spouse	Husband
17	37	Craft & repair	Some-college	Private	11	Married-civ spouse	Husband
18	56	Prof-specialty	Masters	Self-empl-inc.	16	Married-civ spouse	Husband
19	41	Prof-specialty	Some-college	Private	11	Married-civ spouse	Husband
20	56	Executive Mgmt	HS-grad	Private	10	Married-civ spouse	Husband
21	38	Executive Mgmt	Some-college	Private	11	Married-civ spouse	Husband
22	28	Sales	Assoc-acad	Private	13	Never married	?
23	35	Craft & repair	Vocational	Private	12	Married-civ spouse	Husband
24	34	Admin incl. clerical	Bachelors	Private	14	Never married	Own child
25	43	Admin incl. clerical	HS-grad	Federal government	10	Married-civ spouse	Wife

Figure 4-6: Representative census data

There are 14 columns and roughly 3,600 rows, or approximately 166,000 pieces of data. How many can a PivotTable handle? Well, it depends on how much memory your computer has, which version of Excel you happen to be running, and how many unique entries you have for a given report field (that is, how many distinct items for a given column). Older versions of Excel would support up to 8,000 items for each PivotTable Report. Excel 2003 now supports up to 32,500 unique items in a PivotTable field. It seems that Excel 2003 has moved up in the world rather nicely.

I'm not going to show you all the features of PivotTables. Instead, I want to hint at the possibilities and at the same time give you practical suggestions and tools you can apply to your own datasets. Particularly, it is not necessarily easy to take a bunch of data and transform it to a useful working PivotTable. Enough of the preliminaries; let's get to the fun stuff.

As you can see in Figure 4-6, the top row of the dataset has descriptive headers. Immediately below the headers are row after row of data. To transform your data to a PivotTable, use the PivotTable Wizard. Click one of the cells containing the data you want to bring into a PivotTable. Select PivotTable and PivotChart Report from the Excel Data menu. When you summon the wizard, you will be given a choice of where you want to get the data from and whether you want a PivotTable by itself or accompanied by a PivotChart (see Figure 4-7).

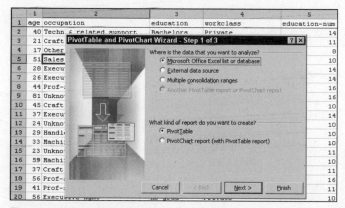

Figure 4-7: PivotTable Wizard

Right now, accept the default settings of getting your data from the underlying spreadsheet. Before getting bogged down with charts, stay with the PivotTable option only. Click the Next button. The wizard tool will reach down to the data below it and "guess" the region of data you want to use (see Figure 4-8).

Figure 4-8: Defining the region of data to be used

If you are unhappy with its guess, simply click the spreadsheet data appearing behind the wizard tool and select the region you want included. Sometimes, you'll want to select a specific region of data for your PivotTable, which the wizard tool fails to correctly guess and which is clumsy for you to point to with your mouse. You can use a user-defined name instead. You may be creating multiple PivotTable reports off of one region of data. Alternatively, your spreadsheet could have multiple worksheet tabs, each populated with different data. You might want to create a separate Pivot Table for, say, each subsidiary in a multicompany organization. Your work could be made easier and more intuitive if you use named references instead of cell coordinates.

BEST PRACTICE If you plan on making multiple Pivot reports or charts from a single spreadsheet, define named references for the regions of data and use these named references instead of physical cell coordinates.

The last step of using your wizard tool involves where you want to put the PivotTable report and specify any type of layout or specific options (Figure 4-9).

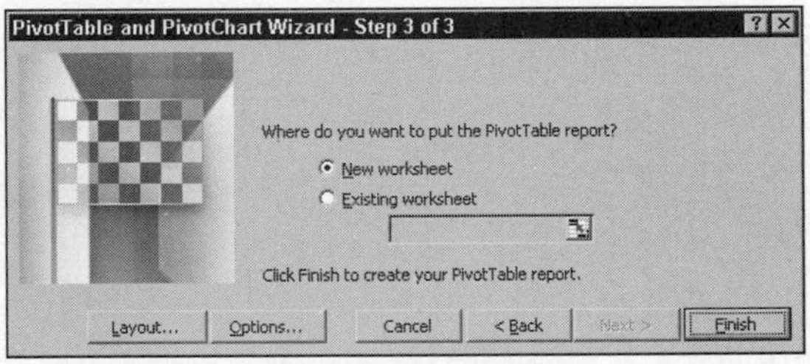

Figure 4–9: Final step of the wizard tool

For now, don't worry too much about these options or the layout. You'll be able to adjust these when you have the generated PivotTable. Because you picked all the default settings when running through the wizard, it would have sufficed to click the Finish button in one of the earlier steps. In any case, go ahead and press the Finish button now. You should see a screen like that shown in Figure 4-10.

On the right side of your "pivot" worksheet, you will see the list of headers from the dataset you specified. You can click-and-drag these over to the drop area on the left. As you drag an item and move it over the drop area, note how your mouse pointer changes appearance.

In any case, drag the "age" item over to the region labeled Drop Row Fields Here. When you drop the field item into this region, all the distinct values for "age" in your dataset will be displayed (Figure 4-11).

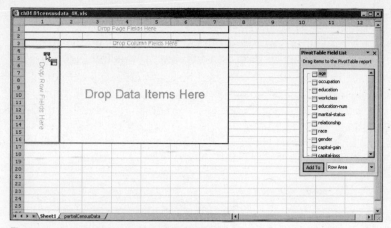

Figure 4–10: Initial state of your PivotTable

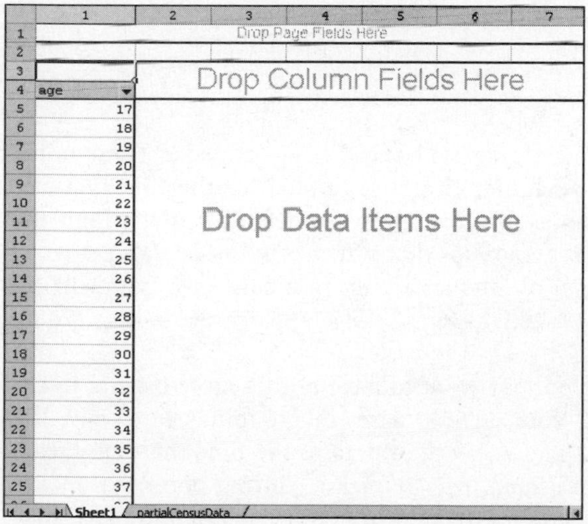

Figure 4–11: All the distinct values of your data, such as
the "age" category are enumerated.

You get to see *all* the distinct values portrayed in the data. Wow! Can you imagine what would happen if you dropped the "income" instead of the "age" item here? Each and every salary figure would be displayed. To make better sense of all these individual pieces of data, you may want to "fold" them into categories or groups that make sense. Take "age," for instance. The youngest person surveyed and included in this data is 17 years. The oldest is 90.

Data grouping

It would be natural to divide the age categories into groups spanning a range of 15 years. Right-click on "age" in the drop area and select Group (see Figure 4-12).

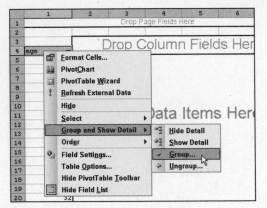

Figure 4–12: Items in your PivotTable can be grouped.

In this particular dataset, the lowest age is 17 and the highest is 90. These minimum and maximum values will be automatically suggested for the "Starting at:" and "Ending at:" values for grouping. If you select the default settings (and the "By:" interval is set to 10), you will get groups that start at the lowest value of your data and work their way up in terms of interval. In this particular case, you will, by default, get the following groups: 17–26, 27–36, 37–46, 47–56, 57–66, 67–76, 77–86, and 87–96.

This may be okay, but I think you may want to have a little more control in the process. Basically, you're locking yourself into a set of groupings for which the division is determined by the first known piece of data at the time that you create the grouping. This seems rather arbitrary. Instead, pick a starting point that makes sense for your data analysis. Also, you may want a wider interval than the one suggested by Excel. Try the starting value of 1 instead of 17 and an interval of 15 instead of 10 (see Figure 4-13).

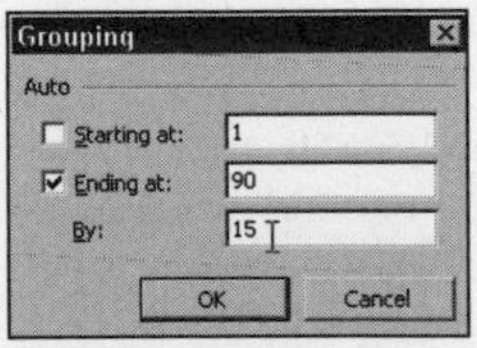

Figure 4-13: Adjusting the default group settings

Now the groups you will get will be the following: 16– 30, 31– 45, 46– 60, 61– 75, and 76– 90. From your PivotTable Field List on the right side of the spreadsheet, drag the "age" item once more to your drop area, but this time drop it into the `Drop Data Items Here` region. You will see the count of the number of people in your dataset by age group (see Figure 4-14).

	1	2	3
1	Drop Page Fields Here		
2			
3	Count of age		
4	age ▼	Total	
5	16–30	1192	
6	31–45	1381	
7	46–60	773	
8	61–75	241	
9	76–90	23	
10	Grand Total	3610	
11			

Figure 4–14: Breakdown of surveyed population by age

SOME THINGS YOU SHOULD KNOW ABOUT GROUPING PIVOT DATA

Are you happy with the groupings? Do they seem to be an appropriate set of ranges? What happens if you get some new data that falls out of this range? When the PivotTable is "refreshed," the underlying data may be changed. You might have a correction to an age value from 17 to 15. When the PivotTable is refreshed, a new grouping of 1–15 will suddenly appear, and the count for 16–30 will be reduced by 1, from 1192 to 1191, and will correctly correspond to the change in the underlying data.

In this dataset, if there were no one between the ages of 61 and 75, how would this PivotTable appear? The whole row would be entirely missing. You would see the grouping "46–60." The grouping on the next row below would appear as "76–90." This would appear pretty weird if you had a nice-looking presentation except for an apparent gap in your groupings. Fortunately, this glitch is easily corrected. You can make the gap disappear by adjusting the settings. To do so, right-click the "age" field (in this example) in the drop area; then choose Field Settings... and select "Show items with no data" (see Figure 4-15).

Refreshing Pivot data

When you click a cell in your PivotTable, you should see a PivotTable toolbar hovering nearby. One of the icons on the toolbar is a red-colored exclamation mark. Click this exclamation mark and the PivotTable is updated to reflect the current values of the underlying data. You can also use the Excel Data menu to choose the Refresh External Data option. (That menu option will be grayed out unless you click a cell in your PivotTable.)

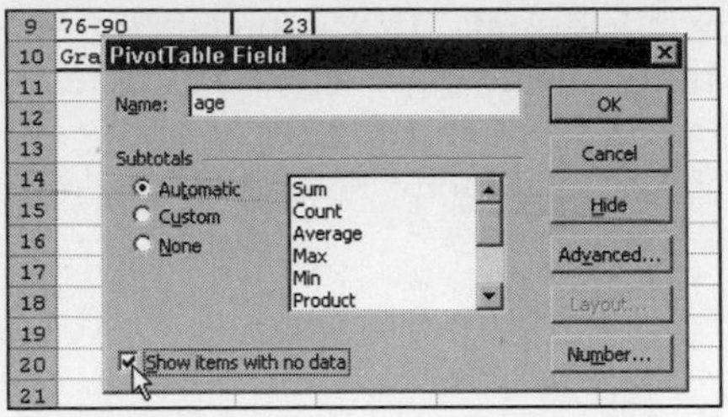

Figure 4–15: Select "Show items with no data."

A count of quantities is not the only way to characterize the members of a field. You can also use Sum, such as when accumulating revenues or expenses. You can use Average for tracking the rate of activity over a period of time. There are other techniques, such as the use of Minimum and Maximum. The PivotTable Field settings allow you to customize the use of these capabilities.

Now all the category groups that you defined are displayed. Even if no data exists within the range of 1–15 or 60–75, these categories will be shown. Along with showing all the groupings, the extremes outside your specifically defined range are also displayed. You will see a category grouping of <1 as well as a grouping for >91 (see Figure 4-16).

A couple of things seem peculiar. These extremes (>91 and <1) never seem to have any data. If you refresh your data that contains an altered value, say 140, the new value is parked into a group range of the range 136–150. All the intervening ranges between 91 and 135 will appear, and so will a new group >151.

Personally, I like having the > and < extremes being accounted for even though they never hold any data. Here comes the weird part. Staying with the original dataset, you see the grouping 76–90 and then >91 (see Figure 4-16). Where is the group that would include 91?

	1	2	3
1	Drop Page Fields Here		
2			
3	Count of age		
4	age ▼	Total	
5	<1		
6	1–15		
7	16–30	1192	
8	31–45	1381	
9	46–60	773	
10	61–75	241	
11	76–90	23	
12	>91		
13	Grand Total	3610	
14			

Figure 4–16: No category grouping exists that includes the value "91".

But wait, this gets weirder! Alter your data. Change the first entry under the "age" column of your source data (a value of 40) to 91 and perform a pivot refresh (see Figure 4-17).

	1	2	3
1	Drop Page Fields Here		
2			
3	Count of age		
4	age ▼	Total	
5	<1		
6	1–15		
7	16–30	1192	
8	31–45	1380	
9	46–60	773	
10	61–75	241	
11	76–91	24	
12	>91		
13	Grand Total	3610	
14			

Figure 4-17: A grouping anomaly: The grouping interval 76–90 has been changed to 76–91.

Rather than park the value into the 91–105 group, the PivotTable alters the grouping 76–90 to 76–91. *It appears that PivotTables bend the rule on the interval size in the groupings.*

If you thought that we're through with all this weirdness, look again. Once more, temporarily alter one of the other "age" values (change the 21 value, the second item under the "age" header, to 92) and then click Refresh Data on your PivotTable toolbar or choose Refresh Data from the Excel Data menu. Figure 4-18 shows that Excel "reclassified" the 91 value and grouped it together with 92 in the grouping of 91–105.

	1	2	3
1	Drop Page Fields Here		
2			
3	Count of age		
4	age ▼	Total	
5	<1		
6	1–15		
7	16–30	1191	
8	31–45	1380	
9	46–60	773	
10	61–75	241	
11	76–90	23	
12	91–105	2	
13	>106		
14	Grand Total	3610	
15			

Figure 4-18: Grouping interval altered once more

The moral of the story is thus: *If you're intending to use PivotTables to classify and group financial information, be aware that Excel can "reclassify" a given item from one grouping to another based on the data that is fed into the PivotTable.*

Some people might think I'm splitting hairs. Well, perhaps. But imagine that your business has a service support contract whose fee structure is determined by the number of incidents per week over six months or a year. Instead of "age," the counts from Figure 4-17 could be incidents per week per branch office aggregated for all offices in the continental United States. A report exhibiting "reclassifica-tions" of counts per grouping could be misleading.

Now that I've alerted you to this anomaly, you can quickly spot the misclassifi-cation. The grouping of 76–91 is bogus and needs to be adjusted. The problem is that the PivotTable is going to continue classifying the data the way it wants. If it's also computing fee structures incorporating PivotTable info, the computed fees may have to be reworked.

Forgive me if I've spent more time on this quirky feature than you care to know. People will be using PivotTables in financial analysis and reporting. A lot of data flies by with PivotTables. So, anything that could materially misstate financial information should not be taken lightly.

More folds in the data

It's pretty nice to get the breakdown of people by age, even if the grouping mecha-nism is a bit quirky. The breakdown could be more meaningful if you could see the split in breakdown by gender. Accomplishing this is easy. Drag the "gender" item from the PivotTable Field List to the column axis in the drop area (directly above the word *Total*, as shown in Figure 4-14). Your PivotTable should be similar to Figure 4-19.

Things are starting to get interesting. With the table appearing as shown in Figure 4-19, try dragging the "occupation" item to the drop area (directly to the right of the "age" column and to the left of the counts for gender). Your PivotTable should look like Figure 4-20.

Here are some things you can do to further refine your PivotTable:

◆ You can nudge the specific order of items in a list. Try nudging "Executive Mgmt" to the top of the list of members of the "occupation" item (you would do this the same way you normally can drag and drop cells in Excel).

◆ The item "Unknown" in the "occupation" column is something you may want excluded from your counts. Right-click the label "Unknown" and select "Hide" from the pop-up menu.

◆ Try dragging the "gender" label directly above "Female" and "Male," over to the left of the "age" label in the PivotTable.

After you perform these steps, your PivotTable should appear similar to Figure 4-21.

When you import data to your PivotTables, you may have a few rows right near the header that have some explanatory remarks such as the type of currency directly below a "sales" or "income" header. This explanatory text appears as "noise" because it adds to your counts. You can exclude the data by right-clicking and selecting Hide. Such noise, even if hidden, will always prevent you from grouping the remaining portions of data. This could place a significant handicap on your PivotTable.

You can fix this problem by deleting the offending rows and performing a Pivot Refresh (see the sidebar "Refreshing Pivot data," earlier in the chapter).

	1	2	3	4	5
1		Drop Page Fields Here			
2					
3	Count of age	gender ▼			
4	age ▼	Female	Male	Grand Total	
5	16-30	490	702	1192	
6	31-45	427	954	1381	
7	46-60	238	535	773	
8	61-75	84	157	241	
9	76-90	5	18	23	
10	Grand Total	1244	2366	3610	
11					

Figure 4-19: Breakdown by both age and gender

	ch04-01censusdata_4K.xls									
	1	2	3	4	5	6	7	8	9	10
1		Drop Page Fields Here								
2										
3	Count of age		gender ▼							
4	age ▼	occupation ▼	Female	Male	Grand Total					
5	16-30	Admin incl. clerical	106	55	161					
6		Agriculture & Fishery	1	20	21					
7		Craft & repair	4	105	109					
8		Executive Mgmt	40	67	107					
9		Handlers & cleaners	7	59	66					
10		Machine operators	12	52	64					
11		Other service	88	78	166					
12		Private household srvc	6	1	7					
13		Prof-specialty	72	69	141					
14		Sales	79	73	152					
15		Security services	6	21	27					
16		Techn & related support	21	22	43					
17		Transportation and moving	4	26	30					
18		Unknown	44	54	98					
19	16-30 Total		490	702	1192					
20	31-45	Admin incl. clerical	94	52	146					
21		Agriculture & Fishery	2	26	28					
22		Craft & repair	10	181	191					
23		Executive Mgmt	63	184	247					
24		Handlers & cleaners	8	28	36					
25		Machine operators	28	60	88					

PivotTable Field List ▼ ×
Drag items to the PivotTable report
- ☐ age
- ☐ occupation
- ☐ education
- ☐ workclass
- ☐ education-num
- ☐ marital-status
- ☐ relationship
- ☐ race
- ☐ gender
- ☐ capital-gain
- ☐ capital-loss

Add To | Row Area

Sheet1 / partialCensusData /

Figure 4-20: Breakdown by age, occupation, and gender

Data that can be grouped must consist of all numbers or all dates. You can't mix numbers with dates; you can't mix dates with numbers. The appearance of text or even empty cells in a column of numbers or a column of dates will destroy the ability of the PivotTable to perform data grouping.

Charting and interpreting data

Charting a PivotTable is a one-step process. Click the Chart Wizard icon in the PivotTable toolbar. Your PivotChart will instantly appear on a new Worksheet and reflect *all* the data in your PivotTable.

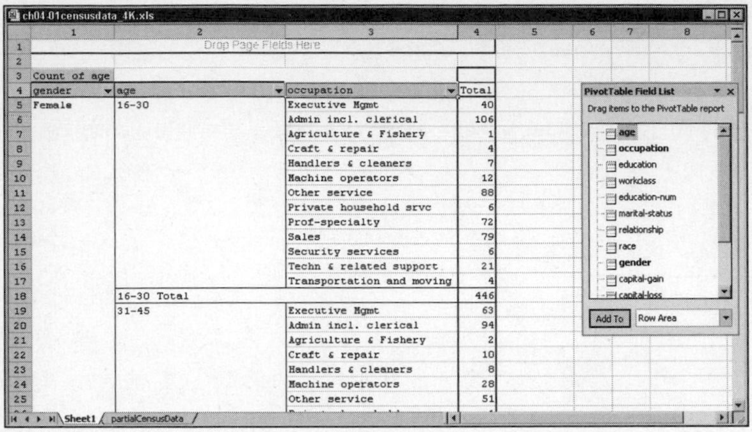

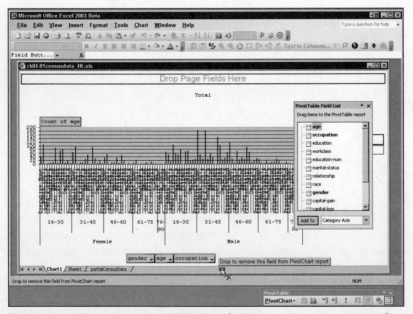

Figure 4-21: Breakdown by gender, and then age, and then occupation (with Executive Mgmt on top and Unknown excluded)

REMOVE THE BALLAST

Be careful, the chart is quickly flooded if the breakdown is too detailed (see Figure 4-22 for an example).

Figure 4-22: An overly saturated PivotChart (with some fields being removed)

Note, in Figure 4-22, that the three fields, gender, age, and occupation, are labeled near the bottom of the chart. To remove a label, just click and drag it off the chart. As you do this, you will see an *X* painted next to the mouse pointer (refer to Figure 4-22).

Go back to your PivotTable on the previous sheet. Changes you make (such as removing a field) are instantly reflected in the PivotTable. The converse is also true. Changes to the PivotTable are instantly reflected in the PivotChart. This is because they are different views of a common data representation that Excel manipulates. When you alter the data represented behind one of these views, you are really altering both.

CONSTRUCTING A MEANINGFUL CHART

Going on a fishing expedition using PivotCharts is difficult at best. It is usually easier to start with the PivotTable and explore your data there. When you see a relationship that you want to demonstrate visually, find a way to simplify the representation so that it lends itself to being shown on a chart.

The best place to start is with a well-defined set of questions. Here's one to consider:

> Given the census data for this PivotTable, does a gender-related difference exist in the proportion of people who achieve an upper level of income, and can you show this graphically?

 The data used in this example derives from a very limited portion of data that is relatively old and dated. The data from this census survey should not be construed as statistically representative of the domestic population today. So, please do not interpret the results of this analysis seriously. If you are interested in doing a more realistic analysis, get the updated data from the U.S. Census Bureau (follow the link provided earlier or go to www.census.gov).

With your defined question in hand, you can now decide which decision variables you will need. They are going to be "income" and "gender." With an empty PivotTable, drag these over to the drop area. Apply grouping to "income." It will suffice to set the interval to 33333. This way, counts of income will fall into one of three groups: those with 33,333 or less, those between 33,334 and 66,666, and those higher than 66,666 (see Figure 4-23).

Does this PivotTable represent enough detail? It does not appear revealing enough to resolve the issue on gender-related differences in income level. What you need to do is compare apples to apples. Right now you're combining apples, pears, tangerines, oranges, bananas, and kiwi. Just as it would be hard to discern one fruit flavor from another (well, maybe you could pick out the kiwi), you don't know the makeup of the individuals surveyed by "occupation."

Drag the "occupation item" to the left of the income label on the drop area (Figure 4-24).

	1	2	3	4	5
1	Drop Page Fields Here				
2					
3	Count of income	gender			
4	income	Female	Male	Grand Total	
5	1-33333	884	1165	2049	
6	33334-66666	265	747	1012	
7	66667-99999	95	454	549	
8	Grand Total	1244	2366	3610	
9					

Figure 4-23: Breakdown by income and gender

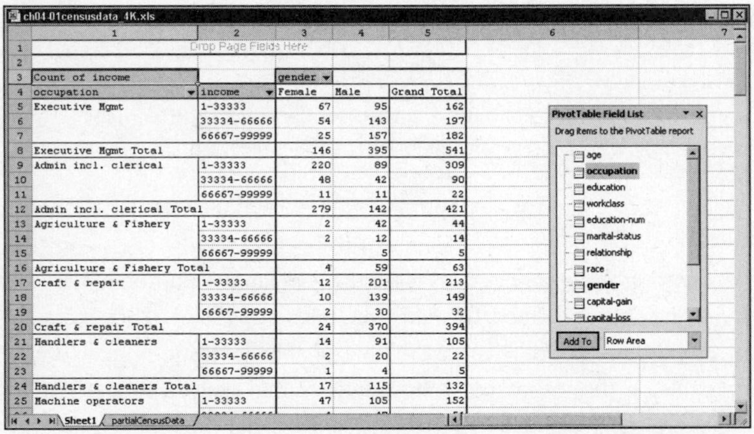

	1	2	3	4	5
1	Drop Page Fields Here				
2					
3	Count of income		gender		
4	occupation	income	Female	Male	Grand Total
5	Executive Mgmt	1-33333	67	95	162
6		33334-66666	54	143	197
7		66667-99999	25	157	182
8	Executive Mgmt Total		146	395	541
9	Admin incl. clerical	1-33333	220	89	309
10		33334-66666	48	42	90
11		66667-99999	11	11	22
12	Admin incl. clerical Total		279	142	421
13	Agriculture & Fishery	1-33333	2	42	44
14		33334-66666	2	12	14
15		66667-99999		5	5
16	Agriculture & Fishery Total		4	59	63
17	Craft & repair	1-33333	12	201	213
18		33334-66666	10	139	149
19		66667-99999	2	30	32
20	Craft & repair Total		24	370	394
21	Handlers & cleaners	1-33333	14	91	105
22		33334-66666	2	20	22
23		66667-99999	1	4	5
24	Handlers & cleaners Total		17	115	132
25	Machine operators	1-33333	47	105	152

Figure 4-24: Breakdown by occupation, followed by income and then gender

Aha! There are some gender-related differences. Look at the how the proportion of females who earn in the upper-income bracket among executives when compared to males.

How about showing this graphically? Click your Chart Wizard icon and the PivotChart will appear (Figure 4-25).

Note that "gender" is stacked, which corresponds to the column labels of the PivotTable in Figure 4-24.

The key factor that you want to focus on is just "Executive Mgmt." You can simplify your chart. Look at the top of Figure 4-25, where it shows the text "Drop Page Field Here." You've seen this text in the PivotTables. Up to now, I haven't told you what purpose it serves, but now I will: The chart would be a lot easier to view if you were looking at one occupation type at a time, particularly "Executive Mgmt." So, go ahead and drag the "occupation" label at the bottom of the chart (Figure 4-25) and place it where the "Drop Page Fields Here" Text appears. In place of that text, you will now see a simplified stacked chart that allows you to "page through" the individual occupation types (see Figure 4-26).

To see the relationship more clearly, you can change the Chart type (see Figure 4-27) the same way as you would with a regular Excel chart (right-click the chart area and then select and preview the Chart type that you want).

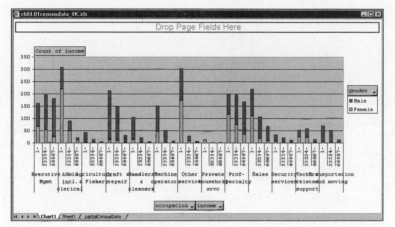

Figure 4-25: Stacked chart with breakdown, but still too much being displayed

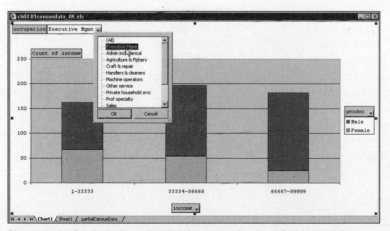

Figure 4-26: Stacked chart that has been greatly simplified by enabling you to "page through" the individual occupation types

Before moving on to the discussion of pivot formulas that follows, you should be aware that you cannot create an XY Scatter PivotChart. You can make a regular Excel chart from a PivotTable. Doing so is discussed in the next section.

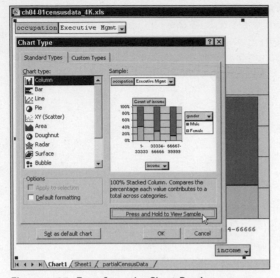

Figure 4-27: Even from the Chart Preview, you can see that as income increases, the proportion of females achieving higher income thins considerably.

Pivot formulas

The sheet holding a PivotTable is not a regular Excel worksheet. You can't simply expect to select a region of data in the PivotTable and create a regular Excel chart. If you try to do that, Excel will create a PivotChart.

There's a simple way to get around this. Create a new Excel worksheet. From one of the cells in the new worksheet, start entering a formula by typing an equal sign (=) in the Excel Formula Bar and then clicking the top-left cell of the PivotTable. Then press Enter. Replicate the formula in this cell down the rows and across the columns. Now your new worksheet has all the values of your PivotTable. It may not look very pretty, but you will be able to create normal Excel charts, XY Scatters included, from this worksheet.

Another way to retrieve the values is to use the Excel GETPIVOTDATA function.

GETPIVOTDATA

This is a little bit of a complex function. GETPIVOTDATA has the following syntax:

```
GETPIVOTDATA(data_field,pivot_table,field1,item1,field2,item2,...)
```

You can use it in a formula outside a PivotTable to retrieve values inside a PivotTable. This can be a useful facility. Rather than try to explain the syntax, let me give you some examples of how it works.

```
=GETPIVOTDATA("income",R3C1,"gender","Female")
```

The GETPIVOTDATA function answers the questions *what*, *where*, and *which*. In Figure 4-28, the numbers in column 6 are obtained by using GETPIVOTDATA and retrieving values as though they were inside the PivotTable. They are flanked on the right side by a listing of the formulas used to compute the respective values, as follows:

◆ The number 1153 is determined by first asking *what* is being counted:

[Count of income.]

◆ Next, *where* is it being tabulated:

[Inside the PivotTable, which starts on R3C1.]

◆ *Which* Item(s) you are looking for:

[The field that holds the item is "gender." The item held inside the field is "Female."]

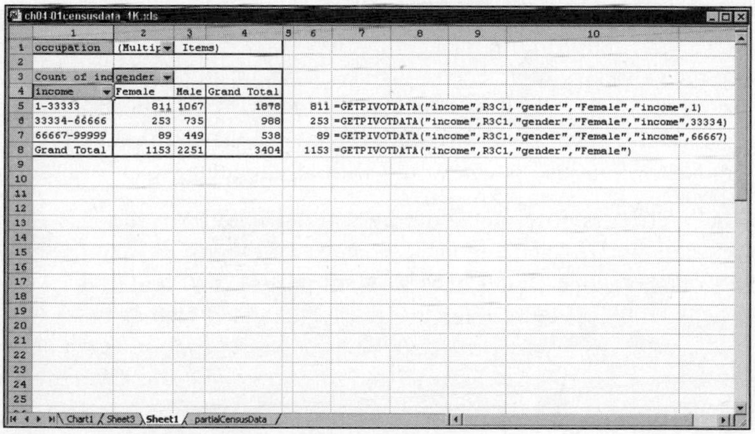

Figure 4-28: GETPIVOTDATA sample usage

If you wished to burrow in deeper, you would tack on more fields and items. To get the "89," you would type:

```
=GETPIVOTDATA("income",R3C1,"gender","Female","income",66667)
```

You need to specify the extra field and item. Fields and items, by the way, always come in pairs when using GETPIVOTDATA.

There are some unusual features of GETPIVOTDATA:

◆ If your PivotTable is not populated (as in the way it was shown in Figure 4-10), you will get an error if you use GETPIVOTDATA to retrieve data inside the PivotTable.

◆ If you remove a field that is displayed inside the PivotTable and it is referenced in your `GETPIVOTDATA` formula, you will get an error.

◆ When retrieving data by burrowing in through multiple fields, you have to follow the order visually displayed in the PivotTable. Suppose you create a PivotTable and then specify a `GETPIVOTDATA` formula outside your PivotTable to retrieve a value. This formula works fine. Now you drag another field from the PivotTable Field List into your drop area. Watch your `GETPIVOTDATA` formula break.

◆ The way you create a GET `PIVOTDATA` is to enter an "=" symbol on the Excel Formula Bar and click the cell containing the data value inside the PivotTable. Instantly, the whole formula for accessing the data value is inserted into the Edit line of your Formula Bar. You can then manually edit this formula to tweak it further.

◆ `GETPIVOTDATA` does not retrieve the field "containers," only the values held inside them. For example:

```
=GETPIVOTDATA("income",R3C1,"gender","Female","income",66667)
```

will retrieve the value 89. There is no `GETPIVOTDATA` formula that can be used to retrieve the `66667-99999` group label. Don't worry too much about this. You can use a regular Excel formula to reference the cell that contains the group `66667-99999` just as you would with any regular Excel formula.

◆ `GETPIVOTDATA` retrieves only the values held and displayed in the PivotTable. Guess what? The Page Field elements at the top of the PivotTable worksheet (and PivotCharts) are not part of the PivotTable. Therefore, `GETPIVOTDATA` can't reference these Page Field elements.

Pivot data drill-down

This is a short and simple topic. As you rummage through your PivotTables, you might want to see the underlying data that contributes to the information summarized in the PivotTable. Just double-click the cell and a new worksheet will appear with a copy of the data.

Preparing Your Data

You will soon find that much, if not most, of the time and complexity demanded by your spreadsheet activities consists of getting your data into shape. Do a poor job of this and you'll be continually hobbling along. Do a good job and you'll be quickly involved in the detailed data analysis instead of puzzling over how you can express certain kinds of information you know exists within your dataset.

Data redundancy

Among the things you will learn here is that a little redundancy in your data can be a good thing. You may have noticed that the sample census dataset contained both "education" and "education-num." One of these is descriptive and the other is numerical. For ordered sorting, the numerical representation works better. If you are zeroing in on just one of the education members (such as Doctorate) or a specific subset, the narrative descriptions may be more convenient to work with. Notice that I chose not to apply this kind of redundancy with every field in the dataset.

Data redundancy in your Pivot Fields can be useful, but be careful not to overuse it.

Data substitution

Sometimes, when you receive data from third-party sources, you will be given all your data as pure numeric information and a separate set of conversion tables for their descriptive or narrative equivalents. As an example, countries might be represented by numeric code. The code "57" might signify the United States. This type of identification makes the data more compact and less prone to minute variations. It also makes the data harder for humans to read and interpret. If you were to have a PivotTable that contained both country of origin and age, and you saw "57," you could easily get confused and not be sure whether you were looking at an age or a country code. For such reasons, it will help you to perform a data substitution before you bring the data into your PivotTable.

Data substitution could become complex, because you may have multiple columns of data along with multiple worksheets. The file ch04-03substitute tool.xls, located on your CD-ROM, shows you how to perform a basic substitution like the one described in this section. This Take-Away spreadsheet should help to get you started because it contains the basic lookup mechanism.

The basic formula for the substitution is as follows:

```
=VLOOKUP(LookupValue,LookupTable,2,FALSE)
```

Dataset pre-consolidation tool

As you can see in Figure 4-7, data used for the PivotTables can come from external data sources, such as a relational database, or from multiple consolidation ranges.

Getting data from external databases is great because your PivotTable can be regularly refreshed. Besides, someone else may be doing the hard work of preparing the data.

You can also get data from multiple consolidation ranges as well as other PivotTables, if they are currently open at the time that you are creating a new PivotTable.

I'll leave you to explore these options on your own.

As an alternative to consolidation ranges, you may want to "pre-consolidate" your data and bring this into your PivotTable in the same way as you regularly would, as shown earlier in the chapter. To that end, I provide a Take-Away tool (open the spreadsheet file ch04-04pivotgenerator.xls on your CD-ROM). This tool is almost identical to the SQL Generator tool presented in the previous chapter (see Figure 4-29).

The tool contains sales data located on the Sheet2 worksheet. The Sheet1 worksheet generates data into individual records, where the data items are separated by commas. Unlike the tool of the previous chapter, this tool generates all the data one year at a time. You can increment the year by pressing the Spinner Control button.

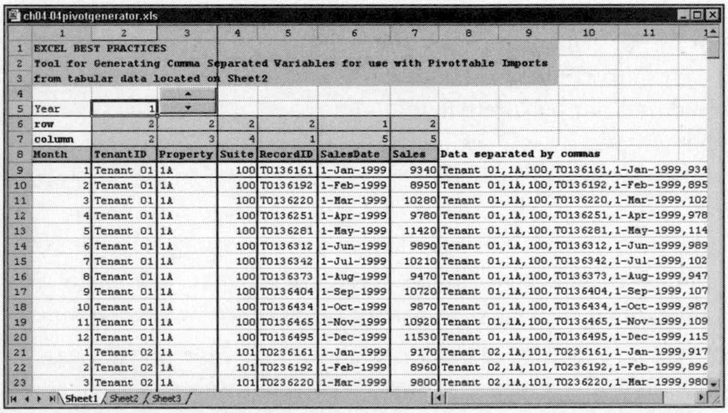
ch04-04pivotgenerator.xls

	1	2	3	4	5	6	7	8
1	EXCEL BEST PRACTICES							
2	Tool for Generating Comma Separated Variables for use with PivotTable Imports							
3	from tabular data located on Sheet2							
4								
5	Year	1						
6	row	2	2	2	2	1	2	
7	column	2	3	4	1	5	5	
8	Month	TenantID	Property	Suite	RecordID	SalesDate	Sales	Data separated by commas
9	1	Tenant 01	1A	100	T0136161	1-Jan-1999	9340	Tenant 01,1A,100,T0136161,1-Jan-1999,934
10	2	Tenant 01	1A	100	T0136192	1-Feb-1999	8950	Tenant 01,1A,100,T0136192,1-Feb-1999,895
11	3	Tenant 01	1A	100	T0136220	1-Mar-1999	10280	Tenant 01,1A,100,T0136220,1-Mar-1999,102
12	4	Tenant 01	1A	100	T0136251	1-Apr-1999	9780	Tenant 01,1A,100,T0136251,1-Apr-1999,978
13	5	Tenant 01	1A	100	T0136281	1-May-1999	11420	Tenant 01,1A,100,T0136281,1-May-1999,114
14	6	Tenant 01	1A	100	T0136312	1-Jun-1999	9890	Tenant 01,1A,100,T0136312,1-Jun-1999,989
15	7	Tenant 01	1A	100	T0136342	1-Jul-1999	10210	Tenant 01,1A,100,T0136342,1-Jul-1999,102
16	8	Tenant 01	1A	100	T0136373	1-Aug-1999	9470	Tenant 01,1A,100,T0136373,1-Aug-1999,947
17	9	Tenant 01	1A	100	T0136404	1-Sep-1999	10720	Tenant 01,1A,100,T0136404,1-Sep-1999,107
18	10	Tenant 01	1A	100	T0136434	1-Oct-1999	9870	Tenant 01,1A,100,T0136434,1-Oct-1999,987
19	11	Tenant 01	1A	100	T0136465	1-Nov-1999	10920	Tenant 01,1A,100,T0136465,1-Nov-1999,109
20	12	Tenant 01	1A	100	T0136495	1-Dec-1999	11530	Tenant 01,1A,100,T0136495,1-Dec-1999,115
21	1	Tenant 02	1A	101	T0236161	1-Jan-1999	9170	Tenant 02,1A,101,T0236161,1-Jan-1999,917
22	2	Tenant 02	1A	101	T0236192	1-Feb-1999	8960	Tenant 02,1A,101,T0236192,1-Feb-1999,896
23	3	Tenant 02	1A	101	T0236220	1-Mar-1999	9800	Tenant 02,1A,101,T0236220,1-Mar-1999,980

Sheet1 Sheet2 Sheet3

Figure 4-29: PivotGenerator tool

Here is how to use the tool:

1. Place your data into the Sheet2 worksheet in the appropriate locations. Change the dates on the top row as appropriate.
2. Create a place that will house the data in its final form that will be used by the Excel Pivot Wizard. You can use Sheet3 on this spreadsheet or an

empty worksheet from another spreadsheet. For purposes of discussion, I just refer to this import sheet as Sheet3.

3. From the Sheet1 worksheet, make sure that the row and column values listed in rows 6 and 7 match the starting row and column location for TenantID, Property, Suite, RecordID, SalesDate, and Sales on Sheet2. Obviously, when you use your data, you will be using different labels than the ones provided in this example.

4. Set the year to 1 (you can use the Spinner Control button or change the contents of R5C2 by hand. Your data should appear in comma-separated form, starting at row 9, column 8 and continuing down through row 236. Select this range (that is, R9C8:R236C8).

5. On Sheet1, copy (Ctrl+C) the range of data (R9C8:R236C8). Switch to Sheet3 (or wherever you plan to place the data); then, click the appropriate location to place your data. If you already have data on this sheet, place it immediately below the existing data. Be sure to use Paste Special, and paste only Values. With luck, you have already read Appendix A and have created a toolbar icon for pasting values only, because that method would be easier than navigating Excel menus.

6. Switch to the Sheet1 Worksheet. If the Year number is less than the number of years for which you have data, increment up by 1 using the Spinner Control button. The region you selected in Step 5 (R9C8:R236C8) should still be selected. If not, make sure that it is. Go back to Step 5. Basically what you're doing is grabbing the data for each of the years and bringing it to Sheet3.

7. Select your data in Sheet3 (you can select the whole column if there is nothing else in the column but your data) and use your Text to Columns facility. This is located on the Excel Data menu. If you use this option frequently, customize your toolbar to have the icon handy (see Appendix A for how to do that). The Text to Columns facility will split out all the items into separate columns. See Figure 4-30 to view the Convert Text to Columns Wizard.

Be sure that the radio button is set to Delimited. Press the Next button. You will then be prompted for the type of delimiters you want to use. Select Comma. The data preview region should display the items into their respective columns (see Figure 4-31).

When using the Text to Columns feature, you have the option to specify a character different from Tab, Semicolon, Comma, or Space. If your delimiter has multiple characters, you should use the Excel Search & Replace feature to change the delimiter to a single, unique character. You can then proceed to use the Text to Columns feature.

Also note that there is an option called "Treat consecutive delimiters as one." This feature is useful when you have multiple spaces appearing between words.

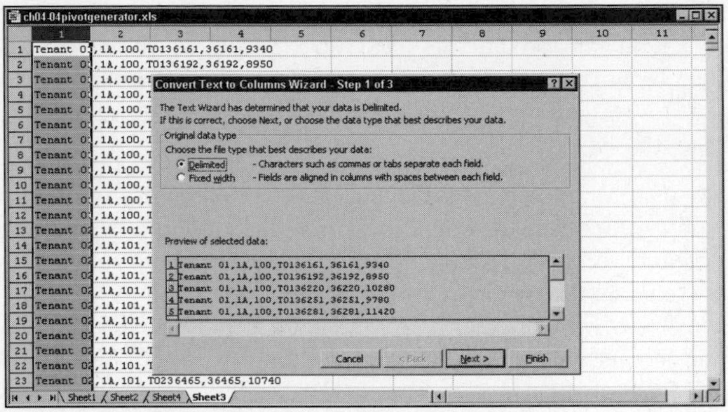

Figure 4-30: Using the text to columns facility

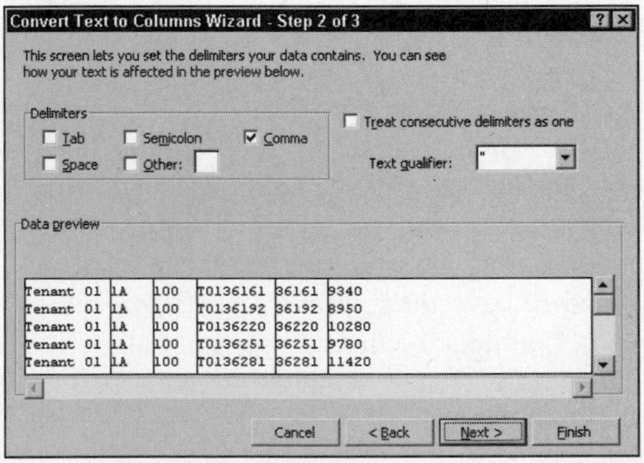

Figure 4-31: Choice of delimiters with Comma selected

Unless you have special formatting needs or want to skip certain columns, just click Finish. The data should now be broken out into separate columns.

8. On the row immediately above the data, place the appropriate labels. If necessary, insert a new row immediately above the data.

Your data should now be suitable for use within a PivotTable or PivotChart. Import it as you normally would. Populate the PivotTable. Apply groupings, and you should be able to have a PivotTable that looks like Figure 4-32.

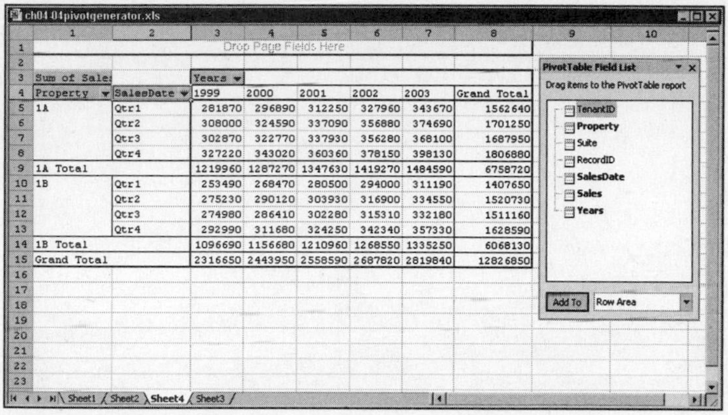

Figure 4-32: PivotTable with multi-level groupings (Years and Quarters)

> **NOTE** Dates in PivotTables and PivotCharts will accommodate multiple groupings. You will be given options to select the grouping interval — such as Years, Quarters, Months, Days, Hours, and so forth. There is no reason to limit yourself to one option if you feel you need more.

If you are really interested in the topic of multi-dimensional data analysis, you may want to explore a product called Muse (www.muser.com). Also look at products from IBM (www.ibm.com), such as its DB2 OLAP Server.

Saving PivotTables as Web pages

Most of the time, you'll want to work with PivotTables inside Excel. There will be times, however, when you will want to publish your PivotTables over the Web and display them inside a browser. This section outlines how to do this. Before I go further, you should be aware of the following:

◆ This procedure is designed to work with the Internet Explorer Browser versions 5.01 (SP2) and later.

◆ Nothing prevents you from placing a spreadsheet file on a Web server and serving the spreadsheet file over the Internet. If users configure their browsers appropriately, Excel will automatically launch when the file is received. Otherwise, they can just save the file to disk and double-click the file.

To save your PivotTable for Web publishing, go to the Excel File menu and select Save As Web Page (see Figure 4-33).

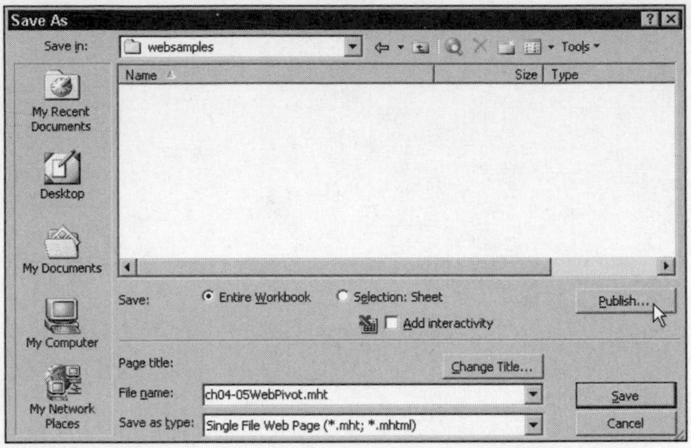

Figure 4-33: The Save as Web Page option (Be sure to press the Publish button.)

After pressing the Publish button, you will be given a number of choices (see Figure 4-34).

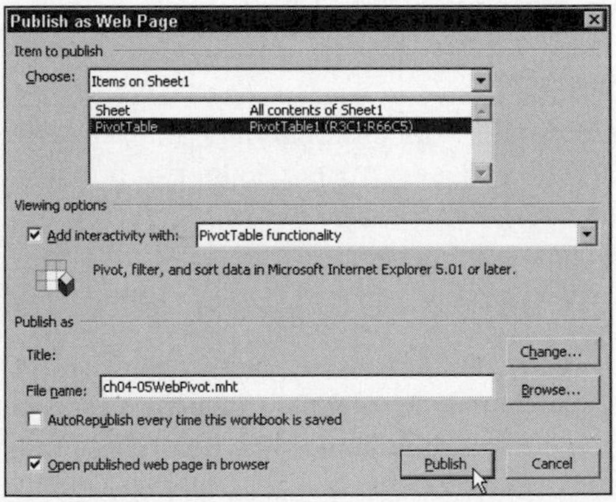

Figure 4-34: Publish your PivotTable with interactivity and PivotTable functionality.

1. In Items to Publish, choose the worksheet that contains the PivotTable.

2. On this sheet, select the PivotTable (which will also display the PivotTable rows and columns). Remember, you can have more than one PivotTable on a worksheet.

3. For Viewing options, select PivotTable functionality.

4. Make sure that the filename and location selected are what you want.

5. You may want to auto republish every time your workbook is saved. If your company is like most that manage a lot of Web content, you will want to explicitly know when the PivotTable is published to the Web. Therefore, you might not automatically want to auto republish.

Figure 4-35 shows what the file looks like.

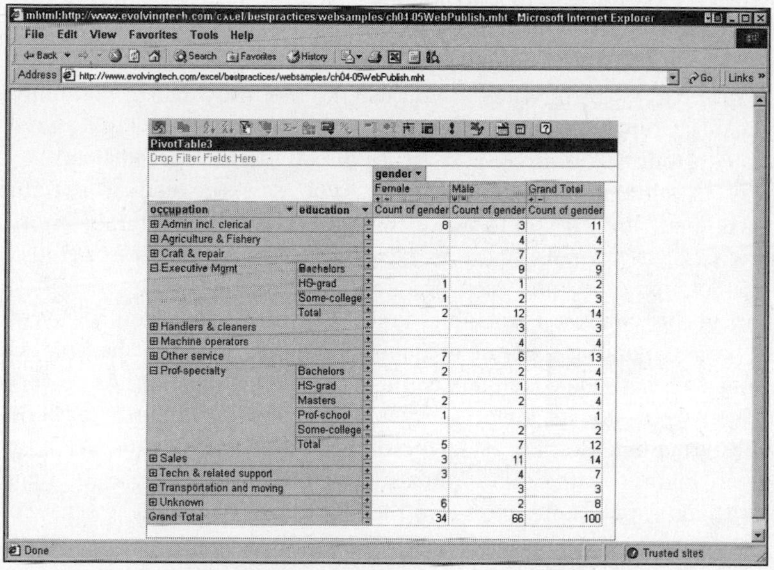

Figure 4–35: Your PivotTable as a Web page

You can individually expand and collapse pivot fields. Note the larger + and – symbols along the extreme left of the PivotTable. These expansion and contraction symbols are housed in unattached boxes. In contrast to these, you should see pairs of +, – symbols immediately above or along the left edge of the Pivot data. Clicking one of these + symbols drills down to the underlying data. Clicking the – symbol returns the Pivot summary data.

> **NOTE** To view the .MHT file, users may have to add your site to their list of trusted sites. This list can be found by going to the Tools menu of Internet Explorer and selecting Internet Options, followed by clicking the Security tab to add the site.

Closing Thoughts

Some people can hardly wait to get their hands on every tiny morsel of data. Others shudder at the thought of toiling through the numbers, trying in vain to align a piece here with a piece there. Either way, you have to ask yourself the question "What am I going to do with this data and how can I turn it into something meaningful?"

These are tough questions to answer. The first part of this chapter gave you a tool and methodology to shuttle PDF financial data into spreadsheet financial data. Somewhere between the skewed alignments, the treatment of formats, and the scaling of the numbers, you had to consciously think about validation, how to alter narrative descriptions and currency/number conversions. These are things you're going to have to face regardless of whether you use the tool provided or manually type a new spreadsheet from scratch. The conversion tool and methodology I gave you forces you to confront and resolve these issues directly in the spreadsheet.

Along the way to adjusting the original data, you saw the use of a Data Overpass. This technique allowed you to make changes, retain your original information, and know explicitly what alterations were made. In addition to having a potentially useful tool, you saw some good practices in action.

The second part of this chapter (PivotTables and PivotCharts) gave you a way to take what could be a staggering amount of data and almost instantly be able to probe, visualize, and summarize the complex connections hidden beneath. As powerful as they are, you were shown some quirky but not obvious features of how PivotTables handle grouping. Putting aside these peculiar features, you saw how effective pivoting or "folding" data can be. You also saw that PivotCharts can become quickly saturated as you throw more items into the mix. It seemed to make sense to tag-team pivot charting with the pivot table capabilities. In retrospect, this is not surprising, because PivotCharts and PivotTables are directly tethered to each other.

As much as this chapter focused on PivotTable analysis, it also addressed the difficulties and issues of getting the data into the PivotTable. Your inability to get the underlying data into some suitable form will only water down your ability to analyze the data later on. If there's a little noise in your data, you'll be unable to perform grouping for those items.

Sometimes, data has to be packaged in a special way to make it suitable for use by PivotTables. To this end, I provided a pre-consolidation tool to assist in this packaging. Other times you may need to substitute one kind of data for another. You found out the basics on how to perform such substitutions.

Finally, you saw how you can publish a PivotTable over the Web so that it can be viewed within a browser.

In the previous chapter I promised to continue harping on the theme of how important and essential it is to become intimate with the numbers and data you are working on. In this chapter, you saw how essential it was to know and understand what your data meant. The next chapter, "Scaling the Peaks of Mt. Data," gives you ideas of how you can tackle the complexities when you're flooded with data.

Part II

Spreadsheet Ergonomics

Chapter 5

Scaling the Peaks of Mt. Data

IN THIS CHAPTER

◆ Introducing the art of data slogging

◆ Importing data

◆ Pruning unneeded data

◆ Making data uniform

◆ Resolving ambiguities

◆ Normalizing portions of your data

◆ Handling violations and anomalies

◆ Enabling search capabilities for your source data

◆ Building increasingly complex summaries

◆ Handling special problems in formula replication

◆ Setting up a list box

◆ Providing graphical summaries with drill-down details

PART I OF EXCEL BEST PRACTICES *for Business* introduced you to the essentials needed for working with spreadsheets. This chapter marks the beginning of Part II, "Spreadsheet Ergonomics." Here, you will be thinking about the overall flow of information moving through your spreadsheets and how the information meshes.

The goal of this chapter is to learn how to plow through mounds of data for a specific set of goals. Along the way, you're bound to be snared by nasty data traps. If you're not careful or thorough enough, they will compromise your ability to complete your tasks as well as the integrity of your completed work. You need to become adept at what I call "data slogging." As much as I can, I will show you how to go about doing this. I hope you'll walk away from this chapter with some definite ideas on how to chisel your data so that it's smaller and more manageable.

You'll also get to see in action things such as the Sentinel Look-Ahead technique of Chapter 3, "Your Handy Reference for Manipulating Data."

The setting for this chapter deals with the restating of some older economic data, expressed in terms of Standard Industrial Classification (SIC) Codes, into its modern form, called NAICS, which stands for the North American Industrial Classification System. Rather than tackle the conversion over all available economic data, you will be dealing a selected subset: Wholesale Trade. This is small enough a task to fit inside a whole chapter, but big enough to be real.

You should be aware that the dataset in this chapter has lots of redundant information and consolidated information that cannot be reconciled with its underlying details. So don't be taken aback if I get a little ruthless with the data, making some seemingly arbitrary and rash decisions. These methods are all necessary to get the data squeaky clean and in useful working order for data analysis.

Are you up to the challenge?

NAICS and SIC are often used to classify economic and financial data. Although the systems are similar, SIC is being phased out. Though SIC Code is no longer in vogue, plenty of data and reports are stated in terms of the old SIC Codes. How do you restate this data using NAICS?

You're going to get your chance to do this data conversion. You will soon discover that you will have to address some subtle and complex issues in SIC/NAICS code conversion. You will also have to be dealing with data substitution, as well as data partitioning/clustering, to make the resulting economic information meaningful.

You will also discover that SIC and NAICS don't mesh perfectly. You will have to make decisions on how you want to "smooth the wrinkles." This entails decisions about specific classifications. It also entails devising a way in your spreadsheet formulas to handle the wrinkles.

The Art of Data Slogging

Those of you who live and work with numbers and data know that the information is fraught with gaps, redundancies, ambiguities, and inconsistencies. Like an 800-pound gorilla, large masses of data can be both stubborn and daunting.

Consider, for the moment, classifying and reporting economic and financial data. There's a numeric classification scheme that was developed by the United States government called the Standard Industrial Classification Code, or SIC Code.

For years, economic and financial data was reported using the four-digit SIC Code. It was the boon and bane of many a financial manager in both the public and private sectors. One of the difficulties in working with SIC Codes is that four digits didn't provide enough granularity to segregate different business categories. Also, as new industry sectors and business classifications emerged, there was no clear choice of the appropriate classification. In the age of NAFTA (North American Financial Trade Alliance), a new system came about, called the North American Industrial Classification System, or NAICS. This system uses six digits, permitting greater detail.

Integrating old and new data

There are good historical summaries of economic data covering a range of years that's still based on the old SIC Code. People in your company may have had their hands on this older data and produced numerous reports. Today, more than ever, there is a wealth of publicly available economic data. This newer data is more up-to-date and comprehensive than the older "company official" datasets you and your colleagues may still have. If you wish to integrate new data with the old, you have two options available:

- ◆ Continue to retrofit all the new data with your company's legacy based reporting framework.

- ◆ Restate your older data with a new, modern attire.

Somehow, I think you'll want to opt for the latter approach. Doing so makes more sense, though it's not so simple. To begin with, there are tons of company reports that have been prepared. Even if you had the time to modernize all these reports, can you be sure that the same set of information and assumptions used to prepare the original reports will be available to you? Even if they are, do you think all the interpretations will still be valid? Nevertheless, it's still important to bridge the old data with current data using a common reporting framework. Fortunately, there's a resolution. The master data files from the original disks have been judiciously archived and preserved. Though no one has pored over the documents in some time, they are still intact. The master data file was economic data downloaded from a governmental agency a number of years back. It contains data for 1992 and 1997. Not only does it contain Wholesale Trade data, the industry relevant to your company, but it also contains data for all industrial sectors.

Your sources for this conversion are two files and a conversion table:

- ◆ E97SIC.txt

- ◆ E97SIC_HeaderInfo.txt

- ◆ An SIC to NAICS conversion table

The files are all on your CD-ROM. The E97SIC.txt file contains all the raw data in comma-delimited form. Because there are no headers in E97SIC.txt, a separate file (E97SIC_HeaderInfo.txt) contains the names of the headers for each of the columns. For the moment, don't worry about the SIC to NAICS conversion table.

Importing data

From Excel, you can open the file E97SIC.txt. You will be presented with the Text Import Wizard (see Figure 5-1).

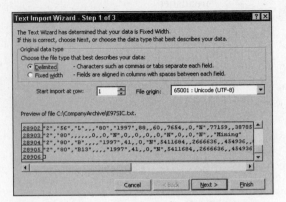

Figure 5–1: Comma–delimited data file for import

Right away, you can see that you're up against a fair amount of data. Scrolling down to the bottom of the preview portion, you can see that you have almost 29,000 rows of data. There are also 25 columns of data. By the way, when I received the comma-delimited file, it came as a .txt file. If the file suffix had been changed to .csv, Excel would have bypassed the Text Import Wizard and immediately opened the file as a spreadsheet.

When you open a comma-delimited file that is named as a .txt file, Excel will automatically present you with the Text Import Wizard. You will have to specify which setting you want in order to complete the import process. If your file doesn't require any special settings other than being a plain-vanilla, comma-separated variable file, you can rename your .txt file to a .csv file. Excel will bypass the custom settings of the Text Import Wizard and immediately open the file as a regular Excel workbook.

If you are given a .csv file and open it up from Excel, you will not be presented with any kind of wizard. Just because Excel thinks you don't need to make use of the Text Import Wizard for a .csv file doesn't mean that you don't. A .csv file can require special processing, such as skipping certain columns or performing additional parsing between commas. You can change the file suffix in the filename from .csv to .txt. In this manner, you can force the Text Import Wizard into action when you open the file from Excel.

Cleaning up the spreadsheet

The first thing you'll want to do is to place meaningful headers in the spreadsheet. Insert a row or several rows at the top of the spreadsheet. Copy and paste the header information from the E97SIC_HeaderInfo.txt file. Your spreadsheet should be similar to Figure 5-2. At first glance, the spreadsheet appears a bit daunting. That's because it is.

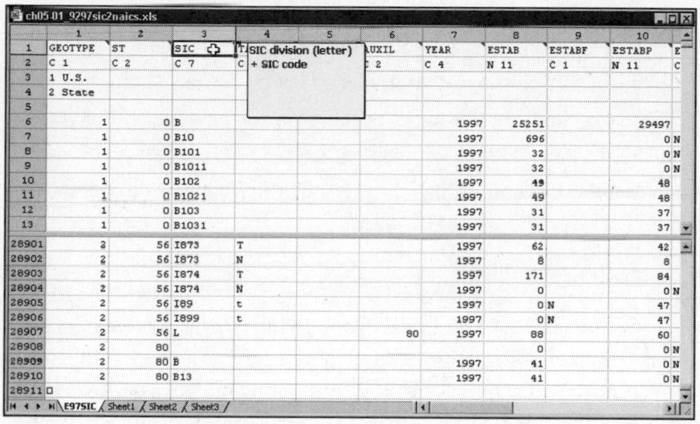

ch05-01_9297sic2naics.xls

	1	2	3	4	5	6	7	8	9	10	
1	GEOTYPE	ST	SIC	T	SIC division (letter)	AUXIL	YEAR	ESTAB	ESTABF	ESTABP	E
2	C 1	C 2	C 7	C	+ SIC code	C 2	C 4	N 11	C 1	N 11	C
3	1 U.S.										
4	2 State										
5											
6	1	0	B				1997	25251		29497	
7	1	0	B10				1997	696		0	N
8	1	0	B101				1997	32		0	N
9	1	0	B1011				1997	32		0	N
10	1	0	B102				1997	49		48	
11	1	0	B1021				1997	49		48	
12	1	0	B103				1997	31		37	
13	1	0	B1031				1997	31		37	
28901	2	56	I873	T			1997	62		42	
28902	2	56	I873	N			1997	8		8	
28903	2	56	I874	T			1997	171		84	
28904	2	56	I874	N			1997	0		0	N
28905	2	56	I89	t			1997	0	N	47	
28906	2	56	I899	t			1997	0	N	47	
28907	2	56	L			80	1997	88		60	
28908	2	80						0		0	N
28909	2	80	B				1997	41		0	N
28910	2	80	B13				1997	41		0	N
28911											

E97SIC / Sheet1 / Sheet2 / Sheet3

Figure 5-2: Imported dataset with header information

PRUNE UNNEEDED DATA

You can chisel away a good portion of the complexity and size. To begin with, your company is only interested in Wholesale Trade (which relates to SIC codes 5012 through 5199, 7389, and 7822). Eliminating all but these codes will greatly reduce the size of your task (it will also make it realistic to handle this project in the space of one chapter). This alone will eliminate close to 20,000 rows of data.

Next, some of the individual columns will not be needed. The following columns have no data, or else no data of relevance:

- Column 11: The flag column for number of establishments in 1992.
- Column 9: The flag column for number of establishments in 1997.
- Column 7: The year (1997) is repeated in every row with data.
- Column 6: Auxiliary has no data.
- Column 4: Tax indicator on profit vs. non-profit is too sparse to be of value.

You can go ahead and safely eliminate columns 11, 9, 7, 6, and 4.

APPLES AND ORANGES

If you look at the column labeled OPTYPE, you will see that there are two classifications. A 00 or 0 (depending upon the settings in place when you imported the file)
implies that data in the given row corresponds to a total of all companies. The 10
designation is specific to Merchant Wholesalers only. As you start to examine and
compare values for these two groups, you will see that Merchant Wholesalers comprises roughly 75–80% of the Totals for Wholesale Trade.

> You can try your hand at creating a PivotTable for this data. This will give you
> a chance to further sharpen the skills you picked up from the last chapter. It
> is a bit of a digression and not the focus of this chapter, however. But if you
> really want to create a PivotTable, you will get better results after you have
> cleaned much of the data. Wait until you get further along in the chapter.

Your immediate task at hand is to get the historically reported economic information restated using NAICS instead of SIC Code. *Your driving principle to accomplish this should be simplification.* Right now, because the data for Totals and
Merchant Wholesalers are comparable and relatively close, it may not be necessary
to keep both sets of data. For the sake of simplifying everything, retain the Totals
data and discard the Merchant Wholesalers data. Those of you who would want to
do the converse (that is, keep the Merchant Wholesalers data and discard the Totals
related data) are free to do so. If you want to keep both sets, you will have increased
complexity, larger files to manage, and may have to improvise as you design the
restated reports based on NAICS.

Removing the rows with the "10" entries in the OPTYPE column will chop the
amount of data to approximately one half. To remove these items, sort your data
using the OPTYPE column as your sort key. After you've sorted, delete the rows containing "10" in this column. You will be left with 4,680 rows with zeros in the
OPTYPE' column and two rows with no entries for this column. These two entries
are for the SIC Codes 7389 and 7822. As with all the other 20,000 rows previously
eliminated, the data for these two rows are already "Totals" because they never had
a "10" designation.

Because everything in the OPTYPE column represents "Totals," there is no need to
keep this column anymore. At this point you should be able to safely delete this
column.

You started with close to 29,000 rows by 25 columns. At this point, you've reduced
it to roughly 4,600 rows by 19 columns (open the file ch05-02_9297sic2naics.xls on
the CD-ROM). Actually, there are still more columns that you can eliminate. Looking at
Figure 5-3, note that you have both the SIC Code number (column 3) and its narrative
description (column 19). As long as you have a separate keyed listing that associates
the SIC Code with its narrative description, you should be able to eliminate the lengthy
text description. Before you do, you need to make sure that no information will be lost
by removing the narrative description.

The sequence of files on your CD-ROM starting with ch05-02_9297sic2naics.xls all the way through ch05-06_9297sic2naics.xls show various snapshots along the way to the final resulting spreadsheet, ch05-07_naics.xls. You should be able to perform all the steps outlined in this chapter in the original file, ch05-01_9297sic2naics.xls and get the end result. These snapshot files will help you to keep your footing and instantly jump ahead to any interim step outlined in the chapter. Also, the filenames and the files' appearance, when opened, correspond to the various screen shots and descriptions in this chapter.

	1	2	3	16	17	18	19	20	21
1	GEOTYPE	ST	SIC	EMPP	EMPPF	STTEXT	SICTEXT	SIC title	
2	C 1	C 2	C 7	N 11	C 1	C 20	C114		
3	1 U.S.								
4	2 State								
5									
4619	2	40	F5199	689		Oklahoma	Other miscellaneous nondurable		
4620	2	41	F5199	1082		Oregon	Other miscellaneous nondurable		
4621	2	42	F5199	3134		Pennsylvania	Other miscellaneous nondurable		
4622	2	44	F5199	403		Rhode Island	Other miscellaneous nondurable		
4623	2	45	F5199	1218		South Carolina	Other miscellaneous nondurable		
4624	2	46	F5199	0 b		South Dakota	Other miscellaneous nondurable		
4625	2	47	F5199	1674		Tennessee	Other miscellaneous nondurable		
4626	2	48	F5199	5986		Texas	Other miscellaneous nondurable		
4627	2	49	F5199	370		Utah	Other miscellaneous nondurable		
4628	2	50	F5199	0 c		Vermont	Other miscellaneous nondurable		
4629	2	51	F5199	2280		Virginia	Other miscellaneous nondurable		
4630	2	53	F5199	1607		Washington	Other miscellaneous nondurable		
4631	2	54	F5199	175		West Virginia	Other miscellaneous nondurable		
4632	a	55	F5199	1786		Wisconsin	Other miscellaneous nondurable		
4633	2	56	F5199	0 b		Wyoming	Other miscellaneous nondurable		
4634	1	0	I7389	523650		United States	Business services, not elsewher		
4635	1	0	I7822	19388		United States	Motion picture and video tape c		
4636									
4637									

H ◀ ▶ H \ E97SIC \ SIC2NAICS \ Sheet2 \ Sheet3 /

Figure 5–3: Both SIC and State/Region information appears redundantly.

RESOLVE AMBIGUITIES

Go to the Worksheet tab labeled SIC2NAICS (see Figure 5-4). There are 72 entries for SIC Codes relating to Wholesale Trade that are mapped to the matching NAICS code. With the exception of 5085, all of them correspond to a unique NAICS number. In this exception, the narrative description is slightly different. Perhaps the wording for the SIC Title that appears in column 19 (Figure 5-3) can provide a clue. The entries for SIC Code 5085 begin in the E97SIC worksheet on row 1982 and continue though to row 2033. Unfortunately, however, the narrative description is even more vague. All it says is Industrial Supplies. Unless you do something about this, you're going to be stuck. Either you have to treat the SIC 5085 entries as a NAICS 42183 or 42184 classification or you have to determine some split between the two classifications. Whatever decision you make, document it.

Right now, because you don't have any information to determine how numbers would be split, lump all the 5085 codes into one of the two NAICS codes. In the absence of concrete information, I suggest that you associate the SIC 5085 code with NIACS 42184 and document this somewhere.

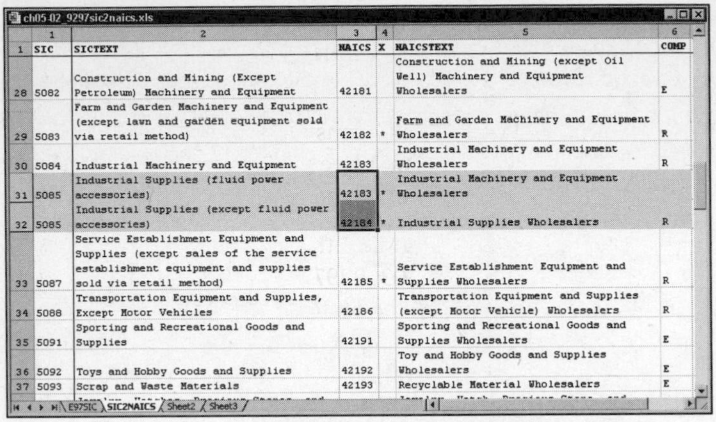

Figure 5-4: One of the SIC Codes (5085) is ambiguously mapped.

At this point, the information provided in the SIC descriptions (column 19 in Figure 5-3) is superfluous. You can go ahead and eliminate the column (you can use the Excel VLOOKUP function to retrieve the descriptions and the appropriate NAICS code).

NORMALIZE PORTIONS OF YOUR DATA

Now you're down to 18 columns. Care to go for more? Column 18 in Figure 5-3 shows the State in its narrative form. There also appears to be an equivalent numeric code in column 2. Do you really need both of these? Maybe it would make sense to retain the numeric listing in the E97SIC worksheet tab. The actual names of the states could be kept on a separate list and looked up as needed. Placing them on a separate list is easy enough to do. How would you go about constructing such a list? How would you know that the list is clean and accurate?

Here's your strategy:

1. Organize the state ID numbers and their names into a long list suitable for using VLOOKUP as a means to retrieve the data.

2. Construct a shortened chart that's valid for general lookups.

3. "Freeze-dry" the shortened lookup table. This will enable you to safely discard the long list without losing access to your data.

4. Now you can safely remove the column containing the State names in their narrative form in E97SIC.

These are the specific steps that you would do:

1. Construct a lookup table in one of the other empty worksheets. Copy columns 2 and 18 to that empty worksheet. Rename the worksheet tab (right-click the Sheet2 tab and select Rename; then type in **StateInfo**).

At the top of the two columns of data, type in some appropriate header labels, such as **StateID** and **StateName**. Sort the data, first by StateID and then by StateName.

To assure yourself that this long list is fully consistent, you can provide a validation formula for the cells in column 3 (see Figure 5-5). The validation formula is a variation of the Sentinel LookAhead formula of Chapter 3.

The value 0 in the validation formula signifies that no errors have been found. To prove this, open the file ch05-03_9297sic2naics.xls and type some erroneous entry in place of one of the State Names appearing in column 2 of the StateValidate worksheet tab. Try it. You will see the row number of the erroneous entry percolate upward. Of course, undo the error.

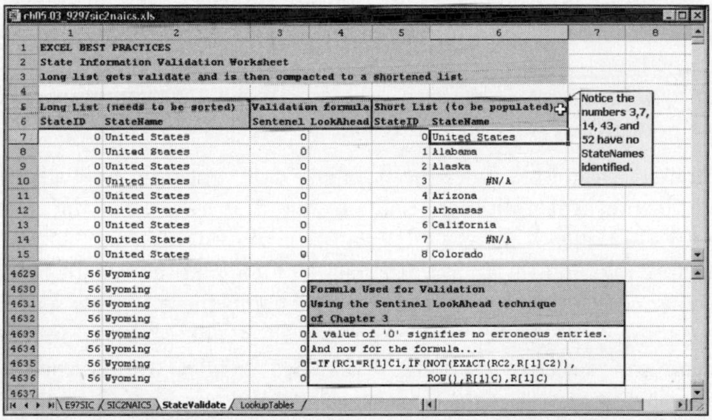

Figure 5-5: State Validation page and construction of shortened list

2. Now that you know that the long list of items in some 4,600 rows are spelled consistently, pull together a shortened list that compacts all the redundant entries. This compacting is displayed in column 6. Note that in Figure 5-5, gaps are appearing for certain StateID numbers. The formula used to pick out the values from the list is as follows:

```
=VLOOKUP(RC[-1],LongList,2,FALSE)
```

Had you not used the optional FALSE parameter in the formula, VLOOKUP would use the last-known good value in the lookup when the requested lookup value is not found. Instead of the errors being signaled where gaps occur, the last good state would appear in place of "#N/A". You would see "Alaska" on both lines 3 and 4. You would see "California" on both lines 6 and 7 and so forth.

There are numbers in the sequence between 0 and 56 that are just not used. Perhaps these were reserved numbers originally intended for use at a future date. These are historical files spanning back over a decade. Those future dates have already come and gone. So unless you have a good reason to keep the "reserved" numbers around, I'm going to blow them away. The dataset shows only information for the 50 states, plus the District of Columbia. This information comprises 51 numbers. There are also a bunch of entries for "United States." It appears to be a nationwide summary of the already existing state data.

The data for lines matching the StateID of 0 (that is, United States) don't exactly match the totals for the individual states. For all you know, the United States designation could also comprise territories, such as Puerto Rico, Guam, and the U.S. Virgin Islands. Because there's no way to discern the underlying information that contributes to the "summarized" United States, it would not seem to make sense to mix the state data with the (irreconcilable) summary data. This was much like the situation of the mixing of Totals with Merchant Wholesalers when information in the rest of the dataset pertained only to Totals.

You may want to hold on to the summary data, but right now, discard it from the spreadsheet. In doing so, you should be aware that the economic data for SIC Codes 7389 and 7822 will be removed, because there is no state data (only national information). Also, the two- and three-digit SIC Codes will be gone. You shouldn't have to worry about these for two reasons: (1) all the information will be expressed in NAICS code, and (2) you'll be able to create summaries over ranges of NAICS/SIC codes. In this regard, you will be able to construct the equivalent of this summary information (with the added ability to drill down to the State level).

3. You could copy the short list lookup table and Paste Special... Values on to a separate worksheet. Look at the worksheet called Region in the file ch05-03_9297sic2naics.xls (also see Figure 5-6). Note that I got rid of the numbers and replaced them with the two-letter abbreviation for the state. I have also added in a regional designation for each state. Later I explain why the state information is repeated in a column on the right.

4. At this point you can turn back to the E97SIC worksheet tab and do a lookup of the two-letter abbreviation given for the state name (see Figure 5-7). The formula to use is the following:

```
=VLOOKUP(RC[-1],Region!R7C1:R57C2,2,FALSE)
```

After you've retrieved the abbreviations for each of the lines, you can copy all the abbreviations (column 19 on this worksheet) and Paste Special... Values on top of itself. With the abbreviation values frozen, you can proceed to safely remove columns 18, 2, and 1.

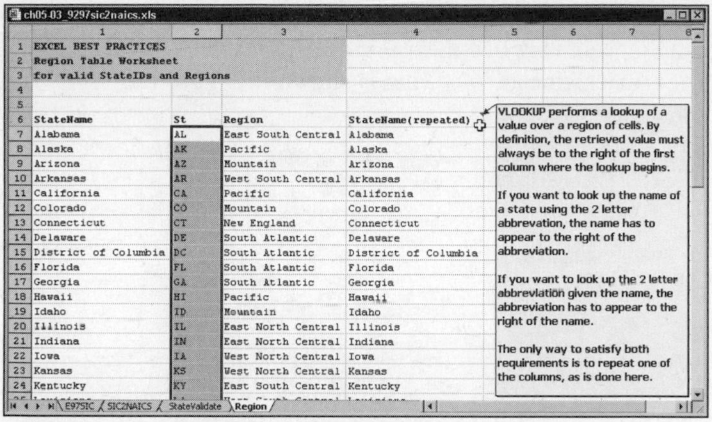

Figure 5-6: Revised State and Regional lookup information with redundant column

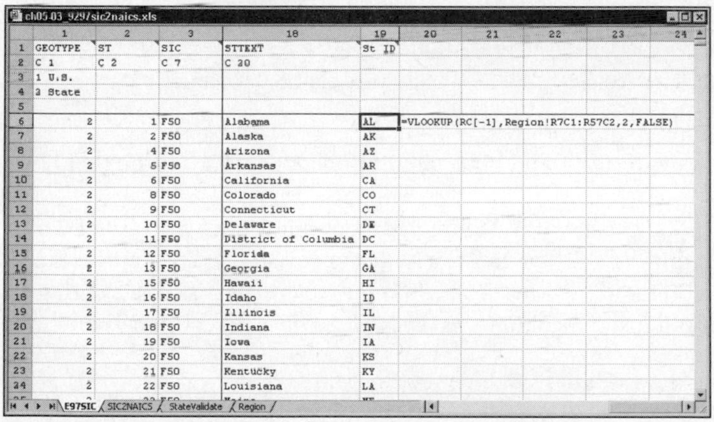

Figure 5-7: A two-letter abbreviation is found for each state.

UNIFORMLY PRESENTED DATA SHOULD NOT MIX SUMMARY INFORMATION WITH UNDERLYING DETAILS

Note that you still have a bunch of two- and three-digit SIC Code entries. These codes comprise summary information that you can prune because you will be able to reconstruct summaries later. Perform the following steps:

1. Insert a new column in column 2 for numeric SIC codes. Populate the cells in column 2 from row 6 through row 4544 with the following formula:

```
=VALUE(RIGHT(RC[-1],LEN(RC[-1])-1))
```

This formula strips away the prefix letter.

2. Sort by the numeric value of SIC (this would be column 2).

Select the rows with two- and three-digit SIC codes. At this point, your spreadsheet should be similar in appearance to Figure 5-8. The file ch05-04_9297sic2naics.xls matches what is shown in Figure 5-8.

	1	2	3	4	5	6	7	8	9	10	
1	SIC	numeric	ESTAB	ESTABF	ECVALUE	ECVALUEF	EVALUEP	EVALUEPF	PAY	PAYF	PAYP
2	C 7	SIC Code	N 11	N 11	N 11	C 1	N 11	C 1	N 11	C 1	N 11
3			1997	1992	1997		1992		1997		
4											
5											
6	F50	50	1. Strip away the prefix letter by using:						0 D		12
7	F50	50	=VALUE(RIGHT(RC[-1],LEN(RC[-1])-1))						255		1
8	F50	50							109		11
9	F50	50	2. Sort by the numeric value of SIC (this would be Column 2).						0 D		5
10	F50	50							0 D		180
11	F50	50	3. Delete the rows with 2 and 3 digit SIC codes (rows 6 through 1025).						725		16
12	F50	50			0 D				0 D		19
1019	F519	519	307	246	0 D		431905		0 D		
1020	F519	519	118	113	0 D		295477		0 D		
1021	F519	519	867	900	0 D		3977628		0 D		2
1022	F519	519	1122	985	0 D		3461074		0 D		2
1023	F519	519	175	184	0 D		396216		0 D		
1024	F519	519	1126	1212	0 D		2951868		0 D		2
1025	F519	519	84	81	0 D		0 D		0 D		
1026	F5012	5012	182	191	1952905		1286815		67884		
1027	F5012	5012	7	8	40527		29376		4234		
1028	F5012	5012	123	104	5061864		770628		53761		
1029	F5012	5012	99	102	745491		636600		38622		
1030	F5012	5012	697	703	61306513		56786390		560963		5

Figure 5–8: Steps for removing the two- and three-digit SIC summary data

3. Delete the rows with two- and three-digit SIC codes (rows 6 through 1025).

After completing the steps shown in Figure 5-8, copy the values in column 2 and Paste Special... Values onto itself. You can safely delete column 1. Your numeric SIC Code shifts over to the left and now resides in column 1. Perhaps it's time to bring in the NAICS codes. You can insert a column for the NAICS codes (in column 2) and use:

```
=VLOOKUP(RC[-1]&"",SicToNaicsTable,3,FALSE)
```

SicToNaicsTable" refers to the data appearing in Figure 5-4, and RC[-1] refers to the numeric SIC codes of column 1.

If you try to look up a numeric value against a text list (even if the text is composed of numbers), you will get an '#N/A' error. To avoid this, you can coerce the lookup value into transforming a number to a text representation. There are two ways to do this:

```
=VLOOKUP(SomeNumber&"",aListOfTextWithDigits,columnN)
```
or
```
=VLOOKUP(TEXT(SomeNumber,"###0"),
          aListOfTextWithDigits,columnN)
```

Note that you cannot use:

```
=VLOOKUP(T(SomeNumber),aListOfTextWithDigits,columnN)
```

If you look back at the original data, you will see that it tried to be everything all at one time while living in a single, two-dimensional grid. It combined national summary data with state data. It had two- and three-digit SIC data summaries with four-digit SIC economic data. It presented a number for the state as well as the state name. On every line, it had both the numeric SIC code and its narrative description. Most significantly, it tried to compare 1992 data side-by-side with 1997 data on every line.

VIOLATIONS IN ATOMIC DATA

This last piece is a big stumbling block. Who is to dictate that you want to look only at 1992 with 1997 figures? Even if you didn't have other data, you might still want to compare equivalent data of one state to another, or against a region. You might want to compare the descriptive statistics for various SIC/NAICS code combinations.

To free yourself from the 1992/1997 tethering, you have to do the following:

◆ Insert a single column for the year that applies to all items in a single row.

◆ Split the data so that all the 1992 data resides on one set of rows while the 1997 data resides on another.

These actions will double the number of rows but halve the number of columns. You can see the result in Figure 5-9. The 1997 data is kept in the top half (from rows 6 through 3524) and the matching 1992 data in the bottom half (from rows 3532 to 7050) in the file ch05-05_9297sic2naics.xls (which you can find on the CD-ROM).

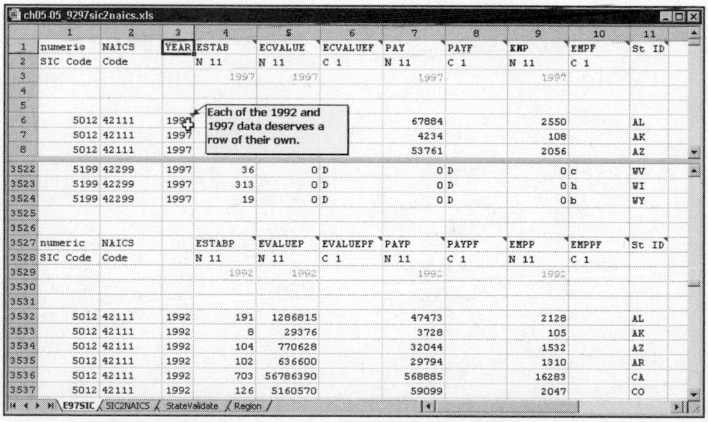

Figure 5-9: Splitting combined 1992 and 1997 data to allow for more flexible comparisons

Here are the basic steps to use to split the data and make it appear as shown in Figure 5-9:

1. Copy the data for all of rows 1 through 3524 and paste it to the cell in R3527C1.

2. In the top portion of the spreadsheet (that is, above row 3525), delete the column data pertaining to 1992 info. To do so, right-click each of the individual 1992 column data, choose Delete, and then choose "Shift cells left." Specifically, delete `R1C15:R3524C16`. Then delete `R1C11:R3524C12`. Next, delete `R1C7:R3524C8`. Finally, delete `R1C4:R3524C4`.

3. Perform the equivalent to Step 2 for the bottom half (everything below row 3524) down to the last row of data, which should be about row 7050. Instead of deleting the 1992 data, delete the 1997 data. Specifically delete `R3527C13:R7050C14`. Then delete `R3527C9:R7050C10`. Next, delete `R3527C5:R7050C6`. Finally, delete `R3527C3:R7050C3`.

4. Insert a column after column2. Label this column "YEAR." In this column, populate the empty cells with **1997** in the top portion (from row 5 all the way down to row 3524) and **1992** in the bottom portion (from row 3527 all the way down to row 7050).

As a final step, you can delete empty rows and headers that sit between the top and bottom portions of the data. You can also erase the references to 1997 that appear in the header portions along row 3.

Believe it or not, you are very close to doing useful analysis with the data. However, just a bit more cleanup is needed.

FLAG ENCODING ANOMALIES

You may have noticed that the file E97SIC.txt contains letter designations for the number of employees. In a certain number of cases, an exact count of employee size is not available, but an estimated range can be provided. Following is the keyed listing of this employee count substitution:

Letter	Range
a	0 to 19 employees
b	20 to 99 employees
c	100 to 249 employees
e	250 to 499 employees
f	500 to 999 employees
g	1,000 to 2,499 employees
h	2,500 to 4,999 employees
i	5,000 to 9,999 employees
j	10,000 to 24,999 employees
k	25,000 to 49,999 employees
l	50,000 to 99,999 employees
m	100,000 employees or more

There's just one thing that's a bit peculiar. What happened to the letter *d*? Because all the data is being "scrubbed," you might as well adjust the flag so that you don't have a missing letter in the range. You do this by shifting the letters *e* through *m* by one letter earlier in the alphabet.

To accomplish this, you can perform a letter substitution using the Excel functions CODE and CHAR, introduced in Chapter 3. CODE, as you may recall, returns the decimal designation representing the given letter. CODE("A") returns 97, CODE("B") returns 98, and so forth. The strategy is to find any of the letters "e through m" and generate new characters one letter earlier in the alphabet using CHAR. The basic formula for this is as follows:

```
=IF(CODE(EmplFlag)>100,CHAR(CODE(EmplFlag)-1),EmplFlag)
```

EmplFlag happens to be the reference to the cell containing the flag for the number of employees. This formula is applicable to roughly 1,800 of the 7,000 rows of data. The remaining 5,200 rows have no flag because the number of employees is known and recorded. The formula needs to take into account whether the flag is empty. Here's a revised version of the formula.

```
=IF(EmplFlag="","",IF(CODE(EmplFlag)>100,CHAR(CODE(EmplFlag)-1),EmplFlag))
```

Before you go ahead and make substitutions, there are two more anomalies to attend to. Some of the time, the EmplFlag letter appears in uppercase (as an *A* instead of an *a*). All the other letters in this column are in lowercase form.

CODE("A") returns 65 and will not work in this formula. You can either:

◆ Perform a search and replace of *A* to *a*, limiting your search to values in this column (Excel gives you options to do this).

◆ Make your substitution formula slightly more complex. If you opt for the more complex formula, here is what it will look like:

```
=IF(EmplFlag="","",
        IF(CODE(LOWER(EmplFlag))>100,
          CHAR(CODE(LOWER(EmplFlag))-1),
          LOWER(EmplFlag)))
```

This formula appears in the file takeaway.txt on the CD-ROM, which you can copy and paste into the Excel Formula Bar.

The second of the two remaining anomalies is that on two of the roughly 7,000 rows, there appears to be a letter *r*. The employee count is non-zero. The *r* indicates a revised estimate on the 1992 figures. This *r* anomaly occurs for just two pieces of data (see Table 5-1).

TABLE 5-1 DATA FOR ANOMALOUS EMPLOYEE FLAGS

SIC Code	NAICS Code	YEAR	ESTAB	ECVALUE	Flag	PAY	Flag	EMP	flag	St ID
5063	42161	1992	809	4183137	R	284515	R	9228	r	PA
5065	42169	1992	555	2409052	R	210722	R	6036	r	PA

For your purposes, just clear the *r* flags appearing in these two rows.

Open the file ch05-06_sic2naics.xls, which is on the CD-ROM (see Figure 5-10). You will see that a column has been inserted just after the EmplFlag column, and the substitution formula has been placed.

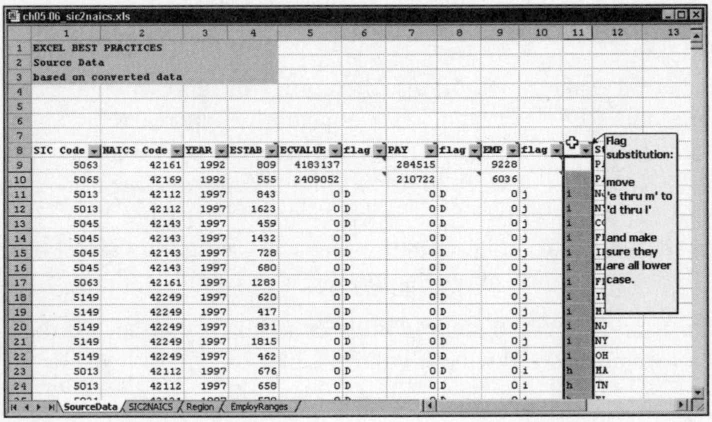

Figure 5-10: Flag substitution

After you confirm that you have the correct flag entries in the revised column, copy the column (column 11) and Paste Special... Values onto itself, so that the values are frozen. Then you can safely eliminate the original and anomalous flag entries (column 10).

Climbing Past the Foothills

Much of the focus and drudgery in this chapter has related to getting the data as clean as possible. Without this, it would not be feasible to probe deeply into the data and provide meaningful summaries. There is a fair amount of data. It would be nice to ask questions such as "How many business establishments were involved with automobile supplies during 1992 by state?" To be able to answer a question of this kind, you need a lookup or search facility.

Search enable your source data

Open the file ch05-07_naics.xls, which is on the CD-ROM, and go to the SourceData worksheet tab (see Figure 5-11).

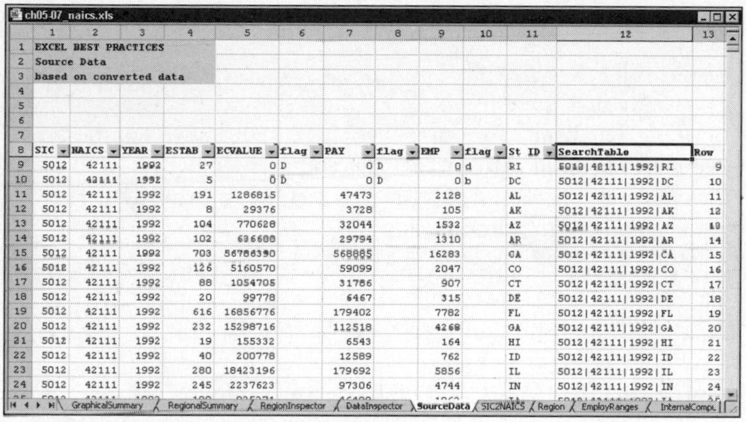
ch05-07_naics.xls

	1	2	3	4	5	6	7	8	9	10	11	12	13
1	EXCEL BEST PRACTICES												
2	Source Data												
3	based on converted data												
4													
5													
6													
7													
8	SIC	NAICS	YEAR	ESTAB	ECVALUE	flag	PAY	flag	EMP	flag	St ID	SearchTable	Row
9	5012	42111	1992	27	0	D	0	D	0	d	RI	5012|42111|1992|RI	9
10	5012	42111	1992	5	0	D	0	D	0	b	DC	5012|42111|1992|DC	10
11	5012	42111	1992	191	1286815		47473		2128		AL	5012|42111|1992|AL	11
12	5012	42111	1992	8	29376		3728		105		AK	5012|42111|1992|AK	12
13	5012	42111	1992	104	770628		32044		1532		AZ	5012|42111|1992|AZ	13
14	5012	42111	1992	102	636600		29794		1310		AR	5012|42111|1992|AR	14
15	5012	42111	1992	703	56786390		568885		16283		CA	5012|42111|1992|CA	15
16	5012	42111	1992	126	5160570		59099		2047		CO	5012|42111|1992|CO	16
17	5012	42111	1992	88	1054705		31786		907		CT	5012|42111|1992|CT	17
18	5012	42111	1992	20	99778		6467		315		DE	5012|42111|1992|DE	18
19	5012	42111	1992	616	16856776		179402		7782		FL	5012|42111|1992|FL	19
20	5012	42111	1992	232	15298716		112518		4268		GA	5012|42111|1992|GA	20
21	5012	42111	1992	19	155332		6543		164		HI	5012|42111|1992|HI	21
22	5012	42111	1992	40	200778		12589		762		ID	5012|42111|1992|ID	22
23	5012	42111	1992	280	18423196		179692		5856		IL	5012|42111|1992|IL	23
24	5012	42111	1992	245	2237623		97306		4744		IN	5012|42111|1992|IN	24

Figure 5-11: Cleaned data plus a SearchTable

The data, including the last two columns, spans 7,038 rows by 13 columns. This is still sizeable but is definitely more manageable than 28,910 rows by 25 columns. Size reduction was one thing. The real improvements came from removing the mixed summary/detailed information and making all pieces of data comparable to one another (each year's data has its own row).

Now that every row of data is on equal footing, it becomes possible to locate any specific data on search criteria and analyze any combination of data.

The key to locating specific data lies in the `SearchTable` column. Every line of data is associated with an SIC/NAICS Code, year, and location. That's what this `SearchTable` constructs. Once you find it, you need only to know what row the data resides in. This is why the `SearchTable` is flanked on the immediate right by row numbers.

The Data Inspector

It's nice to just retrieve values, but what about doing some interpretive analysis? You might, for instance, want to spot some trends such as the Compound Annual Growth Rate in sales or number of establishments over time. The Data Inspector allows you to do this for any NAICS Code and State combination (see Figure 5-12).

Several things are happening in the Data Inspector:

◆ The top Spinner Control button allows you to pick which item from the list of NAICS Codes is retrieved. Pressing the Spinner Control button will increment the item number in the list of NAICS Code. Using OFFSET, you can pluck out the code number, its narrative description, and the respective SIC Code information. You can use essentially the same formula to retrieve these different kinds of information. Just vary the offset column (shown in boldface) in the generic formula

```
=OFFSET(NAICS,DataInspectorNAIC.idx-1,some_column_offset,1,1)
```

◆ The State information is retrieved using the same kind of mechanism you used to get the NAICS related data.

◆ Now that you have the SIC/NAICS, year, and state, you can search the SourceData worksheet to find the specific row containing the data. The formula fragment for finding the row is

```
VLOOKUP(R7C3&"|"&R6C3&"|"&RC1&"|"&R11C4,SearchTable,2,FALSE)
```

or, more descriptively,

```
VLOOKUP(SIC|NAICS|YEAR|STATE,SearchTable,2,FALSE)
```

After you have identified the row, you can use OFFSET to pick the specific item from the SourceData worksheet. This is how the values for the number of Establishments, Sales, Payroll, and Employment figures are retrieved.

◆ Wherever you have the value of an item for two different time periods, you can use the Compound Annual Growth Rate (CAGR) to show how the item has progressively increased or decreased. The formula for computing the CAGR is shown in Figure 5-12. Also shown are the calculated values of CAGR for Establishments, Sales, Payroll, and Employment.

USE SMART FORMATTING TO HIGHLIGHT EXCEPTIONS
A lot of time in the first part of the chapter was spent on dealing with incomplete data. There were roughly 1800 rows with spotty data in the example. It wouldn't make sense to try to compute the CAGR for a particular set of data if one of the pieces had a zero value and were flagged with a letter. If you increment the NAICS Code, you will quickly see that this happens (see Figure 5-13)

Notice that the flag letters suddenly "light up." A formatted table showing the range of employees appears in columns 9 and 10. Because you have zero values for Sales, Payroll, and Empl, you can no longer compute the respective CAGR values. So they disappear.

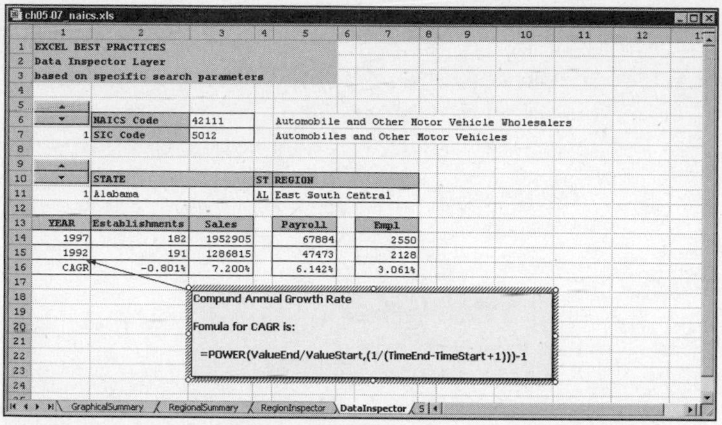

Figure 5-12: View data at two different points in time to determine its Compound Annual Growth Rate (CAGR).

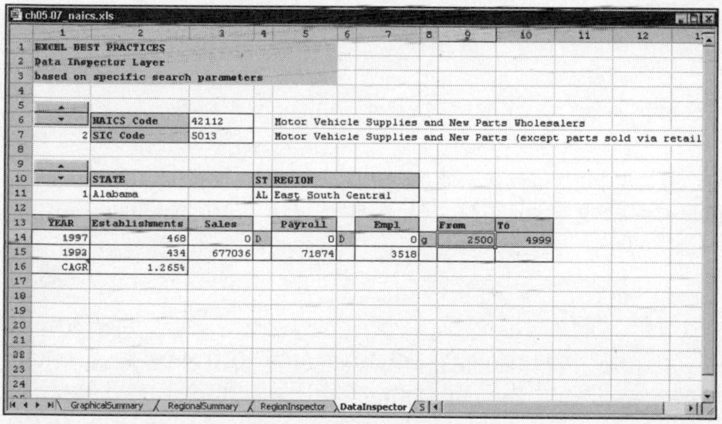

Figure 5-13: Conditional Formatting adjusts the appearance of the Data Inspector.

Figure 5-14 shows how the Conditional Formatting works for one of these cells that light up. You may recall that you can select Conditional Formatting from the Excel Format menu. Instead of selecting Cell Value Is from the drop-down list, select Formula Is. In the Edit Line for each of the conditions, type in a formula (starting with =) that will result in TRUE/FALSE values. Click the Format button to specify the format in which you want the cell to appear when the formula returns a TRUE value. You can adjust the font, borders, and background pattern. If you need to know more about conditional formatting, you'll find plenty of information in Chapter 7, "Creating and Using Smart Data."

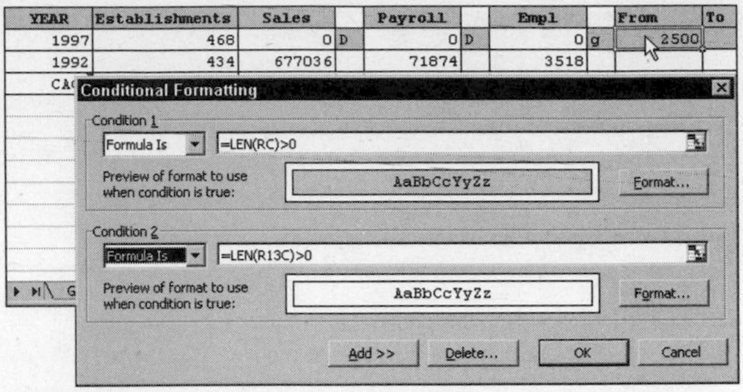

Figure 5–14: Use Conditional Formatting to highlight cells
needing attention.

In these cells that "light up," changing appearance is only one part of the story. Conditional Formatting does not control the values in the cells. You will need a formula that springs to life when an exceptional situation occurs but that otherwise keeps the cell contents empty. The From cell highlighted by the mouse in Figure 5-13 has the following formula:

```
=IF(RC[-1]<>"",VLOOKUP(RC8,EmplFlagTable,2),"")
```

When a flag is signaled, it performs a lookup and retrieves a value. This, in turn, trips the Conditional Formatting to alter the cell pattern and borders. This tag team approach can be very effective.

The Region Inspector

The Data Inspector is good for looking at data for a specific NAICS Code and individual state. There is no provision for combining the data of multiple states. If you're going to aggregate data, it would seem logical to do so by region of the country. After all, each state is already identified with a region.

The Region Inspector (see Figure 5-15) sweeps across the states in any region, performs the calculations handled by the Data Inspector, and then does more. Note the Spinner Control button at the top of column 9. This button controls the type of group calculation done for the region. Right now, it is set to provide the arithmetic sum for the region. At a click, you can change the summary function to yield the minimum, maximum, average, standard deviation, and other kinds of measures. The Excel SUBTOTAL function allows you to do this. Because you have the information by region for both 1992 and 1997, you can perform all the CAGR computations by State and by Region. Scroll down on this worksheet to view the CAGR calculations.

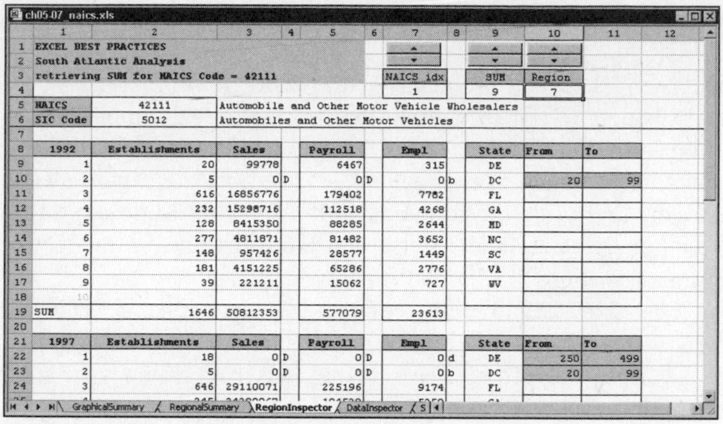

ch05-07_naics.xls

EXCEL BEST PRACTICES
South Atlantic Analysis
retrieving SUM for NAICS Code = 42111

NAICS idx	SUM	Region
1	9	7

NAICS	42111	Automobile and Other Motor Vehicle Wholesalers
SIC Code	5012	Automobiles and Other Motor Vehicles

1992	Establishments	Sales		Payroll		Empl		State	From	To
1	20	99778		6467		315		DE		
2	5	0	D	0	D	0	b	DC	20	99
3	616	16856776		179402		7782		FL		
4	232	15298716		112518		4268		GA		
5	128	8415350		88285		2644		MD		
6	277	4811871		81482		3652		NC		
7	148	957426		28577		1449		SC		
8	181	4151225		65286		2776		VA		
9	39	221211		15062		727		WV		
10										
SUM	1646	50812353		577079		23613				

1997	Establishments	Sales		Payroll		Empl		State	From	To
1	18	0	D	0	D	0	d	DE	250	499
2	5	0	D	0	D	0	b	DC	20	99
3	646	29110071		225196		9174		FL		

GraphicalSummary / RegionalSummary / RegionInspector / DataInspector / S

Figure 5-15: Region Inspector gathers data for each region and computes various types of summary information for each region.

The Regional Summary

As you start to use this spreadsheet, you can begin to see what a difference organized and structured data can make. The separation of the SourceData from the various analysis layers allows you to make your spreadsheet much more scalable.

You have seen that the Region Inspector gathers the needed state information in the space of a dozen or so spreadsheet rows. If you could gather the information for one region, why couldn't you gather the information for all nine regions at one time? Indeed, this is what the RegionalSummary worksheet does (see Figure 5-16). Basically, it replicates the formulas of the Region Inspector in nine separate locations, one for each region. The RegionalSummary worksheet was actually created by duplicating the RegionalInspector Worksheet and retrofitting it, principally replicating the formulas.

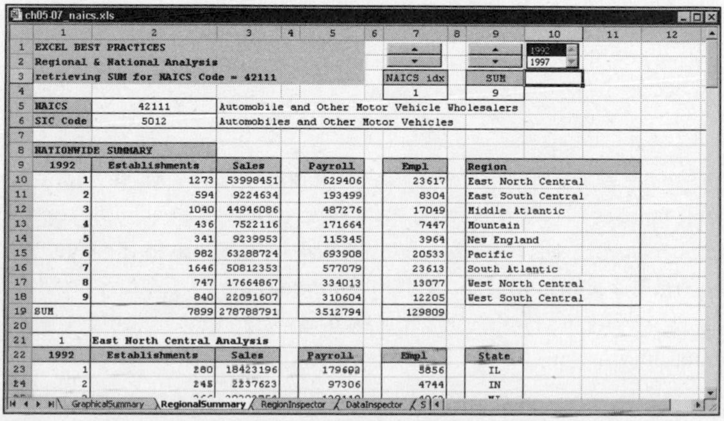

ch05-07_naics.xls

EXCEL BEST PRACTICES
Regional & National Analysis
retrieving SUM for NAICS Code = 42111

NAICS idx	SUM	1992 / 1997
1	9	

NAICS	42111	Automobile and Other Motor Vehicle Wholesalers
SIC Code	5012	Automobiles and Other Motor Vehicles

NATIONWIDE SUMMARY

1992	Establishments	Sales	Payroll	Empl	Region
1	1273	53998451	629406	23617	East North Central
2	594	9224634	193499	8304	East South Central
3	1040	44946086	487276	17049	Middle Atlantic
4	436	7522116	171664	7447	Mountain
5	341	9239953	115345	3964	New England
6	982	63288724	693908	20533	Pacific
7	1646	50812353	577079	23613	South Atlantic
8	747	17664867	334013	13077	West North Central
9	840	22091607	310604	12205	West South Central
SUM	7899	278788791	3512794	129809	

1 East North Central Analysis

1992	Establishments	Sales	Payroll	Empl	State
1	280	18423196	179602	5856	IL
2	245	2237623	97306	4744	IN

GraphicalSummary / RegionalSummary / RegionInspector / DataInspector / S

Figure 5-16: Nationwide Summary Analysis and detailed schedules for each of the nine regions

SPECIAL ISSUES (AND THEIR RESOLUTION) IN REPLICATING FORMULAS

Replicating the formulas poses special problems. With the Regional Inspector you saw two groups of state data, both retrieving data for a common region but for different years. The formulas need to be adjusted for the RegionalSummary worksheet so that the year is common and each of the regions is varied. At the same time, it would be nice to just copy and paste the formulas without having to do anything special. This way, if you decide at a later date to add more regions, you can just casually copy and paste a few more lines.

Unfortunately, the way that formulas are entered to construct the Regional Inspector (or any spreadsheet, for that matter) is not well suited to easy replication. The formulas in the Regional Inspector reference the cells containing year and region number using absolute cell reference locations. This method makes it easy to replicate the same formula for each of the states within a single region. If you duplicate the formulas to another region in the worksheet, however, the absolute references still remain unchanged. The new duplicated formulas are still tethered to the old region and year.

There's a way to get around this problem. Insert two columns on the left. One of these is for region number and the other is for the year. Populate every line in these two columns with the respective region number and year. Adjust the formulas that perform the lookup to use the region number and year found on columns 1 and 2, but for the same row. Now your formulas for each state, in each region, are literally identical. You can freely replicate the 13 or so lines to the space immediately below it for another region. After the eighth replication, you'll have nine regions. Just make sure that you're incrementing the region number along column 1 so that each of the 13 rows picks data for a different region.

The next step is to hide the unsightly appearing columns, repetitively containing the region number and year, row after row. You need to move the data out of this worksheet and onto another worksheet (InternalComputations). Select all of columns 1 and 2, cut the selection (Ctrl+X), click in an empty area of the InternalComputations worksheet, and paste the data there (Ctrl+V). Now go back to the RegionalSummary worksheet (or whatever name you gave to the duplicated Regional Inspector worksheet) and delete the empty columns 1 and 2.

When you glance at the InternalComputations worksheet, you will see right away that it is not at all well structured. In fact, there's a disclaimer at the top of the worksheet that tells you so. I left it this way on purpose to show you how a behind-the-scenes worksheet should *not* be done. All too often, I've seen colleagues prepare fancy spreadsheets and sweep under the rug the messy details that are quickly and easily forgotten.

SETTING UP A LIST BOX

You may have noticed that there's a list box at the top of the RegionalSummary worksheet. Here's how it works.

Make sure that you have your Forms toolbar available. If you don't, select Customize from the Excel Tools menu and check the box called Forms. Move your mouse cursor to the icon called List Box and click it. Your mouse will change into a crosshair. Click and drag on your worksheet, carving out the shape of your list box. Right-click in the empty list box and select Format Control. A window should pop up that looks similar to that shown in Figure 5-17. In the Input range, you need to provide the cell coordinates containing the items that are to appear in your list. The values 1992 and 1997 have been placed in rows 15 and 16 on column 2 of the InternalComputations worksheet. The "Cell link" location identifies where to put the item number of the selected value in your list. Right now, there are only two values, 1992 and 1997. The "Cell link" will place into R14C2 the value 1 or 2, depending on whether you select 1992 or 1997.

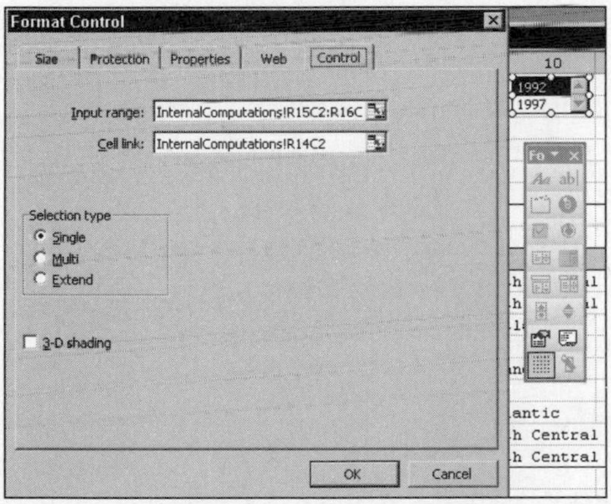

Figure 5-17: Adjusting the Form's List Box control

After you've determined which of the items in the last has been selected, you can pick the value from the list that is to be used as input by using OFFSET:

```
=OFFSET(InternalComputations!R14C2,InternalComputations!R14C2,0)
```

Sometimes a picture is worth a thousand formulas

At this point, there is no reason that you can't pick the numerical information off the Regional Summary and present it visually (see Figure 5-18).

A nice feature of this worksheet is that the chart appears to be interactive and you can instantaneously change which set of data appears in the chart. This is done simply by clicking the Spinner Control button on the left side of the worksheet.

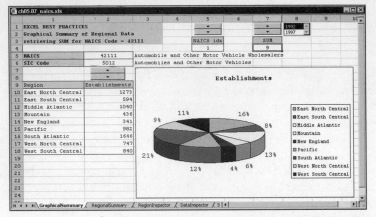

Figure 5-18: Pick and choose which type of information is to be rendered visually.

It will be convenient at times to have the ability to do a context switch in your chart. Excel charts don't automatically allow you to do this context switch. Instead, you have to go into the Chart Settings and manually alter the range of data you're going to chart. This is cumbersome and detracts significantly from the chart's interactiveness.

You can bypass this difficulty. Construct your chart to look at data residing in a placeholder location. Then accomplish a context switch using OFFSET, CHOOSE, or some other appropriate function that pulls the data into the placeholder.

AUTOMATIC DRILL-DOWN

One last point is worth mentioning. As you adjust the Year and NAICS Code in the GraphicalSummary worksheet, the associated detailed information automatically appears in the RegionalSummary worksheet. This gives you an instant "drill-down" ability on a state-by-state basis, nationwide.

Closing Thoughts

In case you're wondering, the data in this chapter, including the problems and pitfalls, are all real. No portion has been modified to create artificial problems. There are enough problems in real-world data that I don't have to go about inventing artificial ones to illustrate a point. An item high on my agenda is to convey to you a realistic sense of:

◆ The sequence of steps you would be going through to acquire, clean up, and make data usable for analysis.

◆ How you can reduce the size of the undertaking and make the data project more manageable.

◆ How to identify the hot spots or potential trouble areas. Often these are found where different parts of a system are joined together. My hope is that you'll start developing a sense of how to confront the difficult decisions, resolve them, document them, and move on.

◆ How to apply a divide-and-conquer strategy that fits directly with the layered pattern approach outlined in Chapter 2, "Mastering Spreadsheet Construction Techniques."

You'll notice that there was no sweeping under the rug any of the difficulties found in the data. You'll also notice that I didn't let go of a problem until I had it resolved and showed you how I resolved it. Data slogging requires that you be tenacious. It is important to pay attention to details. A simple thing such as over-looking the capitalization of the letter *a* can compromise your conversion formulas.

This chapter, "Scaling the Peaks of Mt. Data," was appropriately named. In the first part of the chapter you were approaching the foothills with machete in hand, cutting a trail through dense and seemingly endless foliage. After you got past the foothills, you could proceed to abstract the data into increasingly useful summaries and analyses. This culminated at the peak, where you could graphically display the breakout of any type of data (number of establishments, sales, payroll, or employment numbers), for any NAICS or SIC Code, during any time period (1992 vs. 1997), for all nine regions — coupled with the ability to drill down to the numbers for each state throughout these regions.

It may interest you to know that the U.S. Census Bureau is actively at work on another classification framework called the North American Product Classification System (NAPCS). Don't worry; NAICS hasn't been replaced by this new system (at least, it hasn't as of the time of this publication).

The next chapter, "Let the Data Speak for Itself: Viewing and Presenting Data," takes up the cause of finding additional ways to make your data meaningful and known.

Chapter 6

Let the Data Speak for Itself: Viewing and Presenting Data

IN THIS CHAPTER

- ◆ Automatic organizing and formatting of third-party data that's regularly refreshed
- ◆ Understanding filters, including new features in Excel 2003 such as sorting
- ◆ Replicating content with filtered data
- ◆ Using advanced filters
- ◆ Creating Presentation Tear Sheets
- ◆ Getting the most of Excel's Spreadsheet Comments facility
- ◆ Bullet-proofing your data entry

THE PREVIOUS CHAPTER BROUGHT you through the ins and outs of preparing data and casting it into a useful form for analysis. This chapter focuses on taking data that's been cleaned up and is ready to be cast into reports of various kinds.

You start by using validated data. Although clean, this data may not be how you want it for your regularly published reports. For one thing, you might be dumped with too much information. You may only need a few columns of data. You might have to perform some extra lookup work and reorganize the data. Finally, you'll be able to put on some finishing touches, and voilá! You'll have a polished report.

To add more luster and sheen to your reports, you can give people some "drill-down" capability with AutoFilters. To prepare reports for widespread dissemination, you'll want to make use of Presentation Tear Sheets.

For those of you who are power users, you're going to see some cool things and useful things to do with Advanced Filters.

Finally, to help communicate information in your spreadsheets, you'll discover the ins and outs of the Excel Comments feature. As part of your reward for enduring with the chapter, you will have a useful catalog of colorful swatches and formatted Comment samples that you can just copy and paste.

They Threw In the Kitchen Sink

Have you ever had the situation in which you requested information and got more than you asked for? This is a relatively commonplace occurrence. Sometimes it's just easier to receive everything and pick out what you need. It also avoids having to go back and ask for more data.

When you need data, you can ask the people who regularly send you the data dumps to give you polished reports. I'm sure they'll be happy to comply and happier still to ask you for your cost center code. Being the cost-conscious person that you are, you'll undertake to rework the data yourself. Besides, you understand your business needs far better than the people who just operate the database servers housing the corporate data.

In the real world, there's another wrinkle: time. If you're like most business people who manage some operation, it is quite likely that you will need to send out regular status reports or some other information relating to your department and its activities. The chances are you're a busy person and have more pressing matters to attend to than sending out the same report week after week, one whose contents you already know and that few people will read. If you plan to prepare the report yourself or assign it to your assistant, it's in your interest to do as good a job as you can with the minimum amount of effort.

This effort can be made easier with the ch06-01DatasetPackagingTool.xls file on the CD-ROM with this book.

Start by looking at your data

Your data may contain everything, including the kitchen sink. At the same time it may not have enough of what you need. To help make things concrete, I picked a small piece of data from the previous chapter. Feel free to use your own.

The first 11 columns in Figure 6-1 present data as you might receive it from some third-party source.

Although the data has the essentials, it is missing some things. Your finished report will be easier to read if the state name is fully spelled instead of appearing as a two-letter designation. You may want to provide additional information not contained in the data dump, such as the country region. For this reason it is best to perform a table lookup alongside your source data (columns 12 and 13in Figure 6-1). You can use a formula like the following to retrieve the Region data:

```
=VLOOKUP(RC11,LookupTable01,2,FALSE)
```

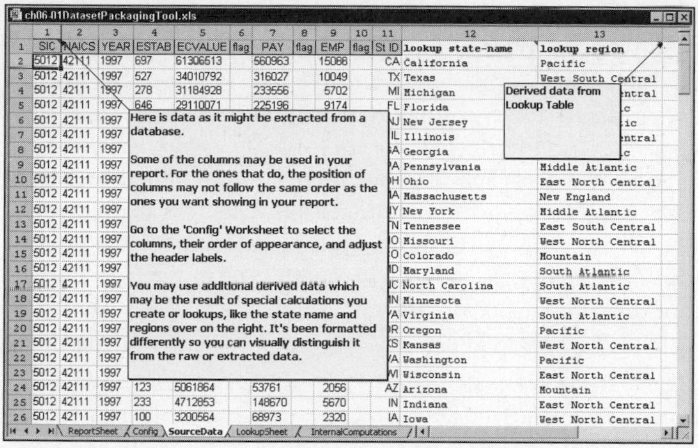

Figure 6-1: The Data Dump with additional derived data supplied by you

The lookup table can be found in the LookupSheet worksheet tab of ch06-01DatasetPackagingTool.xls (see Figure 6-2).

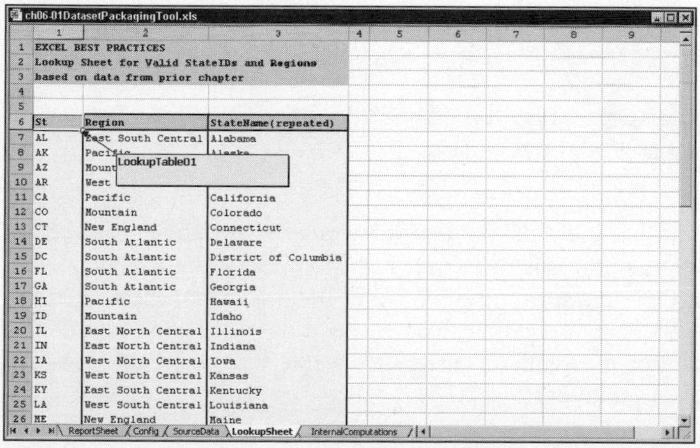

Figure 6-2: Lookup information used to supplement source data

Edit how you want your data to appear

Switch to your Config worksheet tab (see Figure 6-3). On the bottom right, you will see a map that shows you the headers appearing across the top of the Sheet called SourceData. This mapping lists the various items that are available, showing the column header that would appear at the top of a report. If you don't like the way something appears in the Old Item column, type your change in the column to the right (New Item Name). For instance, you may want "YEAR" to appear as "Year." When the data for year appears in a finished report, it will have the column header "Year."

Next, identify which items you want appearing in your report and their preferred order of appearance. You specify this in the Column Order Selection of the worksheet. Inside the column labeled Original Position, type in the number that corresponds to the Old Item # of the mapping section. When you type in the number, the description will appear in the column called "Order of Appearance." For instance, if you type 3 into the Original Position column, you will see "Year" appearing to its immediate right.

	ch06-01DatasetPackagingTool.xls	

EXCEL BEST PRACTICES
Report Configuration Settings
with source data at: 'SourceData'!R1C1

○ A1 Style Coordinates

● R1C1 Style Coordinates

FileName:
Sheet: *SourceData*
Cell or Name: *R1C1*
Complete Name: 'SourceData'!R1C1

Column Order Selection

Original Position	Order of Appearance	Old Item #	Old Item	New Item Name
13	Region	1	SIC	
12	State	2	NAICS	
3	Year	3	YEAR	*Year*
2	NAICS	4	ESTAB	*No. of Establishments*
5	Sales	5	ECVALUE	*Sales*
4	No. of Establishments	6	flag	
7	Annual Payroll	7	PAY	*Annual Payroll*
		8	flag	
	Choose Data Order	9	EMP	*No. of Employees*
	Please type in the 'Old Item #' you wish to	10	flag	
	appear in the	11	St ID	
	'ReportSheet'.	12	lookup state-name	*State*
		13	lookup region	*Region*
		14		

Mapping for top row of 'SourceData'!R1C1

ReportSheet \ **Config** \ SourceData \ LookupSheet \ InternalComputations /

Figure 6–3: Customize the appearance of your report.

Your original data can reside on the SourceData worksheet or any worksheet of any spreadsheet file. Whatever the case is, you need to specify the FileName and Sheet. If the data is located on a separate spreadsheet file, the spreadsheet needs to be open so that its contents are accessible. You can use the cell coordinate or the top-left corner of your data, or a valid user-defined name that points the top-left corner of your data.

If you type in the cell coordinate for the "Cell or Name" entry in the Config worksheet, you have the option of entering the cell coordinate using the A1 Style notation (such as $A1$ or $\$A\$1$), or the R1C1 Style notation. Remember to also select the corresponding radio button on this worksheet (see Figure 6-3).

Bullet-proof your data entry

You will notice that whenever you attempt to type something into the input area of your Column Order Selection, you are prompted with some instructions. This is something you can control using the data validation feature of Excel. Here is how you use it:

First, select the group of cells into which you expect people to enter data. Then select Validation from the Excel Data menu. You will then enter your validation preferences (see the figure that follows) using the three tabs (Settings, Input Message, and Error Alert).

In the Settings tab, you get to specify the type of data you will allow. Depending on which option you select, different validation criteria will be used. As you can see in the next figure in this sidebar, you get to choose among a variety of equality and comparison operations. In the example shown, I've fixed the limits between 1 and 20. Rather than using a hard-wired number like 20, I could have pointed the maximum value to an Excel formula that's computed in the spreadsheet. This approach might be useful if you have an input whose limits could vary. For example, you might have a balance in your checking account of $500. You may want the input for your cell (the amount of a check you can write) to never exceed your balance. Today, it's $500. Tomorrow, it may be $1,500.

You have the ability to prompt the person with some informative message when the input cell is selected (see the following figure).

Continued

Bullet-proof your data entry (Continued)

Data Validation

Settings | [Input Message] | Error Alert

☑ Show input message when cell is selected

When cell is selected, show this input message:

Title:
Choose Data Order

Input message:
Please type in the 'Old Item #' you wish to appear in the 'ReportSheet'.

Clear All   OK   Cancel

Note that in Excel 2003, your Input Message Title is limited to a size of 32 characters.

You also have the ability to customize your response (see the following figure) when an exception to the input entry occurs. As with the Input Message, your Error Alert Title is limited to 32 characters.

Data Validation

Settings | Input Message | Error Alert

☑ Show error alert after invalid data is entered

When user enters invalid data, show this error alert:

Style: Title:
Warning   Please correct your input

⚠   Error message:
                Your input must be between 1 and 20 or otherwise be empty.

Clear All   OK   Cancel

Note that users entering numbers can bypass the alert by pressing the Yes button (see the final figure in this sidebar). You need to be aware of this.

15	2	N
16	5	S
17	4	N
18	7	A
19		
20		
21	bad input	

Please correct your input

⚠ Your input must be between 1 and 20 or otherwise be empty.

Continue?

Yes   No   Cancel

Choose Data Order
Please type in the 'Old Item # you wish to appear in the 'ReportSheet'.

22		11	St ID
23		12	lookup state-name
24		13	lookup region
25		14	

...rceData / LookupSheet / InternalComputations /

I suppose that Microsoft could have chosen to prohibit the bypassing of input constraints. In all likelihood, it is better to give users the option to bypass controls. The prompt "Continue?" doesn't make what's happening all that obvious.

The ReportSheet

The data you specified in Figure 6-3 is now rendered properly in the ReportSheet (see Figure 6-4). The sequence of columns matches your specifications. The column headers use the spelling of the New Item Names listed in Figure 6-3. Note that the Sales and Annual Payroll are formatted to display commas. (The number of establishments does so as well. You're not seeing it because the values displayed haven't numbered into the thousands yet.). This formatting is all done in the ReportSheet. As a presentation layer, the ReportSheet is the appropriate place to do your formatting. Other attributes for you to you adjust here include things such as the font style (boldface for headers, for example) and the use of word wrap.

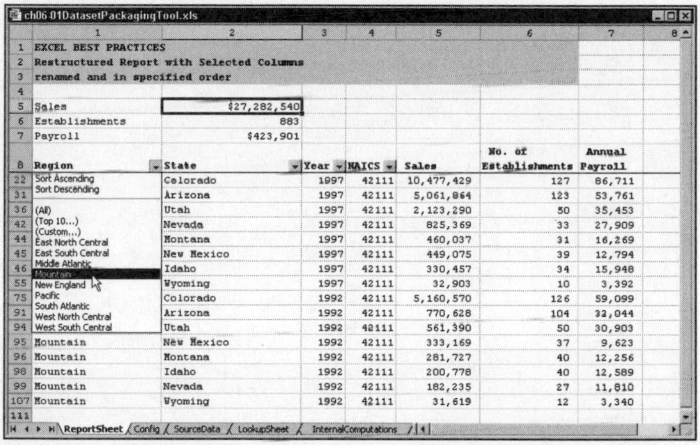

Figure 6–4: ReportSheet uses Excel filters and the SUBTOTAL function.

ADDING MORE COLUMNS OF DATA

As shown, only 7 columns of data are in the report (you can have as many as 20). If you need more columns, perform the following steps:

1. Type in the appropriate column number(s) to your list of columns in the Config Worksheet.

2. Open the ReportSheet and replicate the formulas across so that the appropriate data will be retrieved.

   (As an example, you might copy all of column 7 and paste it into column 8.)

If you do Step 2 before Step 1, you will see a warning message near the top of the unaccounted columns and #REF! errors running down the columns. This is because it is missing the data it needs. You don't have to undo this if you go back and perform Step 1.

EXTENDING THE REPORT SHEET WITH MORE ROWS

To keep the file size of ch06-01DatasetPackagingTool.xls small, the formulas for the Report Sheet go down only as far as row 110. The data you use will likely occupy more than the hundred or so rows. In this case, simply replicate the formulas down as many rows as you need.

INSERTING COLUMNS IN YOUR REPORT SHEET

You may want to insert an empty column in your report so that you can type in your own comments and formulas. Follow these steps:

1. In the list of columns in your Config worksheet, leave one of the cells in your preferred sequence empty (see Figure 6-5).

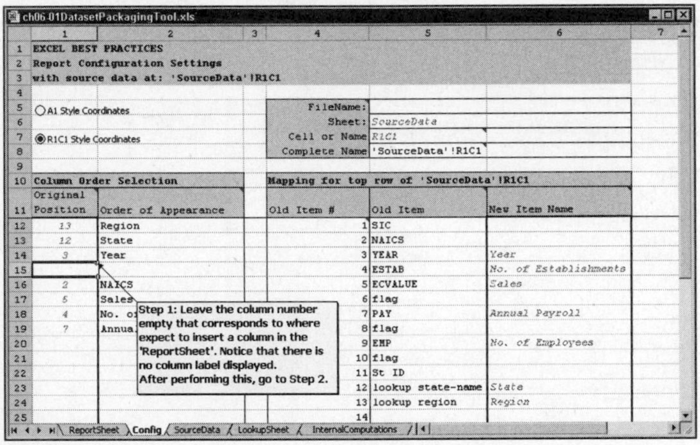

Figure 6-5: Step 1 – Leave your entry blank where you expect to insert a column.

2. When you go to your ReportSheet, you will see a column with a lot of #REF! labels. Just insert a new column where the #REF! labels appear (see Figure 6-6).

3. The labels should go away, and you can type your formulas and comments in this column (see Figure 6-7).

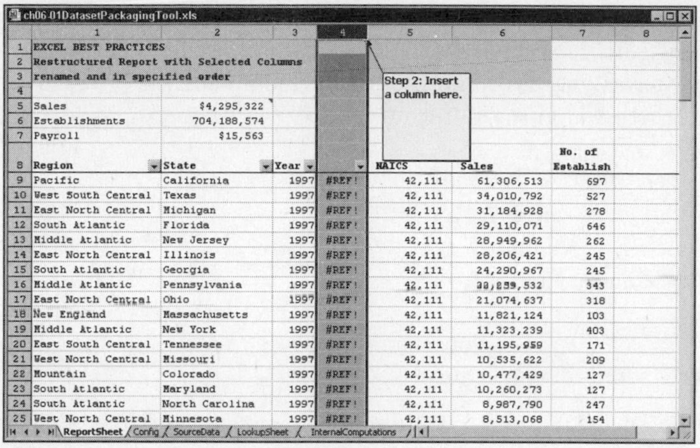

Figure 6-6: Step 2 – Insert a new column.

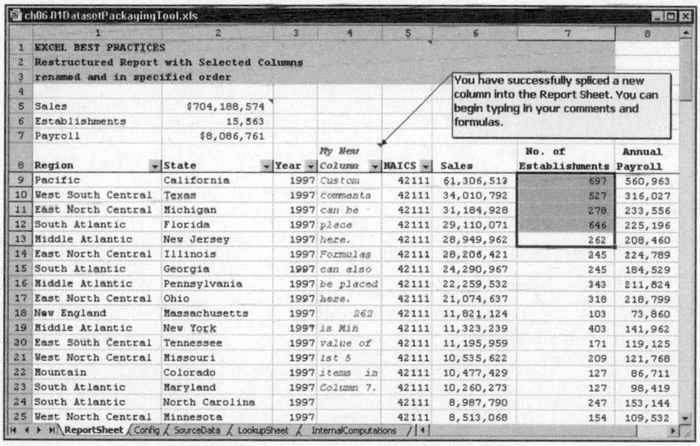

Figure 6-7: Step 3 – Successful splicing of new column into the report

Using Excel Filters

When you view the Report Sheet (refer to Figure 6-4), two items should catch your attention. The worksheet uses Excel filters, and a SUBTOTAL function is available to perform calculations on the filtered data. Read more about SUBTOTAL in the sidebar called "The Swiss army knife of Excel functions."

If you wish to create Excel filters in your data, you can quickly and easily do so. Excel filters work with data arranged in a columnar format like the SourceData or ReportSheet of ch06-01DatasetPackagingTool.xls or like the ch04-01censusdata_4K.xls file from Chapter 4. Select the cells in the header region and then go to the Excel Data menu and navigate to the AutoFilter option via the Filter submenu. You should then see the triangular notches next to the header labels, like those appearing in

Figure 6-4. You should be aware that column widths don't automatically resize when the filtered notches are added. These notches sometimes obscure the column labels. Needless to say, you can resize the columns manually.

Clicking the notch will give you the options for:

- Sort Ascending
- Sort Descending
- Showing All
- Showing the Top 10
- Selecting some custom criteria
- Selecting any of the first 1,000 unique members of the filtered column

The last three need a little more explanation. The Top 10 AutoFilter allows you to control the visibility of items in terms of their frequency of appearance (see Figure 6-8).

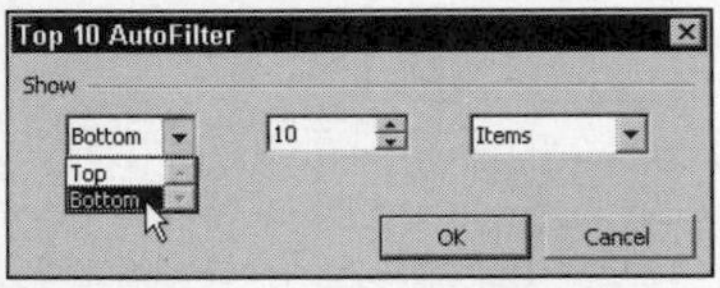

Figure 6-8: Top 10 AutoFilter window gives you more options than 10. You can select Items or Percentage (hidden), and Top or Bottom, and adjust the threshold.

Custom criteria give you the ability to select items from your list with simple Boolean criteria (see Figure 6-9). The right side of the drop-down lists show members of the column. You can use an asterisk (*) to represent any number of characters and a question mark (?) to represent only one character. It is important to remember that the Custom AutoFilter cannot combine more than two queries. To go beyond this limit, you need to use Advanced Filters.

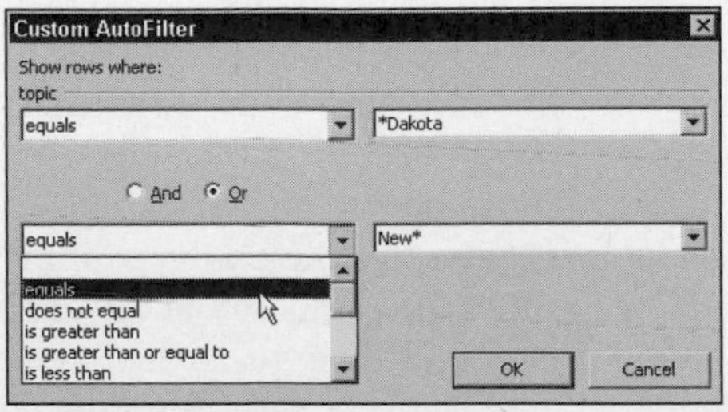

Figure 6-9: Custom AutoFilter can apply two separate queries to filter your data.

There are several things you should know about Excel Filters:

◆ In Excel 2003, the Filter drop-down list will display, at most, 1,000 unique or distinct members. The items displayed will be the first thousand unique items it finds. *If there are more than 1,000 unique items, you will not be warned that the filtered drop-down list is truncated. Watch out!*

Operations such as sorting, custom selection criteria, or picking one of the members from the drop-down list will operate on all the data, not just the first thousand.

◆ If you have multiple filter columns and select a member from one of the columns, the drop-down lists for the remaining filter columns will display only the items belonging to the filtered data. This feature effectively provides you with a "drill-down" capability. For example, if you select Middle Atlantic from the drop-down list in the Region column, the drop-down list for State is immediately shortened from 51 members to only three: New York, New Jersey, and Pennsylvania.

◆ Sorting actually changes the physical order of the rows. If the cells being sorted contain formulas, they may not work properly after the sort is performed.

This is the case with the Report Sheet (it uses `OFFSET`). You can work around this difficulty by pre-sorting your source data.

The Swiss army knife of Excel functions

At first glance, the Excel `SUBTOTAL` function appears to be more complex than it ought to be. It turns out to do some very useful things and really comes in handy, though. In a sense, `SUBTOTAL` is kind of like a Swiss army knife for Excel functions.

`SUBTOTAL` has the following syntax:

`SUBTOTAL(function_num, cellreference1,cellreference2,...)`

You can have up to 29 cell references that can be supplied as input arguments. Each of these cell references can be a range of cells, an individual cell, or a named reference. Unlike `SUM`, the cell reference in `SUBTOTAL` cannot be a regular Excel formula that returns a number. The numerical value of `function_num` tells `SUBTOTAL` what kind of function you want to operate on the cell references. Prior to Excel 2003, `SUBTOTAL` used a `function_num` range between 1 and 11 (see the table that follows). Starting with Excel 2003, the `function_num` scheme has been both revised and expanded.

Continued

The Swiss army knife of Excel functions (Continued)

Function Type	function_num showing both hidden and visible cells	function_num showing only visible cells
AVERAGE	1	101
COUNT	2	102
COUNTA	3	103
MAX	4	104
MIN	5	105
PRODUCT	6	106
STDEV	7	107
STDEVP	8	108
SUM	9	109
VAR	10	110
VARP	11	111

If you want to compute the sum of a range of cells, you might enter something like:

```
=SUBTOTAL(9,R5C3:R104C3)
```

So, what advantage does SUBTOTAL confer over SUM? After all, you could have just written:

```
=SUM(R5C3:R104C3)
```

As is, there isn't a special advantage. However, if you change the function_num from 9 to 109, there is a significant difference. This difference is vital when it comes to Excel filtered data.

Beware of a bug

As this book went to print, Excel 2003 contained a glitch that you need to be aware of. If you use the SUBTOTAL function, this could be important. Excel's SUBTOTAL function has the following syntax:

```
=SUBTOTAL(function_num, OneOrMoreCellReferences)
```

Older versions of Excel (prior to Excel 2003) would accept `function_num` with a value between 1 and 11. Depending on the value of `function_num`, the behavior of `SUBTOTAL` would be different. If `function_num` had the value 1, `SUBTOTAL` would return the `AVERAGE` of the "visible cells" in `OneOrMoreCellReferences`. If `function_num` had the value 9, `SUBTOTAL` would return the `SUM` of the "visible" cells in `OneOrMoreCellReferences`. This `SUBTOTAL` function plays an important role in Excel Filters (which controls the visibility of cells).

Excel 2003 has the same syntax for `SUBTOTAL` as did the previous versions of Excel. The documented specification is quite different, however. It changes the meaning of the old `function_num` values 1 through 11 and introduces a new set of `function_num` values of 101 through 111. The documentation says that `function_num` 1 through 11 are supposed to operate on both "visible and hidden" cells, whereas `function_num` with values between 101 and 111 are supposed to operate only on "visible" cells.

If the documentation is correct, Microsoft has done a switch-a-roo on Excel users. Old Excel spreadsheets will behave differently when opened in Excel 2003. If a spreadsheet is created in Excel 2003 using `SUBTOTAL` and has a `function_num` in the hundreds range, it will generate an error when opened up with older versions of Excel.

To make matters interesting, a beta release of Excel didn't conform to the written spec of `SUBTOTAL`. It accepted `function_num` with values of 1 through 11 as well as 101 through 111. No matter which grouping, it operated on "visible" cells only. It didn't follow the documented spec and I have the feeling that the documented spec may get revised.

As we go into press, I have been waiting with bated breath to know the verdict. By the time this book reaches your hands, this will likely be resolved. I will be posting some updated information on the resolution at the Excel Portal Page:

`http://www.evolvingtech.com/excel`

Additional features you need to know about filters

Filters are a nice way to take large amounts of data and present rows of data containing only those items you want. If you plan on utilizing filtered data extensively, you need to know some additional things. Some of these pertain to copying and pasting data. Others pertain to the use of advanced filters. You need to know that:

◆ Some kinds of information can be lost when you paste cells containing filtered data.

◆ There are workarounds to avoid information loss when replicating information on worksheets containing filtered data.

Replicating content with filtered data

Copying and pasting filtered data actually filters out the formulas in the pasted cells. This can be both a good and bad thing. If you have 2,000 rows of data and your filter isolates the four rows you are interested in, when you copy and paste the filtered data, the pasted content will contain only the visible cells that you selected. If there are only four filtered rows of data visible, you won't be able to paste the intervening rows. What's more, the pasted content will carry over only cell values and formatting information whenever any of the filtered content is hidden. All formulas will be lost in the pasted content, as will all the hidden cells.

This result is fine because it will allow you to take a snapshot of your filtered data and, say, paste it into a report that you plan to e-mail to a colleague or a manager.

You might copy and paste other portions of the worksheet that have nothing to do with the filtered data. Will its formulas carry over, or will they, too, be lost? The answer is: It depends.

If the range of cells you are copying does not reside in the rows containing filtered data, the formulas will carry over and get pasted. Otherwise, all formula information will be lost in the pasted cells. Also, nonvisible cells such as those within a collapsed column (columns with zero width) will not survive the ordeal.

Suppose that you want to duplicate a worksheet that contains filtered data and you want to preserve the other formulas on the worksheet. There are two ways you can accomplish this:

♦ Show all the data so that the filtered data is effectively "unfiltered"; then, perform the regular copy and paste process.

♦ Clone the worksheet.

In the first approach, you would select the (All) option for each of the filtered notches for AutoFilter data. Alternatively, you could select Show All in the Filter submenu of the Excel Data menu, which is how you would show all items using Advanced Filters.

When you copy and paste, the behavior will be like a regular copy and paste, preserving formulas, column widths, and row heights. The filtering information will not be carried over.

If you need to replicate the formulas and filtering information, you might as well clone the whole worksheet. Here's how to clone a worksheet:

1. Locate the worksheet tab for the sheet you want to clone and right-click the tab label. A list of pop-up options will appear (see Figure 6-10). Select Move or Copy.

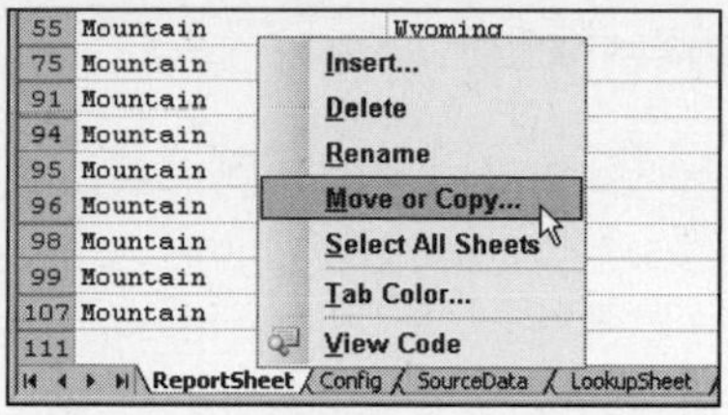

Figure 6–10: From your worksheet tab, you can copy your
worksheet to a new sheet on your current workbook,
another open spreadsheet, or a new workbook.

2. You will be presented with a Move or Copy window and will see a list of
   worksheets in your current workbook along with "(move to end)." You
   will also have a check box option to create a copy. Make sure that you
   check this box. Click the drop-down list to view the various spreadsheets
   you can copy your worksheet to. This list consists of "(new book)," the
   current workbook you are cloning from, and whatever spreadsheets happen to be open at the time. Select the file of your choosing (see Figure
   6-11). If you select "(new book)," a new workbook will be instantaneously
   created with your cloned worksheet.

Figure 6–11: Remember to check the
box for the Create a copy option.

After you select one of the other destination spreadsheets, you see its list
of worksheets. This will be your opportunity to insert the cloned worksheet where you want it to appear. Press the OK button.

3. If the formulas in your cloned worksheet have no formulas with references
   to other worksheets, your work is done. If the formulas are dependent on
   other worksheets, you will likely see some #REF! errors. You can correct
   these errors by pasting the values from your filtered data to your cloned
   worksheet.

Presentation Tear Sheets

On occasion, you'll be asked by a colleague or business acquaintance for a soft copy of your spreadsheet. You know you'll have to comply but don't want to give them the full spreadsheet. It may be too complex or dangerous to put into the hand of a naive user. You may not want to reveal your "secret" formulas. In such situations, you can use a Presentation Tear Sheet.

The technique is really simple.

1. Open your original spreadsheet (the one whose contents you wish to disseminate as a tear sheet).

2. Make a copy of your worksheet by right- clicking the worksheet tab (using the technique described previously). You can put it on a new spreadsheet or place it wherever you want (I'll refer to this as the "cloned tear sheet").

3. Go back to your original spreadsheet and select all the cells in the worksheet (Ctrl+A will do it, as will clicking the top-left corner of the worksheet just above and to the left of the first cell). Copy the contents using Ctrl+C (or from the Excel Edit menu). Now click the cloned tear sheet. Select the cell in the first row and column (that is, R1C1 or A1, depending on how you like to view your spreadsheets), and perform a Paste Special... Values.

4. At this point everything will be copied over except the formulas. This includes the formatting, electronic Comments (the sticky messages I left for you on some of the spreadsheets), and page setups, with the headers and footers. If you defined named ranges in your original spreadsheet, they will be carried here. You can safely remove them by choosing Insert→Name→Define. Unless you have a reason to keep these named references, you can click each of the names and safely delete them.

The use of a Presentation Tear Sheet can serve a practical purpose. Your original spreadsheet may contain a formula that points external data residing on another spreadsheet, file, or database not accessible to the recipient of your cloned tear sheet. What you're doing is removing any of these dependencies. Of course, you can put them back in on a controlled basis, one at a time, by hand. You may need to need to reintroduce some macros.

Whenever you clone a worksheet, regardless of whether it has to do with Presentation Tear Sheets, Excel will copy only the first 255 characters in any of the spreadsheet cells. Though Excel is polite in warning you when this happens, I don't want you to be caught by surprise. An easy workaround is to clone the worksheet and identify the spreadsheet cells that have been truncated. Then copy and paste the individual cells that require fixing.

Let me give you one more thought before closing this topic. Presentation Tear Sheets effectively lobotomize the spreadsheet. If your cloned tear sheet happens to fall into the hands of a crafty competitor, there may be enough information to reverse-engineer the worksheet and reconstruct the essential formulas. If this is a concern, you can password-protect your spreadsheet. First, choose Save As→Tools (see the mouse pointer in Figure 6-12).

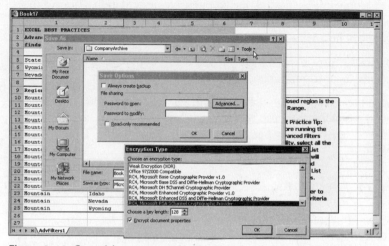

Figure 6-12: Spreadsheet password protection, available with the Tools option from the Save As menu

Next, choose General Options. This will give you the Save Options that allow you to set your password. If you want strong encryption, click the Advanced button to get the different encryption options. Excel will likely default to Office 97/2000 Compatible. Whichever option you deem appropriate, push your encryption key length beyond 40 bits; 128 bits should be more than sufficient.

Keeping up with the passwords

If your spreadsheet is important to you and not just another tear-away worksheet, carefully safeguard your passwords. It's best if you have a specific reason to password-protect your documents; that is, don't do it gratuitously. There are some very practical reasons for this. If you're security conscious, chances are that you will be regularly rotating passwords. If you start preparing plenty of spreadsheets, then every time you revise your password, you'll have to update the password on each and every spreadsheet file. Over time, the list of files is going to grow. You are faced with the option of synchronizing a vast number of files or keeping track of a growing number of passwords. Neither option is very appealing. If you *have to* protect a large number of files, a simple way of doing it is to zip them up as a single file and password-protect that file.

If you're not super trusting of the person you are giving the document to, you can throw another monkey wrench into the gears. Consider turning your spreadsheet into a PDF file.

There are some very specific advantages associated with PDFs:

◆ You can attach other non-spreadsheet files to the PDF document. This allows you to construct a single composite document. PDF files give you the ability to create a highly interactive and media intensive presentation. Packing the presentation with numbers and summary information in the form of a spreadsheet can be a very persuasive sales and communications tool.

◆ It's a politically correct way to give others a soft copy of a spreadsheet that prevents them from looking at the formulas.

◆ If you have the need, you can prevent someone else from having the ability to copy and paste. You can also prevent someone else's ability to print. These measures won't prevent someone from doing a screen capture, however.

Advanced Filters

Sometimes you'll want to select data based on a more complex set of criteria than is possible with AutoFilters. Advanced Filters give you this capability, but it comes at a price of reduced interactivity (the triangular notches disappear).

First, I want to tell you how to set up and specify an Advanced Filter, and then I'll show you a couple of special cases that are not immediately intuitive.

Advanced Filters setup

You must set up two locations on your worksheet:

◆ Criteria Range

◆ List Range

Your Criteria Range effectively replaces the drop-down list of items you had in the triangular notches. The List Range contains the data and their headers that will be filtered.

The top line of the Criteria Range will generally include names of the column headers appearing across the top of the List Range. The cells immediately underneath list the actual filter or search criteria.

It helps to draw a rectangular outline around the Criteria Range for easy visual identification and then to select the cells of your List Range (see Figure 6-13).

You can open the file ch06-02AdvancedFilters.xls and try out the examples.

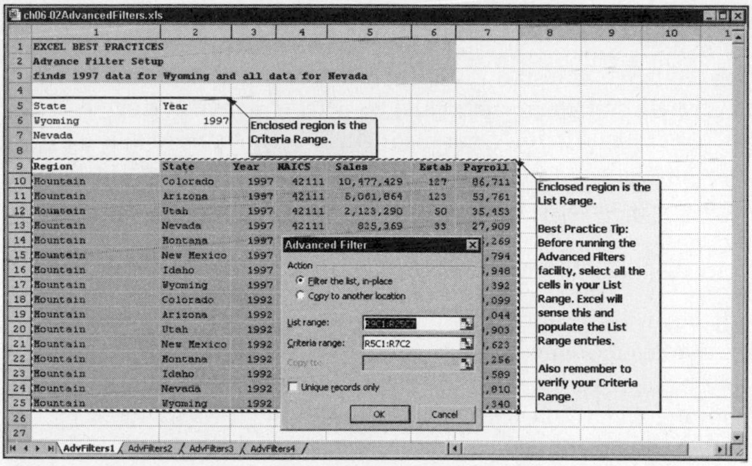

Figure 6-13: Advanced Filter defining a List Range and a Criteria Range

Multiple criteria for a single filter

The way to interpret the Criteria Range is to think of the AND criteria running horizontally across and the inclusive OR criteria running vertically down Criteria Range.

If you said, "I'll take any data for which the number of Establishments is between 105 AND 40, OR happens to be related to the State of Idaho," the Criteria Range would appear as it does in Figure 6-14. This is not the only way to represent the Criteria Range. You could have swapped the order of the data appearing in rows 6 and 7; that is, Idaho would appear on row 6 whereas <105 and >40 would appear on row 7. Note that swapping the order of the columns in the Criteria Range doesn't affect the outcome.

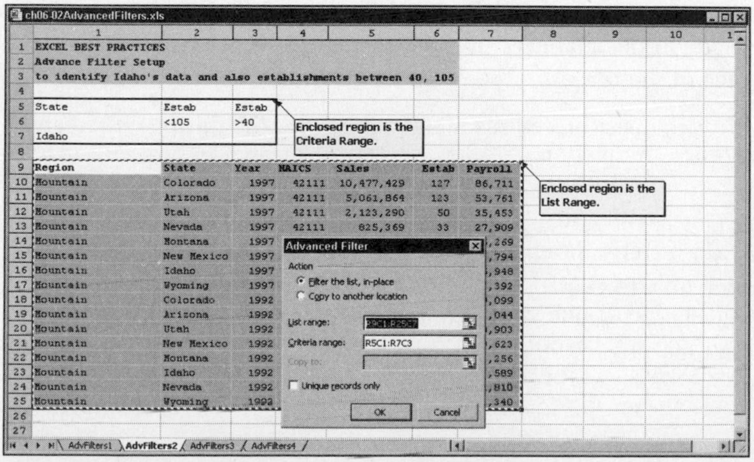

Figure 6-14: Applying multiple criteria, even for a single filter

You can use formulas in your Advanced Filters

Here is where Advanced Filters can start to pick up a little steam. Suppose you want to identify all data for which Sales are more than 25 percent above average over all years aggregated together (that is, you don't distinguish between years).

To handle this, you would need a formula in your Criteria Range. Setting this up is not trivial. There are several rules you must abide by:

1. The Criteria Label must be empty.

2. The formula below this empty label must point to the first row of data using a relative reference on the row. The rest of the formula has to be using absolute references or references referring to the same row. This is because the formula has to cycle through each of the rows in the List Range, holding all other factors fixed.

3. The result of the formula as it cycles through each row must be either a TRUE or a FALSE value.

Here is how you would set up an Advanced Filter for identifying sales that are more than 25 percent above the average of 1992 and 1997 sales combined.

As usual, start by defining your two regions: the List Range and the Criteria Range (see Figure 6-15).

◆ The Criteria Labels are all presented except for one: the Sales.

◆ The formula below the empty Criteria Label refers to the first cell in the List Range using a relative Reference R[4]C. This allows the Advanced Filter facility to cycle through each of the rows below. The formula used is

```
=R[4]C>AVERAGE(R10C5:R25C5)*1.25
```

The rest of the formula, namely the Excel AVERAGE function, uses absolute cell references. In this manner, Advanced Filter facility can safely cycle through each of the rows.

◆ Because the > comparison returns a TRUE or FALSE, the third requirement is satisfied.

This use of formulas in the Advanced Filters takes a little getting used to. By the way, the threshold for 25 percent above average sales combined over the years is $2,131,448. There are only three rows that can satisfy the requirement. Try running the example in your file and you'll see this to be the case. The value of $2,123,290, though close, doesn't make it.

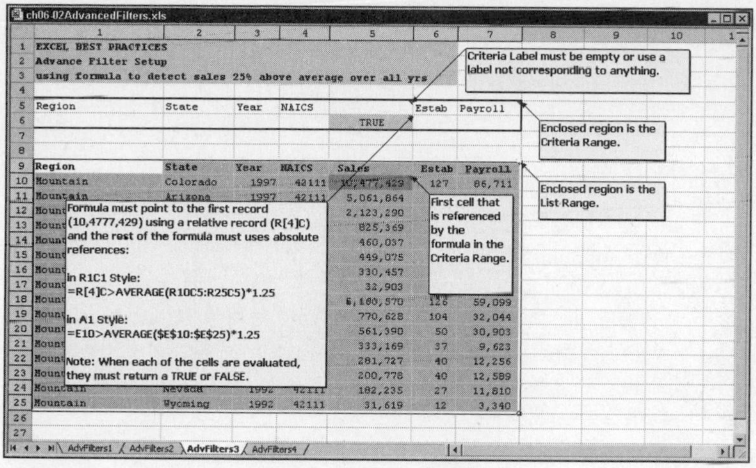

Figure 6-15: Setup of criteria involving formulas

Some of you who regularly use AutoFilters may be quick to point out that this could be done using a Custom filter and supplying the hardwired value of 2,131,448. Although this could work, I have to point out that you have to do some external calculations (finding the average and then bumping it up by 25 percent), and then hand-feed the value to the AutoFilter. You will have to do this each time the underlying data changes. This is not the case with an Advanced Filter.

There's another important reason you should not be too quick to dismiss the benefits of using Advanced Filters. The problem I gave you used only one criteria. In your line of work, you may need 10 or 15 criteria to cull specific data from a list of thousands of rows. You will quickly outstrip the AutoFilter's capability.

You don't need 10 or 15 criteria to outstrip the AutoFilter's capability. One will suffice. To prove the point, I'll ask a simple and very reasonable question: "Which data corresponds to above-average sales *for each individual year?*" In other words, what is above average for 1992 and what is above average for 1997?

Figure 6-16 shows you how it is done (this is the fourth worksheet tab of ch06-02AdvancedFilters.xls). Construct a separate table of lookup values (in this case, Table01, which tabulates the average sales for each year). When the Advanced Filter cycles through each row, it uses OFFSET to find the year (two columns over to the left), performs a lookup, and compares this average value to the Sales value for the particular row.

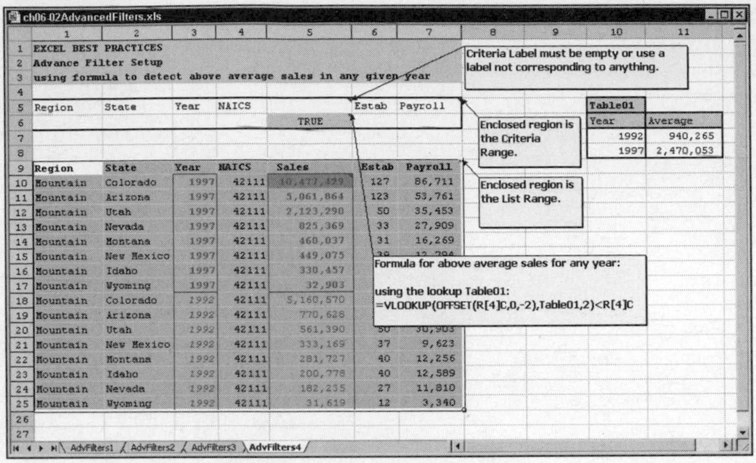

Figure 6-16: Auxiliary lookup technique for an Advanced Filters formula

Tips for Spreadsheet Comments

You may have noticed that when you opened some of the spreadsheets on the CD-ROM with this book, several of the electronic notes were automatically open in some of the worksheets. You can control this sticky behavior and, in general, put this commenting facility to good use.

Use the Comments Catalog

As a first practical step, it helps to have a catalog of Excel Comments that you can easily view, copy and paste into your spreadsheets. Open the file ch06-03Electronic-CommentsCatalog.xls (see Figure 6-17).

As you move your mouse across the various cells, you will see comments appearing that describe the settings for each type of pop-up comment.

If you see any you like, just copy the spreadsheet cell and paste it to your spreadsheets. You can also perform a Paste Special... Comments. Pasting comments is especially useful if you have a group of cells for which you want a consistent look-and-feel for the comments (in terms of their size, position, color, font, and so on).

In the catalog, you will see three different types of comment patterns. Most of you are probably familiar with plain patterns, consisting of solid patterns with light or dark contrasting fonts. You will see that some of these work well; they are pleasing to view and easy to read and print.

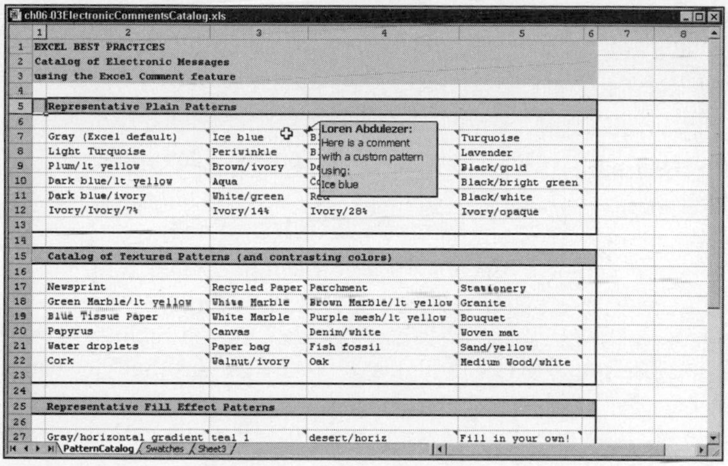

Figure 6-17: Your catalog to copy and paste differently formatted electronic comments for your immediate use

Print settings

You can choose among different print settings for comments. Go to Page Setup for your worksheet, click the Sheet tab (from Page, Margin, Header/Footer, and Sheet). Look for the Comments: drop-down list. You will see that there are three options:

♦ **(None):** This is the default setting for Excel. When you print a worksheet, the comments do not appear.

♦ **At end of sheet:** This setting accumulates all of the comments into one place. This option is particularly useful if you are preparing a financial statement and want to turn this set of comments into notes that accompany the statement.

♦ **As displayed on sheet:** Be careful not to have too many visible comments, because doing so could quickly overpower your printed document.

If you wish to edit an existing comment, double-click the cell. If the cell doesn't have a comment, double-clicking won't create one (you will have to right-click and select Insert Comment to create one).

Good practices

If you have more than just a short passing comment in your spreadsheet (such as detailed explanatory notes incorporated in financial statement analysis), the chances are good that the reader of your spreadsheet will want to print out the comments. All that is provided in the printout are the physical cell coordinates and the actual comments.

In your printout, the listing of physical cell coordinates may not be enough to identify where the comment is located. The following format is often useful:

1. Topic heading

2. Descriptive location on spreadsheet (not just the physical coordinates)

3. Narrative description

Generally, the briefer the comment, the more useful it will be. Explanatory information like the Management Discussion & Analysis should be handled elsewhere, probably off the spreadsheet. Mostly, use the sticky notes as mental reminders that you want to keep at the forefront of your thoughts, or specific items that you want to draw attention to.

It may be helpful to provide in your comments some identifying location or cell name so that the context or antecedent is known by the reader.

Keep in mind that your spreadsheet may one day be opened from an XML or Web-based browser. When you edit your comments, you have the ability to specify Web attributes. Your Web alternative text can be read by search engines.

Coloration

Depending on your need, you can vary the background color of the note or the color of the font (as well as the style). Unless your procedures are highly specialized or you are using a shared document, it is not usually necessary to vary the colors or the appearance of a note. Most of the time, you should do this for the purpose of enhancing readability, that is, clearly distinguishing between an Excel Comment box and a spreadsheet cell.

Try to avoid dark or strong background colors that might compete with the text in the comment.

You can alter the appearance of a comment to make it semi-transparent. Having a tinge of transparency can make a spreadsheet look sophisticated, but it comes at a price. Adding transparency makes the comment harder to read. I would discourage the use of transparency in comments unless you have a good reason to introduce it into your spreadsheets. There are some samples of semi-transparent comments in the Comments Catalog file.

Unless you want people to take notice of specific information *every time* they open your spreadsheets, try not make comments "sticky" (that is, be the very first thing a person sees when the worksheet is made active). I suspect that some readers will think I overstepped my bounds by overusing the sticky property. You're probably right. There's a reason I switched on the Show Comments feature; you can control where the comments appear. If you just leave them to pop up only when the mouse passes over, they almost always position themselves in a way to obscure useful information, or off to the side where they can't be seen (this is especially true when comments are close to the right edge of the worksheet).

Formatting comments

The quick way to format a cell containing a comment is to double-click the cell so that the comment can be edited. Then, double-click the boundaries of the comment so that you can customize the format attributes.

You can adjust many things when you format a comment. Your bang for the buck will be in the Color and Lines (see Figure 6-18). In particular, go straight to the Fill Effects option. This will open a window in which you can set the Gradients, Textures, and Pictures options. The Comment Catalog file has representative samples of these.

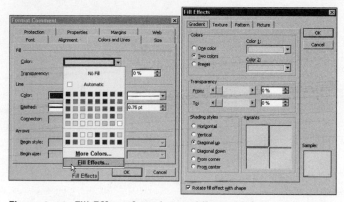

Figure 6-18: Fill Effects for colors and lines and font settings are the most important attributes to set.

You may have noticed that I left out Patterns. Chances are they'll make you dizzy and give you eyestrain. In any case, you have a lot to explore on your own with comments.

Closing Thoughts

This chapter provided you with a tool for reorganizing and restructuring data. After the setup was completed, which was largely a matter of some definitions, all you had to do was to copy and paste your data, or just point to where the source data resides, and your report was done. A little elbow grease up front takes the grunt work out of endless updates to the same report, week after week.

You also had an opportunity to see first-hand some of the features (and quirks) of filters. Presentation Tear Sheets offer a way of freeze-drying a spreadsheet and making it accessible (with filters). There are pragmatic reasons to remove the inner workings. If your complex spreadsheet ties into 17 sub-schedules or worksheets, how are you going to extricate the summary results so that you can send them to the Executive Vice President and not have to prepare a detailed written manual on how to use the spreadsheet? Your spreadsheet should be self-explanatory. If it's not, you can rely on Excel's Comments feature to guide the way. Clearly, the Comments feature lacks the interactive capability that's so beneficial in the other portions of a spreadsheet, though.

In the next chapter, "Creating and Using Smart Data," you will see that visual information can be tied to what's going in the spreadsheet numbers in a very tactile and interactive manner.

Chapter 7

Creating and Using Smart Data

IN THIS CHAPTER

- ◆ Using anchor cells
- ◆ Putting Conditional Formatting to good use
- ◆ Using the Phantom Formatting Technique and Four Color tables
- ◆ Using two numbers to adjust a sequence of data
- ◆ Adjusting the background color when text spills into adjacent columns
- ◆ Using the override and un-erase technique
- ◆ Peeking under the hood on some very effective techniques
- ◆ Creating tables with self organized borders

THIS CHAPTER INTRODUCES the use of Smart Data. Some of you may think of Smart Data as Conditional Formatting on steroids. To be sure, it does some definite bench pressing when it comes to dynamic formatting. The valuable lessons you'll gain from this chapter will not only include techniques, but also a keen sense of when and how to combine Smart Data with the rest of your spreadsheet.

The chapter starts out with Smart Data and the way it can be used with anchor cells. In this example you will see that Smart Data is not only a visual presentation facility but also can be used to alert you to potentially costly spreadsheet errors.

Next, you learn the basics of Conditional Formatting. Then you find out what they didn't teach you in the textbooks: You can achieve four conditional formats when Excel provides only three conditional tests. You'll also get some valuable tips on preparing tabular data.

You will also discover that Smart Data does not need to be tethered to the physical cell on which the Smart Data is defined.

You will be able to do some clever things with Smart Data. One of these will let you override computations with manually prepared values. When you erase the manually prepared values, the prior set of formulas instantly re-emerges.

Finally, the chapter gives you a clear idea on some of the limitations of Smart Data as well as ways to put it good use.

What Is Smart Data, Anyhow?

Put simply, Smart Data is data that is aware of what's going on in the spreadsheet. There are practical reasons for having "self-aware" data and data cognizant of other cells. Some events may alter how a spreadsheet works. Smart Data can help you to identify when certain changes have taken place and may give you suggestions to correct them. The use of Smart Data with anchor cells should make this clear and is also a good starting point to get acquainted with Smart Data.

Smart Data used with anchor cells

Some of the spreadsheets in the previous chapters count the number of rows relative to an "anchor cell." An anchor cell is a fixed point of reference. If you inadvertently move the Anchor Cell, other spreadsheet formulas may get thrown off and compute the wrong results. Sometimes you won't immediately realize there's an error in the computations.

As an example of this alert capability, go to one of the spreadsheets files from a previous chapter. Open the file ch05-07_naics.xls on your CD-ROM. This file uses an Anchor Cell with Smart Data capabilities built in. Before making a change that would signal an alert, go to the worksheets like RegionInspector or the GraphicalSummary. Jot down or note some of the summary values. After you've done this, locate the SourceData worksheet tab and do something that will reposition the top left hand cell. Try inserting a row in the way shown in Figure 7-1. The cell content of the Anchor Cell previously in the top-left corner of the worksheet has suddenly changed from EXCEL BEST PRACTICES to a fairly visible warning message.

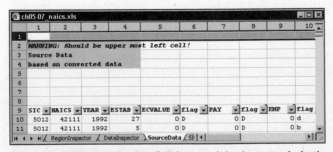

Figure 7-1: When an Anchor Cell is moved, it alerts you in both its format and text content.

Now go back to the summary worksheets, such as RegionInspector or the GraphicalSummary, and look at the numeric values. The computed numbers are now altered. If you didn't have an alert built into the Anchor Cell and didn't take note of the original values in the summaries, would you have immediately spotted a change? Unless you use a Smart Data facility to alert you, you might not catch the changes in your computations until well after the fact.

Perhaps you are thinking that anchor cells are not that pervasive. It may interest you to know that the Anchor Cell in this particular spreadsheet is referenced in the formulas 778 times (see Figure 7-2).

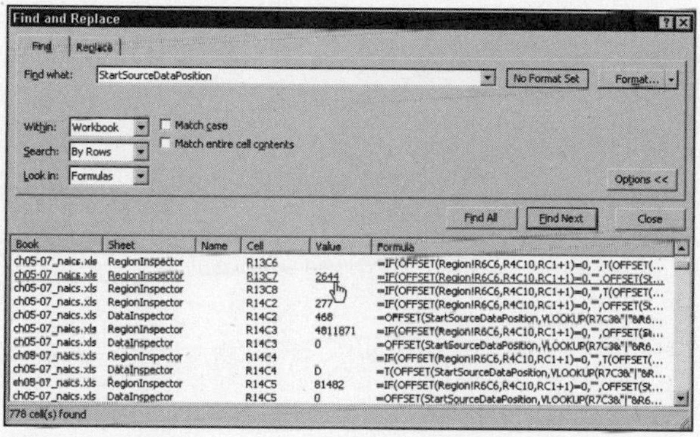

Figure 7-2: You can find cell references by pressing Ctrl+F, searching within the workbook, selecting the Options>> button, and then pressing the Find All button.

Anchor cells are not automatically imbued with Smart Data properties. They are placed there by design. The design of anchor cells calls for three features:

1. An Anchor Cell has a defined cell location. Usually, it is given a user-defined name, such as StartPosition or something similar.

   If you are using more than one Anchor Cell, it is a good practice to use a specific name that clearly identifies where and what the Anchor Cell is for, for example, StartSourceDataPosition. Nothing stops you from using absolute cell coordinates such as R1C1 or $A$1 instead of user-defined names. However, physical cell coordinates tend to make your formulas harder to read.

   One last point: The defined name should be for a single cell and not a range of cells.

2. The Anchor Cell is there for the benefit of other cells so that they can determine their position relative to a fixed point. Being that the Anchor Cell normally doesn't need to perform a calculation to justify its existence, it has an untapped capability to perform a useful computation. This spare capability could be put to use to ensure its well-being. Give the Anchor Cell a formula like:

```
=IF(AND(ROW()=1,COLUMN()=1),"MY STARTING POSITION IS PROPERLY
LOCATED","WARNING: Should be upper most left cell!")
```

Think of this kind of computation as your "insurance policy."

3. Anchor cells can and should have some Conditional Formatting property
   that works independently of the cell formula but simultaneously tag teams
   with it. The Conditional Formatting would display something like that
   shown in Figure 7-3.

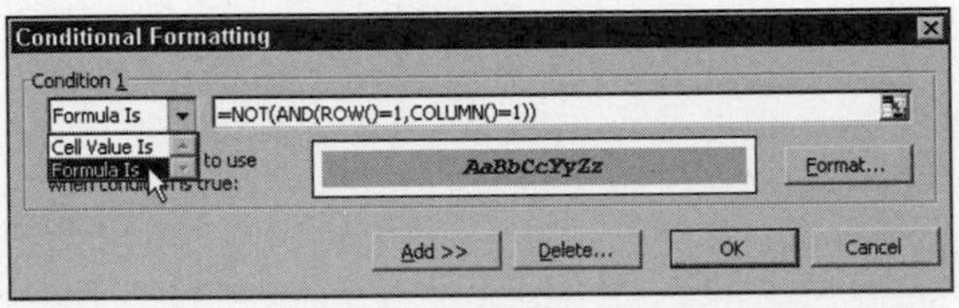

Figure 7-3: Use a Conditional Formatting formula instead of a cell value.

Conditional Formatting

The setup of Conditional Formatting for your selected cells is accessed through the
Excel Format menu. Conditional Formatting can test for three separate conditions.
The Conditional Formatting window, shown in Figure 7-3, starts out with one conditional test. You can add additional tests by pressing the Add>> button. You will
max out at three conditions. Notice that each condition can separately test for
either Cell Value Is or Formula Is.

Let me try to explain the difference between the two. When you select Cell Value
Is, you are always explicitly comparing your current cell value to some external
value or computation in another cell or group of cells. The current cell value takes
center stage in Conditional Formatting when you select the Cell Value Is option.

With the Formula Is option, there is no such built-in dependency on the current
cell value. Instead, you can construct a free-form formula subject to the requirement that it always return a TRUE or FALSE. *The free-form formula does not have to
include the current cell in any of its computations.* These free-form conditional formulas make it easy to construct digital dashboards.

Constructing a "digital dashboard"

Consider constructing a digital dashboard that "lights up" when certain overall
conditions occur. The cells that light up can display messages or values that do not
need to be correlated to the cell's value.

You might have a portfolio consisting of various funds, performance information, and investment objectives. Your portfolio dashboard could highlight one or
more input cells for designated funds. The input cells that get highlighted might
suggest additional investments for specific funds. It's your job to type in the
amount to be maintained in the specific fund.

A digital dashboard can work much like a Spreadsheet Portal (a topic taken up in Chapter 12, "Spreadsheet Portals, XML, and Web Services").

Rules of the road

Before you go on your merry way trying to create gobs of Smart Data, you need to understand some basic rules:

♦ The formulas in the Conditional Formatting window can refer only to values or cells in the current worksheet. References to user-defined names and cell coordinates referring to non-local worksheets are strictly off limits. (You will see that a workaround exists for this.)

♦ The results for any condition defined in the Conditional Formatting window always needs to be expressed as a value of TRUE or FALSE. This is so whether you select Formula Is or Cell Value Is. With conditional formulas (for example, Formula Is), you must explicitly return the value TRUE or FALSE. When you select Cell Value Is, the current cell is always being compared to something else and implicitly returns a TRUE or FALSE.

♦ The length of a formula in a Conditional Formatting window cannot exceed 255 characters. Regular spreadsheet formulas can be much longer. Although this might not seem like a significant limitation, long user-defined names and functions requiring multiple inputs can quickly eat up this available capacity.

♦ Conditional Formatting can test up to a maximum of three conditions. It proceeds to test them in sequential order, starting with Condition 1. If it evaluates to FALSE, it tests for Condition 2. Failing that, it tests for Condition 3. Upon encountering a TRUE result, it immediately stops any further testing and applies the formatting associated with the condition. Condition 1 can preempt Conditions 2 and 3, even if any of them would return a TRUE. Likewise, Condition 2 can preempt Condition 3 in a similar manner. If no condition evaluates to TRUE, no conditional formatting is applied.

♦ When you construct formulas in a Conditional Formatting window and make use of the technique of pointing and clicking on cells to construct a formula, the cell references always show up as absolute coordinates. If you need to convert these to relative or hybrid cell coordinates, remember to use the F4 key to cycle through the absolute, hybrid, and relative cell references.

The Phantom Formatting technique and Four-Color tables

Excel's Conditional Formatting allows you to test for three conditions (see Figure 7-4). Just because you are permitted three tests doesn't mean that you are limited to three formats. What if all tests fail? You could have an underlying "phantom" format that, if not overridden, will become visible.

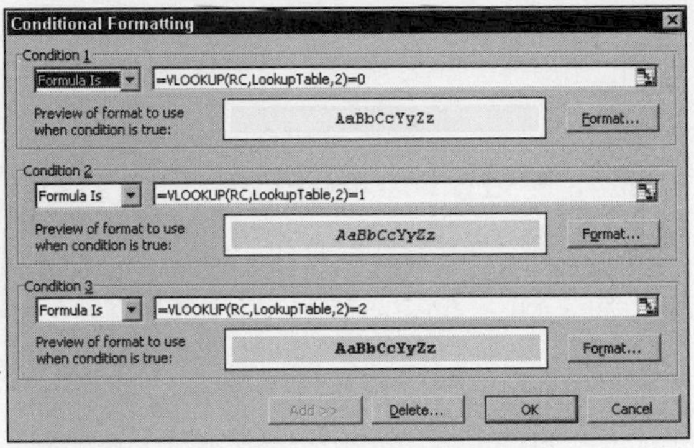

Conditional Formatting

Condition 1

Formula Is ▾ | =VLOOKUP(RC,LookupTable,2)=0

Preview of format to use
when condition is true: | AaBbCcYyZz | Format...

Condition 2

Formula Is ▾ | =VLOOKUP(RC,LookupTable,2)=1

Preview of format to use
when condition is true: | *AaBbCcYyZz* | Format...

Condition 3

Formula Is ▾ | =VLOOKUP(RC,LookupTable,2)=2

Preview of format to use
when condition is true: | **AaBbCcYyZz** | Format...

Add >>   Delete...   OK   Cancel

Figure 7–4: Three separate conditional tests

To see this in phantom format in action, open the file ch07-01_4ColorOption-Pricing.xls (see Figure 7-5). Although the table computes the call option values using the Black-Scholes option-pricing model, it is an illustration of a "Smart Table" that knows how to make full use of colorized bands to display information effectively. Notice that the fourth format in the option-pricing table has a font style that is both boldface and italicized. The background pattern is colored Rose (it would be too difficult to distinguish the text from the background had the pattern been colored Red). This format was applied to the whole table of call value option prices. After applying the format, Conditional Formatting as shown in Figure 7-4 was overlaid. The conditional format tests look up the call value option price on the user-defined LookupTable to determine which color band should be applied. If the value isn't a 0, 1, or 2, then the phantom format emerges.

 To make proper use of a phantom format, all of the conditional formats need to be explicitly set for *both* the Font Style and the Pattern color. Note that the first conditional format uses a Regular font. It is important to explicitly set this font. Otherwise, the conditional format will adopt the font style of the phantom format.

The LookupTable evenly splits the range of values between minimum and maximum call option values. As you adjust various inputs that affect the option value, the minimum, maximum, and intermediate values are automatically recomputed.

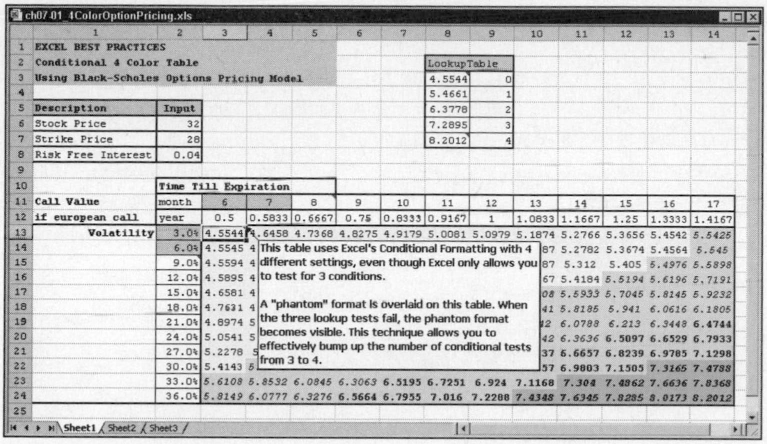

Figure 7-5: Smart Tables provide separate color bands and allow for visual classification.

Automatic adjustment for a range of data

When you look at the spreadsheet (Figure 7-5), you will see that the Stock Price, Strike Price, and Risk Free Rate of Interest are individual numbers. In contrast, the Time Till Expiration and Volatility require inputting a range of values. For the range of numbers, it would be nice to input the first two numbers and have the others automatically continue the progression of numbers along the row or column.

It's nice to know that you can. The technique involves creating a linear sequence of numbers that follows the progression. For example, if you start out with the number 9 and the next number is 11, the next number would be 13, and the one after that would be 15. Notice that 13 equals (2*11)-9 and that 15 equals (2*13)-11. This operation can be put into a spreadsheet formula. For the cells running across, you can use:

```
=2*RC[-1]-RC[-2]
```

This is how the progression of months is computed in the spreadsheet shown in Figure 7-5, running across row 11; starting from the third value in the range. The gray cells containing 6 and 7 do not contain formulas. They are just straight numbers. When you adjust these numbers, the progression continues across.

The progression of cells running down the column for Volatility work the same way, except that the progression formula looks at the previous rows above. The cells running down the column use:

```
=2*R[-1]C-R[-2]C
```

Again, I've highlighted the starter numbers in gray (3.0% and 6.0%).

Smart formatting for overextended text

On occasion, the amount of text you might have for a cell is longer than the size of the cell width. Your cell may format text a certain way. For instance, the text may be boldface or have a certain color. When the text extends beyond the cell boundary, all of the text retains its formatted appearance. The background pattern of the cell never extends beyond the edges of the cell. You can see an example of this in the first row of ch07-02FormatSample.xls file, found on the CD-ROM with this book (see Figure 7-6).

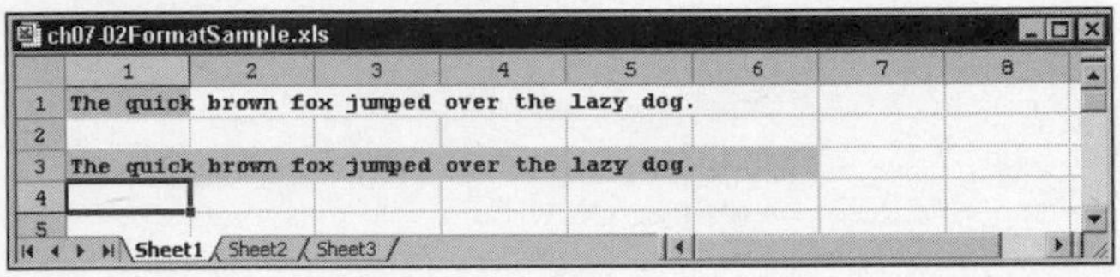

Figure 7-6: Extending the format beyond the cell's boundary

Of course, you can extend the cell's format to stretch over a range of cells to make it look more like the cells in row 3. This is fine for now, but what happens when you later resize the column widths to adjust for something else in the spreadsheet? Depending on what you do, the number of cells with a gray background may amount to too many or too few. It would be much nicer if the gray background were to automatically extend as far as is necessary to provide a colorized background for the text. This is in fact what is done for the text appearing in the third row. Go to the spreadsheet and try typing in something else. If the text is shorter, the number of cells with a gray background will be smaller. If the text is longer, the number of gray cells will be increased, up to a maximum of 8 columns.

Basically, the cells in column 2 through 7 are watching what is typed into the cell on the first column, and they "judge" whether they need to colorize themselves. The file ch07-03SmartFormatExtend.xls is provided on the CD-ROM so that you can directly copy and paste the formats to your spreadsheets (see Figure 7-7). This file contains various combinations: gray background only (right and left margin justified), and colorized backgrounds (right and left margin justified).

As in the case of the Smart Table (refer to Figure 7-5), the printed versions of the colorized cells are always discernable when printed in black and white (that is, you can always distinguish between plain text, italics, boldface, and combined boldface and italics).

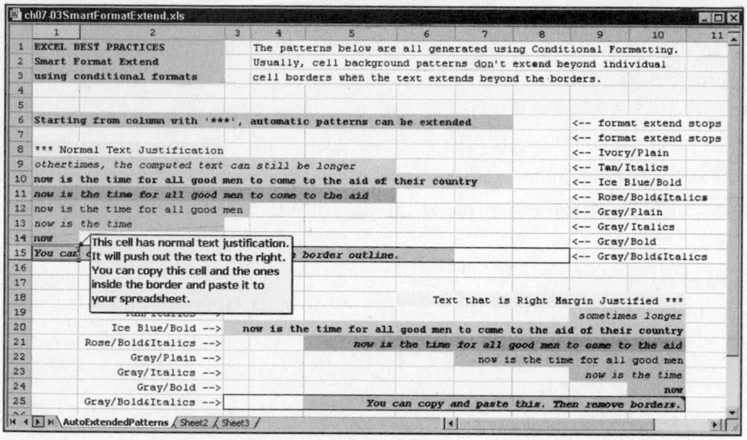

Figure 7–7: You can copy and paste formats from this page to enable Smart Format Extend on your spreadsheets.

From RAGs to Riches: An Interactive Array of Colors

It seems that the corporate standard for project managers is to report the status of projects and activities using a Red, Amber, or Green classification. How do you go about making such an assignment of Red, Amber, or Green? If you're like most busy managers and business professionals, the project status reports that you disseminate are constantly undergoing change. With many things flying around, you need to be able to fulfill the following in your report:

1. Put the essential decision information in one place.

2. Apply objective criteria for your classifications.

3. Override any of the computed information and simultaneously give yourself the ability to "un-erase" the overrides.

4. Subdue distractions in your report.

The information often tracked for a given project or task typically includes a task ID, project description, project leader, budget amount, priority level, due date, and project status (often a Red/Amber/Green code). Feel free to add or remove items on this list.

Assume for the moment that the project status is principally dependent upon how much time is left till the task is due for completion. You or your company management might have some objective criteria that you can use to classify the status of your projects. If it's time-based and you want to automatically compute the project status, then you'll need an additional piece of information: the date you are using to count how much time is left for each of the projects/tasks. You will also need quantitative criteria to determine what gets classified as Red vs. Amber vs. Green.

Red/Amber/Green provides useful information for active projects. What about projects that are already completed? It seems that you will need to account for recently completed projects as well as the status of active and ongoing projects.

Preparing your status report

Essentially, the information you need to assemble for each task will include the due date, days remaining, and project status. You will also need an "As of Date" to compute the days remaining and project status. Figure 7-8 shows you one way in which you might present such a report.

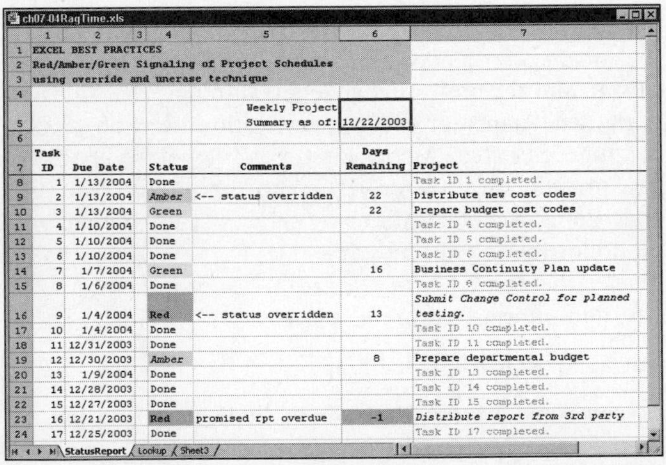

Figure 7-8: Status report using the override and un-erase technique

To see how well the report addresses the four things needed for the status report, open the file ch07-04RagTime.xls. The information such as the due date for each of the tasks is listed. Given the due date and the AsOfDate you can determine how many days are remaining before a given task needs to be completed. There is a separate table on the Lookup Worksheet that tells you what gets classified as a Red vs. Amber vs. Green. It seems that the essential information is in one place.

The lookup table provides a mechanism to apply a uniform set of criteria across all projects. More important, you can revise the criteria by updating your lookup table. This updating allows you to avoid doing surgery on your formulas.

It seems that the first two items have been fulfilled. The next one on the list is interesting. Assume that you have some objective criteria for determining the status. It could be a formula like:

```
=VLOOKUP(DueDate-AsOfDate,TableOfDaysRemainingWithStatus,2)
```

Though this kind of formula would do a nice job of computing the status, there might be some circumstances that would point to an entirely different status. You could override the formula by manually typing your revised classification, but doing so would be frustrating for a couple of reasons.

Whenever you overwrite a formula with hardwired text, you are potentially losing information. If you wanted to reinstate the original formula, you could clone it from one of the neighboring cells. What makes you so sure that the neighboring cell would contain the correct formula, or even any formula (its original formula may have been wiped out as well)?

You could have the formula that computes the status and your overridden value, side by side. Displaying both creates clutter and will be confusing to the reader of your spreadsheet.

Having the best of both worlds

What if you could have a formula that computes the status? What if you could type a value into the Status column and the computed status went away? What if the moment that you erase the manually typed value, the computed value instantly reappears? That's exactly what happens in this spreadsheet. Here's how it works.

Two columns are used and are effectively overlaid one on top of each other. One of these allows you to type in a value into the status column. The other one watches to see whether you've typed in anything. If you have, it does nothing. If you don't type in a value or un-erase a hardwired value, the spreadsheet automatically computes the status and displays it so that it appears to be located in the same status column. Though it relies on an illusion, it's an effective one.

- It renders correctly on the screen so that you don't see the status in two different locations.

- It prints correctly so that the status, whether overridden or computed, appears in a single column.

- Conditional formatting is correctly applied for each status type.

- The override and un-erase features allow you to switch back and forth as often as you like between hardwired values and formulas, without loss of information.

- The other cells can interpret the combined information of hardwired status and computed status as an unambiguous single value.

Despite how well the override and un-erase feature works, it does have some serious drawbacks. One of these is that the column in which the status is computed must have a certain fixed width that is dependent upon the font size and type (and must use a monospace font).

Superimposing two columns into one is not a best practice. Sometimes you have to bypass the best practice or theoretically elegant way to get things done, however. If your approach really does the job well, you certainly shouldn't lose any sleep over the fact that you were imaginative in your approach.

GOING EASY ON THE EYES

I mentioned that four items need to be fulfilled. The last one is to remove unneeded distractions. There are several things worth noticing in Figure 7-5. When a project has achieved the status "Done," the number of days remaining is instantly eliminated. This helps to get rid of the clutter.

If you have important information to communicate in a complex spreadsheet, reduce the noise level of anything unessential. In this manner, a subtle variation in format could suffice to make important information noticed. There is no need for important information to have to compete with the rest of your spreadsheet for your attention.

Notice that certain of the project descriptions are kind of grayed out. This effect occurs only for the projects that are "Done." By forcing completed projects into the background, the active ones are thrust to the forefront without oversaturating the report. It you want to coax the spreadsheet cells to grab your attention, you need only do a little prodding. Notice that the project description for tasks 9 and 16 are in italics. This is because these particular projects have a status of Red. Task 9 is Red because it is overridden. Task 16 is Red because it was the value computed based on the dates.

Peeking under the hood

If you are curious to know how this all works, you should spend some time examining the conditional format settings for columns 3, 4, 6, and 7. For your reference, here are the settings and some of the essential formulas.

Column 3 computes the status using the following formula:

```
=IF(LEN(RC[1])>0,""," "&VLOOKUP(RC[-1]-AsOfDate,Table01,2))
```

The formula looks to see whether you typed anything into the Status column on its immediate right. If you have, it leaves the cell empty. If you haven't typed in anything, it will perform a lookup of the days remaining and produce a value of Red, Amber, or Green. It staggers this over two spaces to the right. If you collapse this column to a zero width, Excel will treat it as a "hidden" column and suppress the visibility to the computed value. Shifting the status two spaces over to the right superimposes the text into the Status column.

The text for the computed status is formatted (see settings in Figure 7-9) to match the formatting of text that would be used if you typed the equivalent by hand into the Status column (that is, column 4).

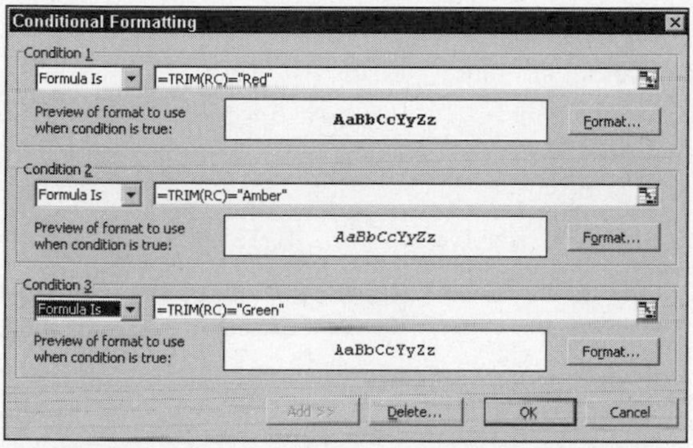

Figure 7–9: Conditional Formatting for the computed status (column 3)

THE PING-PONG EFFECT

Things start to get interesting here. You type something into column 4 to override the computed status (alternatively, you can leave it blank). Column 3 watches what you do. If you do nothing in column 4, column 3 computes a value and superimposes the computed status over column 4. Now column 4, which contains your overridden values, adjusts its formatting based on the combined computed value of status and the overridden value (see Figure 7-10).

You have created a ping-pong effect starting with column 4, going to column 3, and going back again to column 4, all in the space of a single calculation cycle.

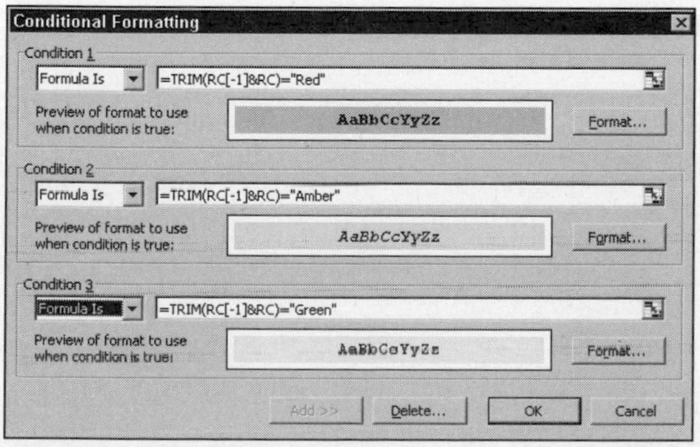

Figure 7–10: Conditional Formatting for the overridden value (column 4)

I will leave you to peruse on your own the formulas and Conditional Format settings for columns 6 and 7.

If you have more time (and the inclination)

You could generalize and improve on this report tool. Here are some things you may want to consider:

- ◆ You could expand on the available status categories to gray out or colorize project descriptions for other categories, such as Inactive, On Hold, Canceled, or Transferred.

- ◆ You might want to generalize your criteria to include project priority, budget priority, or other factors. You may also find it helpful to separate out the logic for the computed status (column 3) and perform detailed computations in another worksheet.

- ◆ You could remove the hardwired number in the Conditional Format settings. For example, the Conditional Formatting in column 6 uses hardwired values. It could be replaced with a computed value or a user-defined name, referring to cells on the same sheet.

Perimeter Surveillance: Smart Borders

So far, all the discussion of Smart Data has been silent on the dynamic adjusting of cell borders. It's time to look at how borders can come into play.

At some time or another, you or anyone else in your office must have had to prepare a table containing data that was complex and could have benefited from appropriate placement of borders. Perhaps, in addition to being complex and constantly changing, the table also incorporated live computations.

Okay, it's not too difficult to format a table. Someone gives you the data. You format the table (by hand). Two days later, the data has been revised and is given to you again. Some new rows have been added, others deleted. Some of the content in the text has been changed. In fact, there are changes scattered all over the place.

You ask yourself, "Do I revise the beautiful document that I slaved over, risking errors or omissions, or do I start from scratch and beautify the new document I just received?" Wouldn't it be nice if you needed only to copy and paste the values, have the table auto-formatted, perhaps have it tweaked just slightly, and be done with it?

Well, you can. That's what the "auto-bordering" spreadsheet is all about. In the Take-Away file (ch07-05PerimeterSurveillance.xls) on the CD-ROM with this book, you will find a description of what it does, the steps you will need to use it, some caveats on its usage, and the specific instructions to extend it (see Figure 7-11).

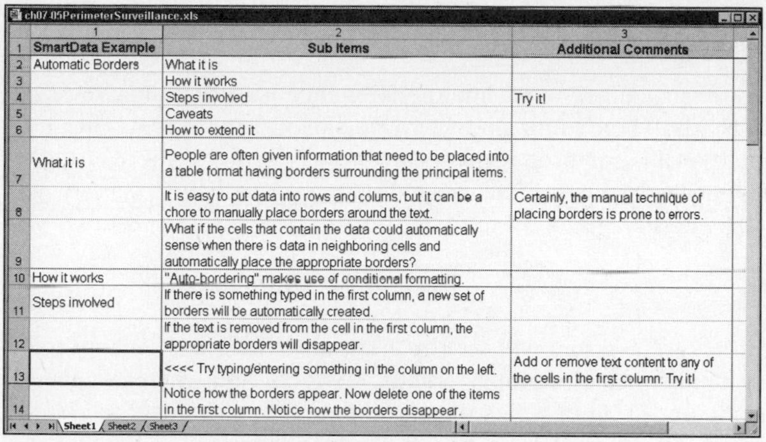

Figure 7-11: Smart Borders sense the positioning of your text.

The technique to create automatic borders is relatively simple. Once again, Conditional Formatting is called into play. Figure 7-12 shows you the basic idea, and here are the main points:

◆ If the cell in the first column is not empty and is not a terminating mark (in this case, an isolated character space), then surround the cell on three borders: left, top, and right.

◆ If there is nothing in the first column, continue the left and right borders on the sides of each cell.

◆ If a terminating mark is sensed (a character space), then place a border on the top of this cell. Because this line is a terminating line, placing the border on top is really helping to put the bottom line on the region of cells having automatic borders.

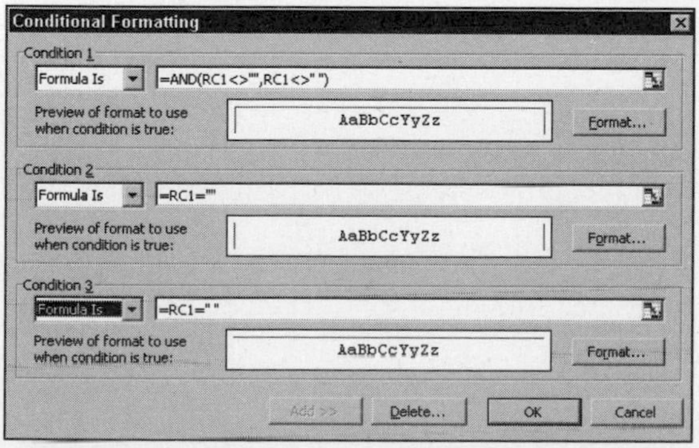

Figure 7-12: Conditional format settings used for Smart Borders

Miscellaneous Topics

By this time, you probably know more about Conditional Formatting than you ever thought you would. Alas, there's one more item you should know about. The "formulas" in the Conditional Formatting windows are incapable of directly referring to cells residing in other worksheets. You can enlist the aid of helper cells to get around this obstacle. Finally, you need to think about some scalability issues.

Helper cells

If you flip back to Figure 7-4, you will see that cell names such as "LookupTable" can be used in a conditional formatting formula. It works fine when the named range is on the same worksheet in which the conditional format is being set. It will not work if you try to reference data residing on another worksheet.

The easy way to bypass this obstacle is to create a "helper cell." Helper cells reside on the same worksheet as do your conditionally formatted cells. These helper cells can use conventional spreadsheet formulas to retrieve the values from another worksheet. After the value can be accessed on the local worksheet, it is fair game for a conditional formatting formula. The file ch07-06HelperCellExample.xls provides a working illustration of how Conditional Formatting can make use of data residing in a separate worksheet (see Figures 7-13 and 7-14).

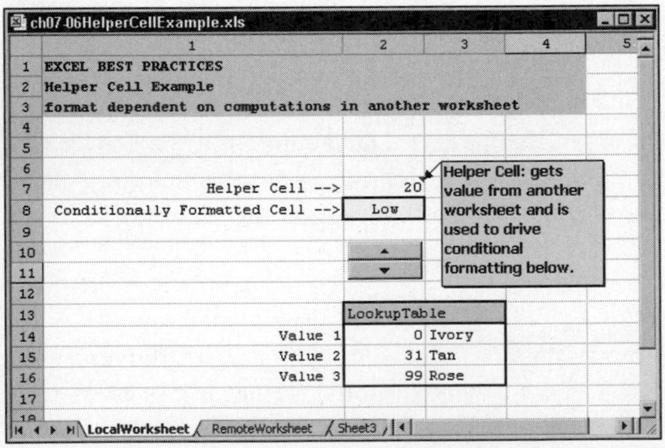

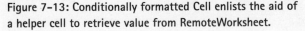

Figure 7-13: Conditionally formatted Cell enlists the aid of a helper cell to retrieve value from RemoteWorksheet.

The helper cell retrieves a value computed from another worksheet. Its formula is

```
=ch07-06HelperCellExample.xls!ForeignValue
```

ForeignValue is obtained through a computation. You can go to the RemoteWorksheet and manually enter the value of one of the cells. The cell ForeignValue will amplify this value by a factor of 10. You can then switch back to LocalWorksheet to see that Helper_Cell has picked up this amplified value. The Conditionally Formatted Cell uses Helper_Cell to dynamically determine its format (see Figure 7-14).

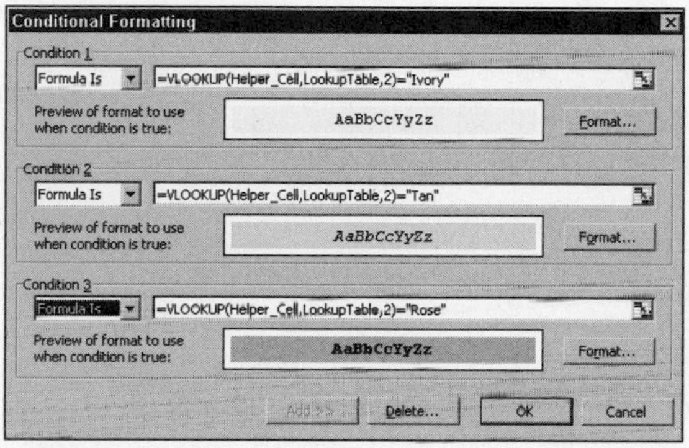

Figure 7-14: Formulas based on the Helper_Cell value

The key point in all of this is that you can "pierce the worksheet veil" if you absolutely need data from a remote worksheet to dynamically drive the conditional format on your local worksheet.

Enlisting the aid of helper cells can be quite advantageous, but it comes at a price. One of the benefits of having multiple worksheets is that you can hide the behind-the-scenes computations. Helper cells will necessarily dredge up some of this information onto the local worksheet. This could complicate the layout of your spreadsheet presentation on the screen and when it's printed.

Scalability issues

Smart Data and Conditional Formatting is great, but you won't want to overuse it. Aside from creating visual clutter, if you apply conditional formatting to every cell in your worksheet, the performance of your spreadsheet computations goes down quickly.

So, here is some simple, good advice:

◆ Separate your presentation layer from the rest of your spreadsheet.

◆ Apply these fancy formatting techniques only to the specific portions of your presentation layer where they will improve communication of information you want people to notice.

Choose the best match

The Excel functions `CHOOSE` and `MATCH` work well together. Look at how this is used to compute the values "Low," "Medium," and "High" in the following formula of the helper cell example:

```
=CHOOSE(MATCH(Helper_Cell,ValueList),"Low","Medium","High")
```

The formula takes the `Helper_Cell` value and finds its pecking order in the list of values (0, 31, 99). Depending on which one is appropriate, it doles out the appropriate characterization (of Low, Medium, or High).

Closing Thoughts

I'm sure that Smart Data has "colored your thoughts" (pun intended) on making your spreadsheets snazzier. Remember the following things:

◆ The use of Smart Data can be a significant digression, both for you while you are creating the spreadsheet and for your audience, who may not be tuned into your presentation but is trying to look beyond it to see what the numbers mean. So, make your use of Smart Data succinct and purposeful.

◆ The key feature that sets Smart Data apart from conventional conditional formatting lies in the tight coupling between what is happening in the spreadsheet and the responding visual signals.

◆ A key factor for achieving the tight coupling is that a specific context is assumed. You are the person who is going to be deciding what that context is. The truly effective use of Smart Data is more readily achieved when you have a focused, single-purpose reason to employ its use.

In this restricted context, you can make assumptions about how your data will behave. Your ability to bank on those assumptions is what allows you to achieve the tight integration between the data's behavior and its visual representation. After you start to change your spreadsheet, the assumptions you made can quickly unravel. For this reason, the specific use of Smart Data tends to take the form of a one-of-a-kind application.

It's perfectly fine to choose not to use Smart Data. You shouldn't forgo one of its key lessons: getting different parts of a spreadsheet to work together in harmony. To gain a better understanding of how to tightly connect the data across a large and complex spreadsheet while keeping the components loosely coupled and independent, look at the first part of the next chapter, specifically the discussion on analysis of data and the Data Viewer tool. It provides a wonderful illustration of the layered pattern approach outlined in Chapter 2, "Mastering Spreadsheet Construction Techniques."

Chapter 8

Analyzing Data

IN THIS CHAPTER

- Understanding Seasonal Data

- Working with and customizing the Data Viewer Tool

- Getting the basics on Stochastic and Markov Processes

- Using Fast Fourier Transforms in Excel and a sample spreadsheet tool

- Quantifying Uncertainty: Techniques and Rules

- Crafting data with the Excel Goal Seek and Solver Tools

- Obtaining more precision from the Excel goal-seeking facility

- Understanding the basics of optimization and the art of data sculpting

- Working through an optimization problem

- Interpreting the Answer, Sensitivity, and Limits Reports in the Excel Solver facility

THIS CHAPTER HAS A BIT more mathematical heft than the rest of *Excel Best Practices for Business*. It is also a relatively long chapter. If you are like most readers, you will want to turn your attention to the sections about seasonal data and the Data Viewer tool. The treatment of this essential topic is nonmathematical and will provide you with practical techniques and an enjoyable tool for analyzing seasonal trends. It also contains some important and indispensable techniques you need to know. I assure you, you will have fun using the Data Viewer tool.

Did you ever need to do "fuzzy" math? There are surely some of you who will be interested in how uncertain data mixes and meshes with the rest of your spreadsheets. If you have two or more numbers that are only approximately known, how do you add or multiply them together? How do you quantify the combined uncertainty? There's a whole section that gives you a concrete way, once and for all, to quantify uncertainty and place it on firm ground. You will find a detailed, worked-out example of how these techniques can be used in analyzing financial statements when the data contains approximate information. Aside from having working techniques, you will see that uncertainty can be treated using specific mathematical rules. The techniques outlined here will play a role in the chapters concerning spreadsheet auditing.

The next part of the chapter deals with a topic I call "data sculpting." Traditional spreadsheet formulas can go only so far in analyzing data. People often resort to efforts outside the spreadsheet to address some essentially quantitative problem. In the hopes that they got the best answer, they proceed to plug the numbers into the spreadsheet to see whether they've improved their situation. If you run a business operation and are trying to cut costs without sacrificing quality of service, how and where are you going to do it? How much will you be able to save? How do you know that the solution you picked will offer the best savings? Although this is at root, a business and management problem, it is also a quantitative problem that could reside firmly in the domain of optimization.

Excel has a tool called the Solver that lets you analyze problems of this kind. The facility can be extremely powerful. It gives you the opportunity to state your problem as a free-form spreadsheet, analyze the numbers and relationships, and mold or recast your decision data to provide the best possible outcome.

This tool, although powerful, is nontraditional in the spreadsheet sense. It behaves differently, has its own terminology, and has to be told specific kinds of information. I introduce you to useful practices so that you will have some reasonable idea of how to use the Solver tool. These include techniques for setting up your spreadsheets for use with the Solver, including real-world assumptions that you will need to incorporate into your spreadsheets. I show you how to more efficiently explain your business problem to the Solver. The Solver can come up with a supposedly optimal answer. It can also provide you with supplementary reports that will help you to determine how realistic the solution may be. If you decide to use the tool, you need to be able to meaningfully interpret these supplementary reports. I give you some pointers that will get you on the road to using this tool.

Does this chapter seem interesting? Regardless of how much time you care to spend on analyzing data, read through the section about seasonal data and the Data Viewer tool. Make sure you try using that tool.

Charting Your Course in a Sea of Data

Data comes in many different varieties. They are far too numerous to classify comprehensively or systematically. Of particular interest is time series data.

In broad strokes, time series data can be categorized into the following groups, each of which lends itself to a different kind of analysis:

◆ Seasonal data analysis

◆ Stochastic and Markovian data analysis

◆ Fourier Transforms and Fourier Analysis

I discuss cyclic and seasonal data and the use of moving averages to ferret out basic trends (generally referred to as "deseasonalizing" data). In this regard, I've provided a general purpose spreadsheet tool for you to use to deseasonalize your own data. You'll want to pay attention to the structure of this tool because it can enable you to manage much more complex sets of data and considerably improve your agility in the use of moving averages.

Detailed coverage of Stochastic and Markovian processes is beyond the scope of this book. Because this is an important topic, I still want to describe some of the basic properties so that you have at least a sense of what these processes are. Also provided is a spreadsheet that simulates these processes to model stock price behavior.

Those of you wishing to push the pedal to the metal may want to explore the Excel Fast Fourier Transform tool. This chapter provides a brief example, enough to get you started and see how it could be useful. However, I do not pursue this topic at any real level of detail.

It's important to look at the section that follows on seasonal data analysis. If you are not mathematically inclined, don't concern yourselves with Stochastic and Markovian processes, or for that matter, Fourier Transforms.

Seasonal data

Often, the data that you look at (especially Web and economic data) is cyclical or seasonal in nature. There are two aspects to understanding cycles. One of these is to anticipate the rollercoaster swings. Swings are important because they indicate the actual peaks and troughs. In some sense, these swings are "noise" to a deeper undercurrent. The other aspect is the underlying trend independent of the swings. Moving averages can often be used to eliminate the swings. The key is to find the magic interval or time duration that makes that cyclical behavior "disappear" so that you can see what is really going on behind the scenes.

The Excel Analysis ToolPak sports a Moving Average facility. This traditional facility is not nearly agile enough to elucidate the patterns you might seek. To be sure, you can absolutely use the Analysis ToolPak. But each time you run through the analysis, you will have to specify the interval, or how many pieces of data are to be included in the moving average. How are you going to "discover" the magic interval where the cyclic effects disappear unless you happen to "stumble" upon the right combination of parameters? Wouldn't it be nice if you could just click a spinner control button to adjust the interval? Why stop there? You may have tons of data and might want to concentrate on selected portions. Why not give yourself more control to do just that? This is what your Data Viewer tool (see the file ch08-03DataViewer.xls on the CD-ROM with this book) provides.

The Data Viewer tool

Figure 8-1 shows a four-day moving average that's superimposed over actual data taken at some point in time. The chart in Figure 8-1 displays only one of two pieces of data that's being tracked over a duration exceeding a year. If you go to the worksheet tab labeled SourceData, you will see a list of dates beginning with 12/1/2003 and extending to 1/14/2005. It is flanked on the right by two columns containing data for each of these dates.

This tool follows the blueprint of layering that is outlined in Chapter 2, "Mastering Spreadsheet Construction Techniques." If you haven't read Chapter 2 or feel the need to refresh your memory, go and review the section on complex spreadsheets; it's important.

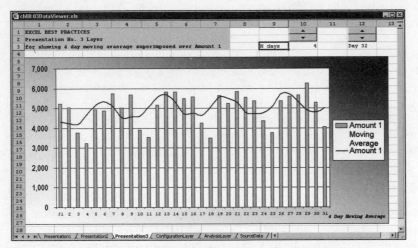

Figure 8-1: Stream of serial data and a four-day moving average

Notice the various worksheet tabs in the Data Viewer tool. The Analysis Layer is separated from the Source Data (they are on different worksheet tabs). The Analysis Layer contains the computationally heavy formulas. It minimizes overhead by retrieving only the data that it needs, and it performs specific calculations on only a limited portion of data at any time. This calculation engine also reads values from a separate ConfigurationLayer worksheet tab (which contains such data as the level of precision and information about where the source data can be found). The presentation layers (of which there are three) know nothing about how the data was computed. They retrieve data only from the Analysis Layer and allow the user to select a starting point on the timeline and the interval to be used for moving averages. Because all the handy work is done behind the scenes and the presentation layers are fully interactive, the presentation layers double as de facto analysis tools.

THE SOURCE DATA LAYER

I specifically want you to pay attention to the fact that layering permits you to handle large amounts of data and simultaneously keep things simple. Your SourceData worksheet could contain more than two columns of data. There's no reason why you couldn't place 20 or 30 columns of data. For that matter, you could place as many as 255 columns of data instead of the two that are there now. On the ConfigurationLayer worksheet, you can specify which two columns you want to pull in for analysis. Nothing limits you to only 411 rows of data. You could populate your SourceData worksheet with thousands of rows of data. Of course, you probably wouldn't want to bloat your spreadsheet with too much data, because the disk space required for your spreadsheet would become large. Because of the layered approach, adding more data to the spreadsheet doesn't add much overhead to the spreadsheet. It only takes up more disk space.

THE ANALYSIS LAYER

The Analysis Layer does all the complex computations in the spreadsheet, as follows:

◆ It pulls in two of the sets of data as specified in the Configuration Layer. The data it retrieves spans a 31-day interval plus data for an additional number of days as needed for the computation of moving averages.

◆ It pulls in the dates listed for the 31-day interval and transforms these dates to day numbers for the particular month. If the date is the first of the month, it inserts the first letter of the month in front of the 1. This column is used in Excel charts in the various presentation layers. Look at the series of day numbers along the bottom of the chart in Figure 8-1. Notice that January 1st is labeled J1. Predictably, February 1st would be labeled F1.

◆ It computes the moving average for these 31 selected days. The spinner control buttons on the various worksheet tabs allow you to move up and down the timeline, as well as change the interval of the moving average. The interval can be dynamically adjusted from 1 day up to 31 days.

The total number of computations handled by the Analysis Layer is 253. That's it. It doesn't matter whether you have 60 or 16,000 rows of data in your SourceData worksheet. The number of computations performed in the Analysis Layer still remains 253. Talk about bang for the buck; you have a very scalable spreadsheet.

When you look at the Analysis Layer, you will see that is not terribly pretty; it's not meant to be. It leaves the pretty graphics and charts up to the presentation layers.

THE PRESENTATION LAYERS

There are three presentation layers. You've already seen one of them (Figure 8-1). Before looking at the others, notice the gradation in the background pattern of the Chart area. This was created using Fill Effect. Pay particular attention to the fact that the gradation moves in a diagonal direction, away from the vertical and horizontal axes. This design aids in the visibility of the numbers and labels along each of the axes. An alternative strategy would be to adjust the appearance of the numbers and labels associated with the axes. You may need to adjust the appearance so that it renders well on the screen *and* is clear when printed in black and white.

The three presentation layers all have a reasonably consistent look and feel. In each of them (as with the Analysis Layer), you can move up and down the timeline. In two of the three presentation layers, you can adjust the interval of the moving average. Looking at Figure 8-2, note that when the moving average is adjusted to an interval of 21 days, the cyclical bumps all disappear. Now you can see the real trends of how the data is changing over time. This process of smoothing out the data is called "deseasonalizing."

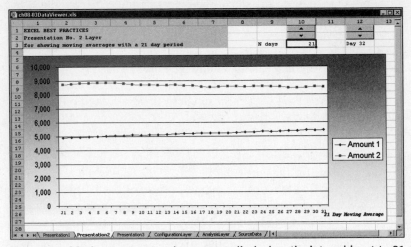

Figure 8-2: Moving average trends are noncyclical when the interval is set to 21 days.

Actually, the moving averages appear as smooth lines on 7-, 14-, 21-, and 28-day intervals. This should come as no surprise. However, there is no guarantee that *your* data will behave with this kind of regularity.

The two items appearing in the legend in Figure 8-2 are dynamically determined by accessing the information contained in the ConfigurationLayer worksheet. The label "21 Day Moving Average" is dynamically determined as well. Both of these labels were prepared using essentially the same process. This technique is described in a later section of this chapter (see the Best Practice Tip in the section on Fourier Transforms). There are two good reasons to use dynamic labeling in charts:

1. Labels involving computations can correctly reflect information that is displayed in the chart (for example, as you adjust the moving average interval using the spinner control button, the label embedded inside the chart is adjusted accordingly).

2. You may have multiple charts that refer to a common label. If they are all mapped to a common location, you need only adjust that label from one location to instantly update all the charts. Because you won't have to touch the charts to adjust the labels, you effectively remove the risk of accidentally clobbering a legend, title, or some other part of a chart.

When you put your own data in the SourceData worksheet, I doubt that you will want to keep the labels Amount 1 and Amount 2 in the legends for the various charts. Rather than manually edit the charts, you can just go the ConfigurationLayer worksheet and adjust the labels there.

One more observation is warranted before moving on to the formalization of metrics in data analysis. The spinner control buttons are linked to a common point. The `MovingAveragePeriod` is set in `R3C10` of the Presentation2 worksheet. The `ItemNumber` (the starting position in your timeline) is set in `R2C11` of the Presentation1 worksheet. These could have been placed in the ConfigurationLayer worksheet instead. Although doing so would be logical, it might not be practical. You want to jump ahead in the timeline from day 32 to day 320. While you're in the Presentation1 worksheet, you can type over the number 32 to make it 320. You will instantly jump to day 320 without having to click the up arrow of the spinner control button 288 times.

Where you place specific pieces of data that is referenced from multiple locations is a design decision. Centralizing such data (such as in the ConfigurationLayer worksheet) might be a logical approach, but there can be valid and good reasons to place the data in other locations.

Stochastic and Markov processes

Data that behaves stochastically is said to change over time in a way that is uncertain. Sometimes, only the current value of stochastically driven data can influence subsequent values. Prior historical trends cannot become reliable indicators of future outcomes. Processes that govern such data are known as Markov processes. A good example of this is the behavior of stock prices. If the lack of predictability were not the case, you and I could easily predict future outcomes based on past history and could make ourselves quite rich in the stock market.

In any case, it will be quite convenient to associate the behavior of stock prices with "random walks," or Brownian motion. Random walk simulations help to capture important mathematical properties. Particularly, in random walks, the drift, `delta z` is:

```
delta z = epsilon * SQRT(delta t)
```

where `epsilon` is a random value generated from a standard normal distribution. This quantity (`epsilon`) can be generated using `NORMINV(RAND(),0,1)`. For short walks, use this:

```
mean of delta z = 0
standard deviation of delta z = SQRT(delta t)
variance of delta z = delta t
```

You may wish to take a look at the file ch08-01RandomWalk.xls on your CD-ROM. It shows how a stock price can vary. Every time that a calculation is performed, a new random walk is taken. You can force recalculations in Excel by pressing Crtl+=.

If you want to generate values that simulate random values having a Normal distribution (that is, centered around a mean of `average_value` and a standard deviation of `std_dev`), you can use the formula:

`=NORMINV(RAND(),average_value,std_dev)`.

Fourier Transforms and Fourier Analysis

There are many occurrences in nature and in business that can appear quite complex. Sometimes, the major contributors giving rise to elaborate behavior may be limited to a small number of underlying components. These components can be thought of as individual heartbeats, each with its own cycle. When combined, the merged behavior is remarkably similar to the original system.

Specific mathematical techniques have been devised to decompose time series data into underlying components. Specifically, a technique known as Fast Fourier Transforms (FFT) translates time domain patterns (such as time series data) into a frequency domain spectrum.

Excel comes equipped with this FFT capability. To get you started, I want you to become familiar with how you can use the tool. I am not going to cover any of the details behind the FFT algorithm or its mathematics.

What follows is a sample usage of the FFT tool. Rather than take an example from a typical business setting, I find it much easier to illustrate the use of the tool by taking data from an entirely different subject domain. The data set you will be working with is sunspot activity collected over a couple of centuries.

Those of you who understand the theory behind Fourier Transforms will quickly see how you can use the tool and supplied spreadsheet. Those of you who are entirely unacquainted with Fourier Transforms may find the topic of sunspot activity more entertaining and won't mind the digression. Even if you're not interested in Fourier Transforms or sunspot activity, I hope that you'll read on. I want to acquaint you with some useful spreadsheet techniques.

USAGE OF FOURIER ANALYSIS IN EXCEL AND A SAMPLE SPREADSHEET TOOL

Open the spreadsheet called ch08-02FFT.xls on the CD-ROM with this book. You will find time series data of sunspot activity from 1747 to 2002. This file comprises 256 data points. The FFT facility of Excel will munch on data only in groups of 2 to a given power. For instance, it will be happy with 32, 64, or 128 data points. It will complain if you try to give it, say, 63 or 65 data points. Excel has a limit on how many data points the FFT facility will accept (the maximum for Excel 2003 is 4096 data points).

The raw data from the ch08-02FFT.xls spreadsheet file was obtained from the National Oceanographic and Atmospheric Administration FTP site:

`ftp://ftp.ngdc.noaa.gov/STP/SOLAR_DATA/SUNSPOT_NUMBERS`

The data is publicly available information, and I encourage you to explore the site.

LOADING EXCEL ADD-INS

To generate the Fourier Transforms, you will first need to ascertain that the Analysis ToolPak is loaded in Excel. Choose Tools →Add-Ins→Analysis ToolPak. While you're at it, you should also select the Solver Add-In option. The Solver will be used later in the chapter. You should be aware that the Add-Ins window displays an Analysis ToolPak - VBA option. Don't confuse this with the Analysis ToolPak option immediately above it. Unless you're planning to do a whole bunch of Visual Basic programming, you won't find this VBA option necessary. It won't hurt, either, although loading additional Add-ins will increase the overall overhead of running Excel.

In any case, when you have the Analysis ToolPak option added, you should be able to select Data Analysis from the Tools menu. Fourier Analysis should be about the ninth item in a list of close to 20 different kinds of data analysis facilities. After selecting Fourier Analysis, you should see a screen similar to Figure 8-3.

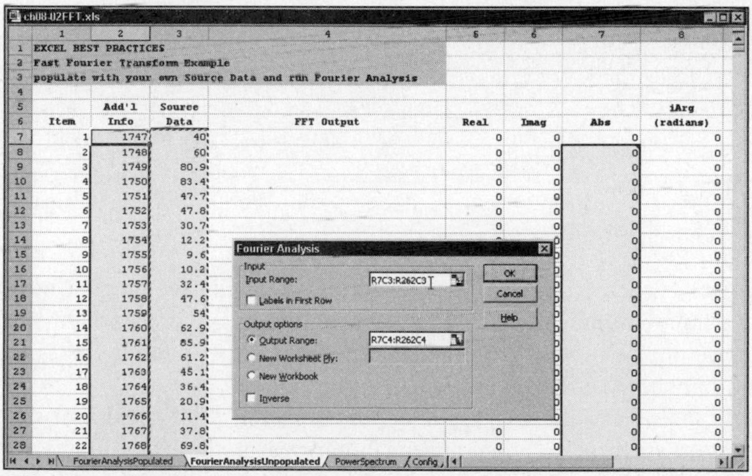

Figure 8-3: Generating Fourier Transforms

You will be prompted for an input range. This range will consist of your serial sequence of data that occupies a single column. From the standpoint of the FFT tool, the column representing years (ranging from 1747 through 2002) flies right out the window. The FFT tool is *only* interested in the *consecutive sequence* of source data, such as the sunspot counts. It will *not* take into account the year or the time duration spanning between any two adjacent points of data. Remember, the number of data points that you specify in your Input Range must be an exact power of 2, and is not to exceed 4096.

You will be given a number of output options. You can have Excel place the output in an entirely new spreadsheet (that is, a new workbook). Or, you can create a new worksheet in an existing workbook. You will be given a chance to specify the name for the new sheet. Alternatively, you can specify an output range, placing it, for example, alongside where the data is sitting (see Figure 8-4). When you specify the range, it will have to match the number of data points in your input range.

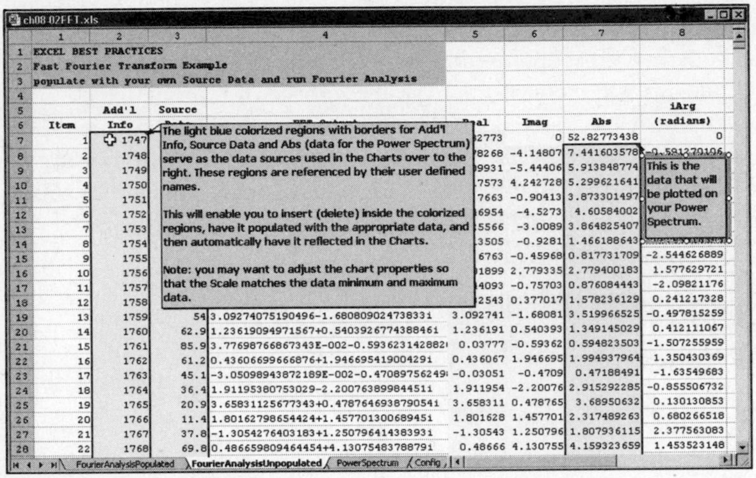

Figure 8-4: Generated FFT data

If you're successful in correctly specifying the data, you should see the FFT output as a group of complex numbers identifying the real and imaginary parts of the complex numbers. Do not fret about the numbers being Complex or about what the terms *complex* and *imaginary numbers* mean.

In the worksheet shown in Figure 8-4, the columns on the right break out the complex number into their respective real and imaginary parts (the Excel functions IMREAL and IMAGINARY accomplish this). The next column over to the right provides the magnitude or contribution for each frequency in the Power Spectrum. (This is the "Abs" data that appears in Figure 8-4. It is plotted as a Power Spectrum in the bottom chart of Figure 8-5.)

Take a look at the Best Practice Tip you will find useful in preparing an Excel chart like the top one in Figure 8-5.

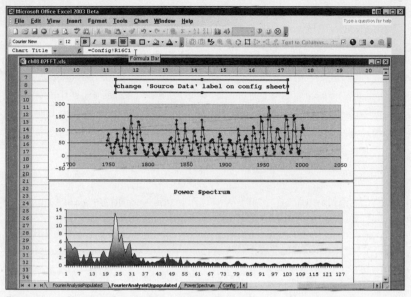

Figure 8–5: Charting Source Data and the Power Spectrum, and customizing chart titles

When you prepare an Excel chart and include a chart title, you enter only a text phrase. If you want the title to be dynamic, you're out of luck — unless you go through the back door. Here's how you do it:

Create a chart title as you normally would. Select the chart title (like the one shown in the upper chart of Figure 8-5). Click the Edit line in the Formula Bar. Create a new formula, because none has been provided. You do this by entering a formula that specifies the cell containing the information that you want to display in the chart title. Excel will now automatically pick up the contents of that cell and display it in the chart title.

Note: The "formula" you enter is not a true formula. You cannot use it to perform computations such as

```
=2*3
```

or

```
=Config!R16C1&" "&TEXT(TODAY(),"m/d/yyyy")
```

Though you can't enter a true formula that performs a computation, nothing stops you from performing the computation in a regular spreadsheet cell and then using a pseudo-formula to dynamically display its value In your charts.

A detailed discussion of Fourier Transforms and their applications in business, engineering, or medicine is beyond the scope of this book. Consult the end of this chapter for suggested further reading.

In the Output Range, you can check the Inverse box to tell Excel that you want to perform an Inverse Fourier Transform. This will allow you to take a complex set of frequency components and generate a sequence of data that corresponds to this set of frequencies.

Before I move on to quantification of uncertainty, you should be aware that the Excel Fourier Analysis facility allows you to compute Inverse Fourier Transforms. Refer back to Figure 8-3. Note that there's a box you can check for the inverse operation. Unless you specifically need to perform an Inverse Fourier Transform, leave this box unchecked.

Quantifying Uncertainty: Techniques and Rules

The prior section of this chapter showed you how to uncover hidden trends in time-varying and seasonal data. It is satisfying when you have a practical technique that you know will work for a well-defined and frequently occurring problem. What about situations that are clearly understood and quantifiable, but the data that drives the spreadsheet results is not readily available?

Consider the preparation of a pro forma income statement. The spreadsheet you create will have all the standard features of an income statement. Your revenue less the cost of selling goods will give you the gross profits. Take away the operating and other expenses and you'll have the income before taxes. There's no uncertainty in specifying the principles for this kind of a spreadsheet or in the specification of the formulas used.

What is uncertain is the numbers that feed into the spreadsheet. The actual quantities have yet to happen. There is no way to be absolutely certain how many units of product X you will be selling over the next three quarters. You might have a contract, but contracts can be broken. Your ability to sell an assembled product may be dependent on third-party suppliers. You know how reliable they can be. The cost of various components may fluctuate depending upon market conditions. Even if you price it aggressively, the marketplace may suddenly veer in a different direction, leaving you to sit with merchandise that doesn't move.

One of the reasons that you would be using a spreadsheet is to model the economics of decisions you make. The unit purchase price of an item could be dependent upon the extent to which you engage in volume purchasing. You buy too little and you don't achieve the economies of scale that your competitor enjoys. There may be missed sales opportunities because you can't produce needed quantities of the product on a timely basis. Purchasing more means that you will incur a greater outlay in expenses. Your spreadsheet model will enable you to quantify a variety of different scenarios and determine the impact to your bottom-line profitability. There may be too many uncertainties, each of which can independently alter your bottom line.

Quantifying uncertainty: The technique of Adding in Quadrature

At first glance, "quantifying uncertainty" may seem to be a contradiction of terms. Actually, it's not. Start off with some simple examples.

Suppose that the selling price of a product is $100.00. Your sales department has been asked by the company CFO to estimate the number of units that will be sold as well as "realistic" upper and lower limits on quantities sold. Your department expects to sell 1,000 such items plus or minus 100 items during the next quarter. This means that your sales could range anywhere between the range of $90,000 to $110,000. You could easily quantify uncertainties of this kind in your spreadsheet.

Your company is highly diversified. Suppose that one of the other divisions is selling an entirely unrelated product to a different market. That division's product sells for $150 and they anticipate selling 1150 ± 200 items during the next quarter. Their revenue could be anywhere between $142,500 and $202,500. As does your sales department, the other company division uses "realistic" estimates for uncertainty. They can easily quantify uncertainties of this kind in their spreadsheets.

I would like to add a little wrinkle. The company CFO wants to prepare a forecast of total company sales and expenses for the next quarter. The CFO will be combining the high, middle, and low estimates across all company departments and divisions. Assume that the sales and expenses for each of the product lines are quite unrelated to one another. How would you combine the uncertainties in a meaningful way?

WHEN TWO AND TWO DON'T ADD UP TO FOUR

Think of it the following way (especially if you want to be "counting pennies"). Your sales department expects to sell a certain amount. There is a 50 percent chance that you will meet or do better than you project, and a 50 percent chance that you will not do as well as you project. It's essentially a toss-up. Another company division is in the same boat with regard to projected estimates. So are a third and a fourth division.

What are the chances that all four divisions will all surpass projected estimates? Remember that all the products are *unrelated* to one another. The estimates of sales for each of these products will vary randomly within a given range.

If they all independently vary in a random or uncertain manner within their respective range, it is less likely that they will all exceed their projected estimates than that they will produce a mixed response. By the same token, it is less likely that they will all under-perform.

Some notes on mathematical notation

Certain formulas, functions, and notations are used in this section. If you are unfamiliar with these, follow the explanations in this sidebar.

The Excel function ABS returns the positive value of a number, regardless of whether the number is positive or negative. The following should be evident:

```
=ABS(234)                          returns 234
=ABS(-25)                          returns 25

=ABS(0)                            returns 0
```

Exponents are shown the way they would be entered in a spreadsheet formula. The following should be evident:

```
=9^2                               is the same as 9*9

                                   and returns 81
```

The Greek letter delta, signified by δ, denotes the amount of change or variation in the item that immediately follows it. It is purely used as a shorthand notation.

THE WHOLE IS LESS THAN THE SUM OF ITS PARTS

To help you grapple with all this uncertainty, there is a technique called *Adding in Quadrature*. It states the following:

> If you have a group of variables, each of which is normally distributed (that is, on a bell curve) and are independent of one another, then the variation of the combined variables will follow certain rules.

The variables can be the things such as the number of units sold, selling price per unit, purchases, and so forth. Until the information has come to pass, there is uncertainty surrounding each of these quantities. Each of these is equally likely to vary within some range. Mathematically, you can express these as:

$$X \pm \delta X$$
$$Y \pm \delta Y$$

If X and Y are added to or subtracted from one another, and their variations δX and δY are random and independent of each other, then the combined variation for $X \pm Y$ is

Listing 8-1: Uncertainty for $X \pm Y$

$$\sqrt{(\delta X)^2 + (\delta Y)^2}$$

If X and Y are multiplied together, the combined variation for X*Y is:

Listing 8-2: Uncertainty for X*Y

$$ABS(X \cdot Y)\sqrt{(\delta X)^2 + (\delta Y)^2}$$

To illustrate this, the combined revenues of your product (X) and the other division's product (Y) would likely be including the combined variation (see Table 8-1).

TABLE 8-1 COMBINED UNCERTAINTY BASED ON THE ADDING
            IN QUADRATURE TECHNIQUE

Item	Projected Revenue	Uncertainty	Lower Range	Upper Range
Product X	100000	10000	110000	90000
Product Y	172500	30000	142500	202500
Combined revenue	272500	31623	240877	304123

The uncertainty amount of $31,623 is calculated in the following way:

$$= SQRT\left(10000^2 + 30000^2\right)$$

The number is rounded to the nearest dollar. Notice that uncertainty of $31,623 is less than the $40,000 (the linear sum of $10,000 and $30,000). The upper and lower ranges are just the combined projected revenue of $272,500 plus or minus $31,623, respectively.

Adding in Quadrature: A real-world example

There are specific rules for adding in quadrature. I'll explain these soon enough. Right now, I'd rather continue with a detailed application of this technique. You might want to open the file ch08-04UncertaintyAnalysis.xls on the CD-ROM (or see Figure 8-6) to follow along with the example in this section.

This spreadsheet shows a pro forma statement that projects the income and profitability in some quarter that has yet to happen. For this reason, an Uncertainty column appears to the right of the Amount column. Note that some of the cells are colorized. Those colorized regions are the projected amounts and their basic uncertainties. Table 8-2 reproduces these values. No formula is involved in the determination of the uncertainty for these colorized cells. It is just a given value. Somewhere along the way, a determination was made that the *basic* uncertainties shown in the table are all equally likely (that is, no amount is overstated or understated in relation to the others).

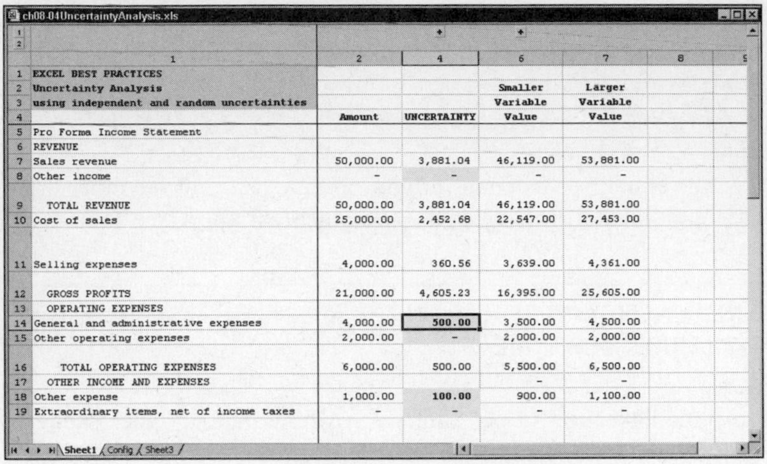

	1	2	4	6	7
1	EXCEL BEST PRACTICES				
2	Uncertainty Analysis			Smaller	Larger
3	using independent and random uncertainties			Variable	Variable
4		Amount	UNCERTAINTY	Value	Value
5	Pro Forma Income Statement				
6	REVENUE				
7	Sales revenue	50,000.00	3,881.04	46,119.00	53,881.00
8	Other income	-	-	-	-
9	TOTAL REVENUE	50,000.00	3,881.04	46,119.00	53,881.00
10	Cost of sales	25,000.00	2,452.68	22,547.00	27,453.00
11	Selling expenses	4,000.00	360.56	3,639.00	4,361.00
12	GROSS PROFITS	21,000.00	4,605.23	16,395.00	25,605.00
13	OPERATING EXPENSES				
14	General and administrative expenses	4,000.00	500.00	3,500.00	4,500.00
15	Other operating expenses	2,000.00	-	2,000.00	2,000.00
16	TOTAL OPERATING EXPENSES	6,000.00	500.00	5,500.00	6,500.00
17	OTHER INCOME AND EXPENSES			-	-
18	Other expense	1,000.00	100.00	900.00	1,100.00
19	Extraordinary items, net of income taxes	-	-	-	-

Figure 8-6: Pro forma statement along with uncertainty estimates

TABLE 8-2 PROJECTED AMOUNTS AND THEIR BASIC UNCERTAINTIES

Line Item	Projected Amount	Basic Uncertainty
Other income	0	0
General and administrative expenses	4,000.00	500.00
Other operating expenses	2,000.00	0
Other expense	1,000.00	100.00
Extraordinary items, net of income taxes	0	0
Selling Price	12.50	0.25
Units	4,000.00	300.00
Beginning inventory	10,500.00	0
Purchases	20,000.00	500.00
CGS percentage factor	0.50	0.03
Selling Price per unit	1.00	0.05
Tax rate	0.40	0

Uncertainty estimates that are non-colorized are *derived* uncertainties computed in a manner similar to that of the $31,623 of the previous section. To better understand how the derived uncertainties are computed, you can click the plus (+) symbol at the top of the spreadsheet. This will expand the column and show you a copy of the formula that was used to compute derived uncertainties (see Figure 8-7).

As you can see, the colorized or basic uncertainties are just plain numbers. The non-colorized or derived uncertainties use formulas based on those shown in Listings 8-1 and 8-2, shown previously.

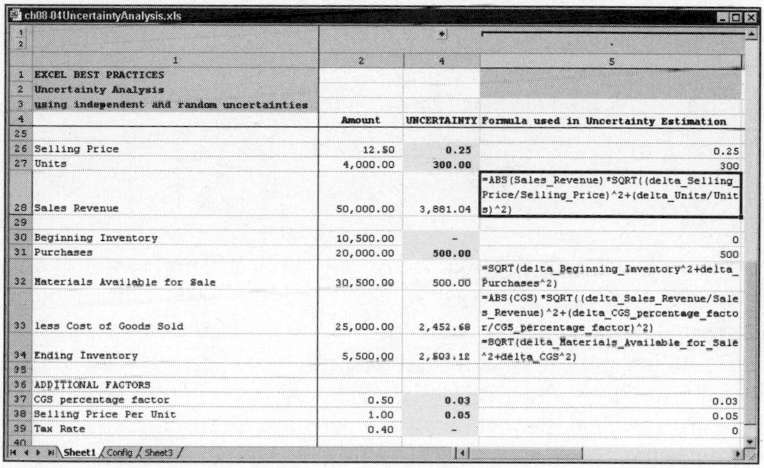

Figure 8–7: Underlying formulas for estimating derived uncertainties

Consider, for the moment, Sales Revenue. It is based on:

$$= Selling\_Price * Units$$

The uncertainty of Sales Revenue uses the formula in Listing 8-2, earlier in the chapter. The formula for derived uncertainty of Sales Revenue is

$$= ABS(\text{Sales\_Revenue}) * \sqrt{\left(\frac{\text{delta\_Selling\_Price}}{\text{Selling Price}}\right)^2 + \left(\frac{\text{delta\_Units}}{\text{Units}}\right)^2}$$

On rows 27 and 28 of Figure 8-8, you can see that the uncertainty of the selling price or delta_Selling_Price is 0.25. The selling price is 12.50. Accordingly, (0.25/12.5)^2 is 0.0004. The uncertainty of the number of units sold, or delta_Units, is 300. The number of units is 4000. Accordingly, (300/4000)^2 is 0.005625. The sales revenue is 50000. The formula becomes:

$$= ABS(50000) * SQRT(0.0004 + 0.005625)$$

This returns a result of $3,881.04, rounded to the nearest cent.

The formulas are a little tedious to apply, but the technique will give you a handle on analyzing uncertainty in your spreadsheet.

When preparing your spreadsheet for uncertainty analysis, you should consider giving all your relevant cells user-defined names. Do the same for the uncertainty estimates. This way, as you click cells to construct your formulas, you will see meaningful cell names, such as:

```
delta_Selling_Price/Selling_Price
```

instead of:

```
R26C5/R26C4
```

This will make your formulas much easier to understand and validate.

Uncertainty rules

If you've read up to this point, you've already covered the basics on how to quantify uncertainty. This section is a reference guide. It is laced with mathematical equations. If you are not mathematically inclined, don't worry about this section. If you feel you need to go beyond the basics, then read on.

Unlike the rest of *Excel Best Practices for Business*, this section is steeped in mathematics. There are a couple of equations using calculus. Those of you who are ambitious but do not toil with equations on a daily basis may want to take a look at the sidebar entitled "A crash course on differential calculus."

Listings 8-1 and 8-2, along with the spreadsheet example, give enough of a basis for you to do some competent uncertainty analysis on your own. This section spells out uncertainty rules a little more formally and identifies limiting constraints when independence of the uncertainties cannot be guaranteed.

The given set of variables x_1, x_2, x_3, ... may have uncertainties δx_1, δx_2, δx_3, ...

Likewise, think of an additional set of variables y_1, y_2, y_3, ... which have uncertainties δy_1, δy_2, δy_3, ...

The following rules (Listings 8-3 through 8-9) apply when the set of variables x_1, x_2, x_3, ... and y_1, y_2, y_3, ... are combined. The first rule relates to uncertainty of a quantity x raised to a given power or exponent (see Listing 8-3).

Listing 8-3: Uncertainty in a power

```
given
```

$$q = x^n$$

δq is the uncertainty

$$\delta q = ABS(n \cdot q) \frac{\delta x}{ABS(x)}$$

Listing 8–4: Uncertainty with a quantity multiplied by an exact quantity

given

$$q = A \cdot x$$
$$\delta q = ABS(A) \cdot \delta x$$

δq is the uncertainty

$$q = f(x) \qquad q \text{ is a function of } x$$

Listing 8–5: Uncertainty in a function of a single variable x

given

$$q = f(x) \qquad q \text{ is a function of } x$$

δq is the uncertainty

$$\delta q \approx ABS\left(\frac{dq}{dx}\right) \cdot \delta x$$

The following applies to Listing 8-6.

If you are determining the uncertainty relating to the addition and/or subtraction of many individual items, you can use the Excel SUMSQ function instead of squaring and adding each of the individual terms. For example, if the individual uncertainties are located in two distinct regions, R5C3:R15C3 and R5C6:R15C9, you can compute the combined uncertainty as:

```
=SQRT(SUMSQ(R5C3:R15C3,R5C6:R15C9))
```

If these cells have user-defined names, you can use the names instead.

Listing 8–6: Uncertainty for $x_1 + x_2 + x_3 + \ldots -(y_1 + y_2 + y_3 + \ldots)$

given

$$q = x_1 + x_2 + x_3 + \ldots -(y_1 + y_2 + y_3 + \ldots)$$

δq is the combined uncertainty

$$\delta q = \sqrt{(\delta x_1)^2 + (\delta x_2)^2 + (\delta x_3)^2 + \ldots + (\delta y_1)^2 + (\delta y_2)^2 + (\delta y_3)^2 + \ldots}$$

when $x_1, x_2, x_3, \ldots, y_1, y_2, y_3, \ldots$ are not all independent, then:

$$\delta q \leq \delta x_1 + \delta x_2 + \delta x_3 + \ldots \delta y_1 + \delta y_2 + \delta y_3 + \ldots$$

The following applies for both Listings 8-7 and 8-8.

If you are determining the uncertainty relating to repeated multiplication and/or division of individual items, you can use the Excel `SUMSQ` function in combination of entering an array, instead of individually dividing the uncertainties by their respective base number, squaring it and then performing the sum.

For example, if you are taking the product of numbers in the range `R5C2:R15C2` and their respective uncertainties are in the immediately adjacent column (`R5C3:R15C3`), you can compute the product of `R5C3:R15C3` as:

`=PRODUCT(R5C3:R15C3)`

You can compute the combined uncertainty as:

`=ABS(PRODUCT(R5C2:R15C2))*SQRT(SUMSQ(R5C3:R15C3/R5C2:R15C2))`

Because you are applying a division between two sets of cell ranges, you will have to enter this formula as an array; otherwise, you will see a `#VALUE!` error message. To enter this formula as an array, you must select the Edit line of the Formula Bar and press Ctrl+Shift+Enter. Your error message should disappear and your formula should be surrounded with curly braces, like the following:

`{=ABS(PRODUCT(R5C2:R15C2))*SQRT(SUMSQ(R5C3:R15C3/R5C2:R15C2))}`

Remember, if the cells within your range have user-defined names, you can use the names instead. This will make your formula easier to read.

Listing 8–7: Uncertainty for $x_1*x_2*x_3*\ldots$

`given`

$$q = x_1 \cdot x_2 \cdot x_3 \cdot \ldots$$

δq is the combined uncertainty

$$\delta q = ABS(x_1 \cdot x_2 \cdot x_3 \cdot \ldots) \cdot \sqrt{\left(\frac{\delta x_1}{x_1}\right)^2 + \left(\frac{\delta x_2}{x_2}\right)^2 + \left(\frac{\delta x_3}{x_3}\right)^2 + \ldots}$$

when $x_1, x_2, x_3, \dots$ are not all independent, then:

$$\delta q \leq ABS(x_1 \cdot x_2 \cdot x_3 \cdot \dots) \cdot \left(\frac{\delta x_1}{ABS(x_1)} + \frac{\delta x_2}{ABS(x_2)} + \frac{\delta x_3}{ABS(x_3)} + \dots \right)$$

Listing 8-8: Uncertainty for $(x_1{}^*x_2{}^*x_3{}^*\dots)/(y_1{}^*y_2{}^*y_3{}^*\dots)$

given

$$q = \frac{x_1 \cdot x_2 \cdot x_3 \cdot \dots}{y_1 \cdot y_2 \cdot y_3 \cdot \dots}$$

δq is the combined uncertainty

$\delta q =$

$$ABS\left(\frac{x_1 \cdot x_2 \cdot x_3 \cdot \dots}{y_1 \cdot y_2 \cdot y_3 \cdot \dots} \right) \cdot$$

$$\sqrt{\left(\frac{\delta x_1}{x_1}\right)^2 + \left(\frac{\delta x_2}{x_2}\right)^2 + \left(\frac{\delta x_3}{x_3}\right)^2 + \dots + \left(\frac{\delta y_1}{y_1}\right)^2 + \left(\frac{\delta y_2}{y_2}\right)^2 + \left(\frac{\delta y_3}{y_3}\right)^2 + \dots}$$

when $x_1, x_2, x_3, \dots, y_1, y_2, y_3, \dots$ are not all independent, then:

$$\delta q \leq ABS\left(\frac{x_1 \cdot x_2 \cdot x_3 \cdot \dots}{y_1 \cdot y_2 \cdot y_3 \cdot \dots} \right) \cdot$$

$$\left(\frac{\delta x_1}{ABS(x_1)} + \frac{\delta x_2}{ABS(x_2)} + \frac{\delta x_3}{ABS(x_3)} + \dots + \frac{\delta y_1}{ABS(y_1)} + \frac{\delta y_2}{ABS(y_2)} + \frac{\delta y_3}{ABS(y_3)} + \dots \right)$$

Listing 8-9: Uncertainty for a differentiable function of more than one variable

given

$$q = f\left(x_1, x_2, x_3, \dots \right)$$

δq is the uncertainty

$$\delta q \approx \sqrt{\left(\frac{\partial q}{\partial x_1} \cdot \delta x_1 \right)^2 + \left(\frac{\partial q}{\partial x_2} \cdot x_2 \right)^2 + \left(\frac{\partial q}{\partial x_3} \cdot x_3 \right)^2 + \dots}$$

when $x_1, x_2, x_3, \dots$ are not all independent, then:

$$\delta q \leq ABS\left(\frac{\partial q}{\partial x_1} \right) \delta x_1 + ABS\left(\frac{\partial q}{\partial x_2} \right) \delta x_2 + ABS\left(\frac{\partial q}{\partial x_3} \right) \delta x_3 + \dots$$

Listings 8-5 and 8-9 involve derivatives and partial derivatives. To better understand these two listings, you may want to explore the sidebar "A crash course on differential calculus." If and when you need to apply the rules in Listings 8-5 and 8-9, you will have to either:

◆ Calculate the derivatives and/or partial derivatives separately and insert them into your spreadsheet formulas where appropriate.

◆ Or use third-party tools such as MathematicaLink with Mathematica (products from Wolfram Research) to perform the calculations and insert the results into your spreadsheet. The detailed implementation steps lie beyond the scope of this book.

A crash course on differential calculus

A number of you may be interested in applying the uncertainty rules but may not be quite sure how to compute a "derivative" or have the slightest idea of what to do with it. If you're one of those people, read on.

I want you to learn three things:

◆ How to calculate certain types of derivatives

◆ How to insert these expressions into your uncertainty formulas

◆ What derivatives can be used for

A hitchhiker's guide to computing derivatives

This bare-bones guide will give you a vastly oversimplified approach on how to compute a derivative of a function. Rather than state formal rules, I give you some examples and state some generalizations that are easy to remember.

Function of the variable (x)	Derivative you will compute
55	0
$x + 55$	1
$13x + 55$	13
x^2	$2x$
x^3	$3x^2$
x^{20}	$20x^{19}$
$2 \cdot x^{20} + 13 \cdot x + 55$	$40 \cdot x^{19} + 13$
$(1 + x)^4$	$4 \cdot (1 + x)^3$

In general:

- The derivative of any constant (such as the number 55) is always 0.

- The derivative of a sum of a bunch of expressions is the sum of the derivatives of each of the individual expressions, as in:

$$\text{Derivative}(A + B + C) = \text{Derivative}(A) + \text{Derivative}(B) + \text{Derivative}(C)$$

- A derivative of a constant value (such as the number 13) times some expression is equal to the constant times the derivative of the expression:

  Derivative of x^n is $n \cdot x^{n-1}$

  where n is a constant value (such as the number 3)

  $$\text{Derivative}\left(A^n\right) = n \cdot A^{n-1} \cdot \text{Derivative}(A)$$

  where n is a constant value (such as the number 3).

- If A is some function of x and B is some other function of x, then

  $$\text{Derivative}(A \cdot B) = A \cdot \text{Derivative}(B) + \text{Derivative}(A) \cdot B$$

This last equation is called the Chain Rule. Don't worry if the generalizations seem a bit abstract. Just stick to the sample examples and you'll do fine.

Computing derivatives for your spreadsheet uncertainty formulas

Suppose you are computing compounded interest rates in some fund you are planning to invest in. You are asked to hold on to your investment for a period of three years. The rate of return will be some number that is computed at a future date. You are expecting a 5 percent rate of return, compounded annually. You are not absolutely certain that the fund will perform as anticipated. The variation in the interest rate could be as much as 0.5 percent. If you invest $10,000 today, how much do you stand to gain or lose on your investment?

Your formula for compounded interest is

$$q = \text{InvestmentAmount} \cdot (1 + x)^n$$

In the formula, I used "x" instead of a more conversational name such as "r" or "rate'" to make it clear that this is a function of just one variable, x. You can compute the variation δq using Listing 8-5, as demonstrated by the following sequence of steps:

$$\delta q \approx ABS(dq/dx) \cdot \delta x$$

Continued

A crash course on differential calculus (Continued)

$$dq/dx = \text{Derivative InvestmentAmount} \cdot (1+x)^n$$
$$= \text{InvestmentAmount} \cdot \text{Derivative}\left((1+x)^n\right)$$
$$= \text{InvestmentAmount} \cdot n \cdot (1+x)^{n-1} \cdot \text{Derivative}\,(1+x)$$
$$= \text{InvestmentAmount} \cdot n \cdot (1+x)^{n-1} \cdot \text{Derivative}\,(x)$$
$$= \text{InvestmentAmount} \cdot n \cdot (1+x)^{n-1} \cdot 1$$
$$= \text{InvestmentAmount} \cdot n \cdot (1+x)^{n-1}$$

So, the estimate for δq is given by:

$$\delta q \approx ABS\left(\text{InvestmentAmount} \cdot n \cdot (1+x)^{n-1}\right) \cdot \delta x$$

Because all the values are positive, the Absolute Value function is not necessary.

$$\delta q \approx \text{InvestmentAmount} \cdot n \cdot (1+x)^{n-1} \cdot \delta x$$

You are now at the stage at which you can incorporate the expression for computing δq directly in your spreadsheet. Open the ch08-05UncertaintyAnalysisDeriv.xls spreadsheet file. Note that it has the following formulas and values:

Location	Formula	Displayed Value
X	0.05	0.050
N_Years	3	3.000
Function	=Invest*(1+X)^N_Years	11576.250
delta_X	0.005	0.005
delta_Q	=ABS(Invest*3*(1+X)^(N_Years-1))*delta_X	165.375
Invest	10000	10000.000

Your return at the end of three years is approximately $11,576 ± 165. Stated differently, your return is likely to be between $11,411 and $11,741.

Other uses of derivatives

A derivative of a function of some variable x is the rate of change of that function. Try to visualize what *rate of change* actually means.

Imagine yourself driving a car up a hill. Your car is "sloped" upward as your elevation increases. When you get to the top of the hill, your slope is leveled, or zero. As you continue moving past the top, your car slopes downward (that is, is negatively sloped). The steeper your slope, the faster your elevation decreases as you move forward. Finally, as you approach the bottom of the hill, your slope levels out once again (the slope will be zero). Your elevation will not decrease unless you drive somewhere where there is a downward (negative) slope in the road.

This notion of inclines, and slopes, and reaching the maximum/minimum points is the crux of what differential calculus is all about. So, how do you calculate these slopes? Well, you've been doing it all along. It's called the *derivative*.

Let me give you a trivial case and then I want you to tackle something much harder and more relevant.

Suppose I give you a function $y = x^2+3$. You know from high school algebra that this is a parabolic-shaped curve (much like a hill but turned upside down). Applying the techniques in this sidebar, you can figure out that `Derivative(`x^2`+3)` is $2 \cdot x$. When x is greater than zero, the derivative, or slope, is going to be a positive number. When x is less than zero, the derivative, or slope, is going to be a negative number. When x is zero, the derivative, $2 \cdot x$, will be zero. This is the point at which the curve bottoms out and can't get any lower.

If you can figure out what value of x will give you a zero slope or derivative, then you will uncover one of the minimum or maximum points in the curve. So, what's the big deal? A curve is just a curve. Right? Well, not quite. Imagine that your parabolic curve, or whatever shape it happens to be, represents a combination of various costs and expense factors. If you could pump out a derivative for your cost function, just as you pumped one out for x^2+3, and further determine the value of x that will make the derivative zero, you might just be able to minimize those costs.

You're going to take and apply this thinking to an important problem in inventory management known as Economic Order Quantity, or EOQ. Imagine that you operate a large warehouse that stores a ready supply of electronic chips. Your company uses 50,000 ASIC chips each year and purchases them at $12.50 each. It costs $300 to process and receive each order. Your carrying cost for housing and maintaining the inventory is $1.50 per chip per year. How many chips should you order each time and how many times a year should you place orders to minimize costs?

Your total costs (TC) are made up of your ordering costs (OC) plus your carrying costs (CC) plus your purchase costs (PC).

$$TC = OC + CC + PC$$

$$\text{Derivative}\,(TC) = \text{Derivative}\,(OC) + \text{Derivative}\,(CC) + \text{Derivative}\,(PC)$$

To get your minimum costs, you will want to drive the derivative of TC to 0. In other words:

$$\text{Derivative}\,(TC) = 0$$

This is the same as:

$$0 = \text{Derivative}\,(OC) + \text{Derivative}\,(CC) + \text{Derivative}\,(PC)$$

Continued

A crash course on differential calculus (Continued)

Figure out the specifics for each of these three, solve for the value of x so that the derivatives add up to zero, and you'll be well on your way to solving a classic and important economics problem.

Begin by chiseling at the problem. Your purchase costs (PC) are going to be based on the overall price paid per unit times the total number of units purchased per year. The number of units is 50,000 and the purchase cost is $12.50 per unit. It really doesn't matter what the numbers are. The purchase costs remain "CONSTANT" no matter what you do. When you try to calculate `Derivative(PC)`, you will be calculating a derivative of a constant. The derivative of any constant, including 625,000, is zero ($12.50 per unit * 50000 units = $625,000). No matter what the purchase costs are, so long as they are unchanging, the `Derivative(PC) = 0`.

Your ordering costs are going to be the cost per order CPO, times the total units in a year TU (a constant number) divided by the order size of x unit. The cost per order, CPO, is also a constant number regardless of the order size. Stated mathematically, the ordering cost, OC is

$$OC = CPO \cdot TU/x$$

$$= CPO \cdot TU \cdot x^{-1}$$

$$\text{Derivative}(OC) = \text{Derivative}\left(CPO \cdot TU \cdot x^{-1}\right)$$

Because CPO and TC are constants

$$\text{Derivative}(OC) = CPO \cdot TU \cdot \text{Derivative}\left(x^{-1}\right)$$

$$= CPO \cdot TU \cdot (-1) \cdot x^{-2}$$

$$= -\frac{CPO \cdot TU}{x^2}$$

When you keep a ready supply in inventory, there are bound to be costs such as storage, handling, insurance, spoilage, and so forth. These carrying costs will be based on the "average" inventory level times the per-unit carrying cost (PUC). The average inventory level (that is, number of items you generally have on stock) will be the midway between your high point in the inventory (order size x) and your low point (zero, or at least very close to zero). This midway point is x/2. Mathematically speaking, your carrying cost is

$$CC = \frac{PUC \cdot x}{2}$$

Because PUC is a constant number

$$\text{Derivative } (CC) = \frac{PUC}{2} \cdot \text{Derivative } (x)$$

$$= \frac{PUC}{2} \cdot 1$$

$$= \frac{PUC}{2}$$

Now you can string these three derivative expressions together to obtain Derivative(TC). If you can find the value of x so that

$$\text{Derivative } (TC) = 0$$

you will have found the order quantity that will minimize your total costs.

$$\text{Derivative } (TC) = \text{Derivative } (OC) + \text{Derivative } (CC) + \text{Derivative } (PC)$$

$$\text{Derivative } (TC) = -\frac{CPO \cdot TU}{x^2} + \frac{PUC}{2} + 0$$

Setting the Derivative(TC) to 0, you have:

$$0 = -\frac{CPO \cdot TU}{x^2} + \frac{PUC}{2}$$

Rearranging the expressions, you have:

$$x^2 = \frac{2 \cdot CPO \cdot TU}{PUC}$$

So then x becomes:

$$x = \sqrt{\frac{2 \cdot CPO \cdot TU}{PUC}}$$

You just solved an important and classic problem in inventory management using just a touch of differential calculus. By the way, the number of chips that you should purchase with each order is approximately 4,472 [=SQRT(2*300*50000/1.5)].

Data Sculpting: Crafting Data with the Excel Goal Seek and Solver Tools

Unlike the situation of uncertainty, in which you don't have control over specific and important quantities in your spreadsheet, you might find yourself having complete control over a variety of factors that have to satisfy a complicated set of constraints and objectives.

Somehow, implicit in the formulas of your already populated spreadsheet are adjustments you can make to your data that get the numbers work together the way you want. The typical "what if?" approach to trying different numbers to see what fits may require countless number of guesses to get the numbers the way you want.

It will be helpful to eliminate some of the guesswork. Excel provides you with two facilities to do this.

One of these is a built-in facility labeled Goal Seek on the Tools menu. There's nothing complicated about using this tool. However, you'll sometimes want a little more precision than the tool normally provides. I'll show you how to gain that extra precision.

The other tool is an Excel Add-In called the Solver. It can be an extremely useful and powerful tool if you know how to set up your problems. I'll give you some guidance on how to do this and show you some of the kinds of problems you can solve.

The Goal Seek tool

The goal seeking facility is a simple tool that you can access by selecting Goal Seek from the Tools menu to open the Goal Seek dialog box (see Figure 8-8). This dialog box prompts you for:

◆ The cell location of your "target cell" whose value you want changed.

◆ The "target value" you want it to become.

◆ The location of the "changing cell" that you will allow Excel to freely vary so that the target cell's value closely matches the designated target value.

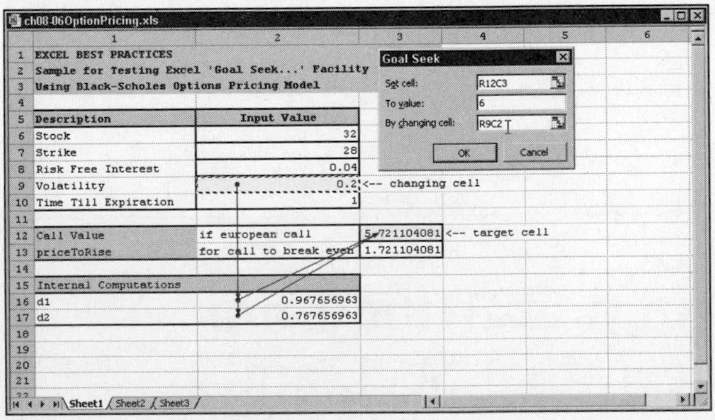

Figure 8-8: Goal Seek option settings

For this to work, your target cell must contain a formula that in some way depends upon the value of the changing cell. The relationship between the changing cell and the target cell can be indirect. If you have read through Appendix A, you may have noticed that there are toolbar icons to trace dependents. You can use this facility to visually identify which set of cells are "dependent upon" a given spreadsheet cell. Specifically, when you click the Trace Dependents icon or choose it from the Formula Auditing submenu of the Excel Tools menu, Excel will draw blue arrows from the currently selected cell to all the dependent cells. You can find more information on dependencies in Chapter 11, "Spreadsheet Auditing: Challenging the Numbers of Others."

Figure 8-8 shows these Trace Dependent arrows starting from the changing cell and leading up to the target cell.

Use the Trace Dependents toolbar icon (see Appendix A for setup) to see immediately affected or dependent cells. Press the toolbar icon repeatedly to view the cascading effects of changing your cell. Alternatively, you can start with your target cell and work your way backwards to all cells that contribute to the target cell. Clicking the Trace Precedents toolbar icon allows you to view the cells that can affect the value of your current cell.

From looking at Figure 8-9, you can see that the goal-seeking facility finds a value for the changing cell (Volatility) that gets the target cell (Call Option Price) reasonably close to your target value (6).

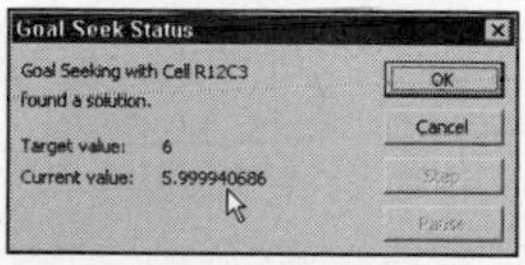

Figure 8-9: Goal Seek gets
Current value reasonably
close to Target value.

SQUEEZING WATER FROM A STONE

Note that the current value of the Call Option Price is 5.99994 and not 6. In many situations, this precision in Goal Seek may be sufficiently accurate. In some situations, the precision may not land you as close as you need to get.

If you need finer precision, magnify the difference and use that magnified difference as the target cell instead of using your original target cell (which was your Call Option Value).

The spreadsheet file ch08-06OptionPricing.xls shows you how to do this (Figure 8-10).

Your target value (the "To value" in your Goal Seek dialog box) should be pegged at 0. Although the Goal Seek tool gets your target value down to -0.0004, your computed Call Option Value becomes *exactly* 6 (instead of 5.99994).

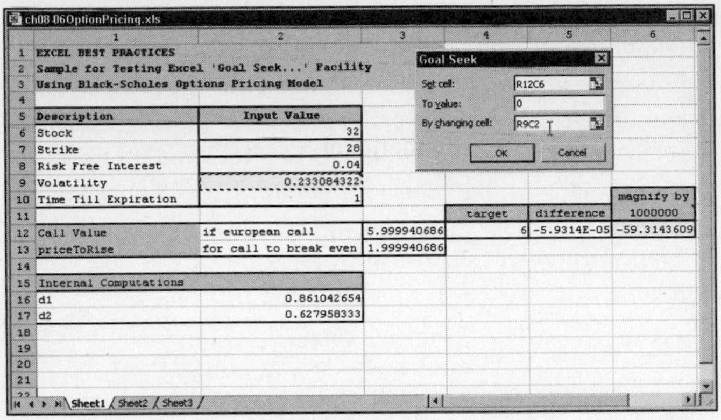

Figure 8-10: Use Goal Seek on magnified difference and try setting it to the value of 0.

SOME THINGS YOU NEED TO BE AWARE OF

Before moving on to a description of the Solver tool, you should be aware of several things:

- ◆ Sometimes, your formulas that contribute to the target cell are not "stable" enough for the goal seeking facility to render a solution even though a solution exists.

- ◆ It is also possible that there is no value in the changing cell that will satisfy the target cell's constraint value.

- ◆ Often, more than one value of the changing cell will satisfy the needed value for your target cell. Consider the equation $øxpx^2+x$. If your target value is 40, two values of x can be found by the Goal Seek facility. If your changing cell (x) starts of with a positive number like 5, the goal-seeking facility will find the value 5.8442891840903. If your changing cell (x) starts off with a negative number such as -6, the goal-seeking facility will find the value -6.8442875672353. Both of these are correct. You need to be aware that Goal Seek will uncover only one such value at a time. The value obtained can be dependent upon the initial starting value for your changing cell.

Two ideas to keep in mind:

◆ You will need to choose an appropriate starting value for your changing cell when more than one possible value exists that satisfies the Goal Seek constraints.

◆ You may need some separate mathematical analysis to determine how many real valued solutions exist. If It is unclear as to whether a closed form analytical solution exists, you can try repeating the goal-seeking process using different starting values for the changing cell.

The goal seeking facility can be a very effective tool when you need to vary only one spreadsheet cell. Certain circumstances may preclude the use of the goal seeking facility:

◆ You may have a whole bunch of independent cell values that you need to vary at the same time.

◆ The target cell needs to be the maximized or minimized instead of set to a fixed target value.

For situations of this kind, you need to turn to the Solver tool.

Optimization and the art of data sculpting

Mathematical optimization can quickly become esoteric. There needs to be an optimization tool that is accessible to the rest of us. The Solver is one such tool. It permits you to optimize your spreadsheets without having to acquire more than a modicum of concepts, terminology, and practical techniques.

The rest of this chapter is intended to give you some of that know-how so that you can take frequently encountered decision problems you normally don't associate with spreadsheets, and use spreadsheets to solve them.

The Solver really doesn't work inside the spreadsheet formulas. Instead, the Solver plucks out numbers from the worksheet, uses the criteria you feed it, and will try to adjust certain cells so that your constraints and objectives are met.

My principle goal is to give you guidance on two things:

1. How to set up a spreadsheet to use the Solver.

2. How to interpret the results.

THINGS THE SOLVER WILL WANT TO KNOW

To take advantage of the Solver, you need to clearly characterize your optimization problem. This is a good thing for both you and the Solver. Specifically, you have to tell the Solver the following:

◆ What value or objective you are trying to achieve

◆ Which cells you will allow the Solver to adjust (these cannot be formulas)

◆ Specific constraints you don't want the Solver to violate

You may also need to identify specific options before you tell the solver to go run off and do its calculations.

SAMPLE OPTIMIZATION PROBLEM

It's time to open your spreadsheets. Find the file ch08-07LPSolverExample.xls on your CD-ROM (see Figure 8-11).

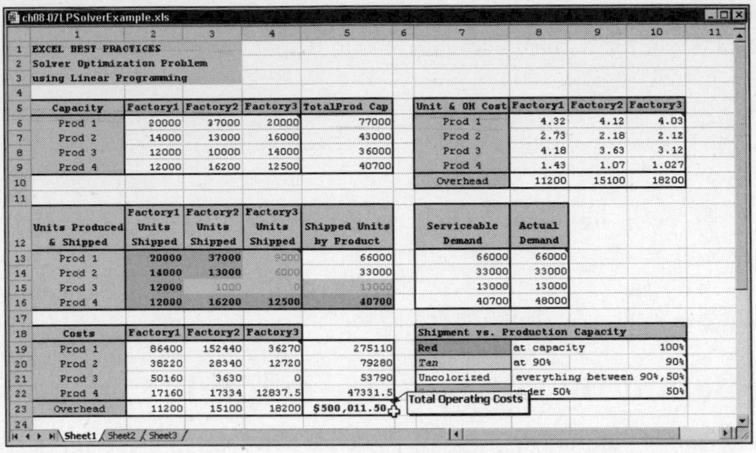

ch08-07LPSolverExample.xls

	1	2	3	4	5	6	7	8	9	10	11
1	EXCEL BEST PRACTICES										
2	Solver Optimization Problem										
3	using Linear Programming										
4											
5	Capacity	Factory1	Factory2	Factory3	TotalProd Cap		Unit & OH Cost	Factory1	Factory2	Factory3	
6	Prod 1	20000	37000	20000	77000		Prod 1	4.32	4.12	4.03	
7	Prod 2	14000	13000	16000	43000		Prod 2	2.73	2.18	2.12	
8	Prod 3	12000	10000	14000	36000		Prod 3	4.18	3.63	3.12	
9	Prod 4	12000	16200	12500	40700		Prod 4	1.43	1.07	1.027	
10							Overhead	11200	15100	18200	
11											
12	Units Produced & Shipped	Factory1 Units Shipped	Factory2 Units Shipped	Factory3 Units Shipped	Shipped Units by Product		Serviceable Demand	Actual Demand			
13	Prod 1	20000	37000	9000	66000		66000	66000			
14	Prod 2	14000	13000	6000	33000		33000	33000			
15	Prod 3	12000	1000	0	13000		13000	13000			
16	Prod 4	12000	16200	12500	40700		40700	48000			
17											
18	Costs	Factory1	Factory2	Factory3			Shipment vs. Production Capacity				
19	Prod 1	86400	152440	36270	275110		Red	at capacity		100%	
20	Prod 2	38220	28340	12720	79280		Tan	at 90%		90%	
21	Prod 3	50160	3630	0	53790		Uncolorized	everything between 90%,50%			
22	Prod 4	17160	17334	12837.5	47331.5			under 50%		50%	
23	Overhead	11200	15100	18200	$500,011.50						
24											

Total Operating Costs

Sheet1 / Sheet2 / Sheet3

Figure 8-11: Optimization example involving minimization of operating costs

This spreadsheet depicts a manufacturing operation of four different product lines from three factories.

Factory 1 is the oldest manufacturing plant. Though it has a lower monthly overhead, the per-unit manufacturing costs are the highest.

Factory 3 became operational just three or four months ago and is poised for expanded production capacity. You want to be mindful of whether a given facility will be well utilized after shipping assignments are made. Therefore, color coding of capacity utilization has been added to the spreadsheet, even though color coding is not a part of the optimization problem. It is not a bad practice to pack your spreadsheets with useful supplementary information.

Your optimization strategy is to minimize the total costs by adjusting the units shipped for each product line at every factory location. You need to tell the Solver these things. In addition, you need to tell it some common-sense constraints that you and I know but that the computer isn't smart enough to figure out on its own. One of these is that the number of units assigned for shipping can't exceed the production capacity. The other is that the units shipped for each product line should match the demand.

SUMMON THE SOLVER

Summon the Solver from the Tools menu. If the Solver option does not appear on your Tools menu, you need to load the Solver Add-in (see the "Loading Excel Add-Ins" section, earlier in this chapter).

With the Solver loaded and ready to go, you need to begin feeding it some information (Figure 8-12).

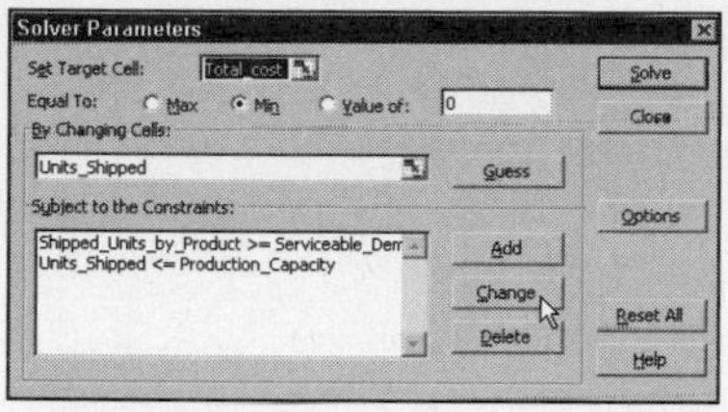

Figure 8-12: Primary screen for setting
the Solver parameters

First, you tell it to set the target cell. Your "Objective Function" (the spreadsheet cell you wish to optimize) is the "Total_Cost." You define this in the Set Target Cell box. Click in this box and then click the spreadsheet cell containing the total cost value. If the cell has a user-defined name such as Total_Cost, the cell name rather than the cell coordinate will be picked. Your Target Cell (that is, Objective Function) can be only a single cell and not a range of multiple cells. The cell you reference must contain an Excel formula. It cannot be a cell value or an empty cell.

You will have to tell the Solver whether you want to maximize the Objective function, minimize it, or try to get it reasonably close to a value that you designate. This last option mimics the goal-seeking facility with some extra bells and whistles (you can define more than one changing cell and specify constraints). The value you supply must be an integer or decimal value.

> **NOTE** If you type a number in the "Value of:" box, remember to click the radio button for this option and not that for the Max or Min option; otherwise, the Solver will ignore the number that you specify and perform an unintended optimization.

Next, you tell the Solver which cells you will allow it to adjust. These are referred to as the adjustable or adjusting cells. You are given the option of having the Solver "guess" which cells you want adjusted to accomplish your optimization. Would you want a third-party software tool to "guess" the constraints for a carefully formulated, multimillion dollar optimization problem? Somehow, I don't think you would.

The cells that the Solver can adjust are specified in the By Changing Cells: region. You indicate these cells by clicking in the input region and then typing in the specific cell references, or just by clicking the appropriate regions of your spreadsheet. Figure 8-12 shows that a group of cells called "Units_Shipped," has already been selected. They correspond to the cell range R13C2:R16C4. You can specify more than one group of cells. Use a comma (,) to separate each group. If you give it cells containing formulas instead of values, the Solver will blow away the formulas when it tries to adjust the cell values.

Important gotcha: If you will be using user-defined names, do not use names that could be construed as cell coordinates in *either* the A1 or R1C1 styles. The Solver tool is easily confused!

After you have specified the adjusting cells, tell the Solver about your constraints. Each constraint is created using the Add button. If you wish to revise an existing constraint, click the particular constraint and then press the Change button, as shown in Figure 8-12. You will see a Change Constraint dialog box, which identifies the cell reference and some formulated constraint (see Figure 8-13). There are five types of constraints.

Figure 8-13: Specifying cell constraints

The first three types of constraints are the following: less than or equal to; equals; and greater than or equal to. The "Cell Reference:" entry must be an actual cell or a range of cells. The "Constraint:" entry can be either a number or cell reference. A valid constraint could be something like this:

```
Units_Shipped<=20000
```

If the Constraint: entry is a cell reference, each of the cells must map to the Cell Reference: entry. The size and shape of the respective cell references have to be the same. For instance, in the constraint:

```
Units_Shipped<=Production_Capacity
```

the cells for `Units_Shipped` maps to `R13C2:R16C4`. `Production_Capacity` maps to `R6C2:R9C4`. Both of these entries occupy a swatch of four rows by three columns.

One thing appears somewhat peculiar. The Constraint: entry always starts with an equal (=) symbol. This has nothing to do with the constraint relationship that you select from the drop-down list.

The last two of the five constraint types are `int` and `bin`. For these two types, you must provide a Cell Reference: entry and leave the Constraint: entry blank. `int` means that the cell reference needs to be restricted to an integer value (basically, a whole number such as 2 or 23). If the constraint type is `bin`, the cell reference must be a 0 or 1.

Care must be taken when specifying integer or binary constraints. The Solver can treat these as integer or binary constraints from the standpoint of its floating-point representation. Having a constraint that's approximately restricted to 0 or 1, or to approximately a whole number, can have significant impact on the optimization outcome!

Fair warning should be given. The Solver cannot solve every kind of problem it is given, even if the problem is well formulated. Also, there are no guarantees that the solution the Solver produces will be the best, or even correct. More often than not, incorrect solutions are the result of giving the Solver incorrect assumptions or mistakenly specifying incorrect Solver options. In any case, you should *always independently verify* the correctness of the Solver's solution. This is a critical step that you should never overlook.

Binary constraint workaround

In some of your optimization problems, you might specify a binary or integer constraint. Sometimes the Solver will provide you with a solution that incorporates a floating-point approximation instead of an exact binary or integer representation. Although the Solver may apply optimization techniques that can tolerate floating-point approximation, such as 0.99999998 instead of 1, the formulas in your spreadsheet that impact the objective function may not be nearly so forgiving.

Here is a technique to treat a number "close enough" to some value as "exactly" that value. It involves using the exact value in place of the approximation when the approximation is close enough. The technique has two parts:

◆ Convert a close-enough approximation of an adjustable cell to an exact value that the rest of your spreadsheet can use.

◆ Signal to the Solver when the binary or integer constraint is deemed to be satisfied.

Such a formula for the first part of this technique might be:

Listing S-1: A test formula with the user-defined name 'Binary_Twin'

```
=IF((ABS(Almost_A_Binary-0.5)-0.5)^2<0.0000001,ROUND(Almost_A_Binary,0),9999)
```

Continued

Binary constraint workaround (Continued)

Assume `Almost_A_Binary` is one of the adjustable cells the Solver can change. The test formula given the user defined name `Binary_Twin` can have one of three possible values: 0, 1, or 9999. It assumes a 0 if `Almost_A_Binary` is reasonably close to zero. It assumes a 1 if `Almost_A_Binary` is reasonably close to one. Otherwise, it will be some alternate value like 9999, to let you know it is nowhere close to being a zero or one. If 0 or 1 is returned, it is up to you to use the exact binary number in your spreadsheet, rather than the `Almost_Binary_Number` that the Solver is allowed to adjust. You will also have to figure out what to do when `Binary_Twin` is 9999.

You need to signal to the Solver when the binary constraint is satisfied (i.e., you only care to know if the `Binary_Twin` is not a 0 or 1). Listing 8-11 will provide this signal.

Listing S-2: Second test formula with the user-defined name 'Binary_Satisfied'
```
=IF(Binary_Twin=9999,10,20)
```

You let the Solver know whether the adjusted cell is good enough by setting one of the constraints to be

```
Binary_satisfied=20
```

Now you have the best of all possible worlds. In your spreadsheet, you can use the exact binary number in place of the approximate one when the approximation is close enough. You also get to tell the Solver precisely when the adjustable cell doesn't require further adjusting. There are two important points to keep in mind:

1. The Solver may still return a floating-point value instead of an exact binary value. At least your spreadsheet can incorporate exact binary values in its place.

2. Depending on how you prepare your optimization spreadsheet, the use of an almost binary or almost integer workaround could be altering your optimization problem to the point at which your resulting solution corresponds to a different problem than the one you think you're solving.

If you decide to use the workaround, apply it with *extreme caution*.

You should be aware that if you select the int or bin type in any of your constraints, you immediately forgo any of the three reports that the Solver can generate after providing a solution. These reports are the Answer Report, Sensitivity Report, and the Limits Report. I explain these shortly.

Before moving to the "Solve" portion of the Solver, I want you to take a look at the Solver options (see Figure 8-14).

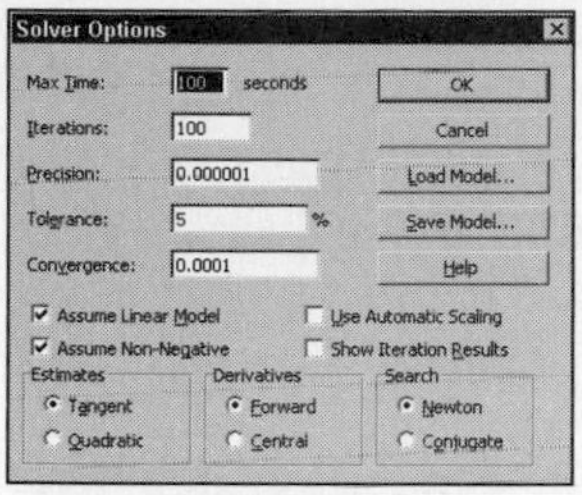

Figure 8-14: Remember to check the boxes
of the Assume Linear Model and Assume
Non-Negative options when performing
linear programming optimizations.

When working with linear programming types of problems, remember to check the boxes for non-negativity and linearity. The optimization problem in the file ch08-07LPSolverExample.xls on the CD-ROM is linear; so make sure that both of these boxes are checked. Non-negativity means that the adjustable cells must be equal to or greater than zero. Non-negativity is a reasonable assumption. In the spreadsheet example, you are not going to have a negative number of units shipped. It turns out that the standard form for all linear programming problems assume non-negativity in the decision variables (that is, adjustable cells). If you don't check the box, you will need to enter the non-negativity conditions in your constraints, which can be a tedious process.

The Show Iteration Results can be useful. As the Solver performs its optimization, it pauses to show you its progress and the various feasible solutions along the way. You can take snapshots of these possibilities and save them as alternative scenarios for later consideration during a side-by-side comparison using the Excel Scenario Manager.

Press the OK button in the Solver Options window. You are now ready to press Solve (see the top-right corner of Figure 8-12). After you press Solve, a Solver Results window pops up and indicates whether a solution was found (see Figure 8-15). Provided that you don't have int- or bin-type constraints, you will have the option to select the Answer, Sensitivity, and Limits Reports.

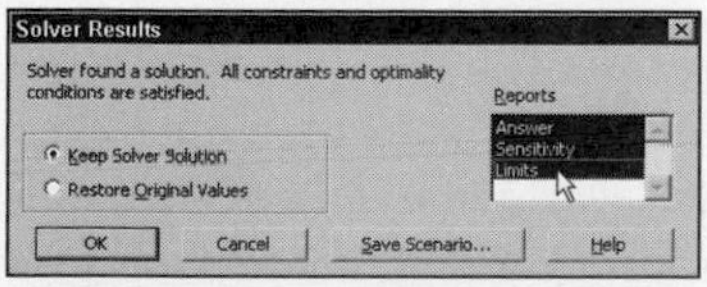

Figure 8-15: The Solver Results
window displays the solution status.

As you view the Solver Results window, you can see your optimization spread-sheet underneath. Sometimes when the Solver Results are reported, you know that the optimization didn't work. You might, for instance, see all the cells in your spreadsheet suddenly jump to zero, or something else that you know cannot be possible. Of course, you can press Cancel or select Restore Original Values and then press 'OK.' Either action will roll back your spreadsheet to its original state – well, almost. You'll recoup your original formulas and values. Whatever mistake you made in the Solver settings that caused the problem still remains. In fact, all the changes you make to settings in the Solver are remembered, *even if you don't run the optimization*. When you closed the Solver Parameters window, it didn't ask whether you wanted to save changes; *it saved the changes without telling you*.

THE SOLVER SEES ONLY ONE WORKSHEET

The Solver "lives" on the worksheet it's associated with. This fact has several important implications:

- ◆ The Solver keeps separate settings for each worksheet in your spreadsheet. You can have as many Solver instances as you have worksheets.

- ◆ Because the Solver constraints and assumptions are local to the worksheet, it cannot directly reference a spreadsheet cell or named reference if that item happens to reside on another worksheet.

This second property of the Solver can be a nuisance. Most of the time, you can write a spreadsheet formula that refers to a name or cell reference in another worksheet, even another spreadsheet. As with conditional formatting, cell references have to be local to the current worksheet.

If you need to reference a cell from another worksheet in your Solver constraints or objective function, you will have to prepare a formula for use in your local worksheet that retrieves the value from the remote worksheet to your local worksheet, and then refer to the local cell in your constraints or objective function. You cannot adjust the cells in another worksheet.

Figure 8-16 shows the optimized solution. Note that you now have worksheet tabs for Analysis Report 1, Sensitivity Report 1, and Limits Report 1.

The good news is that you definitely shaved some dollars off the projected operating costs by shifting the allocation of shipments. This should be visually evident from the shifted colored boxes near the center of the spreadsheet.

REAL-WORLD ADJUSTMENTS

You need to be aware of an important subtlety. One of the optimization constraints was that the Units Shipped by Product is constrained to the Serviceable Demand and not to the Actual Demand. Had you tried running it against the Actual Demand, your optimization run would have failed. This is because the actual demand for the fourth product line is 48,000 units. The respective production capacity is only 40,700. The constraint would not be satisfied.

In real life you're still going to ship out all you can produce, even if you can't meet the Actual Demand. For this reason, serviceable demand caps at the production capacity. This is why the constraint refers to Serviceable Demand.

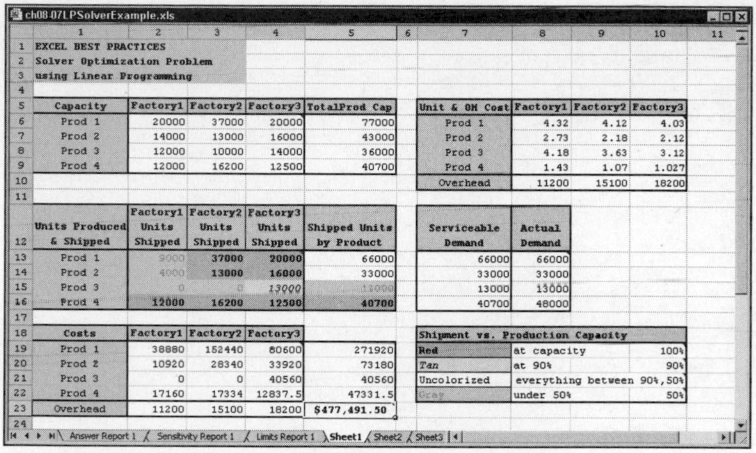

Figure 8-16: Optimized solution and the three reports

You will find that the optimizations you perform in your line of work will likely entail the "real world" adjustments of this kind. A substantial portion of getting the optimization to work correctly lies in nailing down the constraints.

THE ANSWER REPORT

The supplemental Answer, Sensitivity, and Limits reports provided useful information. To make heads or tails out of it, you need to understand what is meant by some of the terminology.

The Answer Report (see Figure 8-17) identifies three groups of information:

♦ The objective function or target cell value (not shown in Figure 8-17) and optimization type (Min, Max, or Value of)

♦ Adjustable cells along with their original and final values.

♦ Constraints along with their formulas, status, and slack.

Note that the Answer Report picked up the row and column labels for the various cells and constraints. This way of labeling your various cells is also applied in the other Solver reports. When you prepare your next optimization run, think about how you might want the labels to appear.

The Constraints "Cell Value" refers to the "Cell Reference:" entries of Figure 8-13 and not the "Constraints:" entries. A non-zero slack indicates that there was an available resource that is not used. There is a slack or spare availability of 11,000 units for product line 1 in factory 1. This is because the production capacity for this product at this location is 20,000 units and only 9,000 would be shipped in the optimal solution. Because there is a non-zero slack, the Status is "Not Binding." If the Status is binding, there will always be a zero slack.

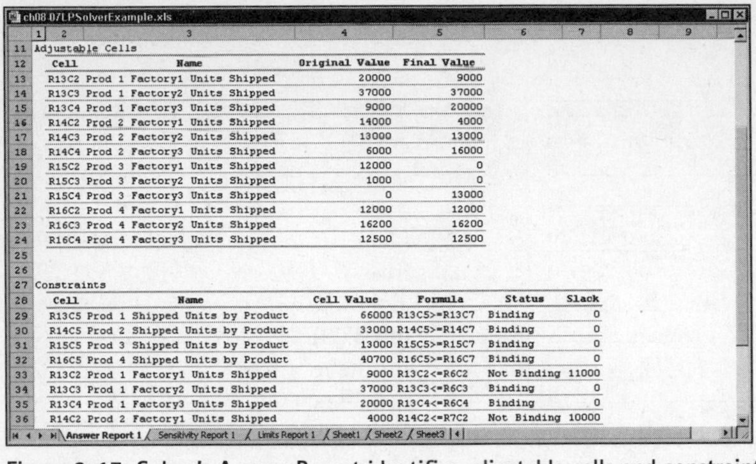

Figure 8-17: Solver's Answer Report identifies adjustable cells and constraints along with the status and slack.

THE SENSITIVITY REPORT

The meaning of most of the information in the Answer Report was self-evident. You can easily figure out what is binding and how much slack there is just by eyeballing your optimized spreadsheet. The situation with the Solver's Sensitivity Report is different. A lot more is going on there.

Let me explain some of the terminology and alert you to things you need to know. Although your solution may be optimal, how good will it be if some of your data is not exactly the way you presented it? You need to know how stable the optimal solution is.

Look at the Adjustable Cells region for product line 1 (see Figure 8-18). In Factory 1, the cost per unit is $4.32. This is the Objective Coefficient. You can also verify this on your Sheet1 Worksheet. Notice that Final Value is 9,000 units. Although 20,000 are available, production from the other two factories is preferable, because their costs are cheaper. If you adjust the unit price of $4.32 to a figure slightly higher or lower, it isn't going to change the Final Value of units produced and shipped. Its Reduced Cost is 0.

In Factory 2 for the same product line, the Final Value is 37,000 units. This is the total number of units of this product to be produced and shipped from Factory 2. It costs $4.12 per unit (the Objective Coefficient). It has a Reduced Cost of –0.2 per unit. This means that as long as the $4.12 per-unit cost doesn't increase by more than 20 cents, you will still select 37,000 as the number of units from Factory 2 in your optimal solution. The total operating costs may rise, but it still makes sense to allocate the same number of units. If the per-unit price goes up by 21 cents, the new price would be $4.33; making the Factory 1 price of $4.32 a more attractive alternative.

Likewise, Factory 3 has an Objective Coefficient of $4.03. Its price would have to increase by at least 29 cents, before you would consider changing your allotment of 20,000 units.

The Final Value of product line 3 at Factory 1 is 0. This is because it is over-priced. Its Objective Coefficient is $4.18. This would have to be reduced by at least $1.06 (the Reduced Cost) before it could be considered competitive.

A word needs to be said about the Objective Coefficient. It matches the Unit_Costs in the Sheet1 Worksheet. Your spreadsheet could easily contain a more complex cost structure; resulting in the Objective Function being a combination of multiple items instead of one.

The Allowable Increase and Decrease identifies how much the Objective Coefficient of each Adjustable Cell can change without altering the optimal solution. Take, for instance, product line 1 at Factory 1. Its Objective Coefficient is $4.32, the most expensive of the three factories (the others are $4.12 and 4.03). The Allowable Decrease is 0.2. This means that the Objective Function would have to dip below $4.12 before there would be reason to produce and ship more than 9,000 such units.

You'll notice that the Allowable Increase is a large number (1E+30). This signifies price insensitivity. The demand for product line 1 items is 66,000 units. Factories 2 and 3 combined can produce only 57,000 units. The remaining 9,000 units have to come from Factory 1. It doesn't matter how much the Objective Coefficient for this product at Factory 1 is raised. A price of, say, $10.00 per unit won't change the allocation (though it will have significant impact on the total operating costs).

ch08-07LPSolverExample.xls

Microsoft Excel 11.0 Sensitivity Report
Worksheet: [ch08-07LPSolverExample.xls]Sheet1
Report Created: 5/18/2003 2:40:47 PM

Adjustable Cells

Cell	Name	Final Value	Reduced Cost	Objective Coefficient	Allowable Increase	Allowable Decrease
R13C2	Prod 1 Factory1 Units Shipped	9000	0	4.32	1E+30	0.2
R13C3	Prod 1 Factory2 Units Shipped	37000	-0.2	4.12	0.2	1E+30
R13C4	Prod 1 Factory3 Units Shipped	20000	-0.29	4.03	0.29	1E+30
R14C2	Prod 2 Factory1 Units Shipped	4000	0	2.73	1E+30	0.55
R14C3	Prod 2 Factory2 Units Shipped	13000	-0.55	2.18	0.55	1E+30
R14C4	Prod 2 Factory3 Units Shipped	16000	-0.61	2.12	0.61	1E+30
R15C2	Prod 3 Factory1 Units Shipped	0	1.06	4.18	1E+30	1.06
R15C3	Prod 3 Factory2 Units Shipped	0	0.51	3.63	1E+30	0.51
R15C4	Prod 3 Factory3 Units Shipped	13000	0	3.12	0.51	3.12
R16C2	Prod 4 Factory1 Units Shipped	12000	0	1.43	1E+30	0.36
R16C3	Prod 4 Factory2 Units Shipped	16200	-0.36	1.07	0.36	1E+30
R16C4	Prod 4 Factory3 Units Shipped	12500	-0.403	1.027	0.403	1E+30

Constraints

Cell	Name	Final Value	Shadow Price	Constraint R.H. Side	Allowable Increase	Allowable Decrease
R13C5	Prod 1 Shipped Units by Product	66000	4.32	66000	11000	9000
R14C5	Prod 2 Shipped Units by Product	33000	2.73	33000	10000	4000
R15C5	Prod 3 Shipped Units by Product	13000	3.12	13000	1000	13000
R16C5	Prod 4 Shipped Units by Product	40700	1.43	40700	0	12000

Answer Report 1 \ **Sensitivity Report 1** / Limits Report 1 / Sheet1 / Sheet2 / Sheet3

Figure 8-18: Solver's Sensitivity Report

The top portion of the Sensitivity Report (Adjustable Cells) tells you how much sensitivity there is to price or cost changes without affecting the optimal solution. It's important to know how stable your optimal solution is.

Although you have an optimal solution, there are bound to be tweaks after you've already come up with an optimal solution. This is what the bottom portion of the Sensitivity Report (Constraints) addresses. Rather than try to define terms, I'll give you a scenario that will make clear what is meant by terms such as "shadow prices."

Suppose your manager tells you that although the optimal solution is great in bringing down the operating costs from a half a million dollars to $477K; there isn't enough money in the budget to cover these costs. Another $50,000 needs to be shaved from the costs. Your manager wants you to trim only the most expensive costs from each of the product lines. Where are you going to going to find the savings? You can start by going to the product with the most expensive shadow price. This is product line 1. You can decrease your production and shipment of 9,000 units at the shadow price of $4.32 per unit. Right away, you have a savings of $38,880. Next, look at product line 3. You can cut out a 1,000 units at the shadow price of $3.12 per unit. You have an additional savings of $3,120. So far, you've got $42,000 of the $50,000 target. Your next $8,000 savings will come from product line 2. You can cut out 2,931units at the shadow price of $2.73 per unit. Your total savings is $50,001.63.

Before moving to the Limits Report, you should be aware that if you don't check the Assume Linear Model box in your Solver Options (Figure 8-14), the Solver will be using a different algorithm to perform the optimization. This different algorithm is accompanied by a slightly different Sensitivity Report. When you see the term "Reduced Gradient," think of "Reduced Cost." You will also see the term "Lagrange Multiplier"; for that one, think of "Shadow Price."

LIMITS REPORT

The Limits Report (see Figure 8-19) shows how the objective value of an optimal solution would be altered by tweaking one adjusting cell at a time. Each adjusting cell is set to its minimum and maximum value, while the others are held constant.

The Limits Report can help to isolate how changes to individual decision variables (adjusting cells) can affect the outcome of an otherwise optimal solution.

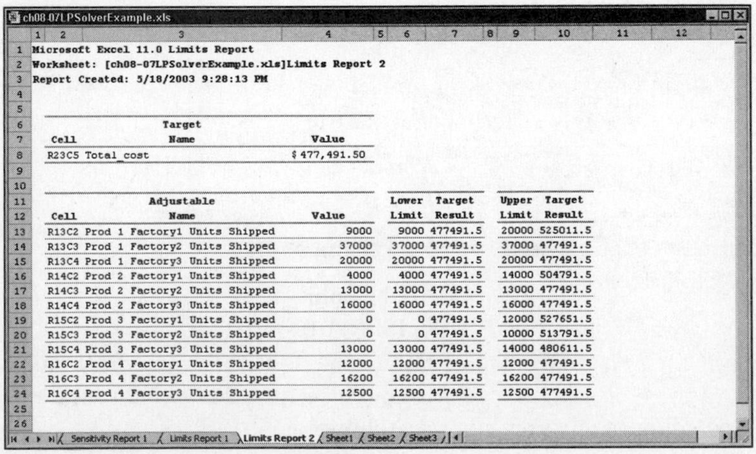

Figure 8-19: The Solver's Limits Report

One minor note: Sometimes, when you generate the Limits Report, you will see a bunch of #N/A errors in the limits and target results. Try rerunning the Limits Report by using the Solver from Sheet1 once more. Generally, the second time around, the Limits Report is generated without error.

A last word on the Solver

The Solver that is bundled in with Excel is actually produced by a third-party company (Frontline Systems, Inc.). The bundled version is not as full featured and powerful as its bigger brother and sister. If you need to tackle much bigger and more complex optimization problems, you should definitely explore the products from companies such as Frontline, Lindo Systems, or Wolfram Research.

On another note, this is a book about spreadsheet practices and techniques. The spreadsheets used in the examples show things you can do with a spreadsheet and are provided for illustration purposes only. There is no assurance, or representation of any level of assurance, that the spreadsheets and concepts presented will work other than to explain the ideas presented in the book. As with anything else, any spreadsheets you use, adapt, or create should always be independently verified for accuracy, correctness, and appropriateness.

Suggestions for Further Reading

This chapter covers a variety of topics. Although many of you no doubt have had your fill, some of you will need to explore some topics in greater detail. If so, you may want to peruse the following books:

Fourier Transforms

◆ *Excel for Engineers and Scientists*, by S.G. Bloch. John Wiley & Sons; 2nd Book and CD-ROM edition (January 2003), ISBN: 0471256862

◆ *Fourier Analysis of Time Series: An Introduction*, by Peter Bloomfield. Wiley-Interscience; 2nd edition (January 2000), ISBN: 0471889482

Stochastic and Markov Processes: Options Pricing and Derivative Securities

◆ *Options, Futures, and Other Derivatives*, by John Hull, Prentice Hall College Div; 5th edition (July 3, 2002), ISBN: 0130090565

Error Analysis

◆ *An Introduction to Error Analysis: The Study of Uncertainties in Physical Measurements*, by John Taylor. University Science Books; 2nd edition (April 1997), ISBN: 093570275X

Closing Thoughts

One of the most compelling reasons for using Excel in business is its superior data analysis capabilities. Chapter 1, "A Foundation for Developing Best Practices," extols the virtues of the Excel computational capabilities and the ability of people to interactively "program" business problems in a rectangular grid of numbers and formulas. If Excel is so capable, why is its use in business so anemic when it comes to the analysis of data?

In preparing this chapter, I set out to respond to this question by giving you the following notions:

♦ One of the obstacles faced with "power tools" such the ones discussed in this chapter is: "How do I get my arms around this topic?" Sometimes, all that is needed is for someone to explain in clear and simple terms how the specific tool is best used, where it would be purposeful, and what some of its hidden gotchas are. My goal has been to jump-start you in getting past the "hand waving" stage and working almost immediately doing some useful and powerful things.

♦ The topic of data analysis is vast and complex. It's also a well-defined discipline. I want to bring you to the doorstep of some of these disciplines so that if you enter and pursue a specific technical area, you can start off with a clear grasp of the basics. For this reason, I have also included suggestions for further reading. There are so many books and they're all so expensive! Your time is precious. Rather than waste your time and money, I want you to start with some of the best stuff.

♦ One of my goals in this chapter was to arm you with tools and methodologies that you're just not going to find elsewhere.

■ The Data Viewer Tool is unique. It gives you a way of analyzing trends and seasonal data the way it was meant to be used: interactively and visually. This tool doubles its value by showing you how to construct a large and complex spreadsheet that's scalable and works. The documentation I provided in how it works is basically a description of its internal architecture. For the Data Viewer tool, how it's used is synonymous with how it works.

■ The quantification of uncertainty is a difficult topic. A great divide separates users who can quantitatively interpret information when there is uncertainty from the rest of us who do some hand waving and can only muster up a best-case, worst-case, and most-likely, middle-ground scenario. I wanted to bridge this gap with a technique that puts the estimation of uncertainty on firm ground. The technique of Adding in Quadrature, although well known in the technical community, is not generally well known in financial data analysis and has not been integrated with spreadsheets to the extent covered here.

I hope that this chapter holds enough that's of real value. If you find that you need more info, you will find some supplementary material at my Web site: `http://www.evolvingtech.com/excel`.

The next chapter, which is also the final one in this part of the book, addresses the thorny issues that arise with "messed-up data," a.k.a. "MUD." It attempts to give you practical strategies and tools to help get you out of the MUD.

Chapter 9

How Not to Get Stuck in the MUD (Messed-Up Data)

IN THIS CHAPTER

- ◆ Working with ambiguous and incomplete data
- ◆ Working with inconsistent data and computations
- ◆ Working with data that has to be restructured
- ◆ Using a data overpass
- ◆ Spotting data mirages

THE PURPOSE OF THIS CHAPTER is to address the thorny issues that can arise when data is poorly stated. For the situations described, alternative approaches and methodologies are presented.

Rarely is there ever a single, clear-cut procedure that is appropriate in all circumstances.

This chapter reviews four situations and ways to deal with them:

- ◆ Ambiguous or incomplete data
- ◆ Inconsistent data and computations
- ◆ The square peg/round hole scenario
- ◆ Analyses/reports built on too much white noise or static

Like it or not, decisions have to be made in the absence of information. Elaborate and formal techniques have been built to work with incomplete information. Portfolio Selection Theory and Game Theory are two examples, to name a few.

The collection of such "theories" is far more esoteric than the "incompleteness" issue I wish to pick up here. Instead, consider being presented with information that is subject to multiple interpretations. Each interpretation can point to different conclusions. Alternatively, the decision outcome may remain unchanged. In either case, knowing what the outcome would be will not help you to determine whether one interpretation is more valid than the other. In this regard, you will see a mundane but nonetheless relevant situation of data ambiguity and a strategy that effectively mitigates the difficulties.

On the other end of the spectrum, you have data that points to clear contradictions. I introduce ideas about how some of these come about and point to a number of different ways to deal with them. I expand on these techniques in Chapter 11, "Spreadsheet Auditing: Challenging the Numbers of Others." I also show you ways in which you can compare source data from one spreadsheet to another.

A third scenario that arises is that of being supplied with source information that you know must be revised, yet you need to keep the original information intact. To that end, I show you how to use a "data overpass."

A fourth scenario that arises is when some pattern appears that is not a true pattern. These are known as "data mirages."

Ambiguous and Incomplete Data

Ambiguities and problematic situations often come up when working with spreadsheets. Automating the conversion of a list of numbers into dates is a good example. You might be working with a list of dates obtained on a Web site or a search engine from the Internet. It might have been generated from a server, perhaps running a language translator, and the divider marks such as a slash (/) or hyphen (-) got dropped in the process. Let me outline a slightly different but similar scenario.

An example scenario

Suppose you work in an organization that is merging with another. It may be that the other organization has not historically computerized its personnel data. Your department has requested electronic records. The other company's response, albeit lame, was to supply your department with OCR scanned documents. This would be fine, were it not for the fact that the delimiter that normally separates months from days and years did not get picked up in the scans. So, now you have a listing of employee birth dates represented as a series of digits.

You are saddled with a twofold task. One of these is to prepare a spreadsheet that determines *who* is eligible for retirement benefits based on their birth dates. The other is to determine as of a given point in time *how many* people will be eligible for retirement benefits. To further complicate matters, you have been asked to prepare this information by Monday morning at 9 a.m. It is late Friday afternoon, so whomever you could ask to redo the scans has already gone for the weekend.

Admittedly, this situation sounds a bit contrived. But I'm willing to bet that at one time or another you have faced the equivalent of this and have been asked to magically pull a rabbit out of a hat.

MORE DETAILS

Before I start talking about the details of this assigned task, let me tell you both some good and bad news. The good news is that you know the dates of birth appearing in the scanned data file, appear as the sequence of month number followed by the day of month and then followed by the year (represented as a two-digit number). Now for the bad news. . . . The digits for the day number show up as a two-digit number only if the number is 10 or greater; otherwise, it appears as a single digit. The equivalent is true for the month number. In other words, a birth date of April 8, 1945, would appear as 4845.

Obviously, additional information needs to be provided to determine eligibility for retirement. Such information includes the minimum age. You will also need to check whether the employee meets the eligibility criteria "as of" a specified date. This *as of* date will also need to be provided.

APPLY SOME COMMON SENSE

So far, all is well and good. Suppose a date appears as 123172. When looking at this number, you can readily surmise the date to be December 31st of 1972. This is fairly clear because the year 2072 hasn't yet happened. And it's very unlikely that anyone born in 1872 is still alive. Also, 72 can't be confused with a month number or day number because the month number will never be greater than 12 and the day number will never exceed 31. By the same token, 31 appearing in 123172 can't be confused with the month number.

Still, so far, so good. What if the first digit is represented by 1 instead of 01? You might see the number 13172. Could you unambiguously determine the date? Here, too, you're okay. Either the month is 1 and the day is 31, or the month is 13 and the day is 1. There is no 13th month of the year. So, it would appear that this date must be 1/31/1972.

Try another example. Suppose you are shown the number 1172. Because this number contains four digits and the year takes up the last two digits, unless there's missing data, the first digit has to represent the month (January) and the second digit has to represent the day of the month. So, this would correspond to a date of 1/1/1972.

Based on the examples just shown, you could design a spreadsheet that computes the correct date even if leading zeros in the days or months are omitted. Will you always be able to discern the correct date?

NOW, FOR SOME OF THE AMBIGUITIES. . .

Suppose you are shown the number 12172. This number could mean either 12/1/1972 or 1/21/1972. It is ambiguous. Without some further information, it is impossible to deduce which is the correct date.

Other issues may be at stake. Because the original list ignores leading zeros in the digits (for example, 1 instead of 01), it may ignore some other things. Consider the date 22997. What's wrong with this number for representing a date? After all, 22 can't represent a month, so you can easily discern that this date could be taken to mean February 29, 1997. Right? Even if you were absolutely certain that the year could not possibly mean 1897 or 2097, you still have a problem. 1997 and, for that matter, 1897 and 2097 are not leap years. *There is no February 29th in the years 1897, 1997, or 2097!*

If your list of birth dates is exceedingly short, consisting of maybe a half-dozen or so names, you might be lucky enough to avoid conversion conflicts. Unless everyone on your list was born in a month other than January, October, November, or December, don't count on it.

Consider a situation in which you have been given a list of approximately a thousand such numbers and have to convert them to proper dates. Your task would be made really easy if they all had proper leading zeros, making them exactly six digits long. Life has a way of complicating things. This hard-luck case is the one I want you to follow here.

Devise a plan

Sometimes, you'll know exactly what you're going to do. In most cases, however, the plan is not immediately evident. Begin by limiting the scope of what has to be addressed. See whether you can classify or break out the big problem into smaller sub-problems, each of which would be more manageable than the previous.

YOUR FIRST LINE OF ATTACK: SIMPLIFY THE PROBLEM

Your common-sense observations can certainly lead to some simplifying assumptions. The employees would be too young if they were born in the 21st century. As a first simplification, none of the birth dates occurs in the 21st century. It is also reasonably safe to assume that none of the dates correspond to the 19th century. You can also be reasonably safe in assuming that the last two digits of the date number refer to the year.

Making these assumptions strips away having to concern your self with multiple interpretations of the year. Right now, this doesn't seem like much to have accomplished, but every simplification you make gets you that much closer to a working solution.

Where necessary, appropriate, or reasonable, make simplifying assumptions that further restrict the scope of the problem.

Look at the sample list in the SourceData worksheet tab of the file ch09-01Date-Conversion (find it on the CD-ROM with this book). The first few lines of this file are shown in Figure 9-1.

If the list were only as long as the first few lines, you could afford to manually edit it. This list, however, contains a thousand dates. This would be too time consuming to do by hand and the effort would be prone to errors.

	1
1	**InputString**
2	122952
3	3643
4	122750
5	92047
6	92552
7	92749
8	22948
9	121851
10	52747
11	51753

Figure 9-1: Dates without delimiters

In addition to the SourceData worksheet tab, the file ch09-01Date-Conversion.xls contains two other worksheet tabs. One of these uses named ranges that should aid in understanding the formulas. The other uses cell coordinates. When providing formulas for this example, I give you the version with names. If you prefer to work with cell coordinates instead of the version with named ranges, simply flip to the worksheet tab called CellCoordinateVersion. Table 1-1 will help you to translate the coordinates and named ranges used in the spreadsheet.

TABLE 1-1 NAMED RANGES AND THEIR CORRESPONDING CELL COORDINATES

Name used in formulas	Cell Coordinates
AsOfDate	R6C1
BestConversion	R10C5:R1009C5
Conclusion	R10C8:R1009C8
CutOffDate	R7C1
Format_0mddyy	R10C6:R1009C6
Format_mm0dyy	R10C7:R1009C7
InputString	R10C1:R1009C1
Layer1	R10C3:R1009C3
Layer2	R10C4:R1009C4
MinRetireAge	R5C1

CLASSIFY YOUR PROBLEM INTO ITS PARTS

Looking at your data, you should clearly see that some dates are not uniform in appearance (the number of digits varies). Your goal is to get all the numbers in the list on equal footing (say, to a format of mmddyy) and then to convert everything to a properly formatted date (for example, mm/dd/19yy). From there, you will be able to perform the necessary date arithmetic to determine who is eligible for retirement.

As a first step, give yourself a visual aid and classify the data in terms of its length. It will be 4, 5, or 6 digits long. So, in column 2 of this spreadsheet, you can use the formula:

```
=LEN(InputString)
```

You can adjust the cosmetic appearance of the cells in column 2 using conditional formatting (see Figure 9-2).

 Remember that when you apply conditional formatting, you should set up the formatting so that each condition is rendered distinctly and unambiguously when printed in black and white.

Cells having Condition 1 are italicized. Cells having Condition 2 are in bold-face. Those cells having Condition 3 do not have any style adjustments to the font, though the cell's background is colorized.

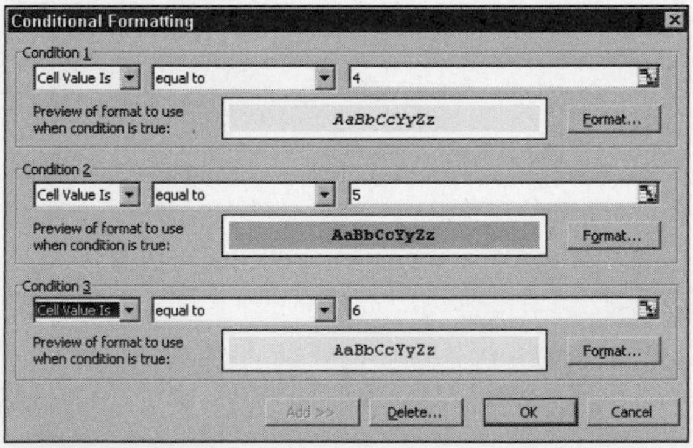

Figure 9-2: Apply different font styles and pattern colors for conditional formatting.

Now that your second column identifies the length and is colorized, you can see what you're up against (Figure 9-3).

	1	2
9	InputString	len
10	122952	6
11	3643	4
12	122750	6
13	92047	5
14	92552	5
15	92749	5
16	22948	5
17	121851	6
18	52747	5
19	51753	5

Figure 9-3: Dates without delimiters
and their respective length

Although column 2 is useful as a visual aid, the real work starts in column 3.

At first glance, you can see that some numbers you want to convert are already in the form you want. As an example, 122952 already has six digits, so there's nothing to do. Other numbers are four digits long. These are in the form mdyy and need to be converted to 0m0dyy. Don't worry yet about those that are five digits long.

State or write your algorithm in plain English before writing out complex formulas.

Rather than start with the Excel formulas, first state what you want to do in plain English. Your logic is as follows:

1. If the string in column 1 is already six digits, you don't need to tweak it at this time.

2. If it is four digits, slip in a leading zero before the second digit and a leading zero before the first digit, thereby making this a proper six-digit number.

3. Otherwise, it is more likely a five-digit number. The only thing you can do at this stage is to throw your hands up in the air. Signify this unresolved situation by labeling the cells in column 3 as FALSE.

Your first attempt at cleaning up the numbers appears in column 3 (see Figure 9-4).

	1	2	3
9	InputString	len	Layer1
10	122952	6	122952
11	3643	4	030643
12	122750	6	122750
13	92047	5	FALSE
14	92552	5	FALSE
15	92749	5	FALSE
16	22948	5	FALSE
17	121851	6	121851
18	52747	5	FALSE
19	51753	5	FALSE

Figure 9-4: Four-digit numbers are
restated in their six-digit form.

The description that was given in plain English translates directly to the following Excel formula:

```
=IF(LEN(InputString)=6,
    InputString,
    IF(LEN(InputString)=4,
        "0"&LEFT(InputString,1)&"0"&MID(InputString,2,3),
    FALSE
    )
  )
```

Rather than keep the preceding formula in the form of a long continuous line as it exists within Excel, I have indented and broken it into multiple lines for readability.

Aside from the overall logic, the most challenging part of this Excel formula is to convert a four-digit string in the form of mdyy to a properly formed six-digit string of the form 0m0dyy. The formula glues "0" to the first digit on the left (as obtained by the LEFT function); glues another "0"; and then glues the remaining three digits of the four-digit number. The portion of the formula that accomplishes all this gluing is as follows:

```
"0"&LEFT(InputString,1)&"0"&MID(InputString,2,3)
```

Next, I want you to walk through the calculation for a specific piece of data. On row 3 column 1, the string you would want to convert is the four-digit number 3643. Try evaluating the results returned by the LEFT and MID Excel functions.

```
LEFT("3643",1)        returns 3
MID("3643",2,3)       returns 643
                      (i.e., starting from second character
                      of "3643", retrieve 3 digits).
```

Therefore, you get:

```
"0"&"3"&"0"&"643"          which is 030643
```

In the next layer of conversion, you need to decide what to do with five-digit numbers. These can appear as mmdyy or mddyy. If the first two digits are greater than 12, it cannot be a valid month. So, you must conclude that the format is mddyy and the number should be converted to 0mddyy.

This logic would translate to the formula:

```
=IF(Layer1=FALSE,IF(VALUE(MID(InputString,1,2))>12,
                  "0"&InputString,FALSE),Layer1)
```

Therefore, either everything is a six-digit number or it is labeled FALSE. The troublesome five-digit dates that will be labeled FALSE will correspond to:

101yy	111yy	121yy
102yy	112yy	122yy
103yy	113yy	123yy
104yy	114yy	124yy
105yy	115yy	125yy
106yy	116yy	126yy
107yy	117yy	127yy
108yy	118yy	128yy
109yy	119yy	129yy
110yy	120yy	

The letters "yy" can be any year you decide to substitute. So, a date given as 12754 (where 54 is substituted for "yy"), can be taken to mean 1/27/1954 or 12/07/1954. Clearly, this result is ambiguous.

Everything at this stage of analysis (Layer2) is either a six-digit number or is labeled FALSE. It now makes sense to convert the six-digit numbers to dates (BestConversion). The Excel DATE function will help you to accomplish this. The syntax for this function is

```
DATE(4_digit_year,month_no,day_no)
```

The month_no starts with 1 and works its way up to 12 (as opposed starting with 0 and working up to 11).

The specific formula you would use for BestConversion is

```
=DATE("19"&MID(Layer2,5,2),MID(Layer2,1,2),MID(Layer2,3,2))
```

The BestConversion works perfectly for 878 out of the thousand birth dates. The remaining 122 cannot be reduced to an absolute date. These ambiguities may not be all that troublesome when determining retirement eligibility.

Suppose the cutoff for retirement is 55 years of age. If you choose an "as-of" date to be 12/31/2003, anyone born after 12/31/1948 would not be eligible for retirement (that is, they would be younger than 55 years of age as of 12/31/2003).

A person with a date given as `12754` would have one of two possible birth dates: 1/27/1954 or 12/07/1954. In both cases they occur *after* 12/31/1948. The person with a birth date signified by `12754` could not be eligible for retirement on 12/31/2003. There is no ambiguity about this.

HERE IS THE STRATEGY

Because ambiguous dates have two possible interpretations, evaluate the retirement eligibility for both possible interpretations of dates. This sounds simple enough. Split the ambiguous dates into two columns, with one interpretation in one column and its alternative in the other. If both alternatives are after the cut-off date, then the person is too young to be eligible. If both alternatives occur on or before the cut-off date, then the person is eligible for retirement. Otherwise, no resolution can be made.

What about the 878 people who don't have birth dates subject to more than one interpretation? Do you have to use a whole different set of logic? The answer is no. Split the unambiguous date into the same two columns you would use for the ambiguous dates. Now you can uniformly apply one set of logic to all the dates.

HERE ARE THE IMPLEMENTATION DETAILS

Create two columns. Call one of these "`Format_0mddyy`" and the other "`Format_mm0dyy`." The formulas in each of these are

```
Format_0mddyy
=IF(ISERROR(BestConversion),DATE("19"&MID(InputString,4,2),
    "0"&MID(InputString,1,1),MID(InputString,2,2)),BestConversion)
```

```
Format_mm0dyy
=IF(ISERROR(BestConversion),DATE("19"&MID(InputString,4,2),
    MID(InputString,1,2),"0"&MID(InputString,3,1)),BestConversion)
```

Note the use of the Excel `ISERROR` function. Basically, these formulas say, "If there was an error in determining the BestConversion, apply some special logic; otherwise, simply use the BestConversion." The special logic has been highlighted.

Looking at Figure 9-5, you can see that the ambiguous dates are spotted and their alternative interpretations are correctly computed in the two rightmost columns.

To bring closure on all this, you will need to compute the cut-off date. This involves some date arithmetic. Basically, you need to construct the cut-off date from the "as-of" date less the number of years for the minimum retirement age. Here is the formula for the cut-off date:

```
=DATE(YEAR(AsOfDate)-MinRetireAge,MONTH(AsOfDate),DAY(AsOfDate))
```

	1	2	3	4	5	6	7
9	InputString	len	Layer1	Layer2	BestConversion	Format_0mddyy	Format_mm0dyy
10	122952	6	122952	122952	12/29/1952	12/29/1952	12/29/1952
11	3643	4	030643	030643	3/6/1943	3/6/1943	3/6/1943
12	122750	6	122750	122750	12/27/1950	12/27/1950	12/27/1950
13	92047	5	FALSE	092047	9/20/1947	9/20/1947	9/20/1947
14	92552	5	FALSE	092552	9/25/1952	9/25/1952	9/25/1952
15	92749	5	FALSE	092749	9/27/1949	9/27/1949	9/27/1949
16	22948	5	FALSE	022948	2/29/1948	2/29/1948	2/29/1948
17	121851	6	121851	121851	12/18/1951	12/18/1951	12/18/1951
18	52747	5	FALSE	052747	5/27/1947	5/27/1947	5/27/1947
19	51753	5	FALSE	051753	5/17/1953	5/17/1953	5/17/1953
20	9655	4	090655	090655	9/6/1955	9/6/1955	9/6/1955
21	21148	5	FALSE	021148	2/11/1948	2/11/1948	2/11/1948
22	101543	6	101543	101543	10/15/1943	10/15/1943	10/15/1943
23	10552	5	FALSE	FALSE	#VALUE!	1/5/1952	10/5/1952
24	31549	5	FALSE	031549	3/15/1949	3/15/1949	3/15/1949

Figure 9-5: 10552 on row 23 interpreted as either 1/5/1952 or 10/5/1952

If the "as-of" date is 12/31/2003 and the minimum retirement age is 55, then the cut-off date is 12/31/1948. You can see this in Figure 9-6.

ch09-01DateConversion.xls

	1	2	3	4	5	6	7	8
1	EXCEL BEST PRACTICES							
2	Number to Date Conversion							
3	when date interpretation could be ambiguous							
4								
5	55	Minimum Retirement Age					242	Meets Age Criteria
6	12/31/2003	As-of date					758	Not Eligible
7	12/31/1948	Cut-off date					0	AMBIGUOUS
8								
9	InputString	len	Layer1	Layer2	BestConversion	Format_0mddyy	Format_mm0dyy	Conclusion
10	122952	6	122952	122952	12/29/1952	12/29/1952	12/29/1952	Not Eligible
11	3643	4	030643	030643	3/6/1943	3/6/1943	3/6/1943	Meets Age Criteria
12	122750	6	122750	122750	12/27/1950	12/27/1950	12/27/1950	Not Eligible
13	92047	5	FALSE	092047	9/20/1947	9/20/1947	9/20/1947	Meets Age Criteria
14	92552	5	FALSE	092552	9/25/1952	9/25/1952	9/25/1952	Not Eligible
15	92749	5	FALSE	092749	9/27/1949	9/27/1949	9/27/1949	Not Eligible
16	22948	5	FALSE	022948	2/29/1948	2/29/1948	2/29/1948	Meets Age Criteria
17	121851	6	121851	121851	12/18/1951	12/18/1951	12/18/1951	Not Eligible
18	52747	5	FALSE	052747	5/27/1947	5/27/1947	5/27/1947	Meets Age Criteria
19	51753	5	FALSE	051753	5/17/1953	5/17/1953	5/17/1953	Not Eligible
20	9655	4	090655	090655	9/6/1955	9/6/1955	9/6/1955	Not Eligible
21	21148	5	FALSE	021148	2/11/1948	2/11/1948	2/11/1948	Meets Age Criteria
22	101543	6	101543	101543	10/15/1943	10/15/1943	10/15/1943	Meets Age Criteria
23	10552	5	FALSE	FALSE	#VALUE!	1/5/1952	10/5/1952	Not Eligible
24	31549	5	FALSE	031549	3/15/1949	3/15/1949	3/15/1949	Not Eligible

NamedRangesVersion / CellCoordinateVersion / SourceData

Figure 9-6: Completed number-to-date conversion and tallies of eligibility for retirement

The conclusion is computed using the following:

```
=IF(AND(Format_mm0dyy>CutOffDate,Format_0mddyy>CutOffDate),
    "Not Eligible",
    IF(OR(Format_mm0dyy>CutOffDate,Format_0mddyy>CutOffDate),
        "AMBIGUOUS",
        "Meets Age Criteria"
    )
)
```

I used a little trick here. I first checked to see whether both birth dates occur after the cutoff date. After you eliminate the possibility that both have not occurred, you need only to check and see whether any of the birth dates occur after the cutoff date. The OR function returns TRUE if any combination of the alternatives, including both of them, occur. You know they can't all be true, because you eliminated that possibility when you tested for both dates.

As you can see in Figure 9-6, the highlighted line identifies the first occurrence of an ambiguous date. Whether you choose to interpret 10552 as 01/05/1952 or 10/05/1952 doesn't make any difference for retirement eligibility. Both these birth dates occur after the cut-off date. The employee in this range has not reached age 55 and is not eligible as of 12/31/2003.

The Excel COUNTIF function is used to determine how many people match each of the three different outcomes (Not Eligible, Meets Age Criteria, or AMBIGUOUS). The formula used in rows five through seven in column 7 is

```
=COUNTIF(Conclusion,RC[1])
```

The formula is looking through the range Conclusion (or R10C8:R1009C8) and counts how many employees match Not Eligible, Meets Age Criteria, or AMBIGUOUS.

By the way, using this technique, the list of 122 ambiguous dates has been reduced to 0 in terms of whether or not age criteria have been met. There is no guarantee that with different data all ambiguities will be eliminated. But for a thousand birth dates, of which 122 were troublesome, bringing the list down to zero or even a small handful of troublesome entries is a great step forward.

In summary, the overall approach is to first flag the ambiguous or incomplete data. Next, find some way to systematically handle these troublemakers so that they can be on the same footing as the rest of the presumably good data. Then continue performing whatever you would regularly be doing with your complete data set.

What happens if some of the data is still ambiguous or incomplete? Well, there's a three-part process for handling exceptions in the next section of this chapter, "Inconsistent Data and Computations."

The lesson to be learned

In this example you were asked to provide a head count of how many people are eligible for retirement (thereby answering the question, "What is the bottom-line financial impact to the company?") and also provide a list of who's eligible. If you had complete and accurate information on the birth dates as well as the cut-off retirement age and as-of date, you could answer these questions completely. Notice that even in the presence of ambiguous birth dates (incomplete information), it was possible to answer the questions. Although there is no ironclad guarantee that you would be able to complete the tasks, you could at lease reduce the scope to the point at which you would need to chase after only a handful of dates.

What this technique has done is to get you out of a tight squeeze and bought you some time. With any luck, you will have enough time to go back and get fully unambiguous data.

Inconsistent Data and Computations

It is one thing to have incomplete or ambiguous information. It is entirely another to have data or a spreadsheet containing portions that are flatly wrong. Let me outline some instances in which you might find inconsistent data.

Data presented might be contradictory

I want to present a true story. Some time ago when I was quite young, the Postal Service first began assigning nine-digit ZIP Codes instead of the usual five-digit numbers. I did not know what the last four digits of my address would be. Not long afterward, I received a piece in the mail from the Postal Service mailed to my home with the full nine digits. The last four digits were 3412. I was very happy and immediately had mailing labels made up with the full nine-digit ZIP Code. Soon afterward, I started receiving other mail that, more often than not, showed a different ZIP Code (the last four digits ended with 3453 instead of 3412). To this day I still get mail with both codes (and, I might add, from the U.S. Post Office). It would be nice if everyone settled on only one of these. Maybe I could get lucky and receive only half the junk mail!

Although you might not find this kind of inconsistency an issue, think again. It's certainly not a real problem for me. However, imagine trying to redistrict zones based on estimated population or resident counts by ZIP Code. This could potentially lead to a significant difference if the tabulated populations based on the nine-digit code contained an appreciable number of people included two or more times because of differences in the last four digits of their ZIP Code. So, do you think this was a ploy by some crafty politicians to use inflated population counts and get more funding for their districts? I am somehow quite doubtful of this as a real possibility.

In any case, accurate and consistent numbers are important in many walks of life. Tolerance specifications and safety data for instrument certification, data collected during clinical trials, and irregularities in accounting information reported by a public company are just a few examples.

If there is inconsistent data, how would it likely appear and how does it manage to slip under the radar screen? Data that's inconsistent or spreadsheets with inconsistent computations often go unnoticed because the conflicting portions appear on different spreadsheets or reports. Give your colleagues the benefit of the doubt and presume that inconsistencies are the result of unintentional errors.

Start with some almost trivial cases where mistakes happen. You might have, for instance, a list of employee names along with their start date, cumulative years worked for their employer, age, birth date, and, you guessed it, their ZIP Code.

All of this information is subject to considerable change. I won't even speak again about the vagaries of ZIP Codes. There are plenty of other things to concern ourselves with.

People get married and, all too often, divorced. A new name appears on the employee roster. Other datasets are revised to reflect this, but the old name still remains.

The age will continually change. So, anything filled out in a form is bound to be quickly dated.

Believe it or not, I've filled out plenty of government forms for which I've been asked to provide both my date of birth *and* my age. Being that I have to sign and date the form, the simultaneous disclosure of age and date of birth is not really necessary. What happens if the age reported doesn't agree with the reported date of birth and the date the form was signed? It would be hard to know which of the two differing pieces of information is correct. Perhaps only one of the two is recorded in a database or spreadsheet. If they're both recorded, what guarantees exist that a consistency check is actually performed? After all, many of the forms we sign ask us to acknowledge under penalties of perjury that everything is truthful and accurate.

In the end, there is nothing that really prevents a person from providing conflicting information.

Even if information is accurately provided, it is still possible to have conflicting information. Consider two examples: information splintering and version tracking.

INFORMATION SPLINTERING

Suppose there is an employee listing that accurately indicates the number of years the employees have been working for a company. This repository contains a whole bunch of other stuff, including social security number, dependents, and other sensitive information. You may need to prepare a report that makes use of the employee names and how long they have worked in the company. Because of the obvious confidentiality of the employee records, unless you happen to be in the Human Resources (HR) Department, you may not have access to the database. A colleague might e-mail you only selected information. You need the information in a rush. Your friend doesn't have time to generate a whole new report or the system is down. A recent report, almost identical to what you need, was prepared a week ago. This gets e-mailed to you. You're grateful for the timely response. The report is largely accurate. Unbeknownst to you, recent changes have been made that are not reflected in your copy of the information. Thus begins the splintering of information. Pretty soon, it becomes a complicated and tedious affair to straighten out the inconsistent information.

VERSION TRACKING

Let's change the venue. Perhaps you work in one of the Information Technology (IT) departments for a very large company. As part of a cost-cutting initiative, you are in the process of trying to consolidate the number of software licenses to a limited number of vendor products, platforms, and versions. Your first step is to gather information. Good luck! Unlike the situation with personnel data, no up-to-date and accurate centralized repository exists that identifies all the different software licenses out there. You're bound to have conflicting information and you're still charged with providing reports to a broad distribution of executives and managers for the next quarterly meeting. Of course, people know that this type of information is soft (that is, an approximation) and that it is very difficult to get concrete information. No one wants to be left holding the bag if information is later revealed to be incorrect — least of all yourself. The situation is even more extreme when it comes to financial and accounting information.

Enough discussion; it's time for some practical techniques and guidelines.

What to do when you find an exception

There are three easy steps to take to limit your exposure:

1. Document the exception.

2. Perform an analysis pertaining to the exception and possible ways of treating it.

3. Based on your professional judgment, draw and state your conclusion(s) as well as the results of your analysis. Document this all within the body of the noted exception.

Find a way to make sure that these noted exceptions travel with the spreadsheets, as well as exist in the form of separate analyses and communications.

Identify differences in almost identical data

There are two ways to compare data on different spreadsheets, different worksheets, or in different regions of the same worksheet. One technique is to "eyeball" the data. The other is to perform a "swatch" comparison.

THE EYEBALL COMPARISON

Although visual comparison is not particularly precise, the human eye can spot complex and minute variations that could not be readily achieved with formulas. This is especially true when you're viewing data that is not necessarily identical but possesses complex relationships and patterns. To assist in the process, you can use the "Compare Side by Side with" feature found on the Window menu of Excel. Of course, you have to have at least two windows open simultaneously: Doing so provides you with synchronized scrolling. Before I further describe this synchronized scrolling, I must tell you that you can do a synchronized scroll on the same worksheet despite the fact that it appears that you cannot. To do so, while your spreadsheet is open and active (that is, displaying the topmost window), choose New Window from the Excel Window menu. With this new view of your spreadsheet open, go ahead and choose Compare Side by Side with: from the Window menu (see Figure 9-7).

Now you can view and synchronously scroll different worksheets on the same spreadsheet or even different regions on the same worksheet (see Figure 9-8). You can adjust the scroll position to affect only one of the worksheets by toggling the Synchronous Scrolling from the Compare Side by Side toolbar.

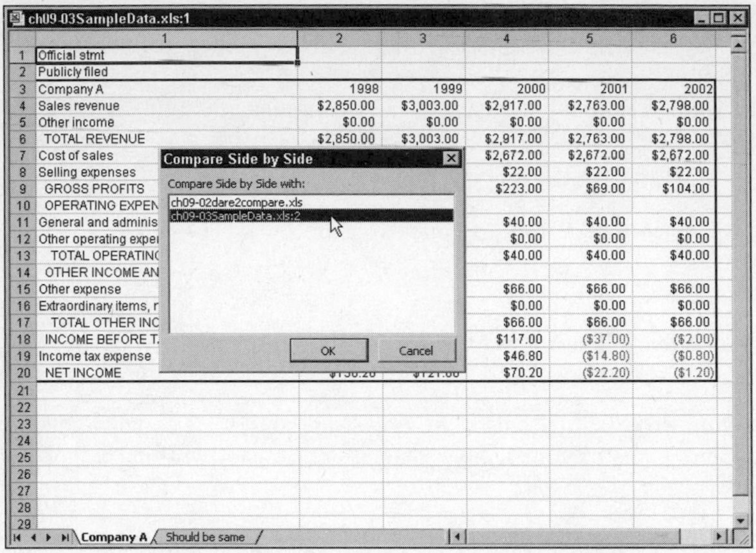

Figure 9-7: A side-by-side comparison between a spreadsheet and another view of the same spreadsheet

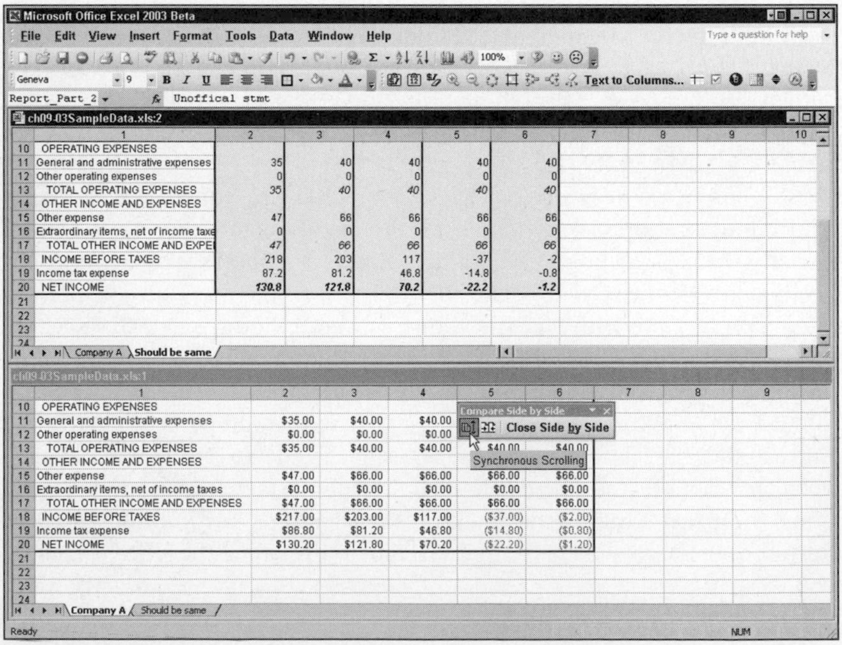

Figure 9-8: Synchronous scrolling can be turned on and off from the Compare Side by Side toolbar.

There's nothing sophisticated about the use of synchronized scrolling. It's just that simple things such as this type of facility can make your work easier.

THE SWATCH COMPARISON

Occasions may arise when you will want to compare one region of a spreadsheet to another to verify that they are precisely identical. Doing so may not be so easy if the numbers you are comparing contain messy numerical calculations going out to many decimal places.

For this purpose, I am providing a Take-Away tool in the file called ch09-02 dare2compare.xls (see Figure 9-9). Basically, you specify two regions you want to compare. If the region is on another open spreadsheet, type in the filename as well as the worksheet name. Make sure that the referenced spreadsheet is open. You can use a cell coordinate or a named range. As you can see in Figure 9-9, a comparison is being made between the Sheet1 worksheet of the actual tool and the "Should be same" worksheet of a separate spreadsheet file.

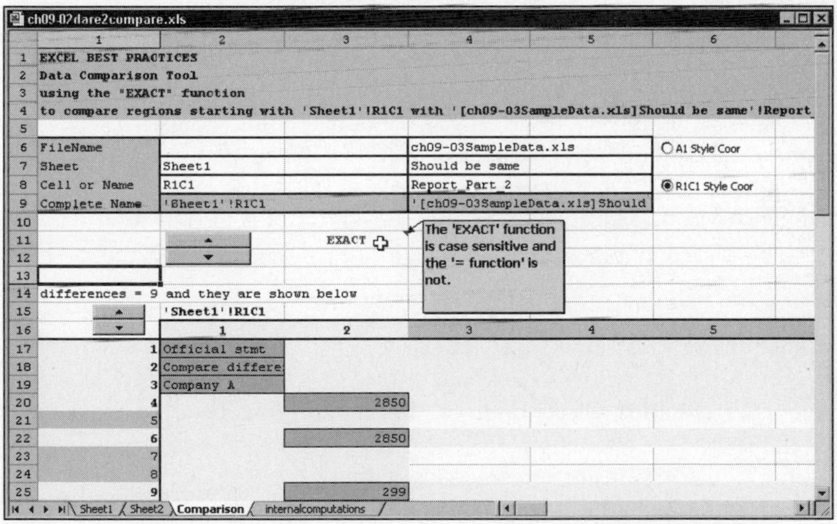

Figure 9-9: Data comparison tool, being used to spot differences between local data on Sheet1 and named reference on another spreadsheet, "Should be same"

As you can see from Figure 9-9, the tool contains a number of different settings. To begin with, you can adjust the style you want to use when referencing coordinates. Those of you desiring to use the A1 style should select the A1 Style Color radio button. Then you can use cell coordinates such as A1 or $A$1 instead of R1C1 (see Figure 9-10).

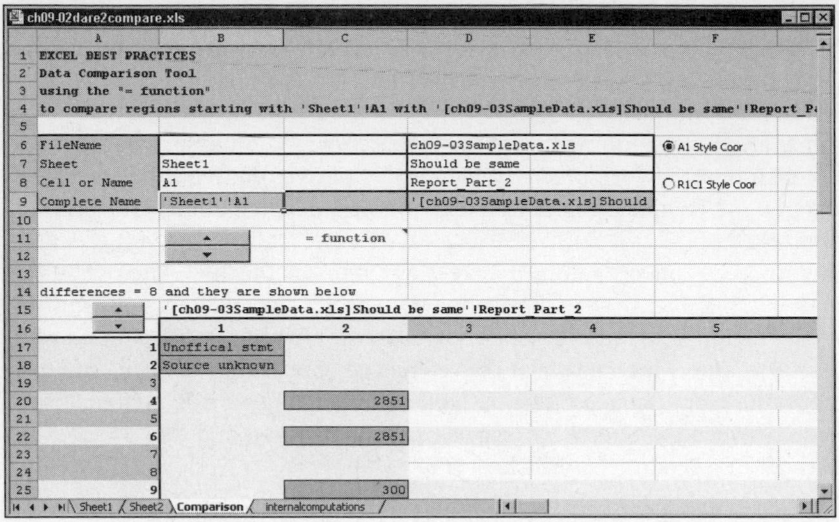

Figure 9-10: Data comparison tool, being used with slightly different settings (comparison is now case insensitive and coordinate style has been set to A1 instead of R1C1 style)

I have switched the settings so that you can see how the tool works. The specific changes were the following:

♦ Changed the Spreadsheet Options so that everything is displayed in A1 Style.

♦ Toggled the radio button to A1 Style Color.

♦ Changed the cell reference from R1C1 to A1.

The spinner control button visible on rows 11 and 12 toggles between the equality function = and the EXACT function. The equality function is not case sensitive. If you look on line 14 of the spreadsheet, you will see that it picks up eight differences, which are shown in Figure 9-10. If you toggle the function back to EXACT, you will see there are nine differences, as shown in Figure 9-9. Toggle your comparison operator depending on whether or not you want to distinguish the case sensitivity between expressions.

The "swatch" comparison spans a region of cells 50 rows by 50 columns. With luck, this is a large enough region to be useful for you.

Square Peg/Round Hole Scenario

All too often, data reports are prepared in such a way that some nips and tucks are required to get correct results. Meanwhile, the underlying structure of the spreadsheet may be unable to withstand mild to moderate scrutiny. In this day and age, when the reliability of budgets and financial estimates are called into question, you have to start looking at what can be done to correct or mitigate internal flaws.

Using a data overpass

Chapter 4, "Compiling, Managing, and Viewing Your Data," introduced a "data overpass" to make changes to financial statement information that was brought in from a PDF file. Here, I want to show you a more generic data overpass. As does the previous section of this chapter, the overpass covers a region of 50 rows by 50 columns (see Figure 9-11).

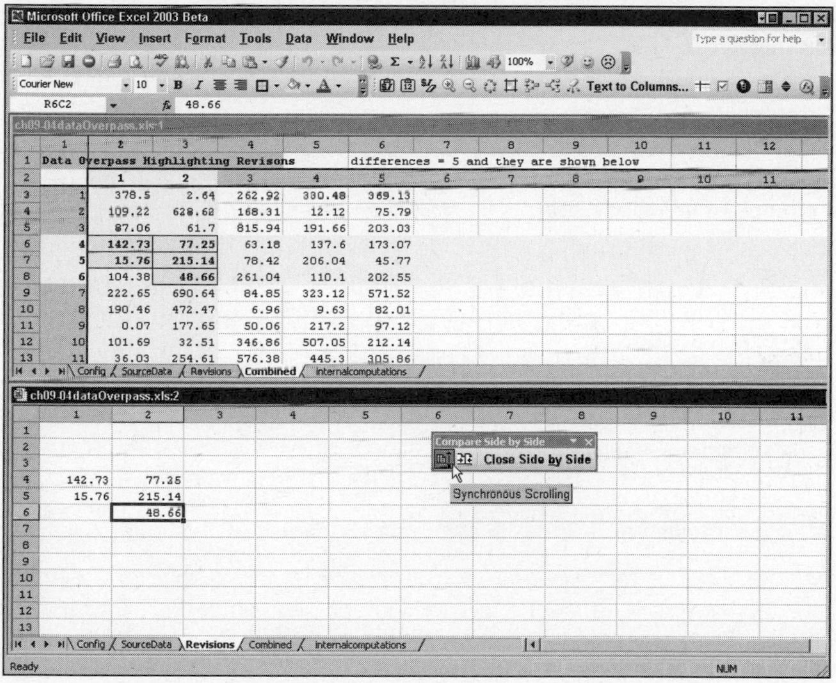

Figure 9-11: Generic data overpass tool with synchronized scrolling

When you open the file ch09-04dataOverpass.xls, you will see two spreadsheet windows open. Be sure to select the Compare Side by Side option on the Window menu. This synchronous scrolling ability will make your life a lot easier. As does the previously discussed data comparison tool, this spreadsheet allows you to configure where the source data and revision sheets reside (see Figure 9-12). You can also see, as shown in Figure 9-12, that the SourceData worksheet tab is populated with a mass of numbers. The Configurator identifies its location as well as the location of where the revisions will take place. After data is properly referenced, you can view the Revisions and Combined worksheet tabs using synchronous scrolling, as shown in Figure 9-11. Just make your changes within the Revisions tab and see the highlighted changes in the Combined tab.

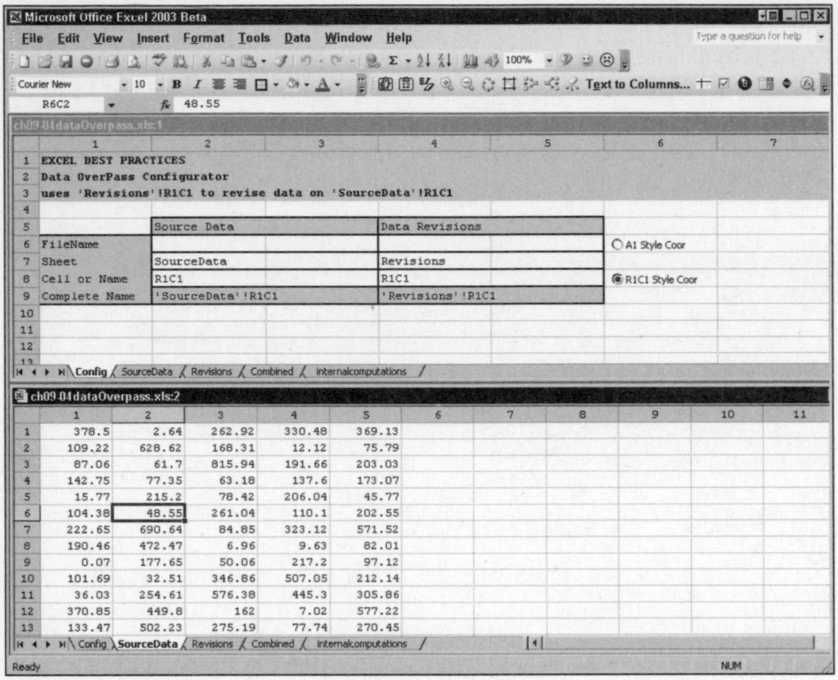

Figure 9-12: Data overpass Configurator and Source Data facilities

There are some things you should be aware of in the use of this data overpass tool:

◆ This tool is mainly designed to revise numbers as opposed to long strings of text and dates.

◆ The data appearing on the Combined worksheet does not preserve any of the original formulas from the source data or revisions you make.

◆ To get data from the Combined Worksheet tab reintegrated back to your original spreadsheet, use Copy and Paste Special... Values. No other means is provided here. Attempting to do so would require making too many assumptions about how you are using your source data. Such assumptions and ways to reintegrate data can be spelled out for specific circumstances and uses. Chapter 11 on spreadsheet auditing in Part III addresses this topic.

What this spreadsheet buys you is the ability to explicitly separate your revisions from the underlying source data. This will help you to preserve original content and document revisions, and to leave an audit trail when and where you find exceptions.

Analyses/Reports Built on Too Much White Noise or Static

Another scenario that happens quite often is the tendency to build spreadsheets that compute results built on assumptions or estimates that are simply not there.

Understanding "data mirages"

To help get the point across, here's a fun exercise. Go out and buy the very cheapest calculator you can get your hands on. Find one of those four-function calculators (+, -, *, /). With this ultra-cheap calculator, try entering the following keystrokes:

`10/9=`

You will get something like `1.111111111`. Try squaring this result using

`*=`

You will get something like `1.234567900`. Then multiply this result times 8:

`*8=`

You will get something like `9.876543200`.

   There is an almost irresistible urge to want to blame the details in the last few decimal places on the cheapness of the calculator. You would think that the last result should have been closer to `9.87654321` and the second-to-last result should have been `1.23456789` instead of `1.2345679`. Well, actually, the calculator is correct. We humans tend to anthropomorphize things and assume a pattern that just isn't there.

   Recognizing patterns and relationships in a mass of data is an important human strength. The value of this skill should not be discounted. In the context of spreadsheets, recognizing a pattern can be easy. Applying or extrapolating the pattern can be easier, still. There's a middle step that's easiest to omit. *It is establishing the validity of the pattern.* This omission gives rise to what is known as a "data mirage."

Strategies for assessing whether you have a data mirage

There are several approaches to dealing with these mirages:

   ◆ Apply the Trace Precedents facilities (see Appendix A for setup) to identify and isolate what factors or spreadsheet cells specifically contribute to a specific critical result you wish to validate. Remember to apply the Trace Precedents repeatedly. Each time you do, the additional precedents are identified. Continue doing this till you identify the root inputs that affect your end results.

◆ For these root inputs, perform some sensitivity analysis by varying your data slightly, and measure the variations in your spreadsheet results. The Scenario Manager, as presented in earlier chapters, could be used for this purpose. There are alternative ways to vary the root inputs. One of these is to construct a data overpass and re-attach the cells depending on root data to your Combined worksheet of the data overpass. In this manner, you could try revising some of the root input numbers and see how doing so affects your spreadsheet results.

◆ Another approach would be to try using some third-party Monte Carlo simulation tools, such as Crystal Ball (a product of Decisioneering).

◆ The techniques on quantifying uncertainty outlined in Chapter 8, "Analyzing Data," will allow you to conduct some sensitivity analysis.

Closing Thoughts

You have seen some thorny issues when there is not enough data, forcing you to impose some interpretation. The strategy of dividing and conquering can be effective in simplifying your tasks and reducing the impact of portions you cannot solve.

The opposite of not enough information is also a problem. Two pieces of data that should be identical are not. They can come about by information splintering. They can also come about because some of the computations are done incorrectly or approximations are made and not uniformly applied. The Data Comparison tool should help you spot that needle in a haystack.

This chapter and Chapter 4 (in the PDF conversion tool) introduced the data overpass facility. A data overpass can be important even if the alterations to the data are relatively modest. There may be reasons for you to keep your original data intact. Some of these could entail legal considerations. Whatever the reason, a data overpass allows you to preserve original data, make isolated revisions, and combine the revisions to produce a revised dataset.

As can be expected, data mirages are illusive. There are two direct routes to discerning a data mirage. One of these relates to formula dependencies. Tracing precedents will help you to objectively understand what can influence a spreadsheet cell. This topic is further addressed in Chapter 11. Also important is the ability to do some sensitivity analysis to see how much something can change when there are variations in the cell inputs or predecessor cells. This topic was covered in the previous chapter in the section on quantifying uncertainty. This theme is taken up further in Chapter 11 in the section on testing the reasonableness of spreadsheets.

Chapter 10, "Going for the Facelift: Spreadsheet Makeovers," introduces a practical framework for reengineering spreadsheets when they are up for major revision. The chapter walks you through a complete, end-to-end makeover.

Part III

Special Topics: Getting the Numbers Right

Chapter 10

Going for the Facelift: Spreadsheet Makeovers

IN THIS CHAPTER

♦ Understanding principles of spreadsheet makeovers

♦ Understanding the pros and cons of alternative strategies in the makeover

♦ Mapping the existing spreadsheet structure

♦ Identifying important computations

♦ Tracing dependencies to those computations

♦ Identifying and validating correctness in the formulas

♦ Identifying and making explicit, hidden exceptions to the rule

♦ Unearthing errors in the computations

♦ Making improvements and simplifications to formulas

♦ Constructing and designing useful worksheet layout

♦ Harnessing positional arrangements of information to manage data

♦ Special techniques in date arithmetic

THE PURPOSE OF THIS CHAPTER IS to introduce techniques to practice reworking existing spreadsheets, whether they were originally developed by you or inherited from others.

In any business, you may find yourself having to work with complicated spreadsheets that others developed. Alternatively, you may have developed some spreadsheets a long time ago and don't remember all the details. Perhaps the spreadsheet was appropriate in the past but no longer fits the situation today. Whatever the case, you can avail yourself of useful techniques to reengineer spreadsheets. This chapter introduces such techniques and runs through a complete end-to-end conversion. The emphasis is on fulfilling the requirements in the most expedient way possible.

Spreadsheet makeovers involve the following important tasks:

◆ Identify the business requirements related to the spreadsheet and keep those requirements clearly in sight.

◆ Take apart the existing spreadsheet by identifying the structural layout, determining functionality (what's happening), tracing dependencies, and understanding how specific issues were handled (and whether they were resolved in a clean way).

◆ Decide on a makeover strategy that includes how to rework formulas, change formatting for consistent appearance, and develop optimizations. Updating your spreadsheet may entail cleaning up the existing spreadsheet or scrapping it in favor of a total rewrite. In any case, you will have to think about scope limitations. You will need to decide on how much historical data you expect to incorporate into your spreadsheet, and whether you are planning major new innovations to the previously existing spreadsheets.

This chapter is organized into two parts: a condensed summary of practices and techniques you are likely to employ in a spreadsheet makeover, and a complete conversion of an existing set of spreadsheets that applies these principles. Focus your efforts on reading through the end-to-end conversion and use the first part of this chapter as a reference of points to remember.

A FEW WORDS OF ADVICE

In addition to perhaps having to fix formulas, improve on formatting, or document assumptions, be prepared to do an extensive amount of data scrubbing when you perform any kind of spreadsheet makeover. The common tendency is to receive data from third parties that's not consistently validated and prepared — data whose names and category phrases are entered with trailing spaces, for instance. This type of problem is bound to foul things up when counting occurrences of such records.

Spreadsheet Makeover Techniques

Here are the techniques and skills you will learn in this chapter:

1. Set efficient goals (in the reworking of spreadsheets).

2. Perform a spreadsheet review and understand the complexities of doing so.

3. Determine what's happening in the spreadsheet (without needing to look at the individual formulas):

   ■ Take an aerial view and identify the broad sections or portions of the spreadsheet.

   ■ Determine what portions of the spreadsheets have formulas and what portions have been etched out by hand or are otherwise hardwired.

- Trace the formula dependencies.

- Look for weaknesses in the formulas and identify ways to correct them.

4. Determine your makeover strategy: "Do I rework the existing spreadsheets or prepare new ones from scratch?"

5. Perform the mechanical steps of the makeover.

6. Be aware of further optimizations: Things you might do if you had more time on your hands.

Some preliminaries

A makeover is different from starting a new spreadsheet project from scratch. When you start a new spreadsheet, you have the option of building anything you want from the ground up. You are free to place whatever constraints you want on the spreadsheet. You are not always afforded such luxuries with spreadsheet makeovers. Like it or not, much of the structure, and likely, the expectations of the existing spreadsheet, is already set. It will be your starting point for the makeover. Just because much may have already been built doesn't mean you must stay with the existing design.

Among accountants and auditors there's a known term called SALY, which refers to 'Same As Last Year'. Auditors find that accounting practices of many companies are carried out year after year in the same manner. When someone gets around to asking the company's financial staff why the particular practice is followed, they often reply "Because that's the way it's always been done." In reality, the person who originated the specific practice may have had a very good reason, even though it is not necessarily understood by his or her successors. On the other hand, the practice may have originated simply because it was convenient at the time.

The situation with spreadsheet makeovers is really no different. Just because the existing set of spreadsheets handled something one way, doesn't mean that it's necessarily correct or will be appropriate going forward.

One of the key questions to ask yourself when preparing to do a spreadsheet makeover is whether you expect to continue some existing practice or spreadsheet framework, or whether you're starting something entirely new. Starting something new or doing a major redesign of an existing spreadsheet can be a lot of work. In fact, it may be more work than you have time for. If you plan to stay with the prior design, then you owe it to yourself and your colleagues to carefully validate that the existing spreadsheet design you are inheriting from others is really on solid footing.

By the way, accountants and auditors view SALY-based practices in accounting with skepticism. I look at SALY-based practices with spreadsheets in the same manner. This healthy skepticism is balanced by the fact that although I view the spreadsheet projects you may take over as important, I fully recognize that you may have additional responsibilities and priorities which are entirely unrelated. Because of the multitude of responsibilities and obligations, taking over the spreadsheet project may not be your number one priority. As such, you do not plan on spending more time on this project than is absolutely necessary.

I will be presenting spreadsheet makeovers from the "doing only what's absolutely necessary" perspective so that you can quickly move on to your next set of priorities. Although expediency and practicality have been the principal drivers in the makeover process, it is always guided by the requirement of assuring correctness of the reworked spreadsheets. Never lose sight of this, or you will end up short-changing yourself and your colleagues who depend on the work you produce.

Review the existing spreadsheets while taking into account complexities

Most spreadsheets that are used in general reporting are not terribly complex. Sometime, long ago, someone probably took what was handled by pencil and paper, and perhaps a few e-mails, and turned it into a spreadsheet. If it was done a really long time ago, that spreadsheet might have been someone's first foray into preparing spreadsheets. Give that person credit for preparing the original spreadsheet nicely.

Spreadsheet technology today is different from what it was in the past. The business circumstances today are different from those of a few years ago. There may be different reporting requirements. Your company may have merged or your department may be consolidated with another department. Whatever your circumstances are, enough may be different to warrant a reworking of spreadsheets even if you didn't suddenly inherit a project from someone else.

GOAL SETTING

So where do you begin? Start by asking yourself these questions:

- ◆ What are the spreadsheets supposed to do?

- ◆ Will the spreadsheet be distributed to others? Will the report appearance/branding play an important role? Are just the bottom-line numbers all that's needed?

- ◆ Is any complex math involved in the spreadsheet computations?

- ◆ How often will the spreadsheet need to be updated and distributed?

- ◆ Is anything new being asked of you with respect to what the spreadsheet should perform?

- ◆ Do you need to validate work previously prepared? Can you accept the consequences if prior work contains errors, but use it only as your starting point?

- ◆ As you prepare the new spreadsheet, how important is it to prepare detailed documentation? If detailed documentation is a requirement, do you have to adhere to a corporate change control policy? Is the scope of the work important enough that the spreadsheet must be accounted for in a business continuity plan?

- ◆ Do you expect to expand the scope of the previously prepared work?

◆ How exact will the spreadsheet have to be? Can numbers be estimates? Is it necessary to perform any sensitivity analysis?

◆ Have you been given all the information you need to take the spreadsheet project forward? Is all the data that goes into the spreadsheet readily (and reliably) available? Is there documentation on the spreadsheet (or notes embedded inside the spreadsheet)?

◆ Is there something that requires correcting before going forward?

Asking and answering questions such as these will help you to spell out your makeover requirements. Often, your business environment and management practices will dictate much of the makeover requirements and scope.

Sometimes you'll be able to forego some of the elements in your spreadsheet. If the Human Resources department is supposed to be supplying you with personnel data, it's not your responsibility to ensure that the employee data is accurate. However, you will have to make sure that the data supplied is uniformly represented. Imagine being provided a list of names and contribution amounts to specific employee funds. If the HR department sends the data to you in a word processing document, you might think that you can directly copy and paste that text into your spreadsheet. The list may, however, have trailing spaces at the end of some of the names, or show names occurring both with and without middle initials. This causes no confusion to the HR department, because it can tie back the information to a unique social security or employee ID number. Somehow, HR has neglected to send this additional information to you. You may need to factor in problems such as these when preparing your spreadsheet.

Finally, when thinking about reworking a spreadsheet, you have to ask yourself, "Am I making more work for myself than I really need to?"

First steps in the makeover

The answers to all your initial questions may not be known. Your predecessor may have left the company and a manager may have arbitrarily decided to hand the responsibility of managing the spreadsheet and its reporting over to you, saying, "Here it is. Go figure out what to do." Sound familiar?

In such a situation, here are some of the things you can do:

◆ Determine what's happening in the spreadsheet (without even bothering to look at the formulas).

◆ Try to determine its basic inputs and outputs.

◆ Try to determine what cells in the spreadsheet are computed and what are just given values.

◆ See whether the numbers in the spreadsheet seem to make some obvious sense.

◆ Identify any possibly complex or tricky formulas. Later, you will want to scrutinize these.

◆ See whether you can identify any portions of the spreadsheet that appear to drive the computed results (such as interest rates or tax rates).

◆ Identify whether the spreadsheet contains a clearly delineated portion with the "report" portion. If it does, see whether any of the formulas contain "hidden inputs."

After this analysis, you may determine that everything is in tip-top shape and you need to do very little other than to pick up where the other guy left off. Right? Yeah, right!

Sometimes you may get lucky and be spared the task of doing a spreadsheet makeover, or at least find that the original preparer of the spreadsheet is still around for consultation. But what if he or she is not available? What if you have to go it alone and are faced with a pressing deadline? Well, that's one of the reasons you've chosen to buy this book and I hope that it will prove to be of value to you. But keep in mind that your key to a successful spreadsheet makeover is to get intimate with the numbers. Unless you are willing to roll up your sleeves and delve into the details of your spreadsheet, you won't get very far in the makeover process.

Although every spreadsheet makeover can be different, there are some common tasks and activities you can do.

MAP THE PORTIONS OF THE SPREADSHEET THAT SHOULD HAVE BEEN FORMULAS WHEN IT WAS HARDWIRED

Tag the cells containing formulas so that they are separately identified from cells that contain only text data or are otherwise empty. You can do this by clicking Edit → Goto ... → Special → Formulas and then, after you select the cells you want to mark, you can format those cells to give them an easily identifiable appearance (you might alter the color and/or font, for example).

IDENTIFY OBVIOUS PORTIONS OF THE SPREADSHEET THAT NEED REVISION

Start identifying what portions of the spreadsheet need to be updated. For starters, if the spreadsheet contains a range of dates, chances are that you'll either continue extending those dates or revise the starting date and carry the dates out over the appropriate range. Depending on how complex your spreadsheet is, date arithmetic may or may not be needed.

FORMULA DEPENDENCIES

One of the earlier steps was to determine which cells contain formulas. What about how they interrelate? You can trace formula dependencies using the Trace Dependencies toolbar buttons or clicking Edit → Goto ... → Special → Dependents. (If you haven't already performed the Excel setup suggested in Appendix A, now would be a good time, paying particular attention to the setup of the Excel toolbar. Having the toolbar buttons available is much more convenient than manually going through the equivalent menu options. There's no need to tax your memory and slow yourself down when a toolbar button can save you work.)

LOOK FOR WEAKNESSES IN THE FORMULAS AND IDENTIFY WAYS TO CORRECT THEM

Table 10-1 lists common mistakes made when preparing spreadsheets.

TABLE 10-1 COMMON FORMULA ERRORS

Situation	Description
Over-specified formulas	This type of situation usually manifests itself in the form of a SUM of a SUM. Sometimes you'll be able to spot a formula that appears to be more complicated than you know it ought to be. Another tell-tale sign is when there's a group of cells that should be using identical or similarly structured formulas and you find out they are not. For example, if you were to replicate the formulas across a range of cells and you find that doing so breaks the spreadsheet when it shouldn't have, then clearly, some formulas are in need of fixing.
Missing Logic	Assumptions built into formulas that lack the logic that determines why they are what they are and how they should change.
Incorrect Ranges	Formulas that might specify incorrect ranges. Sometimes a formula might take a range that extends too far. You might, for instance, have a sum of the values in the next 12 rows when Excel should be summing only the next 10 values. If the two remaining cells are blank, then there's no harm done. Right? Wrong! It's just a time bomb waiting to explode. One day, one or both of those empty cells may be populated with a value or formula. Oops, there goes the correctness of your original SUM formula, and out the window goes your spreadsheet.
Census Type Errors	There is a tendency to group or sum numbers incorrectly.
Apples and Oranges Errors	Apples are grouped with oranges when the two groups should remain completely separate.
Normalization Errors	Everything should add up to 100 percent but doesn't because some things are under- or over-represented. This usually happens with two groups: logical errors and rounding errors. By far, the more common of the two are rounding errors.

Continued

TABLE 10-1 COMMON FORMULA ERRORS *(Continued)*

Situation	Description
Comparison Errors	Arise when two independent sets of data are on a spreadsheet which should add up to the same total. In fact they don't. Since they are assumed to add up to the same number, only one set is actually added. The total of the alternate set is never added; hence the error goes undetected.

FORMULA CLEANUP

Often, you'll encounter spreadsheets that have historically produced correct results but may not work correctly or be easily maintainable going forward.

The most obvious case is when a spreadsheet that was designed to handle a limited amount of data now has an accumulation of additional data, which is more than the spreadsheet can handle. Usually, this problem can be addressed mostly through a cleanup formula.

Another problem occurs when a formula produces correct results but does not replicate correctly.

Be sure to eliminate any "ghosts" that might appear in your spreadsheet. A ghost item is one that shows a non-zero value in a given cell when only a value of zero should be displayed.

DATA ARRANGEMENT

All too often, spreadsheets clump the assumptions, the input data, the analysis, and the reporting portions into one complex, nearly inscrutable worksheet. A little reorganization can go a long way toward cleaning up this kind of mess. A number of different approaches are available to deal with this. You may want to consider separating the different functions and having each appear on a different tabbed worksheet. In addition to isolating the logic in each of these four categories, you'll find the spreadsheet easier to maintain. You'll find that separating the reporting portion from the rest of the spreadsheet facilitates the automation of reports.

MAKE SOME HARD DECISIONS

If the spreadsheet is not originally yours and people who know its inner workings aren't available, you will have to think carefully about whether to retrofit the spreadsheet you've been given or redesign it altogether. The correct answer to this choice is, "It depends."

SAVE YOUR SUPPLEMENTAL TASKS FOR A RAINY DAY

When you're doing your spreadsheet makeover, you'll be discovering the items that you *must have* versus those things that are *nice to have*. Early on, try to decide which tasks belong in which category.

CHART YOUR ROAD MAP

As with anything else that's potentially complex and involved, you would do well to identify on paper what it is you're expecting to accomplish. In this particular case, paper does actually have an advantage over an electronic format for preparing your plan. After being committed to paper, the pieces of your plan aren't subject to revision that leaves no audit trail. This will force you to keep on target with your original goals and stay aware of any changes to your original plan. One by one, implement each of the items in your plan and cross it off your (essentially fixed) list.

A Hands-On Example of a Spreadsheet Makeover

The first part of this chapter summarized a list of items and tasks that are generally involved in a spreadsheet makeover. They've been included here chiefly to serve as a reference source. The best way to understand how to do a spreadsheet makeover is to go through the steps of doing one. The remainder of this chapter is focused on doing just that.

By way of spreadsheet formulas, basically nothing new is introduced in this example. All the emphasis is on technique. In other words, it's all in the flick of a wrist. So get ready to roll up your sleeves and start analyzing, redesigning, and creating some really decent spreadsheets.

Keep in mind that the makeovers do not represent the only way to rework the spreadsheets. The goal is to quickly fix what needs changing and go on to the next order of business, whatever that might be. The idea here is not to get caught up in attempting an overly ambitious project.

The scenario

Place yourself in this situation: Your company has been making cutbacks on the operating budget within your department as well as others. To complicate matters, the person who has been managing budgets is no longer working at your company, and you just inherited his responsibilities. You must track the salaries for administrative and clerical staff and their impact on the operating budget. The salaries are based on a pre-established operating budget and the number of hours your staff is expected to work. Because fewer than twenty people are in the group, this could all be done on pencil and paper. There's no rocket science here. It's just tedious. Sound familiar?

Your predecessor prepared budgets and reports that exist primarily in the form of a few e-mails, word processing documents, and several spreadsheets. Before your predecessor left, he prepared a pro forma budget on a spreadsheet as a template so that others could carry on his work. Unfortunately, he left no documentation. The only information you have to go on, aside from your general knowledge, are those e-mails and spreadsheets from the prior year that are populated with what is now old data.

Your basic objective is to prepare a report on a bi-weekly basis that shows what percentage of the set operating budget has been consumed and how much has been spent for each employee in relation to his or her allocation. Because you are interested only in the budget for the current operating period and you inherited many other responsibilities, you have little or no interest in validating the work done in the prior years (leave that to the auditors!). Nor do you have any real interest in turning this into an expanded project or application. Basically, you want to produce the expected information in a timely manner on a regular basis, without going crazy and with confidence in your numbers. Because you've been saddled with many other responsibilities, you really cannot afford to work harder than you need to.

One saving grace is that the information you provide can be reported in any format of your choosing. No one is expecting any fancy reports with charts and graphs. No complex or sophisticated analysis is required. People on a certain distribution list need the budget information that's accurate and provided to them on a bi-weekly basis. Overall, they've been happy with what they've been getting from your predecessor. They are not expecting anything significantly different.

Another thing you can be thankful about is that the raw data that would be incorporated into your budget analysis/reports is readily available. That is, you have the names of all the people in your department, you know what their hourly rates are, and you have good records of how many hours they've worked for any given week.

Now for some of the wrinkles...

Aside from possible issues in reworking the budget spreadsheet, there's bound to be some turnover of personnel during the overall operating period. Also, from time to time, hourly rates for various people can change during the overall operating period.

Historically, employees never received raises more than once a year. So for budget purposes, you would normally need to consider at most two rates: one before and another after the raise. Raises are based on how long employees have been working in the company. Therefore, when they do happen, raises occur on different dates for different people.

This year is unusual. Most of the employees we're talking about belong to a union that is just completing contract negotiations. Additional raises are expected for most of the staff beyond the regular raises they would normally receive. Thankfully, you've just been given the updated hourly pay rates by HR and don't have to worry about how to compute them.

Review of the prior year's budget

Are you up for the challenge? Start looking at the spreadsheets. There are two of them: one for a prior year (ch10-01LastYearBudget.xls on the CD with this book) and one for this year (ch10-02CurrentYearProforma.xls). The spreadsheet for the current year has no hourly data because the fiscal year hasn't yet started. Your predecessor gave this to your boss and said it was ready to go.

VIEW OF THE SPREADSHEET FROM 14,000 FEET

Take a look at the spreadsheet for the prior year. All the work is on one worksheet. First, don't even bother looking at the formulas and computations. Instead, zoom out to an aerial view of 25 percent or 10 percent magnification (Figure 10-1); you'll get a pretty clear picture that the spreadsheet has three distinct portions.

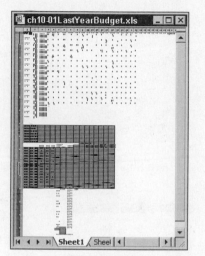

Figure 10–1: View of entire spreadsheet at 10 percent magnification

The first few lines of this spreadsheet are shown in Figure 10-2. This info for the list of employees begins on row 1 and continues down through row 71. It displays data of hours logged for individuals.

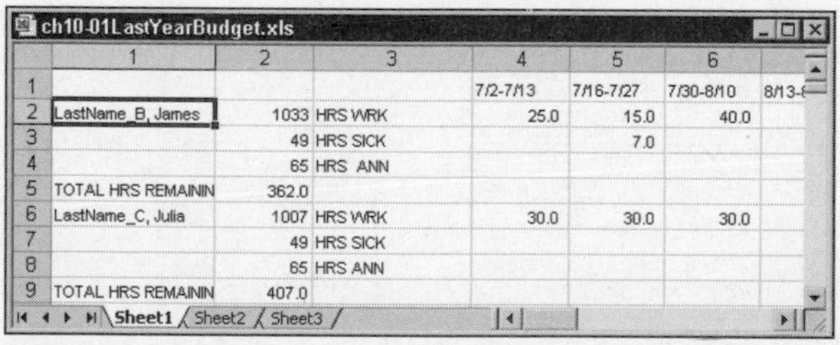

	1	2	3	4	5	6	
1				7/2-7/13	7/16-7/27	7/30-8/10	8/13-8
2	LastName_B, James	1033	HRS WRK	25.0	15.0	40.0	
3		49	HRS SICK		7.0		
4		65	HRS ANN				
5	TOTAL HRS REMAININ	362.0					
6	LastName_C, Julia	1007	HRS WRK	30.0	30.0	30.0	
7		49	HRS SICK				
8		65	HRS ANN				
9	TOTAL HRS REMAININ	407.0					

Figure 10–2: Top portion of spreadsheet containing names and hours worked

The middle portion of the spreadsheet (starting at row 72), as shown in Figure 10-3, shows a budget allocation and how much of it has been consumed (only $43.25 was left in the budget for the prior year).

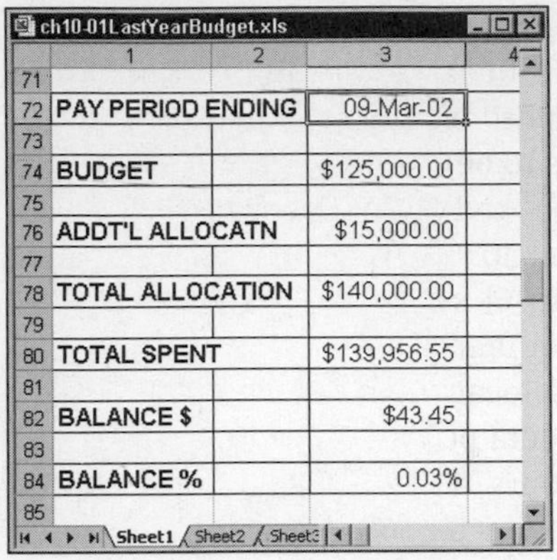

	1	2	3
71			
72	PAY PERIOD ENDING		09-Mar-02
73			
74	BUDGET		$125,000.00
75			
76	ADDT'L ALLOCATN		$15,000.00
77			
78	TOTAL ALLOCATION		$140,000.00
79			
80	TOTAL SPENT		$139,956.55
81			
82	BALANCE $		$43.45
83			
84	BALANCE %		0.03%
85			

Figure 10-3: Middle portion of spreadsheet summarizing aggregate budget totals

It is then followed by the allocation for the specific individuals (Figure 10-4).

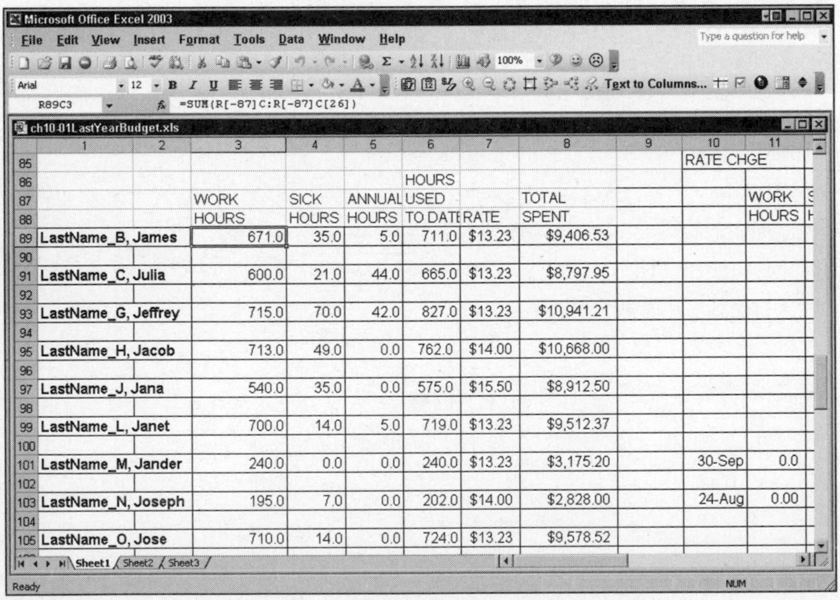

	1	2	3	4	5	6	7	8	9	10	11
85										RATE CHGE	
86						HOURS					
87			WORK	SICK	ANNUAL	USED		TOTAL			WORK
88			HOURS	HOURS	HOURS	TO DATE	RATE	SPENT			HOURS
89	LastName_B, James		671.0	35.0	5.0	711.0	$13.23	$9,406.53			
90											
91	LastName_C, Julia		600.0	21.0	44.0	665.0	$13.23	$8,797.95			
92											
93	LastName_G, Jeffrey		715.0	70.0	42.0	827.0	$13.23	$10,941.21			
94											
95	LastName_H, Jacob		713.0	49.0	0.0	762.0	$14.00	$10,668.00			
96											
97	LastName_J, Jana		540.0	35.0	0.0	575.0	$15.50	$8,912.50			
98											
99	LastName_L, Janet		700.0	14.0	5.0	719.0	$13.23	$9,512.37			
100											
101	LastName_M, Jander		240.0	0.0	0.0	240.0	$13.23	$3,175.20		30-Sep	0.0
102											
103	LastName_N, Joseph		195.0	7.0	0.0	202.0	$14.00	$2,828.00		24-Aug	0.00
104											
105	LastName_O, Jose		710.0	14.0	0.0	724.0	$13.23	$9,578.52			

Figure 10-4: Bottom portion of spreadsheet, apparently containing some type of rate calculation

A quick inspection reveals that hours used to date is the sum of work hours plus sick hours plus annual hours (that is, hours for personal days). The rate seems to be an hourly rate and total spent is the hourly rate multiplied by the hours used to date for the given individuals. Over to the right, there seems to be a section for rate change.

It seems that two employees (Jander and Joseph) had rate adjustments occurring on September 30th and August 24th (lines 101 and 103 of Figure 10-5).

The bottom part of the spreadsheet (Figure 10-6) shows a list of names. The names appear as first names only and are shown in familiar form (for example, Jim versus James). It further appears that the total allocation could be based on the number of hours available. For example, the top data portion of the whole spreadsheet shows that Jim has available 1,007 work hours, 49 sick hours, and 65 hours of personal time, adding up to 1,147 hours. This correctly matches the total allocation for Jim. The rate of $13.23 matches his hourly rate.

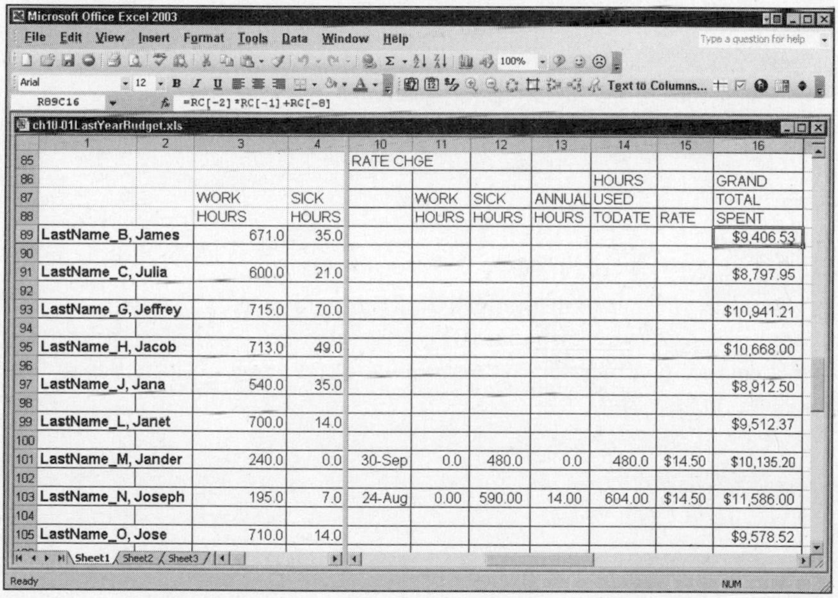

Figure 10–5: Special section of spreadsheet attempting to compute rate adjustments

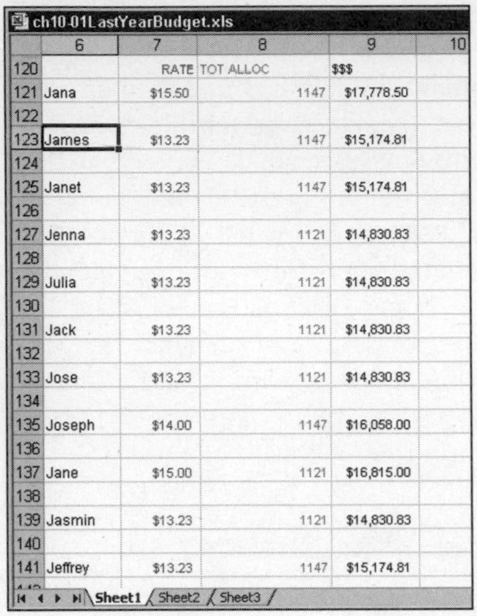

Figure 10-6: Bottom portion of spreadsheet showing informal supplemental analysis; appears to be a kind of scratch pad

DETERMINE THE USE OF FORMULAS VS. THE HARDWIRED PORTIONS

Start digging in a little deeper to distinguish between data entered manually versus cells that contain spreadsheet formulas. The easy way to do this is to choose Go To ... → Special and then pick the option to have Excel select all formulas in the current worksheet (Figure 10-7).

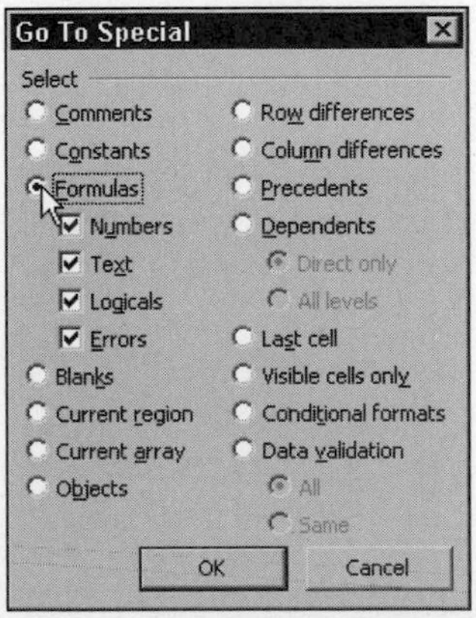

Figure 10-7: Excel menu options for Goto... → Special → Formulas

The spreadsheet now highlights only those cells in the current worksheet that have mathematical formulas (that is, these are all cells beginning with an equal sign (=) followed by some arithmetic computation).

If you scroll through your spreadsheet *without clicking inside* any of the cells, you will see which ones have formulas and which ones don't (Figure 10-8). So, scroll down to row 120 and look at columns 6 through 9. The only ones that have formulas are the cells with dollar currency values appearing in column 9. Apparently, the allocation of hours and hourly rates have been entered manually (they are not tagged as having formulas).

	6	7	8	9
120		RATE	TOT ALLOC	$$$
121 Jana		$15.50	1147	$17,778.50
122				
123 James		$13.23	1147	$15,174.81
124				
125 Janet		$13.23	1147	$15,174.81
126				
127 Jenna		$13.23	1121	$14,830.83
128				
129 Julia		$13.23	1121	$14,830.83
130				
131 Jack		$13.23	1121	$14,830.83
132				
133 Jose		$13.23	1121	$14,830.83
134				
135 Joseph		$14.00	1147	$16,058.00
136				

Figure 10-8: Cells containing formulas are now highlighted with colorized shading.

If you really want to keep track of which cells have formulas, choose Select Special... Formulas and then change the appearance of those cells so that they are visually marked. You might, for instance, change the font to a readily distinguishable color such as lime green. While you're at it, make the font boldface so that it's easily identified if it is printed in black and white.

Try summarizing observations about the work that was done in the prior year's budget spreadsheet. Remember, this has been used successfully and is populated with lots of data. This analysis can serve as the starting point of assessing the current year's budget. Analyzing the current year budget in a vacuum could prove to be difficult because the fiscal year hasn't begun, so no real data has accumulated in the spreadsheet.

For the prior year's budget, the dates (starting from 7/2/2001) appearing on the first row show hours booked over a two-week interval beginning on the Monday of the first week and ending on the Friday of the following week (see Figure 10-9). This information has been entered by hand, a method that is prone to error (see whether you can detect any errors). If you want, you can use some date arithmetic to have this computed automatically.

4	5	6	7	8	9
1	7/2-7/13	7/16-7/27	7/30-8/10	8/13-8/24	8/27-9/7	9/10-9/21
	25.0	15.0	40.0	12.0	50.0	40.0

Figure 10-9: Peculiar date intervals labeled along the top of the spreadsheet

TRACE THE FORMULA DEPENDENCIES

The computation for the hours remaining seems to have some problems. Look at the formula for the Total Hrs Remaining in R5C2. What happened to the Hrs Sick? It looks as though the formula for R5C2 definitely needs some fixing. The same can be said for the Total Hrs Remaining that's computed for the remaining fourteen or so individuals. You can visually confirm this using the Trace Precedents tool (Figure 10-10). To clear the visual arrows and markers brought about by the trace dependency tools, you can use the Remove All Arrows toolbar icon to remove all the arrows and markers.

	1	2	3	4	5	6
				7/2-7/13	7/16-7/27	7/30-8/10
1						
2	LastName_B, James	1033	HRS WRK	25.0	15.0	40.0
3		49	HRS SICK		7.0	
4		65	HRS ANN			
5	TOTAL HRS REMAININ	362.0				

Figure 10-10: Excel Trace Precedents tool highlights cells used to compute total hours remaining

LOOK FOR WEAKNESSES IN THE FORMULAS AND IDENTIFY WAYS TO CORRECT THEM

Specifically, the formula for the Total Hrs Remaining has a problem with the usage of the summation formula SUM (Figure 10-11). It's over-specified, using a SUM inside another SUM:

```
= SUM(R[-3]C-(SUM(R[-3]C[2]:R[-3]C[28])))
```

	1	2	3	4	5
87			WORK	SICK	ANNUAL
88			HOURS	HOURS	HOURS
89	LastName_B, James		671.0	35.0	5.0
90			=SUM(R[-07]C:R[-07]C[26])	=SUM(R[-06]C:R[-06]C[25])	=SUM(R[-05]C[-1]:R[-85]C[24])
91	LastName_C, Julia		600.0	21.0	44.0
92			=SUM(R[-85]C[1]:R[-85]C[26])	=SUM(R[-84]C:R[-84]C[25])	=SUM(R[-83]C[-1]:R[-83]C[24])
93	LastName_G, Jeffrey		715.0	70.0	42.0
94			=SUM(R[-83]C[1]:R[-83]C[26])	=SUM(R[-82]C:R[-82]C[25])	=SUM(R[-81]C[-1]:R[-81]C[24])

Figure 10-11: Calculations of Work Hours, Sick Hours, and Annual Hours are computed differently for each employee when they should all be the same.

Someone has gone to a painstaking amount of effort to prepare a specific formula for each and every person, calculating the total number of work hours, total sick hours, and total annual (personal absence hours). These formulas would not lend themselves to automatic formula replication. In other words, you couldn't just copy and paste formulas for each additional employee you add to your list. To make this problem evident, I have co-opted the use of the empty rows (90, 92, 94) to show you what the actual formulas are for the immediate cells above. By way of example, the value of 671.0 that appears in row 89, column 3 of Figure 10-11 was actually computed using the formula

```
=SUM(R[-87]C:R[-87]C[26])
```

If you look closely, you will see that although the formulas in Figure 10-11 are similar in structure, no two are alike for work hours, sick hours, or annual hours for *any* of the employees appearing in the spreadsheet.

Historically, this usage of formulas has been problematic. What happens to the formulas when you take out some employees or add others? Because the formula for each employee is different, this has been a nightmare to manage. This problem can be resolved rather easily, however. First, you need to wait to see if it has already been fixed in the pro forma spreadsheet. Your predecessor claimed that he had already resolved this — at least, that's what your boss says. You'll need to judge this for yourself.

On another note, remember that two employees have had rate adjustments (Jander and Joseph on 9/30/2001 and 8/24/2001, respectively). So, although this spreadsheet can handle two rates, it appears that some additional modifications to the formulas are being made for these employees to account for the hourly rates in the different time periods. Preparing spreadsheets with (hidden) exceptions for individual employees is definitely a practice to avoid. At the very least, if an exception is made, some documentation should identify that an exception exists and how it was handled. After all, that is what the sticky notes are for (Figure 10-12).

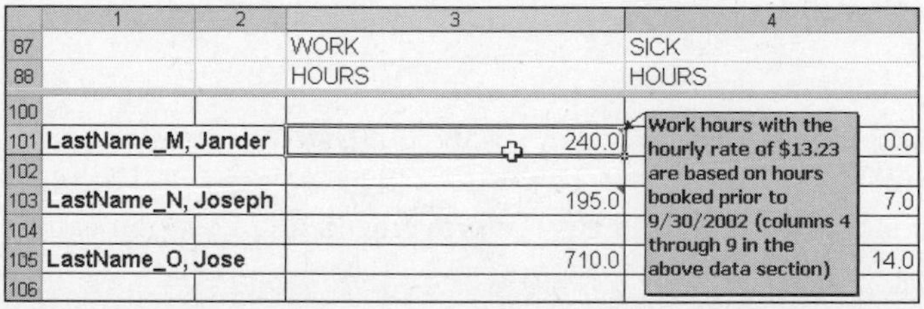

	1	2	3	4
87			WORK	SICK
88			HOURS	HOURS
100				
101	LastName_M, Jander		240.0	0.0
102				
103	LastName_N, Joseph		195.0	7.0
104				
105	LastName_O, Jose		710.0	14.0
106				

Note: Work hours with the hourly rate of $13.23 are based on hours booked prior to 9/30/2002 (columns 4 through 9 in the above data section)

Figure 10–12: Use of sticky notes to highlight (hidden) exceptions

The next problem is in the calculation of Total Spent. The problem is not one of correctness, but rather one of avoiding over-specification (see Figure 10-13), which can ultimately work against you as you build larger and more complex spreadsheets.

	1	2	6	7	8
86			HOURS		
87			USED		TOTAL
88			TO DATE	RATE	SPENT
89	LastName_B, James		711.0	$13.23	$9,406.53
90					=RC[-2]*R89C7
91	LastName_C, Julia		665.0	$13.23	$8,797.95
92					=RC[-2]*R91C7
93	LastName_G, Jeffrey		827.0	$13.23	$10,941.21
94					=RC[-2]*R93C7
95	LastName_H, Jacob		762.0	$14.00	$10,668.00

Figure 10-13: Different formulas for each employee are used to compute total spent when only one formula was needed for all the employees.

Look at the formulas for Total Spent for the first three people listed:

```
Row 89: =RC[-2]*R89C7
Row 91: =RC[-2]*R91C7
Row 93: =RC[-2]*R93C7
```

Can you suggest a change to the formulas? They're *almost* identical. It would be nice if they could be expressed as a single relationship (that is, hours used to date * hourly rate for the particular person). They should be and can be expressed that way, instead of in the form of a unique formula for each row.

Remember the discussion in Chapter 1, "A Foundation for Developing Best Practices," which explained that when the row number matches the current row, specifying the specific row is redundant. In other words, a reference to R89C7 on any cell in row 89 is the same thing as saying RC7 on any cell that resides on row 89. So, as a first step, you can make all the formulas identical:

```
Row 89: =RC[-2]*RC7
Row 91: =RC[-2]*RC7
Row 93: =RC[-2]*RC7
```

Now that the formulas are identical, you can easily replicate them without the heavy potential for errors.

Sounds as though this was a simple and easy improvement, and now you can be on your way.

But wait, there's more!

The column references in the formula mix a relative reference (two columns to the left) with an absolute column reference (column 7). It probably would be cleaner to make everything relative:

```
Row 89: =RC[-2]*RC[-1]
Row 91: =RC[-2]*RC[-1]
Row 93: =RC[-2]*RC[-1]
```

Or, make all the column references absolute:

```
Row 89: =RC6*RC7
Row 91: =RC6*RC7
Row 93: =RC6*RC7
```

Both are equivalent, cleaner, and preferable to the hybrid usage of relative/absolute column references. As long as you've gone this far, then what the heck? Why not really do it right? State the formulas in simple terms: The total spent for each employee is the hours used to date * hourly rate. Define a name called Hours_Used. It begins in column 6 on row 89, where the first name (James) appears and continues all the way down that column till the last name appears (Jarrod, which is in row 119). If you want a visual marker for this named range, just format the cells spanning this range with a different color.

You can do the same for the hourly rate. Give it a name such as Initial_Hourly_Rate. Remember, you're dealing with more than one hourly rate. So now you have a simple formula that works anywhere between rows 89 through 119 (that is, for whatever rows hours used and hourly rates are defined). This formula is as follows:

```
Row 89: =Hours_Used*Initial_Hourly_Rate
Row 91: =Hours_Used*Initial_Hourly_Rate
Row 93: =Hours_Used*Initial_Hourly_Rate
...
Row 119: =Hours_Used*Initial_Hourly_Rate
```

The obvious additional advantage is that anyone who will be working on this spreadsheet or auditing it can quickly understand it.

Before moving on to the current year pro forma budget, note that all the different components on the spreadsheet were combined onto a single worksheet. Because people are regularly added and removed from the list all the time, it would probably make more sense to separate out the personnel information on one sheet and have the computations done on another.

REVIEW OF THE CURRENT YEAR PRO FORMA

At first glance, the current year budget looks very similar to the completed budget of last year. The primary difference is that no hours have been booked for any of the employees. So, the areas containing plenty of entries spanning the weeks in last year's budget now sit empty for this year.

The second part of the spreadsheet shown in Figure 10-14 reveals a budget allocation of $120,000, with an additional $10,000, making for a total allocation of $130,000. This is a reduction from last year's budget.

Something appears a bit strange. The total spent is already $1,494.00 before we're out of the starting gate (Figure 10-14). How can this be? No employee has time booked. Uh-oh — someone made a mistake. Look at the formula for Total Spent and see what contributes to it.

The total spent is

```
=SUM(R[12]C[5]:R[46]C[5])
```

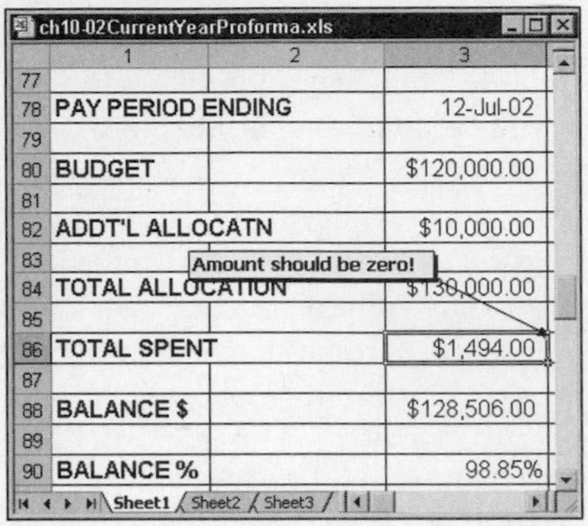

Figure 10-14: Appearance of a ghost: The total spent at start of year should be zero, but $1,494 is already reported to have been spent!

To see this formula a little more clearly, use the Trace Precedents feature (see Figure 10-15).

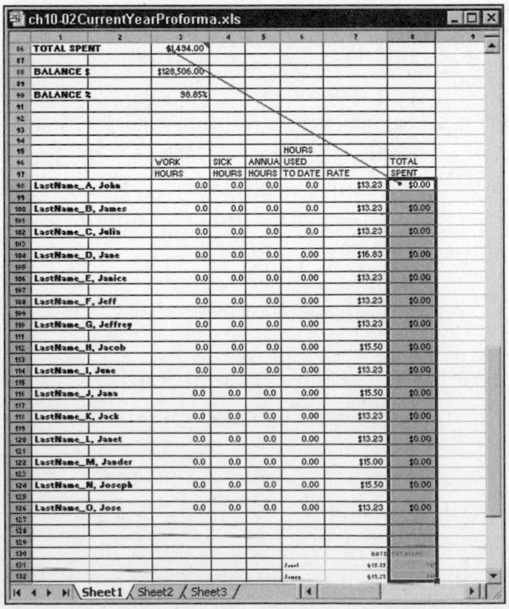

Figure 10-15: Oops! The summation range stretches beyond the list of names.

The summation range appears to be a bit over-extended. It actually dips into another set of data having nothing to do with the total spent for any employee (Figure 10-15). On the spot, you can fix this formula. It should at least be the following:

```
=SUM(R[12]C[5]:R[41]C[5])
```

In looking further at the formulas for the Total Spent, you see that they contain pretty much the same features as the prior year's budget. However, this spreadsheet doesn't even have a provision for dealing with a second or third hourly rate. So the claim made by your predecessor was faulty. You'll still need to address the issue of multiple hourly rates.

Performing the actual makeover: Part One

Rather than rework the pro forma spreadsheet as it stands, go ahead and create a new spreadsheet to try to do everything properly from scratch. It's simpler than you might think, because the concepts and basic computations have already been worked out.

1. Open a blank workbook.

2. Select the Sheet3 worksheet on the bottom tab. Double-click it and rename Sheet3 to EmployeeTime.

3. For each person there should be a line for time booked, sick time, personal time absent, rate for the current period, and the amount spent. This makes five lines for each name.

4. Copy the names of the people (LastName, FirstName) from your list of names, whether that list resides on a separate word processing document or in one of the two spreadsheets that you've been working on. Remember to choose Paste Special - Values so that you don't copy over any formatting.

5. In the first column, start the first name on row five, the second name on row 10, the third on row 15, and so forth.

6. Adjust the column width (Figure 10-16).

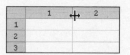

Figure 10-16: Adjusting the column width

Place your mouse pointer between columns 1 and 2 just over the top of the spreadsheet cells so that the pointer turns into a cross-hair with horizontal arrows. Double-clicking the pointer in this state will automatically resize the width of column 1 so that the width of the column matches the longest name in your list.

7. In the second column on row five, type **Time Spent**. On row 6 on the same column, type **Sick Time**, row 7, **Personal Time**, row 8, **Hourly Rate**, and row 9, **Dollars Spent**. If you move down to the cell just underneath where you typed Dollars Spent, you'll be on row 10, just next to the second name. Place the following formula in the cell for R10C2:

```
=R[-5]C
```

8. Copy and paste this formula all the way down to four rows past the line where the last name appears. Now if you decide that you want to change the label "Time Spent" to "Time Spent (hrs)," you need to change it only in the first line in which it appears. The same can be said for all the other labels.

If you haven't already done so, you can go ahead a resize the column width for column 2. Your spreadsheet should begin to look the way it appears in Figure 10-17.

	1	2
1		
2		
3		
4		
5	LastName_A, John	Time spent
6		Sick time
7		Personal time
8		Hourly rate
9		Dollars Spent
10	LastName_B, James	Time spent
11		Sick time
12		Personal time
13		Hourly rate
14		Dollars Spent
15	LastName C, Julia	Time spent

Figure 10-17: Your spreadsheet's appearance at this stage

Start filling in the dates across the top row. The reality is that in the workplace, you're not too likely to have spare time to fiddle around with sophisticated date arithmetic techniques. I won't waste your time trying to push you into developing something you might have neither the time nor inclination to use. For those of you who are interested, I've included a brief sidebar at the end of the chapter along with some Take-Away formulas.

9. Right now, you can go ahead and copy the dates listed in the pro forma spreadsheet and the Paste Special...Values to row 1 column 3 in the EmployeeTime worksheet. Do this by opening the pro forma spreadsheet and clicking the first date, which should be R1C4. While holding down the Ctrl+Shift keys, press the → key. With this, you should have the whole range of dates selected. Copy the selected cells (Ctrl+C). Open the new spreadsheet, click the tab for EmployeeTime, and then click the cell on row 1, column 3. Now you can choose Paste Special...Values.

10. Compute the dollars spent as an aggregate of time spent, sick time, and personal time. Go to row 9, column 3. The formula for this cell is the rate (located one row above) multiplied by the sum of the time spent plus sick time plus personal time (that is, the sum from four rows above through two rows above):

```
=R[-1]C*SUM(R[-4]C:R[-2]C)
```

Just replicate this formula over to the right for the next 26 columns across or however many columns the dates span. You may wish to clean up the labeling for the dates based on the previous footnote. However, I'll leave this to your discretion.

Note: The date values that were obtained from the pro forma spreadsheet were originally prepared manually and do contain some errors. In that spreadsheet, you will see the dates on column 17 spanning from 12/30/2001 through 1/10/2002. In column 18 they span from 1/6/2002 through 1/17/2002. It is clearly not logical to have the beginning date in column 18 start before the end date in column 17 has finished! This underscores the importance of keeping your attention on details. Perhaps it might not be such a bad idea to employ some date arithmetic, after all.

11. Copy the formula that's used to compute the total spent and paste it to the appropriate cells for the other names in the list. Go to row 8 column 3 and place a dollar value for the hourly rate. In keeping with the data from the prior spreadsheets, a good value to use would be $13.23. For now, just put this number in. As soon as HR supplies you with the updated values, you'll be able to place them into the spreadsheet. Move over one column to the right (you should be in cell R8C4). Type in this formula:

```
=RC[-1]
```

12. The value for the rate for the prior period is now adapted to the current period (in this case, spanning 7/15/2002 through 7/26/2002). Continue to copy this formula all the way to the right for the next 25 columns or however many columns the dates span. Replicate the rate value and formulas to each of the other employee names.

For the moment, put some test values into the hours booked to verify that the formulas are working correctly. The resulting worksheet should now look something like Figure 10-18.

	1	2	3	4	5	6	7
1							
2							
3							
4			7/1-7/12	7/15-7/26	7/29-8/9	8/12-8/23	8/26-9/
5	LastName_A, John	Time spent	35	42	42	35	
6		Sick time	7			7	
7		Personal time					
8		Hourly rate	13.23	13.23	13.23	13.23	13.2
9		Dollars Spent	555.66	555.66	555.66	555.66	
10	LastName_B, James	Time spent	42	42	42	21	
11		Sick time				14	
12		Personal time					
13		Hourly rate	13.23	15	15	15	1
14		Dollars Spent	555.66	630	630	525	
15	LastName_C, Julia	Time spent	39	42	42	42	
16		Sick time					
17		Personal time	4				
18		Hourly rate	13.23	14	14	14	1
19		Dollars Spent	568.89	588	588	588	
20	LastName_D, Jane	Time spent	40	35	42		
21		Sick time		7			
22		Personal time					
23		Hourly rate	13.23	14	14	14	1
24		Dollars Spent	529.2	588	588	0	
25	LastName_E, Janice	Time spent	21	21	43		
26		Sick time	14	7			
27		Personal time		7			

Sheet1 / Sheet2 \ EmployeeTime /

Figure 10-18: Current snapshot of your new spreadsheet with some made-up test values

13. You may recall that the reporting requires separate accounting of the total time spent, total sick time, and total personal time for each individual employee. You can compute this now using the SUMPRODUCT formula.

Insert a blank column between columns two and three on the EmployeeTime worksheet.

To compute the total dollars for time spent for the first employee, go to the blank cell on row 5 column 3. In that cell, type in the following formula:

```
=SUMPRODUCT(RC[1]:RC[27],R[3]C[1]:R[3]C[27])
```

SUMPRODUCT multiplies identically structured ranges that are separated by commas.

As an aside, you could choose to always use SUMPRODUCT, specifying only a single range and no commas. This would compute the same result as the SUM formula. In addition to making the formula harder to read, SUMPRODUCT incurs a greater overhead of processing resources than does SUM.

Tests on a Pentium 4 based CPU clocked at 1.7GHz running Windows 2000 shows a requirement of at least a 50 percent more CPU time for the equivalent computation when using SUMPRODUCT.

Obviously, if the range of dates spans more than (or fewer than) 27 columns, you will need to adjust the formula so that the cell references match. That is, take all the values of hours booked for time spent, which appear on the next 27 columns, and multiply them by their respective hourly rates to get the aggregate dollars for time spent for this employee.

You'll do something similar for computing the sick time and personal time. Also sum these three values to get the total dollars spent for the employee. Here is what the formulas look like:

```
Row 5: =SUMPRODUCT(RC[1]:RC[27],R[3]C[1]:R[3]C[27])
Row 6: =SUMPRODUCT(RC[1]:RC[27],R[2]C[1]:R[2]C[27])
Row 7: =SUMPRODUCT(RC[1]:RC[27],R[1]C[1]:R[1]C[27])
Row 8: [leave this cell blank]
Row 9: =SUM(R[-4]C:R[-2]C)
```

The SUMPRODUCT formulas have their row references highlighted to show how they differ. As you can see, all the formulas use relative references. The reason is simple: The relative referencing makes replicating these formulas for all the other employees easy. Just do a simple copy by selecting rows 5 through 9 on column three and pasting this data into the cell in row 10 of the same column, paste again on row 15, again on row 20, and so forth until this has been done for all the employees in the list.

14. At this point the spreadsheet is beginning to appear dense with all the formulas and numbers. You may want to tidy up the formatting to make the display more palatable.

    Click column 3 (see Figure 10-19) and adjust the formatting so that numbers in this column are reported in dollars and cents (after the column is selected, choose Format → Cells and specify formatting for numbers).

		1	2	3
1				
2				
3				
4				
5	LastName_A, John	Time spent	$2,037.42
6		Sick time	$185.22
7		Personal time	$0.00
8		Hourly rate	
9		Dollars Spent	$2,222.64
10	LastName_B, James	Time spent	$2,130.66

Figure 10-19: Selecting columns and adjusting formats

If you haven't deselected column 3, you can immediately select all of rows 8 and 9 in much the same way you did for column 3 (except that now your selection will span a horizontal range instead of a vertical column). Upon selecting, click Ctrl+Y to repeat the formatting you previously did.

15. In case you did something (for example, saved your spreadsheet) before attempting to repeat the formatting, Excel will have forgotten the very last step. You will have the option to copy a cell with the currency formatting (that is, pretty much any cell on column 3, because it is already formatted for dollars and cents), perform a horizontal select of the row for rate and dollars spent (rows 8 and 9), and click Paste Special...Format.

After you've done this for rows 8 and 9, you can repeat or apply the paste formatting for the next occurrence of rate and dollars spent (which is on rows 13 and 14), then again for the next occurrence of rate and dollars spent (which is on rows 18 and 19), and so forth.

The spreadsheet should look like Figure 10-20.

Figure 10-20: Current appearance of your new spreadsheet

By now, you're probably thinking that if you had formatted the cells for rates and dollars spent while you were still writing the mathematical formulas for those cells, you wouldn't have to go through the formatting for these rows now. The formatting would have been replicated along with the formulas and you could have avoided this step. Right you are! This is all part of the learning process. Next time, you'll know better and will be more adept at organizing and planning your spreadsheet construction. It's all about technique.

16. Go ahead and do some quick formatting and finishing touches before proceeding to the report section. Your worksheet should end up looking like Figure 10-21.

This worksheet is a lot more readable than the original spreadsheets given to you. To make your worksheet appear this way, here's what you should do:

a. Make the labels for time spent, sick time, personal time, and rate and dollars spent easier to read by adjusting the capitalization and revising the wording, where appropriate, to make it more descriptive. (You need do this only on rows 5–9, because they should be duplicated all the way down the column.)

b. Make all the text in the first column boldface.

c. Move the contents of the dates listed from the first to the fourth row.

d. Put in a descriptive title for Budgeted Amounts and resize the column width as necessary.

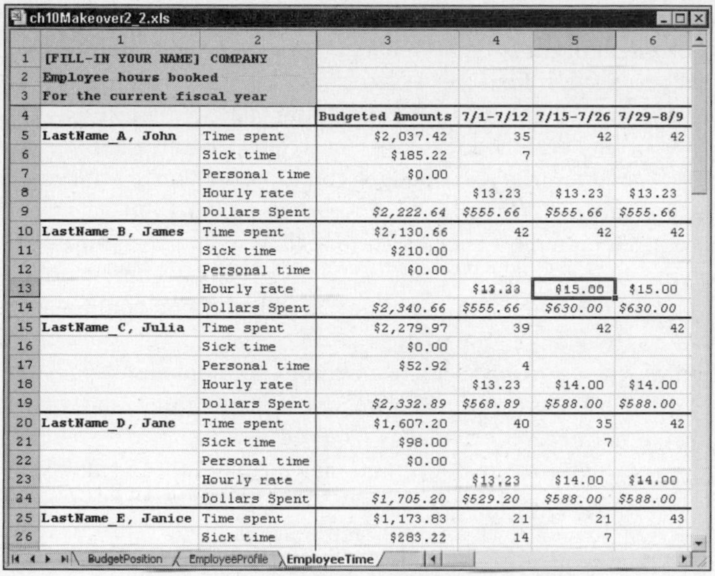

ch10Makeover2_2.xls

	1	2	3	4	5	6
1	[FILL-IN YOUR NAME] COMPANY					
2	Employee hours booked					
3	For the current fiscal year					
4			Budgeted Amounts	7/1-7/12	7/15-7/26	7/29-8/9
5	LastName_A, John	Time spent	$2,037.42	35	42	42
6		Sick time	$185.22	7		
7		Personal time	$0.00			
8		Hourly rate		$13.23	$13.23	$13.23
9		Dollars Spent	*$2,222.64*	*$555.66*	*$555.66*	*$555.66*
10	LastName_B, James	Time spent	$2,130.66	42	42	42
11		Sick time	$210.00			
12		Personal time	$0.00			
13		Hourly rate		$13.23	$15.00	$15.00
14		Dollars Spent	*$2,340.66*	*$555.66*	*$630.00*	*$630.00*
15	LastName_C, Julia	Time spent	$2,279.97	39	42	42
16		Sick time	$0.00			
17		Personal time	$52.92	4		
18		Hourly rate		$13.23	$14.00	$14.00
19		Dollars Spent	*$2,332.89*	*$568.89*	*$588.00*	*$588.00*
20	LastName_D, Jane	Time spent	$1,607.20	40	35	42
21		Sick time	$98.00		7	
22		Personal time	$0.00			
23		Hourly rate		$13.23	$14.00	$14.00
24		Dollars Spent	*$1,705.20*	*$529.20*	*$588.00*	*$588.00*
25	LastName_E, Janice	Time spent	$1,173.83	21	21	43
26		Sick time	$283.22	14	7	

BudgetPosition / EmployeeProfile / EmployeeTime

Figure 10-21: Worksheet with finishing touches applied

e. Format the totals appearing on row 9 in italics.

f. Place a thick outline border starting at R5C1 and ending on R9C30 (or whatever column the date ranges end).

g. Copy this region and choose Paste Special...Format.

h. Select the range from the descriptive title Budgeted Amounts through the last date label (i.e., R4C3:R4C30) and create a thick border around this range.

i. On the top-left corner of the spreadsheet, type in identifying information such as the company name, type of report for this worksheet, and period covered. To make this portion readily identifiable, colorize the background with a light shade of gray.

j. Create horizontal and vertical panes that intersect between rows 4, 5 and columns 2, 3 and apply the freeze panes feature to lock in the split panes.

Surely, by now, you should be able to do all this on your own. If you find you are still having problems, you can go back to some of the earlier chapters (to get a better handle on the use of formulas and cell references).

If you want, you can add whatever additional formatting that you like. You could, for instance, define custom headers or footers for the worksheet. You might want to adjust the Page Setup preferences so that the report will render nicely on a printout.

Remember, this section is just a table of data values and interim computations that will be used for the more important reports that summarize where your department stands on the budget. So, all this formatting is just for your benefit. It will make it easier on your eyes and help you to avoid potential clerical mistakes.

You're facing two important design decisions. One relates to the hourly rate structure. The spreadsheet for the prior year budget could accommodate, at most, two hourly rates for any employee. When an employee had a change in pay rate, the formulas for computing the amount spent for the specific employee had to be manually edited, applying one rate for the sum of a given set of columns and another for the remaining set of columns. It might not be so bad if you could avoid manual editing of formulas (which is prone to error).

The technique used in the new spreadsheet allows you to accommodate as many changes in the hourly rates as you please. You do not have to think about the process, and no manual editing of any formulas is required.

The other design decision pertains to the intentional positioning of employee summary data on specific rows and columns. This positioning will play a key role in retrieving data for the Employee Profile and Budget Reports.

You may have noticed that the data for any given employee spans a block of five rows. The data for the first employee begins on row 5. The data for the second employee begins on row 10, the third on row 15, and so forth. Imposing such regularity will make it easy to collect the data that will be used for the summary reports.

Performing the actual makeover: Part Two

This section explains a powerful and elegant technique for those of you who are ambitiously inclined or actually encounter the need for this technique.

Those of you who are not prepared to follow the details might still want to read through the beginning portions of this section to understand the other options available, and then skim through the remainder to get a sense of the technique and its benefits, in case a need for this technique eventually arises.

RETRIEVING RELATIONALLY POSITIONED INFORMATION

This makeover chapter is based on a real-life example that contains the kinds of spreadsheet errors and stylistic tendencies you might expect to find when you inherit a predecessor's work. Every now and then, you'll be thrown a curve ball. In the next step of this makeover, you'll encounter one of these curve balls.

Rather than change the makeover assignment to a made-up scenario or try to sugarcoat the analysis and computations, I show you how to address the challenge head on. I also present some alternative approaches.

Take a brief moment to review what's required. You will see that you need to provide information summarizing to date each employee's time spent, sick time, and total time. You already have this information in the EmployeeTime worksheet. It's just spread out. No one seems to care very much about how it is presented; your colleagues just want consolidated summary figures. So, if you want, you can copy the first three columns of this worksheet and perform two paste specials onto a new worksheet: once for pasting the values, and once for pasting the format (that is, you will forgo the use of formulas on the new worksheet). There's an advantage with this approach: It is simple. There's just a bit of elbow grease in the copy and pasting. You can easily e-mail the resulting spreadsheet.

The advantages, however, don't extend further than this. To begin with, you still need to compute the total amount spent to date in order to show your financial position and what percentage of the budget has been consumed. Of course, you can pluck out the numbers of the fifteen or so employees. This strategy veers toward electronic pencil pushing (something I would prefer that you avoid). If it's expedient and you're in a one-time situation, it may be called for. However, this report needs to be prepared every two weeks. Also, this approach does not scale particularly well. What if your task was to track more than 150 employees, maybe even 1,500 employees?

So, in a pinch, this "one-off approach" is workable but not recommended, and certainly does not follow best practices. The section "The alternative one-off approach," which you'll find a little later in this chapter, summarizes this alternative (but not recommended) approach.

THE RECOMMENDED APPROACH

You are a surprisingly short distance away from completing the basic makeover. The approach is both powerful and elegant.

The key to completing this step essentially entails the use of one Excel function, OFFSET. With this function you can leverage all your hard work and pick the data you want from the EmployeeTime worksheet in one fell swoop. It's a bit involved, so I'll go through this slowly.

The methodology for this is straightforward if you think about it visually. Recall that on your EmployeeTime worksheet, the name of the first employee appears on row 5. The name of the second employee appears on row 10. No doubt you can guess on what row the name for the third employee appears.

The strategy for retrieving data for each of the employees is to locate where the desired data resides for the 1st employee. Once it is found, look exactly five rows down and in the same column you will find the equivalent data for the second employee. Look another five rows down and you will see the same type data for the third employee. Continue with this pattern and you will be able to retrieve data for all of the employees.

If all of these lookups shared a common reference point, you could use a common formula for doing a lookup and you'd need only to identify which employee's data you want (that is the first, second, third, and so on).

If you've been linearly reading through the chapters in the book, you'll probably guess that the likely Excel function candidate to use is OFFSET, which has the following syntax:

```
OFFSET(basePosition, numberRowsDown, numberColumnsRight)
```

OFFSET, as you may recall, retrieves the contents of a cell that is positioned a given number of rows down and columns across, relative to some base position. Use the top-left corner (R1C1) of the EmployeeTime worksheet as the starting point.

From the base position of R1C1, you see in Figure 10-22 that the dollar amount for time spent for the first employee is located over to the right by two columns (which takes you to column 3), and is located four rows down (which takes you to row 5).

Go another five rows down and you will find the cell displaying the amount for time spent for the second employee. Relative to R1C1, you have moved a grand total of 9 rows (=(2*5)-1) down.

Because every employee is uniformly spaced in five-row intervals, starting on row five, you can retrieve the names and their data based on their positional arrangement on the worksheet. Everything seems to work in multiples of 5.

So, here are the steps:

	1	2	3	4	5	6	7
1	R1C1 - base pos.						
2							
3							
4			Budgeted Amt	Date1	Date2	Date3	Date4
5	1st name	Time Spent	$2,037				
6		Sick Time					
7		Personal					
8		Hourly Rate					
9		$ Spent					
10	2nd name	Time Spent	$2,130.6				
11		Sick Time					
12		Personal					
13		$ Spent					
14		Hourly Rate					
15	3rd name	Time Spent	$2,279.9				
16		Sick Time					
17		Personal					
18		Hourly Rate					
19		$ Spent					
20	4th name	Time Spent	$1,607.20				
21		Sick Time					
22		Personal					
23		Hourly Rate					
24		$ Spent					
25	5th name	Time Spent	$1,173.83				
26		Sick Time					

Figure 10-22: Pinpointing offsets from top-left corner of the worksheet

1. Rename Sheet2 to EmployeeProfile.

2. On the EmployeeProfile worksheet, type in the numbers 1 through 15 in a vertical column starting from R6C1. This can be a straight list of numbers without any formulas, or you can employ a formula such as:

   ```
   =1+R[-1]C
   ```

   You can choose which approach you prefer.

3. As shown in Figure 10-23, define an Excel name for this region of cells (that is, R6C1:R20C1) with a name like Employee_Sequence_No (see Figure 10-23).

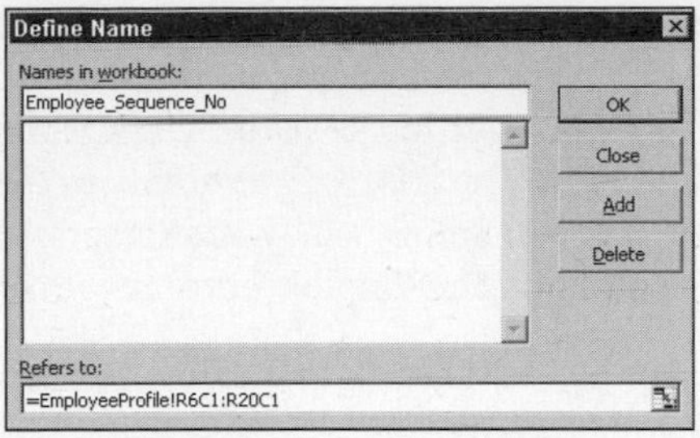

Figure 10-23: Define a range for `Employee_Sequence_No`.

4. Retrieve the names of the first few people. On the EmployeeTime worksheet you'll see that:

   `LastName_A, John` is located on `R5C1`

   `LastName_B, James` is located on `R10C1`

   `LastName_C, Julia` is located on `R15C1`

   The specific offsets relative to `R1C1` of the EmployeeTime worksheet are

   ```
   =OFFSET(R1C1,4,0)
   =OFFSET(R1C1,9,0)
   =OFFSET(R1C1,14,0)
   ```

As you can clearly see, you are retrieving subsequent names in increments of five rows at a time. The first employee name is four rows beneath `R1C1`. It's just one short of being five rows. The second employee name is nine rows beneath `R1C1`. It's just one short of being ten rows. The third employee name is fourteen rows beneath `R1C1`. It's just — you guessed it — one short of being fifteen rows beneath `R1C1`.

So, the pattern that's emerging is this:

```
row offset is (5 * Employee_Sequence_No) - 1
```

You saw that employee names and their respective data are laid out in blocks of five rows. Had they been spaced six rows apart, you would be using 6 instead of 5 in the formula.

An interesting thing has happened. When you used specific offsets to retrieve the employee names, you had to enumerate every offset. Clearly, that was inefficient. If you used the formula instead of hardwired numbers for row offsets, you would need only one formula:

```
=OFFSET(R1C1,(5*Employee_Sequence_No)-1,0)
```

You almost have the complete formula to retrieve any of the employee names. This formula would work fine if `R1C1` cell were on the same worksheets as the one you're computing from. The `R1C1` I've been referring to is on the *EmployeeTime* worksheet. We're doing our computations on the *EmployeeProfile* worksheet. So, basically, you must define the `R1C1` reference unambiguously with respect to worksheets. Here is the final formula that appears on the EmployeeProfile worksheet for each of the cells in `R6C2:R20C2`.

```
=OFFSET(EmployeeProfile!R1C1,(5*Employee_Sequence_No)-1,0)
```

Figure 10-24 shows what the spreadsheet looks like (with the formulas spelled out for your convenience). The label `Name` is placed above where the names appear.

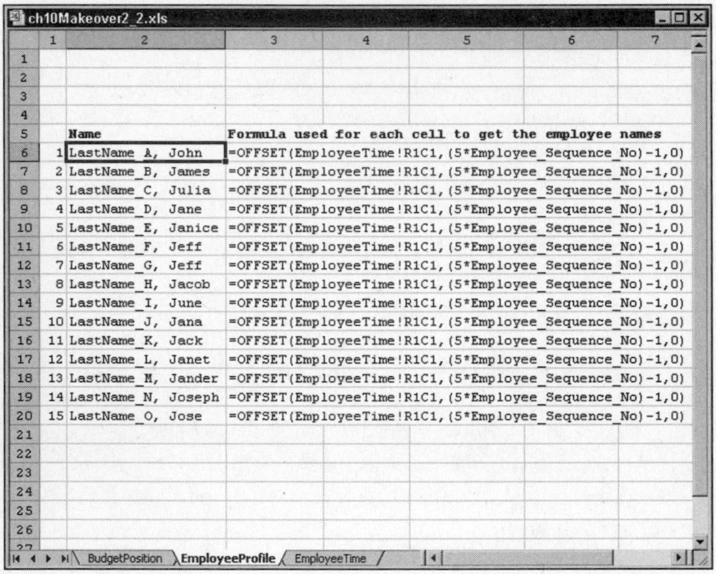

	1	2	3
5		Name	Formula used for each cell to get the employee names
6	1	LastName_A, John	=OFFSET(EmployeeTime!R1C1,(5*Employee_Sequence_No)-1,0)
7	2	LastName_B, James	=OFFSET(EmployeeTime!R1C1,(5*Employee_Sequence_No)-1,0)
8	3	LastName_C, Julia	=OFFSET(EmployeeTime!R1C1,(5*Employee_Sequence_No)-1,0)
9	4	LastName_D, Jane	=OFFSET(EmployeeTime!R1C1,(5*Employee_Sequence_No)-1,0)
10	5	LastName_E, Janice	=OFFSET(EmployeeTime!R1C1,(5*Employee_Sequence_No)-1,0)
11	6	LastName_F, Jeff	=OFFSET(EmployeeTime!R1C1,(5*Employee_Sequence_No)-1,0)
12	7	LastName_G, Jeff	=OFFSET(EmployeeTime!R1C1,(5*Employee_Sequence_No)-1,0)
13	8	LastName_H, Jacob	=OFFSET(EmployeeTime!R1C1,(5*Employee_Sequence_No)-1,0)
14	9	LastName_I, June	=OFFSET(EmployeeTime!R1C1,(5*Employee_Sequence_No)-1,0)
15	10	LastName_J, Jana	=OFFSET(EmployeeTime!R1C1,(5*Employee_Sequence_No)-1,0)
16	11	LastName_K, Jack	=OFFSET(EmployeeTime!R1C1,(5*Employee_Sequence_No)-1,0)
17	12	LastName_L, Janet	=OFFSET(EmployeeTime!R1C1,(5*Employee_Sequence_No)-1,0)
18	13	LastName_M, Jander	=OFFSET(EmployeeTime!R1C1,(5*Employee_Sequence_No)-1,0)
19	14	LastName_N, Joseph	=OFFSET(EmployeeTime!R1C1,(5*Employee_Sequence_No)-1,0)
20	15	LastName_O, Jose	=OFFSET(EmployeeTime!R1C1,(5*Employee_Sequence_No)-1,0)

Figure 10-24: Formulas for retrieving names from the EmployeeTime worksheet (Note: They all have identical formulas!)

To get the other data for each employee (time spent, sick time, and personal time), you will apply the criteria exactly as stated before:

The strategy for retrieving data for each of the employees is to locate where the desired data resides for the first employee. After it is found, look exactly five rows down and in the same column to find the equivalent data for the second employee. Look another five rows down and you will see the same type data for the third employee. Continue with this pattern and you will be able to retrieve data for all of the employees.

Take a closer look to see how the data is relationally positioned. In Figure 10-25, the formatting has been altered to highlight the information you will want to retrieve.

	1	2	3
1	[FILL-IN YOUR NAME]	COMPANY	
2	Employee hours booked		
3	For the current fiscal year		
4			Budgeted Amounts
5	**LastName_A, John**	Time spent	**$2,037.42**
6		Sick time	**$185.22**
7		Personal time	**$0.00**
8		Hourly rate	

Figure 10-25: Information to be retrieved is highlighted.

You already have the basic formula for retrieving the employee name:

```
=OFFSET(R1C1,(5*Employee_Sequence_No)-1,0)
```

The 'Time spent' of $2,037.42 is two columns over to the right (relative to R1C1). So, change the column offset from 0 to 2. Everything else remains the same.

```
=OFFSET(R1C1,(5*Employee_Sequence_No)-1,2)
```

Use this formula for every cell in row 6, column 3 down through row 20, column 3. Then label R5C3 as Time Spent.

If you really want to get fancy, you can use an OFFSET formula to retrieve the label of Time Spent from the EmployeeTime worksheet.

The position for data specifying the monetary amount of the employee's sick time ($185.22) is only one row further down than the data for time spent. This translates to a row offset that is 1 + the row offset for time spent. The –1 and +1 cancel each other out, so you have:

```
=OFFSET(R1C1,(5*Employee_Sequence_No),2)
```

Use this formula for every cell in row 6, column 4 down through row 20, column 4. Then label R5C4 as Sick Time.

The row offset for personal time is 1 + the row offset for sick time. Hence, the data for personal time for each given employee is

```
=OFFSET(R1C1,(5*Employee_Sequence_No)+1,2)
```

Use this formula for every cell in row 6, column 5 down through row 20, column 5. Then label R5C5 as Personal Time.

To get the Total Spent, take the arithmetic sum of time spent + sick time + personal time. This should appear in each of the cells from row 6, column 6 through row 20, column 6. Add the appropriate formatting and labeling information, and you should have something like Figure 10-26, which gives you a bird's eye view of all the employees.

ch10Makeover2_3.xls

	1	2	3	4	5	6	7
1	[FILL-IN YOUR NAME] COMPANY						
2	Employee Summary Profile						
3	For the current fiscal year						
4							
5		Name	Time spent	Sick time	Personal Time	*Total time*	
6	1	LastName_A, John	$2,037.42	$185.22	$0.00	*$2,222.64*	
7	2	LastName_B, James	$2,130.66	$210.00	$0.00	*$2,340.66*	
8	3	LastName_C, Julia	$2,279.97	$0.00	$52.92	*$2,332.89*	
9	4	LastName_D, Jane	$1,607.20	$98.00	$0.00	*$1,705.20*	
10	5	LastName_E, Janice	$1,173.83	$283.22	$98.00	*$1,555.05*	
11	6	LastName_F, Jeff	$1,574.37	$92.61	$0.00	*$1,666.98*	
12	7	LastName_G, Jeff	$1,815.66	$0.00	$0.00	*$1,815.66*	
13	8	LastName_H, Jacob	$1,691.97	$0.00	$52.92	*$1,744.89*	
14	9	LastName_I, June	$1,607.20	$98.00	$0.00	*$1,705.20*	
15	10	LastName_J, Jana	$1,173.83	$283.22	$98.00	*$1,555.05*	
16	11	LastName_K, Jack	$1,574.37	$92.61	$0.00	*$1,666.98*	
17	12	LastName_L, Janet	$1,815.66	$0.00	$0.00	*$1,815.66*	
18	13	LastName_M, Jander	$1,691.97	$0.00	$52.92	*$1,744.89*	
19	14	LastName_N, Joseph	$1,607.20	$98.00	$0.00	*$1,705.20*	
20	15	LastName_O, Jose	$1,173.83	$283.22	$98.00	*$1,555.05*	
21							
22							
23							
24							
25							
26							

BudgetPosition / **EmployeeProfile** / EmployeeTime

Figure 10-26: Completed summary profile

You really are at the home stretch. If you haven't given a name to your Sheet1 worksheet, name it BudgetPosition. It should look like Figure 10-27.

ch10Makeover2_3.xls

	1	2	3	4	5	6	7
1	[FILL-IN YOUR NAME] COMPANY						
2	Budget Position Report						
3	For the current fiscal year						
4							
5	PAY PERIOD ENDING	7/12/2002					
6							
7	BUDGET	$120,000.00					
8							
9	ADDT'L ALLOCATN	$10,111.00					
10							
11	TOTAL ALLOCATION	$130,111.00					
12							
13	TOTAL SPENT	$27,132.00	=SUM(EmployeeProfile!C[4])				
14							
15	BALANCE $	$102,979.00					
16							
17	BALANCE %	20.9%					
18							
19							
20							
21							
22							
23							
24							
25							
26							

BudgetPosition / EmployeeProfile / EmployeeTime

Figure 10-27: Position Report (Note: Total Spent captures all employee data from EmployeeProfile since it takes the sum of the whole column)

The BALANCE $ is the difference between the TOTAL ALLOCATION and the TOTAL SPENT. The BALANCE % of funds used is just the ratio of TOTAL SPENT to TOTAL ALLOCATION, formatted as a percentage to 1 decimal point of a percent.

The essential item to note is that the formula for the TOTAL SPENT takes the sum of the whole column from the previous worksheet (EmployeeProfile). The formula for this is

```
=SUM(EmployeeProfile!C[4])
```

The completed spreadsheet is provided on the CD-ROM in the file ch10_Makeover2_2.xls.

Those of you who apply the alternative one-off approach, described later in this chapter, will have to use a different formula. You will have to calculate the total spent directly on the EmployeeTime worksheet. If that calculation is located on R3C3, you can retrieve that value by using the following formula in your Budget Position Report:

```
=EmployeeTime!R3C3
```

Alternative Approaches

In working through this makeover you have three strategies available, and I've asked you to take the middle-of-the-road approach. One of the two alternative approaches is to exceed your original scope and perform further optimizations if you have additional time or specific needs. The other alternative is the exact opposite. It assumes, on this go-round, that you are really strapped for time and need a quick, one-time solution, which, of course, is not a best practice.

Further optimizations: Some things you could do if you have the time or the need

In this chapter I spoke of utilizing date arithmetic and conditional formatting to highlight changes in the hourly rates. Both of these have been incorporated into an enhanced spreadsheet enclosed on the CD-ROM in the file ch10_Makeover2_3.xls.

RATE CHANGE COLORIZATION

Using Conditional Formatting, you can colorize changes to the hourly rate for any and all employees. As shown in Figure 10-28, when the hourly rate for a given employee is different than it was for the prior period, it is colorized.

Formulas for the date arithmetic

Recall that the date ranges are shown to start from a given Monday and end on Friday of the following week. The date 7/1/2002 is the start date on this spreadsheet and happens to fall on a Monday. Note that this appears on R3C2 (as shown in the figure that follows). When you type in the date in any cell, Excel automatically stores it as the number of days since January 1, 1900, but applies the default date format, making the number easy for humans to read.

	1	2		3	4	5
1	[FILL-IN YOUR NAME] COMPANY				Formula is used to predict these date ranges	
2	Employee hours booked					
3	As of week beginning:	7/1/2002				
4	Start			Budgeted Amounts	7/1-7/12	7/15-7/26

Starting Date used for computing subsequent dates is highlighted

Select the cell R3C2 and type in **7/1/2002**.

Excel will automatically re-edit what you just typed and convert it to the value 37438 (July 1st, 2002, is 37,437 days since January 1st, 1900).

Recall that you can convert a number into a custom formatted text representation using the Excel TEXT function. A text string of "7/1" can be constructed from the following:

=TEXT(37438,"d/m")

The number 37438 is stored in R3C2. So you can use:

=TEXT(37438,"d/m")

to construct the string "7/1". 7/1/2002 falls on a Monday. Friday of the following week is eleven days later. To get the string "7/12", you can use the formula

=TEXT(37438+11,"d/m")

Equivalently, you can use

=TEXT(R3C2+11,"d/m")

To construct the string "71/-7/12", you can perform a string concatenation (using the & symbol):

=TEXT(R3C2,"d/m")&"-"&TEXT(R3C2+11,"d/m")

This is the string that's been computed in R4C4. To compute the next string ("7/15-7/28") in R4C5, you need only to advance the start and end date by 14 days. The next string ("7/29-8/9") that appears in R4C6 is essentially computed the same way, only you are adding another 14 days. It would mean that every time you shift a column to the right, you need to advance your beginning and end dates at 14. If you count the number of columns beyond 4 and multiply it by 14, you will get the correct number of days to add to R3C2 for the beginning date and R3C2+11 for the end date.

The correct formula is now

```
=TEXT(R3C2+14*(COLUMN()-4),"m/d")&"-"&TEXT(R3C2+14*(COLUMN()-
4)+11,"m/d")
```

Starting from column 4, this will produce the following list of sequences:

```
7/1-7/12
7/15-7/28
7/29-8/9
8/12-8/23
...
```

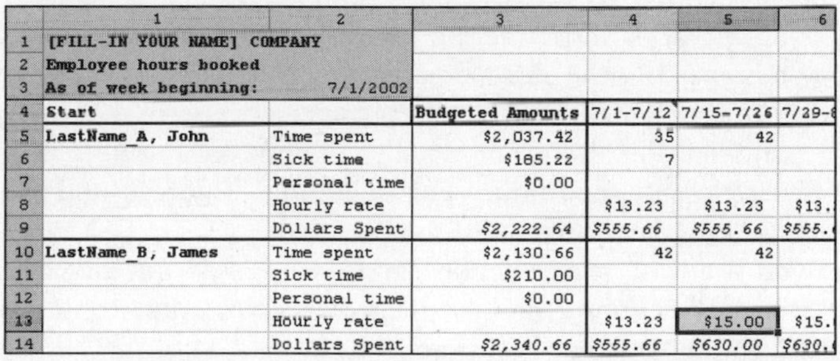

	1	2	3	4	5	6
1	[FILL-IN YOUR NAME] COMPANY					
2	Employee hours booked					
3	As of week beginning:	7/1/2002				
4	Start		Budgeted Amounts	7/1-7/12	7/15-7/26	7/29-8
5	LastName_A, John	Time spent	$2,037.42	35	42	
6		Sick time	$185.22	7		
7		Personal time	$0.00			
8		Hourly rate		$13.23	$13.23	$13.
9		Dollars Spent	$2,222.64	$555.66	$555.66	$555.
10	LastName_B, James	Time spent	$2,130.66	42	42	
11		Sick time	$210.00			
12		Personal time	$0.00			
13		Hourly rate		$13.23	$15.00	$15.
14		Dollars Spent	$2,340.66	$555.66	$630.00	$630.

Figure 10-28: Automatic colorization of altered data

This is done using conditional formatting of the hourly rates for each of the employees (columns 4 - 30 on rows 8, 13, 18, 23, 28, 33 ... 78). The logic of the formula for conditional formatting is as follows: If the current cell is different from the cell on its immediate left and the cell on the immediate left is not empty, then colorize the current cell). Here is how it appears when you make the entry for a conditional format. Note, the drop-down list specifies Formula Is rather than Cell Value Is (see Figure 10-29).

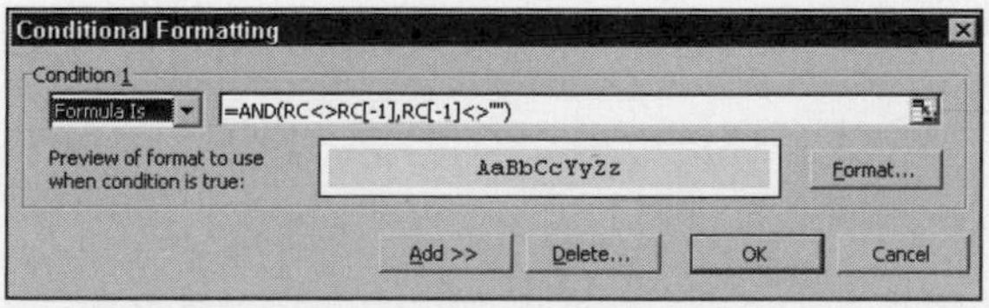

Figure 10-29: Conditional formatting based on cell
formulas rather than cell values

The reason that you would want to see whether the cell on the immediate left is empty is because the cell to the immediate left of the leftmost hourly rate is empty.

If you don't take this into account, the leftmost entry for any employee would be gratuitously colorized. This is an artifact you do not need.

The alternative one-off approach

Earlier in the chapter, "Recommended Approach" outlined a very elegant and powerful technique. Its use entailed an Excel function called OFFSET. Also discussed was a methodology for picking out the locations of specific data you might want to retrieve. I have to imagine that some readers will have neither the time nor the inclination to delve into the level of detail or complexity entailed by that approach.

This discussion has been prepared for those of you who do not want to bother with the more sophisticated route. The approach stressed here favors "quick-and-dirty" over best practices, when the two conflict. This approach will get the assignment of tracking budget totals done. After all, that is the objective, right?

The quick-and-dirty approach has its merits. You don't have to apply sophisticated Excel functions, but you will still get the job done. Just remember that this time next year, you may be repeating the same exercise you're about to do. Every time you have employee turnover, you'll need to rework and recheck your formulas. You'll also see that you won't be able to produce the Employee Profile report with this approach. If that report is important, your hand will be forced and the quick-and-dirty approach will not be viable.

By comparison, had you used the recommended approach, you'd get all three reports. You would have to adjust only a few numbers and your work would be almost done. That's central to the theme of best practices.

In a nutshell, here's a summary of what you're about to do:

Recall that the EmployeeTime worksheet is already done. Ultimately, you will need to prepare a Budget Position Report that compares Total Allocation with Total Spent. The allocation is a given number. There's no computation for you to perform.

The Total Spent is a different story, however. You have the information, but it's in piecemeal form. A little piece of it is tabulated with each employee. You will garner this information by tabulating the aggregate amount spent for each of the individual employees and plugging this number into the Budget Position report.

If you want to prepare the Employee Profile report to be similar to what was prepared earlier in the chapter, you're out of luck. There's no easy and direct way to do it other than through the recommended approach previously described. I suppose you could work out all the individual formulas. If you have several hundred employees to track, then you're definitely using the wrong techniques and most certainly the wrong technology for the tasks at hand.

Follow these steps:

1. Recall that the EmployeeTime worksheet tabulated the time spent, sick time, personal time, and dollars spent for each employee. Go to row 3, column 3 (see Figure 10-30) and type in the following formula:

   ```
   =R[6]C+R[11]C+R[16]C+R[21]C+R[26]C+R[31]C+R[36]C+R[41]C+R[46]
   C+R[51]C+R[56]C+R[61]C+R[66]C+R[71]C+R[76]C
   ```

This formula is included in the takeaway.txt file on the CD-ROM for this book, so you can just copy and paste the formula into Excel.

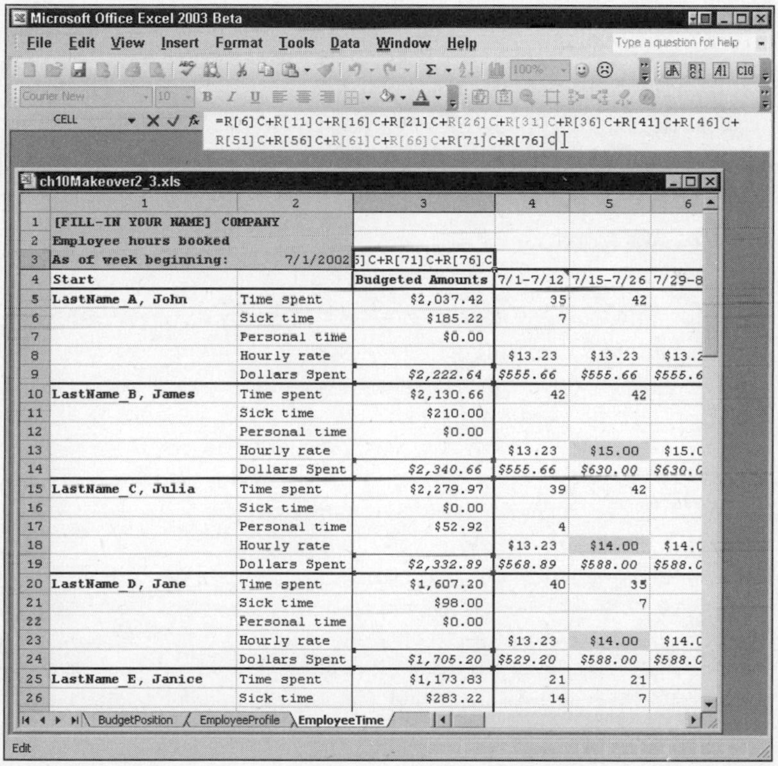

Figure 10-30: Tabulating total spent by adding up the dollars for each of the individual employees

If you're planning on tabulating data for more than 15 employees, you will need to extend the formula to reference the data for the additional employees. In this layout, employees are spaced every five rows. The terms in your formula should reflect this. Five rows lower than 76 rows down is 81. The next term in your formula would be R[81]C. The one after that would be R[86], and so forth.

Keep in mind that this approach will start to get unwieldy after about 25 or so employees. Also, Excel has a limit on the number of characters permitted in a cell formula. This limit is likely to surpass your ability to correctly type in a lengthy formula by hand.

2. As shown in Figure 10-31, prepare the Budget Position report as described earlier in the chapter, with the following difference. Rather than use the formula

```
=EmployeeProfile!RC[4]
```

you would type

```
=EmployeeTime!R3C3
```

into row 13 column 2 of your Budget Position Report (see Figure 10-31).

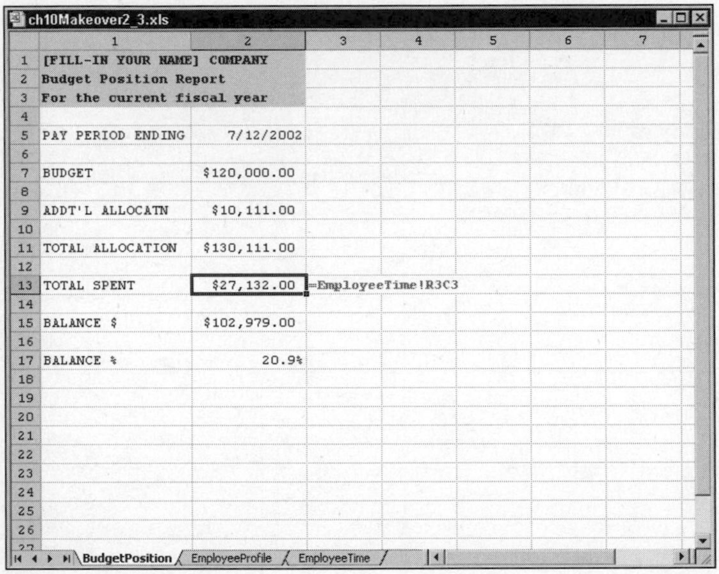

Figure 10-31: Budget Position report with revised formula for Total Spent

Closing Thoughts

The chief goal of this chapter is to learn how to reengineer spreadsheets that have been previously developed. To facilitate things, I have walked through an end-to-end conversion of an existing set of spreadsheets. The focus was on fulfilling the requirements in the most expedient way possible.

This chapter covered four important tasks:

> Task 1: When performing a spreadsheet makeover, whether yours or someone else's, identify the requirements and keep those requirements clearly in sight throughout your decision-making.

Task 2: Learn how to take apart a spreadsheet in terms of its structural layout, identify functionally what is happening, trace dependencies, and develop an understanding of how specific issues were handled and whether or not it was resolved in a clean way.

Task 3: Develop a strategy for how to rework formulas, change formatting for consistent appearance, and develop optimizations.

Task 4: Decide whether you'll clean up the existing spreadsheet or create a new one from scratch or a template, import data, re-apply formulas and so on. Important to guiding this decision is the scope limitation. You may have to decide how much data you will use and how far back you will go. Along with this, you will need to determine whether to take the high road or the low road on the challenging part(s) of the spreadsheet.

The next chapter, "Spreadsheet Auditing: Challenging the Numbers of Others," picks up where this leaves off and addresses how to go through a spreadsheet to help validate the correctness and reliability of its results.

Chapter 11

Spreadsheet Auditing: Challenging the Numbers of Others

IN THIS CHAPTER

- ◆ Understanding the basics of structural analysis of Spreadsheets

- ◆ Testing your skills on structural analysis

- ◆ Watching out for common spreadsheet mistakes

- ◆ Recognizing "off-spreadsheet" analysis

- ◆ Compensating for off-spreadsheet results with State Transition Analysis

- ◆ Using the Interpretive Reconciliation Worksheet

- ◆ Testing the reasonableness of spreadsheets

IF YOU ARE LIKE MOST busy managers, you may easily have half a dozen new spreadsheets coming across your desk every week. Most of these are likely to be simple summaries supplied as attachments to internal memos. Every now and then you'll come across some that are more complex. They require your careful and thoughtful examination. These big-ticket items are the ones you cannot afford to misjudge.

If your work entails due diligence, you will no doubt want to marshal the resources at your disposal to evaluate the data contained in the spreadsheet and the spreadsheet itself. This chapter is aimed at giving you techniques and some tools to assist you in the task.

In a nutshell, here's what this chapter is about. There are four aspects to auditing spreadsheets:

- ◆ Performing explicit structural analysis of spreadsheets

- ◆ Recognizing implicit relationships contained within the data but not actually encoded in the spreadsheets (a.k.a. "off-spreadsheet" analysis)

- ◆ Performing State Transition Analysis

- ◆ Performing tests of reasonableness of assumptions and formulas used

It seems to me that there are several things you need to be concerned with. The starting point is spreadsheet correctness, a mechanical but nevertheless important concern. I can't tell you how often I've come across spreadsheets that have been purported to quantify some information but miss their mark. I would find things such as formulas not accounting for 100 percent of some quantity. Sometimes, units would be mixed. Formulas would be hardwired. Whatever the case may be, you don't have to look very hard to uncover something in the spreadsheet formulas that can harpoon the basic integrity of the numbers produced.

Assuming that the spreadsheet is structurally sound, a more practical issue looms. Chances are, if the spreadsheet is at all complex, there are factors present that are not explicitly encoded within the spreadsheet formulas but nonetheless play into the spreadsheet results and interpretations. You need to uncover these implicit relationships.

Spreadsheet auditing, it turns out, has much to do with your interpretive analysis. Unless you can bring to bear your professional background and expertise, you may have a bit of a challenge trying to take apart and reassemble spreadsheet information to arrive at some meaningful interpretation. The burden of analyzing and interpreting shouldn't be totally upon you. The spreadsheet should be a tool to allow you to pry open data and complex relationships.

The data could be a set of numbers, such as financial information. It's presented one way. Then a quantum leap takes place and you have a new set of numbers. It sometime eludes us as to how the transition takes place; yet we know it occurs in a series of smoother, more finely grained increments. Uncovering these finer-grained increments can shed light on the underlying dynamics.

State Transition Analysis (STA) comes into play in all sorts of disciplines. Basic financial interpretation, root-cause analysis, and forensic accounting are a few that come to mind. It often turns out that the chief benefit of STA is to identify leads for inquiry and further investigation.

To show you what is possible, I provide a reference implementation of an STA tool called an Interpretive Reconciliation Worksheet (IRW.) Reference implementations are not meant to rise to production-quality standards. This tool is certainly not meant to replace software applications you may already be using for financial analysis. The tool's chief purpose is to show how a tool of this kind allows you to integrate your professional knowledge and business acumen with the spreadsheet's analytical capabilities.

Finally, even after you validate a spreadsheet's structural soundness, have identified that it is consistent with assumptions and constraints, and know how you got from one set of numbers to another, how do you know that the spreadsheet results are reasonable? This chapter provides the means to evaluate your results with that question in mind.

Structural Analysis of Spreadsheets

Many things can cause a spreadsheet to be incorrect. Some of these are obvious. Others are subtle and buried deeper inside the spreadsheet.

Test your skills

Take a look at the ch11-01LeaseAnalysisForReview.xls on the CD-ROM with this book. This spreadsheet presents the analysis of expenses projected for various real estate properties that will be leased (see Figure 11-1). The actual spreadsheet was set up to look at two different properties and some variations on information assumed for each of the two properties.

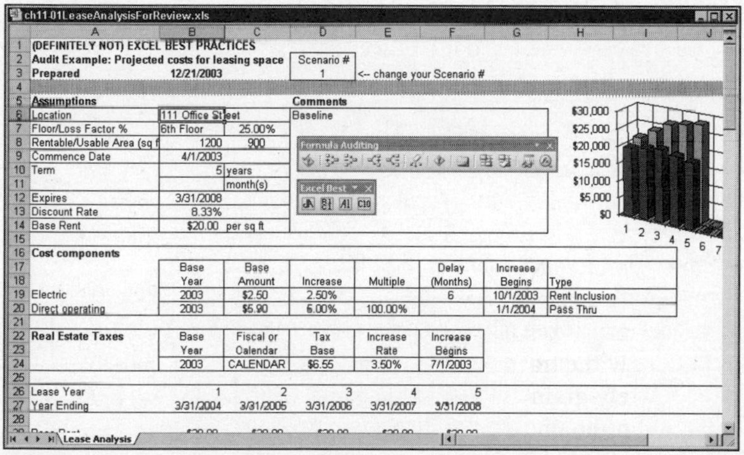

Figure 11-1: Sample spreadsheet to audit

The moment you open the file, you will notice that the spreadsheet may not be perfect. You will see a warning message (Figure 11-2). This message indicates that there is an external link.

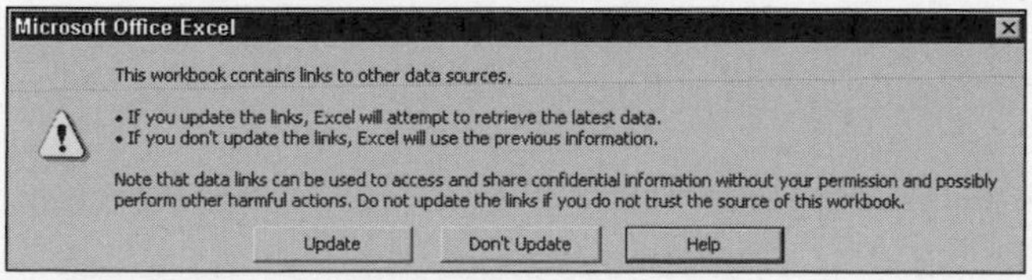

Figure 11-2: The external link alert

When you're opening a file with external links, there are good reasons to *not* choose the update feature. At the top of the list of these reasons is that you may be receiving the spreadsheet but lack the proper connectivity to retrieve the external data. The result can be cascading errors throughout your spreadsheet. If for any reason your spreadsheet gets saved, it will save all the errors that were just generated. A safer strategy would be to select the Don't Update option. You can now examine the spreadsheet without seeing the potential external link errors.

Choose Save As to save the spreadsheet to a new file. Close the current spreadsheet. Open the new spreadsheet that you just created. This time, click Update. If you do get errors and the file is inadvertently saved, you at least have your original file intact.

You may want to press the Help button. Excel 2003 has some useful information on whether or not to update.

After clicking Update, if one or more of the links cannot be updated, you will be presented with the option of Editing Links or just Continue. If you choose to edit the links, you will be given the option to break the link. Doing so will remove the formula but keep the last known value. If you don't want to lose the formula, you are better off closing the Edit Links window and revising the offending formula yourself.

Interestingly enough, when you enter into the spreadsheet, everything looks okay. Actually, it's not. Before reading further, please look at the file ch11-01LeaseAnalysis ForReview.xls and see whether you can find the mistakes and problems with the spreadsheet. You shouldn't need to spend more than 15 minutes or so to develop a rough idea of the problems and issues with the spreadsheet. As a starting point, you can apply some of the techniques presented in the previous chapter, "Going for the Facelift: Spreadsheet Makeovers." Instead of trying to improve on the spreadsheet style in this case, review it to detect what's wrong with it.

You may want to avail yourself of an Excel Add-In that may help you to examine spreadsheets. See the sidebar "Installing the Data Audit tool." *Note:* Please follow the specific instructions for installing the Add-In instead of double-clicking the Audit01.xla file.

Installing the Data Audit tool

Your CD-ROM that accompanies this book contains a file called Audit01.xla. Installing this file will display an *Excel Best Practices* toolbar on your screen.

Place the Audit01.xla file into your Excel Add-Ins directory. To find out where the Add-Ins directory is, go to your Tools menu and choose Add-Ins. When you're prompted with the Add-Ins dialog box window, click the Browse button. This will bring you to the Add-Ins directory. Take note of the directory location and press Cancel. Now copy your Audit01.xla file to this directory. Click Browse to bring up the Add-Ins directory, and you should see the Audit01.xla file listed there. Select it and click OK. The option Simple Audit Tool should appear. Make sure that there is a check mark next to this option. Click OK and you're in business.

You will see a floating toolbar with four icons. They are as follows:

- ◆ dA — A simple data audit "toolet"

- ◆ R1C1 — Used for converting the presentation of your spreadsheets to R1C1 style

- ◆ A1 — Used for converting the presentation of your spreadsheets to A1 Style

- ◆ C10 — Used for converting the font of your actively displayed worksheet to Courier New font, size 10

The dA icon is a data audit tool that will generate a map of user-defined names in your current workbook. Pressing the dA icon will cause Excel to look at your spreadsheet. If Excel sees user-defined names, it will open a new worksheet and populate it with information about the various user-defined names, their locations or ranges, and the formula or value if the named range is a single cell.

Note that the cell reference generated by the dA toolbar icon follows the prevailing cell reference convention (A1 or R1C1 style, whichever you've selected).

If you want to examine or extend the macros used in the Add-In, you can go into the Excel macro mode (instructions for working with and using Excel macros are provided in the next chapter). The macros for Audit01.xla are password-protected to keep the code out of harm's way. In case you want to look at the code or extend it, the password is the word "password" in lowercase.

Some observations for beginning your assessment

As a first step, you should gather ideas of what is going on in the spreadsheet and how it works. When you type in a Scenario Number (cell D3), you will see that information from the appropriate property in a lookup table that appears on row 55 below is retrieved and analyzed. This works nicely, but does it work correctly?

Note that some of the cells between B6 and D14 contain formulas that refer to named ranges. You can find out the location of the cells they refer to by just double-clicking them. Try it. B6 has the formula:

```
=location
```

Double-clicking it takes you to B58.

 When you double-click a spreadsheet cell, it will appear highlighted and bring you to its predecessor cells. This is a quick way to trace what feeds into a formula.

Double-clicking to backtrack your formulas will take you only so far. The moment that your backtracking highlights more than one predecessor cell, you will have difficulty double-clicking the range of cells.

Obviously, this double-clicking technique is limited, and you need better ways to trace the flow of formulas. There are several ways you can do this. Did you notice, for example, the Formula Auditing toolbar in Figure 11-1? You can make this toolbar appear by choosing Tools→Customize Toolbars and then checking the Formula Auditing option. I'm hoping that you've already installed the Excel Best Practices toolbar (see the sidebar "Installing the Data Audit tool" if you want to do that now). Make sure that the check box for this toolbar is also checked.

Once the Formula Auditing Toolbar is installed, click the Trace Precedents icon. Doing so results in a blue arrow showing you the flow of numbers from the originating cells to the destination cell. Clicking Trace Precedents again will extend the backtracking further. You can continue clicking the Trace Precedents until you've reached all the original cells that affect the current cell in question. If you are dealing with a complicated spreadsheet, you may have a tangle of lines and have a hard time discerning whether you traced back to all the predecessor cells.

There's another way to get to all the predecessor cells. Click Ctrl+G or choose Edit→Go To. Then click the Special button. You will then be presented with a variety of options (see Figure 11-3). Choose Precedents→All levels.

Figure 11-3: Specialized cell selection

Figure 11-3 shows you a variety of options. It is worth your time to explore the other selection options.

The submenu options Numbers, Text, Logicals, and Errors displayed in Figure 11-3 are applicable to both Formulas or Constants.

At this point you're probably curious about the Excel Best Practices toolbar, and the dA icon in particular. Go ahead and click the toolbar icon with this spreadsheet open. A new worksheet will be generated that provides a mapping of the named ranges along with their locations and the formulas they hold (see Figure 11-4).

	A	B	C	D
1	Name	Location	Formula	
2	area	='Lease Analysis'!$B$60	1200	
3	Base_Amount___Dir._Op.	='Lease Analysis'!$B$68	=INDEX(table,ROW()-ROW($B$56),$D$3)	
4	Base_Amount___Electric	='Lease Analysis'!$B$67	=INDEX(table,ROW()-ROW($B$56),$D$3)	
5	Base_Rent	='Lease Analysis'!$B$65	=INDEX(table,ROW()-ROW($B$56),$D$3)	
6	Base_Year	='Lease Analysis'!$B$66	=INDEX(table,ROW()-ROW($B$56),$D$3)	
7	Baseline	='Lease Analysis'!$B$76	=INDEX(table,ROW()-ROW($B$56),$D$3)	
8	Bldg_Op_Cost	='Lease Analysis'!$B$109	=(B107*B105+B108*B106)/12	
9	Calendar	='Lease Analysis'!$B$73	=INDEX(table,ROW()-ROW($B$56),$D$3)	
10	commense_date	='Lease Analysis'!$B$61	=INDEX(table,ROW()-ROW($B$56),$D$3)	
11	Comments___line2	='Lease Analysis'!$B$77	=INDEX(table,ROW()-ROW($B$56),$D$3)	
12	Comments___line3	='Lease Analysis'!$B$78	=INDEX(table,ROW()-ROW($B$56),$D$3)	
13	Comments___line4	='Lease Analysis'!$B$79	=INDEX(table,ROW()-ROW($B$56),$D$3)	
14	Comments___line5	='Lease Analysis'!$B$80	=INDEX(table,ROW()-ROW($B$56),$D$3)	
15	Comments___line6	='Lease Analysis'!$B$81	=INDEX(table,ROW()-ROW($B$56),$D$3)	
16	Comments___line7	='Lease Analysis'!$B$82	=INDEX(table,ROW()-ROW($B$56),$D$3)	
17	Comments___line8	='Lease Analysis'!$B$83	=INDEX(table,ROW()-ROW($B$56),$D$3)	
18	Comments___line9	='Lease Analysis'!$B$84	=INDEX(table,ROW()-ROW($B$56),$D$3)	
19	Comments1	='Lease Analysis'!$B$76	=INDEX(table,ROW()-ROW($B$56),$D$3)	
20	Delay___Electric	='Lease Analysis'!$B$72	=INDEX(table,ROW()-ROW($B$56),$D$3)	
21	dir_op_cur	='Lease Analysis'!$B$105	=13-MONTH($B$9)	
22	dir_op_next	='Lease Analysis'!$B$106	=MONTH($B$9)-1	
23	Discount_Rate	='Lease Analysis'!$B$64	=INDEX(table,ROW()-ROW($B$56),$D$3)	
24	electr_cur_yr	='Lease Analysis'!$B$101	=IF(B$26=0,0,12-MOD($F$19,12))	
25	electri_from_next	='Lease Analysis'!$B$102	=IF(B$26=0,0,MOD($F$19,12))	
26	electric	='Lease Analysis'!$B$103	=$C$19	
27	floor	='Lease Analysis'!$B$59	=INDEX(table,ROW()-ROW($B$56),$D$3)	

Figure 11-4: Mapping of named ranges and their formulas, as generated by the data audit toolet

The spreadsheet contains about 50 different user-defined names. The formulas are listed in column C. Wait a minute. They should all be formulas, right? Then why is the term `area` listed as a number (with the value of `1200`) instead of a formula? It should be a full-fledged formula. You've found one of the errors. There are more.

If you want a visual representation, here's what you can do:

1. Pick some important summary numbers in the spreadsheet. The data that is graphed is picking up the numbers from rows 123 and 124. This data shows the projected rental lease expense as well as its present value. Essentially, all the relevant numbers in the spreadsheet should contribute to these numbers; so these numbers serve as a good starting point.

2. Select the cells `B123:K124`; then, choose Go To, click Special, and select Predecessors to All Levels. After those cells are identified, change the selected cells to some background color, such as gray.

3. With these predecessor cells selected, choose Go To again, click Special; and then this time select Dependents to All Levels. With these cells selected, change their background pattern to a contrasting color, such as yellow.

The spreadsheet should look something like that shown in Figure 11-5.

	A	B	C	D	E	F	G	H	I	J
	ch11-01LeaseAnalysisForReview.xls									
55	Look Up Table									
56	Scenario No.	1	1	2	3	4	5	6	7	
57	Date Prepared	12/21/2003	12/21/2003	12/21/2003	11/20/2003	11/21/2003	1/20/2003	1/20/2003	1/20/2003	1/20/2
58	Location	111 Office St	111 Office St	111 Office St	55 Office St.	56 Office St.				
59	Floor	6th Floor	6th Floor	6th Floor	22nd Floor	23rd Floor				
60	Rentable Area	1200	1200	1200	1100	1101	1200	1200	1200	1
61	Commence Date	4/1/2003	4/1/2003	4/1/2003	4/1/2003	4/2/2003	4/1/2003	4/1/2003	4/1/2003	4/1/2
62	Term (yr)	5	5	5	5	6	5	5	5	
63	Term (months)									
64	Discount Rate	8.33%	8.33%	7.69%	8.33%	8.70%	9.00%	9.00%	9.00%	9.0
65	Base Rent	$20.00	$20.00	$20.00	$15.00	$18.00	$18.00	$20.00	$20.00	$20
66	Base Year	2003	2003	2003	2003	2003	2003	2003	2003	2
67	Base Amount - Electric	$2.50	$2.50	$2.75	$1.75	$2.75	$2.75	$2.25	$2.25	$2.25
68	Base Amount - Dir. Op.	$5.90	$5.90	$5.90	$5.00	$5.90	$5.90	$5.90	$5.90	$5.90
69	Incr. - Electric	2.50%	2.50%	2.50%	2.50%	2.50%	2.50%	2.50%	2.50%	2.50%
70	Incr. - Dir. Op.	5.00%	5.00%	5.00%	5.00%	5.00%	5.00%	5.00%	5.00%	5.00%
71	Multiple - Dir. Op.	100.00%	100.00%	100.00%	100.00%	100.00%	100.00%	100.00%	100.00%	100.00%
72	Delay - Electric	6	6	6	6	5	1	1	1	
73	R.E. Tax - Calendar/Fiscal	Calendar	Calendar	Calendar	Calendar	Calendar	Calendar	Calendar	Calendar	Calenda
74	R.E. Tax - Tax Base	$6.55	$6.55	$6.55	$6.00	$6.55	$6.55	$6.55	$6.55	$6.55
75	R.E. Tax - Incr. Rate	3.50%	3.75%	3.50%	3.50%	3.50%	3.50%	3.50%	3.50%	3.50%
76	Comments - line1	Baseline	Baseline	An alternate	Another prop	An alternate				
77	Comments - line2			of scenario 1		of scenario 3				
78	Comments - line3									
79	Comments - line4									
80	Comments - line5									
81	Comments - line6									
82	Comments - line7									

Figure 11–5: Color highlighting can reveal anomalies in your formulas.

Notice that something different is going on with the numbers `1200`, `5`, `5.00%`, and `3.50%`. Unlike the other cells in yellow in the same column, these numbers are frozen at fixed values. They should be picking up values based on the scenario number. They are not.

When you look further, you should notice another anomaly. The data in columns E and F are shifted by a value of 1. Look over the following:

Item	Column E	Column F
Date Prepared	11/20/2003	11/21/2003
Location	55 Office St.	56 Office St.
Floor	22nd Floor	23rd Floor
Rentable Area	1100	1101
Commence Date	4/1/2003	4/2/2003
Term (yr)	5	6

Obviously, something is wrong here. It appears that the person preparing the spreadsheet used the Excel "handle-bar" (the rectangular notch at the bottom-right region of selected cells) to duplicate cells from one column to the next. Although extending ranges using a handle-bar will duplicate formulas, the handle-bar will increment values wherever it finds a number. Excel even went so far as to change the abbreviation from the word 22nd to 23rd. Copy and pasting would have worked better than using the handle-bar.

Because the two properties make use of five-year leases, the mistaken value of a six-year lease should be noticed. Unfortunately, it goes unnoticed, because the value for the lease term (cell B62) is the frozen number 5. Also note that the month portion for the lease term, although picked up in B63, is not carried forward into B11.

Formula evaluation

In the Formula Auditing toolbar, you may have noticed an icon that says Evaluate Formula. Clicking this icon allows you to see just exactly what Excel 2003 is calculating, each step of the way for any individual cell. Figure 11-6 shows you how Excel computes the cell F46.

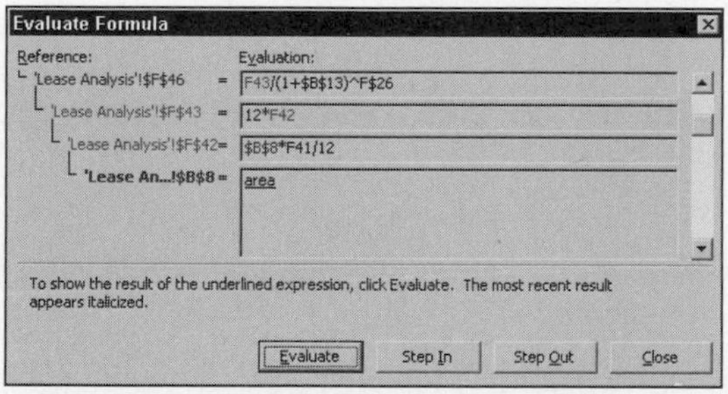

Figure 11-6: Excel is evaluating the application of a formula to an individual cell.

This Evaluate Formula tool comes in handy when a formula returns an error and you don't know where the error originated. The offending cell(s) need not have errors. You may have a formula like this:

```
=A1*LOG(A2)+A3/(A4-A5)+A6/(A7-A8)
```

A4 and A5 may be perfectly well-behaved except when the two values equal each other, in which case you would be attempting division by zero. This, of course, is not a valid arithmetic operation and will generate an error. The same can be said about A7 and A8. The Evaluate Formula tool will help you to discern where in the formula you have a problem.

A partial checklist for discerning mistakes

Despite all the good things in this spreadsheet, plenty of other mistakes in it could impair its integrity.

I will leave you to find these on your own, but here are some general questions to ask and things to do. I hope you will extend this list with questions of your own.

- ◆ Does the spreadsheet you are examining contain any time-changing information? Some information, such as risk-free rate of interest, may require updating from time to time. Other information may be inherently changing moment by moment, such as age. With the latter, you could record the date of birth. You could compute the current age by taking the difference between the current date and the birthdate. If the data represented in the spreadsheet is mapped to a specific as-of date, you might compute the age from the difference between the as-of date and the birthdate.

- ◆ Are assertions being made without their underlying assumptions being stated?

- ◆ Have you checked for splintered data? Data splintering will often occur when a spreadsheet has more than one worksheet containing copies of the same data (copying and pasting data from one worksheet to another can do this).

- ◆ Is the spreadsheet too simplistic? You will often see a best-case, middle-case, and worst-case scenario side by side. Do these scenarios consist of point estimates as opposed to weighted averages?

- ◆ Is there anything that would lead you to believe that the preparer of the spreadsheet is getting lost in the numbers?

- ◆ Are any of the formulas "hardwired"? For example, you might have a formula like this:

`=(1+0.045)^4`

instead of a formula like this:

`=(1+InterestRate)^TotalYears`

If the spreadsheet does have hardwired formulas, are there any that may not be accurate or up-to-date?

◆ Have you found any discrepancy between a single number and a list of numbers that when summed, should add up to that single number? If so, is the difference between these two sets of numbers an exact multiple of nine? This may be an indication of a transposition of digits. Look at the file ch11-02NumberTranspose.xls for some examples of these transposition errors.

◆ Would the spreadsheet "break" if you started varying some of the underlying assumptions? For example, say that the term of the lease in all the data is five years. Would the spreadsheet have any problems producing results if one of your scenarios had a lease of eight years? (Try it.)

◆ Do any of the formulas contain external links? Do you have any trouble connecting to those links? Concerning the preceding example, you may wish to check the formulas on line 27. (Hint, hint.) If you do find a problem, how can you correct it?

◆ Do you see any evidence of some of the data being double or triple counted?

◆ Does the spreadsheet appear to be mixing apples and oranges? For instance, if incidents in a production environment are being tracked, you might see a formula for cost to the firm as:

```
=IncidentsPerMonth+TimeForResolution+OutOfPocketExpenses
```

Though an increase in any of these factors will always correspond to an increased cost to the firm, it is not a good measure. It mixes different kinds of costs. A better formula would be the following:

```
=HourlyBurnRate*TimeForResultuion*IncidentsPermonth+
OutOfPocketExpenses
```

This formula converts everything to dollars and then adds up the dollar amounts.

◆ When the spreadsheet is handed to you, do you find yourself filling in the blanks, insofar as the assumptions are concerned? Even if all the assumptions are provided, do you believe any to be incorrect?

Clearly, this list isn't even close to being exhausted. It is a good starting point. Work on developing your own methodology to address these and other issues you feel are important. Note that I've worded the checklist so that a "YES" answer implies something that should capture your attention or require follow-up action.

Off-Spreadsheet Analysis

The previous section addresses issues that you can uncover just by looking at the structure of the spreadsheet without regard to what the spreadsheet is actually modeling. That's the easy side of spreadsheet auditing. The hard part is when things are happening outside the confines of the spreadsheet — things that would affect the validity of the results presented.

Those of you familiar with the Sarbanes-Oxley Act and issues related to disclosure of "Off-Balance Sheet Arrangements" will appreciate the discussion that follows. Unfortunately, there is no mandated requirement that spreadsheets (or accompanying documentation) supply all supporting information for data incorporated into the computations. It's very hard to accept or reject the validity of a spreadsheet when only the end results of an analysis have been incorporated into the spreadsheet.

Sometimes a spreadsheet can be complete, but the numbers used in the spreadsheet might be obeying some set of rules not encoded in the spreadsheet. A spreadsheet might contain a schedule that depicts a portfolio of funds you are planning to invest in. Because of the way your investment portfolio is structured, you may need to maintain certain margin requirements. If you prepare a schedule listing the current holdings and planned investments by asset type, the spreadsheet you might assemble wouldn't necessarily need to incorporate specific formulas that assure that margin requirements are obeyed. You could, if you so choose, be on the "honor system" and make sure that the amounts you invest do not violate these margin requirements. All the logic on investment amounts, in this case, is done outside the spreadsheet. The spreadsheet can apply only the assumptions and formulas you give it in order to produce a report.

A spreadsheet, after all, is nothing but a fancy calculation tool that will take numbers on one end, apply certain formulas, and produce numbers on the other end. Unless you or someone builds in specific formulas or uses Smart Data (see Chapter 7, "Creating and Using Smart Data") that tests some of the underlying assumptions (and subsequent calculations), the spreadsheet will sit silently as inappropriate information is pumped into it.

One for the history books

Thomas Jefferson, quill in hand and writing the Declaration of Independence, is an unassailable image. But some of his most enduring phrases were the result of editing. Most notable is the phrase "We hold these truths to be self-evident," revised so eloquently by Ben Franklin. Apparently, even the words of an icon of the American Revolution needed a little clarification, so what's to stop us from questioning the assumptions in a spreadsheet?

We hold these truths to be self-evident . . .

The preparer and often the recipient (possibly yourself) can be expected to make reasonable assumptions about information in a spreadsheet. If you're looking at a balance sheet as of a given date, you would expect that, when properly prepared, its list of total assets would match its tally of total liabilities (including stockholders' equity). If the balance sheet is presented in the form of a spreadsheet, then there *should* be a numerical matching of total assets to total liabilities. Unless specific safeguards are built in, nothing prevents the spreadsheet from being "out of balance." Of course, the likelihood is that even a partially diligent effort on the part of the preparer would make an issue of this kind a rather unlikely event.

The reality is that these "self-evident truths, "although duly observed and respected by spreadsheet preparers, are rarely encoded into the spreadsheets. Unless you apply the kinds of techniques such as those presented in Chapter 7, you won't see spreadsheets waving red flags when the numbers are out of whack. As a result, most reports prepared as spreadsheets go out the door without proper safety nets. Blatant disregard for safety nets. . . . Hmmm, haven't you seen this somewhere before? When was the last time you changed your password for a critical resource you need to keep protected? Systems of any kind without safety nets are ticking time bombs. In the case of spreadsheets, unchecked verification of specific constraints or guidelines undermines reliability when the spreadsheet starts to get large and complex. It's way too easy for things to get lost in the shuffle.

So, part of spreadsheet auditing entails verification and corroboration of "self-evident truths" that have not been encoded in the spreadsheet.

The mind-reading game

The thinking behind some spreadsheets is obvious. A balance sheet always matches assets to liabilities (and stockholders' equity); the distribution of sales by territory, product group, or market segment should always add up to 100 percent — not more, not less. Some truths are self-evident. Spreadsheets for other kinds of purposes can hold murky depths, however. Assumptions and decisions are too often deeply hidden, whether by neglect or design.

Consider that someone provides you with a projection of revenues for the next several quarters, such as the following:

```
Projected Revenue
Quarter 1    Quarter 2    Quarter 3    Quarter 4    Total
21600        26400        33600        38400        120000
18.0%        22.0%         28.0%        32.0%        100.0%
```

When you review the formulas for projected revenue for each of the quarters, you see that they are built on a set percentage of Total Projected Revenue (that is, 21600 is 18 percent of 120000; 26400 is 22 percent of 120000; and so forth). This method makes things easy for the spreadsheet preparer. To produce a low, medium, and high estimate for each of the quarters, the preparer needs only to change the Total Projected Revenue.

But a problem arises with this picture. Putting aside the assumption that expected percentages for each of the quarters will remain constant regardless of the level of projected revenues, how did the preparer come up with the number 120000 in the first place? What objective criteria were used? This number does not contain a self-evident truth that can be inferred, as can, for example, a statement such as "Units manufactured cannot exceed production capacity." The reader of a spreadsheet gets locked into a mind-reading game the moment that decision criteria are not encoded into the spreadsheet or communicated through separate documentation.

I bring up the point of insisting on properly prepared information for a good reason. A recent study reviewing more than 350 large and complex spreadsheet applications revealed that roughly 25 percent contain material errors. This is quite a substantial number of errors. Errors can be purely spreadsheet-related ones, of the kind discussed much earlier in the chapter. Or they can relate to the murkier kind, arising from information being misinterpreted because the spreadsheet contains nothing to substantiate it.

State Transition Analysis

When a spreadsheet doesn't have all the information you would like to see regarding how the numbers presented were obtained, it doesn't necessarily imply that something is wrong the spreadsheet or that its validity is suspect.

A common situation that occurs in financial analysis is that of following some set of information that changes over time. You might have two snapshots, one of which characterizes the beginning state of a system or entity and the other of which characterizes the ending state. Though you have a complete description of the beginning and ending state, the question of the day is, "How did the entity evolve from one state to the other?"

The framework for dealing with this kind of question is known as State Transition Analysis. To help make this topic concrete, consider two balance sheets for a company that are spread a year apart. Basically, these balance sheets represent the financial state of a company over two snapshots in time. Somewhere along the way, a variety of incremental events nudged the entity from one state — that of a starting balance sheet — to another, with information having accrued over the course of the year. Much of the relevant information on the specific changes is buried in the financial statements, the footnotes to the financial statements, the Management Discussion & Analysis, various disclosures found in the 10-K and 10-Q reports, and possibly other filings with the SEC.

The key to performing the State Transition Analysis is to combine your knowledge of accounting and finance with the analytical capabilities of the spreadsheet to develop a composite picture.

USING THE INTERPRETATIVE RECONCILIATION WORKSHEET (IRW)

To follow along with an example of using this facility, open the ch11-03IRW.xls. You should see a comparative balance sheet for two periods: 12/31/1994 and 12/31/1995 (see Figure 11-7).

	A	B	C	D	E	F	G
	ch11-03IRW.xls						
1	EXCEL BEST PRACTICES						
2	Comparative Balance Sheet						
3	sample data for 12/31/1995 and 12/31/1994						
4							
5	BALANCE SHEET						
6	ASSETS (000$)						
7	FISCAL YEAR ENDING	12/31/1995	12/31/1994				
8	CASH	3,910	9,880				
9	MRKTABLE SECURITIES	3,000	0				
10	RECEIVABLES	24,805	18,677				
11	INVENTORIES	2,200	0				
12	RAW MATERIALS	0	0				
13	WORK IN PROGRESS	0	0				
14	FINISHED GOODS	0	0				
15	NOTES RECEIVABLE	0	0				
16	OTHER CURRENT ASSETS	856	135				
17	TOTAL CURRENT ASSETS	34,771	28,692				
18	PROP, PLANT & EQUIP	26,443	22,109				
19	ACCUMULATED DEP	6,100	3,509				
20	NET PROPERTY & EQUIPMENT	20,343	18,600				
21	INVEST & ADV TO SUBS	0	0				
22	OTHER NON-CUR ASSETS	0	0				
23	DEFERRED CHARGES						
24	INTANGIBLES	26,557	30,155				

AcctBrowser / AcctRecon / JLEntries \ BS / IS / InternalComputations /

Figure 11-7: Comparative balance sheet for a fictitious company

Note that this spreadsheet contains Income Statement data on another worksheet tab. The question to be asked is what transpired to cause the transition from one balance sheet state (at 12/31/1994) to another (at 12/31/1995)? The framework for addressing this is to use a reconciliation worksheet like the kind in Figure 11-8. Notice the various account names in column B, ranging from Assets to Liabilities, Income, and Expense. You can see the ending balances for each account in the two periods in columns D and E.

 TIP If you want to use this tool with your own data, you can start by overwriting the data in the balance sheet and income statement. The current and prior period ending balances in the Reconciliation worksheet of Figure 11-8 (columns D and E) read the numbers directly from the balance sheet and income statement.

Columns F and G summarize debits and credits made to each of the accounts from a general journal. Column H serves as a reconciliation column, identifying the net adjustment need to transition from the beginning account balance to the ending account balance.

To achieve a full reconciliation, you will need to add journal entries (see Figure 11-9).

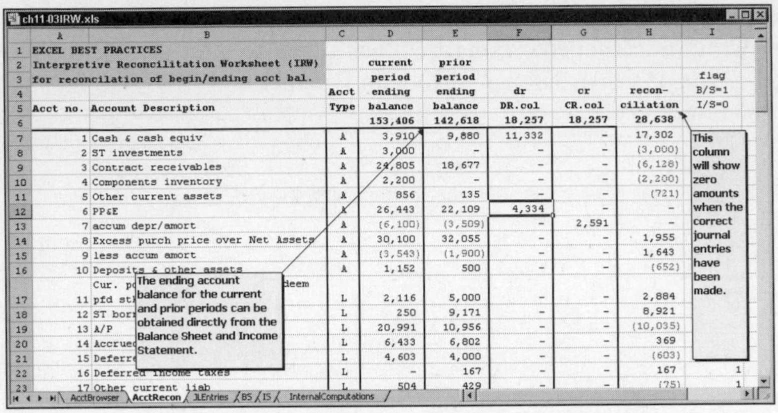

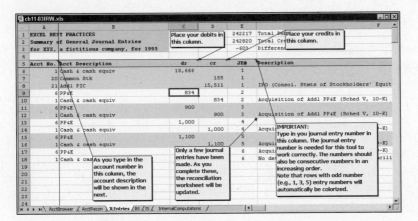

Figure 11-8: Reconciliation worksheet that is partially populated

Figure 11-9: Preparing the journal entries

The accounting entries you make are dependent on the various financial disclosures made. If Schedule V of the 10-K report details the acquisition of seven properties, you could make a separate journal entry for each of them. As luck would have it, the schedule has provided details for only four of the seven. Somehow you have to make do with the information you have. The first four properties are no problem. You can enter individual journal entries for each of the four properties. They may be debits to PP&E in the amount of $834,000, $900,000, $1,000,000, and $1,100,000, and credits to cash in the same amounts. The acquisition of the remaining three properties would have to be represented by a journal entry that aggregates the three properties. It might be, say, a debit to PP&E in the amount of $500,000 and credit to cash in the same amount.

All this information is recorded in the JLEntries worksheet (see Figure 11-9). Note that all information in the spreadsheet is shown in thousands of dollars. As the journal entry information is being entered, the total debits and credits for each account are automatically updated. You can verify that this is happening. The debits to PPE& is $4,334,000, which is the sum of $834,000, $900,000, $1,000,000, $1,100,000, and $500,000. Figure 11-8 shows that the total debits for PP&E is $4,334,000 (column F, line 12).

If you had information available to you as an insider, not only might you have access to the purchase amounts for the individual properties, you would likely have a breakdown of the PP&E data by stage and component, permitting a more detailed analysis.

As you enter information into the journal, net differences between debits and credits are highlighted. Also as you enter the journal entry numbers, the rows are automatically colorized for easier viewing. (Try entering some journal entries of your own to test this functionality.)

You can use the Account Browser worksheet (see Figure 11-10) to drill down to any journal entry of any of the accounts.

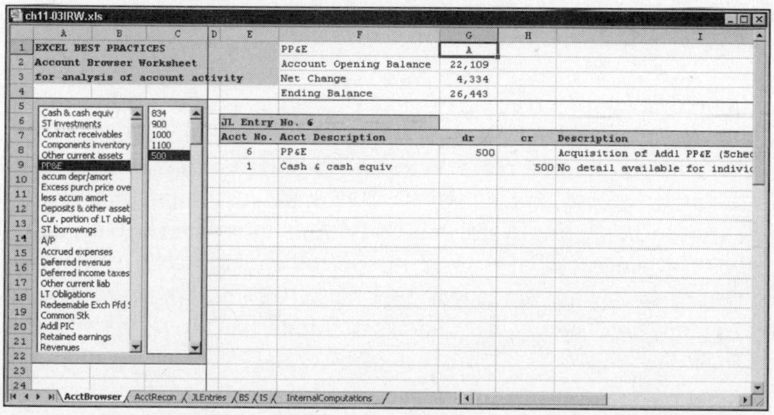

Figure 11-10: Account Browser gives you a quick snapshot of the net change in any account, as well as a detailed display of the changes and access to the complete journal entry.

This framework of browsing data is very interactive. You will be tempted to put all your data in a system of this kind. Keep in mind that spreadsheets have their limitations. The system shown here will work nicely with several hundred entries and accounts. If you want to use the facilities of a spreadsheet to analyze data when the number of entries is on the order of thousands, you should consider using a "Spreadsheet Portal," such as the kinds described in Chapter 12, "Spreadsheet Portals, XML, and Web Services." Chapter 12 also describes the interface components in greater detail.

USES FOR TOOLS OF THIS KIND

The IRW is a very specific kind of tool. You should think about constructing similar kinds of tools for other purposes. In particular, three areas come to mind:

- Examination of revenue recognition
- Accruals
- Business combinations

How might you adapt a tool of this kind to spot improperly timed revenue recognition? What about improper valuation or fictitious revenue? Is there a way to examine inventories to assure that the cost of goods sold is properly set?

My goal is not to answer these particular questions but rather to get you thinking about new and different ways of using spreadsheets as an analytical and assistive tool.

Testing the Reasonableness of Spreadsheets

This chapter and indeed much of *Excel Best Practices for Business* are centered on carefully examining spreadsheets and the data they contain, and identifying problems and issues. At some point you'll make a clear determination as to whether the spreadsheet is structurally sound and contains valid data. Assuming that everything appears okay up to this point, I ask you: Is there is any chance that you're skating on thin ice by accepting what is presented in the spreadsheet? Although I could drive this discussion toward statistical hypothesis testing, I want to take a different tact. Put plainly and simply, are the assumptions that drive the spreadsheet results reasonable?

Sometimes it's a matter of semantics

I want to get back to an issue I brought up in Chapter 8, "Analyzing Data," an issue relating to the quantification of uncertainty. Let me revisit this by playing out a scenario.

The V.P. of Sales for a company is attempting to project product sales into the next season. He asks the product-line managers of three different divisions to provide the anticipated level of sales for each of the products in their divisions as well as a realistic best-case and worst-case scenario for each product. The managers comply and send the information (see Figure 11-11, or open the file ch11-04Reasonable.xls).

There's a problem with the data as represented. The uncertainty that would cause a variation in the number of units sold for each of the products is a combination of two factors. One of these is correlated (or systematic) and the other is uncorrelated (or random). When the managers are giving the estimates for the projected sales volume, the estimate will take into account overall economic conditions (which is highly correlated) as well as uncorrelated variations for each of the products.

ch11-04Reasonable.xls

EXCEL BEST PRACTICES
Test of Reasonableness
initial information on projected sales volume

			Units(000)		
		Unit	Worst	Middle	Best
Divison	Product	Price	Case	Case	Case
Medical Prod Div	Med A	10.23	45	50	55
Medical Prod Div	Med B	4.95	38	42	46
Medical Prod Div	Med C	10	47	54	61
Software Prod Div	S/W 1	50	3.5	5	6
Software Prod Div	S/W 2	139	2.1	3	3.6
Publications Div	Text X	19.99	22	28	34
Publications Div	Text Y	89.99	4	5	6
Publications Div	Text Z	105.33	3	4.5	6

Sheet1 / Sheet2 / Sheet3

Figure 11-11: Systematic and random uncertainties are mixed together.

The problem is that no information is provided that could tell you whether the best and worst-case scenarios are purely a matter of random variation, or arise from inherent industry and related economic conditions, or are some specific combination of the two. Look at Sheet2 in this spreadsheet (Figure 11-12), which shows that two very different outcomes are possible depending upon whether the uncertainty is correlated.

ch11-04Reasonable.xls

EXCEL BEST PRACTICES
Test of Reasonableness
two very different outcomes in sales depending on degree of correlation

			Units(000)				Sales(000)		
		Unit	Worst	Middle	Best	Uncertainty	Worst	Middle	Best
Divison	Product	Price	Case	Case	Case	in sales	Case	Case	Case
Medical Prod Div	Med A	10.23	45	50	55	51.15	460.35	511.5	562.65
Medical Prod Div	Med B	4.95	38	42	46	19.8	188.1	207.9	227.7
Medical Prod Div	Med C	10	47	54	61	70	470	540	610
Software Prod Div	S/W 1	50	3.5	5	6.5	75	175	250	325
Software Prod Div	S/W 2	139	2.1	3	3.9	125.1	291.9	417	542.1
Publications Div	Text X	19.99	22	28	34	119.94	439.78	559.72	679.66
Publications Div	Text Y	89.99	4	5	6	89.99	359.96	449.95	539.94
Publications Div	Text Z	105.33	3	4.5	6	158	315.99	473.99	631.98
Projected Sales if 100% Correlation & No Random Variation						*708.98*	2701.08	3410.06	4119.03
Projected Sales if Individual Product Sales are Uncorrelated						*276.82*	3133.24	3410.06	3686.88

Sheet1 / Sheet2 / Sheet3

Figure 11-12: Not specifying degree of correlation results in two very different interpretations and outcomes.

On a product-by-product basis, the variation in sales of individual products remains the same. When you start aggregating the sales of the various products, the degree of correlation plays an important role in the total sales. You can see that the variation in projected sales could be plus or minus $277,000 (for uncorrelated product sales) versus a swing of $709,000 (when the sales are correlated). This is a difference of close to half a million dollars in either direction.

The moral of the story is that despite the fact that the data in a spreadsheet may be correct, and that the spreadsheet may be free of arithmetic errors, unless you get all the assumptions laid down on the table, the results and outcome of the spreadsheet may not be reasonable.

Closing Thoughts

Because this is Chapter 11, I was tempted to present a spreadsheet containing sample data relating to bankruptcy. I felt, however, that I should stress a more positive note for this chapter. The goal here is to help you secure some sure footing with respect to the validity and integrity of the spreadsheets you receive.

It is very hard to prove unequivocally that a spreadsheet is producing correct and reliable results. It is much easier to identify the errors and possibly correct them.

Thankfully, spotting common spreadsheet errors is not too difficult. You saw the ease with which this can be done with the first spreadsheet provided in the chapter. Although presentation style in a spreadsheet should not be an audit issue, lack of style or utter disregard for organizing and structuring information into some coherent form can lead to mistakes in more complex spreadsheets. A poorly presented spreadsheet may be indicative of deeper issues to investigate.

Along these lines, the preparer of a spreadsheet may, whether by habit or design, be analyzing some information outside the context of the spreadsheet and fail to fully incorporate that information into the spreadsheet. I refer to this oversight as "off-spreadsheet analysis." Just because the preparer of the spreadsheet segregated his or her thinking from the spreadsheet doesn't mean that the disconnects forever separate you from the underlying details. Sometimes you can reconstruct information from direct and indirect evidential matter. Why bother doing this with pencil and paper when you can marry your professional skills and knowledge to computer-based tools (such as a spreadsheet)? You saw how this works through the use of an Interpretive Reconciliation Worksheet (IRW).

It should be pointed out that you may not be able to "reconnect" all the data. A frequent goal in examining data with a tool of this kind is to identify leads for further investigation, rather than to provide the answers.

If you find yourself in need of greater computational resources than an interactive tool such as an IRW can provide, consider using spreadsheet portals, the subject of the next chapter. Spreadsheet portals give you the benefits of online access to industrial-strength databases, Internet connectivity, the ability to send and receive XML data, and all the computational facilities of regular Excel spreadsheets.

Before leaving the topic of spreadsheet auditing, I want to point out that when people ask for information, they often get exactly what they asked for instead of what they meant (or needed). Spreadsheets, without the proper foundations or driving assumptions, can't go anywhere. If they do, they may have done so at the cost of a misinterpretation.

Chapter 12

Spreadsheet Portals, XML, and Web Services

THE PROMISE OF XML IN Excel (and in the Microsoft Office Suite) has been long awaited. As you will soon see, you stand at the precipice of a very expansive territory. Because the technology is so new and changing so rapidly, and your business needs can be so diverse yet specialized, I won't give you an exhaustive presentation of the topic. Instead, I want to help you accomplish two things:

- ◆ Quickly familiarize yourself in working with XML in Excel, enough to take advantage of some of its new capabilities as well as new uses of previous capabilities.

◆ Understand the concept of a Spreadsheet Portal. *Excel Best Practices for Business* has been pretty much ambidextrous when it comes to the version of Excel that you use. This chapter stands out as a clear exception because many of the spreadsheets do not work with earlier versions of Excel. Some, however, do, and I point those out along the way. Meanwhile, if you haven't yet upgraded to Excel 2003, you now have good reason to do so.

This chapter begins with a simple framework for presenting information in what I call a Spreadsheet Portal. The Spreadsheet Portal is based on the concept of a traditional Internet portal but commandeers it into something wonderfully suited for spreadsheets. This adjustment paves the way for a whole new set of applications, which I call Desktop Client Portals (or DCPs). DCPs and, in particular, Spreadsheet Portals can harness Web capabilities including XML and Web Services. As with mainframe computers, desktop applications are not going to whither on the vine; instead, they will continue to re-invent themselves. The Client Portal concept is just one of these reinventions.

After I whet your appetite with an introduction to Spreadsheet Portals, you'll want to lift up the lid to see to how they work. You'll find two things that are new and different. One is a new kind architecture for spreadsheet design, based on the layered pattern approach originally introduced in Chapter 2, "Mastering Spreadsheet Construction Techniques." The other is that the spreadsheet is Web-enabled through XML. In the second part of this chapter, I introduce you to various ways of Web-enabling your spreadsheets. I show you two Spreadsheet Portals. One of these gives you a portal page that lets you participate in an online survey. With this, you can design a portal page to support bidirectional communication. The second Spreadsheet Portal allows you to fuse separate information flows into a single view.

Next, you will dive into the newer XML capabilities of Excel. I introduce it from a hands-on perspective and show you an example that hints at the real potential. I also present some aspects of XML that indicate how the technology still has a ways to go.

For all its potential, XML can only be a mechanism for the encoding and exchange of information. A framework is needed that can be overlaid on top of XML to enable a vast array of computers and network devices to work together. That framework has become known as Web Services. It is built upon three independent but cooperating pillars. One pillar serves as a mechanism for discovery of services. Another is the mechanism that tells the various computers how and where to access the services available from other computers. The third pillar provides a protocol for exchanging requests and responses between the computers. And what's the underlying language for communicating all three of these facilities? You guessed it: XML.

Spreadsheet Portals and Desktop Client Portals

This chapter introduces the concept of a Spreadsheet Portal and provides several reference implementations. Some of you may already be familiar with Internet-based portals. The concept is simple. You, the user, connect using your browser to a portal page on some remote server. You set your preferences and the remote server gathers data from even more remote locations. You don't worry about what goes on behind the scenes. You just tell it, by selecting from among its options, what you want. The portal pipes in the appropriate data onto your page and hands it to you.

This traditional view regarding portals is way cool, but is it the only way or necessarily the best way to accomplish what it does? Obviously, the answer depends upon your goals. To be sure, the traditional portal is a technology whose value should not be discounted. However, it needs to make way for the new kid on the block: Desktop Client Portals (DCPs). Interestingly enough, DCPs can, like Spreadsheet Portals, tag team very effectively with traditional portal servers, making for a very effective partnership among the technology components.

Just as a traditional portal can aggregate and channel multiple sources of information and consolidate them onto a Web page, so can a Desktop Client Portal accomplish these feats. The question you have to ask yourself is whether a specific advantage is conferred by using a DCP. Depending on the desktop application you choose, the advantages can definitely be there. In the case of a Spreadsheet Portal, the spreadsheet can create a seamless integration between remote data and the computations in your spreadsheet.

Simple Client Portals

The framework of a Spreadsheet Portal is rather simple, as is shown in Figure 12-1.

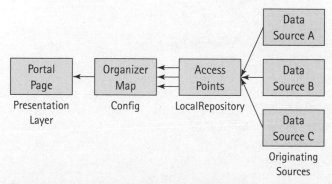

Figure 12-1: Simple Spreadsheet Portal schematic

An example of a Spreadsheet Portal page is shown in Figure 12-2. You can also open the file ch12-01PortalConceptNonXML.xls, on the CD-ROM with this book. This file will work perfectly well with Excel 2003 and earlier versions.

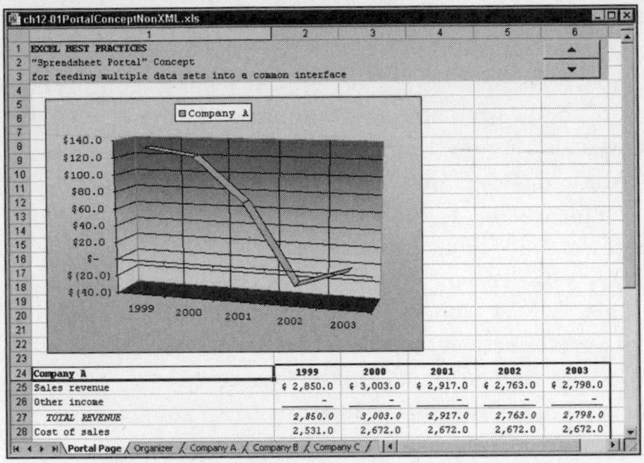

Figure 12-2: Simple Spreadsheet Portal example

A Spreadsheet Portal has a portal page that assumes the role of the Presentation Layer. This layer is graphically driven. Notice the Up/Down arrow button in the sample Spreadsheet Portal (Figure 12-2). Clicking the arrows on this button allows you to cycle through and select the specific company data you desire.

The Portal page itself really has no idea how or where the data is coming from. To get this information, it looks to the Organizer (Figure 12-3).

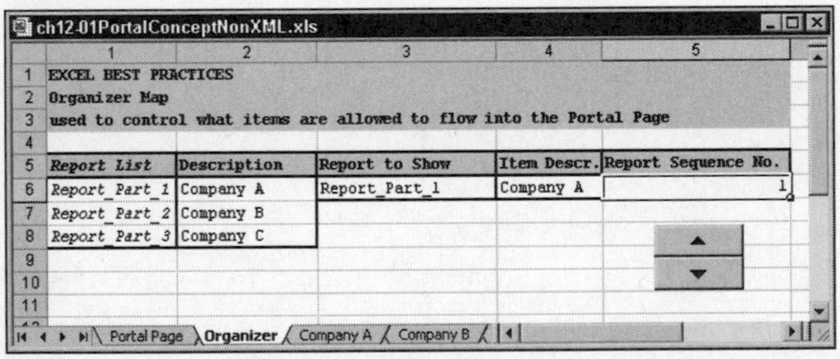

Figure 12-3: An Organizer map allows you to select which items in your reports will flow into the Portal page.

The Report List identifies various named regions in your spreadsheet. Report_Part_1 corresponds to the top-left corner of the financial data for Company A. The Description fields listing the names, Company A, B, and C, are purely a cosmetic convenience so that you can quickly view each of the names to which the Report List refers. The spinner control button appearing on this page is the same as the one for the Portal page. As you click the up and down arrows, the Report Sequence number is adjusted. The changing of this sequence number adjusts the Report to Show. Listing 12-1 provides the formula for this.

Listing 12-1

```
=OFFSET(ReportSection1,Section1SeqNo,0)
```

The Organizer simply identifies the name of the information requested from the Portal page. Think of your Organizer as a table of contents for your spreadsheet.

The Portal page takes the name listed within this table of contents and uses the Excel INDIRECT function to reference the actual cell represented by that name. If you're retrieving just a single value, then you don't need to go though this craziness to get a single number. However, if you want to get all the data over a range of cells, such as a whole financial report, then this framework makes a lot of sense.

THE BENEFITS

For the moment, forget about the Internet- and Web-enabling aspects of your spreadsheet. Consider the following scenario: You work in a "new ventures" group at a bank and are conducting the due diligence for potential portfolio companies. You are working with the data for 45 or so companies and preparing 45 spreadsheets.

During one of the conference calls, several V.P.s, all of whom like your prepared spreadsheets, would like to see them done differently (for example, they'd like you to prepare a financial ratio such as Profit Margin [net income / sales] and use a bar chart instead of the 3D line chart you already have).

If you've prepared 45 separate spreadsheets, chances are you'll be busy for the next couple of days reworking them. However, if you use a Spreadsheet Portal, you need adjust only the Portal Interface, and you're done. Thankfully, because you're using the Spreadsheet Portal, you have little to do other than to print the reports and spend your time further analyzing the data to determine which company should make it to the next round of financing.

I should point out that with a Spreadsheet Portal you can also take advantage of Web connectivity to automatically retrieve up-to-the minute data.

Whatever the case may be, a Spreadsheet Portal gives you the advantage of streamlined efficiency and a uniform interface for a wide selection of data.

Complex Spreadsheet Portals

Complex and larger Spreadsheet Portals broaden the definition and elevate the capabilities of a Spreadsheet Portal by several notches. To be effective, the Spreadsheet Portal must be facile with managing data.

The data I am speaking about is online Web data that is continually changing over time. The data is found on Web servers, database servers, and who knows how many other sources. Decision analysis no longer takes place over the course of weeks or days, but in Internet time. These accelerated demands place increasing reliance on the ability of technology to adjust to minute-by-minute changes in data.

Interactive participation in an evolving survey

For a concrete example of continuously changing circumstances, imagine a community of people who work collectively on a worldwide basis, participating in a survey for which feedback is nearly instantaneous. Such an interactive survey might be similar to Figure 12-4. Here, the items in the drop-down lists as well as the questions are all updated whenever someone clicks the Connect button. Based on the participant's responses, blanket messages or specifically targeted messages can be placed into the interactive survey.

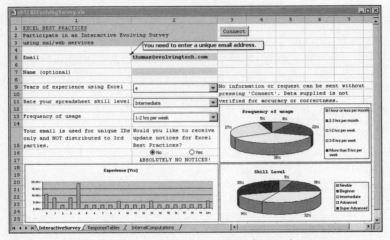

Figure 12-4: A Spreadsheet Portal as an evolving interactive survey

A couple of other things in Figure 12-4 are worth noting. To begin with, an Excel HYPERLINK function at the top-left corner of the interactive survey is determined dynamically. When old versions of the spreadsheet are detected, links to a current version can be instantly inserted here.

Basically, the content and delivery of information in the form of a spreadsheet can be personalized, making this framework a true portal service. Unlike a browser-based version, the Spreadsheet Portal has the ability to integrate any and all of Excel's calculation and graphing capabilities. Because the spreadsheet is Web-enabled, users can also extend the portal interface of their spreadsheets to connect to additional data sources.

Another interesting feature of this Spreadsheet Portal is that the process of retrieving data is synonymous with the process of supplying information, thereby making bi-directional communication effective and efficient.

I encourage you to try out this Spreadsheet Portal (open the file ch12-02Evolving Survey.xls on the CD-ROM with this book).

This interactive survey facility works only with Excel 2003. Earlier versions of Excel will not work with it.

HOW THE EVOLVING SURVEY WORKS

Leaving out the technical details, here is what happens:

1. The items you enter into the Interactive Survey, such as your identity or the items you select from the drop-down lists or the preferences are encoded into a parameter string. This string provides supplied information to a "servlet" running on a remote server. The back-end server can be as simple as an Apache Tomcat Server or as full featured as a WebSphere Portal Server.

2. When you click the Connect button, an Excel macro kicks into action and sends a URL request to the servlet.

3. The servlet validates the URL request it receives. If the request is from a person who is new to the survey, it creates a new database record and stores appropriate information into the record. If the request comes from a person already registered in the survey, the database record for that person is updated.

4. After adjusting the database record, the servlet specifically composes a response message specific to the individual, encodes this as an XML message, and sends it back to the Spreadsheet Portal.

5. The Spreadsheet Portal receives the message and deposits it into a location that has been defined by an XML Map. This map knows how to interpret and lay out the data.

6. After the information has been sent back into the spreadsheet, the individual components of the XML message are parceled out into separate pieces of information. Each of these is transformed into one of several lookup tables. These lookup tables correspond to the various components that appear on the Portal Page called InteractiveSurvey. In this manner, the contents of the survey are dynamically driven.

Use a Spreadsheet Portal to braid information

Business information often has to be made in Internet time, requiring you to take different kinds of information from a variety of sources and weave them into a coherent picture. For an example, consider the following scenario.

Imagine that you work for a large, multinational company and have the responsibility of reviewing the financial activity of overseas operations. Basically, for a given range of dates, you want to compare any two companies or subsidiaries side-by-side. Although you may have daily financial activity for each subsidiary, your one big problem is that each subsidiary is located in a different country; hence, each subsidiary records its information in a different currency.

Say there are 19 subsidiaries. (Why 19? There's no particular reason other than to illustrate that the problem is realistic but readily solvable.) Now, each subsidiary reports results of its operations on a daily basis. The subsidiaries that are comprised of some kind of a trading operation base their contract for the settlement of the trade on the published Spot Exchange Rate for the currency on a specific day.

So, you are dealing with 19 operations having 19 exchange rates published daily. Over a period of seven calendar days, you may have as many as 5*19*18, or 1,710, side-by-side comparisons. By the way, the number being multiplied is 5 instead of 7 because currency exchanges operate only five days out of a seven-day week. Additionally, no exchanges occur for specific dates such as New Year's. Furthermore, you're multiplying 19*18 because each of the 19 subsidiaries can be compared to only 18 of the remaining subsidiaries. In any case, it doesn't matter how many calculations there are – the point is, there are a great many.

Your challenge is made interesting by the fact that the Spot Exchange rates are published separately from the historical financial data of each subsidiary. For all of the 19 or so different currencies, the published exchanged rates are provided only in the conversion of the currency to U.S. dollars.

If you want to compare the operations of an entity in Sweden (whose financial information is recorded in kronors) and an entity in South Africa (whose financial information is recorded in rands) from the 3rd through the 10th of January 2000, you would have to look up the currency exchange rates for each of the business days, perform a bunch of conversions and apply them to the amounts for each of the contracts for the given dates.

I suppose you could download all the currency and financial info to your computer and do everything locally on your machine. Suppose that the financial information for each subsidiary may be more than a single number for any given day? It could be that your company's accounting system has a hundred or many hundreds of items in the Chart of Accounts.

Whatever the situation, it may not be feasible to do everything on your single desktop machine. Nothing stops you from retrieving smaller parcels of information, however, and performing the analysis you want on your local Spreadsheet Portal.

Figure 12-5 shows you a possible Portal page that would handle this. At the click of a mouse button, you could select any set of subsidiaries to compare, choose a start date and duration, and instantly compare financial date in a common currency. This is information on demand. The key factor is that you are always working with the amount of information you need to analyze – and no more. This approach enables you to circumvent the info-glut problem altogether.

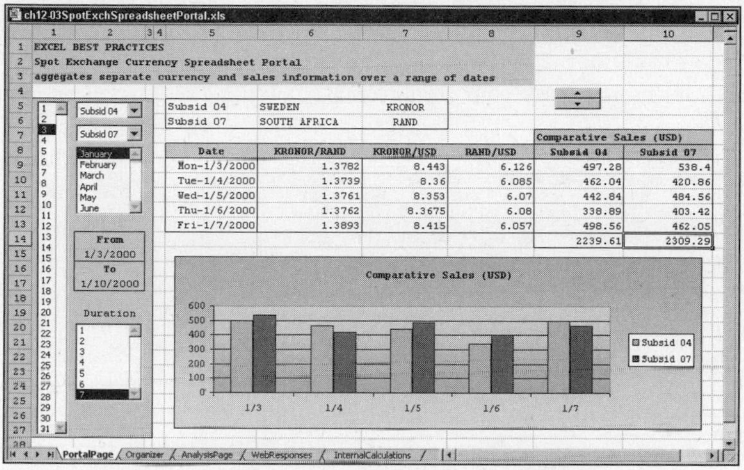

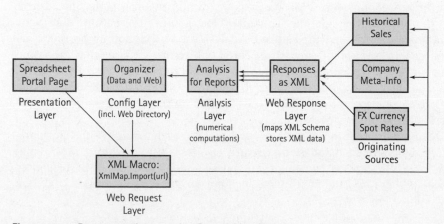

Figure 12-5: Multi–currency comparative financial analysis

HOW THE BRAIDED-STYLE SPREADSHEET PORTAL WORKS

Figure 12-6 provides a basic schematic for this specific type of portal, but is also representative of typical large and complex Spreadsheet Portals. Notice this portal is inherently similar to the simple Spreadsheet Portal shown previously (refer to Figure 12-1).

Figure 12-6: Representative complex Spreadsheet Portal

You know what the Presentation Layer looks like (Figure 12-5). If you try working with the sample file (ch12-03SpotExchSpreadsheetPortal.xls on the CD-ROM),
you will see that when you jump between dates, the Portal is fetching the data from
remote sources. Your mouse-clicking action fires some XML macro. I get to the
specifics of the macros soon enough. Right now, I'm just concentrating on what's
going on.

The macro reads information from your Organizer (see Figure 12-7).

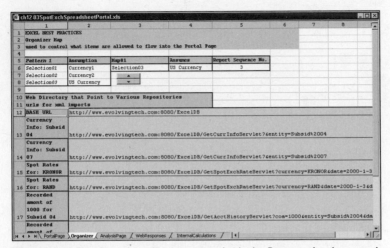

Figure 12-7: The Organizer sheet supports both the Presentation Layer and
the XML macros.

Your Organizer now serves a dual role. As occurs in the simple Spreadsheet
Portal, the top portion of the Organizer maps the information that your
Presentation Layer will be lifting off the Analysis Layer. The bottom portion contains the URL info that the Spreadsheet Portal will retrieve. Notice that the information supplied in the URL is tethered to the selected items from your Portal page.
It is, in fact, driven by your actions and inputs on the Portal page. Because the
macros are event-driven, they read the information on the Organizer and fetch the
information from remote locations.

The requests are sent to a variety of servlets. The servlets retrieve the appropriate information from a database and return responses as a stream of XML data.
The Excel macro that is making the requests intercepts the XML responses
and deposits them into the appropriate location on the Web Responses page (see
Figure 12-8).

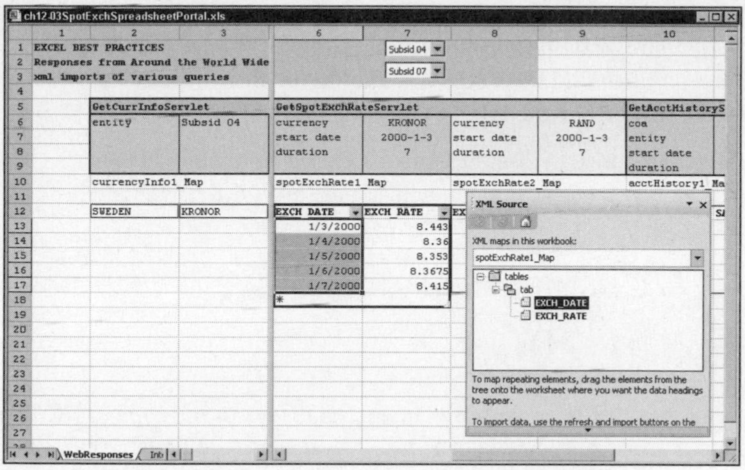

Figure 12–8: XML data is imported to specifically mapped locations.

AND NOW A WORD FROM OUR SPONSOR (ME!)

In using this demonstration Spreadsheet Portal, you need to be aware of several things:

> This system has been prepared FOR DEMONSTRATION PURPOSES ONLY. Although currency conversion information is displayed, this information has *not* been reviewed for any level of accuracy or correctness and should *not* be relied upon for any kind of business decision whatsoever. The example in this section is meant to serve for illustrative purposes only, to outline the architecture of a Spreadsheet Portal.

◆ In a production environment, back-end services such as retrieval of foreign currency conversion info that would likely be obtained from a different server than the one that has company financial history. Because the system explained here is a demonstration system, they both happen to reside on the same server. For the sake of keeping things logically distinct, each kind of information is sending the request to a different servlet.

◆ To keep the system simple, I've limited the data to a range of dates spanning six months (from January 3 through June 30, 2000).

◆ I've capped the range of dates for comparative analysis at seven calendar days (or five business days). My objective in mind was not to create a production system, but rather to provide a standard reference implementation that you can use to develop Spreadsheet Portals of your own.

◆ As was true in the previous demonstration, the Spreadsheet Portal described here will not work if your version of Excel is earlier than Excel 2003. However, at least in Excel XP, you should be able to open the spreadsheets and examine the various formulas.

◆ From time to time, I may revise the Spreadsheet Portals and URL locations. In such cases, I will post some additional info on my Web site: `www.evolvingtech.com/excel`

XML in Excel 2003

You may have noticed that I've been inching closer and closer to the topic of XML. Although Spreadsheet Portals rely heavily on the XML features of Excel 2003, I've introduced them separately because the architecture for a Spreadsheet Portal is essentially independent of the specific XML features, even though it makes significant use of XML.

You have seen the insertion points where XML comes into play with Spreadsheet Portals. Understanding this conjoining will help to get a handle on how to work XML into your spreadsheets.

You have seen that almost every time I've brought out XML, I mention it in the context of some macro. XML and macros do not have to be a macro-only facility.

My goal in this section is to catapult you directly into using XML in some useful manner. Basically, I am making the assumption that you have some Web-based applications which send you XML data and you want to create a seamless integration between your spreadsheet and the remote applications. The example in this section is an application that uses Amazon Web Services to search for books (see Figure 12-9).

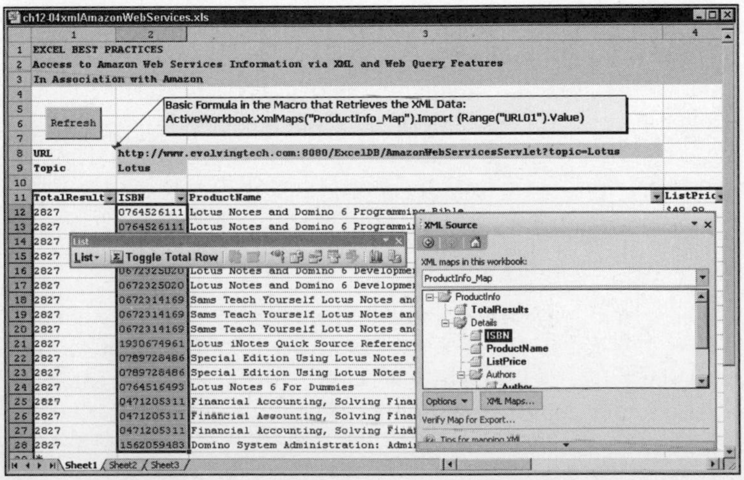

Figure 12-9: Internet online search

You'll find the completed file for this example, ch12-04xmlAmazon WebServices.xls, on the CD-ROM that accompanies this book.

Here are the initial thoughts you need to concern yourself with:

1. You have to fill in the blanks on the specifics for how requests are going to be sent from your spreadsheet and how information will be received.

2. You have to tell Excel how the data is to be structured and what to do with it.

3. You want to automate the interaction between Excel and the remote server.

4. You want to build the other parts of your spreadsheet application to work with this XML-based facility.

The following sections provide the details for each of these steps.

Step 1: Communicate with the server

In your spreadsheet application, type in a search term and press the Refresh button (see the top-left area of Figure 12-9). The spreadsheet then sends a request to a remote server. That server, in turn, adds parameters and sends a full request to the search engine at Amazon. Amazon performs the search and transforms the response into a specified XML structure relying on an eXtensible Style Language (XSL) sheet. After the search result is transformed, the result is sent back to the originating server and the server returns the results as XML to the spreadsheet.

To set the formula for the URL in your spreadsheet, define two named ranges. Give one of these the name Topic and place it in a suitable location (in the completed application, it is in row 9, column 2). This is where you will enter in you search term. Define another range as URL01. This will contain the following formula:

```
="http://www.evolvingtech.com:8080/ExcelDB/AmazonWebServicesServlet?
topic="&Topic
```

This formula pulls your search term directly into the URL string. If for some reason the URL for this servlet changes, I will post it on my Web site at: www.evolvingtech.com/excel.

At this stage, you haven't yet constructed much of a spreadsheet. You can still test the URL, though. To do so, type a search term into the Topic field and then copy the URL01 cell (click Ctrl+C) that is in your spreadsheet, go to your browser, and paste it (Ctrl+V) directly into the edit line of your browser. Press the Enter key, and you should get back an XML string. The MIME type for the content returned is "text/xml", so your browser may not show anything intelligible unless you select View Source from the browser View menu.

Step 2: Tell the spreadsheet application how to structure the received data

If you look back at Figure 12-9, you will see an XML Source Pane that outlines the schema of XML received. Basically, the XML Map is an inverted tree representation of the expected XML content. Notice that some of the names in the XML Map, such as `TotalResults`, `ISBN`, `ProductName`, and `ListPrice`, appear in boldface. The same names are running across the top of the spreadsheet region that is populated with XML data. Also notice that when you click in or select any region in the XML Map, the corresponding portion of data in the spreadsheet is also highlighted.

So, how do you get the XML Map to appear? There are several ways. Here is one of them, which is easy to do if you want to run in auto-pilot mode. From the Menu bar, choose Data → Import External Data → New Web Query. When you're prompted for a URL, type it in or paste it from the plain text that you copied previously. The "sample" URL used in this case is

```
http://www.evolvingtech.com:8080/ExcelDB/AmazonWebServicesServlet?to
pic=Lotus
```

Now press the Go button (see Figure 12-10).

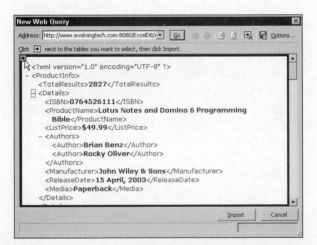

Figure 12-10: Importing XML and its schema from a New Web query

You can see the XML content. To the left of the content you should see one or more horizontal, colored arrows. Clicking the arrow will signal to Excel 2003 that you want this portion of content imported. This example shows only one region. After you click the arrow, the page will be highlighted and you can press the Import button. Also notice the minus sign (–) to the left of some of the tags. These minus signs signify tags that can contain sub-tags. Clicking the – will collapse the tag and minus sign will change to a plus sign (+).

 The Web Query facility assumes a static URL request. If you attempt to refresh from the Excel Data menu or through one of the toolbar icons, the exact same query will be run. In this case the search term is "Lotus." The Web Query data refresh will now be fixated on Lotus. Although the resulting XML Map *may be* suitable, you will have to rely on some other facility pump in the XML data if you want be running dynamic queries.

Upon importing through the Web Query, Excel 2003 will immediately sense that this is XML data. If no schema definition is referenced in the XML file, Excel will attempt to construct its own XML Map based on the content (see Figure 12-11).

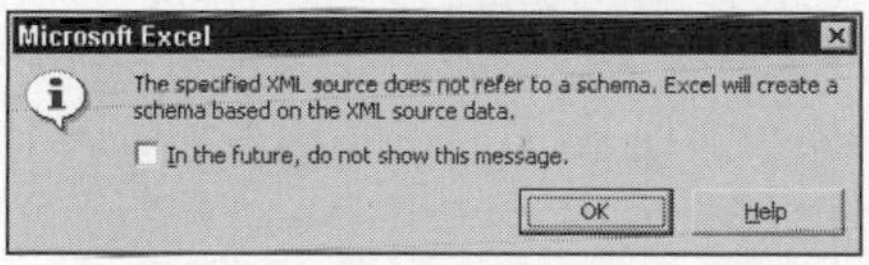

Figure 12-11: On-the-fly XML Map creation

In addition to creating an XML Map, Excel 2003 will then prompt you for a place to park the imported data (see Figure 12-12). While you're setting the location of the data, you have the opportunity to adjust some of the properties of the XML Map. Excel will construct the name of the XML Map by taking the name of the "root" element in the XML content and adjoining it to "_Map." Notice in Figure 12-10 that the root element in ProductInfo. The name `ProductInfo_Map` is automatically created. A spreadsheet can have more than one XML Map, because you can import more than one XML document into a spreadsheet.

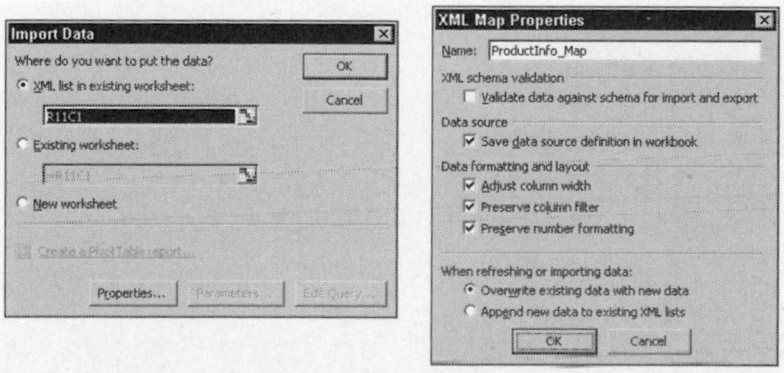

Figure 12-12: The Import Data window allows you to set the XML Map properties.

The XML Map names for a given spreadsheet have to be unique. So, what happens if two XML documents are imported into a single spreadsheet and have the same tag for the root element? Excel simply appends a unique number at the end of the XML Map name. As an example, the second XML Map of an XML document containing the root element `ProductInfo` would automatically be named `ProductInfo_Map1`. The third would be named `ProductInfo_Map2`.

The XML Map Properties settings provide the option to turn off "Adjust column width by unchecking the item." If you plan to display other data along with the XML content on the same worksheet, you may want to keep this turned off. Also, when refreshing or importing data, you have the option to append the imports instead of overwriting.

The creation of an XML Map is basically a one-time process. It isn't something that gets changed the way regular data does. If you will be preparing XML Maps based on a single example file, you had better choose the sample data wisely; otherwise, you will get errors like the kind shown in Figure 12-13.

Notice that in the `ISBN` tag, the values displayed consist of a pure series of digits. Excel 2003, being spreadsheet-centric, is predisposed to treating content like this as a pure number. If all the ISBN content in the "sample" import has no letters, Excel is going to treat the ISBN as a number data type when it defines the XML Map. Further, it will not tell you that it is making such an assumption. This could lead to unexpected and undesired results. Figure 12-13 shows you the kind of error you might get.

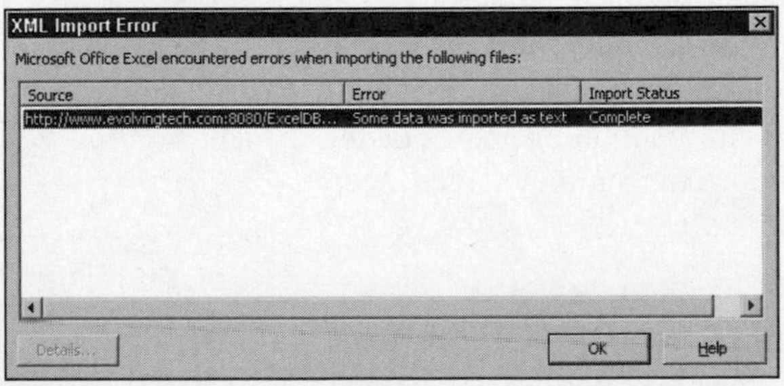

Figure 12-13: Import error owing to an overly restrictive data type defined in the XML Map

GETTING THE SCHEMA DIRECTLY

As is often the case, the XSD Schema file can be obtained directly from the Web site or server. The schema file for the servlet in this example can be downloaded from

`www.evolvingtech.com/ExcelDB/AmazonWebServicesServlet`

Schema definitions and namespaces

XML affords some nice advantages. One of these is that you can invent XML tags on the fly. As long as you are consistent about your usage of tags, and the XML documents you create or use are well formed, you can make use of the XML documents as much as you like. What if you want someone to send you information that conforms to your way of preparing the XML document? There might be certain conventions regarding organization and structure of the XML document that need to be preserved. To communicate these governing conventions to others, you can make use of a special kind of XML document called an XSD Schema (XSD stands for eXtensible Schema Definition).

The tag names defined in your schema can make use of "namespaces" so that the meaning and rules of interpretation for a specific tag name do not collide with a tag of the same name in a different XML document. For instance, your tag called "invoice" might require specific elements such as customer ID, customer address, date, product name, product model number, product price, quantity, and so forth. Someone else's invoice tag might just have name, date, service type, billed hours, and billing rate. The use of namespaces allows you to specify which of these invoice tags you mean when invoice info is encountered.

An XML document can reference an XSD Schema that specifies the specific schema for that document. Software applications that are savvy enough can put this information to use when creating new XML documents on the fly. Generally, the XML document will refer to the schema document location using a URL. Remember, there is no requirement that a schema document has to be referenced in or supplied with the XML document. As long as your XML documents are well formed, it may suffice to continue using and working with the XML documents without a separate schema file.

When Excel 2003 imports an XML file, it looks at the structure of the XML and searches to see whether a schema definition exists. If not, it will create its own schema definition, which takes the form of an XML Map. When an XSD Schema is specified, Excel 2003 will use the schema definition instead of constructing one of its own.

Note: If you use your browser to retrieve this file, you may need to save the content to a text file having the .xsd suffix or else tell your browser to "View Source" from the browser's View menu, and then you can copy and paste the content to a text editor, where you can save the contents as an .xsd file.

After the file is saved, you can go straight to your XML Source Pane and click the XML Maps button. When the dialog box for XML Maps appears, click Add and you'll see a window indicating Multiple Roots and asking you to identify the root node. When you complete this process, your XML Map will be added (see Figure 12-14).

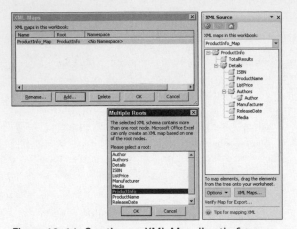

Figure 12-14: Creating an XML Map directly from
a Schema (XSD) file

GENERATING THE SCHEMA WITH THIRD-PARTY TOOLS

If no XSD file can be found anywhere and you want better control over preparing
your XSD file, you can make use of any of a number of third-party tools. Figure
12-15 shows the WebSphere Studio Application Developer being used to generate
the XSD file.

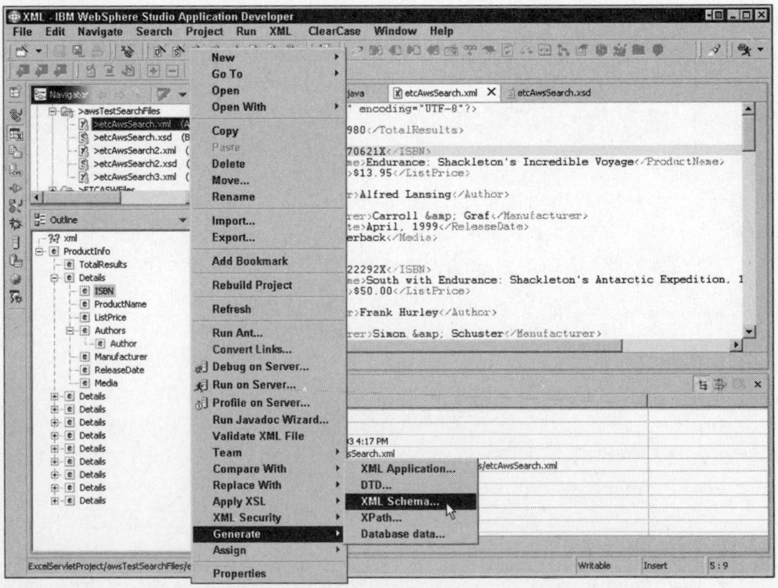

Figure 12-15: XML Schema generation

After you have generated the XSD file, you can tweak it manually for the appropriate data types and bring it into Excel as described previously.

TURNING YOUR MAP ELEMENTS INTO LISTS

You may recall your experiences in assembling PivotTables. The behavior is similar here. You just drag and drop the elements of your choosing (see Figure 12-16). You can mix and match any of the elements into just about any of the columns of your spreadsheet. You can drag one item at a time or hold down the Ctrl key and click any set of elements in your XML Source Pane. You can then "group drag" these items onto your spreadsheet.

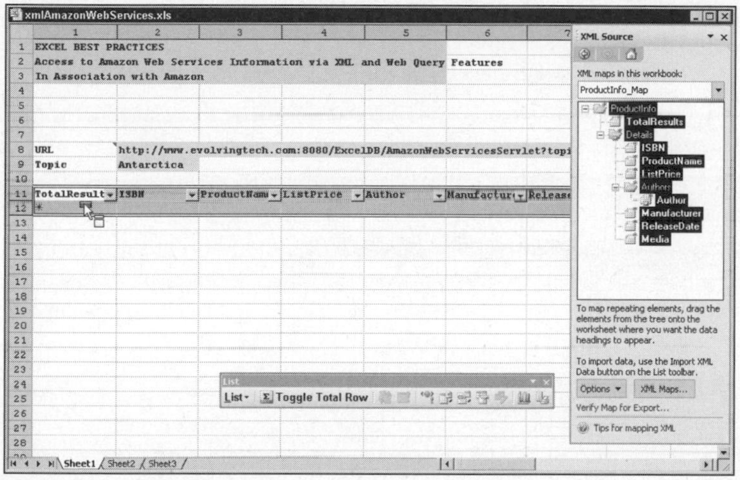

Figure 12-16: List creation

I want you to pause now and take a moment to understand the primary changes brought on by the introduction of Excel 2003. There are essentially only two. One of them relates to XML and the other relates to the Excel List structure.

The role that Lists play as enabling components in Excel 2003 is significant. In a nutshell, Lists are the containers that will hold, manage, and display your XML content. If you achieve a good handle on Lists, then your ability to manage XML content will significantly improve.

LISTS AND XML LISTS

Lists in Excel 2003 are designed to provide enhanced structure to a range in a worksheet. Lists have distinct columns and column headings, as well as an insert row for adding more data (signified by the blue asterisk appearing in the last row of the bounded region that surrounds the List). An XML List is one whose columns map to an associated XML schema element. Whenever you drag one or more repeating elements from an XML Map onto your worksheet, an XML List is automatically created.

Step 3: Interaction between Excel and the remote server

Your next step is to bring data into the List structure. You can do this by creating an Excel macro.

To go into macro mode, press Alt+F11. (This works as a toggle: Pressing Alt+F11 again will allow you to return to Excel mode.) While you're in macro mode, you will add some code similar to that appearing in Figure 12-17. If you don't see a VBA Project window, you can make the Project Explorer visible by pressing Ctrl+R. In the Project Explorer, you will see a listing of all open Excel workbooks, including those hidden. Select the one for the XML workbook you've been working on and expand the tree to see whether it contains a module. You should be able to double-click the module to open the code window. If the window doesn't appear, though, open the Visual Basic Insert menu and select Module.

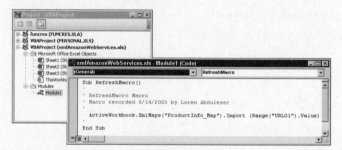

Figure 12-17: A Visual Basic macro for importing XML data

In the code window, type in the code shown in Listing 12-2.

Listing 12-2

```
Sub RefreshMacro()
' Place some informative comment here
  ActiveWorkbook.XmlMaps("ProductInfo_Map").Import _
(Range("URL01").Value)
End Sub
```

Some Visual Basic syntax and elementary concepts

In case you're not used to working in Visual Basic, here are some quick tips on syntax:

◆ A single quotation mark (') at the beginning of a line will turn the whole line into a comment. When you are experimenting with alternative variations on a line of code, you can comment out some lines and not others to achieve the effect you want to test and validate.

◆ The code window does not wrap the text. When you have long lines of code that stretch well beyond the length of the window, you can safely split the line by adding a line continuation mark. This is signified by an isolated underscore character (_) appearing at the end of the line where the code breaks and wraps to the next line. An example of this usage is shown in Listing 12-2.

◆ Sometimes you will want to concatenate, or join, two strings of text. The concatenation operator in Visual Basic is a plus symbol (+) The following two strings have the identical effect:

```
"ProductInfo_Map"
```

```
"ProductInfo" + "_Map"
```

Notice that Visual Basic uses a + operator to join strings, whereas your regular Excel spreadsheets use the &'

◆ If you intend to copy and paste code from a document you find on the Internet, be sure to watch out for unusual character mappings. From one respected journal article, I found an expression like this:

```
"ProductInfo_Map˜
```

Visual Basic will not treat this like a regular quoted expression.

◆ Sometimes you may want quote characters to appear inside a character string. It is done the same way you would do it in an Excel formula. Basically, you type two sets of quotes for the appearance of each quote inside the string. For example, the following:

```
"Please input ""THE VALUE"""
```

would render as: `Please input "THE VALUE"`

◆ On occasion, you will want to insert individual characters, such as a space or carriage return. You can do this programmatically using the `Chr` function. For example, the following two lines are equivalent:

```
"Input a value:"
```

```
"Input" + Chr(32) + "a" + Chr(32) +"value:"
```

The Visual Basic `Chr` function is the same as the Excel workbook function `CHAR`. Refer to Chapter 3, "Your Handy Reference for Manipulating Data," for more information on the various character codes.

◆ When you create subroutines in Visual Basic, they will automatically be visible in your selection of available macros unless you declare them `Private`. To do so, here is how the code would appear:

```
Private Sub SomePrivateMacroFunction()
' Replace this line with your code for the subroutine.

End Sub
```

Visual Basic uses an Object Model to refer to the various entities in its world. `ActiveWorkbook` is an entity the holds a collection of `XmlMaps`.

`ActiveWork.XmlMaps("ProductInfo_Map")` refers to the specific XML Map whose name is `ProductInfo_Map`.

`ActiveWorkbook.XmlMaps("ProductInfo_Map").Import (SOME_URL)` tells Visual Basic to go to `SOME_URL`, retrieve XML data, and import it. Instead of hard-wiring the value `SOME_URL` with something like this:

```
"http://www.evolvingtech.com/ExcelDB/AmazonWebServicesServlet?Topic=Antactica"
```

you can lift the value from a defined range using:

```
Range("URL01").Value
```

Go back to your regular Excel mode (press Alt+F11) and run the macro you just created. To do so, choose Tools → Macros → Macros. Somewhere along the way, you should have saved your spreadsheet. Excel will not allow you to run a macro if its contents are not attached to a saved workbook. Excel may force you to save your workbook.

 If you have a spreadsheet that you want to preserve as is, but you want to experiment with variations in the macros, you would do well to first save the file under a different name. Otherwise, you might alter your original file in a manner you didn't intend.

At this point, you should be able to run your macro (Figure 12-18). Sometimes your list of macros may be long, especially if you have other workbooks open that contain macros. In the Macros in: drop-down list, set your option to This Workbook and then select the appropriate macro and click Run.

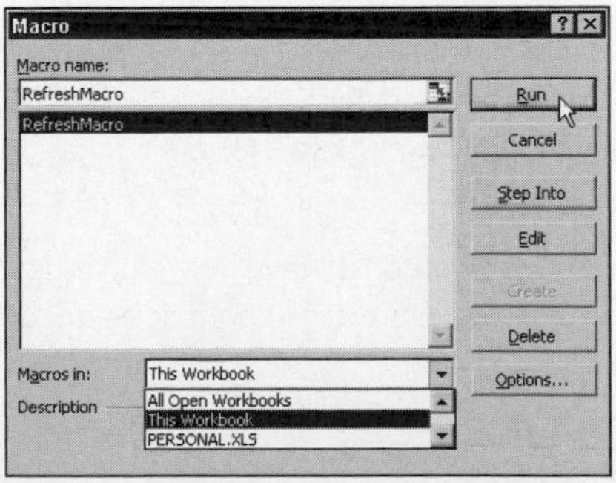

Figure 12-18: Running the RefreshMacro

You may have noticed that the Macro submenu gives you the ability to record new macros. Basically, Excel will watch what you do and translate these steps into Visual Basic code. You can use this capability decisively to your advantage. There are times when you might be trying to construct some Visual Basic and are uncertain of the correct syntax. A useful strategy is to turn on the macro recording and perform some of the actions manually, such as selecting named ranges, copying and pasting cells, making formatting changes, and so forth. After you stop recording, you can toggle to your macro mode (press Alt+F11) and edit your macros by incorporating code generated from your actions.

You should be aware that whenever you populate a List structure, the cells below the list get pushed down. This may have some impact on your spreadsheet formulas. Excel 2003 will give you an appropriate warning (Figure 12-19).

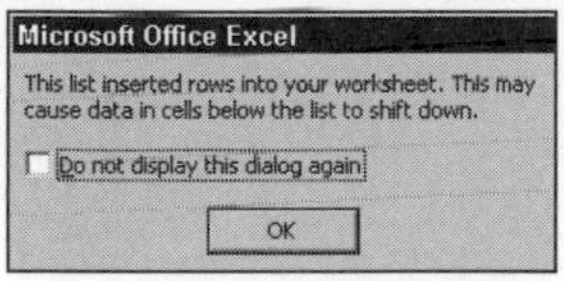

Figure 12–19: List structures insert rows
that can have undesired consequences

Finally, you will get some data into your spreadsheet (Figure 12-20).

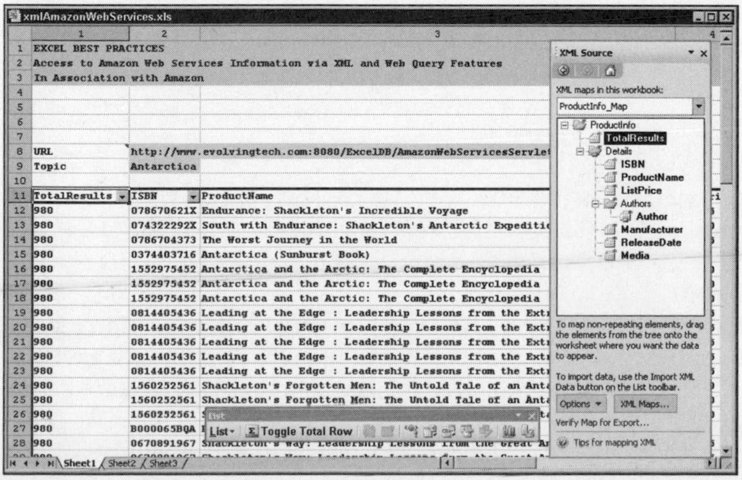

Figure 12–20: Populated list

Calling the macro from a menu is awkward. You can automate the interaction by adding a Forms button. If you don't have the Forms toolbar open, choose Tools → Customize and then, in the Toolbars tab, check the Forms option. Click the Button option and drag the outline of a button to some appropriate place on your worksheet. You should instantly be prompted to assign it to a macro. Select the appropriate macro in the Assign Macro window and click OK.

You should now have a button like the kind shown in Figure 12-21. You should be able to adjust the properties of the button by double-clicking its borders. When you deselect the button, clicking inside the button will activate the macro. If you wish to alter the properties or assign a different macro, right-click inside the button to select it without activating the macro and pull up your context menu options.

Figure 12-21: Button created from a Forms Toolbar

Step 4: Interaction with the other parts of your spreadsheet application

You have two possible approaches for interacting with the populated Lists containing XML content:

♦ You can keep everything on one worksheet.

♦ You can separate the XML Lists from the remaining portions of the spreadsheet.

THE ALL-IN-ONE WORKSHEET

Having an all-in-one worksheet, in which the XML content appears with the rest of the worksheet items, is fine for smaller-sized spreadsheets when the data you receive is not particularly complex. The Amazon search tool shown in this chapter is one such example.

Keep in mind that the size of the XML List can grow or shrink. It would be good to keep nothing below the XML List. The default setting in Excel 2003 is to have the column width vary each time in accordance with the data that gets imported. You can turn this setting off in the XML Map Properties. You can access the XML MAP Properties settings by choosing Data → XML → XML Map Properties.

The menu item for XML Map Properties is accessible only if your active cell resides physically, so to speak, within the XML List. Also, when you make the change to the Map Properties, it applies to the whole Map. For example, you won't be able to make the width of some List columns fixed and others variable.

XML Lists provide a number of conveniences:

♦ You can have them automatically total a column.

♦ At the top of each list is an Auto Filter tab. These basically work the same way that conventional filters do in Excel. As an example, in Excel 2003 you can sort your filtered data. The same is true with XML filters.

♦ Adjacent formulas are contagious. You will notice in the ch12-04xmlAmazonWebServices.xls file that there are Excel HYPERLINK formulas to the immediate right of the XML Lists. Notice that as the number of rows in the List expands or contracts, so does the formula containing the hyperlink.

In your spreadsheet formulas, you can insert hyperlinks. The following example should make it clear:
`=HYPERLINK("http://www.wiley.com","Wiley Publishing")`

A LAYERED APPROACH FOR A SPREADSHEET PORTAL

When your spreadsheet application gets to be more complex, as it does with Spreadsheet Portals, the XML data content you may be receiving may be more complex and terse than you would want for presentation purposes. For this reason it makes sense to adopt a layered pattern approach for the portal.

Increased complexity arises from the fact that:

♦ You could be receiving XML content from multiple sources, each of which has a fundamentally different type (recall the example in which currency information and company financial history data were coming from two different servlets).

♦ Even if the data feed originates from only one source, the content may be complex and context-dependent (for example, error messages may use a different set of tags than those used by the regular stream of data).

♦ In the translation from the XML content to a spreadsheet list content, Excel "denormalizes" the data. You may have noticed this in the book search example. When the search for books related to "Lotus" was returned, every row in the spreadsheet had a `TotalResults` column that was filled with a count of `2827` books (the spreadsheet in the chapter example displays only the first 10 titles). In the actual XML content received, the `TotalResults` info appears only once (see Figure 12-22). Data denormalization in Excel 2003 is not specific to Spreadsheet Portals; it can occur with simple XML data.

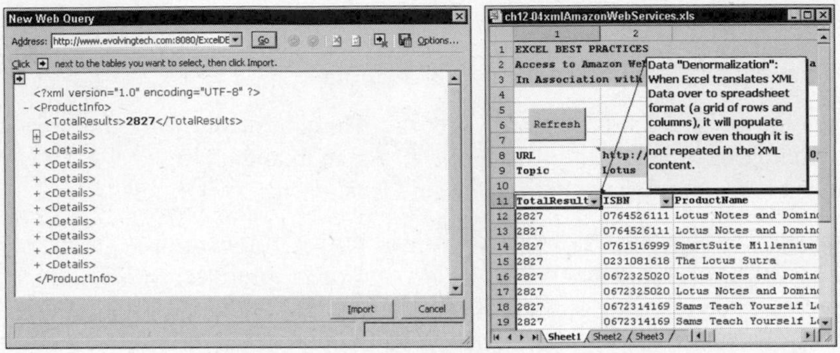

Figure 12-22: Data denormalization: When Excel 2003 converts the hierarchical structure of an XML document to a list on the spreadsheet, it repeats each of the elements in the hierarchy.

To make effective use of XML Lists for the layered approach, you need to do three things:

1. Centralize your XML/Web content onto a single worksheet and make sure that you lay out your XML Lists side-by-side, running horizontally across your worksheet. Flip back to Figure 12-8. It's an excellent example of how to layout the XML Lists for six different XML feeds.

   ■ Line 5 of Figure 12-8 shows the name of the servlet that feeds in the XML data.

   ■ Lines 6–9 of Figure 12-8 show the relevant parameter to each of the six XML feeds.

   ■ Line 10 of Figure 12-8 identifies the name of the XML Map for the XML Lists contained below.

   ■ All the XML Lists start at line 12 of Figure 12-8 and work their way downward. There is nothing to interfere with how the number of rows they occupy grows or shrinks.

2. The Web Response sheet like the kind shown in Figure 12-8 doesn't really do anything other than get the data into a well-known location. Because this page is isolated, you need a way to retrieve the information, be it for computational analysis or for presentation purposes. Either way, there are

two mechanisms you can use. You can use an OFFSET formula similar to Listing 12-1 at the beginning of this chapter. A more complex and real-world version of this formula can be found on both the PortalPage and the AnalysisPage worksheets of the file ch12-03SpotExchSpreadsheetPortal.xls. There are times you'll have name/value pairs that you'll want to look up. VLOOKUP can be used for this purpose. Look at the formulas for the ResponseTables worksheet of the ch12-02EvolvingSurvey.xls file. These techniques serve different purposes, but each performs its job well. Follow these examples.

3. To improve upon the interactiveness of your portal pages, you may want to have some interface components such as drop-down lists, which may need to be populated with values derived from your XML content. Construct regions in a dedicated location that retrieve the values from the XML Lists. Do not read the information directly from the XML Lists into your forms and interface components. There is good reason not to do this. The extra layering allows you to keep your presentation and interface components simple. They don't have to know anything about how to interpret the underlying data. Suppose you are retrieving some calendar date and the XML data isn't formatted correctly? Your interface components or portions of your Presentation Layer aren't designed to deal with all the data complexities and exception handling. Keep this complexity away from your portal pages or presentation layers. This separation will allow you to manage this complexity without being distracted by the visual presentation.

The XML "Staircase" Problem in Excel 2003 (and Other Things to Keep in Sight)

The integration of XML into Excel 2003 is not a light undertaking. Think about it for a moment. A spreadsheet is a tabular grid of rows and columns of numbers and formulas. By contrast, XML is a structure of text whose only restrictions are certain rules of syntax and, if need be, a prearranged schema. The use of namespaces permits a virtually endless lexicon of tags.

Many challenges can affect you if you intend to be working with XML in Excel 2003. Bringing XML data into Excel is one thing. Exporting it back out to its original state is entirely another. Sometimes Excel will complain that it cannot export your XML (Figure 12-23). This can come from either of two basic reasons, one of which you've already seen:

◆ The XML List is denormalized.

◆ The XML content is structured as a list of a list.

The key feature to keep in mind is that when you start working with lots of XML data in Excel, you may face the possibility of not easily being able to send the data back out. For a concrete example, imagine that someone sends you an XML file, and you examine it and make some changes within Excel. You may not be able to send your revised file back out making it look similar to the way you received it or have been working with it.

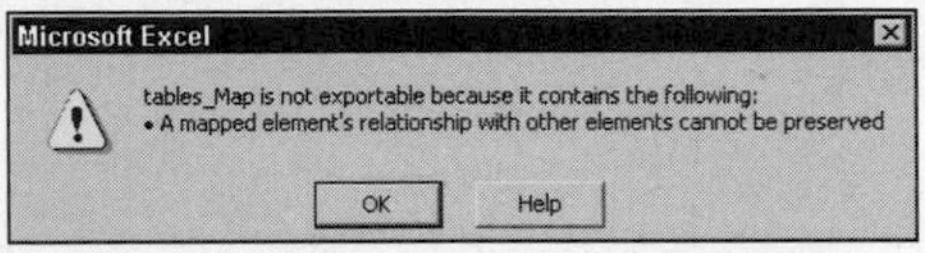

Figure 12-23: XML Export difficulties

Another problem that you're sure to encounter and will doubtless find frustrating is one that I call the "staircase" problem. Fortunately, I can provide you with a solution for this one.

Sometimes — actually, quite often — you will encounter XML data that looks like the following:

```
<?xml version="1.0" encoding="UTF-8"?>
<A>aaa</A><B>bbb</B<A>aaa</A><B>bbb</B><A>aaa</A><B>bbb</B>
```

This seemingly innocuous string composed of an `<A>` tag followed by a `<B>` tag followed by repeated sets of A and B tag is something that Excel has a hard time putting into a column of A's alongside a column of B's. Excel puts all the A's in one column. When it gets to the B's, it starts a row below the end of the A's (see Figure 12-24).

If you had some tags with C's following the pattern `ABCABCABC` instead of `ABABAB`, you would see a third "step" in your data when it is brought into Excel. Need I tell you what the pattern is going to look like if you have a sequence of `ABCD` tags?

Having data come in running diagonally down your spreadsheet as a series of steps is unwieldy, to say the least. As if to add insult to injury, the Excel Filter feature is rendered useless. But wait, there's more! If you click Verify Map for Export in the XML Source Pane, you will get the error message as shown in Figure 12-23.

The data can be altered slightly to get around this pathology. If you place a tag enclosing each `AB` pair, the line items will pair up properly (see Figure 12-25). Now there is no more staircase to contend with, the Filters work fine, and the structure of the data as it was imported is still preserved. The only loss is that the data is slightly more verbose.

There is still another way to bring in the data. This one involves attributes and is definitely more compact (see Figure 12-26).

As in the case of the first solution, everything lines up, the filters work, and the data is fully exportable. Notice that the XML Map for both Solutions 1 and 2 are identical in structure.

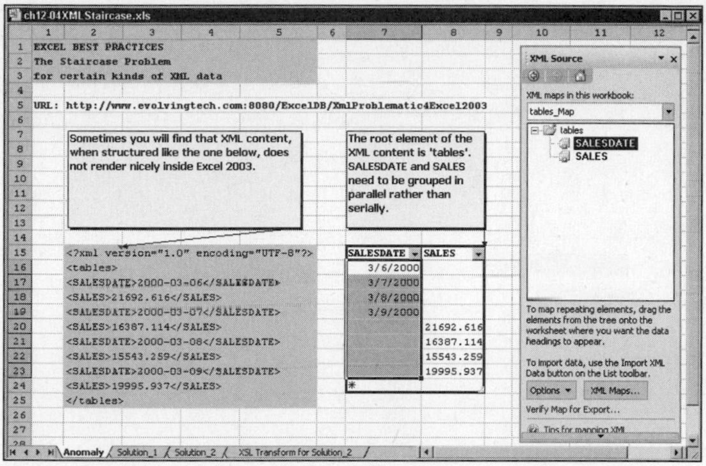

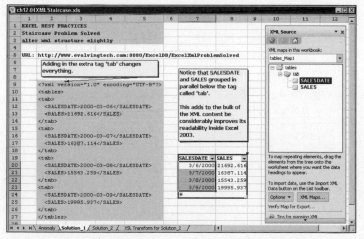

Figure 12–24: Excel is unable to align the columns of data, giving instead the appearance of a "staircase" as more columns of data are added.

Figure 12–25: A happy solution to the XML staircase problem

You may have to face yet one more obstacle. The XML data may come from a third-party source. You may not be able to tell that source to alter its XML structure for your convenience. To get around this problem, you need access to an XSLT server for doing some style sheet transformations. Basically, you would have to provide an XSL file to the server that tells it how to transform one kind of XML to another. How to set up an XSLT server is beyond the scope of this book, but if you have one accessible to you, you could provide it with an XSL style sheet like the one presented in Listing 12-3 and have the XSLT request the XML content, transform the XML on the fly, and punt it over to your Excel.

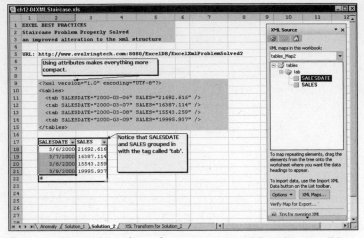

Figure 12–26: A second (happy) solution to the XML staircase problem

Listing 12–3

```xml
<?xml version="1.0" encoding="UTF-8"?>
<!-- Copyright 2003, Evolving Technologies Corporation -->
<xsl:stylesheet xmlns:xsl="http://www.w3.org/1999/XSL/Transform"
version="1.0">
  <xsl:output method="xml" />

  <xsl:template match="/">
    <tables>
      <xsl:for-each select="tables/SALESDATE">
        <xsl:variable name="pos" select="position()" />
        <tab>
          <xsl:attribute name="SALESDATE">
            <xsl:value-of select="/tables/SALESDATE[$pos]" />
          </xsl:attribute>
          <xsl:attribute name="SALES">
            <xsl:value-of select="/tables/SALES[$pos]" />
          </xsl:attribute>
        </tab>

      </xsl:for-each>
    </tables>
  </xsl:template>

</xsl:stylesheet>
```

Another possibility you might want to explore is to bring the data into Microsoft Access 2003. Access will be able to export content as XML using XSL style sheets that you provide.

I'll leave you to explore this on your own, but be aware that Excel 2003 has some useful macros related to XPath. In a nutshell, XPath gives you the ability to programmatically search and retrieve your XML data. Rather than use conventional spreadsheet formulas to search the rows and columns of an XML list, XPath uses the XML structure or "path" to retrieve data. If you'll be searching for data based on where it is logically located rather than by row and column location, you will definitely want to explore the XPath-related macro facilities.

By the way . . .

Most of the pre-release documentation I found on Excel 2003 focused almost exclusively on opening XML files from the C:\ drive. There was virtually nothing on receiving and sending data over networks and the Internet. I don't know about you, but to me, the whole purpose of using XML with spreadsheets is to enable spreadsheets to become first-class citizens in the Internet-driven generation of software.

Before I bring up the topic of Web Services I should really mention that Excel 2003 gives you the ability to open an XML file just about as easily as you can open a regular spreadsheet. When you open an XML file from the Excel File menu, you are provided with three options (see Figure 12-27).

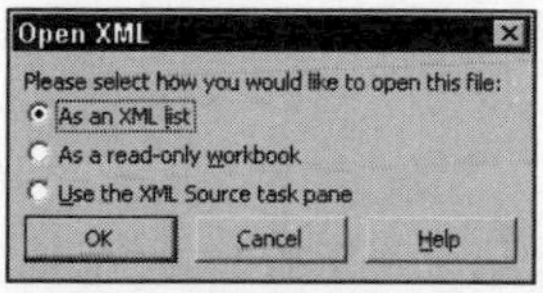

Figure 12-27: Options available
when opening an XML file

- ◆ The first option instructs Excel to read the XML file. If no predefined schema exists, Excel creates one on the fly. Additionally, it creates an XML List on your worksheet and populates the list with the file data.

- ◆ The second option allows you to browse the XML file content without saving it.

- ◆ The third option allows you to create only an XML Map based on the schema.

One last point needs mentioning. Excel provides the ability to copy or move worksheets. This was covered in some detail during the topic of Presentation Tear Sheets (see Chapter 6, "Let the Data Speak for Itself: Viewing and Presenting Data"). You should be aware that XML Maps and schema definitions are independent of the worksheet location. As such, they are not duplicated when a spreadsheet is copied. Though the Lists on the worksheets do get copied, the copied lists are no longer bound to the schema definitions. When the XML data is refreshed, the copied worksheets will not get updated.

Web Services — with a Twist

You've already seen Web Services being used in conjunction with Excel spreadsheets. You even constructed one of these spreadsheets (the Amazon Web Services search facility). The way the Web Services worked was so subtle that you didn't notice it was at work. That subtlety was intentional.

The Web Services capability of connecting into and searching for books came to you *after* you pulled Excel 2003 out of the shrink wrap and installed it on your computer's hard drive. More important, that specific service came to you without involving the product development folks at Microsoft to build in a feature to support online book searches. The next couple of dozen Web Services that you tap into with your spreadsheets won't entail additional product development costs on the part of Microsoft. The equivalent would be true for any vendor offering Internet-enabled software products.

This is a very significant shift in the economic landscape of producing software. In my mind, this is the key ingredient that sets apart Web Services from the crowd.

In the sample spreadsheets where you were using Web Services, the Web Services portion wasn't really happening inside your computer. You were just seamlessly connecting to a Web service. Care to bring some of this capability a little closer? What follows is an example of how you can tap directly into a UDDI Registration Service Node from your spreadsheet.

Web Services — a simplified explanation

It should come as no surprise to you that Web Services uses XML as its alphabet. It has three principal components:

- ◆ SOAP: Simple Object Access Protocol
- ◆ WSDL: Web Services Description Language
- ◆ UDDI: Universal Description Discovery & Integration

Let me outline a scenario of what typically happens with Web Services:

You may have a business that buys parts for use in your manufacturing and assembly operations. Automating this process would greatly improve your company's competitiveness.

You decide to Web-enable the exchange of purchasing information and product model data. Your operation is small and specialized. You need to place emphasis on purchasing automation and secondarily on the exchange of product model data.

You could spend a lot of money for a license to use a software package that implements a full STEP system (STEP, which stands for Standard for the Exchange of Product Model Data, is an ISO standard [ISO-10303] and is very comprehensive). Instead, you decide to go with preparing a streamlined version of the standard using your own home-grown application as a starting point, and make it available using Web Services.

If your internal application is written in Java, you could make your application accessible online. You could use a SOAP engine such as Axis, which is freely downloadable. Axis will allow you to receive and send SOAP messages. The SOAP messages themselves are composed of XML structured a certain way. To deploy your Java code, you need only to place your source file into a specified directory of your Axis server and rename the 'java' file to a 'jws' file. Axis will take care of the rest. If your Axis server is visible on the public Internet, you now have your Web Services available to the world.

Now anyone running a SOAP client who knows what kind of a SOAP request to make and where to send it to can use your Web service. I suppose you could e-mail instructions on how to make use of this service that's now online. Doing so would reach only the people you know. There may be plenty of others who you can't reach this way. Okay, you could post a notice of the information on the home page of your Web site for all to read. Doing so would be discriminatory. Although people could read the information and take further actions, machines could not. The whole idea of making Web Services available is to automate the seamless connection from machine to machine without involving people.

So, what do you do: publish a how-to manual online for other computers to read? Yes, that's precisely what you do. You provide a special type of XML file called a WSDL file. It tersely but formally describes what Web Services are provided, the data types used, how to converse with the Web Service, and where on the Internet or network it can be found. Though you could manually prepare this WSDL file, there is really no need to do so. There are software tools that will look at your source code, ask you a few questions, and generate the file for you.

So now you have this terrific Web service available to every Web Services client on the Internet. Your Web Services also happens to be the world's best-kept secret. It would be nice if there were some kind of an Internet phone book for computers to use to look up and find out about what Web Services you offer, who you are, and how and where to connect to your Web Services. You're in luck. There is such a facility. It is called a UDDI registry and provides three kinds of "Internet phonebooks":

◆ White pages: Includes general information about specific companies such as company name and contact info

◆ Yellow pages: Includes general classification data such as geographic location of the company or the NAICS code describing the kind of business activity the company is engaged in

◆ Green pages: Includes technical information about the Web service and a pointer of where to go to get the specifics on your Web Services.

It should come as no surprise that you can automate the registration of your Web Services whenever you create new services or update existing ones.

Accessing the UDDI Registry from your Spreadsheet

This section has several points to convey:

- From your spreadsheet, you can tap directly into and interact with the facilities used in Web Services using software running only from your computer.

- You can do that without having to use the latest version of Excel (2003).

- You can put to use a wide variety of technologies that allow you to add functionality to Excel. One of these is Java.

- There is a tool provided here that you can extend on your own to make further use of Web Services.

Figure 12-28 shows you what the spreadsheet looks like.

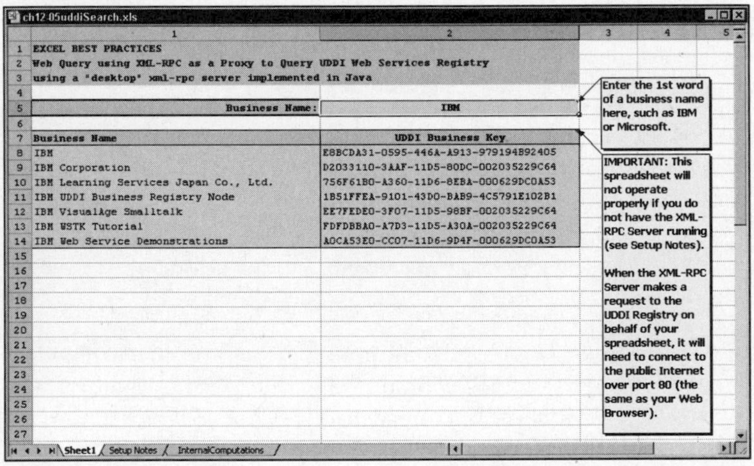

Figure 12-28: Spreadsheet that connects to a UDDI Registry via XML SOAP messaging

To use the registry, just complete the procedures outlined in setting up an XML-RPC Server that's described a little later in the chapter. After the setup is completed and you have your proxy server running, open the file ch12-05UddiSearch.xls on the CD-ROM (see Figure 12-28) and then type in the business name and press Enter. The information is looked up and placed in the blue region below. That's all there is to it.

Every business that is listed in the UDDI Registry has a unique UDDI business key. If a Web Services client is looking up where to find a service for a particular business, it will use this unique business key. Your application spreadsheet application is tapping into the Application Programming Interface (API) to make a request for the business key. If you feel so inclined, you can review the UDDI4J API and documentation and adjust some of the Java code to get other kinds of information. Hyperlinks for all the software used are available in the Setup Notes worksheet of the file ch12-05UddiSearch.xls on the CD-ROM. See the next section of this chapter for more detailed information.

SETUP INFORMATION

This spreadsheet does not require Excel 2003. Earlier versions of Excel will work fine. They just need the ability to issue Web queries via a POST mechanism.

To get this to work, you need to be able to run some Java programs on your machine. Figure 12-29 shows you a schematic of how it works.

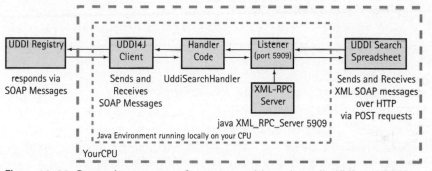

Figure 12-29: Personal proxy server for your spreadsheet that talks XML and SOAP

Basically, you are going to set up a "personal proxy server" on your computer. This personal proxy server speaks only XML and performs remote procedure calls (hence the name XML-RPC Server). Your spreadsheet will issue requests to the XML-RPC Server every time you type in a new business name to search.

When the request is received, the XML-RPC Server calls into action a registered handler. This handler code knows what to do with the request. To complete the request, it can enlist the help of other Java code. In particular, it makes use of a well-established utility called UDDI4J that can send and receive SOAP messages.

All the Java code used here is free. Your Setup Notes worksheet has hyperlinks to the download sites and up-to-date information. The JAR files and their licenses for distribution are located on the CD-ROM with this book. These files have been set up to work in the Java 1.4 environment.

SETTING UP THE XML-RPC SERVER

Follow these steps to set up your XML-RPC server:

1. Make sure that you have a Java SDK environment set up (you should use SDK 1.4 or later). You can do this from the command prompt (run the command.exe program that is a part of Windows). To determine the version you have, type **java -version** at the command prompt:

```
C:\>java -version
java version "1.4.1_01"
Java(TM) 2 Runtime Environment, Standard Edition (build
1.4.1_01-b01)
Java HotSpot(TM) Client VM (build 1.4.1_01-b01, mixed mode)
```

If your machine is not running Java, go to the Sun site to download the appropriate machine environment:

```
http://java.sun.com/j2se/
```

Although you can download the JRE (Java Runtime Environment), I strongly suggest that you download the full SDK. You may need to make some source-level changes and recompile the code.

Note: you're the CD-ROM with this book contains a Java 1.4.2 installation file ("j2sdk-1_4_2_01-windows-i586.exe") for the Windows platform. Although you can use this to install a Java environment, the download site may contain a more up-to-date version of the installation software.

2. Place the following JAR and DLL files into a common directory of your choosing:

```
activation.jar
mail.jar
org_w3c_dom.jar
soap.jar
COMProvider.dll
uddi4j.jar
xercesImpl.jar
xercesSamples.jar
xml-apis.jar
xmlParserAPIs.jar
xmlrpc-1.2-b1.jar
```

If you want to be running the software with the latest version files, be sure to download them (the Setup Notes worksheet of your spreadsheet file 12-05UddiSearch.xsl has hyperlinks to these files).

Though supplied on the CD-ROM for this book, you should be aware that one of the Java packages (org.w3c.dom) can be obtained online through a CVS Server but is not generally available via FTP or through a Web server.

If you wish to download updates, you will need CVS client software to download versions of this package. You can pick up the latest release from http://www.cvshome.org.

3. Place the following source and compiled files on the CD-ROM into the common directory:

```
UddiSearchHandler.java
UddiSearchHandlerStringArray.java
XML_RPC_Server.java
UddiSearchHandler.class
UddiSearchHandlerStringArray.class
XML_RPC_Server.class
```

4. Start the XML-RPC server.

The takeaway.txt file on the CD-ROM contains the line of code that you need for this. You can copy and paste this code into your command line (right-click at the command prompt to paste the content):

```
C:\testdrive>java -cp
.;activation.jar;mail.jar;org_w3c_dom.jar;soap.jar;uddi4j.jar
;xercesImpl.jar;xercesSamples.jar;xml-
apis.jar;xmlParserAPIs.jar;xmlrpc-1.2-b1.jar XML_RPC_Server
5909
```

When the server is properly started, you will see:

```
XML-RPC Server running on port 5909 is ready...
```

You are now ready to try out your spreadsheet. If you decide to change your port number to something other than 5909 and you do not make the appropriate adjustment in the spreadsheet macro, you will see an error like the one shown in Figure 12-30.

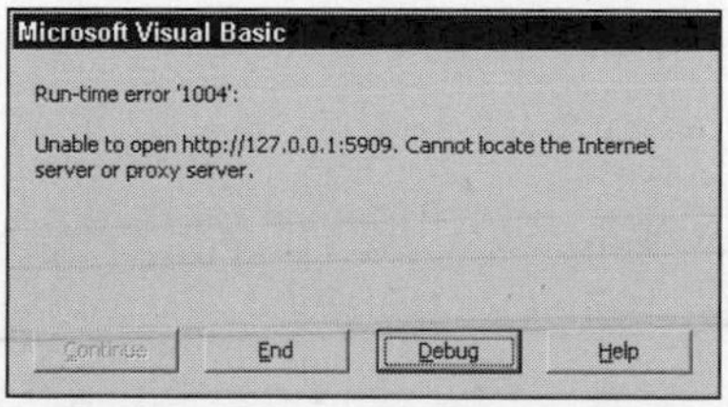

Figure 12-30: An error you might get when your ports are not properly matched

Debug will bring you into the mode in which you can make changes to the macro. After you make the change to the port number, close the Excel debugger window and retry.

FINE-TUNING YOUR SOFTWARE

As you experiment with this software, you will want to add handler code of your own so that the XML-RPC Server will run additional Java code you tell it to handle. Basically, you'll have an RPC `WebServer` object (I've named it `rpcws`). You'll tell `rpcws` to add an instance of a Java class that you want it to handle. Using the `addHandler` method, you will supply a descriptive name and new instance of a class, as in the following code snippet:

```
//Register your Handler Code:
rpcws.addHandler("aLabel", new JavaClassOfYourChoosing());
```

With the handler registered, you can run a method defined in `JavaClassOfYourChoosing` by making a call in your Excel macro similar to that shown in Listing 12-4.

Listing 12-4: Pseudo Code for Running yourMethod (namedRange) on an Instance of JavaClassOfYourChoosing

```
Sub URL_Post_Query()
    With Worksheets("Sheet1").QueryTables.Add( _
    Connection:= _"URL;http://127.0.0.1:5909", _
    Destination:=Worksheets("Sheet1").Range("ExternalData_1"))
    .PostText = "<?xml version=""1.0"" encoding=""ISO-8859-1""?> _
        <methodCall><methodName>aLabel.yourMethod</methodName> _
        <params><param><value><string>" + _
        Worksheets("Sheet1").Range("namedRange").Value + _
        "</string></value></param></params></methodCall>"
    End With
End Sub
```

It is worth your time to go to the actual `URL_Post_Query` macro to read through the code. There are some commented alternatives to the code listed.

Two noteworthy and useful features about the way the Excel Web Query is handled are the following:

◆ It shows you how to make a request to a server using an HTTP POST method. Generally, most published examples of Excel Web Queries examples describe how to issue requests using only the HTTP GET method.

◆ Instead of the usual `?param1=...&param2=...` generated from an HTML form, you have a pure XML message without parameters of any kind being sent to the XML-RPC Server.

While you are looking at the macros, take a moment to see how event manage-ment is handled. Look at the Worksheet_Change macro for Sheet1.

```
Private Sub Worksheet_Change(ByVal Target As Excel.Range)
    Dim VRange As Range
    Set VRange = Range("Business")
    For Each cell In Target
        If Union(cell, VRange).Address = VRange.Address Then
            Application.Run "URL_Post_Query"
            Range("Business").Select
        End If
    Next cell
End Sub
```

Two things you should observe:

◆ It senses when the named range "Business" is changed, and calls a sequence of actions.

◆ It shows you how a macro can run another macro.

RECOMPILING

If you adjust the .java source files, you will need to recompile using the following:

```
javac -classpath
.;activation.jar;mail.jar;org_w3c_dom.jar;soap.jar;uddi4j.jar
;xercesImpl.jar;xercesSamples.jar;xml-
apis.jar;xmlParserAPIs.jar;xmlrpc-1.2-b1.jar *.java
```

Note: Some of the methods are deprecated, so you will get a compiler warning. You can use the -deprecation flag to get the details. Be sure to place this in front of -classpath, not after.

```
javac -deprecation -classpath
.;activation.jar;mail.jar;org_w3c_dom.jar;soap.jar;uddi4j.jar
;xercesImpl.jar;xercesSamples.jar;xml-
apis.jar;xmlParserAPIs.jar;xmlrpc-1.2-b1.jar *.java
```

Closing Thoughts

If you think that Excel 2003 is just another one of those office productivity prod-ucts of the "shrink-wrapped generation," think again. We are quickly making the transition to a world in which XML will become ubiquitous for every kind of busi-ness communication. The tight coupling of XML to Excel 2003 firmly places Excel at center stage as businesses evolve their thinking of how to use information.

I strongly encourage you to view XML as an enabling technology. It is the ingredient that transforms Spreadsheet Portals from a concept on paper to one that works in practice. It is also the enabling technology for Web Services. The interesting thing about Web Services is that it's built from readily available off-the-shelf components. The phenomenal thing about Web Services is the dramatic shift in the economic landscape of product development costs and the significantly lower costs of putting information technology to good use.

You may have noticed that I walked you through how to use XML and make it work in a Web-centric environment. It was necessary to plumb into the depths of Excel macros. But instead of becoming mired in the macros, you discovered specific techniques for creating Spreadsheet Portals.

So, what's the import of this chapter? Several things:

♦ You saw a whole new way of looking at how spreadsheets can be used to process information in a network-based world in Internet time.

♦ You were introduced to a consistent architecture for Spreadsheet Portals, premised on the Layered Pattern framework first introduced in Chapter 2.

♦ You were given several good reference implementations of Spreadsheet Portals and provided with implementation details to help you build your own.

♦ You were given practical methodologies for working with XML in a Web-centric world.

♦ Mostly, the boundaries of what constitutes (spreadsheet) applications and the practices involved in working with them have been dramatically redefined.

The next chapter further solidifies these redefined boundaries by introducing Assistive Portals.

Chapter 13

Assistive Technologies and Assistive Portals

IN THIS CHAPTER

- ◆ Shattering preconceptions about economics of making electronic information accessible

- ◆ Understanding challenges facing individuals with disabilities

- ◆ Leveling the playing field for individuals with disabilities

- ◆ Setting up and getting acclimated with a screen reader

- ◆ Understanding JAWS concepts: a training-wheel approach

- ◆ Understanding how to build an accessible spreadsheet

- ◆ Teaching a screen reader to intelligently speak spreadsheet structures

- ◆ Making graphical components accessible

- ◆ Creating an accessible UserForm in a spreadsheet

- ◆ Working with UserForms

- ◆ Employing an important design strategy: the Abstraction Layer approach

- ◆ Working with compound interfaces

- ◆ Using the Assistive Portal tool to make a complex spreadsheet accessible

- ◆ Using an Assistive Portal for an industrial-strength spreadsheet application

RECENTLY, I ATTENDED A conference on assistive technologies. The speaker in one of the presentations started discussing the detailed requirements and standards of various governmental regulations relating to disabilities. The speaker went on and on, citing one regulation subsection after another. I kept thinking to myself, "Why am I here?"

Actually, I knew quite well why I was there. The conference and this speaker's presentation did cover important topics. It did help to crystallize some thoughts I had been formulating.

Not long afterward, I was invited by a colleague to a smaller gathering, at which various assistive technologies were being presented and discussed. I particularly recall an older gentleman whose vision was, at best, very limited. He was accompanied by his wife and a relative or friend of the family. They had him trying out some screen magnifier software, going through the ins and outs of its various settings. He was just beginning to grasp the sheer dimensions of the world suddenly about to open up. So here I was, a total stranger to these people sitting halfway across the room. I never shared a conversation with them prior to, during that day, or even afterwards. That relatively understated but important moment was to me what the significance of Assistive Technology is all about.

One of my goals for this chapter is to shatter a preconception about Assistive Technology and the promise it holds in the business world. Clearly, as the above story indicates, overcoming disabilities and making the information world accessible is important. No one denies that. With recent amendments to Section 508 of the Rehabilitation Act, the Federal government is stepping up to the plate and taking a responsible position to make information in electronic form accessible to all communities of individuals despite challenges and obstacles faced by individuals with disabilities. Many state governments and the vendors serving these communities are rallying in good faith to uphold these standards, even if not bound by the covenants the federal government has set for itself.

So, what preconception needs to be shattered?

Myth: It is not cost effective to produce and distribute the primary document for business, quantitative, and financial analysis (that is, spreadsheets) in a form that is truly accessible.

Intended audience and basic goals

I've directed this chapter specifically at corporations, governmental agencies, and organizations that are actively preparing or thinking about preparing accessible spreadsheets and documents. More important, this chapter is specifically directed at organizations both large and small that have counted themselves off the list of organizations and have tentatively concluded that they can forego the preparation of accessible documents. I want to show you that the economics of making 508 compliant and truly accessible documents can be made cost effective (on a level not previously considered). Doing so requires the use of Assistive Portals, a special type of Spreadsheet Portal designed to make the contents of other spreadsheets accessible.

I want to give you to a hands-on implementation guide that accomplishes the following:

◆ Drives home the issues and challenges for both individuals with disabilities and for your organization (for both managers and implementers)

◆ Shows you how the economics of preparing accessible documents is altered with Assistive Portals

- Provides a hands-on guide to starting to work with screen reader software

- Shows you the basic do's and don'ts for preparing accessible documents for use with screen readers, and provides working samples of these types of documents

- Shows you how to enhance the ability of a screen reader to speak the contents of a spreadsheet by customizing a settings file for individual spreadsheets or a batch of spreadsheets

- Shows you ways to use graphical interfaces as part of an accessible spreadsheet

- Explains how accessible graphical components fit with Assistive Portals

- Walks you through adding an Assistive Portal to a complex, legacy-based spreadsheet that was not designed to be accessible

Chapter organization

This chapter begins with some background information about various kinds of disabilities and relevant legislation. It goes on to discuss the economics of making widely distributed documents accessible. In particular, I introduce a new concept called an "Assistive Portal" (AP). I identify the basic strategy behind Assistive Portals and show how an AP alters the economics of producing and maintaining accessible spreadsheets. For the sake of demonstration, I have focused on a specific disability. The examples chosen illustrate the use of preparing Assistive Portals designed to work with screen readers.

The rest of this chapter walks you through the specific steps and issues you will face when setting up a screen reader. After you have a screen reader set up, you'll begin to work with the basics of organizing a spreadsheet to make its contents readily accessible. To give the spreadsheet a little more *oomph,* I show you how to incorporate accessible graphical components.

This will give you the basics for preparing generally accessible spreadsheets for use with screen readers. These basics should serve you well even without incorporating Assistive Portals.

The next step is to understand what Assistive Portals are, how they are structured, and how to implement one. Stated concisely, an Assistive Portal is a simple spreadsheet portal page designed for a specific disability. An Assistive Portal provides access to spreadsheets that lack the navigation aids and accessibility friendly features (a.k.a. electronic curb cuts) and makes large, complex spreadsheets accessible without having to perform surgery on them.

Though one disability is discussed in detail, the overall steps outlined apply in general to preparing an Assistive Portal regardless of the type of disability. Also, nothing precludes you from broadening the concept of an Assistive Portal beyond the use of spreadsheets.

Background

Although many readers of this book may be familiar with assistive technologies and the nature of disability issues, others may not. What follows is a brief outline of these topics.

Disabilities

There's a wide range of disabilities; in fact, far too many to comprehensively address here. I will try, however, to give you representative examples so that you can begin to develop an orientation.

Before you dive into the background, I want you to have a clear understanding of what the real challenges are. Individuals with disabilities face four challenges:

1. They have to contend with their own disabilities. A person with motor skills challenges, aside from dexterity issues and restricted range of movement, may become quickly fatigued.

2. The assistive software or adaptive devices may not be as quick, interactive, or easy to use as the regular application software.

3. The assistive software may not recover 100 percent of the capabilities of the operating system features and applications software. Unless you are aware of the specific gaps, you may be throwing a curve ball at some users.

4. Sometimes spreadsheet design (and, for that matter, any document design) can mar the effectiveness of an otherwise accessible document. Specifically, data in a spreadsheet can be "orphaned." Think about a user who is visually impaired. How is such a user going to find relevant data located at the cell coordinates of AZ1024? Unless the user was specifically told that there is data in this location, or the data is adjacent to other data being used by the user, the chances are pretty slim that the user will easily find the data in the normal course of his or her work.

The challenges in numbers 3 and 4 are what you need to be concerned with and what I address in this chapter.

MOBILITY IMPAIRMENT

The obstacles presented by disabilities can range from the relatively mild, such as carpal tunnel syndrome, to extremely severe, when the only means to interact with a computer is for the user to blink his or her eyes in response to "scanning" software that highlights a portion of the screen or indicates a pending action.

All sorts of adaptive technologies have been designed to compensate for mobility issues. These range from oversized keyboards to single-handed keyboards, body keyboards, external track pads, track balls, joysticks with lock and unlock capabilities, and the head mouse.

Devices are just devices. By themselves, they cannot provide a complete solution. Take, for example, a head mouse. It is a pointing device mounted on a person's head, which can move a mouse with relative ease and precision. But what about clicking a button or clicking and dragging a group of items? That capacity depends upon the specific disability. A person may be able to reliably tap a button on some keypad with a finger. Then again, a person might not have any such options and may have to rely on some timing delay mechanism. Only when the pointing device is hovering for a long enough time around a specific location, such as a button, is the action interpreted as a click. This managing of mouse click events handled through one software package would need to be integrated with the head mouse or other adaptive devices.

There are also keyboard filters that can compensate for things such as hand tremors or can remap the arrangements of keys on a keyboard.

Not everything has to be super specialized. Often, conventional software packages can be used as part of an accessibility solution. Take, for instance, speech recognition software. It can be used effectively if a person has a clear and consistently uniform voice. This might be a viable option for a person who does not have effective use of his or her hands to use a standard keyboard, but has clear speech.

In the more extreme cases, a person may be restricted to communicating through a binary or on/off device. An example of this is a Sip and Puff device. Hardware of this kind must be used with scanning software that serves as the liaison between the person with the device and what's happening inside the computer.

As you can see, the available devices and technologies are widely diverse. For many people, however, achieving a true accessibility solution may entail mixing technologies that were not specifically designed to work together. To put this in perspective, accessibility solutions almost always involve:

◆ A case-by-case custom adaptation for each person's specific disability and needs. Disabilities are almost never a one-size-fits-all situation.

◆ The solution couples software with hardware.

◆ The solution generally requires "training" the software and/or hardware to function effectively.

Speech recognition software serves as a case in point. Those of you who have dabbled or regularly use such software for dictation will appreciate what it takes to "train" the software. How many pages of text did you have to read to train your speech recognition software to respond accurately to your voice? It's one thing to have to correct misspelled words in a paragraph of text you've dictated. It's entirely another to deal with the consequences of having told an application to save a file before closing it and it thinks you answered No instead of Yes.

DEAFNESS AND HEARING IMPAIRMENT
Traditional desktop applications such as Word and Excel don't generally pose problems for the deaf community. The extent of the adjustment may entail providing visual cues when the computer makes a beep.

So, for the most part, you may not have much to do to make spreadsheets accessible for the deaf community. Keep in mind that the information age is becoming increasingly multimedia intense. The day is not too far off when a spreadsheet may be incorporated into a kiosk that kicks multimedia clips into action. The multimedia components may need to include additional info for deaf or hearing-impaired individuals. This extra information may include some form of signing, such as American Sign Language (ASL), or captioning. You may want to explore on your own some of the advances made in this area.

Regarding captioning technology, check out the work of:

◆ WGBH

◆ Apple Computer's QuickTime Pro (for both Windows and Mac)

◆ Macromedia's Flash

Concerning ASL, check out the work of the NYC Department of Education's *StreetSigns: A City Kid's Guide to American Sign Language.*

See the "Useful links" sidebar for the URLs of numerous sources providing further information.

VISION IMPAIRMENT

Vision impairment manifests itself in three forms: color blindness, low vision, and blindness.

People who are color blind often don't even know that they are color blind until they are well into their adult years. In terms of spreadsheets, color blindness does not pose significant issues except for in the realm of Excel charting. Certain color combinations may be hard to distinguish. For example, red and green combinations pose a problem for people who have deuteranopia.

You can compensate for color blindness in two ways:

◆ Label the items in your Excel Charts.

◆ Adjust the visual appearance of the chart Series Data for a specific pattern, border, gradient fill, or texture.

As a quick check to verify that custom-prepared patterns are unambiguous, print your spreadsheet on a black-and-white printer.

Low vision refers to a condition in which a person who, even with glasses, cannot see standard print. Screen magnifier software can compensate for this. The current Windows and Macintosh operating system software provide basic capabilities of magnifying the screen as well as putting the screen into a high-contrast mode. In Windows you will find the options for screen magnification in the Accessibility Options submenu of the Control Panel. On the Macintosh platform, you will find these options in Universal Access settings of the System Preferences. These system software options allow the user with low vision to control various settings, such as foreground and background color, icon size, font size, etc. to meet individual visual needs.

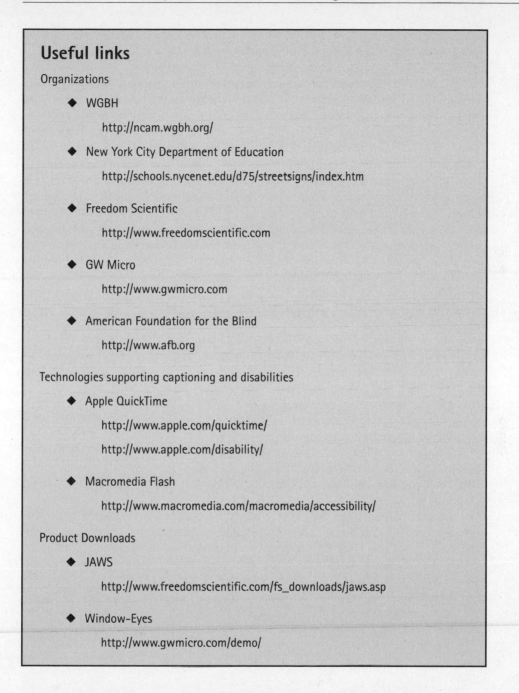

Useful links

Organizations

◆ WGBH

  http://ncam.wgbh.org/

◆ New York City Department of Education

  http://schools.nycenet.edu/d75/streetsigns/index.htm

◆ Freedom Scientific

  http://www.freedomscientific.com

◆ GW Micro

  http://www.gwmicro.com

◆ American Foundation for the Blind

  http://www.afb.org

Technologies supporting captioning and disabilities

◆ Apple QuickTime

  http://www.apple.com/quicktime/

  http://www.apple.com/disability/

◆ Macromedia Flash

  http://www.macromedia.com/macromedia/accessibility/

Product Downloads

◆ JAWS

  http://www.freedomscientific.com/fs_downloads/jaws.asp

◆ Window-Eyes

  http://www.gwmicro.com/demo/

Some commercial software packages also provide these capabilities, and much more. Screen magnification software can include multiple custom magnification settings combined with screen reading (and spelling) of selected text.

People who are blind or who have low vision use screen reader software to translate text and graphic symbols into spoken words. This area of technology is particularly challenging for such individuals.

People with unimpaired or adequately corrected vision can look at a screen and have little trouble making sense of it. Take, for instance, a table of numbers. It is easy to look along the column headers as well as the row descriptions and find the intersection for the number buried in the table. For a sighted person, reading a table means locating a simple triangulation of three spreadsheet cells.

When a screen reader reads the contents of a spreadsheet aloud, how does it know that it has reached a table region? Assuming that a spoken cell is part of a table, will the screen reader know where to find the appropriate row and column headers? What if you have stacked headers, much as those in a PivotTable? Even if you can tell the screen reader where to find the headers, won't it become tedious and time consuming for it to repeat the column header information as it moves up and down the same column?

Fortunately, problems like these have been elegantly solved.

Legislation you should know about

Although there are many pieces of legislation relating to disabilities, you should at least be aware of Section 508 of the Rehabilitation Act.

SECTION 508

Section 508 refers to a statutory section in the Rehabilitation Act of 1973 (which can be found at 29 U.S.C. 794d). There were some amendments to the 73 Act during 1998, which updated and significantly enhanced section 508.

Federal executive agencies such as the Department of Agriculture, Department of Commerce, Department of Education, and NASA, must all provide access to and make available the use of electronic and information technology to individuals with disabilities.

Whenever such agencies distribute electronic information, they must make the contents of the electronic information accessible. Accessible is taken to mean "comparable" to what would be regularly available to individuals without disabilities. This comparable access is not required if it imposes an "undue burden" on the agency. Though an agency can claim an undue burden exception, it's still on the hook to provide the information and data to individuals with disabilities by an alternative means of access. As an example, if a document is not accessible in its electronic form, a hard copy, perhaps in Braille, might be provided.

Although state agencies are not obliged to follow the federal statutes, the growing trend is to adopt Section 508 as a guideline or adopt some similar form of legislation.

The Economics of Making Spreadsheets Accessible

There's a big problem here. The problem applies both to governmental agencies striving for 508 compliance and businesses trying to take a responsible position with regard to disabilities. Preparing accessible documents is a costly affair. Add to this the pressure of preparing business documents under tight deadlines. Complicate it further by trying to accommodate the needs of multiple communities, each with its own specific kind of disability. How can you possibly satisfy all these constraints and manage to keep operating costs manageable? For many organizations, this is a losing proposition.

To better appreciate the issues and help develop a workable approach, try think-ing about spreadsheets in a little more detail. Imagine that you are preparing a pen-sion fund calculator in the form of a graphical spreadsheet. This spreadsheet will be distributed to the employees of your company. Think of your company as being reasonably large — more than, say, 25,000 employees. Employees can input their individual financial information and select the percentages of their portfolio that would be allocated to equities, real estate, fixed income, and money market funds. The spreadsheet is slightly complex. It draws upon each individual's specific data, as well as retrieves historical performance of the various funds.

This spreadsheet that you are preparing will have some pretty charts. It will also have considerable interactive capability via some GUI widgets such as List Boxes or spinner control buttons. Individuals with a disability such as blindness or signifi-cant mobility impairments may not be able to access the full graphical capabilities of the spreadsheet.

The accessibility needs within each of these broad groups of disabilities can be varied; hence, they will not be the same across the board. To make your spreadsheet accessible, you have two immediate options available to you:

- Prepare a spreadsheet that is completely accessibility-friendly.

- Prepare equivalent versions of the same spreadsheet that addresses, and is optimized for, each community of individuals.

Which of the two makes more sense? The first option, albeit highly laudable, shoots for the lowest common denominator. It defeats the benefits of the tech-nology you want to put to use in the first place. What if there is no common denominator? It may turn out that two different kinds of disabilities have conflict-ing accessibility implementations. So, making your semi-complex spreadsheet accessibility-friendly for all may not be a viable option. You risk watering it down to the point of drowning it.

What about the next option? You certainly could prepare a special version of the same spreadsheet for each community of individuals. This will solve the issue of potential conflicts previously identified. It does so, however, at the cost of adequate efficiency. It quickly becomes unwieldy to manage. Think about what would be involved in managing, say, five versions of the same spreadsheet.

Both these approaches have their merits but suffer from significant drawbacks. So, how do you make your spreadsheet accessible without detracting from its original form? Basically, you don't. The key is to let the spreadsheet be what it needs to be, largely unfettered by multiple accessibility requirements. The accessibility issues are then addressed through the use of individualized Assistive Portals that know how to look at and drive the original spreadsheets.

The Assistive Portal approach

An Assistive Portal is just like the Spreadsheet Portals introduced in the previous chapter. Instead of connecting to a remote back-end server, it connects to whatever spreadsheet you want to make accessible. For the regular spreadsheet user, it's business as usual. However, those with disabilities are provided an additional portal spreadsheet that accesses and drives the primary spreadsheet. This allows an individual with disabilities to access and use the primary spreadsheet even though the primary spreadsheet may not have been designned to be accessible.

This approach has several advantages:

◆ Users who prepare the primary spreadsheets need only follow simple guidelines to make the spreadsheet accessible.

◆ Assembling an Assistive Portal that taps into the original spreadsheet and makes its features accessible to the specific disability is a relatively straightforward process.

◆ A separate portal page can be prepared for each kind of disability.

◆ The portal page allows users with disabilities the same access to the whole spreadsheet contents as that afforded to regular users.

◆ After the Assistive Portal is prepared, it can be readily adapted to access other similar spreadsheets. This alters the economics of making spreadsheets accessible into one of regular reuse of templates.

The best way to understand this approach is to walk through a hands-on example. As noted previously, many kinds of disabilities and special purpose software applications and adaptive technologies are available, but the examples developed in this chapter focuses on screen readers. The chapter examples have been prepared using JAWS (a product of Freedom Scientific). You should also investigate Window-Eyes (a product of GW Micro). Both these products are popular in the visually impaired community. If possible, you should become familiar with both of these packages. Additional information regarding screen readers, screen magnifiers, and related accessibility technologies can be found at the American Foundation for the Blind Web site (www.afb.org).

Setting Up a Screen Reader

To fully benefit from the examples in this chapter, you will need to set up a screen reader.

Please note that the coverage presented here is directed at sighted individuals who anticipate preparing accessible spreadsheets for people with blindness. Although products such as JAWS and Window-Eyes have extensive support for Braille devices, discussion of Braille devices and their support is beyond the scope of this chapter.

Also note that individuals with partial vision may simultaneously make use of both a screen magnifier and a screen reader. The discussion in this chapter makes the assumption that only screen readers are being used.

Though the steps of creating accessible spreadsheets for the visually impaired can be done without a screen reader, I strongly recommend that you obtain a screen reader to become familiar with and better understand its nuances. Also, you will need to test what you're developing on a level comparable to what a user with blindness would experience.

Before sending out your document, you would do well to have a user with blindness test the spreadsheet for accessibility.

Please download one of the major screen reader packages of JAWS and/or Window-Eyes. Links to Web sites with evaluation versions of both these packages can be found in the "Useful links" sidebar. The evaluation software for both products are full featured.

Though the basic presentation here is applicable to screen readers in general, the examples throughout the remainder of the chapter are specific to JAWS.

The version of JAWS presented here is 4.51. This book went to press before version 5.0 was available.

Getting acclimated to a screen reader

Working with screen readers takes a little bit of getting used to. Keep the following in mind:

◆ Screen readers are keyboard intensive. Remember, the functionality of a mouse must be available through a keyboard.

◆ During most of the time when working with JAWS, the Num Lock key on your keyboard's numeric keypad is switched off. If you're in the habit of using the keys on the numeric keypad when you work with spreadsheets, be prepared to either constantly turn the Num Lock on and off or get used to using the number keys immediately above the QWERTY keys. The latter is likely to be easier.

◆ Screen readers such as JAWS provide full support for two keyboard layouts: desktop and laptop. Although the mappings for both keyboard layouts are similar, there are some differences in the keystroke sequences. All the examples presented in this chapter assume a desktop layout.

◆ Screen readers intercept every keystroke you make. It should not be surprising that your CPU will have some performance degradation. Although this should not cause problems for your computer, I recommend against installing a screen reader on a production-based machine, such as a Web server or database server that others connect to.

◆ There are two ways of operating a screen reader such as JAWS. One of these is as a service and the other is as a standalone application. The choice you make is dependent entirely upon your specific set of circumstances. If you run JAWS as a standalone application, you may want to adjust the properties of the JAWS Windows shortcut icon so that you can launch JAWS using a designated keystroke sequence while in any Windows application (I've set mine to Ctrl+Alt+J).

When you're running JAWS as a standalone application, I recommend that you launch it before launching Excel 2003 or Word 2003.

◆ If you share your office with co-workers or work in an open area such as a cubicle, you may want to hook up headphones to your computer. The constant chattering from your computer can be a distraction to others. More important, as you are first getting used to working with a screen reader, your self-consciousness will impede your learning curve. It's better to work in privacy.

Before I get into the specifics of configuring and working with your screen reader, consider the following. The activity of preparing an Assistive Portal amounts largely to business as usual for spreadsheets regularly going out the door. The spreadsheet preparers for these conventional spreadsheets need only follow a few simple guidelines, elaborated on shortly. If the guidelines for the conventional spreadsheets have been followed, a separate Assistive Portal would be separately prepared. It would make sense to have one of the people in your office develop proficiency with a screen reader and be the designated person to construct the Assistive Portals.

The essential point here is that to prepare and regularly distribute spreadsheets in an accessible form, you don't have to get everyone in your office reworking their regular practices. *Providing accessible spreadsheets should involve only a limited number of individuals instead of your whole staff.*

Preliminary JAWS concepts: A training-wheel approach

I want you to start using JAWS with "training wheels." There's no overriding need to turn off the power switch of your computer monitor or throw away your mouse. By the same token, if you don't start revving up the keyboard to explore the ins and outs of the screen reader facilities; you won't attain the proficiency you really need. For this reason, try to get used to doing things by keyboard, and when you get stuck, or are working on non-Excel applications, use the mouse.

Even in this training-wheel mode, you'll find that when you work with spreadsheets, you really won't have to use the physical mouse, but may instead opt for a "virtual mouse cursor," generally known as the "JAWS cursor." On your keyboard, you invoke this cursor by pressing the `NumPadMinus` key. (This is the key with the – symbol on the top-right corner of your numeric keypad. Make sure that the Num Lock key is in the "off" position.) Once you're in the JAWS cursor mode, the arrow keys will actually move the mouse that appears on your screen. As it moves, JAWS will speak the items it is passing over. This notion of speaking whatever the cursor happens to be in the vicinity of is integral to how a screen reader works.

Your cursor can be in one of two modes. One of these, as you are already aware, is the JAWS (or Virtual Mouse) Cursor mode. The other is the PC Cursor mode (invoked by pressing `NumPadPlus`, the + key on the numeric keypad). Actually, most of the time, you'll be in the PC Cursor mode.

 When you switch between JAWS Cursor and PC Cursor modes, the spoken voice changes in pitch and tone.

To better understand the difference between these two modes, consider the following. Open your word processor and start typing away. While you are typing, you are in PC Cursor mode. In fact, the cursor position is continually adjusting and moving to keep up with your typing. Now move your mouse anywhere. Notice that your screen is displaying two cursors, one for the mouse and one for the text insertion bar, which appears wherever you've just been typing on the keyboard (PC Cursor). When the mouse is actively being moved, you are in the JAWS Cursor mode. The moment you start typing again, the computer instantly switches back to PC Cursor mode. Notice that when you start moving the mouse again, it resumes from its last known position.

There are times when you need to have the PC Cursor and the mouse in the same location on your screen. You can either bring the mouse over to the PC Cursor using `Insert+NumPadMinus`, or bring the PC Cursor over to the current mouse location using `Insert+NumPadPlus`. This is known as routing the cursor.

Are you starting to feel overwhelmed with all the keyboard commands? Table 13-1 outlines some of the more common keystroke sequences for desktop systems. JAWS also gives you the means to look up all the different keystroke sequences. Don't worry about memorizing all the keystroke sequences.

Sometimes JAWS will launch into motor-mouth mode and relentlessly read just about everything on your screen. You can silence JAWS by simply holding down the Ctrl key. Pressing the Shift key will sometimes achieve the same effect.

As you start working with JAWS, you will notice that many of the keyboard commands begin with the Insert key. The Insert key for JAWS acts much like a Ctrl key for conventional computer programs. The online documentation for JAWS often makes reference to "JAWSKey." The default setting for JAWSKey is the Insert key. A JAWS user can assign a key other than Insert as the JAWSKey. This is important for individuals with motor skill challenges. For the purposes of this chapter and your initial use of JAWS, substitute Insert wherever you see the occurrence of JAWSKey in the product documentation.

TABLE 13-1 COMMON JAWS KEYSTROKE COMMANDS

Script Name	Keyboard Sequence
AdjustJAWSVerbosity	Insert+V
HotKeyHelp	Insert+H
JawsCursor	NumPadMinus
KeyboardHelp	Insert+1
LeftMouseButton	NumPadSlash

Script Name	Keyboard Sequence
MoveToWorksheet	Control+Shift+S
NextDocumentWindow	Control+Tab
PCCursor	NumPadPlus
ReadBoxInTabOrder	Insert+B
RightMouseButton	NumPadStar
RouteJawsCursorToPc	Insert+NumPadMinus
RoutePCCursorToJaws	InsertPadPlus
SayAll	Insert+DownArrow
sayColumnTitle	**Alt+Shift+C**
SayDefaultButton	Insert+E
SayLine	Insert+UpArrow
sayRowTitle	**Alt+Shift+R**
SayWindowTitle	Insert+T
ScreenSensitiveHelp	Insert+F1
ScriptFileName	Insert+Q
SelectCurrentItem	Control+Space
StartJawsTaskList	Insert+F10
WindowKeysHelp	Insert+W

Items in boldface are specific to Excel.

Several of these keyboard commands, such as KeyboardHelp, are toggle switches. The SayAll command may speak the content starting from the current cursor location to the end of the document, rather than from the very beginning of the document to the end. On some systems, the Shift keys on the left and right sides serve different functions. For instance, RightShift+Insert+DownArrow spells words; whereas LeftShift+Insert+DownArrow reads the selected text.

The naming used in Table 13-1 and throughout this chapter matches the actual names used in the JAWS settings files. You will find these files in the JAWS SETTINGS\ENU folder. There are two files you may want to view: default.jkm and excel.jkm. The default.jkm file contains the keystroke sequences that JAWS knows about by default when it is first launched. The excel.jkm file contains information on the specific keystroke sequences that JAWS recognizes when Excel is active.

390   Part III: Special Topics: Getting the Numbers Right

These .jkm files are plain-text files. They associate keyboard mappings with specific scripts that JAWS will run when a specific combination of keys is pressed. Though you can open these up with Notepad, I strongly recommend that you first make copies of these files, place them into another directory such as c:\temp, and open the copied files there.

In case you're wondering, ENU stands for English, United States. However, JAWS comes with multilingual support.

Basic JAWS configuration

Although you can use the factory default settings that are supplied with JAWS, you may want to adjust some of them. In the course of doing so, you will learn plenty about the features and capabilities of JAWS.

When launching an application while JAWS is running, you can navigate through the Windows Start menu solely through the keyboard. Press the Window Start key, which is positioned between the Ctrl and Alt keys. Then, pressing the P key should bring you straight into the list of Windows programs that reside on your computer. At this point you can move through the list one at a time using the Down Arrow key. However, if you press the first letter of the program or program group you want to navigate to, your cursor will jump to the next occurrence of an item in the list that matches the letter. If Microsoft Excel appears inside the group Microsoft Office, for example, you press the letter M.

As JAWS jumps to the next position, it speaks the item. If there are multiple items starting with the same letter, JAWS will speak each one as it gets to it. You don't have to wait for JAWS to complete speaking the word before moving on to the next item using an arrow key or pressing a letter. When you get to the Microsoft Office menu group, JAWS will speak "Microsoft Office *submenu*." The added term "submenu informs you that this is a menu group and you should press the Enter key to choose it. Cycle through the items in the submenu and press Enter to launch the specific application.

GET YOUR WINDOWS START MENU IN ORDER

It will be easier for you to navigate through the Windows menu to your applications (using the keyboard) if the programs are listed in alphabetical order. Sometimes the programs listed in your menu are not in alphabetical order. Here's how you can fix this. (Note that the instructions listed here are for Windows 2000. If you are working with a different version of Windows, there may be a slightly different way of accomplishing the same task.).

Click Start→Settings→Taskbar & Start Menu. Click the Advanced tab of the settings (see Figure 13-1) and then click Re-sort.

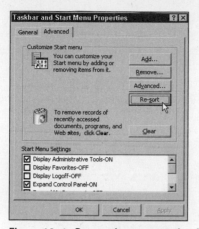

Figure 13-1: Re-sort items appearing in your Windows Start menu by clicking the Re-sort button.

VOICE SETTINGS

Bring JAWS to the forefront of your applications. You can either press Alt+Tab and cycle through the list with your arrow keys, or you can press Insert+F10 to be presented with a "Windows List Dialog" of active applications. This dialog window is generated by JAWS and is not a Windows facility.

When the JAWS program is active, you will be able to configure and set your JAWS application settings. Press Alt+O (you could use the mouse to navigate the application menus, but this way will help accustom you to using the keyboard) and navigate to the Voices submenu. There, select the Global Adjustment settings (see Figure 13-2).

Notice two settings: a Global Adjustment and an Individual Voice Adjustment. Right now, just stay with the Global Adjustment. After you select the Global Adjustment, you will see a Global Voice Settings window similar to the lower half of Figure 13-2. To cycle through the various items press the Tab key. JAWS will speak each of the items. When it gets to the slider, JAWS will provide additional instructions. For example, to move the slider, you can use the Left and Right Arrow keys. At this point you should adjust the rate of speech. The default factory setting for rate is 57. Personally, I like setting it at a somewhat faster rate (77). Experienced JAWS users often like to set this at a *much higher* rate.

The Eloquence Speech Synthesizer that comes supplied with JAWS is exceptionally clear and crisp when the speech rate is fast. This is also true of the speech synthesizers for the other major screen readers.

JAWS will speak what you are typing, as you are typing. To help discern what you are typing, the pitch of the spoken voice is bumped up slightly, as you type capitalized letters. The factory setting for this is 20. I can easily discern this when the pitch is set to 15. Pick whatever values work for you.

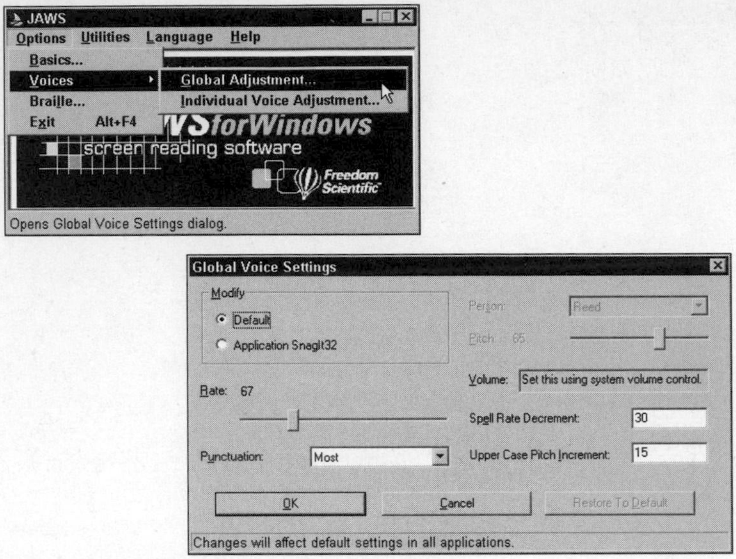

Figure 13-2: Adjusting the basic voice settings

JAWS supports individualized voices. You can select from a palette of eight pre-defined voices.

There are four contexts in which JAWS may be speaking to you. These are as follows:

- PC Cursor Voice
- JAWS Cursor Voice
- Keyboard Voice
- Tutor and Message Voice

Of these, the JAWS Cursor Voice is, by default, set to a different voice than the others. You can change the voice for each of the contexts; however, having too many different voices will become quickly disorienting.

As noted previously, JAWS has support for multiple languages. These synthesizer languages include:

- American English
- British English
- Castilian Spanish
- Latin American Spanish
- French

- ◆ French Canadian

- ◆ German

- ◆ Italian

- ◆ Brazilian Portuguese

- ◆ Finnish

You can set the language through the JAWS Language menu. Keep in mind that the synthesizer language you select for JAWS needs to match the text of words appearing on the screen and dialog boxes. Otherwise, you will have a difficult time discerning what is being spoken. Because language synthesizers for British English and American English are so similar, you can set the language synthesizer to either of these two when you have English text and easily understand what is being spoken. You may in fact prefer to have the speech synthesized in British English mode.

JAWS UTILITIES
Within the JAWS Utilities menu you should examine the Keyboard Manager (see Figure 13-3). As mentioned earlier, the keyboard settings are stored in a .jkm file. There are plenty more than just the default.jkm and excel.jkm files. This is important to know so that you can identify the specific sequences of keystrokes that JAWS recognizes.

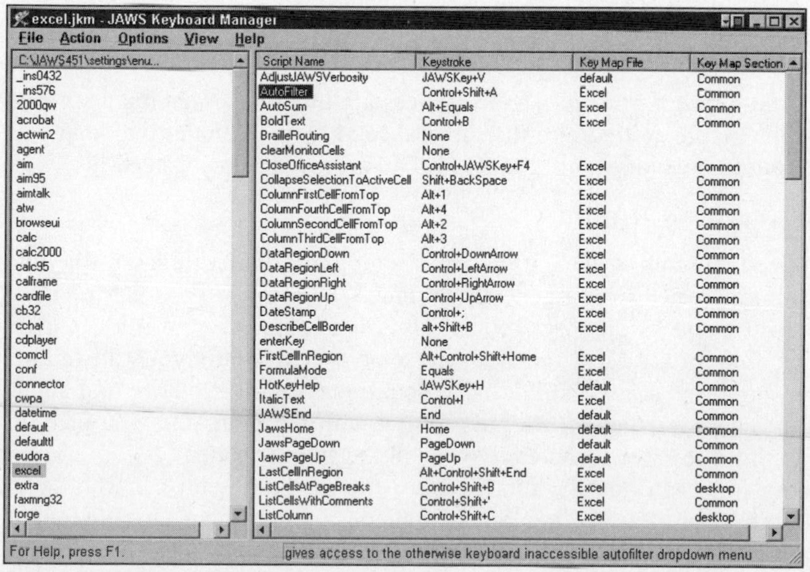

Figure 13–3: The Keyboard Manager allows you to define, for any application, new keystroke sequences and associate them with scripts that can be run by JAWS.

The Keyboard Manager associates specific keystrokes with individual script names. When the specific keystroke sequence is pressed, the appropriate script from a corresponding key map file is run by JAWS. The script may invoke JAWS to speak some phrase. Key map files contain the .jss suffix in the filename.

Before moving on to working with spreadsheets with screen readers, you need to be aware of some of the facilities in the Configuration Manager (found in the Utilities menu of JAWS). You don't need to make any changes here, but you should take a peek at some of the configuration settings related to user options, verbosity, and text processing.

Spreadsheets with Screen Readers

Users who are experienced with screen readers are likely to be familiar with the major PC programs such as Excel and Word and could navigate their way through a spreadsheet if they are given clear-cut information and a well-organized spreadsheet. *Your first and most important steps to make a spreadsheet accessible via a screen reader are to make navigating the spreadsheet easy.*

There are simple techniques for making navigation easy. Open the ch13-01AccessibleSpreadsheetTemplate01.xls. But first, get your screen reader software up and running. You won't get much benefit of using this spreadsheet if you don't. If you haven't downloaded and installed your screen reader software, now would be a good time to do so.

The design features of an accessible spreadsheet

Several important design principles and practices are integral to making a spreadsheet accessible. Before getting into the spreadsheet, here's an analogy to help you understand what you would want to build into an accessible spreadsheet.

THE BASIC FRAMEWORK
A well-organized museum is likely to have a Visitor's Information Center. On your first visit, you are greeted with a general welcome. You are told basic information about the museum and its purpose. You are also given some ground rules to keep you out of trouble. In the museum there are some specific tours you can follow. These will be found in various exhibit halls. Before proceeding, you are told about some of the museum highlights. After dispensing with the highlights you pick up the floor plan that shows you where to go for all the specific tours.

At this point you can go to a specific tour. Alternatively, you can choose to bypass pre-established tours and explore the galleries on your own. On subsequent visits to the museum, you may want to bypass the general welcome greeting and proceed straight to the museum highlights, main tours or some specific exhibit.

Basically, the experience of using an accessible spreadsheet should really be no different. In fact, this would be an excellent way to think about how you would communicate business information to a general audience.

THE STARTING POINT

When you open a spreadsheet in Excel, it normally opens up with the same work-sheet and active cell as when it was last saved. Though you can specifically position the active cell to a preferred starting point before saving, you will likely find that such a technique of pre-positioning the active cell is not very reliable.

A straightforward way to guarantee that the spreadsheet will open to a predeter-mined location is to use an "auto open" macro. Whenever the spreadsheet opens, the spreadsheet will automatically run whatever is in the auto open macro.

 The user can prevent the auto open macro from running by holding down the Shift key when opening the spreadsheet.

Although it is a good practice to start from the same location every time the spreadsheet is opened, a user may have good reasons to open from a different location.

If you want, you can have the best of both worlds. You can have the spreadsheet open to a specified location whenever an auto open macro is used. You can give the user the ability to revise where the spreadsheet opens without having to touch the auto open macro. The user can even turn off the starting position feature so that the spreadsheet will remember to open where it was last saved.

Here's how to do it: Rather than provide it with a hardwired location, you pro-gram the auto open macro to read configuration information from the spreadsheet to determine where to open when first launched. The ch13-01AccessibleSpreadsheet-Template01.xls spreadsheet makes use of this method. The macro code used is shown in Listing 13-1.

Listing 13-1: Macro Code for ThisWorkbook in the VBA Project

```
Private Sub Workbook_Open()
'    The names ConfigOpenOnSheet and ConfigOpenOnCell
'            need to be defined in your spreadsheet.
     StartingSheet = Range("ConfigOpenOnSheet").Value
     StartingCell = Range("ConfigOpenOnCell").Value
     On Error Resume Next
     Sheets(StartingSheet).Select
     On Error Resume Next
     Range(StartingCell).Select
End Sub
```

This auto open macro reads the names of cell locations from the Config work-sheet. You simply need to type in the physical cell coordinates or cell name in the Value column defined in the Config worksheet.

Those of you who are new to Excel macros and want to tinker with Excel's scripting capabilities will find some information on VBA (Visual Basic for Applications) in the previous chapter. Look at the supplemental listing in the takeway.txt file to see how exception handling is applied. For help with doing some serious work with VBA and macro facilities, I recommend *Excel 2003 Power Programming with VBA* by John Walkenbach, Wiley Publishing, Inc.

At the risk of stating the obvious, I should note that you can rename the template ch13-01AccessibleSpreadsheetTemplate01.xls to a filename of your choosing by opening the spreadsheet and choosing →File→Save As to save it to a different filename. When the new file is opened in Excel, the auto open feature will work the same way as it did for the original template.

OVERALL SPREADSHEET ORGANIZATION

Your accessible spreadsheet should provide some basic information on what is contained in the spreadsheet, how to navigate the workbook, some key highlights, and all the basic navigation points the user can follow.

You can place all this explanatory information on one worksheet. Give the worksheet a descriptive name such as "InformationCenter". Don't worry about the fact that there is no space separating "Information" from "Center." JAWS will recognize and speak the words with no difficulty.

In addition to the InformationCenter worksheet, you'll need a worksheet for storing configuration information, such as the auto open data. Use whatever names you like for these worksheet tabs; just remember to apply a consistent practice of whatever naming convention you choose.

One or more worksheets should provide the actual information or computations that the user would be interested in. In the sample template, I provided a worksheet called OutlineOfTechniques to serve as this page. The naming of worksheets that contain the "guts" of the spreadsheet is purely a matter of choice. Financial information spreadsheets could have worksheet names such as AnnualReport, IncomeStatement, BalanceSheet, or ManagementDiscussionAndAnalysis.

CREATE EASY-TO-FIND SIGNPOSTS

There's no complicated science to this. Simply create a list of user-defined names as described in Chapter 1.

Here are some simple steps to follow:

◆ Give appropriate user-defined names to various cells in the spreadsheet so that they are easy to pick from a list when the user selects the GoTo command (Ctrl+G). Figure 13-4 shows you some representative names.

Figure 13-4: Representative organization of user-defined
names suitable for an assistive-friendly spreadsheet

◆ Choose names for these locations so that when arranged in alphabetical order, the important user names are at the top of the list when Ctrl+G is pressed.

◆ Choose a consistent naming convention. If you have a series of assumptions, you may want to precede the name of the assumption with the word *Assumption*, thereby winding up with names such as `AssumptionForFixedExpenses`, `AssumptionForVariableExpenses`, and so forth.

◆ Navigation points or signposts appear at or near the top of the list because they are preceded with the prefix AccessTo. The prefix gives meaning and establishes an order for the user-defined names.

◆ User-defined names are not allowed to have spaces in the names. A user-defined name can consist of compound words. When using compound words, capitalize the first letter of each word in the name and leave the rest in lowercase form (numeric identifiers are permitted as well). JAWS will recognize this method and correctly speak the word and number, if you've included one. For example, `AssumptionForExpenseCategory1` will be spoken as "assumption for expense category one."

A spreadsheet cell can have more than one user-defined name, such as `InterestRate` as well as `AssumedInterestRateForSenario1`. You are free to choose the shorter or longer of the names when you incorporate it into a spreadsheet formula. This flexibility allows you to design your spreadsheet formulas for clarity and at the same time preserve accessibility.

The key factor here is that the enhancements in accessibility shouldn't come at the cost of the overall clarity and design of the spreadsheet.

You should be aware that JAWS allows you to define what it calls "monitor cells." Such cells can facilitate spreadsheet navigation within a worksheet. Monitor cells do not allow you to navigate between separate worksheets. (You'll find more details about monitor cells a little later in this chapter.)

PROVIDE A TRAIL OF BREAD CRUMBS

It's one thing to establish the starting position that the user lands on when the spreadsheet is first opened. It is entirely another to clue the user in on where to find the start and end points of new information. In contrast to a sighted person, a person who is blind has no way to determine at a glance where information begins and where it ends. There are four things you can do.

◆ Let your spreadsheet data and content hug the leftmost column (column A) so that a user can sequentially move down the spreadsheet a row at a time. The presentation should progress as the user sequentially moves through the spreadsheet.

◆ Get into the habit of providing an empty separator row (or column) between two groups of data. In this way, a user can search to the edge of a group data using a Ctrl and arrow key combination. This will make for easier navigation.

◆ From time to time, you may have a series of blank lines as a result, for example, of a null result having turned up in a computation. It would be helpful to inform the user of how far away the next relevant information is. A user might want to skip introductory information and jump straight to the main data or analysis. Telling the user how many rows down to go, or the actual row number of some information, makes things easier.

◆ On every worksheet, provide a standard text message such as "End of worksheet" to signify that the worksheet contains no more data or content below a given line.

These items may seem trivial, but neglecting them will make the spreadsheet harder to navigate. Also consider the inconvenience of a person with visual impairments having to tentatively explore the layout of data by trying to "cover the territory" and spend time to re-map the data you've already prepared.

Some of you may be thinking that a spreadsheet will be harder to maintain if you have to start accounting for the actual row positions of information. Indeed this would be a nightmare if the row positions have been listed as hardwired numbers and you have to manually edit the numbers each time you insert or delete rows. Fortunately, a quick and easy way around this exists. Make use of the Excel ROW function to tell a user where specific information can be found. It is tremendously liberating for a user to have a tactile feel of the spreadsheet layout.

Consider the following formula, which generates the greeting message when the ch13-01AccessibleSpreadsheetTemplate01.xls is first opened.

Hyperlinks

Excel 2003 supports hyperlinks. The Excel hyperlink feature works much the same as those on Web browsers. Though the Excel HYPERLINK function is specifically targeted at Internet URLs, it can be used to navigate from one location of a spreadsheet to another as well. For most of us, moving around a spreadsheet is a mundane affair. But hyperlinks can be useful to someone who is partially sighted and works with a screen magnifier.

Here is the basic syntax for navigating from one open spreadsheet to another:

```
=HYPERLINK("[FileName]SheetName!CellReference","Text Label")
```

For the HYPERLINK function to work, you need to provide the filename, which must be enclosed by the square brackets. The sheet name needs to be specified, followed by the exclamation mark and then the cell reference. The cell reference can be a physical cell coordinate, such as $A$20 or A20. It can also be a user-defined name, such as AccessToNavigationTips. The following provides a more realistic example of how a HYPERLINK function would be used.

```
=HYPERLINK("[SpreadsheetFileName]InformationCenter!AccessTo
NavigationTips","Click here to navigate to Navigation Tips
located on row "&ROW(AccessToNavigationTips))
```

One more point is worth mentioning. Users who work with a screen reader instead of a screen magnifier will have to switch over to JAWS Cursor mode, position the mouse directly over the link, and then press NumPadSlash. Though this will work, it is cumbersome. As a general rule, build your spreadsheets so that users can do everything while in PC Cursor mode. Leave the hyperlink features for users who have no problems using a physical mouse, such as a user with low vision.

```
="Information Center Worksheet. The cell on row "&ROW(A2)&" contains
    some introductory information."
```

The resulting message is spoken:

```
Information Center Worksheet.
The cell on row 2 contains some introductory information.
```

It is fairly straightforward to associate that the row corresponding to A2 is row 2, or the row corresponding to A29 is row 29. The column letters have nothing to do with the row numbers. Because it's so easy to specify the row numbers, why not hardwire it into the narrative statement? It's certainly easier to type this information out by hand than to splice a formula. However, what's easier now may not be easily maintainable. As you build your accessible spreadsheet, you may find yourself inserting, moving around, and deleting rows of data. You are bound to do endless tweaking to your spreadsheet. The hardwiring of data will only saddle you with additional responsibilities. Also remember that this is a template that's meant to be reused. Hardwired information will be of little benefit when it comes time to reuse the spreadsheet.

VISIBILITY CONSIDERATIONS

When you prepare a spreadsheet, keep in mind that different users will have different computer configurations. Consider the implications of a person with visual impairments whose Screen Monitor is 640 x 480 or 800 x 600 pixels.

Though it should not make a difference to a person with blindness and cannot see the screen, it actually does make a difference. The screen reader software may be in a mode in which it reads what is visible on the screen as opposed to the contents of the spreadsheet cell. In such a situation, if text from a spreadsheet cell extends beyond the edge of the screen, the text may be truncated when read by the screen reader. This, of course, is dependent upon many factors pertaining to how the user may be using the screen reader, the user's CPU configuration, and the way the spreadsheet is set up. The spreadsheet, for instance, may not automatically open to the full window size.

When you test a spreadsheet for accessibility, take these factors into consideration. As an aside, users who have smaller-sized screens often compensate by decreasing the magnification of their spreadsheets to shrink everything to fit in one screen. The screen reader generally isn't affected by the font size. The point is, if you're going to be packing a lot of text into single spreadsheet cells that would run beyond the edge of the screen, you may want to reconsider your design or alert the user that there is a lot of text.

Not every user will be using up-to-date software. There are still plenty of users working with Windows 98, Office 2000, and earlier versions. The screen reader may not be the latest. When you send out the accessible spreadsheet, identify the minimum system requirements.

Spreadsheet Structure

You are now aware of some basic techniques to make a spreadsheet accessible. To get better utilization with a spreadsheet, you need to make use of spreadsheet structure.

Defining spreadsheet regions

When a sighted person reads data from a spreadsheet table, he or she is looking at row and column headers and reading the data at their intersections. That is, the information touches not just one cell, but extends over a region of cells. To enable a person with blindness to have a comparable representation, you need to overlay additional information about the spreadsheet structure. JAWS allows you to do this by defining "regions."

Open the file ch13-02AccessibleSpreadsheetTemplate02.xls and go to the PageWithRegions worksheet. In addition to the introductory material in the first few rows, you should see three regions of data. They are all similar in structure but refer to three different companies, and the range of years for each of these companies is different. How do you get the screen reader to correctly speak the row and column headings when you or a person with blindness moves through the data a cell at a time?

Follow these simple steps:

1. Take your spreadsheet file and save it with the name you intend to use when you distribute the document.

   The reason it is important to choose and save the name as a first step is because your subsequent actions will create a settings file. This settings file will basically match the spelling of your spreadsheet filename.

2. Define a set of regions in your spreadsheet that needs to be read using a table structure. Give each of these regions a user-defined name. When you define each region, it is important that you associate the whole region to the name.

   Three regions are being added. These are associated with the user-defined names RevenueCompanyA, RevenueCompanyB, and RevenueCompanyC. Figure 13-5 shows RevenueCompanyC being added and spans the range of cells from A46:F63.

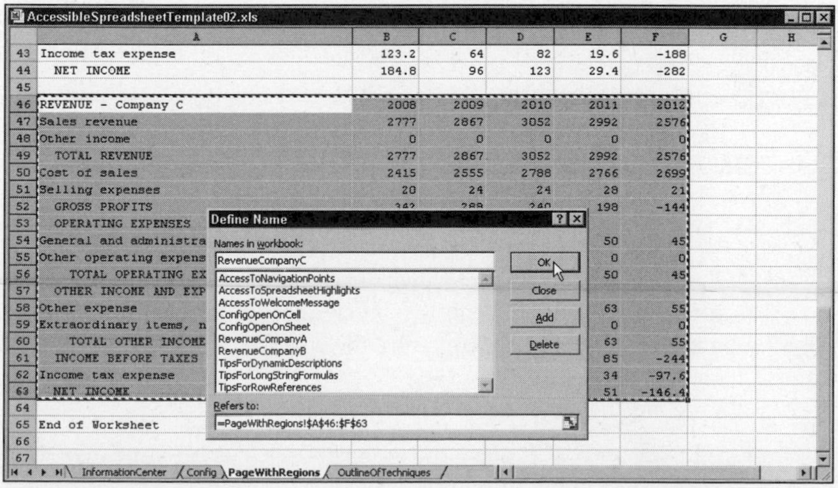

Figure 13-5: When defining a name that will be referenced as a speakable region, remember to select the whole region and not just the top-left cell of the region.

3. Continue preparing the spreadsheet as you normally would, inserting and deleting rows as appropriate. Fix the positions of the named regions you just created.

4. When you're sure that you won't need to reposition the user-defined names, go ahead and define each of the regions. Here are the sub-steps to perform for each separate region:

   a. For the given region, select the range of cells that forms the intersection of the row and column headers you want to read when you move through the region.

      In the example of RevenueCompanyC, the column titles all run across row 46 and the row titles all run up and down column A. Move your cell to the coordinates A46.

      You may have "stacked headers," much like what you would find with a PivotTable. Sometimes you will want two lines to be used for column headers. You could, for instance, have a calendar date on one line and the weekday on the second. Alternatively, you may have the row descriptions on two or more columns. In such cases, select the intersection of the row and column headers. For example, if you had two lines of column header data (rows 45 and 46), you would select A45:A46.

   b. While you have the cursor positioned in the intersection of the row and column headers for the intended region, open the JAWS Verbosity window by pressing Insert+v. A window similar to Figure 13-6 should then open.

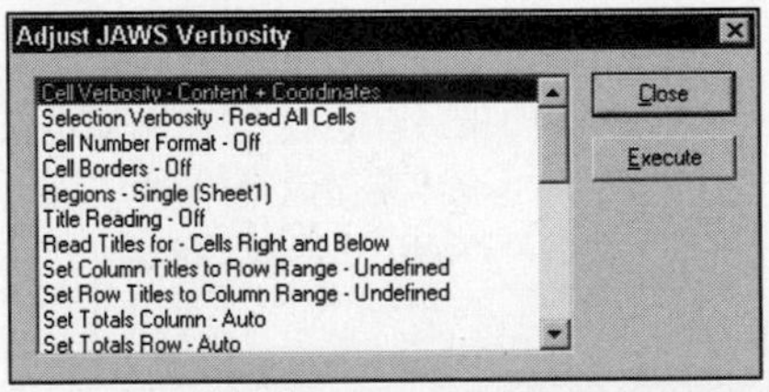

Figure 13-6: Verbosity settings window before settings have been made

      You can use the Up and Down Arrow keys to move through the various items in the list. You can then cycle through the verbosity settings for any item in the list by pressing the spacebar. For instance, you can choose between Contents + Coordinates and Content Only by pressing the spacebar for Cell Verbosity.

   c. I'll leave you to explore the verbosity settings on your own, but first, here are a couple of pointers. Move down to the item called Regions and press the spacebar until Regions is set to Multiple instead of Single.

When it is set to Multiple, the named region should automatically be listed. You should see something like `Current=RevenueCompanyC` or whatever name you defined for the region. Move down to Set Column Titles to Row Range and press the spacebar. You should see Row 46 or whatever row(s) you had selected when you previously pressed Insert+v. Move down to the next line, Set Row Titles to Column Range and press the spacebar. You should see column A or whatever column(s) you had selected when you previously pressed Insert+v. This should look similar to Figure 13-7.

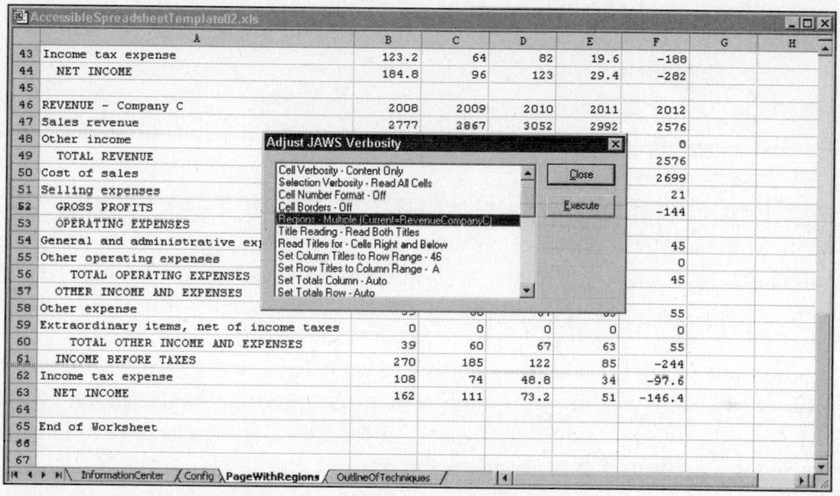

Figure 13-7: Verbosity settings for a specific region

d. JAWS allows you to specify row and column totals. This is convenient for the user who may be in the middle of a region and want the total for the respective row or column read. You should note that the term *total* is only a marker for cells to be read. JAWS doesn't do any computations. It just reads the data that resides in the designated row or column. As an example, nothing prevents you from placing computations of averages into a row that JAWS thinks is a row total. This mislabeling would, of course, throw a curve ball at individuals with visual impairments. Perhaps better terms to have used in the verbosity settings would have been *summarizing row* and *summarizing column*.

e. JAWS allows you to define up to 10 monitor cells. Defining monitor cells allows a user to jump to any of those monitor cells (using Ctrl+Shift+M). A monitor cell can be defined over a range, but when the user jumps to the monitor cell, only the first cell in the range is selected. Note that when the user presses Ctrl+Shift+M to get the list of monitor cells, only cell coordinates are presented – there is no information identifying what the cell coordinates represent. So if you'll be preparing predefined monitor cells for users, consider preparing a mini-table of contents listing what the monitor cells contain.

One of the advantages of using a monitor cell over the simple GoTo cell coordinates or named ranges is that the user can jump back to the previous location before visiting the monitor cell (using Ctrl+Shift+`). This may not seem significant to sighted people, but for an individual with visual impairments, this can make working with a spreadsheet easier.

f. All the items appearing in the verbosity settings below `User Verbosity` are global settings rather than ones that are specific to the particular spreadsheet file.

g. When you press Enter, the settings are activated and the settings file is saved.

IMPORTANT INFORMATION ABOUT VERBOSITY SETTINGS

The JAWS Verbosity Settings offers three possible options: New JSI File, Exact Match, and Best Match. When New JSI File is selected, a file with the current workbook filename but having a prefix of excel_ and a suffix of .jsi will be created in the JAWS settings directory.

When adjusting the verbosity settings for an Excel workbook that doesn't have a settings file, you will be presented with three options: Exact Match No Settings, Best Match, and New JSI File. The option for New JSI File is presented because no existing JSI settings file is keyed to the current workbook name. If you select New JSI File and press Enter, a file with the current workbook filename but having a prefix of excel_ and suffix of .jsi will be created in the JAWS settings directory. The next time you fire up the verbosity settings for this workbook, you will see that it is set to Exact Match but based on the new filename.

If you set it to Best Match, JAWS will know that whenever you open Excel workbooks with similar filenames — even if they are not supplied with their own settings file — it needs to apply this settings file if the names match. You might have a weekly status report with filenames such as IncidentReport01.xls, IncidentReport02.xls, IncidentReport03.xls, and so forth. It uses the same format each time and just uses a different set of numbers, so the Best Match setting will work well.

When you're using Best Match for a specific sequence of files, if you adjust the settings for any of those files, the new settings will apply for the whole sequence. Be careful because it is very easy to unintentionally alter the settings without knowing it has happened.

If you want to modify the verbosity settings for a particular workbook that already uses Best Match settings but you don't want to disrupt the settings for the other workbooks in the sequence, select New JSI File and press Enter. This will exit and save the verbosity settings to a new JSI settings keyed on the current name. Go back to the Verbosity Settings (using Insert+v). Your settings will now be mapped to the current workbook with Exact Match. You can now safely modify the settings for this file without altering the Best Match settings file. If you want to go back to the old settings file you used for the previous Best Match, just select the Best Match option.

 Name collisions for the settings files can occur easily. If you send a financial analyst a spreadsheet and settings file that are keyed to the name IncomeStatement, it will work fine until someone in another company also sends that person a spreadsheet called IncomeStatement along with a new settings file. You can avoid this possibility if you make your filename specific. For example, consider using XyzCompanyIncomeStatement.xls instead of IncomeStatement.xls.

One last point: If you perform an action that creates or modifies a verbosity settings file, you will need to distribute that specific .jsi settings file with your spreadsheet. The spreadsheet will work without the settings file; however, users may have a harder time navigating the spreadsheet. Also, users who use only the Window-Eyes screen reader software will not be able to take advantage of the JAWS settings.

Graphical Components

Spreadsheets filled with rows and columns of data are quite accessible to screen readers. However, it is commonplace for spreadsheets to incorporate graphical components such as List Boxes. Depending on how you design your spreadsheet, the components may be accessible or may not be readily accessible. This section provides some starting concepts so that you can ferret out the issues and spreadsheet design strategies.

A point of confusion can quickly arise, because two broad categories of graphical components can be used in a spreadsheet and are basically identical in appearance. The first group belongs to components found on your Forms toolbar. The other group belongs to ActiveX Controls found on the Controls Toolbox toolbar. Both sets of toolbars are shown in Figure 13-8. Can you figure out which one is which? I bet not. Both toolbars will allow you to place graphical components onto your worksheet. They work differently, and when it comes to screen readers, they do not function equivalently.

Graphical components such as List Boxes and Combo Boxes carry macros with them. Many users set the macro security level options to High, which prohibits the execution of all third-party macros that are not digitally signed.

If you are distributing spreadsheets that contain macros, you should supply some documentation that alerts users to the presence of macros. If the macros are not digitally signed by a trusted Registration Authority, such as VeriSign, users will need to adjust their macro security settings to a Medium level.

You should provide specific instructions outlining on a step-by-step basis how they can set these options. If you are distributing spreadsheets to a broad audience, you should seriously consider making it a standard practice to digitally sign documents sent to third parties.

The vertical toolbar on the extreme right is the Control toolbox. The one to its immediate left is the Forms toolbox. Aside from the slight difference in the selection of icons, the letters *C* and *F* appearing in the title bar portion of the respective palettes helps to distinguish them.

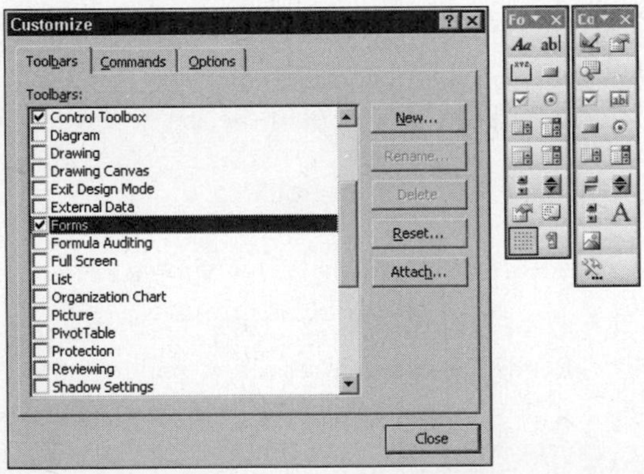

Figure 13-8: The older forms-based toolbar and the newer Control Toolbox toolbar are very similar in appearance.

Try clicking the List Box icon in the Control Toolbox and then dragging a shape onto your worksheet. Pull up the context menu (that is, right-click the List Box you just created) and select Format Control (see Figure 13-9). Unlike the older-style List Box, the Format Control window has no Control tab. This is because everything is handled on a pure scripting level. In the background of Figure 13-9, you can see that the selected List Box has no built-in scroll bars.

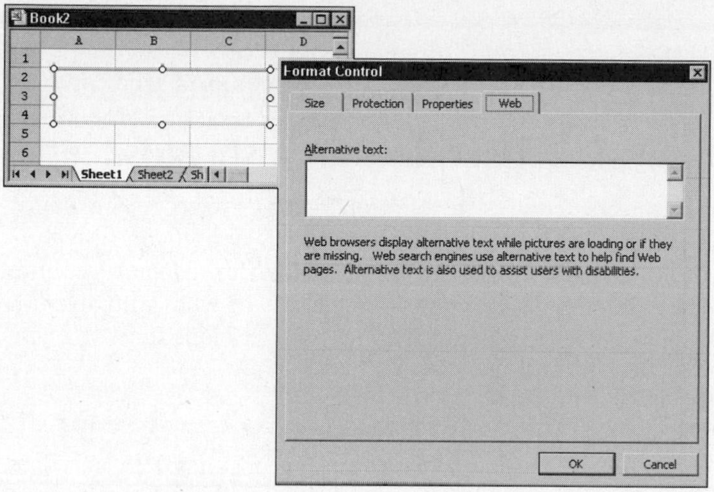

Figure 13-9: List Boxes created from the Control Toolbox no longer have a Control tab; the functionality is handled at the scripting level.

Why am I bringing all this up? I want you to be keenly aware of the differences between these kinds of components, because they work very differently with screen readers. In short, you will need to go the route of working with Control Toolboxes if you want to develop accessible spreadsheets for screen readers.

Road Map for Creating the Assistive Portal

For the rest of this chapter, I focus on some of the basics of creating simple accessible spreadsheets with graphical components that work cleanly with screen readers. You will see that the process entails a certain amount of scripting. If you're not a veteran Visual Basic programmer, it's probably more scripting than you want to do.

Next, I am going to switch gears. Rather than have you create a separate graphical component for each and every list, I provide you with a single interface that can be used for speaking multiple lists, based on parameters you supply on a Config worksheet. If you specify everything properly on the worksheet, you will not have to do any macro scripting to have a working interface for a screen reader. This is because the input information is no longer hardwired in the body of the scripts. Your filling in the Config worksheet tells the portal where to go looking for information and how it's organized. Sound good? Here's something even more compelling. The Assistive Portal you'll be using will be separate from the actual spreadsheet that you want to make accessible. Other than identifying all the inputs that drive the original spreadsheets, carefully mapping out the portions you want displayed for the screen reader, and creating signposts in the form of user-defined names, there will be no changes to your original spreadsheets. That's right: No changes in formulas to your original spreadsheets and no additional scripting.

Creating an accessible UserForm in a spreadsheet

Believe it or not, UserForms created with the Control Toolbox are accessible almost out of the box. In this section, I walk you through the flow of creating one. My purpose in doing so is not to show you anything about macros or catapult you into becoming a programmer. Rather, I want you to get a sense of what's involved in going the scripting route, and the design complexities and decisions for which you should be aware.

DIFFICULTIES WITH "DROPPING" A FORM ONTO A WORKSHEET

The Forms toolbar that some of you may be used to using predates VBA and does not make use of an object model and full VBA support that UserForms provide. It should come as no surprise to you that the older-style Forms interface does not work as well with screen readers. Specifically, the controls that are "dropped" onto a spreadsheet are "floating." To access these components, you need to switch from your PC Cursor context to a Virtual Mouse Cursor mode, such as JAWS Cursor. Accomplishing the switch over to Virtual Mouse Cursor mode entails managing physical placement of a mouse pointer over an object that is not anchored to your spreadsheet and is not tethered to your mouse. As you try to scroll through a long list of items, you'll find yourself easily "rolling off" the graphical component. This can be a frustrating experience. Read on to find out a solution.

WORKING WITH USERFORMS

Popping up a UserForm that incorporates ActiveX Controls is a much better approach. Basically, you're directly interacting with the graphical components, but you never leave your keyboard context. Because you maintain your PC Cursor mode, you can interact with the controls in the dialog box using your keyboard. The biggest challenge for screen reader software is that not all controls are spoken when you interact with them.

It is going to be both easy and hard to work with UserForms. If you're used to working with the older-style controls, you will find the flow to be a bit different and more complex. Rather than drop a control onto the worksheet, you will prepare UserForms and tell them to "show" themselves. You will endow these UserForms with various components or controls.

These controls, such as List Boxes, ComboBoxes, and buttons, maintain state information. You will pack these components with such information. For instance, with a List Box, you will need to supply it with a list of items to make it start. Additionally, you may want to tell it to pre-select a specific item in the list. All this will be done programmatically.

There are events associated with each of these controls, such as every time you click inside a button. Associating events with controls gives you the ability to execute and run macros from any of the components on your UserForm. Even as users cancel or exit a UserForm, specific macros can be run.

Very quickly, you can build complex behavior. You need to be careful in your design, because the technology and design options give you enough rope to easily hang yourself several times over.

♦ The best strategy is to design your facilities so that the elements can be easily reused.

♦ Your next step is to make sure that you're building safety nets.

♦ Your third strategy is to ask yourself whether your design is as simple as it can be made without shortchanging your basic requirements.

♦ Your fourth strategy is to test as much as possible.

♦ Finally, once you get something working, don't be afraid to do it all over again and "get it right." A clean design will serve you far better in the long run than one that works correctly but has hidden wrinkles.

Interface for a List Box and a button

To illustrate the basics, I want to walk you through the construction of an accessible List Box and set of buttons. Open the file ch13-03ListBox.xls (see Figure 13-10). At first glance, it seems to have a rather unassuming appearance. Notice that you are immediately taken straight to a predefined location. This was made possible by the auto open mechanism presented previously in Listing 13-1. Immediately underneath the starting location is summary information about the spreadsheet's contents. Next is a set of instructions for accessing and operating the List Box.

To summarize, you launch the UserForm-based List Box by pressing Alt+F8 to bring up a list of available macros, tabbing over to LaunchUserForm, selecting it, and pressing Enter. (For those of you still in training-wheel mode and not comfortable with navigating solely by keyboard, the Test button will accomplish the same thing. I encourage you, however, to persist with the keyboard/screen reader combination so that you can develop a sense of how the devices and software work together.)

Notice that you can be facile in moving around the List Box with only a keyboard. Not only do you have access to the ↑, ↓, PageUp, PageDown, Home, and End keys, but pressing a letter will also allow you to cycle through all the list items that start with the same letter. As you move through the list, notice that the large button to the immediate right of the List Box is automatically adjusted to reflect the currently selected state and perform a lookup of its geographic region.

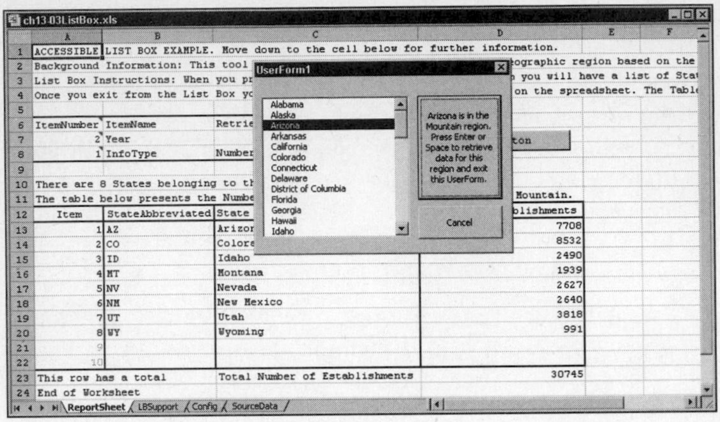

Figure 13-10: A simple accessible UserForm that is "connected" to a spreadsheet application

Exiting from the List Box requires the user to consciously accept the chosen geographic region or press Cancel to return to the original state. A layer of "passive persistence" has been built in. The next time the List Box is relaunched, it automatically selects the same state that was previously chosen. In this sense the memory is persistent. It is passive in the sense that the value is read from a spreadsheet cell whenever it is needed. It is also saved to that spreadsheet cell whenever it needs to be updated. In this case, the persistent item is found on ListItem1 of the LBSupport worksheet (see Figure 13-11).

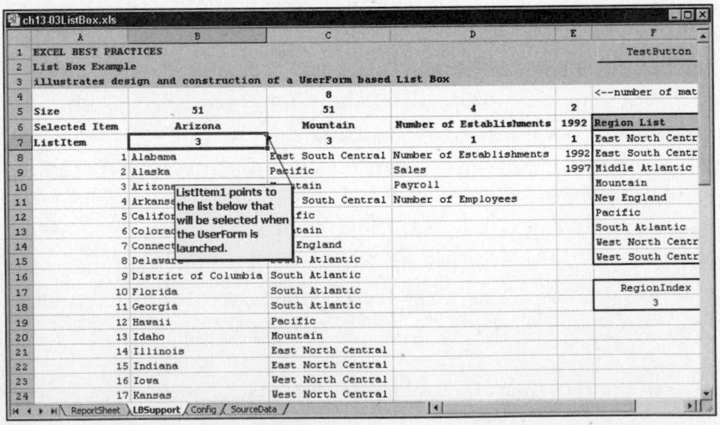

Figure 13-11: List Box Support worksheet contains information that will be read by the UserForm and lookup formulas.

An Important Design Strategy: Remove Hardwired Dependencies

This next step is probably the most important design decision for developing UserForms as an accessible interface. It boils down to the following simple rule:

> If you want to make your interfaces flexible, robust, and easily maintained, remove all (hardwired) dependencies from the macro scripting.

You saw this strategy in action with the auto open macro of Listing 13-1. The macro does not actually hold the specific cell location info, but rather holds a pointer to where the information can be retrieved. By placing the information *outside* the script, the script behavior can be adjusted without touching the script. This is very liberating.

Now comes the challenging part. Can you do this for 100 percent of the scripting code, or at least very close to it? The answer is yes, but the coding style is different from what you may be used to.

I'll start with the list initialization. When you or the user presses Alt+F8 and runs the LaunchUserForm macro, the code displayed in Figure 13-12 is run.

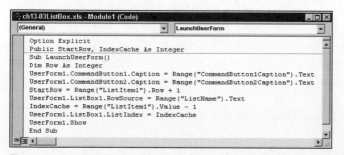

```
ch13-03ListBox.xls - Module1 (Code)
(General)                                    LaunchUserForm

    Option Explicit
    Public StartRow, IndexCache As Integer
    Sub LaunchUserForm()
    Dim Row As Integer
    UserForm1.CommandButton1.Caption = Range("CommandButton1Caption").Text
    UserForm1.CommandButton2.Caption = Range("CommandButton2Caption").Text
    StartRow = Range("ListItem1").Row + 1
    UserForm1.ListBox1.RowSource = Range("ListName").Text
    IndexCache = Range("ListItem1").Value - 1
    UserForm1.ListBox1.ListIndex = IndexCache
    UserForm1.Show
    End Sub
```

Figure 13-12: The Macro that launches the UserForm has to initialize the components.

My goal isn't to get you to delve into the coding. Rather, I want you to gain an understanding of how a script can be written so that changes to its behavior can be done outside of the script. The way you can do this is to create a layer of abstraction.

Abstraction Layer approach to coding

You are facing an important trade-off. You can opt for a simpler, one-time VBA code such as:

```
UserForm1.ListBox1.RowSource = "ListOfStates"
```

or you can write:

```
UserForm1.ListBox1.RowSource = Range("ListName").Text
```

Both of these will do the job. If you are preparing a list that you know will *never* change and you don't care to reuse your components, then hardwiring the values into your code would be easier. If, on the other hand, you would like to have a template that you could plunk into *any* list, whose list size and content may be different each time you launch it, and if you don't want to have to do surgery on the macro code, then the Abstraction Layer approach will serve you better.

This design decision is your judgment call. All I can tell you is that after you have a cleanly designed, accessibility-friendly spreadsheet created using the Abstraction Layer approach, you won't have to go playing with macro code as you continue to customize your spreadsheet. And when you want to use the facility with another set of data, you will only need to update a configuration table to be able to reuse the components. Controls such as your List Box will automatically point to the new dataset without requiring any re-scripting of macros or behind-the-scenes formulas.

This design strategy of using an abstraction layer will give you the basic building block for the Assistive Portal Interface, or "API," as I like to call it. This facility makes a whole spreadsheet accessible without changes to the original spreadsheet.

Compound interfaces

The next task is to design a UserForm which can be used in a wider diversity of situations than a single List Box. The design criteria are as follows:

◆ The interface should allow for selecting and setting an arbitrary number of lists without requiring adjustments to its structure.

◆ Although the behind-the-scenes implementation may be complicated, there should be no macro/scripting needed to use or configure the interface. This includes the ability to customize and add different datasets.

◆ The interface should work in a simple manner that works with screen readers. Navigation should be easy, choices should be easy, and interface design should be consistent and unambiguous. Also, all the trimmings need to be in the spreadsheet, such as:

■ Automatically opening to a pre-specified location on the spreadsheet (with its capacity to be fine-tuned left intact).

■ Automatically resizing the active window and application window to the maximum possible size (and retaining the ability to turn this feature off).

API: Assistive Portal Interface or Application Programming Interface — Which is it?

For many years, programmers have used an application programming interface (commonly known as an API) to connect programs that operate independently of one another. An API enables multiple groups of programs to share information and interact with each other. An Assistive Portal Interface is simply an API for spreadsheets. Rather than interface through programming constructs, it interfaces through conventional spreadsheet constructs such as spreadsheet cells and, through Excel 2003, can make use of XML/Web Services capabilities. Chapter 12 covers the Spreadsheet Portal concept in detail.

The file ch13-04ListBox.xls implements this feature set (see Figure 13-13). This interface is very similar in appearance to the one shown in Figure 13-10, with the addition of a List Box that allows you select from the categories of State, Year, and Info Type (that is, type of Economic Information).

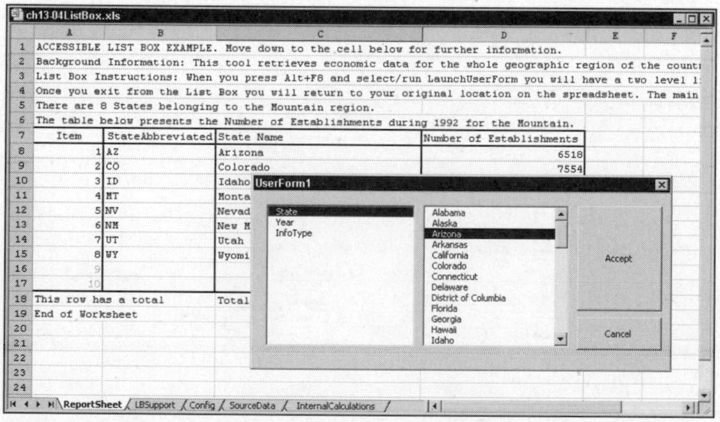

Figure 13-13: Screen reader–accessible two-level List Box

As you move up and down the category list of State, Year and info type, the screen reader speaks the category name and its associated category value, such as the specific state (Arizona, in Figure 13-13). Tabbing over to the second List Box allows you to select the subcategory item. You still have the same navigation facilities afforded from the previous List Box example, including the ability to cycle through all the items beginning with a chosen letter by repeatedly pressing the letter. You can jump to the beginning and end of the list by pressing the Home and End keys. You can also use the PgUp, PgDn, and Up and Down Arrow keys. You can tab over to the Accept and Cancel buttons. Because it is easy to move up and down the categories list and listen to the specific items selected for each category, you don't need to recapitulate the list for the user when he or she reaches the Accept button. Accordingly, the text label of the Accept button is now static. In the earlier example (see Figure 13-10), the Accept button was dynamic. The emphasis here is on simplicity of operation and implementation.

Run through the interface a few times to convince yourself that the operation is smooth and simple.

Implementing the screen reader–accessible two-level List Box

Now for the implementation... I am not going to discuss any macro coding; no need for that. Go straight to the LBSupport Worksheet (see Figure 13-14). First, pay attention to the dotted lines in row 10. To the immediate right of the `State` category is the name of the location that holds the value of the currently selected State. The name of that container is `ListItem1`. All you need to type into the `UpdateLocation` column is **`ListItem1`**. No formula is involved. Into the next column, type **`ListOfStates`**. This happens to be the name of the defined range starting at `E10` and continuing down to `E60`. Again, no formula is involved.

Typing in `State`, `ListItem1`, and `ListOfStates` is all you need to do to properly establish the State category, along with a fully populated sublist and its expected behavior. The same goes for `Year` and `InfoType`. You don't need to contend with any formulas or macros whatsoever.

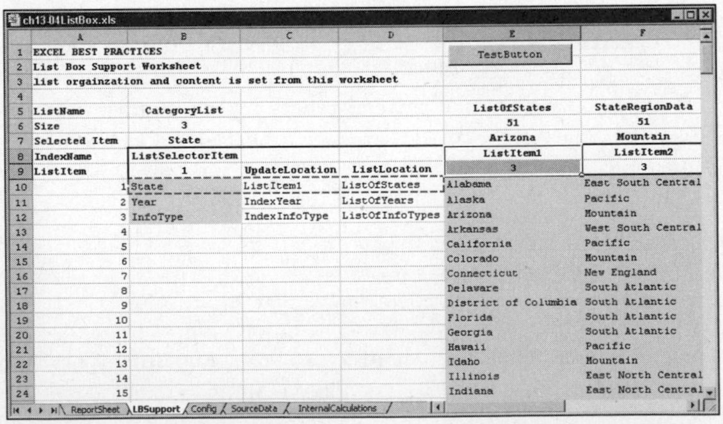
ch13-04ListBox.xls

	A	B	C	D	E	F
1	EXCEL BEST PRACTICES				TestButton	
2	List Box Support Worksheet					
3	list orgainzation and content is set from this worksheet					
4						
5	ListName	CategoryList			ListOfStates	StateRegionData
6	Size	3			51	51
7	Selected Item	State			Arizona	Mountain
8	IndexName	ListSelectorItem			ListItem1	ListItem2
9	ListItem	1	UpdateLocation	ListLocation	3	3
10	1	State	ListItem1	ListOfStates	Alabama	East South Central
11	2	Year	IndexYear	ListOfYears	Alaska	Pacific
12	3	InfoType	IndexInfoType	ListOfInfoTypes	Arizona	Mountain
13	4				Arkansas	West South Central
14	5				California	Pacific
15	6				Colorado	Mountain
16	7				Connecticut	New England
17	8				Delaware	South Atlantic
18	9				District of Columbia	South Atlantic
19	10				Florida	South Atlantic
20	11				Georgia	South Atlantic
21	12				Hawaii	Pacific
22	13				Idaho	Mountain
23	14				Illinois	East North Central
24	15				Indiana	East North Central

ReportSheet / LBSupport / Config / SourceData / InternalCalculations

Figure 13-14: Mapping the List Boxes only involves filling in a table on a worksheet.

What if you want more categories than State, Year, and InfoType? In summary, here are the basic steps to accomplish that:

1. Replicate the basic structure for the detailed items in your new category and define it as a named range along with an update location.

2. Immediately below the CategoryList of State, Year, and InfoType that appear in column B, add new entries for the category label, update location, and list location. Then, extend your CategoryList to include your new entries.

Try an example. First, add a new category called Economic Sector. Go to column H of the LBSupport worksheet of ch13-04ListBox.xls and replicate all of column H onto column I. Next, copy the list of values for this new category from the take-away.txt file (this is the list appearing in the tail end of the file) and paste it directly on top of the first cell where a list would belong in column I. This should be on row 10.

With the 20 or so cells selected, define a named range. A good name would be ListOfEconomicSectors. Notice that the region of blue-shaded cells appears only in the first two rows of your list items. This is because the text appearing in row 5 of column I is referring to ListOfYears instead of the newly defined name ListOfEconomicSectors. Go ahead and change this name to ListOfEconomicSectors (or whatever name you are using). When you do this, the region of blue-shaded cells should extend all the way down the 20 items in the list.

Move down to row 9 of column I and give the cell the defined name IndexSector. You can also change the cosmetic label immediately above IndexYear to IndexSector.

After you adjust the centering alignment to left justification, your spreadsheet should look like Figure 13-15.

Notice that your new list resource column correctly picks up the number of items (20) in the list. Also, the description in the cell I7 correctly matches the IndexSector position in the list. Make sure that you verify this match before moving on to the next step.

Next, go to column B and add a new set of entries that will be used by your category list. Type in the label for your new category in the cell B13. This can be a label of your choosing. In column C, type in IndexSector; in column D, type in ListOfEconomicSectors. Now comes an especially important step: Redefine the cell coordinates to include the additional cell. Edit your named range of CategoryList to include B10 through B13 (see Figure 13-16).

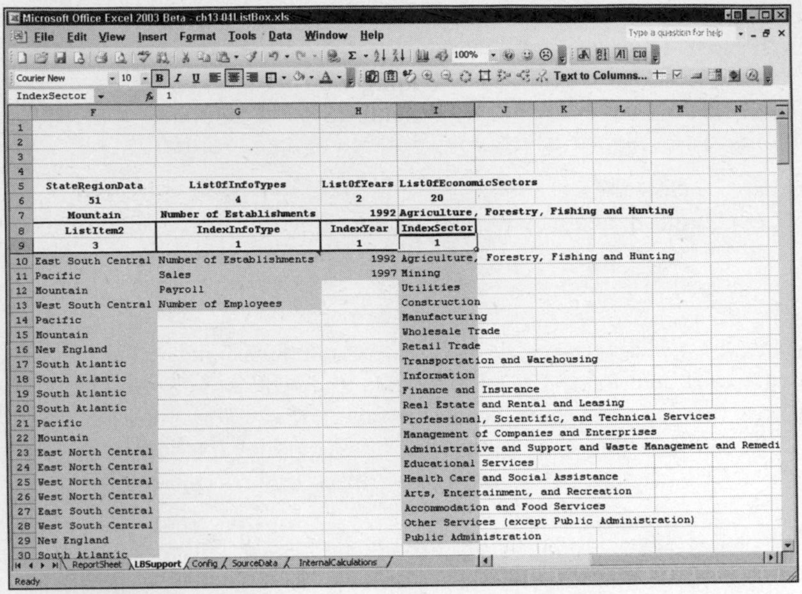

Figure 13-15: Start replicating the structure for existing lists.

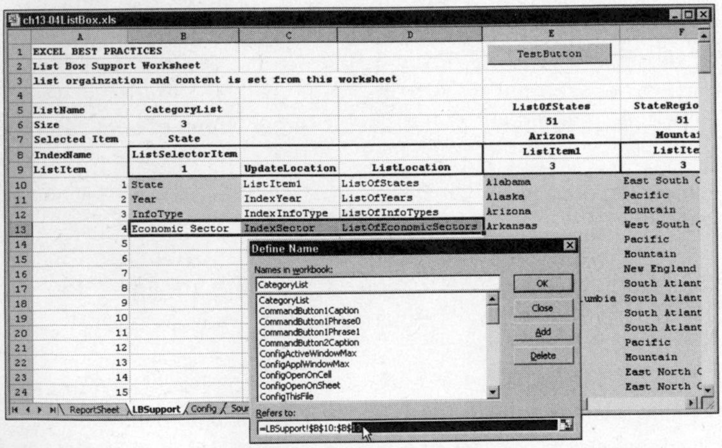

Figure 13-16: Extend your CategoryList by redefining its boundaries.

Although UpdateLocation and ListLocation are directly related to the CategoryList, they are not part of its named range. CategoryList is only one column wide. When you are extending its boundary to include additional categories, you should be extending it only within the same column as the one in which it is defined. In the example in this chapter, this is column B.

After you extend the boundary for the named range of CategoryList, the blue shading should encompass the phrase "Economic Sector" (see Figure 13-17). If you are curious to see how the automatic blue shading works, look at the Conditional Formatting settings from the Excel Format menu. (See Chapter 7 for lots more information on Conditional Formatting.)

	A	B	C	D	E	F
1	EXCEL BEST PRACTICES					
2	List Box Support Worksheet				TestButton	
3	list orgainzation and content is set from this worksheet					
4						
5	ListName	CategoryList			ListOfStates	StateRegio
6	Size	4			51	51
7	Selected Item	State			Arizona	Mountai
8	IndexName	ListSelectorItem			ListItem1	ListIte
9	ListItem	1	UpdateLocation	ListLocation	3	3
10	1	State	ListItem1	ListOfStates	Alabama	East South C
11	2	Year	IndexYear	ListOfYears	Alaska	Pacific
12	3	InfoType	IndexInfoType	ListOfInfoTypes	Arizona	Mountain
13	4	Economic Sector	IndexSector	ListOfEconomicSectors	Arkansas	West South C
14	5				California	Pacific
15	6				Colorado	Mountain
16	7				Connecticut	New England
17	8				Delaware	South Atlant
18	9				District of Columbia	South Atlant
19	10				Florida	South Atlant
20	11				Georgia	South Atlant
21	12				Hawaii	Pacific
22	13				Idaho	Mountain
23	14				Illinois	East North C
24	15				Indiana	East North C

ReportSheet \ LBSupport / Config / SourceData / InternalCalculations /

Figure 13-17: CategoryList, extended to include an additional category, is automatically highlighted.

Your third and final step is to connect the results from your List Box to your spreadsheet reports, such as the ReportSheet. You can use a formula like the following:

```
="The Economic Sector selected is: "&LBSupport!I7
```

Of course, you can give the cell coordinate I7 a more descriptive name. In any case, try out your UserForm interface (see Figure 13-18).

As you move up and down the list of categories, the screen reader will also speak the associated item in the category but may truncate the detailed info based on what is visible. For instance, when you move the Down Arrow key to the Economic Sector category to the associated item Agriculture, Forestry, Fishing and Hunting, the screen reader may say only "Agriculture, Forestry, Fishing a." Don't fret about that. When you tab over to the detailed column, the screen reader will speak the full line of text, with nothing missing.

As a practical measure, you may want to consider readjusting the column widths to make one column narrower and the other one wider.

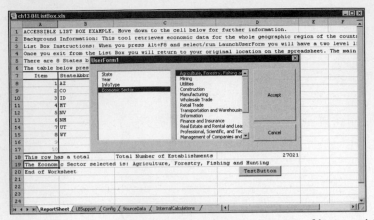

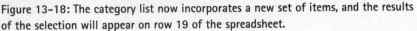

Figure 13-18: The category list now incorporates a new set of items, and the results of the selection will appear on row 19 of the spreadsheet.

An essential point to keep in mind about some interfaces, such as the dual-level List Box in this example, is that this kind of interface is not typical of what individuals with blindness are used to. For example, if not specifically told otherwise, a user might expect to have to retrieve data for a specific region and economic sector by first selecting the desired region and pressing the Accept button. After exiting the UserForm, the user would expect to relaunch it to choose the desired Economic Sector and then press Accept. The user with blindness needs to be told that launching the UserForm twice is not necessary. The user can select both these parameters in one sitting without exiting the UserForm. When users realize this, they quickly shift into high gear.

As you go about preparing and designing your interfaces, think about explaining how to work the interfaces efficiently. Be prepared to perform some user testing with people who regularly use screen readers and redesign your instruction documentation so that users are aware of the features you built in.

OTHER TECHNIQUES

Plenty of other kinds of interfaces can be constructed and made accessible, and different kinds of coding methodologies are available.

The technique of applying abstraction layers, although common in some communities of programmers, may not be as popular in others. In this last example you did see a specific advantage of using the Abstraction Layer Approach. When modifying the interface to accommodate a new category and their detail, at no point did you have to look at or worry about macros and scripting. If a more conventional style had been used, then you would have been doing major surgery on the underlying macros. I think this is a persuasive reason to take the Abstraction Layer approach seriously.

I suspect that some of you who regularly distribute interactive spreadsheets might be concerned that the Abstraction Layered approach exposes portions of the spreadsheet that control its behavior. You may worry that the interface is so reusable that someone could effectively co-opt it for his or her own use. If this is a concern, you can use conventional techniques to hide and protect portions of the spreadsheet from the user. Consult any of the numerous "encyclopedic" reference books on spreadsheets on how to protect Excel spreadsheets.

Delving deeply into other kinds of programming methodologies or interfaces is beyond the scope of this book, but I want to mention two so that you can research these on your own. One of these is a spreadsheet facility and the other is a feature specific to the JAWS screen reader.

If you need to fine-tune the spreadsheet interactivity, you'll definitely want to explore the InputBox facility. Here is an oversimplified version of writing that facility into a macro.

```
Sub GetName()
Range("a1").Value = InputBox("enter your name", "MyTitle")
End Sub
```

There are many variations on InputBox. Also, an InputBox can be Excel-related or VBA related. There are differences. The discussion lies beyond the scope of this book (for further details, consult *Excel 2003 Power Programming with VBA*, by John Walkenbach, Wiley Publishing, Inc.).

On the screen reader side, you may wish to enhance interactivity. With JAWS, there are two approaches. One of these is a non-script–based facility called a Frame (not to be confused with HTML Frames). See Figure 13-19.

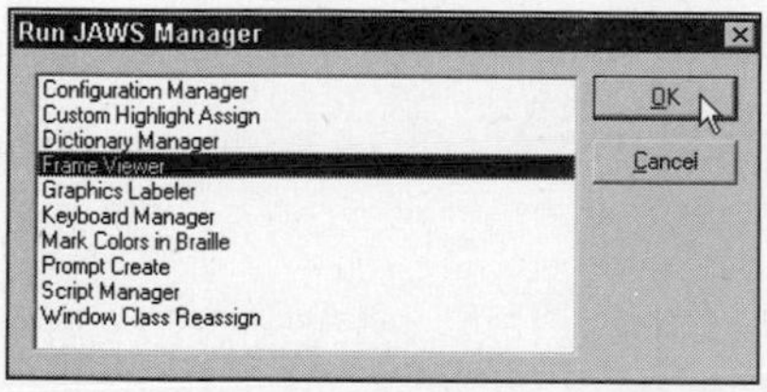

Figure 13-19: The JAWS Frame Viewer can be accessed by pressing Insert+F2.

Frames can filter keyboard events, suppress vocalization, or automatically speak the contents of a defined frame whenever the text of a specific button or widget changes. Frames are defined by their position relative to the screen or a specific window, such as a UserForm.

JAWS also has its own scripting language. Frames and JAWS scripting lie beyond the scope of this book.

Assistive Portals

As you followed along with the List Box examples, you used a graphical interface to point to data that resides on the same Excel workbook or spreadsheet file. What if the data you want to access is located on another spreadsheet that does some rather involved analysis but is not accessibility-friendly?

You could modify that spreadsheet to make it accessible. This may be risky, especially if you are not the original designer of that spreadsheet and may not be familiar with all the subtleties of its formulas or macros. Even if you could retrofit the spreadsheet, the costs, approvals, and validation process you might have to go through to get a new and official version of the spreadsheet could be excessive. Also, what if you need to accommodate more than one kind of accessibility need, and what if they are conflicting?

This is where the Assistive Portal Interface comes into play. Consider the following scenario. As part of your efforts within a Federal government agency, you are preparing an interactive spreadsheet that is quite complex. Section 508 dictates that electronic documents be provided in a fully accessible form, or at least that users with disabilities be provided with comparable access to the electronic information. As a specialist in economic data, you know next to nothing about assistive technologies. Neither you nor your colleagues are equipped to address the accessibility issues. If the spreadsheet is to be made accessible, it will have to be done by a person trained with screen readers or some other adaptive technology. There's a danger here. That person trained in the assistive technologies knows nothing about your discipline and cannot handle the complicated math, spreadsheet formulas, and macros you've prepared. Attempts to rework your spreadsheet may compromise its integrity.

Basic ingredients needed for an Assistive Portal

An Assistive Portal provides a solution to this conundrum. The preparer of the original spreadsheet need only follow certain guidelines:

- Input cells need to be identified so that an action from the Assistive Portal page can remotely adjust the input cells in the original spreadsheet.

- Important spreadsheet results need to be explicitly identified and given user-defined names, thereby making them easy to look up and be displayed in the Assistive Portal Page.

On the Assistive Portal page, more work remains to be done, but it, too, is limited in scope. Here are the important steps:

- Map all the inputs that drive the original spreadsheet and create the equivalent input cells in the Assistive Portal. In the same breath, assure that the input cells are accessible on the Assistive Portal in a manner comparable to the input cells in the original spreadsheet.

◆ Passively tether the Assistive Portal to the input cells of the original spreadsheet. In this manner, the Assistive Portal acts like a remote control device.

◆ Read specific information from the original spreadsheet and display it on the Assistive Portal in a manner that makes it accessible.

◆ Some configuration mapping may be needed to ensure that everything works together properly.

Obviously, you need to perform some testing to verify that the configuration works correctly.

These steps are just an overview, but there really isn't much more to setting up the basic Assistive Portal than what I've outlined. The key to preparing a successful Assistive Portal is to map the data into a simple and logical organization. The next section walks you through a sample implementation.

An Assistive Portal implementation

At this point, you know the basic concept of an Assistive Portal. This section describes a simple Assistive Portal and then provides an industrial-strength example. The simple example is designed to be quickly and easily modified by you.

OVERVIEW

Figure 13-20 shows a spreadsheet that would, for the most part, be accessible if its inputs weren't all controlled by nonaccessible interfaces.

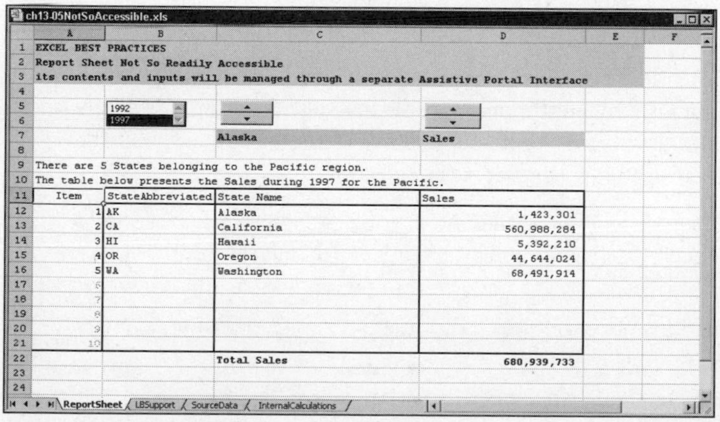

Figure 13-20: A spreadsheet whose inputs are driven by nonaccessible graphical interfaces

By comparison, Figure 13-21 shows the basic appearance of an Assistive Portal. For this example, open the ch13-06AssistivePortal.xls file, but first place the JAWS settings file (excel_ ch13-06AssistivePortal.xls.jsi) into your JAWS SETTINGS\ENU folder. The exact directory depends on the version of JAWS you are running. You'll be able to run the spreadsheet without the settings file; however, the JAWS Screen Reader will not automatically announce the row and column headers when you get to the table areas.

Origin of the Spreadsheet Portal

Some of you may be curious to know how Spreadsheet Portals and Assistive Portals came to be. Interestingly enough, the idea of Spreadsheet Portals and Desktop Client Portals evolved as an offshoot of the Assistive Portal concept.

While thinking about the challenge of adhering to Section 508 — the Federal law requiring government agencies to make electronic information accessible to people with disabilities — I continually asked questions of educators. What are the kinds of problems individuals with disabilities face when trying to use a computer to navigate through the complex information space (as well as the simple ones)?

I quickly came to the realization that the problems and challenges were hard — very hard. In addition to the broad diversity of disabilities and special needs, the issues and challenges are compounded by the nature of technology, which is increasingly complex, constantly changing, and frequently on the verge of some upheaval.

Integrating *electronic curb cuts* throughout a complex spreadsheet with delicate formulas is not only difficult but also time consuming to prepare and maintain. It seemed to me that rather than master the challenges of making a large and complex spreadsheet navigable, it would be far easier to bring the data to an easily accessible and comfortable location (a.k.a. the Assistive Portal Page).

This idea basically inverted the navigation problem by pulling and retrieving data instead of chasing after it through the inner recesses and crevices of the spreadsheet. It is much easier and safer to create a portal page that retrieves the needed information than it is to perform major surgery on a complex spreadsheet to make it accessible.

I found that I could quickly and easily build the prototypes and take advantage of economies of scale to tackle complex problems that seemed unimaginable only a few months earlier.

Spreadsheet Portals and Desktop Client Portals came right on the heels of developing the Assistive Portal. Not long afterward, the concept of Assistive Portals evolved into a general framework for Internet-based Spreadsheet Portals and Desktop Client Portals. Although I was able to develop Client Portals with other technologies such as Flash, close to a year passed before I could get my hands on Excel 2003 and put to use the much promised capabilities of XML.

After you've copied the settings file to the appropriate JAWS directory, you can open the file ch13-06AssistivePortal.xls by navigating to it from the File Dialog window.

 This spreadsheet will open a second file (ch13-05NotSoAccessible.xls), which needs to be in the same directory as the Assistive Portal spreadsheet. Excel also needs to navigate to this directory; otherwise, when it searches for the second file, it may be looking in the wrong directory and return an error. This is why you must navigate to the Assistive Portal spreadsheet through the File Dialog window. After Excel sets the directory path, it will have no problem opening the file.

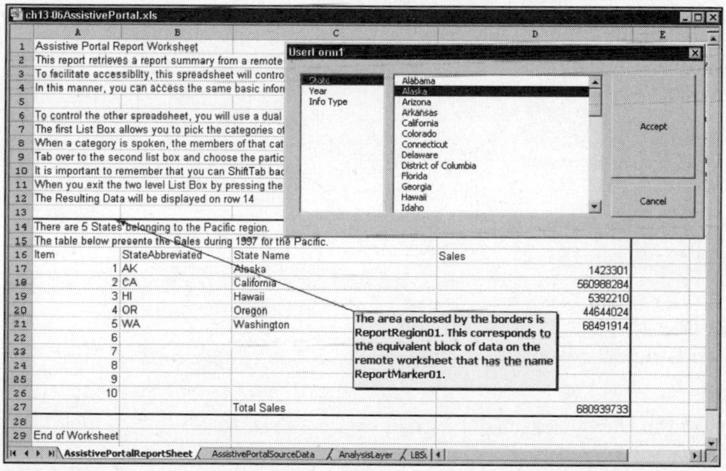

Figure 13-21: The Assistive Portal maps the original spreadsheet content to the Portal page and replaces the nonaccessible interfaces with its own screen reader–friendly version.

The Assistive Portal spreadsheet will:

◆ Automatically open a second spreadsheet file (the one it needs to remotely access)

◆ Automatically resize the spreadsheet and Excel application to take maximum advantage of the screen size

◆ Automatically set the active cell to the default starting point of the Assistive Portal page

Remember, all these features are tweakable (as are many other factors) from the Config worksheet (see Figure 13-22). The Config worksheet allows you to do much more than perform these perfunctory tasks. Specifically, you have the ability to precisely define the input values that will be pushed onto the remote worksheet and drive its behaviors and content. Having these input values embedded in the Config worksheet is not necessary. An item with the name `InputValue01` will be pushed onto the remote worksheet at the location that corresponds to whatever name is typed into the `InputNameOnRepository01` on the Config worksheet. In Figure 13-22, `InputValue01` is 2. This is the value that will be placed into `ListItem1` of the file ch13-05NotSoAccessible.xls.

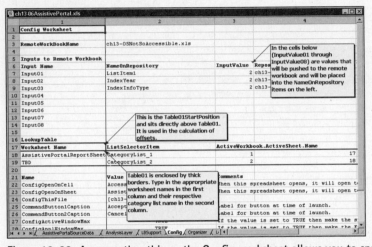
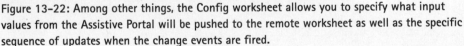

Figure 13-22: Among other things, the Config worksheet allows you to specify what input values from the Assistive Portal will be pushed to the remote worksheet as well as the specific sequence of updates when the change events are fired.

The nice feature of this approach is that this behavior is completely table driven. You don't have to mess around with macros and VBA to adjust this behavior. The sequence of update macros that fire with each update event is table driven.

You may have wondered why there is a lookup table called `Table01` on the Config worksheet. The table exists to perform two functions. One of these is for context switching. There is only one UserForm interface in the whole spreadsheet. Both the content it is populated with and the items it updates are dependent solely upon which worksheet happens to be active when the UserForm (that is, the dual-level List Box) is summoned. A lookup is performed that matches the active worksheet to `Table01`. The match returns a category list. The information for the category list is stored in the right side of the LBSupport worksheet (see Figure 13-23). This worksheet tells the UserForm what lists it needs to get and what items it will modify.

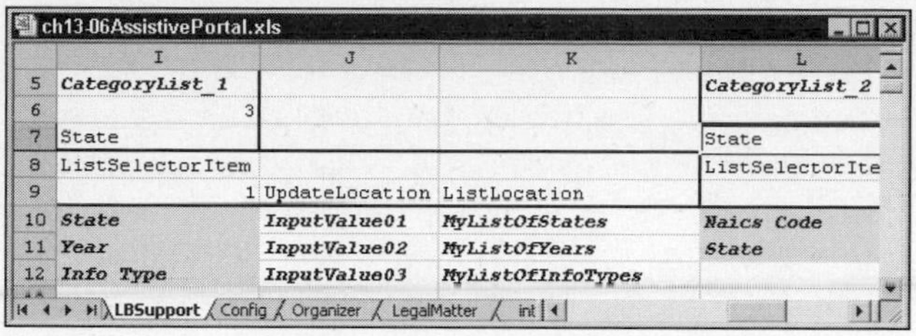

Figure 13-23: The CategoryList structure specifies the list of items that will appear in the UserForm and the values it will set (and correspond to the Config update parameters).

The list that contains items such as MyListOfStates has to be provided from somewhere. Rather than make it a static list, why not make it retrievable from the remote worksheet? This is handled in the left part of the List Box Support worksheet LBSupport (see Figure 13-24). To populate these lists, you need only to provide the names of the lists you want. Note that on this worksheet, the items you would manually type appear in **BoldfaceItalics**.

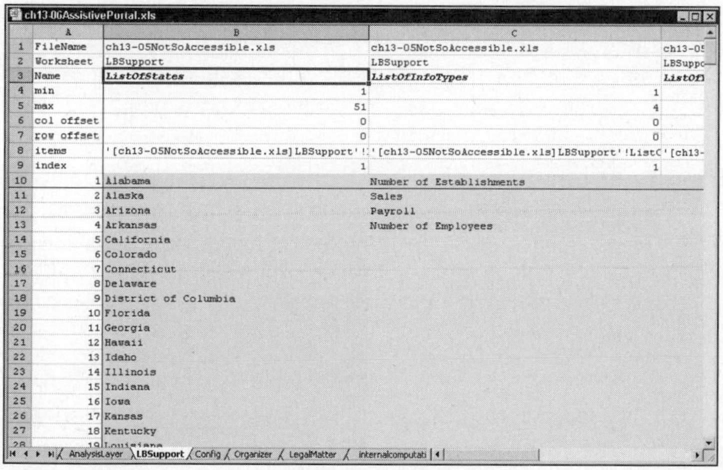

Figure 13-24: You need only to identify the name of the list to retrieve the complete list from the remote spreadsheet.

Row 8 of Figure 13-24 provides the full name needed to retrieve the list of items. The full name needs to specify the remote workbook filename as well as the worksheet it is found in. You could enter the worksheet name manually, but doing so is not necessary. Instead, Excel looks it up using a tool provided in the Organizer worksheet (see Figure 13-25).

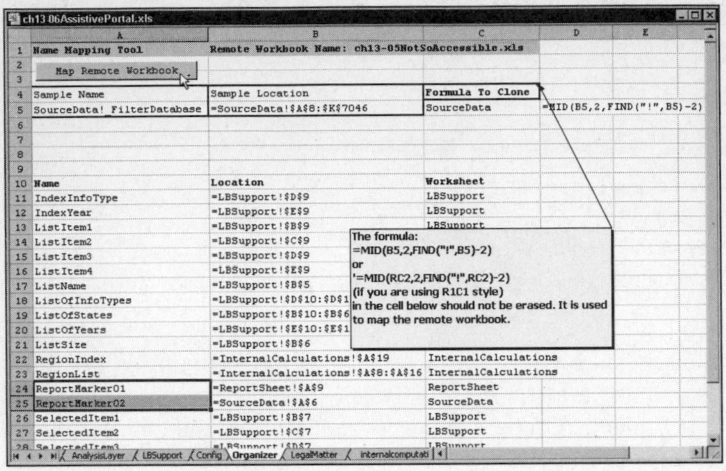

Figure 13-25: The Name Mapping Tool retrieves information about all defined names in the remote workbook.

To run the tool, first make sure that you entered the specific filename for the `RemoteWorkBookName` in the Config worksheet; then run the mapping tool by clicking the Map Remote Workbook button of the Organizer worksheet (alternatively, you can press Alt+F8 and run the `GetRemoteWorkbookNameInfo` macro).

> **NOTE** When you take this Assistive Portal template and set it to retrieve data from another workbook, remember to run this mapping tool. Also, as you define new names/markers on the remote workbook, remember to re-run this mapping tool.

I want to call your attention to two names highlighted and appearing near the bottom of Figure 13-25. These are `ReportMarker01` and `ReportMarker02`. These names have a special significance in relation to the remote workbook. Can you guess what purpose they serve? Go to `A9` on the ReportSheet and `A6` on the SourceData sheet of ch13-05NotSoAccessible.xls. Then take a look at the top-left corners of the bordered areas of the corresponding worksheets in the Assistive Portal pages.

Just as the lists in the LBSupport worksheet need a fully qualified name for an item in the remote workbook, so does the Portal Page, which will display a block of data from the remote workbook. Your spreadsheet constructs the full name and uses it in its computations (see Figure 13-26).

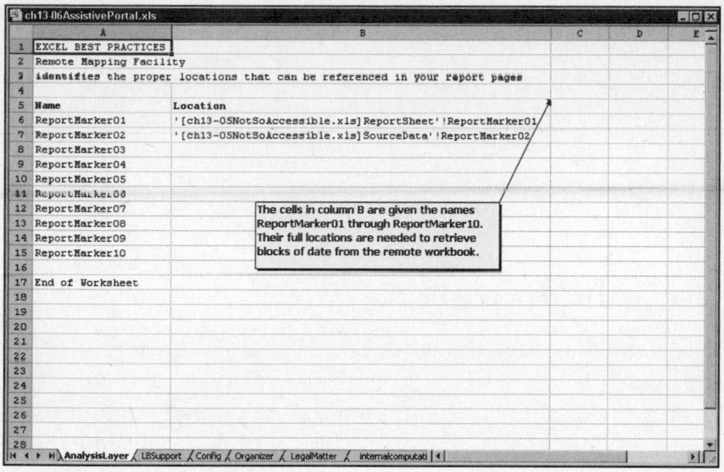

Figure 13-26: Fully qualified names that appear in the Portal Pages are specified in the AnalysisLayer worksheet.

In this example, only two blocks of data that feed into the Portal Pages have been defined. One of these is for the interactive ReportSheet and the other is for the SourceData. The way you specify retrieving data is as follows:

◆ Identify the top-left corner of a location on your remote workbook where you would like to bring over a block of data. On the remote workbook, give it a name in the range ReportMarker01 through ReportMarker10. The defined named range need refer only to a single cell.

◆ On your (local) Assistive Portal page, select a range of cells that corresponds to the same number of rows and columns as the data you want to transfer from the remote spreadsheet. To help distinguish this region, set an enclosing border around the selected cells. This will help to visually identify the region.

◆ For this selected region of cells, define a named range. A good name to use would be ReportRegionXX, for which you would substitute digits that correspond to the ReportMarkerXX on the remote worksheet. For example, if you designated a location on the remote worksheet called ReportMarker03 (which is the top-left of a group of cells spanning three rows by four columns), then you would select a region on your Portal Page extending three rows by four columns and define a named range called ReportRegion03.

- On your Portal Page for all of `ReportRegion03`, you would use formulas like the following:

  ```
  =OFFSET(INDIRECT(ReportMarker03),ROW()-
  ROW(ReportRegion03),COLUMN()-COLUMN(ReportRegion03),1,1)
  ```

  Of course, you would adjust the two-digit suffixes to match them up with one another.

Time to shift into high gear

You've come full circle in walking through the Assistive Portal design and revising it for your own needs. Was it worth it to go through the effort of modifying the Assistive Portal and leaving your original remote spreadsheet virtually untouched? Before you answer that question, you may want to take a peek at an industrial-strength Assistive Portal application.

This example is taken from Chapter 5, "Scaling the Peaks of Mt. Data." It is a good example of a large and complex spreadsheet, and is particularly useful here because the original spreadsheet was prepared with absolutely no preconception that an Assistive Portal would be later involved.

THE ORIGINAL SPREADSHEET

Those of you who read through Chapter 5 and are versed in the art of data slogging will appreciate that you won't have to do it all over again. Open the file called ch13-07OrignalSpreadsheet.xls (see Figure 13-27). The source data on this file contains 7,038 rows by 11 columns of raw data – nearly 75,000 points of data. It takes up almost 2MB of disk space. By comparison, the Assistive Portal is less than 230KB in size.

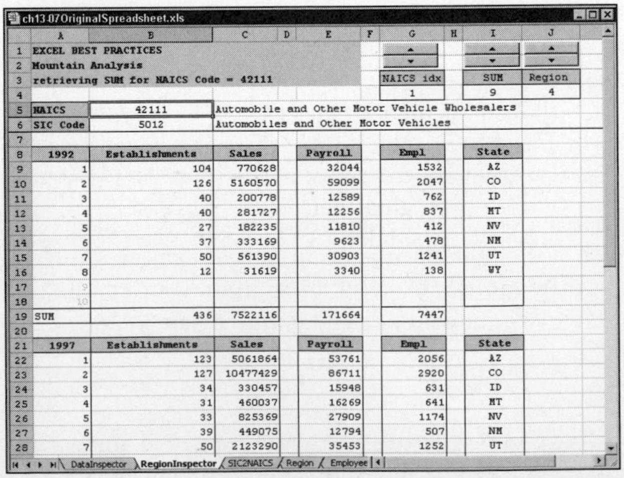

	A	B	C	D	E	F	G	H	I	J
1	EXCEL BEST PRACTICES									
2	Mountain Analysis									
3	retrieving SUM for NAICS Code = 42111						NAICS idx		SUM	Region
4							1		9	4
5	NAICS	42111	Automobile and Other Motor Vehicle Wholesalers							
6	SIC Code	5012	Automobiles and Other Motor Vehicles							
7										
8	1992	Establishments	Sales		Payroll		Empl		State	
9	1	104	770628		32044		1532		AZ	
10	2	126	5160570		59099		2047		CO	
11	3	40	200778		12589		762		ID	
12	4	40	281727		12256		837		MT	
13	5	27	182235		11810		412		NV	
14	6	37	333169		9623		478		NM	
15	7	50	561390		30903		1241		UT	
16	8	12	31619		3340		138		WY	
17	9									
18	10									
19	SUM	436	7522116		171664		7447			
20										
21	1997	Establishments	Sales		Payroll		Empl		State	
22	1	123	5061864		53761		2056		AZ	
23	2	127	10477429		86711		2920		CO	
24	3	34	330457		15948		631		ID	
25	4	31	460037		16269		641		MT	
26	5	33	825369		27909		1174		NV	
27	6	39	449075		12794		507		NM	
28	7	50	2123290		35453		1252		UT	

Figure 13-27: One of the nonaccessible worksheets from a large and complex spreadsheet

Figure 13-28 shows an Assistive Portal page of the same content displayed in Figure 13-27 and an equally capable interface.

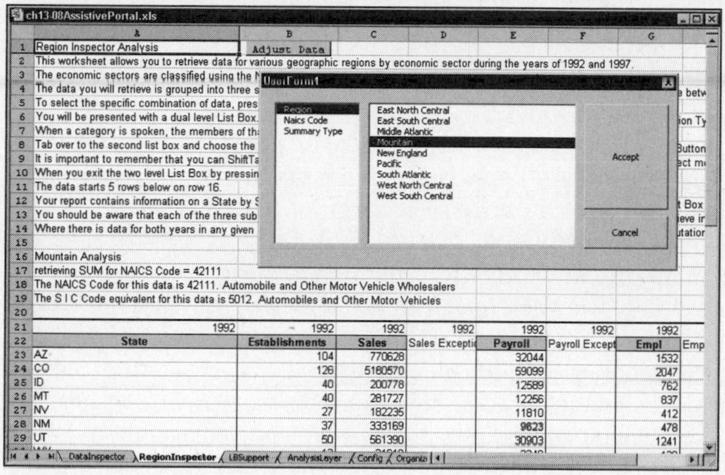

Figure 13-28: The screen reader–friendly version of the Assistive Portal, along with the interface controls, is fully equivalent to the nonaccessible version of Figure 13-27.

It looks as though all the data is on the Assistive Portal. The spreadsheet works as though all the data resides within the Assistive Portal. However, all the source data resides on another spreadsheet. More important, the Assistive Portal is relying on the original spreadsheets to do all the tough computations and cull through the 75,000 data points to get the needed information and perform the numerical computations, such as compound annual growth rate. The Assistive Portal drives the queries, pushes data onto the remote spreadsheet, and then reads the results and puts them in a format that is suitable for a screen reader.

Some people may be tempted to think of the Assistive Portal as an over-glorified interface. It may be so. However, consider this: There are not many interfaces around that can, at the turn of a dime, be pointed to any remote data source, map its inputs and outputs, undertake two-way communication executing specific sets of instructions to perform updates whenever certain events fire, and above all, do all this without performing surgery on the original data source and analysis tool and or writing even a single line of macro code. I don't know about you, but in my book that's pretty impressive.

Closing Thoughts

So what is it going to take for you to decide to press ahead and find some sane way to address these accessibility issues and develop a set of practices you feel comfortable living with? I can imagine that when you read this chapter; your reaction will place you into one of two camps:

◆ Those who think "I had no idea what would be in store. You've given me concrete thoughts and ideas. I now have a sense of what the next steps are. *I never thought there would be a streamlined and direct approach to making spreadsheets accessible.*"

◆ Those who think "I had no idea what would be in store. You've given me concrete thoughts and ideas. I now have a sense of what the next steps are. *I never thought that making spreadsheets accessible would be so difficult.*"

My guess is that more of you will fall into the latter category. In any case, it doesn't matter which of these two polar opposites you identify yourself with. You're wrong!

If you think that the approaches I presented all fit together nicely, think again. They are fraught with complexities at every step along the way. There's a substantial learning curve even if you concentrate and restrict yourself to one assistive technology such as screen readers. The disabilities and special needs generally don't neatly align themselves to well-defined accessibility solutions. The solutions need to adapt to people, and not the other way around. Even if you have the paradigm correct, the implementation is almost always harder to do well. Think about the mundane issues such as how you're going to package and send out your accessible spreadsheets. How are you going to go about user testing? Will your users correctly interpret the supplied documentation? Have you budgeted the time and resources to make sure your Help Desk department can properly field the incoming questions? When you try adapting the Assistive Portal, you may find that when you first start juggling all the different names, your juggling quickly turns into jumbling.

If you think that the approaches I presented are too difficult to successfully address, please reconsider. Remember, individuals with disabilities already have a tough time. Forget about physical access and challenges. Navigating and making meaningful use of spreadsheets can be challenging enough. For a user with blindness, just having the words or some kind of marker that signifies the end of the worksheet can be a major help. One of the practices introduced in the earlier chapters is to have the first three lines of the spreadsheet answer the questions WHO (identifies the company name), What (identifies the name of the report) and when/where (give some context or condition to further distinguish this spreadsheet from others). The last thing you want anyone in the world to do is to leave someone puzzled as to whether they have the right spreadsheet.

These small and simple steps go a long way to making spreadsheets and technology useful. The next step up the ladder is to become facile with the technology components such as screen readers. My goal was to make this kind of technology "accessible" to you. That's why I included all the hands-on setup of the screen reader. Many people are motivated and would take significant steps to learn about it but would not have any idea of where to start or how to go about getting their hands around this topic. I hope that giving you that handle will make it feasible for you to develop accessible spreadsheets that work.

I defined spreadsheets that work as being successful on two levels: one addressing the interface and navigation challenges, the other addressing the economic issues. I sought to remove both these challenges.

Appendix A

Excel Configuration and Setup

BUSINESS PEOPLE POSSESS a widely varying range of skills when it comes to using Excel and spreadsheets. The differentiating factor that separates people in the upper end of the spectrum from those in the lower end rarely has anything to do with intelligence. It more often relates with things such as:

◆ Having to work under pressure with little available time, reinforcing the tendency to adopt a "one-off" style (something that should be avoided).

◆ Continuing to use a spreadsheet in "auto-pilot" mode. We all know the adage "If it ain't broke, don't fix it." Well, this quickly gets people into auto-pilot mode and prevents them from delving deeper into what's going on behind the scenes in a spreadsheet. If the spreadsheet is being maintained in this "continue as you go" fashion, sooner or later it is bound to run aground.

◆ Sometimes, people continue using an out-of-date version of Excel or otherwise don't have their environment configured to best take advantage of what Excel has to offer.

It is principally this last category that I want to address here. Most of you should already have moved to or be thinking about moving to Excel 2003. *Excel Best Practices for Business* has been written with Excel 2003 in mind.

Backward Compatibility

If you already are using Excel 2003, that's great. However, some further configuring could help you immensely. A good many of you may be working with earlier versions of Excel. There are differences between Excel 2003 and its predecessors. With the exception of XML, these differences are not terribly significant as far as best practices are concerned.

This appendix presents configuration/setup information to provide guidance for both Excel 2003 and the earlier versions of Excel, with Excel 2003 as the assumed version. In situations where I am specifically aware of material deviations between Excel 2003 and its earlier versions, I highlight relevant info, where appropriate, using separate sidebars.

433

The spreadsheets supplied on the CD-ROM and examples used throughout the book have all been prepared with Excel 2003. Extensive XML support and client-based Web Services are entirely new and found only in Excel 2003. These features of XML and Web Services are discussed in Chapter 12.

I have tested the spreadsheets using Excel 2003 and Excel 2002. Except as indicated for the XML/Web Services–related material, the spreadsheets all work fine when using Excel 2002. Although testing has not been done for earlier versions of Excel, the spreadsheets that work when using Excel 2002 should also work equally well when using Excel 2000 and Excel 97. Table A-1 summarizes various features of Excel 2003 as presented in the book, along with its backward compatibility with several earlier versions of Excel.

TABLE A-1 SUMMARY OF CONFIGURATION INFO AND TREATMENT IN THE BOOK

Feature	Excel 2003	Excel 2002	Excel 2000	Excel 97
Spreadsheets and examples using XML/Web Services (Ch 12)	Tested	N/A	N/A	N/A
All other spreadsheets and examples	Tested	Tested	Should work fine	Should work fine
Excel menu layout	Covered in the book	Menus should be largely equivalent to 2003	Menus likely to be equivalent to 2003	Menus may be equivalent
Custom toolbars used throughout book	Covered in the book	Essential differences between Excel 2003 and 2002 pointed out	Not covered, but are likely to be similar to Excel 2002	Not covered
Custom toolbars in appendix	Covered in the book	Where appropriate, discussed in sidebars	Where appropriate, discussed in sidebars	Where appropriate, discussed in sidebars
Excel charting	Important techniques are covered in the book, but treatment is not comprehensive	Techniques related to charting for Excel 2003 are applicable to Excel 2002	Not covered, but are likely to be similar to Excel 2002	Not covered

Feature	Excel 2003	Excel 2002	Excel 2000	Excel 97
General Excel formulas	Covered in the book	Essential differences between Excel 2003, 2002 are pointed out	Not covered, but are likely to be similar to Excel 2002	Not covered, but are likely to be similar to Excel 2002
Special Purpose Excel Formulas	Covered in the book	Essential differences between Excel 2003 and 2002 are pointed out	Not covered	Not covered
Excel Macros and VBA	Discussed in Chapter 12 (XML related macros and VBA are specific of Excel 2003 and will not work with earlier versions of Excel) and 13	Discussed in Chapter 13	Not covered in the book	Not covered in the book

Configuring Excel

This appendix presents various steps that are to be followed for configuring Excel. Those of you who feel a greater degree of comfort with spreadsheets should breeze through this material. Pay particular attention to the setup of toolbars, font settings, and cell referencing. These settings will enable you to closely match the book examples without having to stop and configure Excel as you go along.

You will see "Take-Aways" liberally sprinkled throughout the book. To make your reading more enjoyable and productive, these Take-Aways are keyed to files on your CD-ROM so that you can directly copy and paste these portions into your spreadsheet. The good news on these Take-Aways is that, even if you don't fully understand the formulas, you can generally copy and paste them and they should work. Some of these Take-Aways are whole spreadsheets that you can use directly (you'll only need to copy in your data and adjust a few of the titles).

Let's get on the same page

The key starting point to successfully work spreadsheets is for you to have full control from the very start. So, if you already have some spreadsheets open, close them and exit Excel. Don't worry, you'll get back to your own files soon enough.

So, fire up Excel from your menu.

Your screen should look something similar to Figure A-1.

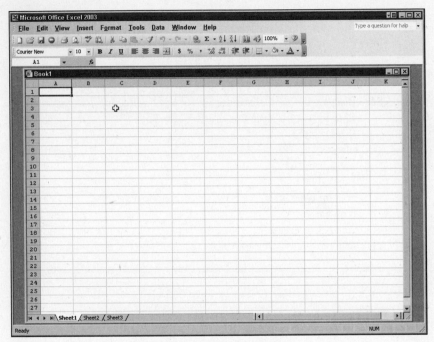

Figure A-1: Basic appearance of Excel when launched

If you start trying to work with spreadsheets without changing any of its default settings, you may quickly conclude that Excel has a mind of its own. Fortunately, this is something you can change.

Changing Additional Settings

Excel allows you to customize your spreadsheet settings. The basic way to adjust your Excel settings is to select Options from the Tools category of you Excel toolbar.

Taming your Office Assistant

Some of you might still be using an early version of Excel. If so, you may find the Paper Clip Office Assistant regularly appearing on your screen. If you would rather not have the Office Assistant appearing unless you summon it, you have two options:

◆ Upgrade your Excel to the current or very recent version (and I heartily recommend that you do).

◆ Follow the instructions in this sidebar (a stopgap measure till you upgrade Excel).

The reason I make a point about adjusting these and other settings is that one of the most important steps you can take to using spreadsheets more effectively is to put yourself in the driver's seat. This means that wherever Excel may have assumed specific settings or behaviors, you should have explicit control on what these settings are and how you want them set. (Be forewarned that some companies' and organizations' software application settings may be controlled from the network. In such situations, the software and application settings may not be permanently configurable from your machine. You may go ahead to change the software setting. Those settings will be retained while you are logged on. If those settings get wiped out the next time you log on, there's not much you can do. Your only real option is to contact your network or system administrator to allow you to make permanent changes to your application.)

Most people who start getting adept at using Excel don't need the animated assistant and find it to be in the way. This becomes a problem for people when they achieve a level of proficiency beyond the rank beginner. There is no obvious choice given to disable or alter the animated assistant. It's kind of like learning to ride a bicycle with training wheels. They remain attached although no longer needed.

So, if you want to tame or minimize the appearances made by your animated assistant, here is what you can do: Double-click your mouse on the Paper Clip and select the Options button when "Clippy" asks you what you would like to do.

You will be taken to a Dialog box that presents a Gallery and Options tab. Press the Gallery tab first (I'll go back to discuss the Options tab in a few moments). As expected you will see your familiar paper clip. Every time you press the button, a new animated figure will appear. Cycle through the figures till you get to the diamond-shaped assistant.

Apparently, at least in some versions of Excel, the different animated office assistants pop on to the screen with different degrees of frequency. The one that is most shy is supposed to be this diamond shaped jigsaw puzzle, which goes by the name of "Office Logo". So, when it does show up or is summoned, it will cause minimal disturbance. Press the OK button.

Continued

Taming your Office Assistant *(Continued)*

The next time you summon up the help wizard, it should appear as the Diamond Office Logo. Go ahead and select the Show the Office Assistant option. Now you will see the diamond logo. Double-click it and select the Options button.

The chances are that you already have many or most of the options checked or switched on. The chances are you will not want every one of them active.

If you look closely, you may notice that some of these have check marks that are partially grayed out and are not solid black. If you click the checkmark once, it will become solid black. If you click once more on the solid black checkmark, it will disappear entirely. Unless you really want to keep the animated assistant around, you can go ahead and remove all the check marks in the Options tab. Disable the Use the Office Assistant the last, as it will gray out all the other options and prevent you from changing the sub options.

Press the OK button, and you can wave bye-bye to the Office Assistant. The next time you start up Excel, you won't find the Paper Clip rushing to greet you. Remember, you will always be free to call the help assistant from the Help menu.

Unless you already have a spreadsheet open, the Options in the Tools menu will be grayed out. You get around this by opening an existing Excel spreadsheet or creating a new one from the File menu. You must have an open spreadsheet to change the options, but the changes you make to the settings apply to all spreadsheets you create — they're not specific to the ones that happen to be open at the time you change the settings. More will be said about opening files. Right now, just open any spreadsheet, even if it is just a blank workbook.

In the Tools menu, select Options (Figure A-2).

When you are presented with the various options, you will notice there are many tabs to press. For the moment, just focus on specific settings associated with the General tab. With the exception of the User Name and Default file location, match up the settings to those shown in Figure A-3.

The user name is kind of obvious. Some of you may be working for large corporations. Sometimes these corporations place the company name or department in the user name setting. In such a case, your employer might have a specific reason why the User Name is set the way it is. It is up to you to determine whether or not you want to change this.

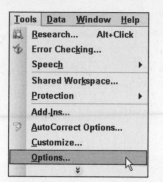

Figure A-2: Select Options from the Excel Tools menu.

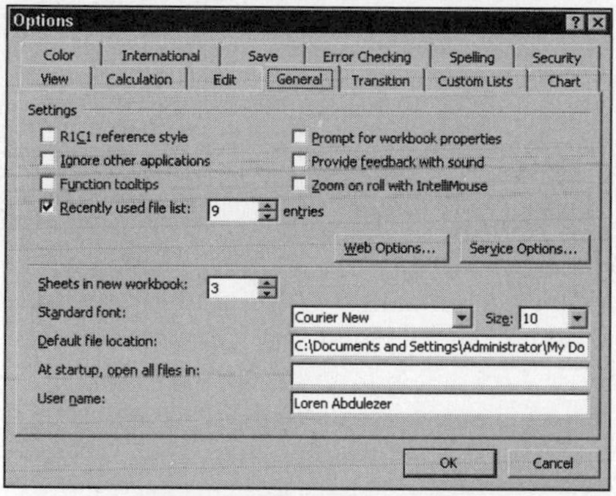

Figure A-3: General options

Next up on the list is the location where you'd like to place files to be automatically launched whenever Excel starts up. Unless you have a specific need to have certain spreadsheets open every time you start Excel, you will not need to utilize this feature.

> **TIP** Keep in mind that these start-up files will only open on *your* computer. So, if you email these spreadsheets to a friend or colleague, they will not automatically open up when Excel is launched on your colleague's computer. Your colleague will have to double-click each of the files from their Windows Explorer or choose to open each one from their e-mail program.

It will be good to remember this auto-launch feature and keep it in your hip pocket. One day you might be called upon to give a presentation. You may find it convenient to place the spreadsheets you want to show in specific folder in your laptop and launch them automatically (You might, for example, have 15 or 20 separate data files and one presentation spreadsheet that summarizes the results from all of them, in which case, you certainly wouldn't want to open them up one at a time during your presentation.).

Fonts

A font is the term that is used to describe the type style of how your text appears when it is displayed on the computer screen and printed. Your text can be used so that it would look like came from a traditional typewriter. Text appearing with this type of font is called monospaced. Letters shown in monospace fonts use the same character width regardless of which letters or punctuation marks appear. An example of a monospace font is `Courier`.

Non-monospace fonts use different character widths based on each character or punctuation mark. An example o f a non-monospace font is Arial.

When Excel is first installed on your computer, the default font that is generally installed is Arial. Probably, those of you who have been working with spreadsheets for some time have gotten used to it and may not see anything wrong with it. Indeed, the choice of which font you pick is just a presentation preference, right? Well, note quite. There are some good reasons for wanting to select a monospace font such as `Courier` or `Courier New`. Some of these reasons are outlined below.

Suppose you are getting data from a third party source, that is, data that's not necessarily originating from your spreadsheet. You might have a list of words or labels that's supposed to be, say, eleven letters long, immediately followed by a three digit number. Figure A-4 shows how they would appear if displayed using a monospaced font such as `Courier` or `Courier New` and how the same words/numbers would appear in a font that is not monospaced, such as Arial.

	1
1	**Monospace Font**
2	`Mississippi 100`
3	`MISSISSIPPI 123`
4	`jijjijjjijj 456`
5	`JijjIjjJIjj 789`
6	
7	**Arial Font**
8	Mississippi 100
9	MISSISSIPPI 123
10	jijjijjjijj 456
11	JijjIjjJIjj 789

Figure A-4: Monospace fonts line up evenly; non-monospace fonts do not.

Notice that the monospace font lines up exactly. This is because they all have the same number of characters and the width for each character is uniform. The same words and numbers appearing in a non-monospace font don't exactly line up. It is almost as if the letters and numbers are drunken!

The spreadsheet shown In Figure A-4 appears in the spreadsheet called: ch00-01fontcompare.xls

So, imagine that you are preparing a report that you are sending to an Executive Vice President in your company. The chances are, you are preparing it under a deadline. You've worked hard to get everything to line up in your report. At the eleventh hour, you find that the corporate guidelines for presentations state that the company name is supposed to appear in uppercase letters. If you had done everything in a monospace font, you wouldn't have to worry about playing around with the format, especially, when you're under pressure. If you had been working with a non-monospace font, you might have some additional formatting adjustments after changing the company name to uppercase.

Aside from the formatting of your reports, you may find that at times you might have to import data, such as government published tables or log files obtained from a server whose data you have to analyze. In such cases, working with a monospace font is a good practice.

Monospace fonts tend to be easier on the eyes when looking at large amounts of data. So why not get it right from the beginning?

The spreadsheet font that is generally used throughout this book is Courier New. Feel free to pick whatever font you prefer, though the examples will be easier to follow if you match your default font options to Courier New with size 10.

Settings for creating new worksheets

When you create or work with an Excel spreadsheet, you are given the freedom to organize and split your work into multiple sheets. This affords a great deal of flexibility. In this book, you will see many uses of how multiple sheets work together.

The default setting that is supplied by Excel for creating new spreadsheets is three sheets. Three or four sheets is a good value to adopt for your setting. So when you select a new workbook from the File menu, you will get a spreadsheet that has several tabs on the bottom of the spreadsheet.

You can change the names on the tabs by double-clicking it. Then you can type in a descriptive name. For instance, you could name the first sheet Summary and the second one Details.

Recently Used File List

This is a simple change. When Excel is first installed, it will remember the last four documents you have worked on. Although it is good to have easy recall to the last four, why not, while we're at it, increase it? Excel allows you to increase the setting so that it can remember nine. Go ahead and do so (you can either directly type in the number 9 in place of where the 4 appears or you can continually click the up arrow, which is situated between the number on the left side and the word *entries* on the right side).

REFERENCE STYLE

No doubt some of you will find all this instruction thorough, comprehensive and a little too detailed. This has been done so every one can get on the same page. This topic I am about to cover is extremely important, so please follow this carefully. There is more detailed information in Chapter 1.

Historically, Excel has provided for two different ways of representing formulas. Excel is a product that succeeded Multiplan, an earlier spreadsheet application program. Multiplan referenced formulas using their row and column numbers. For instance, the cell appearing on the top-left corner of a spreadsheet is, logically enough, on the first row and first column. So, this cell would be referred to as R1C1 (see Figure A-5).

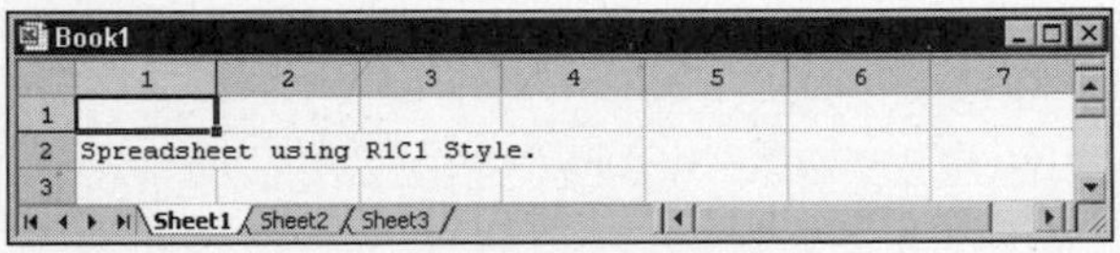

Figure A-5: Spreadsheet using R1C1 Style

A chief competitor of MultiPlan was Lotus123. This product was originally positioned to compete against VisiCalc. In the early spreadsheet wars, Lotus123 successfully captured market share. Like VisiCalc, Lotus123 referenced spreadsheet cell columns using letters instead of numbers. So, in Lotus123, the top-left cell in a spreadsheet would be referred to as A1 (Figure A-6).

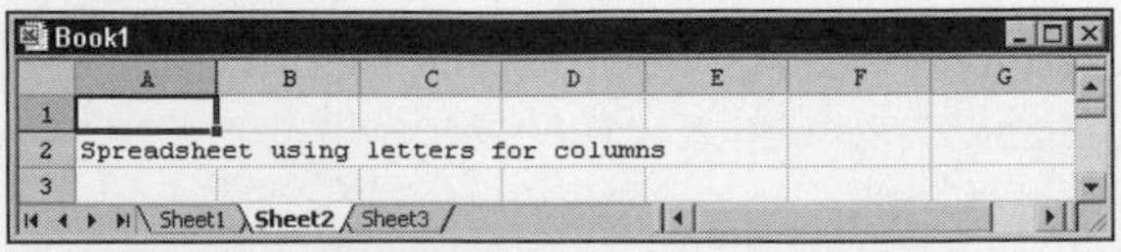

Figure A-6: Spreadsheet using letters for columns

In creating Excel, Microsoft realized the logical appeal of using the Multiplan style of row and column numbers to represent spreadsheet cells and formulas. However, they didn't want to alienate the broad community of users who had been weaned on the Lotus/VisiCalc style for representing rows and columns differently. Microsoft correctly combines both of these and gives you the option to choose which way you want to view your formulas and cell references.

The reason why Microsoft was able to seamlessly combine both formats is because it totally divorces the internal representation of data, cell references and formulas used in its computations from the visual presentation of the cells and formulas. So, at the flick of a switch, you can go back and forth between one style and the other.

Truly this is a win-win situation for you, as you have the choice of representing cells either way and pay no price for switching as often as you please. It also forces a bit of a dilemma (especially, upon the part of the author).

This book is heavily rooted in technique. In particular, the focus in on techniques that allow you to break through the barriers that normally stymies "the rest of us." There are persuasive arguments that can be made for either case of using the row/column number approach or using letter columns/row number approaches.

After much deliberation (and believe me, I wrestled *very* hard with this), the decision was made to favor the approach which will improve your technique. For reasons that will become evident (see the sidebar in Chapter 1), working with row and column numbers (rather than column letters) is vastly more logical and will make replication of your formulas simpler. So go ahead and check the box for R1C1.

One of the approaches I considered was to display both styles for every formula. However, this quickly gets unwieldy, adds considerable bulk to the book, and obscures clarity of thought and presentation. Remember, you always have the option to switch back and forth any time you want. The Take-Away (Figure A-8) provided on the CD-ROM (file ch00-02switchtool.xls) makes this particularly easy.

 If your security settings are set at too high a level you may get a warning. You can adjust your security settings by selecting the Security tab of Excel Option. Click on the Macro Security button and select a lower security level like Medium (I DON'T recommend you set it to Low).

At this point, I've gone through the General Options settings. Once again, the settings should closely match Figure A-7.

Press the OK button.

Because you're changing the standard font, you will get a warning message stating that the font change will take effect only after you quit and restart Excel. Go ahead and do so.

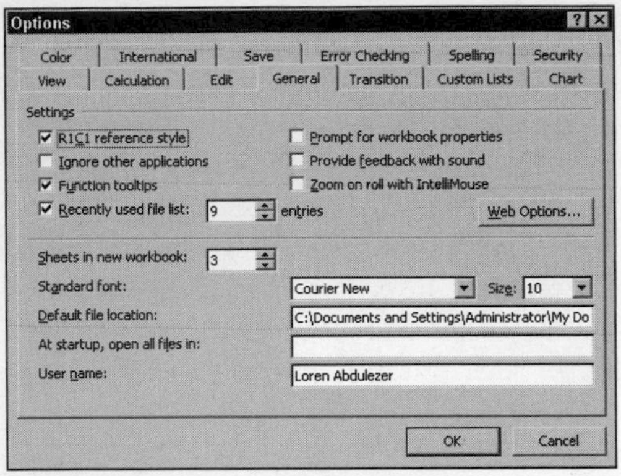

Figure A-7: General Options settings

ON THE CD

Open the spreadsheet supplied on your CD-ROM called ch00-02switch-tool.xls (see Figure A-8). In it you will find two buttons. One says to switch to A1 style and the other says to switch to the R1C1 style. Now going back and forth is as easy as pressing a button!

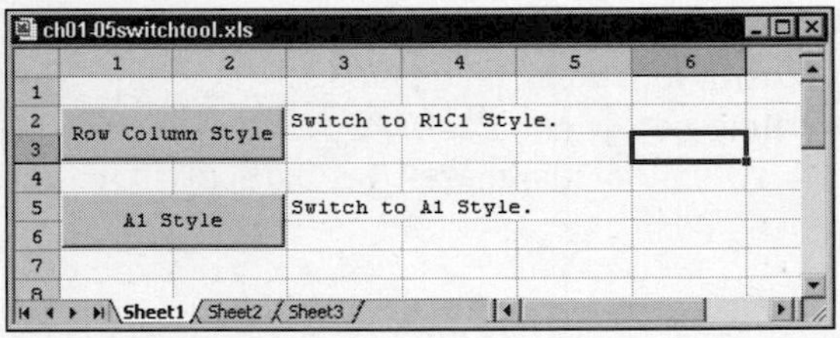

Figure A-8: Take-Away Switch Tool for easy change between referencing modes

SUPPRESSING THE KNEE-JERK REACTION OF EXCEL

Often while you're entering words and text of your choosing in a spreadsheet, Excel may attempt to replace the text as you type with what it thinks ought to be the correct spelling, punctuation or character substitution.

Excel may do things like capitalize the first letter of any day of the week quite literally as you are typing the word. But suppose you wanted to create a spreadsheet where some of the days of the week are shown in uppercase and others are completely lowercase? With the auto-correct feature enabled, you might find this significantly challenging. Certainly, this can be annoying.

Rework some of these items so that you can specifically control when and where such knee-jerk reactions kick in.

Once again, look under the Tools menu for the AutoCorrect Options. You will see a dialog box similar to that shown in Figure A-9.

Figure A–9: AutoCorrect options

The obvious difference between the one displayed Figure A-9 and the one you have on your computer is that probably many, if not all of the AutoCorrect features on your computer may be enabled (that is, checked). Go ahead and uncheck the ones you do not want (especially, the "Replace text as you type" feature).

 Start with maximum controls or restrictions and, bit by bit, loosen the reins.

Excel will also attempt to copy and extend cell formatting and auto-replicate formulas as you are entering them into new cells on the spreadsheet. If you really want control and don't want Excel to decide what you want, you can go ahead and disable this feature. Here is how to do it.

Go to the Tools menu for Options. Select the Edit Tab and make sure that nothing is checked in the box to the immediate left of the extended list formats and formulas.

While you're at it, match up the settings in your Options Edit tab with those shown in Figure A-10.

Unless otherwise specified, auto-correct features will not be turned on for the examples used in this book. Feel free to reintroduce some of these features in a controlled manner after being satisfied that specific sets of features are needed (for example, the Web enablement of spreadsheets).

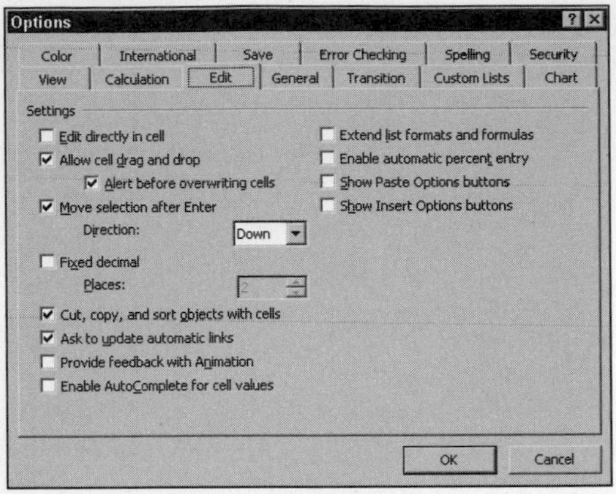

Figure A-10: Options Edit settings

TOOLBARS

At this point I would like you to define some custom toolbars of your own. Ultimately, the ones you select are of your own choosing. Just keep in mind that you'll quickly run out of screen space if you select too many toolbars. I show you some useful ones you may want to keep as part of your standard arsenal. Most of these will get a good workout in the book. I also tell you about others you may want to know exist and, where possible, give you some useful tips. For every toolbar icon I tell you about, there's probably another ten or so additional icons I could be describing. My intention is just to get you off to a good start.

If you have never customized your toolbars, then they may appear similar to Figure A-11.

Figure A-11: Excel Default Settings

You can add to the existing slate of toolbars on your screen. Actually, I would like you to construct your own custom group. First, go to the Excel menu and select Customize. Notice the three tabs running across the top of your Customize window. Make sure that the Toolbars tab is the frontmost tab showing. If it's not, click it. When you see the checklist of predefined toolbars, press the New button to create your own custom toolbar (Figure A-12).

The name can be any descriptive name of your choosing. For now, you can call it Group1. I use the Group1 toolbar that's set up here throughout the book. You are free to create additional groups. You can also mix and match icons among the different groups.

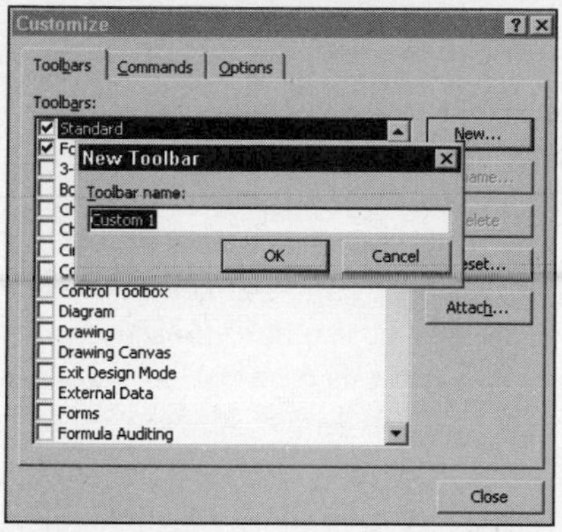

Figure A-12: Give your custom toolbar a name.

Click the Commands tab. You will notice a variety of Categories, including File, Edit, View, and so forth. Click the Edit category. To the right of the Categories are the various commands. Scroll down on the right till you see Paste Formatting (see Figure A-13). Click to select this.

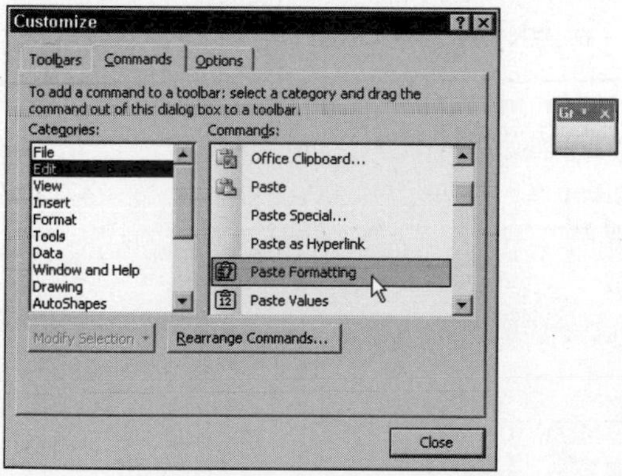

Figure A-13: Select a toolbar icon to add to your custom group.

To add the feature to your Toolbar, simply click the feature you desire to add. Notice that when you press the mouse button down, the arrow pointer will display a small box with an plus sign (+) in it. While you have your mouse button pressed down, drag the icon onto into your empty Group1 Toolbar. When you drag the icon on to the Group1 Toolbar, two things will happen:

1. The + changes to an *x*.

2. A vertical insertion point indicates where the icon will be positioned.

When you release the mouse button inside the Group1 toolbar, you will see the icon deposited there.

For the Edit Category, add the toolbar commands for Paste Values and Clear Formatting. You may have noticed that in addition to Clear Formatting, there is a feature for Clear Contents. Although you could also add this icon to your Toolbar, it won't really benefit you to do so, because you can clear the contents of any cells on the spreadsheet that happen to be selected just pressing by the Del key.

Feel free to experiment and try adding any variety of command icons to your Toolbar that you wish. Whatever helps you to be productive is great. Also keep in mind that unless you have a super-gigantic screen, the real estate space on your computer display can be a precious commodity. After you've had a chance to experiment with the different toolbar icons, pick the ones that are most useful to you (that is, the ones you will use on a regular basis).

To get off to a good start and have in place the icons that will be used throughout the book, add the following to your Toolbar:

- ◆ From the View Category: Zoom In and Zoom Out

- ◆ From the Insert Category: Diagram...

- ◆ From the Format Category: Light Shading

- ◆ From the Tools Category: Trace Precedents, Trace Dependents, Remove All Arrows

- ◆ From the Data Category: Text To Columns

- ◆ From Window and Help: Freeze Panes

- ◆ From the Forms Category: Check box, Button, Combo Box and Spinner

Your Group1 Toolbar should now appear similar to Figure A-14.

Figure A-14: Group1 custom toolbar

There are "space saving" icons that combine the benefits of several toolbar icons. The Diagram icon is one. Icons and menu options that have the ellipsis (...) following them often have this feature. When you click the Diagram icon, you will be able to choose among Cycle diagrams, Radial diagrams, Pyramid diagrams and so forth. Unless you have a specific favorite and use it constantly, you won't really need all the different options in your custom toolbar.

There are times when you will want specific toolbar icons even though you can access the facility through one of the space-saving icons. The Paste Values and Paste Formatting is one such icon. Being able to paste pure values that are devoid of formulas and formatting information is an important feature to have. Likewise, being able to paste formats will facilitate your ability to manage spreadsheet information.

Some of you who are already used to using the Format Painter may be wondering, "Why bother at all with the Paste Formatting when I have the Format Painter?" The Format Painter just clones the format of a selected region of cells at a new location. If, in addition to formatting, you also want to paste the values, then you'll need to do more than just use the Format Painter. You'll have to go back to your original selection of cells and then copy and paste the values. This adds to the number of steps you need to perform and will slow you down. Actually, this issue relates to the discussion of Presentation Tear Sheets in Chapter 6. If you feel tightly wedded to the Format Painter, do not fret. Continue using what you're already adept at. Old habits die hard. Some of them are important to keep. Others should be shed. Ultimately, you're the best person to make that call.

Keep in mind that all of the facilities of these toolbars are generally accessible through the Excel menus.

The Freeze Pane is useful because of how it solves the problem with the Split Pane feature (perhaps better named the "Split Pain" feature, in my opinion). Heavy spreadsheet users in the business world repeatedly neglect to use the Freeze Pane feature (Figure A-15) when they split their screens. Once they know about it, people just love this feature. Use the Freeze Pane icon to have the ability to quickly switch back and forth (Figure A-16).

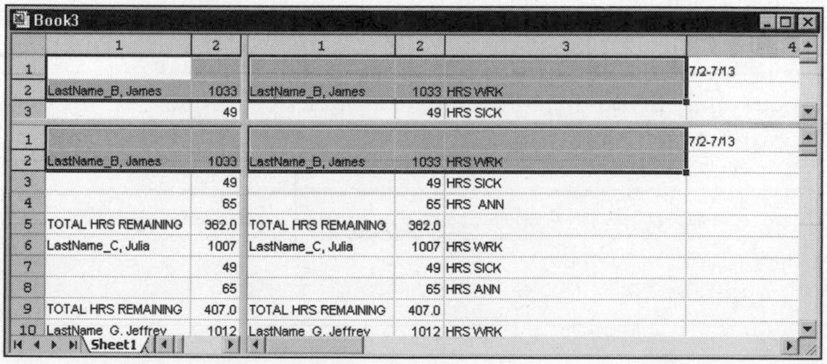

Figure A-15: Confusing use of Split Pane

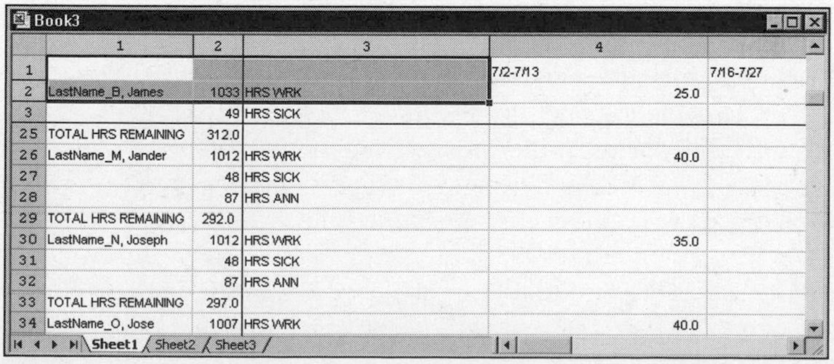

Figure A-16: After you click the Freeze Pane icon, the confusing split pane is gone and the spreadsheet scrolls naturally with a split screen.

BUT WAIT, THERE'S MORE!

Text to Column is a feature that is particularly handy if you're going to be working with data files that's provided from third-party sources, such as government-published information pulled off the Internet. You will see this feature put to use in Chapter 4, "Compiling, Managing, and Viewing Your Data."

Do not confuse the Forms category with the Control Toolbox category. They both have similar icons and is explained in greater detail in Chapter 12, Assistive Technologies and Assistive Portals. The Check box, Button, Combo Box, and Spinner icons should all come from the Forms category (Figure A-17).

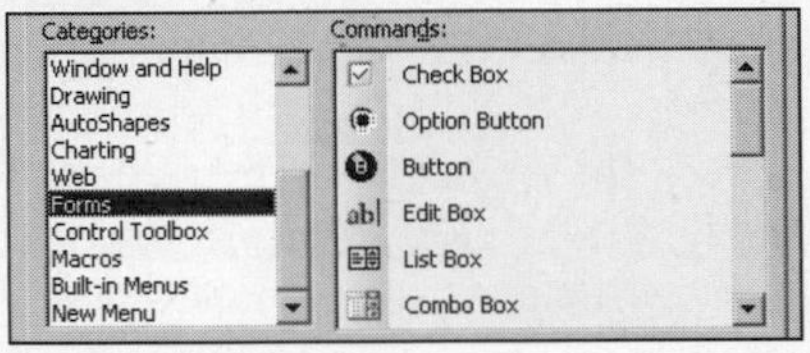

Figure A-17: Select from the Forms category.

Here's the last bit of configuration and I'll be done with toolbars. Right now, your Group1 Toolbar (refer to Figure A-14) is floating somewhere on your screen, because I haven't told you to anchor it to the standard Excel toolbars. Just click the Group1 Toolbar anywhere on the title bar and the mouse point will take on a compass-like appearance. Holding the mouse button down, drag the toolbar over to the other toolbars and the Group1 Toolbar will snap into place (Figure A-18).

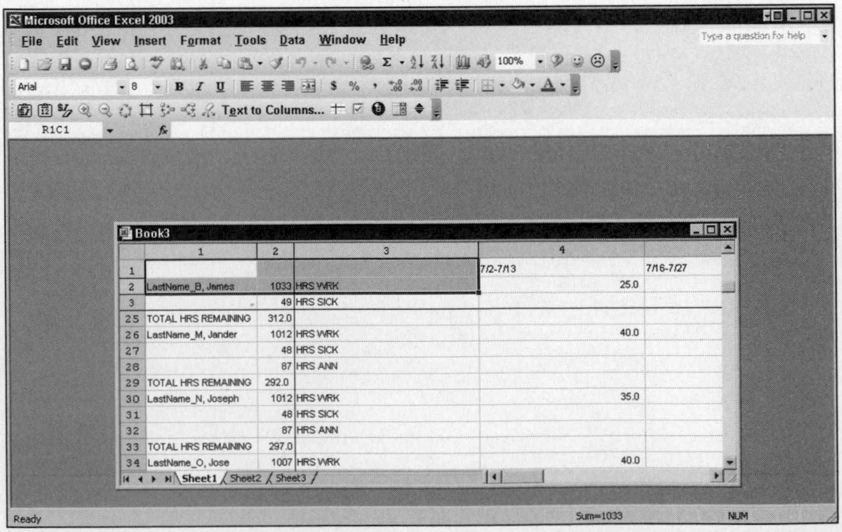

Figure A-18: Three rows of toolbars

Notice that the toolbars take up three rows and there's a fair amount of empty space. Unless you're using a really large screen, you may want to consolidate all the toolbars into two rows. They can be shoved on to the second row, but there is not quite enough space to simultaneously display all of them on a straight horizontal line.

I don't know about you, but I don't particularly like the idea of using second-class icons. If they're out of sight, they're out of mind. Also, what's the purpose of having hidden icons when you already have their underlying capabilities in the Excel menus?

My first way of fixing this is to effectively remove the icons I don't expect to be using. There are roughly about eight of the formatting icons in the second row of toolbars that I haven't used very much in the book (Figure A-19).

Figure A-19: Group of Icons in the Formatting
toolbar that are not used often in this book

There are a number of strategies. You can keep the Group1 Toolbar at its full length and try resizing the formatting toolbar on its left to be a shorter width. This will relegate some of the Formatting Icons to 2nd class. Somehow this is not so palatable.

You could whisk away some of the icons to never-never land dragging and dropping them to the desktop area. By doing so, you would be modifying an Excel standard feature, which I'm not sure you would want to do.

There's another way that's quite safe. Construct a new toolbar called Formatting2 (or whatever name you want to give it). Add to this toolbar the formatting facilities you need and exclude the rest. In the Customize Options menu, deselect the Formatting Toolbar and check the newly created Formatting2 toolbar. Now there are no second-class icons and they all fit on two rows.

Nothing forces you to keep toolbars at the top of the spreadsheet. Aside from having them hover somewhere around, you can park them off to the side.

Configuring Excel Menu Options

You may have noticed at the bottom of the pull-down menus that a vertical double arrow appears (see Figure A-20). If you wait a few moments and move your mouse over the double arrow or click it, the menu will expand to its full size with all its options listed. This is an example of Excel trying to give you the best of all possible worlds. First, Excel presents you with a list of menu options it thinks you're likely to use. If, after some delay, you haven't yet selected an item from its standard list, then it enlarges the list, giving you more options. This goal, although admirable, may fail to be useful for people who do repeated work with Excel.

Figure A-20: Abbreviated menu with double arrow

First off, when you're looking for an item of a given menu, you have to think about whether the item you want lives on the short list or on the expanded list. So now you are thinking about two similar lists instead of one.

Unless you specifically know that the item on the menu resides on the expanded list, you might find yourself pausing a moment or two just to let the list expand. So now you need two mouse clicks on the menu instead of one. This leads to more active menu navigation. All this slows you down.

Okay, the next time you go the menu, you expect to find that item only in the expanded menu. Think again. Excel has now added it to the short list. So not only are you thinking about two lists (the short and expanded version), but the short one changes based on your usage patterns.

You already have enough to think about while constructing a spreadsheet with all its numbers and formulas. You don't need the distraction of these shifting menus!

Instead of using the "accordion style" menus, there are some good reasons to opt for full menus. The menu options are complete and unchanging. This will be easier to memorize as you only have to be thinking about one menu structure. You won't have to be bothering with so many mouse clicks and active navigation. You won't find yourself slowed down waiting for the menu to expand.

Now, are you convinced that you should use full menus?

To set up the option for full menus, here is what you do:

1. Select the Customize feature from the Tools menu.

   The Customize window with its three tabs appears.

2. Click the tab labeled Options.

3. The second check box, "Always show full menus," is not selected. Click its checkbox to make this option active.

4. Click the Close button to accept the changes you made.

Appendix B

Information for Macintosh Users

THE EXAMPLES AND ILLUSTRATIONS in *Excel Best Practices for Business* are all based on the Windows platform. With a few exceptions, however, the techniques and practices presented in *Excel Best Practices for Business* are equally applicable to the Macintosh platform. The differences you will encounter fall into the following categories:

◆ A different set of keystroke sequences are used to accomplish the appropriate set of tasks on the Macintosh.

◆ The directory naming convention on the Macintosh platform (both OS 9 and OS X) does not use backslashes or drive-letter names, which are normally associated with the Windows platform.

◆ Some of the menu options use a different terminology, and the appearance of some of the interface components on the Macintosh platform differs from Windows.

◆ The rendering of fonts on the Macintosh platform is slightly different, so you may need to adjust the column widths of some of the spreadsheets.

◆ You may find differences between the Windows and Macintosh platform when it comes to macros and VBA.

◆ At the time of this publication, Excel 2003 has not been released for the Macintosh platform. Accordingly, Excel 2003-specific features are not yet available.

From the standpoint of techniques and practices, most of these differences are cosmetic.

Keystroke differences

The principal change for Macintosh users is that most of the time when the Ctrl key is specified for the Windows platform, you will use the Command key, marked on your keyboard by a ⌘ or ⌘ symbol. When you see a reference to an Alt key, you use the Option key.

If there is a sequence of keystrokes which work on the Windows platform but doesn't work on the Macintosh, and one of the keys is the Ctrl key, here's what you do: Instead of using the Macintosh equivalent (the ⌘ key), try using the Ctrl key on your Macintosh keyboard. For example, if you want to remove or insert a worksheet, you must Ctrl+click the worksheet tab (⌘+click will not work).

DEFINING NAMES

To define a name, press ⌘+F3. To define a batch of names for cells whose labels are to the immediate left of them, select the labels and the cells and then press ⌘+Shift+F3.

RELATIVE, HYBRID, AND ABSOLUTE CELL REFERENCES

To cycle through relative, hybrid, and absolute cell references, press ⌘+T whenever the F4 key would be used on the Windows platform.

Excel menus on the Macintosh platform

The layout of menu options for the Macintosh platform differs from Windows, but mostly only in minor ways. For the most part, this should not give you too much trouble. There is one significant difference you should be aware of. On the Windows platform, the Options settings appear in the Tools menu. On the Macintosh platform, the equivalent settings are found under the label Preferences, not Options. The Preferences settings also appear in a different menu. For Mac OS 9, Preferences appears within the File menu. On OS X–based machines, Preferences appears within the application menu called Excel (which sits between the menu and the File menu).

Using the spreadsheets on the CD-ROM

The example spreadsheets for this book are meant to exemplify best practices and techniques. In this regard, the vast majority of spreadsheets provided on the CD-ROM for this book will work without modification on the Macintosh platform. There are some differences. I outline the principal ones here and provide some additional notes.

Please remember to load the Analysis ToolPak Add-In. The spreadsheets ch01-06random.xls and ch07-03SmartFormatExtend.xls both use the Excel function RANDBETWEEN. Also the Fourier Analysis facility is a part of the Analysis ToolPak. If the Analysis ToolPak is not loaded, you will not be able to run ch08-02FFT.xls.

Excel 2003 introduces some new functionality that specifically differs with older versions of Excel. In particular, the Excel function SUBTOTAL behaves differently. On the ReportSheet worksheet of ch06-01DatasetPackagingTool.xls, three formulas contain the SUBTOTAL function. These spreadsheet cells will display a #VALUE! error. This is because the first argument or input parameter supplied is in the range of 101 through 111. For example, the value 109 that signifies a SUM will not work on any version of Excel prior to Excel 2003. This is true regardless of whether you are using Windows or Macintosh. To correct this, change the value of "109" to "9" for any version of Excel prior to Excel 2003.

In Chapter 4, concerning the topic of PivotTables, you must use the same convention as that used on the Windows platform if you plan to define Grouped data. Specifically, you would use Ctrl+click, as directed in the chapter. Using ⌘+click will not work. At least on the versions of Excel that I have used on the Macintosh platform, the Pivot Refresh facility does not appear to be fully robust. Though data in the PivotTable is updated, group definitions are not. Your workaround is to ungroup the data and group again. Perhaps this has been fixed since Excel X for Mac Service Release 1.

The Interpretive Reconciliation Worksheet tool of Chapter 11 (ch11-03IRW.xls) uses List Boxes. Though these work correctly, the fonts rendered in a List Box may appear a little scrunched.

In Chapter 12, most of the spreadsheet files are dependent upon features that are exclusive to Excel 2003. As with users of Excel 2002 and earlier, on the Windows platform, you will not be able to put to use the Excel 2003-specific features.

Regarding the XML-RPC Server, I was successful in getting the server up and running. Doing so required a Java 1.4 or later Virtual Machine environment (earlier versions do not work with the JAR files provided on the CD-ROM). I tried testing the Ch12-05UddiSearch.xls file with the XML-RPC server. I encountered some difficulties and will be posting technical notes on my Web site at:

www.evolvingtech.com/excel

The screen reader software described in Chapter 13 (JAWS), as well as Window-Eyes, are Windows-only products and do not work with the Macintosh platform.

Excel Best Practices for Business on the Macintosh Platform

On an overall basis, the spreadsheet construction techniques, concepts relating to the layered approach, the specific tools, methodologies, and thinking that are needed in the business setting are independent of whether you are using Windows or Macintosh.

Perhaps when Microsoft releases Excel 2003 for the Macintosh platform, the Macintosh version will address the challenges and difficulties outlined here.

Appendix C

Excel Best Practice Techniques and Hip Pocket Tips

EXCEL BEST PRACTICES FOR BUSINESS is filled with a substantial amount of information. To make this information convenient and readily accessible, the top 150 best practice techniques and tips from this book are provided here (Table C-1). You can use this reference to quickly locate essential information you may need without having to search through the more detailed book index.

From time to time, be sure to check for updated information on my site: www.evolvingtech.com/excel

TABLE C-1 LIST OF EXCEL BEST PRACTICE TECHNIQUES AND HIP POCKET TIPS

No.	Best Practice Technique or "Hip Pocket" Tip	Ch	Section
1	Accessible (Excel) provided graphical components compatible with screen reader software	13	Interface for a List Box and a Button
2	Adjusting constraints and setup of an optimization problem to take into account real world conditions	8	Real-World Adjustments
3	Adjusting global and individual voice settings (and national language support)	13	Voice Settings
4	Advanced Filters: setup, multiple complex criteria, and usage of formulas within advanced filters	6	Advanced Filters
5	Anatomy of an Assistive Portal Interface	13	An Assistive Portal Implementation
6	Automatic smart borders	7	Perimeter Surveillance

Continued

457

TABLE C-1 LIST OF EXCEL BEST PRACTICE TECHNIQUES AND HIP POCKET TIPS
         (Continued)

No.	Best Practice Technique or "Hip Pocket" Tip	Ch	Section
7	Automatically picking up names of cells and constraints in the Answer Report of the Solver	8	The Answer Report
8	Automating the rearrangement of columnar data	6	They Threw In the Kitchen Sink
9	Basic design of the Assistive Portal Interface	13	Basic Implementation Steps
10	Basic setup of a "Forms" List Box	5	Setting Up A List Box
11	Basic step for setting up web based XML queries	12	XML in Excel 2003
12	Basic steps in performing spreadsheet makeovers	10	First steps in the makeover
13	Basics on Visual Basic	12	Some Visual Basic Syntax and Elementary Concepts
14	Block Sorting (& Scaffolding) Technique	3	Block-sorting
15	Bullet-proofing data entry	6	Bullet-proof your data entry
16	Catching potential errors caused by the Excel handle bar replication	11	Some observations for beginning your assessment
17	Caveat on the use of the Limits Report generated by the Solver	8	The Limits Report
18	Caveats on accessing and adjusting XML Maps	12	The All-In-One Worksheet
19	Caveats on creating and modifying JAWS verbosity settings (new file vs. best match vs. exact match)	13	Things You Need To Know About Settings
20	Common keyboard commands for JAWS and the Excel Application Software	13	Listing 13-1: Common JAWS Keystroke Commands (items in boldface are specific to Excel)
21	Comparing apples to oranges – a classic example	11	A partial checklist for discerning mistakes

No.	Best Practice Technique or "Hip Pocket" Tip	Ch	Section
22	Conditional Formatting: understanding the use of formulas vs. values when used in conditional formats	7	Rules of the road
23	Constructing a SOAP based UDDI4J API call in the XML-RPC Handler	CD	UddiSearchHandler.java
24	Constructing cell references on-the-fly	3	Using Indirect With Concatenate
25	Context switching: example (1) - spinner controls like an up/down arrow button (spinner control sets which dataset gets graphed in the existing chart)	5	Setting Up A List Box
26	Context switching: example (2) - spinner controls like an up/down arrow button (spinner control sets which part of a sequence or timeline gets analyzed and graphed in the existing chart)	8	The Analysis Layer
27	Context switching: example (3) - data feeds in a portal page (managed via an Organizer Map)	12	Simple Client Portals
28	Context switching: example (4) - dual list box	13	An Assistive Portal Implementation
29	Converting tabular data to SQL	3	Data Surgery and Data Manipulation
30	Creating a sequence of digits along a row or column based on the first two numbers	7	Automatic adjustment for a range of data
31	Creating chart titles and captions whose codes can be based on formula calculations in a spreadsheet cell	8	Usage Of Fourier Analysis In Excel And A Sample Spreadsheet Tool
32	Criteria for spotting a data mirage	9	Strategies for assessing whether you have a data mirage
33	Data Overpass: example (1)	4	Dataedit Worksheet
34	Data Overpass: example (2)	9	Square Peg/Round Hole Scenario
35	Defining a batch of user defined names in rapid succession	1	User-Defined Names within Excel Spreadsheets

Continued

TABLE C-1 LIST OF EXCEL BEST PRACTICE TECHNIQUES AND HIP POCKET TIPS
(Continued)

No.	Best Practice Technique or "Hip Pocket" Tip	Ch	Section
36	Defining JAWS custom spreadsheet regions	13	Defining Spreadsheet Regions
37	"Diff" comparison of two spreadsheets	9	The Swatch Comparison
38	Drill down to source data in a PivotTable	4	Pivot data drill-down
39	Essential macro code for opening a spreadsheet to a specific location (and providing for customization without macro recoding)	13	Listing 13-2: The following is placed in the code for 'ThisWorkbook' in the VBA Project for your workbook
40	Essential Web Services concepts explained	12	Web Services -- a simplified explanation
41	Event management technique for running a specific macro anytime a new entry is made in a spreadsheet cell (and reselecting the cell)	12	Fine-Tuning Your Software
42	Excel Lists and their role in rendering, accessing and manipulating XML in worksheets	12	Turning Your Map Elements Into Lists
43	Finding the JAWS configuration and settings files	13	Listing 13-1: Common JAWS Keystroke Commands (items in boldface are specific to Excel)
44	Formula for displaying current filename of a spreadsheet without full path info (and not using any macros)	CD	See the formula for: [ch13-06AssistivePortal. xla]Config'!ConfigThisFile
45	Formula Replication Techniques (Advanced)	5	Special Issues (And Their Resolution) In Replicating Formulas
46	Formula Replication Techniques (Basic)	1	Best Practice Topic: Evolving a strategy toward Absolute vs. Relative vs. Hybrid cell references

No.	Best Practice Technique or "Hip Pocket" Tip	Ch	Section
47	Functions for text manipulation: representative examples using LEFT, MID, RIGHT, REPT, REPLACE, SUBSTITUTE, LOWER, UPPER, PROPER, LEN, TRIM, CHAR, CODE, CLEAN, VALUE, TEXT	3	Some more functions for data manipulation
48	Goal Seek caveats	8	Some Things You Need To Be Aware Of
49	Guide for calculating, understanding, and using derivatives	8	A crash course on differential calculus
50	Guidelines for placing XML Lists in your spreadsheet	12	Step 4: Interaction with the Other Parts of Your Spreadsheet Application
51	Guidelines for print settings (1)	2	Step 6: Refining Your Spreadsheet's Appearance
52	Guidelines for print settings (2)	2	Excel Templates
53	Harnessing positional arrangements of information to manage data	10	The Recommended Approach
54	How to create a .xlt template	2	Excel Templates
55	How to have the programs in your Windows start menu sorted in alphabetical order (for easier navigation with JAWS)	13	Get Your Windows Start Menu In Order
56	Identifying and making explicit, hidden exceptions to the rule	10	Look For Weaknesses In The Formulas And Identify Ways To Correct For Them (located in two parts of the chapter)
57	Identifying and validating correctness in the formulas	10	Look For Weaknesses In The Formulas And Identify Ways To Correct For Them (located in two parts of the chapter)

Continued

TABLE C–1 LIST OF EXCEL BEST PRACTICE TECHNIQUES AND HIP POCKET TIPS
(Continued)

No.	Best Practice Technique or "Hip Pocket" Tip	Ch	Section
58	Identifying important computations	10	[Identify Obvious Portions Of The Spreadsheet That Are In Need Of Revision], and [Determine What Portions Of The Spreadsheets Have Formulas And What Portions Have Been Etched Out By Hand Or Are Otherwise Hardwired]
59	Implementing a dual-level List Box	13	Compound Interfaces
60	Important and subtle issues in using web based queries for importing XML and its Schema	12	Step 2: Tell the Spreadsheet Application How the Received Data is to be Structured
61	Important information about grouping data with PivotTables	4	Some Things You Should Know About Grouping Pivot Data
62	Important navigation design tips for accessible spreadsheets	13	Provide A Trail Of Bread Crumbs
63	Importing XML from a document on your hard drive	12	By the way . . .
64	Importing XML from a URL specified by a spreadsheet cell	12	Step 3: Interaction between Excel and the Remote Server
65	Increasing the precision of the Excel goal seeking facility	8	Squeezing Water From A Stone
66	In-lined (row) counting and "Anchor" Cells	7	SmartData Used with Anchor Cells
67	Installing a .xla file as an Excel Add-In	11	Installing the Data Audit tool
68	JAWS Frames	13	Other Techniques

No.	Best Practice Technique or "Hip Pocket" Tip	Ch	Section
69	JAWS Scripting	13	Other Techniques
70	JAWS verbosity settings	13	Defining Spreadsheet Regions
71	Keyboard command for silencing JAWS when it won't shut up	13	Preliminary JAWS Concepts: a training wheel approach
72	Keyboard navigation to move around spreadsheets at warp speed	1	Keyboard and cursor navigation tips
73	Layered Pattern Approach: a good reference implementation	8	The Data Viewer tool
74	Layered Pattern Approach: architecture/blueprint	2	Creating a "blueprint" for large or complex spreadsheets
75	List of common formula errors	10	TABLE 10-1 Common Formula Errors
76	List of spreadsheet issues to examine	11	A partial checklist for discerning mistakes
77	Making improvements and simplifications to formulas	10	Look For Weaknesses In The Formulas And Identify Ways To Correct For Them (located in second occurrence of section heading for this chapter)
78	Mapping the existing spreadsheet structure	10	[Determine What Portions Of The Spreadsheets Have Formulas And What Portions Have Been Etched Out By Hand Or Are Otherwise Hardwired], and [View Of The Spreadsheet From 14,000 Feet]
79	Mathematical rules for combining multiple quantities whose values are uncertain	8	Uncertainty rules

Continued

TABLE C–1 LIST OF EXCEL BEST PRACTICE TECHNIQUES AND HIP POCKET TIPS
(Continued)

No.	Best Practice Technique or "Hip Pocket" Tip	Ch	Section
80	Naming conventions for accessible spreadsheets	13	Create Easy To Find Signposts
81	New capabilities, features, and limitations of Filters in Excel 2003 (and caveats on its usage)	6	Using Excel Filters
82	Organization of accessible spreadsheets	13	The Basic Framework
83	Overall technique of chiseling a problem - example (1)	5	The Art of Data Slogging
84	Overall technique of chiseling a problem - example (2)	9	Ambiguous and Incomplete Data
85	PC Cursor mode vs. JAWS Cursor mode	13	Preliminary JAWS Concepts: a training wheel approach
86	Phantom Formatting Technique: getting four colors or formats instead of three when using condition formatting	7	The Phantom Formatting Technique and Four Color Tables
87	Practices relating to the Spreadsheet Masthead (Who, What, and When)	2	Step 6: Refining Your Spreadsheet's Appearance
88	Presentation Tear Sheets	6	Presentation Tear Sheets
89	Preventing the auto open macro from automatically running	13	The Starting Point
90	Reading data using OFFSETs: example	3	Reader Offsets
91	Reference architecture for a complex Spreadsheet Portal	12	How The Braided Style Spreadsheet Portal Works
92	Registering new handler code for your personal XML-RPC Server	12	Fine-Tuning Your Software
93	Removing hardwiring from coding: separating hardwired data from your spreadsheet formulas (some examples)	3	The & Joining Operator and Concatenate
94	Removing hardwiring from coding: the Abstraction Layer Approach	13	[An Important Design Strategy], and [Abstraction Layer Approach to Coding]

No.	Best Practice Technique or "Hip Pocket" Tip	Ch	Section
95	Repeat what I just did (and more): cloning print settings	2	The Repeat What I Just Did Feature
96	Repeat what I just did: another example	10	Using The Excel Repeat Facility
97	Running an XML import from a macro	12	Some Visual Basic Syntax and Elementary Concepts
98	Running JAWS in standalone mode and some caveats	13	Getting Acclimated With a Screen Reader
99	Selecting a column of data embedded inside a PDF document	4	Copying and pasting columnar data
100	Sentinel Look-Ahead Technique	3	The Sentinel Look-Ahead Technique
101	Setting the XML Map directly from a schema resulting from a URL request	12	Getting The Schema Directly
102	Setting up a Screen Reader	13	Setting up a Screen Reader
103	Setup of an XML-RPC Server	CD	XML_RPC_Server.java
104	Setup of the Excel Solver for mathematical optimization (defining problems, suggested practices and important gotchas)	8	Summon The Solver
105	Side by side synchronized scrolling	9	The Eyeball Comparison
106	Simple spreadsheet construction: outline of steps	2	Understanding Simple Spreadsheets
107	Simple spreadsheet construction: worked out example	2	Building a Spreadsheet: A Simple Example
108	Simulate random values having a Normal or Gaussian distribution	8	Stochastic and Markov processes
109	Sorting with more than three keyed fields	3	Sorting with more than three columns (or rows)
110	Special techniques in date arithmetic	10	Formulas for the date arithmetic

Continued

TABLE C-1 LIST OF EXCEL BEST PRACTICE TECHNIQUES AND HIP POCKET TIPS
(Continued)

No.	Best Practice Technique or "Hip Pocket" Tip	Ch	Section
111	Spotting where errors occur in a complex formula (when each of its components do not contain errors)	11	Formula evaluation
112	Spreadsheet guidelines relating to color blindness	13	Vision Impairment
113	Spreadsheet Portal reference implementation (1)	12	Interactive Participation in an Evolving Survey
114	Spreadsheet Portal reference implementation (2)	12	Use a Spreadsheet Portal to Braid Information
115	Syntax for Excel HYPERLINK function: (1) Hyperlinks to a URL	12	The All-In-One Worksheet
116	Syntax for Excel HYPERLINK function: (2) Hyperlinks to another part of an Excel workbook	13	Hyperlinks
117	Table summarizing case sensitivity of various Excel functions	3	First Steps to Tidying Up Your Data
118	Technique for extending format of text that is longer than the size of the cell width	7	Smart Formatting for Overextended Text
119	Technique for mapping a remote workbook in an Assistive Portal	13	An Assistive Portal Implementation
120	Technique of "Addition in Quadrature"	8	Quantifying Uncertainty: Techniques and Rules
121	Technique of creating a search key	5	Search Enable your Source Data
122	Technique of gathering data of other worksheets (or spreadsheets) otherwise unavailable for conditional formatting	7	Helper cells
123	Technique of incrementing variables in an XSL transformation	12	The XML "Staircase" Problem in Excel 2003 (and Other Things to Keep in Sight)

No.	Best Practice Technique or "Hip Pocket" Tip	Ch	Section
124	Technique of issuing a POST request from an Excel macro	12	Listing 12-4: Pseudo Code for Running yourMethod-(namedRange) on an Instance of JavaClassOfYourChoosing
125	Technique of managing arrays in an XML-RPC Server (instead of a single value)	CD	UddiSearchHandler-StringArray.java
126	Technique of overriding and un-erasing overrides	7	From RAGs to Riches: turn red, amber green into a rich and dynamically interactive array of colors
127	Techniques for addressing the XML "Staircase" Problem	12	The XML "Staircase" Problem in Excel 2003 (and Other Things to Keep in Sight)
128	Techniques for cleaning up data including: pruning unwanted data, eliminating comparison of apples and oranges, resolving ambiguous data, and assuring data uniformity	5	Cleaning up the spreadsheet
129	Techniques to prepare data before importing to a PivotTable	4	Preparing your Data
130	Techniques, guidelines and catalog of popup comments	6	Tips for Spreadsheet Comments
131	The Input Box interface	13	Other Techniques
132	Tracing dependencies to those computations	10	[Formula Dependencies], and [Trace The Formula Dependencies]
133	Tracing formula dependencies	11	Some observations for beginning your assessment
134	Transforming "approximate" binary constraints to exact binary constraints	8	Binary constraint workaround
135	Understanding shadow prices (and Lagrange Multipliers) reported by the Solver	8	The Sensitivity Report

Continued

TABLE C-1 LIST OF EXCEL BEST PRACTICE TECHNIQUES AND HIP POCKET TIPS
(Continued)

No.	Best Practice Technique or "Hip Pocket" Tip	Ch	Section
136	Understanding the aggregate effect of uncertainties when they are systematic (or correlated) vs. random (or uncorrelated)	11	Testing the Reasonableness of Spreadsheets
137	Understanding the difference between the Controls Toolbox and the older Forms controls	13	Graphical Components
138	Unearthing errors in the computations	10	Look For Weaknesses In The Formulas And Identify Ways To Correct For Them (located in two parts of the chapter)
139	Updating external links	11	Test your skills
140	Use of 3rd party tools to generate an XSD Schema	12	Generating The Schema With Third Party Tools
141	Using capitalization to identify which functions in not properly defined (When #NAME? appears in spreadsheet cells)	1	Entering Formulas
142	Using CHOOSE and MATCH to create a custom pick list in a single spreadsheet cell	7	Choose the best match
143	Using Excel to run Java applications and return results in XML	12	Accessing the UDDI Registry from your Spreadsheet
144	Using JAWS to read custom designed spreadsheet tables (with stacked row and column headers)	13	Defining Spreadsheet Regions
145	Using the TEXT function to render numerical values as dates	3	Contending With Excel's Way Of Representing Dates
146	Using the Text Import Wizard for both .txt and .csv files	5	Importing data
147	Walk-thru of setting up an XML-RPC Server for use with Excel	CD	takeaway.txt

No.	Best Practice Technique or "Hip Pocket" Tip	Ch	Section
148	XML data denormalization	12	A Layered Approach For A Spreadsheet Portal
149	XML export difficulties in Excel 2003	12	The XML "Staircase" Problem in Excel 2003 (and Other Things to Keep in Sight)
150	XML Map creation process	12	Step 2: Tell the Spreadsheet Application How the Received Data is to be Structured

Appendix D

What's on the CD-ROM

THIS APPENDIX PROVIDES YOU with information on the contents of the CD that accompanies this book. For the latest and greatest information, please refer to the ReadMe file located at the root of the CD. Here is what you will find:

- ◆ System Requirements

- ◆ Using the CD with Windows, and Macintosh

- ◆ What's on the CD

- ◆ Troubleshooting

System Requirements

Make sure that your computer meets the minimum system requirements listed in this section. If your computer doesn't match up to most of these requirements, you may have a problem using the contents of the CD.

For Windows 9x, Windows 2000, Windows NT4 (with SP 4 or later), Windows Me, or Windows XP:

- ◆ PC with a Pentium processor running at 120 Mhz or faster

- ◆ At least 32 MB of total RAM installed on your computer; for best performance, we recommend at least 64 MB

- ◆ Ethernet network interface card (NIC) or modem with a speed of at least 28,800 bps

- ◆ A CD-ROM drive

For Macintosh:

- ◆ Mac OS computer with a 68040 or faster processor running OS 7.6 or later

- ◆ At least 32 MB of total RAM installed on your computer; for best performance, we recommend at least 64 MB

Using the CD with Windows

To install the items from the CD to your hard drive, follow these steps:

1. Insert the CD into your computer's CD-ROM drive.

2. A window appears with the following options: Install, Browse, eBook, Links and Exit.

    Install: Gives you the option to install the supplied software and/or the author-created samples on the CD-ROM.

    Explore: Enables you to view the contents of the CD-ROM in its directory structure.

    eBook: Enables you to view an electronic version of the book.

    Links: Opens a hyperlinked page of Web sites.

    Exit: Closes the autorun window.

If you do not have autorun enabled, or if the autorun window does not appear, follow these steps to access the CD:

1. Click Start → Run.

2. In the dialog box that appears, type **d:\setup.exe**, where *d* is the letter of your CD-ROM drive. This brings up the autorun window described in the preceding set of steps.

3. Choose the Install, Browse, eBook, Links, or Exit option from the menu. (See Step 2 in the preceding list for a description of these options.)

Using the CD with the Mac OS

To install the items from the CD to your hard drive, follow these steps:

1. Insert the CD into your CD-ROM drive.

2. Double-click the icon for the CD after it appears on the desktop.

3. Most programs come with installers; for those, simply open the program's folder on the CD and double-click the Install or Installer icon. **Note:** To install some programs, just drag the program's folder from the CD window and drop it on your hard drive icon.

What's on the CD

The following sections provide a summary of the software and other materials you'll find on the CD.

Author-created materials

All author-created material from the book, including code listings and samples, are on the CD in the folder named Author.

At the root level in the `Author` folder you will find a file called `takeaway.txt`. This file contains a variety of code snippets and spreadsheet that you can use with your spreadsheets and examples provided in *Excel Best Practices for Business*.

There are over 75 example spreadsheets in *Excel Best Practices for Business*. All spreadsheet examples described in *Excel Best Practices for Business* are located in the `Spreadsheets` folder. Also in this folder is the file called `readme.xls`. This file lists each of the spreadsheets and has a description of what each spreadsheet does. Also listed are specific dependencies to properly use certain spreadsheets. Most of the spreadsheets have hyperlinks that will allow you to directly open the spreadsheet by clicking on the spreadsheet name in the readme.xls file.

The folder `other_files` contains a PDF file used as an example in Chapter 4 (`orb10Q.pdf`) to show how financial information can be reliably converted from PDF format to a spreadsheet. This folder also contains two text files (`E97SIC.txt` and `E97SIC_HeaderInfo.txt`), which are used in Chapter 5, "Scaling the Peaks of Mt. Data." Also included in this folder is a copy of the *Sarbanes-Oxley Act*, referred to in Chapter 11. This document is in PDF form. The document is rather lengthy. I have placed numerous bookmarks in the file for all the sections and subsections, to help make the document more accessible and readable. There is a text-only version of Chapter 13, "Assistive Technologies and Assistive Portals," called AssistiveText.txt, which is formatted to facilitate readability with screen reader software.

Chapter 13, "Assistive Technologies" has spreadsheets designed to work with Screen Reader software. You will find specific settings files in the folder called `PlaceIntoJAWS_SETTINGS_ENU_FOLDER`. When you install the JAWS Screen Reader as described in Chapter 13, be sure to place these files into its `SETTING\ENU` folder before launching the spreadsheet files for Chapter 13. Otherwise, JAWS will not be able to take advantage of the predefined attributes specific to these files. Instructions on the setup for the JAWS Screen Reader can be found in Chapter 13. When you download the free software, you can, for a nominal fee, purchase audio tapes. These are well worth the price.

The folder called `XML_RPC` contains Java code (both source and compiled), JAR files, a DLL file, and redistribution licenses. To use the software, you need to be running a Java 1.4 (or later) environment. If you are using the Windows platform and are not running Java or are using a version prior to 1.4, you can use the executable file (`j2sdk-1_4_2_01-windows-i586.exe`) to install a Java 1.4 Virtual Machine environment.

The installer file should be compatible with the following system configurations:

- ◆ Windows XP Professional (SP1)   Windows Active and Classic Desktop
- ◆ Windows XP Home   Windows Active and Classic Desktop
- ◆ Windows 2000 Professional (SP3)   Windows Active and Classic Desktop
- ◆ Windows 98 (1st & 2nd Editions)   Windows Active and Classic Desktop
- ◆ Windows NT 4.0 (SP6a)   Windows Active and Classic Desktop
- ◆ Windows ME   Windows Active and Classic Desktop
- ◆ Windows Server 2003, Web Edition   Windows Active and Classic Desktop
- ◆ Windows Server 2003, Standard Edition   Windows Active and Classic Desktop
- ◆ Windows Server 2003, Enterprise Edition   Windows Active and Classic Desktop
- ◆ Windows Server 2003, Datacenter Edition   Windows Active and Classic Desktop

After you have the appropriate Java environment installed, follow the instructions provided at the end of Chapter 12 for the setup of an XML-RPC Server. After you have installed the Java SDK, open a new DOS prompt and type **java –version** and press Enter. You should see a response with a version number of 1.4 or higher.

Please note that when specifying multiple classpaths when running Java classes or compiling them, the separator symbol used on the Windows platform is the semicolon (;). On the Macintosh platform, the separator symbol is a colon (:).

Applications

Shareware programs are fully functional, trial versions of copyrighted programs. If you like particular programs, register with their authors for a nominal fee and receive licenses, enhanced versions, and technical support. *Freeware programs* are copyrighted games, applications, and utilities that are free for personal use. Unlike shareware, these programs do not require a fee or provide technical support. *GNU software* is governed by its own license, which is included inside the folder of the GNU product. See the GNU license for more details.

Trial, demo, or evaluation versions are usually limited either by time or functionality (such as being unable to save projects). Some trial versions are very sensitive to system date changes. If you alter your computer's date, the programs will "time out" and will no longer be functional.

The following applications are on the CD.

ADOBE READER

Adobe(r) Reader(r) free software for viewing and printing Adobe PortableDocument Format (PDF) files on major hardware and operating systemplatforms. Adobe

Reader 6.0 is the newest version of the familiar AdobeAcrobat(r) Reader software. It also replaces Adobe Acrobat eBook Reader, software for viewing high-fidelity eBooks on your notebook or desktop computer.

MATHEMATICA 5

From simple calculator operations to large-scale programming and interactive document preparation, Mathematica is the tool of choice of the frontiers of scientific research, in engineering analysis and modeling, in technical education from high school to graduate school, and wherever quantitative methods are used.

eBook version of Excel Best Practices for Business

My goal in writing this book has been to empower you and provide as much value as possible. To this end, the complete text of this book is available on the CD in Adobe's Portable Document Format (PDF). You can read and search through the file with the Adobe Acrobat Reader (also included on the CD). Appendix C of the book identifies the top 150 best practice techniques and "hip pocket" tips mentioned in the book.

In going this extra length to provide you with an e-copy of the book, I have one request to make of you. When friends or associates want a copy of the book, please insist that they buy the book instead. I think you will agree that the book is not expensive, especially in relation to the value it provides, and that what I am asking of you is fair and worth honoring.

Links

There are several important links you should avail yourself.

AUTHOR'S WEB SITE

Author's Web site:

    http://www.evolvingtech.com/excel

DOWNLOAD SITES

 ◆ JAWS (a product of Freedom Scientific)

    http://www.freedomscientific.com/fs_downloads/jaws.asp

 ◆ Window-Eyes (a product of GW Micro)

    http://www.gwmicro.com/demo/

 ◆ Java SDK (to select the version appropriate for you it may be necessary to navigate to specific links at this site).

    http://java.sun.com/j2se/

    http://www.apple.com/java/

◆ Mathematica and Mathematica Link for Excel (products of Wolfram Research)

```
http://www.wolfram.com/products/mathematica/index.html
http://www.wolfram.com/products/applications/excel_link/
```

◆ Crystal Ball a product of Decisioneering

```
http://www.decisioneering.com/cbpro/index.html
```

◆ Mathematical optimization tools from Lindo Systems

```
http://www.lindo.com/cgi/frameset.cgi?leftproduct.html;
productsf.html
```

◆ Mathematical optimization tools from Frontline Systems

```
http://www.solver.com/exceluse.htm
```

LINKS OF ORGANIZATIONS RELEVANT TO ASSISTIVE TECHNOLOGY

◆ WGBH

```
http://ncam.wgbh.org/
```

◆ NYC Dept of Education

```
http://schools.nycenet.edu/d75/streetsigns/index.htm
```

◆ Freedom Scientific

```
http://www.freedomscientific.com
```

◆ GW Micro

```
http://www.gwmicro.com
```

◆ American Foundation for the Blind

```
http://www.afb.org
```

LINKS FOR THE U.S. CENSUS BUREAU

◆ NAICS

```
http://www.census.gov/naics
```

◆ Source of National Demographic Information

```
http://dataferrett.census.gov/TheDataWeb/index.html
```

Link for the National Oceanographic and Atmospheric Administration FTP site:

```
ftp://ftp.ngdc.noaa.gov/STP/SOLAR_DATA/SUNSPOT_NUMBERS
```

LINKS RELATING TO MULTI-DIMENSIONAL ANALYSIS

◆ DB2 OLAP Server.

`http://www-3.ibm.com/software/data/db2/db2olap/`

◆ Muse

`http://www.muser.com`

LINKS ON INFORMATION ABOUT CONCURRENT VERSIONING SYSTEM (CVS)

`http://www.cvshome.org`

LINKS FOR TECHNOLOGIES SUPPORTING CAPTIONING AND DISABILITIES

◆ Apple QuickTime

`http://www.apple.com/quicktime/`

`http://www.apple.com/disability/`

◆ Macromedia Flash

`http://www.macromedia.com/macromedia/accessibility/`

Troubleshooting

If you have difficulty installing or using any of the materials on the companion CD, try the following solutions:

◆ **Turn off any anti-virus software that you may have running.** Installers sometimes mimic virus activity and can make your computer incorrectly believe that it is being infected by a virus. (Be sure to turn the anti-virus software back on later.)

◆ **Remember to load the Analysis Toolpak Add-In.** Several of the spreadsheets use the RANDBETWEEN function and the Fourier Analysis facility. Be sure to load the Analysis Toolpak for your Excel Add-Ins. Instructions for loading Add-Ins is described in Chapter 8 of *Excel Best Practices for Business*. The option for the Analysis Toolpak in the list of available Add-Ins may not be displayed if you have not completed a full Excel installation.

◆ **Remember to load the Solver Add-In.** The Chapter 8 optimization example requires the use of the Solver Add-In. Be sure to load the Solver Excel Add-Ins. Instructions for loading Add-Ins is described in Chapter 8 of

Excel Best Practices for Business. The option for the Solver in the list of available Add-Ins may not be displayed if you have not completed a full Excel installation.

◆ **Upgrade to Excel 2003 if you are using an earlier version of Excel.** A number of spreadsheets, particularly those for Chapter 12, make use of Excel 2003 features and will not work with earlier versions of Excel. To run these spreadsheets, you will need to upgrade to Excel 2003.

Excel 2003 introduces some new functionality that specifically differs with older versions of Excel. In particular, the Excel function SUBTOTAL behaves differently. On the ReportSheet worksheet of ch06-01DatasetPackagingTool.xls, there appears three formulas where SUBTOTAL is used. These spreadsheet cells will display a #VALUE! error. This is because the first argument or input parameter supplied is "109". The value 109 will not work on any version of Excel prior to Excel 2003. This is true, regardless of where you are using Windows or Macintosh. To correct this, change the value of "109" with "9" for any version of Excel prior to Excel 2003. More information about the SUBTOTAL function appears in the "Swiss army knife of Excel functions" sidebar in Chapter 6.

◆ **You may need to open several of the spreadsheets by navigating through the Excel Open window.** A number of spreadsheets, (particularly, ch09-04dataOverpass.xls, ch13-06AssistivePortal.xls, and ch13-08AssistivePortal.xls) may not behave as intended unless they are opened by navigating through the Excel Open window (by navigating through the File→Open menu).

◆ **Information for Macintosh users.** Please refer to Appendix B for information specific to the Macintosh platform.

◆ **Close all running programs.** The more programs you're running, the less memory is available to other programs. Installers also typically update files and programs; if you keep other programs running, installation may not work properly.

◆ **Reference the ReadMe:** Please refer to the ReadMe file located at the root of the CD-ROM for the latest product information at the time of publication.

If you still have trouble with the CD-ROM, please call the Wiley Product Technical Support phone number: (800) 762-2974. Outside the United States, call 1(317) 572-3994. You can also contact Wiley Product Technical Support at www.wiley.com/techsupport. Wiley Publishing will provide technical support only for installation and other general quality control items; for technical support on the applications themselves, consult the program's vendor or author.

To place additional orders or to request information about other Wiley products, please call (800) 225-5945.

Index

Symbols

& (ampersand) operator, 75, 76

* (asterisk) as wildcard for filter criteria, 168

: (colon) for ranges of cells, 24

δ (delta), defined, 216

... (ellipsis) on toolbar icons, 448

= (equal symbol)
   as equality operator, 69, 71
   starting formulas, 12

> (greater than symbol) for extremes in PivotTables, 112–113

< (less than symbol) for extremes in PivotTables, 112–113

– (minus sign) by XML tags, 348–349

( ) (parentheses), highlighting when entering, 23

+ (plus sign)
   expanding columns, 218–219
   by XML tags, 349

? (question mark) as wildcard for filter criteria, 168

' (single quotation mark) for Visual Basic comments, 354

A

Abdulezer, Loren (*Excel Best Practices for Business*)
   eBook version on the CD, 475
   Web site, 32, 63, 171, 247, 346, 457

ABS function, positive value returned by, 216

absolute cell references
   for Conditional Formatting, 189
   defined, 13
   Macintosh platform, 454
   relative and hybrid references versus, 13–19, 290–291
   switching with relative or hybrid references, 15
   for values in formulas, 16–18

Abstraction Layer approach to coding, 411–412, 418–419

accessibility. *See* assistive technologies; disabilities

Accessibility Options (Windows), 380

accordion style menus, eliminating, 451–452

Acrobat Reader (on the CD), 474–475

ActiveX Controls. *See also* Control Toolbox toolbar
   List Box, 406–407, 409–410
   in UserForms, 408–409

Add-In functions
   Analysis ToolPak for, 39, 205
   complexity of spreadsheets and, 63
   Data Audit tool, 319
   for Fourier Transforms and Fourier Analysis, 211
   loading (overview), 39
   Macintosh platform and, 454
   performance and, 211
   RANDBETWEEN function, 38–40
   sharing spreadsheets and, 40
   for Solver tool, 211, 234

Adding in Quadrature
   combined uncertainty based on, 217
   computing derivatives for uncertainty formulas, 225–226
   formal statement of, 216
   independent variation in random or uncertain manner and, 215
   mathematical notation, 216
   real-world example, 217–219
   technique, 215–217
   uncertainty rules, 216–217, 220–224

Add-Ins submenu (Tools menu), 211

Adobe Acrobat Reader (on the CD), 474–475

Advanced Filters
   benefits of, 179
   Criteria Range for, 176–178

continued

continued

continued

continued

X

continued

Wiley Publishing, Inc.
End-User License Agreement

5. Limited Warranty.

   (a) WPI warrants that the Software and Software Media are free from defects in materials and workmanship under normal use for a period of sixty (60) days from the date of purchase of this Book. If WPI receives notification within the warranty period of defects in materials or workmanship, WPI will replace the defective Software Media.

   (b) WPI AND THE AUTHOR(S) OF THE BOOK DISCLAIM ALL OTHER WARRANTIES, EXPRESS OR IMPLIED, INCLUDING WITHOUT LIMITATION IMPLIED WARRANTIES OF MERCHANTABILITY AND FITNESS FOR A PARTICULAR PURPOSE, WITH RESPECT TO THE SOFTWARE, THE PROGRAMS, THE SOURCE CODE CONTAINED THEREIN, AND/OR THE TECHNIQUES DESCRIBED IN THIS BOOK. WPI DOES NOT WARRANT THAT THE FUNCTIONS CONTAINED IN THE SOFTWARE WILL MEET YOUR REQUIREMENTS OR THAT THE OPERATION OF THE SOFTWARE WILL BE ERROR FREE.

   (c) This limited warranty gives you specific legal rights, and you may have other rights that vary from jurisdiction to jurisdiction.

6. Remedies.

   (a) WPI's entire liability and your exclusive remedy for defects in materials and workmanship shall be limited to replacement of the Software Media, which may be returned to WPI with a copy of your receipt at the following address: Software Media Fulfillment Department, Attn.: Excel Best Practices for Business, Wiley Publishing, Inc., 10475 Crosspoint Blvd., Indianapolis, IN 46256, or call 1-800-762-2974. Please allow four to six weeks for delivery. This Limited Warranty is void if failure of the Software Media has resulted from accident, abuse, or misapplication. Any replacement Software Media will be warranted for the remainder of the original warranty period or thirty (30) days, whichever is longer.

   (b) In no event shall WPI or the author be liable for any damages whatsoever (including without limitation damages for loss of business profits, business interruption, loss of business information, or any other pecuniary loss) arising from the use of or inability to use the Book or the Software, even if WPI has been advised of the possibility of such damages.

   (c) Because some jurisdictions do not allow the exclusion or limitation of liability for consequential or incidental damages, the above limitation or exclusion may not apply to you.

7. U.S. Government Restricted Rights. Use, duplication, or disclosure of the Software for or on behalf of the United States of America, its agencies and/or instrumentalities "U.S. Government" is subject to restrictions as stated in paragraph (c)(1)(ii) of the Rights in Technical Data and Computer Software clause of DFARS 252.227-7013, or subparagraphs (c) (1) and (2) of the Commercial Computer Software - Restricted Rights clause at FAR 52.227-19, and in similar clauses in the NASA FAR supplement, as applicable.

8. General. This Agreement constitutes the entire understanding of the parties and revokes and supersedes all prior agreements, oral or written, between them and may not be modified or amended except in a writing signed by both parties hereto that specifically refers to this Agreement. This Agreement shall take precedence over any other documents that may be in conflict herewith. If any one or more provisions contained in this Agreement are held by any court or tribunal to be invalid, illegal, or otherwise unenforceable, each and every other provision shall remain in full force and effect.